NEW ENGLAND'S
PROSPECT : 1933

NEW ENGLAND'S PROSPECT : 1933

BY

James Truslow Adams, Henry S. Graves, Edward A. Filene, William J. Cunningham, Roy M. Cushman, E. F. Gerish, Orren Chalmer Hormell, R. J. McFall, Lewis Radcliffe, E. W. Morehouse, John S. Keir, Charles E. Artman, William Roger Greeley, I. G. Davis, John F. Sly, H. C. Woodworth, R. T. Fisher, J. L. Hypes, Fred Rogers Fairchild, Gerald A. Fitzgerald, Frederick V. Waugh, Derwent Whittlesey, Alexander E. Cance, Henry F. Perkins, Arthur W. Dean, G. B. Roorbach, and John K. Wright

AMS PRESS

NEW YORK

Reprinted from the edition of 1933, New York
First AMS EDITION published 1970
Manufactured in the United States of America

International Standard Book Number: 0–404–00354–0

Library of Congress Number: 78–111763

AMS PRESS INC.
NEW YORK, N.Y. 10003

CONTENTS

FOREWORD

"I UNDERTOOKE this worke . . . because there hath some relations heretofore past the Presse, which have beene very imperfect; as also because there hath beene many scandalous and false reports past upon the Country, even from the sulphurious breath of every base ballad-monger: wherefore to perfect the one, and take off the other, I have laid down the nature of the Country, without any partiall respect unto it."

These remarks from the foreword to William Wood's "New England's Prospect," published in London in 1634, well describe the motives that prompted the preparation of the present volume, in which Wood's title has been revived. "Some relations heretofore past the Presse" concerning contemporary New England have indeed been "imperfect." New England has suffered from "the sulphurious breath" of a modern breed of "ballad-monger." The several contributors to "New England's Prospect—1933" have attempted to lay "down the nature of the Country, without any partiall respect unto it"—that is, in a detached spirit of scholarly inquiry. They have tried not to advertise New England nor to glorify it, but to see it as it is.

Several broad fields of inquiry were outlined covering social, economic, and governmental conditions and activities in New England. Each contributor is a specialist in one of these fields and, in connection with it, was invited to discuss contemporary movements and issues that have appeared to him of the first importance. He was asked to give particular attention to the progress of investigation and to gaps that further investigation should fill. He was urged, so far as pertinent, to consider not only issues regarding which New England presents a united front but also the divergent interests of the several communities that make up the larger whole. Finally he was requested to bear in mind conditions beyond New England's borders that affect the destiny of its people.

The book opens with five introductory papers. Dr. Adams interprets the character of the New Englander in the light of history. The editor describes the principal regions into which New England may be split and the landscapes found in each. Dr. Artman and Mr. Filene survey New England's industrial prospects and the problem of unemployment, and Dr. McFall presents a statistical analysis of the position that New England's industries hold within the greater industrial region of the northeastern United States.

The main part of the book consists of papers on specific problems: food supply, agricultural production, marketing of farm products, forestry, fisheries, power, manufacturing, transportation, trade, rural and urban sociology. There are also discussions of state and local government and of regional and city planning. Special attention is directed to the geographical circumstances that play an important part in all of these problems.

The two concluding papers, like the second, are more specifically geographical. Professor Whittlesey's analysis and comparison of two representative localities in northern New England exemplifies a modern method of detailed geographical study. In the final paper the editor illustrates some changes that the forces of recent progress are bringing about in the geographical relationships of the inhabitants of New England.

Different as may be the actual topics and points of view of its writers, unifying threads run through the volume. One thread is geographical; another, an interest in the bearings of research; and still another, a concern with the future. Mere encyclopedic description has not been an objective.

The prospect here spread before the reader is far more complex than the prospect seen by William Wood three hundred years ago. The word "prospect" means a "view of things within reach of the eye"; it also means a "looking forward into the future:" In the title of the present book the word carries both meanings. The several contributors have aimed to disclose the broad lay of the land. To paraphrase a couplet addressed to William Wood by a friend:

> And their experience thus a Mount doth make
> From whence we may NEW ENGLAND'S PROSPECT take.

Partly because of its immensity and partly because it is obscured over wide tracts by the mists of ignorance, the entire prospect cannot be revealed. In contemplating the New England of today, however, the writers of the following chapters have sought also for views ahead and here and there have picked out trails that seem to lead into the future.

ACKNOWLEDGMENTS

The American Geographical Society expresses sincere and grateful appreciation to the scholars who have responded generously with their time and thought to the Society's invitation to contribute to this volume. In addition to those whose names appear in the table of contents, Professor M. F. Morgan of the Connecticut Agricultural Experiment Station compiled the soil map and accompanying description, Professor L. A. Wolfanger of Columbia University made helpful suggestions in regard to soils, and Mr. Chapin Hoskins contributed a statistical analysis of manufacturing employment in New England. In preparing their papers, Professor Perkins received the aid of Dr. H. C. Taylor and Mr. Fitzgerald that of Messrs. Wetmore Hodges, Gardner Poole, and W. H. Raye. Miss Marion Eckert and Miss Dorothy Harnden rendered skilled assistance in connection with certain graphs, maps, and tables. With a few exceptions the illustrations were drafted by Messrs. John Philip and E. D. Weldon. Mr. A. A. Brooks read the proofs and made the index.

THE HISTORICAL BACKGROUND

James Truslow Adams

A WRITER on scientific method in a book published a few years ago says that "as a rule it will be found that the historical introduction is very much like the chaplain's prayer that opens a legislative session or a political convention: very little of the subsequent proceedings are decided by reference to it."[1] Yet he admits elsewhere that social phenomena depend in part on historic continuity and cannot be understood without some reference to the past. I agree with him on both counts. The problem is, What references to the complex past may be of use in interpreting specific aspects of the present?

It is clear that so brief an introduction as this to the twenty-eight topics treated subsequently cannot be resolved into a genetic approach to each or all of them. What I shall more modestly try to do will be merely to point to certain traits and developments in New England character and history that may provide a background for the discussions to follow.

For the present purpose our history may be divided into two periods, one of approximately two centuries, from 1630 to about 1830, and the other of one century from about 1830 to 1930. In the first, the psychological character and the framework of social institutions became molded and "set"; in the second, these came into conflict with the new economic and intellectual forces operative in that period in both Europe and America. The resultants, if a curve could be plotted, would bring us to the material and spiritual situation in 1932. Instead of a scientific graph, the historian, unlike the statistician, can offer only tentative suggestions.

The Diversity and the Homogeneity of New England

As contrasted with the rest of America, even in colonial times, New England became a section clearly differentiated from the others socially, economically, and psychologically. The obviousness of this broad differentiation, however, should not lead us to overlook the marked local differences existing within the New England section itself. Other contributors to this volume make clear the fact that only in a limited sense is the section a "region" with common interests. In part these heterogeneous interests derive from obvious factors of location. A fishing community will be found on the coast, whereas a manufacturing city may develop about a water power on an interior

---

[1] M. R. Cohen, *Reason and Nature*, New York, 1931.

I

river, and not vice versa. What I wish to point out is that there are also marked distinctions in character and outlook between some of the subsections that can be derived only remotely, when at all, from their geography. For example, whereas the early settlers of Boston and Newport took advantage of geographical circumstances to develop these towns into the most important ports of the entire section, geography was not at all responsible for the fact that under their several early leaderships Massachusetts should have developed a harsh, dogmatic, persecuting spirit, while Rhode Island should have been our first colony to insist on complete toleration, with all that later stemmed from those contrasting attitudes. When the banished Roger Williams tramped in the winter snow from Boston to establish a new settlement devoted to freedom of spirit, he did not choose Rhode Island with the slightest thought of the type of economic state that might there arise. He went solely because he knew an Indian there. Nor had the divergent physical aspects of Massachusetts Bay and Narragansett Bay anything to do with the vastly different intellectual outlooks, in respect to toleration, of the communities that grew up on their separate shores. Again, Vermont, owing more to the character of its settlers and the accidents of history than to anything inherent in its landscape and position, became a state so much apart that for a while, during the American Revolution, it set up as an independent one internationally and for some time after remained uncertain as to whether it would even enter the American Union.

On the other hand, the inhabitants of all six New England states resemble one another fundamentally much more than they do those of any other section, and we must here concern ourselves with these broad resemblances and not with the minor differences.

The Puritan Tradition

In spite of scattered settlements of fishermen and that of the Pilgrims at Plymouth, the real founding of New England may be dated from 1630 when some two thousand well equipped settlers arrived on the shores of Boston Harbor. By 1640 the population of the New England colonies had risen to about 18,000, thanks to native births and continued immigration. About that date immigration abruptly ceased for nearly two centuries.

The general run of the first immigrants may perhaps have been more strictly Puritan than those of other sections, but a large part of the English people of that period were tinged with Puritanism of varying shades; and the laws of Virginia were practically as Puritanical as those of Massachusetts. Different factors, however, quickly combined to mark the New England colonies as distinctly and very strongly Puritan.

The leaders of the movement to that section, unlike those elsewhere, belonged to what may be called the extreme left wing of Puritanism. They were of the strictest sect of the Pharisees. They felt that they alone possessed the key to eternal truth and were the elect of God. "God sifted a whole nation to send choice grain into this wilderness," said one; and "we are a city set upon a hill," later wrote another. This attitude, communicated to their followers and emphasized through the generations, had several effects. It gave an unyielding, dogmatic tone to the thought of the community. It tended to unite its members in one of the strongest of all bonds, the belief that they formed a class apart and superior. In the case of an aristocracy or, say, the officers of an army or a navy, such a feeling sets a class or group apart from the rest of their society. In the case of New England it set the whole community off as contrasted with the other colonies. The "Middle Colonies" and "the South" were but vague terms. Their citizens were primarily New Yorkers, Pennsylvanians, Virginians, and so on. From the start the inhabitants of Massachusetts, Connecticut, or other New England colonies were primarily New Englanders in the mind of the rest of the country; and this in spite of their local differences.

Speaking broadly, and always keeping such differences in mind, it may be said that the type of immigration, and the subsequent method of settling new towns, also operated strongly to develop the sense of unity and of corporate and community spirit. Whereas, on other parts of the seaboard, settlement was largely by individuals, in New England it was by groups gathered about the kernel of the church organization. Settlements were not fortuitous assemblages of individuals; they were, from their inception, closely organized bodies. The citizen lived, moved, and had his being as a part of a small but tightly knit group, not as a solitary. In church meeting and town meeting (sometimes scarce distinguishable from each other), he grew to consider organized action as normal action. It is, perhaps, not unscientific to link to this condition the fact that, later, the modern business corporation should have first arisen and assumed its distinct legal characteristics in this section.

Everywhere in a new country work takes on a different aspect from what it wears in older lands. In the latter it is a personal affair. In breaking the wilderness, by contrast, the loafer becomes a menace to the community, and the insistence upon every one's working becomes often a subject for legislative enactment. It did so in our South as well as North; but, owing to the strong religious coloring given to all life in New England, work came there, much more than elsewhere, to be considered a moral virtue and idleness a sin. Work having become a virtue, a complying with the will of God, successful results of work or business became God's blessings, not to be idly dissipated on the vanities or follies of this world. Thrift also became a virtue, and "thou shalt scrimp" entered the decalogue.

THE GEOGRAPHICAL BACKGROUND

Added force was lent to this commandment by the land and climate. In the beginning the settlers had had no objection to ease, wealth, or exploited labor. The Pilgrims had first considered emigrating from Holland to Guiana, where they hoped to find gold and easy riches. Winthrop, like others, came to America in part to recover a financial and social position he was losing in England. The Puritans tried to utilize slaves, Indian or negro. It is often said that slavery proved unprofitable because of the nature of the New England "soil and climate." This statement, which contains a truth, is, nevertheless somewhat misleading unless clarified by further analysis.

On the whole, the New England area is, topographically, a minutely rough land, on which much labor is required on a small tract to make it suitable for agriculture. There are, however, a number of topographic depressions, such as the Connecticut Valley Lowland and the Aroostook region in Maine. In these, staple crops can be raised. The Connecticut Valley has long been famous for its fruit and tobacco, and the Aroostook has become so more recently for its potatoes. Why, then, it may be asked, did the generalized factors of "soil and climate" interfere with the raising of these staples in the first century or more of settlement?

Owing to its forested surface and its extremely severe climate, Maine increased very slowly in population. Furthermore, potatoes, which later became its staple crop, were little known or used in the colonies in the first century. It has usually been said that they were not introduced until 1719; and, although this is not so, there was little market for them until well into the eighteenth century.

It is true that tobacco is now a staple in the Connecticut Valley, but several factors combined to prevent its becoming so for the first two centuries. The leaders here and the backers of New England in old England were opposed to its use and cultivation on moral grounds. This served merely as a drag anchor on the industry, for tobacco was used and raised for personal consumption. Its quality for export, however, was not as good as that of the plants raised in the South, and the crop never became important until the nineteenth century, after cigars became popular, when the Connecticut tobacco leaves could be used as wrappers. In addition, although the climate did not preclude its cultivation, it had certain influences on it. The much more severe winters of New England as contrasted with the South imposed special requirements on the northern agricultural worker. For example, he had to have a stouter house, a larger and more varied supply of heavy clothing, more firewood, and so on.

These same factors would make it more expensive for him to maintain his slaves through the cold weather when idle. The negro, unless carefully protected, was less likely to survive the Connecticut than the Virginia winter. The northern agricultural economy was more complex than the southern and so less adapted to negro mental capacity. The New Englander, who was anxious enough to make every penny he could, exported practically no tobacco at all until 1700 and for long after that only small quantities to the West Indies. Probably for the reasons mentioned above, the crop was merely one of the several raised for home consumption in the variegated economy of the farm life of the period.

Slave labor is profitable only in the raising of a staple crop involving comparatively simple processes and under other favoring conditions. It proved unprofitable in New England, where white labor was also extremely scarce. From a combination of factors, geographic and historic, the section thus became, agriculturally, a land of small farms, sufficiently small to be worked by the owner and his family (the only exception being a corner of Rhode Island, where unusual conditions prevailed). In time, this situation was also to set New England off against other sections, as it was to emphasize its small-enterprise type of life. The small farm, the town as the unit of government, the local church governed by its own local congregation— all trained the New Englander to think and work in terms of the small and local group.

THE ACCUMULATION OF CAPITAL

Another factor worked in the same direction. No community can rise above mere subsistence level without the accumulation of capital. In our first century capital was slowly accumulated by the Indian trade in furs, by mills for grinding, by agriculture, and by commerce. The geographical and zoölogical conditions in New England early made the fur trade negligible. In agriculture one-family farms created little or no capital, and after the overthrow of the Stuarts in England, which improved the position of the extreme Puritans, immigrants ceased coming to New England. Puritans no longer had to emigrate, and others preferred the better soil and climate, with less rigorous religious restrictions, of the other colonies as compared with most of New England. Early in the eighteenth century, the Middle and Southern colonies were advancing rapidly in the accumulation of capital from exploiting indented or slave labor on large farms or plantations; and from the rapid influx of English, Scotch-Irish, and German immigrants who took up lands and frequently made large owners, like the Carrolls and Dulanys, rich in a generation.

In New England, balked by soil, topography, climate, and the comparatively stationary population, the people had to turn to other means for the accumulation of capital. Work and thrift were not only virtues but economic necessities. In the absence of large enterprises, of any labor to be exploited, and of new immigration, the New Englander if he wanted to "get ahead" by his own exertions had to make one penny do the work of three as contrasted with his fellow American in more favored sections. All factors—the frontier, religion, land, and climate—thus combined to make the New Englander think long and carefully over the advisability of the least expenditure. Such necessity produces a certain type of character. If it may easily descend to the vice of miserliness, it also makes for self-restraint, strength of will, and extreme conservatism. This conservatism, once thoroughly instilled, comes to operate on everything, from the spending of money on the gewgaws of fashion to the accepting of new-fangled ideas in business or government.

One other road to capital was open to the New Englander—the sea. If there was little profit in tilling his stony, glaciated fields, he could turn to fishing or trade. The cod, the whale, and foreign commerce laid the foundations of the very economical economics of the section. Here again we are met by group organizations and small units. From time immemorial a ship has peculiarly lent itself to ownership in shares. Unlike a farm, mill, or other business venture, the entire capital in ship and cargo may be sunk complete in a moment. Such a risk cried imperatively for distribution in ages when insurance was unknown. Although fishing was mostly conducted from the Atlantic coast, the small vessels carrying the trade of the section set sail from almost every cove of ocean and sound, as well as from villages as far up the Connecticut River as Hartford. Until well through the eighteenth century, the vessels were mostly small, often jointly owned, and the trade with the West Indies and Europe of a huckstering sort. The point is that the growing capitalists were confirmed in their habit of working in small ventures through group action. In the South, with its staple crops and plantation economy, there was little need felt for commerce. In the Middle Colonies, owing partly to the outline of the Jersey coast, commerce tended quickly to concentrate in the two large ports of Philadelphia and New York.

The Growth of Sectional Individuality

In another respect New England was a land apart from the rest of America. Until 1690, when owing to a dispute with the English government the Massachusetts charter was annulled and a royal governor was appointed for that colony and New Hampshire, there had been no such official within the borders of the entire section, nor was there ever to be one in Rhode Island or Connecticut. The long training in self-government, in almost complete independence—the

governor being considered an evil anomaly even in Massachusetts—
gave a character to political life there different from that found
anywhere else in the English colonies. It developed a strong attach-
ment to local forms, a self-consciousness with respect to them, and
a vigorous effort to cling to them, that all emphasized the conservative
trait already noted. Change under the circumstances could mean
only political loss, and the fear of loss and the fear of change became
intertwined.

There was yet another factor that made for sectional difference
and sectional self-consciousness. From 1640 for nearly two centuries
there was no infusion of new blood by immigration. New Yŏrk,
originally Dutch, had always been cosmopolitan, and early in the
eighteenth century twenty-eight languages were spoken there. In
that century, the Middle Colonies and the South had large immigra-
tions of several races. In the South there was also frequent social
and intellectual contact with England by the going thither of young
men to study at the universities or at the Temple. In this regard
it may be questioned, with no attempt at paradox, whether the early
founding of Harvard College at Cambridge in 1636 was not detrimental to the intellectual life of New England. For several generations the institution was scarcely more than a grammar school, but
young New Englanders went to it instead of going to the larger
opportunities of universities in England. Whereas in 1643, 50 per
cent of the New England clergy, who were the intellectual leaders
of that section, were trained at Oxford or Cambridge in old England,
by about 1690, 95 per cent, at least in Massachusetts and Connecticut,
had had only the narrow training of Harvard. Thus, both from
lack of immigration and from the home training of the ablest young
men, there was much less contact with the broader civilization of
the mother country and less healthy stirring of the provincial life than
almost anywhere else in America. New Englanders more and more
came to think of themselves as a race apart, and, as man always
rationalizes his situation agreeably to his self-esteem, they came
to think of themselves and their ways as superior. This again tended
to make them exclusive, provincial, and conservative.

The New Englander was never a "good mixer," and it may be
noted that of the four Presidents whom that important section has
given to the nation, only one, Coolidge, has served for longer than his
first term. It is also notable that the movement for secession from
the British Empire had its origin in New England under the lead
of Samuel Adams; that the first threats of secession from the American
Union came from that section in the first two decades of the nineteenth
century; and that through its spokesman, Josiah Quincy, it bitterly
opposed western expansion and the creation of new states. The
section, strongly self-conscious, has always fought consistently to

defend its own local life whether it felt it threatened from London, Washington, or the new capitals across the Alleghenies.

In the earlier period, in spite of its commerce—which itself, in the absence of any staple products, called for great shrewdness—there was always the danger that the balance of trade would go against New England. For that reason shrewdness had to be developed in another direction, that of satisfying as many needs as possible by home production and contrivance. Yankee ingenuity, as well as Yankee "notions," became a byword. Without staple crops, coal, or ores, the Yankee had to devise every possible article which might be sold to create capital, supply his own wants, bring his foreign necessities, bolster his weak-kneed exchange.

Under stress of that necessity he became not merely a Jack-of-all-trades, a versatile workman, but an unexcelled inventor and a skilled workman. A century or more ago, as a traveler came up the coast from the big easy-going plantations of the South, through the large farms and iron works of the Middle Colonies, and entered New England, he reached the land of small things materially, small farms and landholdings, small towns, small political units, all kinds of small goods manufactured in small plants, a land that wanted a small nation. Incidentally, it was then a land also that had suffered in the Revolution from the exodus of a large proportion of its wealthiest and most liberal-minded citizens, great numbers of whom had been Tories. That many of the most prominent men in Boston and elsewhere in the section were exiled, accounted in part, perhaps, for the dominance in national political life, for a couple of generations, of the "Virginia Dynasty." Possibly it also accounted in part for the increasing touchiness of New England and her fear of the extension of the national domain with the prospect of reducing yet further her national influence.

By the beginning of our second period, roughly that from 1830 to 1930, New England had thus become a clearly marked section, with characteristics quite its own. These had, by that time, become "set," and although they were to come into conflict with the new forces of the nineteenth century, they were only partially to be deflected by them.

THE OPENING OF THE WEST AND NEW ENGLAND AGRICULTURE

The building of the Erie Canal, which was completed in 1825, helped to isolate New England yet more. The cost of transporting freight from the new western country dropped from $100 a ton to $5 a ton between Buffalo and New York. New England at once felt the repercussions. Chenango potatoes, for example, quickly and heavily undersold those from Connecticut in the New York market. With the introduction of farm machinery New England suffered from another handicap in competition. For the most part, the rough and minute topography, of which I have already spoken, made the use of such machinery difficult where not impossible, as contrasted with the large units of low-taxed, low-priced, and easier worked land in the West. Costs, topography, climate, and markets all favored the western farmer. The western country, appearing to offer more profitable opportunities, attracted capital, which, as well as labor, was lacking to the small farmer of New England. At a critical period, the difficulties of large-scale production were insuperable for Yankee agriculture.. From the opening of the Erie Canal, and for long thereafter, there was a rush of farmers from New England to western New York and farther. Owing to poor economic conditions there had already been for many decades such a movement away from depleted New England farms, but under the new conditions this became a veritable exodus. Fostered by the growth of the West, the wealth and activity of New York increased rapidly, and it was not long before there were weekly scheduled sailings from that port to Europe. The regularity and other advantages of the New York service attracted additional business, and by the time the railroad era succeeded to that of the canals, Boston was hopelessly behind.

New England Shipping and the Rise of Manufactures

Meanwhile, there had been a great alteration in New England's economic life. Those who think of the present crisis there as unprecedented, like those who believe the present business depression unequaled in the past, may well calm their minds by a study of history. New England has had her crises before. She had an extremely bad one as early as 1640 when the cessation of immigration, following on the failure of agriculture, nearly wrecked her. She has always been having to adjust herself to what have been called "new conditions." Few of her early settlers had been seafaring in England, but, when agriculture in rocky fields and poor soils proved inadequate to support her economic prosperity, she had to turn to fishing on a grand scale to serve as the basis for an oversea commerce. As a later consequence, she invented the "schooner" and came to lead all nations, easily beating the British, in building the fastest ships in the world, perhaps the most beautiful things, aesthetically, ever created in America. In 1790 the *Columbia* had reached Boston after a three years' voyage on which she had circled the globe, and as a result of the information brought by her the great "China trade" began.

In the first quarter of the nineteenth century, New England was again in a crisis. A port requires a *hinterland* if it is to grow. New England was largely shut off from our rapidly developing West, the produce from which was passing out to sea by way of the Mississippi

River and the Gulf or by way of the Érie Canal through New York.
The years of the Embargo and the War of 1812 had greatly stimulated
domestic manufactures; and, in spite of severe depression following
the conclusion of peace, New England had become heavily com-
mitted to manufacturing and had had a vision of her future. In
particular, a beginning had been made in the textile industry, an
English workman in Rhode Island having succeeded in reproducing
from memory English machines, the export of which was at that
time forbidden. Many merchants who had made money in shipping
turned to the new field of manufacturing. In 1820 shipping was
still supreme, and that sensitive barometer of local interest, a vote on
the tariff, showed New England as still for free trade, that is for the
interests of the merchants. By 1824, however, the manufacturers
had won, except in Massachusetts. They had become more influential
than the shippers and merchants, and the section as a whole, the Bay
State still dissenting, voted, as ever since, for protection of American-
made goods instead of for free trade. If, in a rapidly growing competition, New England could not handle the produce of the West,
she would create her own, not from fields and forests but from looms,
spindles, and other machines.

One of the greatest obstacles had been the labor supply. Although
there was steady emigration and no immigration, population had,
it is true, been increasing, thanks to native fecundity, but more
slowly than elsewhere and much more slowly than was needed for
the creation of factory hands. A "model" factory town, such as
Lowell was considered for a while in the 1830's, had attracted young
women from the farms with the lure of town life for a few years,
the hope of making a dowry, or of helping father pay the mortgage.
American labor might have been induced to enter the mills, but
soon competition caused working conditions to become so much
worse that even the poorest of our farming people turned away.
Native American labor was forced out. By 1846 long black wagons
known as "slavers" cruised through New Hampshire and Vermont
in charge of men who tried to lure girls to the mills, receiving a dollar
a head for all delivered, and more if they were brought from such a
distance as would make it difficult for them to get back. By the
1840's, however, the vast stream of Irish immigration, which was
eventually to make Boston an Irish city, had got well under way.
Uncouth, often half wild, and accustomed to an extremely low standard of living, these poor creatures, willing to work for a pittance, were
exploited by the contractors and mill owners. They solved the labor
problem but created in turn a political problem. I need not here more
than mention the successive waves of immigrants of other nationalities
who came later and who overlie in successive strata the original
Yankee stock. It may be added, however, that that stock, though

hampered politically, is yet dominant in the leadership and ideals of the section. In the past century there have been many dissenting voices, but the character of the section is still that which had become "set" by 1830.

PERSISTENCE OF NEW ENGLAND LOCALISM

The coming of the railroads did little to break down the section's isolation. Whereas great systems gradually developed, leading westward from New York and Philadelphia, New England clung to her old localism. New England capital had concentrated on locally competing lines and could not be induced to enter the western trunk-line field. Charles Francis Adams, the head of the Railroad Commission of Massachusetts, in his Report in 1877 complained of the situation and stated that there could be no free flow of goods between Boston and the West so long as such localistic views prevailed as made the Hoosac Tunnel a mere "tollgate."

The old Americanism had been largely transferred to the Mississippi Valley, in part by emigrants thither from New England itself. From the election of Jackson in 1828 the thought and aspirations of the West were becoming more and more controlling in our national life. Owing to both her physical and mental isolation New England was, for better and worse, largely immune from the contagion of them.

The nation, outside New England, was beginning to think in big terms, in terms of our huge continental expanse, our unexampled natural resources, our unparalleled free-trade market area. From the swift development of the West and the boundless opportunities it offered for making fortunes we derived that buoyant optimism that has remained a national trait. We also derived that characteristic American concept of "bigger and better." To the half-dozen settlers who camped on a village site, "bigger" did legitimately connote "better." Increased population meant not only more business and higher real estate values, it meant neighbors, churches, schools, shops, a doctor perhaps. It meant the difference between stark wilderness conditions and those of a town with such amenities as civilization at that time had to offer. Long after the concept has lost its validity we have continued to carry it in our life far past the point of diminishing returns. The interest for the present essay is that, owing to local conditions, to national isolation, and to innate character, this concept, like some other American ones, carried comparatively little conviction to the stay-at-home New Englanders. They already had their facilities and strong traditions. They preferred on the whole small towns to cities. They clung to the town-meeting form of government even when they had cities, such as Boston with its population of about 45,000, much too large to be thus governed before it was finally given a city government in 1822.

New England Character and the Idea of Mass Production

For similar reasons, the idea of mass production seems never to have taken deep root in New, any more than it has in old, England. In the changing conditions of the day both Englands are facing their new crises, New England especially in the transfer of much of her textile industry to the South. How far should they follow the trend of the times?

In the first place, it may be questioned just what the trend may prove to be in a few more decades; and, secondly, whether it can pay any people to go against the genius of their particular race. In spite of the great religious changes that took place in New England in the early nineteenth century, in spite of the presence there of a vast foreign population, in spite of other changes, I think it clear that in three centuries of growth in a localized and isolated life of strongly marked character, the New Englanders have developed a distinct quality of their own. They have their own idiosyncratic outlook on and reaction to life, their own set of values. In the past they have shown at several crises that they could adapt their economic life to meet the emergency, but a shift to mass production would involve a deeper-seated dislocation of fundamental ideas than any they have yet been called upon to suffer. I speak as a historian and philosopher rather than an economist when I suggest that a shift from quality to quantity production must have a deep influence upon those engaged in it. The training, character, and ideals of New England would appear to be better adapted to the former than to the latter, as they are in old England. When the Rolls Royce Company was considering the establishment of a plant in America, every factor but one pointed to the wisdom of placing it in the West. That factor was a supply of skilled labor for a quality product. That supply could be found only in New England, and the plant was located at Springfield. Skilled labor is in large part a matter of character and tradition.

The production of an ever-enlarging number of units, at a steadily decreasing margin of profit for a steadily enlarged market, involves quite a different mental attitude and outlook from the effort to produce goods of a steadily improving quality. The former attitude and outlook are hostile to New England's traditions. Success does not come to those who do not believe. The other day, one of the most important men in one of the largest mills in New England was reported to me as saying that he was tired of steadily lowering his quality, margin, and price and that he intended to reverse the process, raising quality, margin, and price steadily until he could again take pride in his output. Nor does it seem to me at all certain that he will not find a market as well as satisfaction. In a world constantly growing richer and more and more flooded with low-grade, standardized goods, the demand for quality and beauty may also grow. Better than any other section, New England would be able to meet that demand. At any rate, she would remain true to her own genius.

CONCLUSION

In the brief suggestions that I have thrown out, I would stress three points: first, that a crisis is no new thing in New England's history and that the section has invariably surmounted previous ones; second, that it is very markedly a distinct region of culture with its own peculiar character, abilities, and ways of looking at things, developed in comparative isolation through three centuries; third, that whatever means may be adopted to bring it through its present crisis can be only such as are consonant with its genius of race and place and not a mere attempt to copy methods successful elsewhere. History and heredity are unfashionable just now. We trust to environment and change. But if we force ourselves too far, we are almost certain to become conscious, like the mill owner I have quoted, of a deep dissatisfaction, which is assuredly a bad foundation on which to build even economic success. In planning to make New England once more a happy and prosperous section its past—and its character which is the result of its past—should not be forgotten.

REGIONS AND LANDSCAPES OF NEW ENGLAND[1]

John K. Wright

IN passing through New England the observant traveler by automobile cannot fail to be struck by the rapid changes in the landscape. Within an hour or two the hard-surfaced roads of Connecticut or Massachusetts will lead him past varied scenes. First he may traverse a prosperous agricultural region of lush meadows and well tilled fields, where the houses are freshly painted, the stone walls neat, and there are ample barns and silos. Then the road will enter hills. Here the farms seem run out, walls and fences have fallen into disrepair, and the pastures are grown up to brush. The empty windows of an abandoned house strike a note of melancholy. Not far beyond, the country becomes wild, with forested hillsides, lonely lakes, and moss-lined ledges, or with swamps and scrub-covered sand flats. Then more settled country is reached, and the road enters the elm-lined street of an old village. A graceful steeple is seen through the trees. Facing the grassy "common" stand a few new buildings, usually a business block, a high school built of brick, a marble bank, or a small public library. Otherwise the village seems outwardly much as it has seemed for a hundred years. White wooden dwellings, often exquisite in their proportions and in the detailed work of their doorways and windows, stand apart from one another on shaded lawns. Beyond the village a municipal reservoir may be passed; planted rows of young white pines line its banks. The road then descends into a valley and through a gray mill town, with its massive stone or brick factory buildings.

New England is essentially a patchwork of small regions of varied character; hence the changing aspects of the landscape seen even in the course of a relatively short journey. Nature is partly responsible for these variations.[2] Much of New England is a country of ancient, worn-down mountains, a land of extremely complex rock structure. The ceaseless forces of erosion have etched out a pattern of valleys below the general levels to which the mountains were reduced far back in geological times, and the complexity of the relief reflects the complexity of the underlying rocks. The invasions and retreats of the continental ice sheets did much to accentuate the diversified quality of the surface.[3] The ice scraped off the earth and carried away pieces of rock from countless hillsides; it dropped its load in moraines, damming streams and impounding the waters in lakes and ponds. It turned rivers aside from their older channels. It scattered

---

[1] For notes see below, p. 44.

14

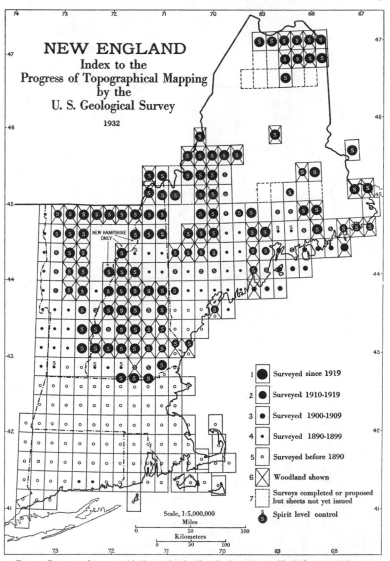

FIG. 1—Progress of topographical mapping in New England by the U. S. Geological Survey to December 1932 (see p. 45). Each rectangle represents a topographical sheet (1 : 62,500) published or an advance sheet (1 : 48,000) issued. Two symbols on one rectangle represent two separate surveys. The sheets covering Massachusetts were published in partially revised form by the Massachusetts Commission on Waterways and Public Lands in 1917. Symbol 1 where it appears in rectangles including the boundary between Massachusetts and New Hampshire indicates that the parts of these rectangles lying within New Hampshire were resurveyed and remapped in 1931. Based in part on unpublished data furnished by courtesy of the U. S. Geological Survey.

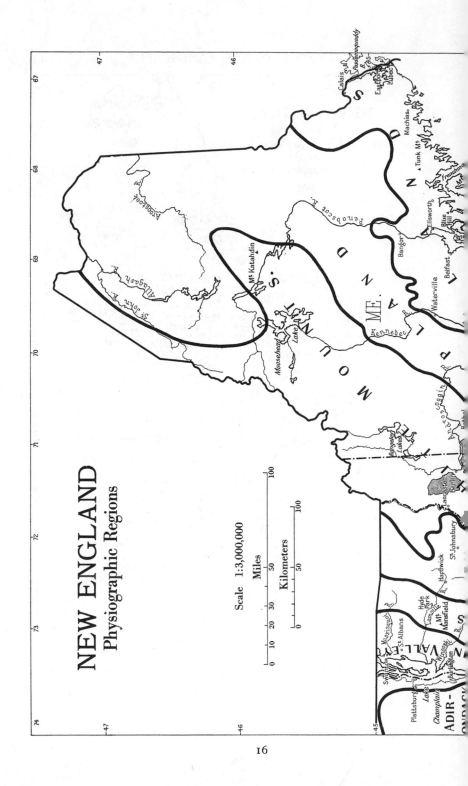

NEW ENGLAND
Physiographic Regions

Scale 1:3,000,000

Miles

Kilometers

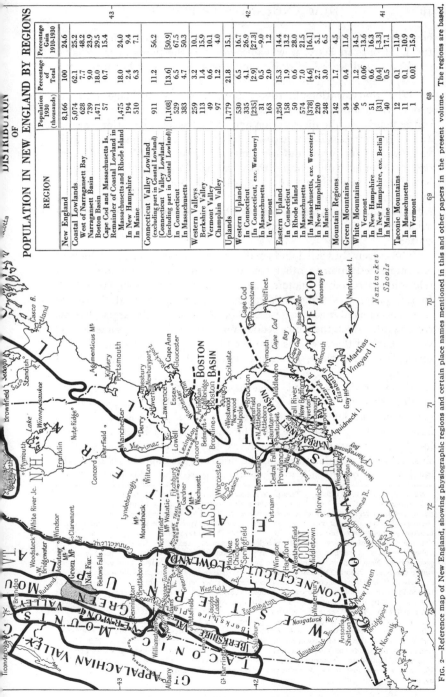

DISTRIBUTION
OF
POPULATION IN NEW ENGLAND BY REGIONS

REGION	Population 1930 (thousands)	Percentage of Total	Percentage Gain 1910-1930
New England	8,166	100	24.6
Coastal Lowlands	5,074	62.1	25.2
West of Narragansett Bay	628	7.7	48.2
Narragansett Basin	739	9.0	23.9
Boston Basin	1,471	18.0	29.5
Cape Cod and Massachusetts Is.	57	0.7	15.4
Remainder of Coastal Lowland in Massachusetts and Rhode Island	1,475	18.0	24.0
In New Hampshire	194	2.4	9.4
In Maine	510	6.3	7.1
Connecticut Valley Lowland (excluding part in Coastal Lowland)	911	11.2	56.2
[Connecticut Valley Lowland (including part in Coastal Lowland)]	[1,108]	[13.6]	[50.9]
In Connecticut	529	6.5	67.5
In Massachusetts	383	4.7	50.3
Western Valleys	259	3.2	10.1
Berkshire Valley	113	1.4	15.9
Vermont Valley	49	0.6	10.1
Champlain Valley	97	1.2	4.0
Uplands	1,779	21.8	15.1
Western Upland	530	6.5	16.7
In Connecticut	335	4.1	26.9
[In Connecticut, exc. Waterbury]	[235]	[2.9]	[27.3]
In Massachusetts	31	0.5	-9.0
In Vermont	163	2.0	1.2
Eastern Upland	1,250	15.3	14.4
In Connecticut	158	1.9	13.2
In Rhode Island	50	0.6	28.0
In Massachusetts	574	7.0	21.5
[In Massachusetts, exc. Worcester]	[378]	[4.6]	[16.1]
In New Hampshire	220	2.7	5.1
In Maine	248	3.0	6.5
Mountain Regions	142	1.7	4.5
Green Mountains	34	0.4	11.6
White Mountains	96	1.2	14.5
In Vermont	5	0.06	-13.6
In New Hampshire	51	0.6	16.3
[In New Hampshire, exc. Berlin]	[31]	[0.4]	[-3.3]
In Maine	40	0.5	17.1
Taconic Mountains	12	0.1	-11.0
In Massachusetts	11	0.1	-10.9
In Vermont	1	0.01	-15.9

FIG. 2.—Reference map of New England, showing physiographic regions and certain place names mentioned in this and other papers in the present volume. The regions are based, with additions and minor modifications of their boundaries, on the map of the "Physical Divisions of the United States" accompanying N. M. Fenneman's article cited in note 2, p. 18. See also footnote on p. 46, below. For "Narraganset" read "Narragansett"; for "Weathersfield" read "Wethersfield."

17

boulders and gravel far and wide. Its melting waters gathered along the ice fronts in lakes, now vanished. On the floors of these lakes sand and mud were laid down, and these deposits today form little plains, often terraced by postglacial streams.

With the variations in topography, soils, and drainage are associated variations in the uses to which the land may be put and, consequently, in the distribution and character of population (Fig. 4) and of industries. Large areas under present conditions are of little value except for forest and are almost entirely unsettled. In Maine one continuous tract larger than the whole state of Connecticut has scarcely more than 500 inhabitants. In southern New England, by contrast, are found some of the most densely peopled areas in the New World, although even here much land stands idle, and forested wildernesses lie within a few miles of the largest manufacturing centers.

The extremely varied and small-scale topography of New England is commented upon in other chapters of this book, and some of its relations to social, economic, and political affairs are pointed out. In this paper New England's topography as nature made it and as man has changed it will be described in terms of certain larger physical regions into which the whole section may be divided. To some degree, within each of these regions human enterprise has assumed distinctive forms, and with these forms are associated characteristic types of landscape.

Professor W. M. Davis in a classic paper on the physiography of New England wrote as follows: "Ascend a hill that reaches the general upland level, and note how even the sky line is on all sides; how moderate the inequality of the surface would be if it were not for the few mountains that rise above it, and the many valleys that sink below it. Looking around the horizon, the slightly rolling high-level surface of one hill after another approaches the plane of the

NOTE ON TABLE ON FIGURE 2—This table is based on the U. S. Census Reports. It shows the approximate population in New England of the several regions outlined on Figure 1 as well as of the portions of these regions lying within the several states. The figures for the Champlain Valley include the part of Vermont shown on the map as lying in the Great Appalachian Valley. Items in square brackets are not counted in the totals. (See also Table III, p. 427, below.)

Three quarters of all New England's population is concentrated in the Coastal and Connecticut Valley Lowlands. Less than one fiftieth is in the Mountain Regions. Gains in population slightly exceeded the New England average for the period 1910–1930 in the Coastal Lowlands as a whole and in the Boston Basin. The most notable gains occurred in the Connecticut Valley Lowland (particularly in Connecticut, where the relative increase (67.5 per cent) was more than twice that of the United States as a whole, 33.5 per cent). Population gained somewhat (15.1 per cent) on the uplands and very slightly in the mountains. The Green Mountain and Taconic Mountain regions, however, lost population. The presence of the cities of Waterbury and Worcester within the uplands of Connecticut and Massachusetts respectively and of Berlin in the White Mountain region of New Hampshire tend unduly to expand the totals for these regions for purposes of comparison. Hence figures excluding these cities are also given for the regions in which they lie. The vicinity of New Haven, Conn., may be regarded as lying either in the Coastal Lowlands or in the Connecticut Valley Lowland. Two sets of figures are therefore given for the Connecticut Valley Lowland, one from which the New Haven area is excluded to avoid duplication in the grand total and the other in which this area is included.

circular sky line. It requires but little imagination to recognize in
the successive hilltops the dissected remnants of a once even and
continuous surface."[4] A large part of New England consists of such
worn-down and dissected surfaces—broken, hilly uplands where most
of the valleys are narrow and above which there rise here and there
the stumps of once lofty mountain ranges.[5]

There are also certain areas where the streams have widened
their valleys and so far destroyed the intervening ridges that lowlands
have made their appearance. Along the coast, moreover, a zone of
varying and indefinite width must also be regarded as a lowland
country. These coastal lowlands merge imperceptibly into the
adjacent uplands and, except for their low altitude and relatively
subdued relief, are indistinguishable from the uplands in physical
character, if not in the facts of settlement and industry.

Four fundamental type areas may therefore be distinguished in
New England, in order of age: (1) residuals of the ancient mountains;
(2) dissected uplands; (3) interior lowlands; and (4) coastal lowlands.

In considering these several regions the reader should bear in
mind the fact that they are but one of many kinds of region into
which New England might be split and that some of the most important interests and connections of society cut arbitrarily across
their boundaries. The physical regions are linked together by a
network of roads and railways, and trade flows freely over them.
In respect to climate, topography, soils, and industry a Cape Cod
village seems far removed from a hill town of the Berkshire plateau,
yet both are united by a lively common interest in the fortunes of the
New York, New Haven and Hartford Railroad and in the quality
of government on Beacon Hill.

The Coastal Lowlands

On the accompanying map (Fig. 2) the line marking the inner
limit of the coastal lowlands has been drawn arbitrarily, following
in a general way the 300-foot contour line. No natural feature sepa-
rates the coastal lowlands from the uplands.

The moderating influence of the Atlantic Ocean and Long Island
Sound affects the climate of the coastal lowlands.[6] The winters are
warmer than in the interior, with less snow. Although in summer,
when the winds are from the south and southwest, even the immediate
neighborhood of the shore suffers from hot waves as extreme as elsewhere in the eastern United States (temperatures as high as 106° F.
have been recorded in Boston), the great heats are often suddenly
broken by sea breezes—Boston's famous east wind. The average
January temperature is over 20° F., and the mercury seldom falls
as low as 10° F. The growing season (Fig. 3) ranges from 130 days
in eastern Maine to nearly 200 days in southeastern Massachusetts

and averages about a month longer on the shore than fifty miles inland
on the uplands. Sea fogs, both in summer and winter, often lie along
the Atlantic coast, especially east of Penobscot Bay and wherever
promontories and islands make out to sea.

Fringing the ocean and Sound, the coastal lowlands are the most
accessible parts of New England from the outer world. All the first
settlements were planted on the seaboard. In colonial days communications by land and water were everywhere easy in the coastal
belt; and no serious obstacles, other than the Indians, hindered the
penetration of colonists to the patches of meadowland not far back
in the interior. Only where the surface of the ground becomes more
rugged as the upland country is approached was the advance of settlement temporarily halted. By 1713 the entire stretch of the coastal
lowlands south of Maine was fairly well peopled, whereas the uplands
of New Hampshire, central and western Massachusetts, western
Connecticut, and, of course, of Maine were still, almost literally,
a howling wilderness.[7]

Thus the coastal lowlands had a head start in settlement. The
advantages of location and topography that they enjoyed in colonial
days later fostered their development into one of the most densely
peopled and highly industrialized regions of North America. Some
5,000,000 people dwell on the coastal lowlands, or 62 per cent of all
the people in New England (Fig. 2, Table); and 18 of the 23 cities
of New England having more than 50,000 inhabitants lie within the
limits of this region.

To the coastal lowlands came the first settlers in colonial times,
and to their most thickly peopled portions have flowed the recent
tides of European immigration (Fig. 7). Only on the outer end of
Cape Cod and along the Maine coast does the Yankee stock still
predominate. In the large, those parts of New England where population is the densest are the parts where foreign-born and their children
comprise the largest fraction of the total population.

For more than a century the sea itself has played a decreasingly
important part in the lives of the dwellers on the coastal lowlands.
Deep-sea fishermen, to be sure, still put out from Boston and Gloucester, and the large-scale fisheries based on these ports have prospered
of late, as New England industries go.[8] There is also a good deal of
longshore fishing for lobsters and shellfish, but the great maritime
industries that were once New England's glory—whaling, oversea
shipping, and shipbuilding—are now little more than memories.[9]
The very factors that have led to the decline of certain industries,
however, have stimulated the growth of others to take their place.
The capital that was accumulated in maritime enterprises and the
executive ability that directed them were turned to the development
of manufactures. Furthermore, the coastal towns that have been

left behind by the march of modern economic progress, owing to remote location or lack of good harbors or poor facilities of communication with the interior of the continent, have preserved, largely from

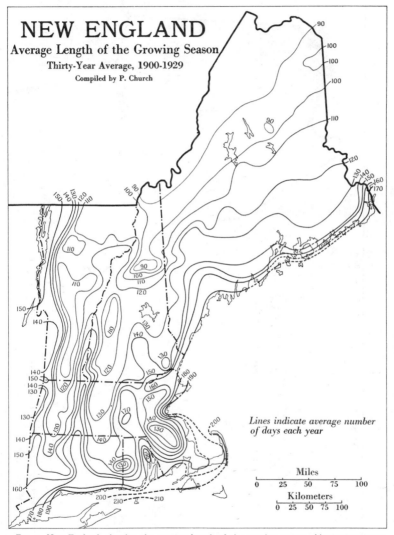

FIG. 3—New England, showing the average length of the growing season, thirty-year average, 1900–1929.

these very circumstances, qualities that now draw visitors from nearly all the cities of the nation. The "recreational industry" has become one of New England's larger sources of wealth. It is not to

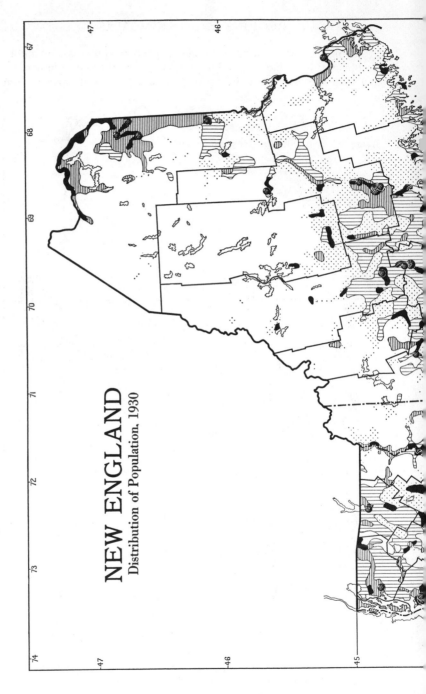

NEW ENGLAND
Distribution of Population, 1930

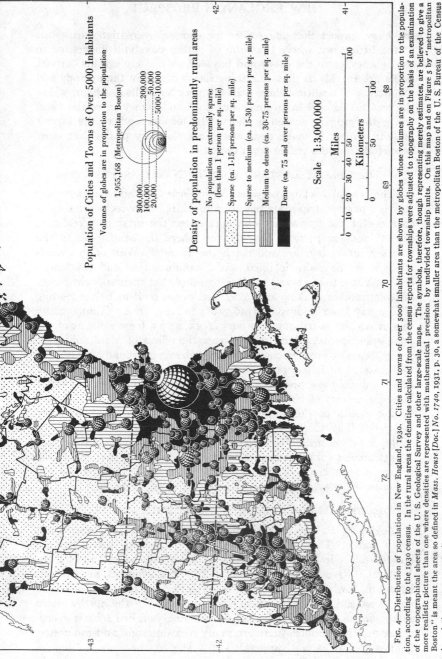

Population of Cities and Towns of Over 5000 Inhabitants

Volumes of globes are in proportion to the population

1,955,168 [Metropolitan Boston]

300,000 ....
200,000
100,000 ....
50,000
20,000 ....
5000-10,000

Density of population in predominantly rural areas

No population or extremely sparse
(less than 1 person per sq. mile)

Sparse (ca. 1-15 persons per sq. mile)

Sparse to medium (ca. 15-30 persons per sq. mile)

Medium to dense (ca. 30-75 persons per sq. mile)

Dense (ca. 75 and over persons per sq. mile)

Scale   1:3,000,000

Miles
0 10 20 30 40 50   100

Kilometers
0   50   100

FIG. 4—Distribution of population in New England, 1930. Cities and towns of over 5000 inhabitants are shown by globes whose volumes are in proportion to the population, according to the 1930 census. In the rural areas the densities calculated from the census reports for townships were adjusted to topography on the basis of an examination of the topographical sheets of the U. S. Geological Survey and other large-scale maps. The symbols, therefore, though representing merely estimates, are believed to give a more realistic picture than one where densities are represented with mathematical precision by undivided township units. On this map and on Figure 5 by "metropolitan Boston" is meant the area so defined in *Mass. House [Doc.] No. 1740, 1931*, p. 30, a somewhat smaller area than the metropolitan Boston of the U. S. Bureau of the Census (population 1930, 2,307,897).

the busy seaport that the seeker for summer recreation turns, but to the little town where the calm of earlier days still lingers, or to the beaches, or to the coves and bays where he may sail his catboat undisturbed. Much the same thing has occurred in the uplands and mountains. Localities where soils are poor and hills rise high, where the weather is cool in summer but cold and snowy in winter, and where the growing season is short—the localities where the farmer finds it hardest to make ends meet—are the very places that most powerfully lure the visitor from the cities.

The Coastal Lowland West of Narragansett Bay

The coastal lowland between New York City and Narragansett Bay is a narrow strip some ten miles in width. The rocks are similar to those of the uplands to the north—for the most part resistant crystallines, except near New Haven where the sandstones of the Connecticut Valley Lowland reach the Sound.[10] West of this sandstone area the shore is lined with manufacturing and residential cities. These towns stand so close together that their suburbs merge into one another, making an almost continuous built-up belt extending all the way from Bridgeport (146,716*) to New York. Commercially this urban belt is tributary to New York, and a large element of the population journeys daily to and from the offices of Manhattan (see p. 473, below). From Bridgeport eastward, except around New Haven, the coastal belt is less populous, although the density within half a dozen miles of the shore greatly exceeds that of the interior. The only large places east of New Haven (162,655) are New London (29,640) at the mouth of the Thames, Stonington (11,025), and Westerly (10,997). The Connecticut River, which leaves the Connecticut Valley Lowland near Middletown, enters the Sound at old Saybrook (1643) amidst rural scenery. Beyond the Thames, particularly on the granitic uplands of Rhode Island that front the open ocean, the coastal landscape becomes bleaker and more wind-swept.

Eastern Massachusetts and Eastern Rhode Island

Beginning at Narragansett Bay the coastal lowlands spread out much wider. Their inner margin turns northward, traversing the middle of Rhode Island and cutting across Massachusetts toward the Merrimac River at Manchester. In Massachusetts and Rhode Island the lowlands fall into two main subregions, a larger one to the northwest and a smaller one to the southeast. In the northwestern subregion, as generally throughout New England, bed rock is everywhere near the surface, there are many rock outcrops, and the underlying structure is well understood.[11] The southeastern subregion, consisting of Cape Cod and the Massachusetts islands, is so deeply

---

*Figures in parentheses indicate population in 1930.

buried beneath glacial deposits that very little is known of its bed rock geology. Well borings, however, have shown that Cape Cod and the islands are underlain by sedimentary deposits similar to those of the coastal plain south of New York City. Cretaceous and Tertiary deposits are disclosed at the surface in the strangely colored cliffs of Gay Head on Marthas Vineyard.[12]

The northwestern subregion is characterized by certain shallow troughs and basin-shaped depressions eroded in large part on weaker Carboniferous conglomerates, slates, sandstones, etc. The higher lands inclosing these depressions are formed by more resistant granites and other igneous rocks. Topographically there is no very marked contrast between these heights, whose general elevation ranges from 100 to 300 feet, and the depressions where the altitude is for the most part less than 200 feet. Two of the depressions, however, the Boston Basin and the Narragansett Basin, are of exceptional size and exceed other parts of the coastal lowlands in population and economic importance.

The Boston Basin. From the top of the Customs House tower, Boston's only genuine skyscraper, an unrivaled view may be had over the Boston Basin.[13] Below lies the blunt peninsula on which the older quarters of the city are built. Here, as has often been pointed out, the crowded buildings and narrow, crooked streets remind one more of an English market town than of an American metropolis. From northeast to southeast the harbor, dotted with grassy islands, opens into the unbroken reaches of Massachusetts Bay. In all other directions the middle distances are filled with roofs spreading away to the low hills that mark the Basin's rim. Southward, where the rounded domes of the Blue Hills rise above the general sky line, and from west to north, where a fretted escarpment extends from Waltham to the sea beyond Lynn, this margin is clearly defined.

Although its low-lying character is apparent in such a view, the Basin is by no means a level plain. On its floor of weak Carboniferous rocks the ice sheet deposited its load of drift. In many places these deposits present the complicated relief of ground moraines; here and there they rise as drumlins—smooth, lenticular hills between 100 and 200 feet in height. Most of the islands in Boston Harbor are drumlins, and, where exposed to the ocean surf, some of them have been cliffed by the waves. Corey Hill in Brookline is an almost perfect example of a drumlin, although its exquisitely curving sky line is now disfigured by buildings. Except for salt marshes there is little really flat ground anywhere in the Basin outside of a small area underlain by glacial clays on the outskirts of Cambridge, Belmont, and Arlington. This area not many years ago was one of the most intensively cultivated market-garden spots in New England, but its greenhouses and vegetable fields are now giving place to suburban development.

Almost no part of the Boston Basin, in fact, has preserved a rural aspect. The entire depression is filled by what is essentially one great city, although broken politically into many independent units

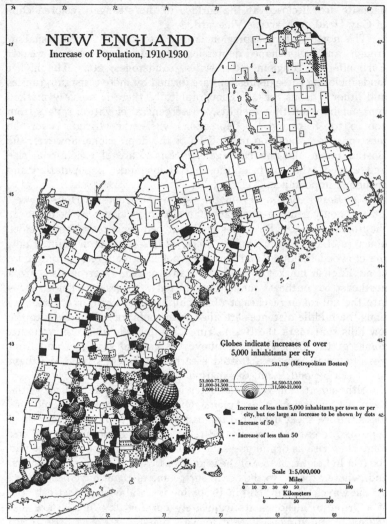

FIG. 5—Increase of population in New England, 1910–1930. This map and the map on the opposite page are directly comparable. Based on U. S. Census of 1930. See caption to Figure 4.

of local government. Throughout the metropolitan region population is everywhere increasing, except at the very core (as is true of nearly all the largest cities of the world). In the peninsular portion of old

Boston there has been a marked decrease in resident population of late years owing to displacement of dwellings by office buildings (see Fig. 3, p. 439).

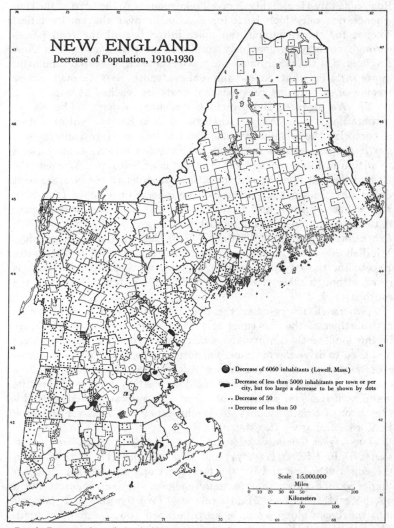

NEW ENGLAND
Decrease of Population, 1910-1930

⊙ = Decrease of 6060 inhabitants (Lowell, Mass.)

Decrease of less than 5000 inhabitants per town or per city, but too large a decrease to be shown by dots

∙∙ Decrease of 50

∙∙ Decrease of less than 50

Scale 1:5,000,000
Miles
0 10 20 30 40 50   100
Kilometers
0   50   100

Fig. 6—Decrease of population in New England, 1910–1930. Based on U. S. Census of 1930.

Metropolitan Boston, moreover, has overspread the limits of the Basin (the population of metropolitan Boston is about 1,955,000, that of the Boston Basin 1,471,000). Its long tentacles lie in the valleys that cut through the Basin's rim and run back into the upland.

Between these tentacles the higher ground is more countrified. An old turnpike, not as yet converted into a through motor highway, runs from Cambridge to Concord. At Belmont, only seven miles from Boston's State House, this Concord pike mounts to the crest of the rim, whence one may look back for a moment over the smoky cities. Thence for the remaining ten miles into Concord the road passes through country as genuinely rural and unspoiled as any in New England. On the other hand, the traveler leaving Boston on the main motor arteries that follow the valleys must pass through many leagues of suburbs before woods and fields are reached at last.

The Narragansett Basin and Its Tributary Valleys. The Narragansett Basin is much larger than the Boston Basin. Not only does it comprise the islands and mainland shores of Narragansett Bay, but it projects as a broad, shallow depression across Massachusetts to within a dozen miles of the Atlantic near Scituate. Whereas the Boston Basin is filled by a single vast metropolis, in the Narragansett Basin the cities are nearly all near the periphery: Providence (252,981), Pawtucket (77,149), and Cranston (42,911) near the western rim; Attleboro (21,769), North Attleboro (10,197), Mansfield (6364), Brockton (63,797), and Whitman (7638) close to the northern edge; Middleboro (8608) to the east; and Newport (27,612) to the south. Except for the city of Taunton (37,355), the heart of the Basin is rural, although more closely settled than the granitic heights to the southeast.

Two small rivers enter the Narragansett Basin from the west and northwest, the Pawtuxet and Blackstone[14] respectively. Early in the nineteenth century the water powers of these streams were first used to drive the machinery of cotton mills, and the valley towns, especially those of the Blackstone (Woonsocket, R. I. (49,376), Lincoln, R. I. (10,421), etc.) now hold a position among the textile manufacturing communities of New England surpassed only by the towns of Bristol County, Massachusetts (i.e. Fall River and New Bedford), and along the Merrimac.[15]

The Higher Grounds within the Coastal Lowland of Eastern Massachusetts. Fall River (115,274) and New Bedford (112,597) stand on the edges of a low and for the most part sparsely settled crescent-shaped granitic area that partially encloses the Narragansett Basin on the east. Between Middleboro and Tiverton this area falls off into the Basin along a gentle scarp between 100 and 200 feet high. The city of Fall River is built on the face of this slope. Some of the mills stand on the upper level, others along the water front at the base of the scarp.[16] The water power of a small stream, the Quequechan (or Fall) River, that once coursed down the scarp, first attracted cotton manufacturers to this site, but now only 7 per cent of the power used in the mills is local water power.[17] Of all New England textile towns Fall River and Lowell have suffered the most from the difficulties encountered by the textile industry during the past twenty years, and both have lost population. The old whaling city of New Bedford, on a fine harbor on the Buzzards Bay side of the granitic area, turned to cotton when whaling declined. Like Fall River, New Bedford has also suffered from the depression in the textiles but has nevertheless held its own in population.

North of Boston, the lower Merrimac from its eastward bend nearly to the sea at Newburyport follows a narrow trough eroded out on Carboniferous rocks. The manufacturing centers in this trough along the Merrimac—Lowell (100,234), Lawrence (85,068), Haverhill (48,710), Amesbury (11,899)—constitute an important secondary nucleus of population. The cotton-manufacturing city of Lowell and the wool-manufacturing city of Lawrence both lost in population between 1910 and 1930; during this period more people moved away from Lowell than from any other place in New England. The other Merrimac cities enjoyed moderate gains.

Between this urban nucleus on the Merrimac and the northern edge of metropolitan Boston lies a tract of truly rural country where population has also been decreasing. Toward the ocean this rural country gives way on the north to salt marshes and dune-covered barrier beaches but farther south extends seaward in the boulder-strewn granite headland of Cape Ann. Here, too, population has dwindled in the coast towns of Gloucester (24,204), Rockport (3630), and Essex (1465). The "North Shore" between Cape Ann and Lynn has been a summer resort of wealthy Bostonians since early in the nineteenth century.[18]

Cape Cod and the Massachusetts Islands. The whole of Cape Cod and the adjacent mainland east of a line drawn from Plymouth to the head of Buzzards Bay, together with the Elizabeth Islands, Marthas Vineyard, and Nantucket, are lands almost wholly made by the continental ice sheet and its melting waters and in part refashioned by sea and wind.[19] The glacial deposits here bear witness to two stages in the recession of the ice. The earlier stage is marked by the terminal moraines and outwash plains of Marthas Vineyard and Nantucket; the more recent by two terminal moraines on Cape Cod— the Cape Cod moraine, which runs along the southern shore of Cape Cod Bay from Orleans as far as the isthmus that joined the Cape with the mainland before a canal was cut through, and the Falmouth moraine, which joins the Cape Cod moraine at this point and passes down the eastern shore of Buzzards Bay to swing southwestward as the Elizabeth Islands. The terminal moraine on Marthas Vineyard attains an altitude of 300 feet, but nowhere do the moraines on the Cape much exceed 200 feet in elevation. Buzzards Bay and Cape Cod Bay were probably occupied by two separate lobes of ice, whose

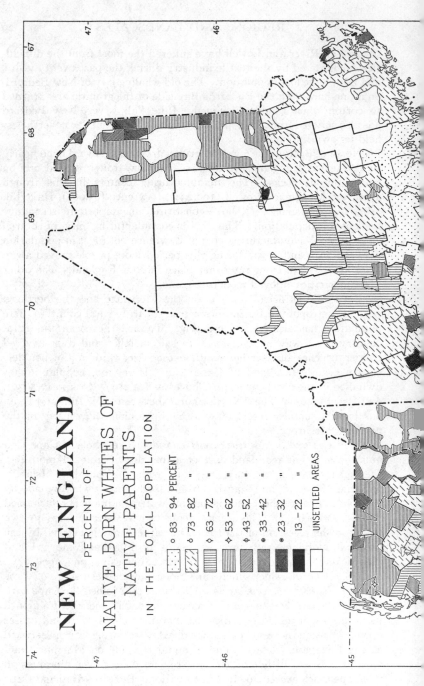

NEW ENGLAND

PERCENT OF

NATIVE BORN WHITES OF
NATIVE PARENTS

IN THE TOTAL POPULATION

- ° 83 – 94 PERCENT
- ◊ 73 – 82 "
- ◊ 63 – 72 "
- ◇ 53 – 62 "
- φ 43 – 52 "
- ⊕ 33 – 42 "
- ⊙ 23 – 32 "
- 13 – 22 "

UNSETTLED AREAS

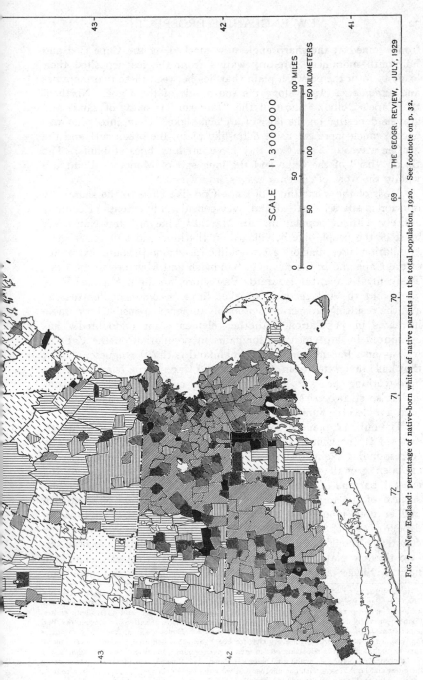

SCALE 1:3000000

0 50 100 150 KILOMETERS
0 50 69 70 71 72 100 MILES

THE GEOGR. REVIEW, JULY, 1929

Fig. 7.—New England: percentage of native-born whites of native parents in the total population, 1920. See footnote on p. 32.

fronts joined at the sharp angle now marked by the Cape Cod and
Falmouth moraines. Melting waters from the ice deposited their
loads to form the outwash plain that lies between these two moraines
and extends eastward along the south side of the Cape. North of
the Cape's "elbow" most of the "forearm" is made of sands and
gravels deposited on the floor of a glacial lake. Here, into what was
once a much more extensive delta-like plain, the ocean surf and the
gentler waves of Cape Cod Bay have cut long lines of bluffs. The
tip or "fist" of the Cape and the long spit of Monomoy Point are
wholly the work of currents, waves, and winds.

Most of the inhabitants of Cape Cod live close to the shore; the
interior is sparsely settled and over considerable extents of country
entirely without population. In Marthas Vineyard and Nantucket
most of the people live in villages on the inner sides of the islands.
Population is receding or barely holding its own on the outer extremity
of the Cape and in the towns of Sandwich and Mashpee to the west.
The central Cape, the Buzzards Bay shore, northern Marthas Vineyard, and the village of Nantucket have become popular resorts,
and the resulting prosperity is probably in part responsible for notable
increases in population. Another element that undoubtedly has
accounted in large measure for gains in population on the Cape as
well as on adjacent parts of the mainland is the Portuguese, a stock
that has immigrated from the Azores and Cape Verde Islands. These
hard-working peasant folk successfully cultivate cranberry bogs
and raise strawberries and vegetables on sandy soils that had long
been avoided by Yankee farmers.[20]

The outwash plains of southern Marthas Vineyard and Nantucket,
exposed to the winds of the ocean, form broad grassy heaths. The
corresponding plains on Cape Cod are clothed over wide areas with
an open growth of pitch pines (*Pinus rigida*) reminiscent of the
coastal barrens of New Jersey and the South. Over the knobby
surface of the terminal moraines spreads a desolation of scrub oak
and stunted pine through which forest fires run wild in times of
drought. Much of the "forearm" of the Cape is a bleak grassy
country, although woods fill the narrow ravines that have been cut
into the low plateau formed by the glacial-lake deposits. The long
narrow village of Provincetown clings to its harbor and would un-

NOTE ON FIGURE 7—This map was published in the *Geographical Review*, Vol. 19, 1929, pp. 482-483.
The U. S. Census reports for 1920 give for counties, cities, and certain towns the number of native
whites of native parentage, native whites of foreign or mixed parentage, and foreign-born whites.
Figure 6 shows by different symbols the percentages of native whites of native parentage in the total
population, *the lighter the tint the higher being the percentage indicated.* The appropriate percentages
for 1920 are plotted separately for every city, for every town that had a population of over 2500 in
1910 or 1920, and for the remaining settled area of every county, unsettled areas (including minor
civil divisions of less than 50 inhabitants) being left blank. It is thus possible from the map to compare
the cities and larger towns with one another and with the less thickly settled parts of each county,
but it is not possible to compare individual small towns. In the 1930 census reports, it should be noted,
data are given from which a map could be prepared showing the percentages for every township.

doubtedly be overwhelmed by the shifting dunes when northeasters sweep the coast were it not for constant vigilance on the part of the Commonwealth of Massachusetts in maintaining an anchoring growth of grass on the state-owned Province Lands that lie between the village and the outer beach.

Along the coves and harbors of Cape Cod Bay, Buzzards Bay, and Nantucket Sound cluster neat villages and hamlets with their old weather-beaten houses. The waters in summer are alive with the sails of yachts, and the beaches with bathers. One may fairly estimate that the population of the Cape in July and August is twice that of winter.

On the outer end of the Cape and the seaward sides of the islands the landscape is wilder. Buildings are scattered—at most a few camps and cottages, with here and there a lonely lighthouse or life-saving station. The Atlantic surf beats on the long yellow beaches.[21] Scarcely a mile of these outer shores has not at one time or other been the scene of a shipwreck.[22]

The Coastal Lowlands of New Hampshire and Maine

North of the Merrimac River the coastal lowlands in New Hampshire and Maine may be divided at the Kennebec River into two subregions. The coast of the southern region runs on the whole fairly straight. Beaches with dunes and tidal marshes behind them succeed rocky headlands as far north as Casco Bay. Some of the beaches have been developed as resorts of the cheaper type. On the headlands stand the cottages of wealthier summer residents. While there are no large cities either on the shore or in the interior, there are many places of between 5000 and 40,000 inhabitants. The principal harbor towns—Portland (70,810), Portsmouth (14,495), and Bath (9110)—like other medium-sized coast towns of New England, give one the impression of age and of a substantial and enduring if moderate prosperity. In the older quarters square wooden dwellings with central chimneys abut directly on the streets; distinguished colonial mansions of the Tory aristocracy stand amidst shady gardens. These towns today suggest what Boston or New York or Philadelphia must have looked like in the eighteenth century.[23]

The inner portions of the coastal lowlands in New Hampshire and southern Maine constitute one of the important secondary industrial areas of New England. There are no great manufacturing centers except Manchester, N. H. (76,834); but on all the larger streams between the Merrimac and the Kennebec mill towns of second and third rank are found where falls or rapids occur. Most of these industrial towns have experienced slight gains in population recently, but the farming communities have almost everywhere declined.

From Casco Bay and the Kennebec eastward the character both

of coast and interior alters. Subsidence of the land has allowed tide waters to enter the valleys of the dissected lowland. Deep fiords run far inland, long narrow promontories jut out to sea, and there is a maze of channels passing among islands. In this region population is concentrated along the coast; there is no industrial zone. But while the essential features of the coast line are alike all the way from Portland to Passamaquoddy Bay, the inland region differs east and west of Penobscot Bay. West of Penobscot Bay one of the principal farming districts of New England spreads back from the coastal lowland into the adjoining uplands, here much less rugged than farther west and south. East of the Bay farming is conducted on a very small scale. The central and northern parts of Hancock and Washington counties are a vast wilderness where blueberry barrens fringe the margins of the forest.

In almost every town of this region, but especially in the communities along the coast, population has long been falling off. Fishing brings but a scanty return. As the forests have been depleted, there are now no longer cargoes for the lumber schooners that formerly put out from many a landlocked harbor.[24] The hope of finding better opportunities has lured away the more ambitious boys and girls from coastwise village and upland farm alike.[25] As far east as Mt. Desert Island the shore has for many decades been a favorite summer resort, and the dwindling native population has derived material benefit from this fact. The slight increase in population in two towns on Mt. Desert, as on parts of Cape Cod, reflects the prosperity brought by summer visitors. Beyond Frenchman's Bay the waters are colder, fogs more frequent, tidal currents stronger, and the region is far from urban centers. Relatively few summer people come to this remote eastern shore, and the old towns are still much as they were a half century ago.

Between Casco Bay and Penobscot Bay the eastbound traveler enters the domain known to foresters as the spruce-hardwoods region (Fig. 1, p. 214, below) and finds that the landscape begins to wear a more northern aspect. This is the "country of the pointed firs"; spruces and firs crown the rocky islets and hilltops. They loom black out of the fog banks or stand sharp against the hard, cold sunsets of northern New England when the northwest wind has swept the fog out to sea.

THE LOWLANDS OF THE INTERIOR

There are six principal lowlands in New England eroded on relatively weak rocks. Two of these, the Boston and Narragansett basins, have already been described. The remaining four form long narrow trenches that run north and south and are enclosed on nearly all sides by uplands. These are the Connecticut Valley Lowland of

Connecticut and Massachusetts and the Champlain, Vermont, and Berkshire valleys along the western border.

The Connecticut Valley Lowland. The Connecticut Valley Lowland is a lens-shaped trench extending from the northern boundary of Massachusetts to Long Island Sound at New Haven. Its extreme southern end, as already explained, lies within the coastal lowlands. Throughout most of its length it is drained by the Connecticut River, but near Middletown, Conn., the main stream turns aside to the southeast to make its way to the Sound through a gorge cut across the southwestern corner of the Eastern Upland.

Weak, red sandstones give a ruddy tint to the soils and to stone walls and buildings where the native rock has been used. As in the similar lowland of northern New Jersey, the uptilted edges of Triassic lava flows and intrusive sills make a succession of narrow curving "trap" ridges that run longitudinally through the lowland.[26] These wooded ridges dominate the landscape, presenting their bolder aspect toward the west where their cliffed borders rise precipitously in places from the lowland floors.

The climate in the Connecticut Valley Lowland is milder than on the uplands to the east and west. The growing season along the Connecticut averages well over a month longer than at stations thirty miles to the east and west (Fig. 3).

The rich soils, the generally level surface, and the favorable climate attracted settlers to the Connecticut Valley long before the stonier, colder uplands were occupied. Hartford, Wethersfield, Windsor, and Springfield were settled before 1637.[27] By 1675 an almost continuous line of farms and villages lined the river from Middletown to Northfield.[28] Communications were easy from Saybrook up the river or from New Haven north. Until the rise of the potato industry in Aroostook the lowland was almost the only large tract in New England where commercial farming could be practiced on anything approaching a grand scale, and the lowland still retains its preeminence as a region of specialized agriculture, producing tobacco, vegetables, and fruits. Farming, however, is now overshadowed by manufacturing. Water power at such points as Greenfield (15,500), Holyoke (56,537), and Chicopee (43,390) was an important factor in the early industrial development of the Connecticut Valley Lowland; but a larger factor has been its location about halfway between two of the largest urban markets in the country—Boston and New York.

As a center of New England's population the Connecticut Valley Lowland stands second only to eastern Massachusetts and Rhode Island. There are three chief nuclei, surrounding Springfield (149,900), Hartford (164,072), and New Haven (162,655). From every economic point of view if not physiographically the busy mill towns of the

Naugatuck Valley, which parallels the Connecticut Valley Lowland a few miles within the margin of the Western Upland, belong in the lowland. As on the map showing the distribution of population (Fig. 4), the lowland and the Naugatuck Valley stand out by contrast with the neighboring uplands on the map depicting the composition of the population (Fig. 7). Factory and field alike have attracted to this region immigrants from eastern and southern Europe.

Except for the textile- and paper-manufacturing city of Holyoke, Mass., no town in the entire Connecticut Valley Lowland lost population between 1910 and 1930, and the gains were nearly everywhere substantial.[29] The region is one of diversified manufactures; and its factory towns, by contrast to the more exclusively textile towns farther east, have enjoyed a stability and conservative prosperity that account in part for their steady growth. Indeed, the relative gain in population that occurred in the lowland during the twenty years 1910–1930 exceeded that of any other region in New England (see Fig. 2, Table).

In its rural aspects the Connecticut Valley Lowland is a little exotic for New England.[30] There is a suggestion of the South in the broad, open meadows, the reddish soils, the tobacco and onion fields, and of Europe in the vineyards and the bronzed foreign women and children at work on the land. The bold green slopes and dark cliffs of the trap ridges add a touch of wildness. Immense cheese-cloth tents spread over the tobacco fields and the great wooden sheds in which the tobacco is stored bear witness to a costly and intensive type of farming different from anything found on the New England uplands.[31] But the manufacturing cities with their tall factory chimneys and endless streets lined with small workers' houses are typical enough of industrial New England.

The Western Lowland Trenches. The Champlain, Vermont, and Berkshire valleys, shut off on the east by the Green Mountains and the high rim of the Berkshire plateau, are somewhat like worlds apart. The Champlain Valley is a segment of the Great Appalachian Valley, a structural depression that extends all the way from Alabama to Canada and is continued northward in the St. Lawrence Valley. During the glacial period the waters of Lake Champlain at various epochs stood much higher than is now the case, and in postglacial times the Champlain Valley was invaded by an arm of the sea that once filled the St. Lawrence Valley.[32] Sedimentary deposits were laid down in these waters. The level floors of these deposits, below which streams in glacial and postglacial times have carved deep ravines, now form one of the most prosperous dairy-farming regions of New England. The Champlain Valley reaches west as far as the Adirondacks, but its New England side is separated from the part in New York state by the southward-tapering Lake Champlain.

From the grounds of the University of Vermont, on the rim of a terrace on which Burlington is built, there is a view of the Champlain Valley that lingers long in the memory of those who have seen it. One may look across the city and the broad expanse of the lake to the bold crests of the Adirondacks. Eastward, beyond a placid farming country rise the "soft and comfortable" shapes of the Green Mountains.

The Vermont and Berkshire valleys are deep trenches eroded along a winding belt of calcareous rocks between the Green Mountains and Berkshire plateau on the east and the long ridge of the Taconics to the west. From Brandon, Vt., the Vermont Valley[33] runs south as far as the Massachusetts line, whence the Berkshire Valley extends to Salisbury, Conn. The northern half of the Vermont Valley is watered by Otter Creek, a tributary of Lake Champlain; its southern half and the northern part of the Berkshire Valley by streams that cut through the Taconics to the Hudson; and the southern Berkshire Valley by the headwaters of the Housatonic. From Pittsfield northward neither valley is anywhere much more than six miles wide, but south of Pittsfield the Berkshire Valley opens out in the meadowlands of Great Barrington, Lenox, and Sheffield. At Salisbury the Housatonic enters into a narrow gorge in the Western Upland.

Owing largely to the tempering influence of the lake, no part of northern New England except the far northeastern coast of Maine has such mild winters, so little snow, and such a long growing season as the Champlain Valley. The Vermont and Berkshire valleys, where the altitude is higher and there is no large body of water, are less favored, but by comparison with the bleak uplands a few miles away they are pockets of warmth.

Except for a few small manufacturing towns—notably Pittsfield (49,677), North Adams (21,621), and Adams (12,697) in the Berkshire Valley, Bennington (10,628) and Rutland (17,315) in the Vermont Valley, and Burlington (24,789), Winooski (5308), and St. Albans (8020) in the Champlain Valley—these western lowlands are a region of dairy farming *par excellence*. Population, although denser than on the adjoining uplands, is far less concentrated than in the Triassic Lowland. Pittsfield enjoyed a substantial gain between 1910 and 1930, and slight gains were recorded in the other larger towns, except Adams and North Adams. The farming communities suffered a decline, though the losses in proportion to the total number of inhabitants were not as severe as those that have generally occurred on the uplands.

Politically within New England, these western lowlands have many historical and economic connections with New York. The advancing frontier of settlement reached them relatively late. Before 1754 people from New England and New York had established a few

isolated communities in the Berkshire Valley, but the two valleys
to the north were still unoccupied.[34] Even at the close of the Revolution the greater part of the Vermont side of the Champlain Valley
was a wilderness.[35] A minority of the settlers in all three valleys came
from New York. In another chapter Dr. Gerish has shown that at the
present time the trade of Berkshire County, Massachusetts, is linked
largely with Albany (p. 398, below). The dairy farms of the entire
region send most of their milk to New York City.

THE UPLANDS

The uplands of New England fall into two belts east and west
of the Connecticut River; the Eastern Upland and the Western
Upland. The southern ends of these belts, as already stated, reach
nearly to Long Island Sound. From here northward to the northern
border of Massachusetts the uplands are separated from each other
by the Connecticut Valley Lowland, but farther north they adjoin
along the Connecticut. While the Connecticut in the northern half
of its course follows a zone of relatively weak slates and slaty schists,[36]
the valley is here more like a narrow slot cut below the upland surface
than like the broad lowland into which it opens to the south.

The dissected surface of the Western Upland ascends as one goes
north and also as one goes west from the rim of the Connecticut
Valley Lowland. The southern part of the upland extends beyond
the Connecticut-New York line almost to the Hudson. In Massachusetts the Western Upland forms a plateau that falls off in an abrupt
escarpment into the Berkshire Valley. This plateau, the higher part
of which is over 2000 feet above sea level, has been deeply cut by
streams flowing southeast to the Connecticut—the Deerfield, Westfield, and Farmington rivers and their branches. The Deerfield in particular has carved for itself an impressive canyon-like valley, whose
floor at the entrance of the Hoosac Tunnel lies some 1200 to 1400 feet
below the plateau surface. Although structurally the bed rocks
of this Berkshire plateau are a southward continuation of the Green
Mountain axis, physiographically the mountain region ends in
southern Vermont near the Massachusetts line. The character of
settlement also differs in the mountain region and on the plateau.
The former is forested, with villages only in the valleys. On the
plateau, farms and hamlets are found almost up to the highest levels
(the villages of Florida and Peru, Mass., are at altitudes of over
2000 feet). In Vermont the Western Upland is a tract of rugged
country that extends north to the Canadian line.

The dissected surfaces of the Eastern Upland rise gradually from
southern Connecticut northward across Massachusetts and New
Hampshire to abut against the White Mountains[37] at altitudes of
between 1000 and 2000 feet. They also ascend from their eastern

and western margins to a series of irregular longitudinal crest lines,[38] above which, in Massachusetts and New Hampshire, rise isolated mountains, the remnants of once much loftier peaks. Monadnock (3166 feet) the noblest of these, has given its name as a generic term for such residuals wherever found.

In Maine the Eastern Upland swings off to the northeast and encircles a great prolongation of the White Mountain region. Over central and eastern Maine the upland surface is less accentuated than farther west and south, and it is perhaps doubtful whether much of this region should, strictly speaking, be regarded as an upland. The farm lands between the Kennebec and the Penobscot lie in a shallow basin that seems to be continued northeastward into New Brunswick.[39] On the southeast this basin is bounded by higher ground overlooked by isolated monadnocks in the vicinity of Penobscot Bay and extending northeastward as the wilds of Hancock and Washington counties. The uninhabited forest solitudes of the Allegash and St. John valleys of far northern Maine also constitute a great shallow basin. The potato country of Aroostook County is formed by the alluvial flats along the middle valley of the St. John and its tributary, the Aroostook River.[40]

In summer there is not a great deal of difference between the climate of the uplands and that of the lowlands, but in winter the contrast is marked.[41] The winters, especially in western Massachusetts and in northern New England as a whole, are long and hard. On the uplands of central New Hampshire and Vermont the first killing frosts wither the gardens early in September; snow flurries come in October; the ground is often covered with its permanent winter blanket by mid-November. Nearly every year during the cold waves of January and February the temperature will fall occasionally as low as 20° or 30° below zero (Fahrenheit). The springs are delayed; the snow does not melt nor the ice break up until late in March; and killing frosts occur into the latter part of May. This represents the average for the uplands; farther north conditions become more severe, farther south less so. The narrow upland valleys are sometimes visited by floods.[42] The flood of November, 1927, was particularly destructive both of life and of property in Vermont and New Hampshire. Such visitations are fortunately rare, and New England on the whole has been spared from natural calamities of the types that work wholesale devastation.

The winters, combined with the stony, recalcitrant soils, and the broken topography, long held population back from the uplands. Not until about 1800 had settlement reached its ultimate borders,[43] which do not, even today, comprise the entire upland zone in Maine. The uplands, moreover, were scarcely occupied before the same factors that had for so long retarded the advance of settlement helped reverse the tide. These physical circumstances, combined with the impact of western competition and the lure of the mill towns, account for the depopulation of the farming communities of almost the entire upland region that has been going on for a century.[44] The last chapters of this often-told story are eloquently summarized by the dots on Figure 6. A map for 1850 showing the distribution of population in the uplands would have presented much less the appearance of a patchwork than does Figure 4, for 1930.[45] The population in 1850 was more evenly spread. Now most of the people dwell in manufacturing towns in the valleys of the larger streams. Two of these towns, Worcester, Mass. (195,311), and Waterbury, Conn. (99,902), are among the larger cities of New England, but they lie so close to the margins of the uplands and in such easy reach of the lowlands that they can hardly be regarded from the industrial point of view as belonging to the upland region. It is not necessary to mention in detail the many smaller cities of the uplands. They are found along the main rivers and many of the branches. Most of them, as will be seen from Figure 4, form centers of small areas comprising one or two neighboring townships in which population has increased of late. It seems likely that these gains are due primarily to the almost universal use of the automobile. In these areas the farmers and their families have found a supplementary source of income by working in the mills, now easily reached by car. Hence they have been less tempted to move out than their neighbors farther back in the hills. Moreover, in some instances mill hands have purchased for residence use farms within twenty miles or so of the factories in which they work. This movement deserves further study.[46] It is symptomatic of a process that in time may be expected to work widespread changes in rural New England.

With the coastal lowlands of Maine outside of the manufacturing centers, the uplands are the regions of purest native stock in New England. This is especially true of the farming communities of Maine and Vermont, except toward the north where French- and British-Canadians have come in. In central New Hampshire, Massachusetts, and Connecticut, where industrial influences are felt, the percentages of foreign stock are considerably higher. In the uplands of Massachusetts and Connecticut, especially, there are many immigrants and their children not only in the mill towns but on the farms.[47] Western Rhode Island forms a curious island of relatively undiluted Yankee stock (Fig. 7).

The uplands of all parts of New England reveal the characteristic small-scale topography. The description of the landscape given in the opening paragraph of this paper would apply with minor modifications to the uplands of New England generally. In the three northern states longer stretches of wild land intervene between the towns than farther south. In central Maine the country seems more open and spacious. The rivers of the north are often filled with floating logs. In the mill towns within reach of the northern forest immense piles of four-foot logs, like miniature mountains, tower above the mill buildings, and the odor of wood and of the chemicals used in reducing wood to pulp hangs on in the air.

In western Maine and throughout New Hampshire the percentage of the total area in farms and crop land is less than in central Maine (see Figs. 1 and 2, pp. 142–143, below). This, perhaps, is largely because the soils tend to be more stony.[48] Hence the countryside appears wilder, and the roads pass for greater distances through second-growth woodland.

The uplands in eastern Vermont are still different. Although the topography is, if anything, more broken, the soils are richer and not so stony as in New Hampshire, and the relative acreage of cultivated ground and pasture is larger. East-central Vermont is a mellow land of narrow valleys and great bulging hills, with pastures running high up their sides. Farther north the hills stand farther apart. One may often look across field and forest to blue mountains.

THE MOUNTAIN REGIONS

These mountains, which the traveler sees rising serenely above the New England uplands, are, as already stated, the worn-down stumps of ranges that were once of Alpine character.

Outside of the Green and the White Mountains they occur only as isolated monadnocks or as short isolated ranges. The White Mountains lie near the center of three great trains of monadnocks, crowning the Eastern Upland. One extends south into Massachusetts, another northeast into Maine where it culminates in the remote ridge of Katahdin (5268 feet), and the third is carried north-northeastward along the international boundary between Maine and Canada. The Western Upland in Vermont is also overlooked by several monadnocks, the most prominent being the sharp peak of Ascutney (3144 feet), which rises above the Connecticut River near Windsor. Scattered monadnocks are also found in the coastal lowlands from the Blue Hills (635 feet) of Massachusetts north. Agamenticus (692 feet) in York County, Maine, commands a wide view of the ocean and White Mountains. There is a cluster in the neighborhood of Penobscot Bay; the bold Camden Hills (1380 feet) form a range along the west side of the Bay; Blue Hill (940 feet) stands alone, dominating the country between the Penobscot Bay and Blue Hill Bay, and Tunk Mountain (1157 feet) with its outlying hills lies to the northeast on the edge of the wilderness. The short steep parallel ridges of Mt. Desert Island (1532 feet), separated from one another by deep mountain lakes and the fiord of Somes Sound, are the highest lands on

the Atlantic coast of the United States.[49] Here the summer visitor
may climb mountains in the morning and enjoy a sail on the open
Atlantic in the afternoon of the same day.

The Green and the White Mountains constitute the only mountain
regions of New England in the strict sense of the term. Here alone
mountains fill the greater part of the total area. In the Green Mountains the principal and loftiest range (maximum altitude, Mt. Mansfield, 4393 feet) runs the entire length of Vermont and is continued
on through Canada as far as New Brunswick.[50] Northward from
central Vermont this main range is paralleled to the east by lesser
ranges. In spite of the fact that the west-flowing Missisquoi, Lamoille,
and Winooski rivers have cut deep valleys through the ranges, the
Green Mountains constitute a very real barrier between the eastern
and western sides of the state. This barrier has figured in Vermont
politics in an old and only recently broken custom of choosing the
Republican candidate for governor (and the Republican candidate
has always been elected) alternately from east and from west of the
mountains.

In a physiographic sense, although not in local terminology,
the White Mountain region (maximum altitude, Mt. Washington,
6288 feet)[51] comprises northern New Hampshire, the northeastern
corner of Vermont (Essex Co.), and the adjacent parts of northwestern Maine. The pronounced range-like character so marked in
the Green Mountains is entirely lacking in the White Mountains, which
consist of a group of short ridges that trend, with many exceptions,
somewhat east of north by west of south. These ridges are surrounded
by deep valleys. The wider valleys, those of the upper Connecticut,
Androscoggin, Saco, and Pemigewasset (upper Merrimac), were
filled with glacial lakes whose flat floors now make meadowlands
locally known as "intervales." The best farm lands in the mountain
region are almost wholly confined to the intervales, where level
hayfields, winding streams, graceful elms, and grazing cattle seem
sheltered by the forested slopes that rise above them on every side.

The climate of the mountain regions requires no special comment.
It is essentially like that of the uplands, though rainier[52] and cooler
in summer and snowier and colder in winter.

Of all parts of New England these mountain regions, together
with the "wild lands" of Maine, have the fewest people. Except for
the wider valleys they are almost without permanent population,
although often the temporary home of lumbermen and much visited
in summer and autumn by sportsmen and trampers.

The even texture of their wooded slopes is in few places broken
by grassland or pasture, and the aspect is somewhat somber except in
spring and in autumn when the forests are aflame with color. On
the mountains of central Europe there are high pastures where cattle

graze at altitudes as lofty as the top of Mt. Washington. In the New England mountains the endless uniformity of the forest is broken only where fire and the logging crew have passed. Recent cut or burned slopes often show as ruddy or brownish scars, but where second-growth hardwoods have come in to heal the scars the lighter greens of the foliage stand out against the dark tints of the conifers.

The crests of Mt. Mansfield in Vermont and of the White Mountains above altitudes of about 4500 feet are bleak wastes of rock, except where scanty accumulations of earth have permitted the growth of arctic plants.[53]

In many mountain regions of the world distinctive types of economic and social activity have developed and with them modes of life quite different from those of the surrounding country. In New England this has not been the case. There are no New England "mountaineers" comparable to the Alpine highlanders or the mountaineers of Kentucky and North Carolina. There are no "mountain industries." The mountain villages of New England are like the villages of the New England uplands generally, and the native of the White or Green Mountains is scarcely distinguishable from his neighbor who dwells outside their limits. If he is a farmer his technique of farming and mental outlook are much the same. His farm generally lies in a valley or on foothills, seldom on the mountain side itself. The heights that look down on his fields and pastures mean little to him except as a place where he may go now and then to hunt or set out traps or pick berries or fight forest fires, or as a lure to the summer boarder whose cash helps him eke out his income.

The only people who derive the greater part of their livelihood from work actually done on the mountain sides are the lumbermen— French Canadians, Nova Scotians, Prince Edward Islanders, Finns, with Yankee overseers—here one year and gone the next. Logging camps are built in the higher forested valleys and on the lower mountain slopes and are connected with the outer world by "tote roads," often of "corduroy" construction, and in places by logging railways. From the camps a network of rough "drag roads" is carried as high as it is feasible to cut. Usually the only virgin forest that has been left is the tangled and almost impenetrable stunted growth of balsam fir and spruce that crowns the upper ridges and peaks. The logs are drawn down the drag roads to yards where they are scaled, sorted, sawed, and whence they are either floated downstream to the mills or shipped out by logging railroad. Twenty or thirty years ago it was customary to "drive" long logs down the streams—great spars 20 or 30 feet in length. These often gathered in formidable jams; and skill, with some heroism, was often required to clear the rivers. Now that the pulpwood is generally cut to more manageable four-foot lengths much of the romance of the log drive has passed.[54]

After the logging operations have been completed, the woods-men move on, the camps fall to ruin, and the logging roads grow up to a tangle of undergrowth. Some roadbeds of the abandoned logging railways, however, have been converted into automobile roads that now afford access to summer camps. A large part of the White Mountain region in New Hampshire and a small area in the Green Mountains have been included in National Forests, and the devasta-tion wrought a generation ago by fire and ruthless cutting has nearly everywhere been checked by the introduction of more adequate fire control and more conservative methods of cutting.

To all the mountain summits except those far from civilization trails have been cut through the forest and marked by cairns on the open ridges. In summer an ever increasing army of climbers toil up these trails. Many years ago a cog railway and a good stage road were built to the top of Mt. Washington. For a few weeks every summer they bring to this culminating peak hundreds of visitors from all parts of the nation to look out across the broad expanses of "New England's prospect."

NOTES

[1] In these notes selected references are given to publications in which the physical features of New England are described and to a limited number of popular works that, by reason of their comprehensive character, their literary charm, or the excel-lence of their illustrations contribute something of substantial value to an under-standing of the outward aspects of the region. This introductory note deals with maps, bibliographies, and general descriptive works.

Maps. The Boston, the Hudson River, and the Montreal sheets of the Inter-national Millionth Map of the World (about 16 miles to the inch) show all of New England except the portion lying north of latitude 44° N. and east of longitude 72° W.—in other words, all but northeastern Vermont, northern New Hampshire, and Maine north of Cumberland County. The Boston and the Hudson River sheets were published by the U. S. Geological Survey in 1912 and 1927, respectively, and the Montreal sheet by the Chief Geographer, Department of the Interior, Ottawa, 1929. These are the best medium-scale maps of New England upon which altitudes are shown (by hypsometric tints bounded by the 100, 200, 300, 400, 500, 600, 800, 1000, 1200, and 1600 meter contour lines).

On the map of the United States, 1 : 2,500,000, first published by the U. S. Geo-logical Survey in 1890, appear contour lines showing elevations of 100, 500, 1000, 1500, 2000, 3000, and 4000 feet. This map was used as a base for the relief as shown in colors on a map (scale about 1 : 1,500,000) accompanying C. E. Artman, *Indus-trial Structure of New England*, U. S. Dept. of Commerce, Bur. of Foreign and Do-mestic Commerce, Washington, 1930 (*Domestic Commerce Ser. No. 28*). The relief as shown on these maps is not accurate.

The United States Geological Survey has published contour maps (contour interval 100 feet) of Connecticut (1 : 125,000), 1893, and of Massachusetts and Rhode Island (1 : 250,000), 1915. The map of Connecticut is a reduction of the sheets on a scale of 1 : 62,500 (see below) and shows roads, buildings, and town boundaries, features that do not appear on the map of Massachusetts and Rhode Island. In H. F. Walling, *Atlas of the State of New Hampshire*, New York, 1877, county maps of New Hampshire will be found on which 100-foot contours are shown, but the latter are far from accurate.

The basic topographical maps for the greater part of New England are the sheets published by the U. S. Geological Survey on a scale of 1 : 62,500, or about one mile to the inch, with contour interval of 20 feet. To date all of the more thickly settled portions of the region and much sparsely settled country have been mapped in this series. A considerable part of northeastern Vermont, small areas in northern New Hampshire and northwestern Maine, most of the forested regions of northern and eastern Maine, and the farm lands of southern Aroostook, Penobscot, and Piscataquis counties, Maine, have not as yet been covered. With the exception of the older sheets for parts of eastern Massachusetts and Rhode Island and Berkshire County, Massachusetts, house dots in rural areas appear on all of these maps, and woodland is indicated on the more recent issues (Fig. 1, p. 15). On the soil maps accompanying the recent *Soil Surveys* published by the U. S. Bureau of Chemistry and Soils (see below, p. 123, Fig. 1, inset) colored symbols showing different types of soils have been superimposed upon the topography of the U. S. Geological Survey sheets. The latter, however, has been corrected to some degree, and house dots have been added.

The National Survey Co. of Chester, Vt., the Walker Lithograph and Publishing Co. of Boston, and Rand McNally Co. have published serviceable commercial maps of New England as a whole and of the several states. The American Geographical Society has also prepared an outline map of the region (1 : 1,500,000) showing town and county boundaries, useful as a base for plotting areal distributions.

Areas. For the benefit of students requiring data on areas of townships, often of use in the preparation of certain types of map, the following references are given: Maine: an unpublished and somewhat inaccurate list of acreages is on file at the State Assessor's Office, Augusta (also at the American Geographical Society, New York City); New Hampshire: mimeographed list entitled *New Hampshire Land and Water Areas, Miles of Highway and Population by Towns and Counties as Compiled in 1924 by State Forestry Department* (square miles, total acreages, and land acreages); Massachusetts: F. W. Cook and W. N. Hardy, *The Population of Massachusetts as Determined by the Fifteenth Census of the United States*, Boston, 1931 ([*Mass.*] *House* [*Doc.*] *No. 1740*), pp. 9–11, table showing net land areas in square miles; Vermont: *Vermont Year-Book & Guide for 1930–31*, Rutland, Vt., 1930 (acreages); Rhode Island: *Know Rhode Island*, compiled by the State Bureau of Information, Office of the Secretary of State, Providence, 1927 (acreages); Connecticut: *Storrs Agric. Exper. Sta. Bull. No. 127*, 1925, pp. 124–133 (acreages).

Bibliographies. There is no comprehensive bibliography of works on the geography of New England. For references to certain general and special bibliographies that open up this field consult J. K. Wright, *Aids to Geographical Research*, New York, 1923 (*Amer. Geogr. Soc. Research Ser. No. 10*), pp. 5–9, 12, 18–21, 24–27, 121, 123, and 129–131. A useful pamphlet, "suggestive rather than comprehensive," is entitled *New England: A Selected List of Works in the Public Library of the City of Boston*, Boston, 1920 (*Brief Reading Lists No. 16*).

General Descriptive Works. Twenty-two years ago the Boston Chamber of Commerce published a coöperative work of somewhat the same character as the present volume (George French, edit., *New England: What It Is and What It Is To Be*, Boston, 1911). There are twenty-two chapters on a wide range of topics, including manufacturing, water power, agriculture and soils, forestry, transportation, commerce, summer resorts, education, religion, publicity, civic work, commission government, the charm of New England, and industrial Boston.

For details in regard to individual towns and localities see *A Handbook of New England*, Porter E. Sargent, Boston, 1921. This is in the form of an automobilist's guidebook; the main emphasis is historical, but much is included on industries and population. Statistics and miscellaneous information about individual towns will also be found in the official and semi-official state annuals, more especially the *Maine Register, New Hampshire Register, Vermont Year-Book & Guide* (formerly *Walton's*

Vermont Register), and *Connecticut Register and Manual*). These are not as comprehensive as the state gazetteers published during the middle years of the last century, which, although now out of date, often contain material of considerable value to the student of historical geography. (John Hayward, *The New England Gazetteer, Containing Descriptions of All the States, Counties, and Towns in New England* . . . Boston, many editions, *ca.* 1840; J. C. Pease and J. M. Niles, *A Gazetteer of the States of Connecticut and Rhode Island* . . . , Hartford, 1819; John Hayward, *A Gazetteer of Massachusetts* . . . , Boston, 1846; Elias Nason, *A Gazetteer of the State of Massachusetts*, Boston, 1874; Zadock Thompson, *History of Vermont, Natural, Civil and Statistical*, Burlington, 1842, Part III, *Gazetteer of Vermont;* A. J. Fogg, *The Statistics and Gazetteer of New Hampshire*, Concord, 1874; G. J. Varney, *A Gazetteer of the State of Maine*, Boston, 1886).

References to state and local histories and to bibliographies covering this field will be found in Edward Channing, A. B. Hart, and F. J. Turner, *Guide to the Study and Reading of American History*, Boston, 1912, pp. 62–89; for current works see G. C. Griffin, *Writings on American History: A Bibliography of Books and Articles on United States and Canadian History* . . . , New Haven, published annually, 1906–1917, and subsequently as supplements to the *Annual Reports of the American Historical Association*, Washington.

Photographs of New England scenes will be found in *National Geographic Magazine*, Vol. 51, 1927, pp. 327–369, Vol. 60, 1931, pp. 257–317; in Wallace Nutting's *States Beautiful Series* (volumes entitled *Maine Beautiful*, etc.), covering Maine, New Hampshire, Vermont, Massachusetts, and Connecticut (Framingham, Mass.. 1922–1924); and in the many pamphlets published by publicity departments of the several states.

Members of the Department of Geography, Clark University, Worcester, Mass., have carried out regional studies of various localities in New England and have prepared the results in the form of masters' and doctors' theses.

[2] For comprehensive descriptions of the physiographic features of New England the following publications should be consulted: W. M. Davis, *The Physical Geography of Southern New England*, in National Geographic Society, *The Physiography of the United States*, New York, 1896, pp. 269–304; Isaiah Bowman, *Forest Physiography: Physiography of the United States and Principles of Soils in Relation to Forestry*, New York, 1911, pp. 636–664 and 681–683; N. M. Fenneman, *Physiographic Divisions of the United States*, in *Annals Assoc. of American Geographers*, Vol. 18, 1928, pp. 261–353; and Douglas Johnson, *Stream Sculpture on the Atlantic Slope; A Study in the Evolution of Appalachian Rivers*, New York, 1931 (presents an important new hypothesis concerning the physiographic history of the region). On individual states, see W. N. Rice and H. E. Gregory, *Manual of the Geology of Connecticut*, Hartford, 1906 (Connecticut, *State Geol. and Nat. Hist. Survey Bull. No. 6*); B. K. Emerson, *Geology of Massachusetts and Rhode Island*, Washington, 1917 (*U. S. Geol. Survey Bull. 597*); J. W. Goldthwait, *The Geology of New Hampshire*, Concord. N. H., 1925 (*N. H. Acad. of Sci. Handbook No. 1*); G. H. Perkins, *Physiography of Vermont*, in *17th Report of the State Geologist* . . . *of Vermont*, 1929–1930, pp. 1–54. There is no comparable study for Maine. On New England shore lines see Douglas Johnson, *The New England-Acadian Shoreline*, New York, 1925.

[3] See Goldthwait, *op. cit.*, pp. 10–59, for a clear description of the glacial features of New Hampshire; also Ernst Antevs, *The Recession of the Last Ice Sheet in New England*, New York, 1922 (*Amer. Geogr. Soc. Research Ser. No. 11*), and R. F. Flint, *The Glacial Geology of Connecticut*, Hartford, 1930 (Connecticut, State Geol. and Nat. Hist. Survey Bull. No. 47; for a revised interpretation of certain conclusions presented in this monograph, see the same, *Deglaciation of the Connecticut Valley*, in *Amer. Journ. of Sci.*, Vol. 34, 1932, pp. 152–156).

[4] Davis, *op. cit.*, pp. 269–271.

[5] See Johnson, *Stream Sculpture*, etc. (cited in note 2).

[6] On the climate of New England generally, see *Atlas of American Agriculture*, U. S. Dept. of Agric., Bur. of Agricultural Economics (formerly Bur. of Farm Management), Washington, Part II, *Climate*, 1918, 1922, 1928; R. DeC. Ward, *The Climates of the United States*, Boston, 1925; Winslow Upton, *Characteristics of the New England Climate*, in *Annals Astron. Observ. of Harvard College*, Vol. 21. Part II, 1889, pp. 265–273; J. H. Weber, *The Rainfall of New England*, in *Journ. New England Water Works Assoc.*, Vol. 42, 1928, pp. 137–149, 278–302, and 414–430; Gragg Richards, *The Rainfall of Northern New England*, in the same, Vol. 42, pp. 431–456; C. F. Brooks, *New England Snowfall*, in *Geogr. Rev.*, Vol. 3, 1917, pp. 222–240; the same, *New England Snowfall*, in *Monthly Weather Review*, Vol. 45, 1917, pp. 271–285.

[7] Map of New England settlement in 1713 in L. K. Mathews, *The Expansion of New England*, Boston, 1909, opp. p. 70.

[8] See the papers on fisheries, by Messrs. Radcliffe and Fitzgerald, in the present volume, pp. 247–277, below.

[9] See S. E. Morison, *The Maritime History of Massachusetts, 1783–1860*, Boston, 1921.

[10] H. E. Gregory and H. H. Robinson, *Preliminary Geological Map of Connecticut*, in Rice and Gregory, *op. cit.*, p. 85; H. S. Sharp, *The Physical History of the Connecticut Shoreline*, Hartford, 1929 (Connecticut, *State Geol. and Nat. Hist. Survey Bull. No. 46*).

[11] Emerson, *op. cit.*, especially the colored geological map of Massachusetts and Rhode Island, scale 1 : 250,000, 1916, accompanying this bulletin.

[12] J. B. Woodworth, *Unconformities of Marthas Vineyard and of Block Island*, in *Bull. Geol. Soc. of America*, Vol. 8, 1897, pp. 197–212. Cretaceous and Tertiary beds have also been found as far north as Third Cliff, Scituate, Mass. (Isaiah Bowman, *Northward Extension of the Atlantic Preglacial Deposits*, in *Amer. Journ. of Sci.*, Vol. 22, 1906, pp. 313–325.

[13] See Laurence La Forge, *Geology of the Boston Area, Massachusetts*, Washington, 1932 (*U. S. Geol. Survey Bull. 839*). A guidebook of the region near Boston, comprehensive and scholarly, though now old, is E. M. Bacon, *Walks and Rides in the Country Round About Boston*, Boston, 1898.

[14] For a regional study of the Blackstone valley see P. E. James, *The Blackstone Valley: A Study in Chorography in Southern New England*, in *Annals Assoc. of Amer. Geogrs.*, Vol. 19, 1929, pp. 67–109.

[15] J. H. Burgy, *The Cotton Textile Manufacturing Industry of New England: A Study in Industrial Geography*, Baltimore, 1932.

[16] *Ibid.*, p. 29.

[17] *Ibid.*, p. 112.

[18] Morison, *op. cit.*, pp. 244–246.

[19] See A. P. Brigham, *Cape Cod and the Old Colony*, New York, 1920, pp. 32–68; the same, *Cape Cod and the Old Colony*, in *Geogr. Rev.*, Vol. 10, 1920, pp. 1–22 (gives references); J. B. Woodworth, *Some Glacial Wash-plains of Southern New England*, in *Bull. Essex Institute*, Vol. 29, Salem, Mass., 1897, pp. 71–119.

[20] *Population and Resources of Cape Cod*, Massachusetts, Dept. of Labor and Industries, 1922, pp. 28–34.

[21] For the impressions of a poet and a lover of nature who has spent many days on the outer beach of Cape Cod see Henry Beston [Sheahan], *The Outermost House*, Garden City, N. Y., 1929.

[22] H. C. Kittredge, *Cape Cod: Its People and Their History*, Boston, 1930, contains a map showing the location of recorded wrecks.

[23] See Hildegarde Hawthorne, *Old Seaport Towns of New England*, New York, 1916.

[24] See the article by Professor Derwent Whittlesey entitled *Coast Land and Interior Mountain Valley*, in the present volume, pp. 446–458, below.

[25] L. O. Packard, *The Decrease of Population Along the Maine Coast*, in *Geogr. Rev.*, Vol. 2, 1916, pp. 334–341; E. P. Morris, *Along the Maine Coast*, in the same, pp. 325–333.

[26] Bowman, *Forest Physiography*, pp. 653–664.

[27] Mathews, *op. cit.*, map opp. p. 22.

[28] *Ibid.*, map following p. 56.

[29] L. E. Klimm has studied from a geographical point of view the trends in population of some of the towns in the Connecticut Valley Lowland in Massachusetts (*The Geographic Basis of Population Changes in Three Massachusetts Counties*, in *Annals Assoc. of Amer. Geogrs.*, Vol. 21, 1931, pp. 130–131, abstract).

[30] See unpublished theses on land utilization in the Connecticut Valley Lowland, Clark University, Worcester, Mass.

[31] See below, pp. 159–160.

[32] Perkins, *op. cit.*, pp. 43–44; H. L. Fairchild, *Post Glacial Marine Waters in Vermont*, Burlington, Vt., 1916 (Vermont, *Report of the State Geologist*, 1915–1916, 10th of this series), pp. 1–41.

[33] S. D. Dodge, *The Vermont Valley: A Chorographical Study*, in *Michigan Papers in Geography*, Vol. 2, 1932, pp. 241–274.

[34] Mathews, *op. cit.*, map opp. p. 98.

[35] *Ibid.*, map opp. p. 136.

[36] Goldthwait, *op. cit.*, p. 8.

[37] A. K. Lobeck, *The Position of the New England Peneplane in the White Mountain Region*, in *Geogr. Rev.*, Vol. 3, 1917, pp. 53–60.

[38] W. C. Alden, *The Physical Features of Central Massachusetts*, Washington, 1924 (*U. S. Geol. Survey Bull. 760-B*).

[39] Fenneman, *op. cit.*, pp. 306–307.

[40] E. M. Wilson, *The Aroostook Valley: A Study in Potatoes*, in *Geogr. Rev.*, Vol. 16, 1926, pp. 196–205.

[41] *Atlas of American Agriculture* (cited in note 6, above).

[42] A. J. Henry, *Floods in New England Rivers*, in *Monthly Weather Review*, Vol. 42, 1914, pp. 682–686; J. W. Goldthwait, *The Gathering of Floods in the Connecticut River System*, in *Geogr. Rev.*, Vol. 18, 1928, pp. 428–445; J. M. Shipman, *Local Phases of the New England Flood*, in *Bull. Geogr. Soc. of Philadelphia*, Vol. 26, 1928, pp. 169–183; *Report of the Committee on Floods*, March, 1930, in *Journ. Boston Soc. of Civil Engineers*, Vol. 17, 1930, pp. 293–464; H. B. Kinnison, *The New England Flood of November, 1927*, Washington, 1929 (*U. S. Geol. Survey Water-Supply Paper 636-C*).

[43] Mathews, *op. cit.*, map opp. p. 140.

[44] See A. E. Cance, *The Decline of the Rural Population in New England*, in *Quarterly Publics. Amer. Statistical Assoc.*, Vol. 13, 1912, pp. 96–101; W. S. Rossiter, *Vermont, An Historical and Statistical Study of the Progress of the State*, in *Quarterly Publics. Amer. Statistical Assoc.*, Vol. 12, 1911, pp. 387–454; the same, *Three Sentinels of the North*, in *Atlantic Monthly*, Vol. 132, 1923, pp. 87–97; *Selective Migration from Three Rural Vermont Towns and Its Significance*, in *Fifth Annual Report, Eugenics Survey of Vermont*, Burlington, 1931; Genieve Lamson, *A Study of Agricultural Populations in Selected Vermont Towns: A Report Prepared for the Committee on the Human Factor of the Vermont Commission on Country Life*, Burlington, Vt., 1931.

[45] See for example *Rural Vermont: A Program for the Future, by Two Hundred Vermonters*, The Vermont Commission on Country Life, Burlington, Vt., 1931, pp. 14 and 15, where two dot maps are presented on opposite pages showing the distribution of population in Vermont in 1850 and 1930.

[46] See H. F. Wilson, *The Roads of Windsor*, in *Geogr. Rev.*, Vol. 21, 1931, pp. 379–397, a study of this movement in the vicinity of Windsor, Vt.; also pp. 144–145 and 464, below.

[47] See below, pp. 189–205.

[48] J. W. Goldthwait, *The Geology of New Hampshire* (cited in note 2, above), pp. 16–25.

[49] E. J. Raisz, *The Scenery of Mt. Desert Island: Its Origin and Development*, in *Annals New York Acad. of Sciences*, Vol. 31, 1929, pp. 121–186.

[50] The orographical relations of the mountains on either side of the international frontier are well shown on the *Physical Map of Canada*, National Development Bureau, Ottawa, 1928 (scale, 1 : 3,801,600). For a guidebook to the Green Mountains see W. C. O'Kane, *Trails and Summits of the Green Mountains*, Boston and New York, 1926.

[51] See A. H. Bent, *A Bibliography of the White Mountains*, Boston, 1911; F. W. Kilbourne, *Chronicles of the White Mountains*, Boston, 1916; *The A. M. C. White Mountain Guide: A Guide to Paths in the White Mountains and Adjacent Regions*, Appalachian Mountain Club, Boston, 7th edit., 1928.

[52] J. W. Goldthwait, *Summer Rainfall on New Hampshire Mountains*, in *New Hampshire Highways*, Vol. 6, Sept. 1928, pp. 1–3; C. F. Brooks, *Mountain Rainfall Measurements in New Hampshire*, in *Bull. Amer. Meteorological Society*, Vol. 10, 1929, pp. 30–31.

[53] See Ernst Antevs, *Alpine Zone of Mt. Washington Range*, Auburn, Me., 1932.

[54] See leading article in Magazine Section, *Boston Evening Transcript*, July 30, 1932.

NEW ENGLAND'S INDUSTRIAL PROSPECTS

Charles E. Artman

WHAT is ahead for New England industry? What are its present needs? What are its major trends? These questions are uppermost in the mind of every business man who has a stake in the region's future. The purpose of this article is to orient the reader, so that he may see the broad relations between the various economic factors that have determined the industrial life of New England and that will continue to shape its destiny.

What is the outlook for industrial New England? To answer this question we must turn to its history and against it mark the developments needed to maintain the region in harmony with changing conditions in the nation.

Let us first consider the outstanding characteristics of industrial New England. From the earliest times it has been forced to depend on other regions for its principal raw materials, as it must today. Its industries were never developed primarily out of native materials. With regions rich in natural goods commerce comes as a consequence and is built up out of these resources. In New England, however, manufacturing was the sequel and the outgrowth of extensive early commerce. Today commerce still provides the life blood for the region's industrial activity. A second characteristic, and one largely traceable to this fact, is the wide diversity in New England industrial life. This was fostered by the very paucity of raw materials, which necessitated that individual initiative for which the Yankee is traditionally famous. A third general characteristic of New England industry is the fact that production in the past was mainly of staple articles, such as textiles, shoes, and mechanical appliances, designed to meet the primary needs of mankind.

PHASES IN INDUSTRIAL DEVELOPMENT

It will help us to judge the present and future place of New England in the life of the nation if we consider the various phases in its development. New England is the birthplace of our industrial system. In the first phase of its development, lasting into the eighties of the last century, New England was the unquestioned leader in the country's industrial growth. This first phase of leadership was followed by a period, of perhaps a generation, in which the rest of the country was catching up with its leader. This second period of national expansion continued into the first decade of the twentieth century.

Following this there has come more recently a third phase, or period, in which the industrial activities of the nation have been undergoing a great deal of regional adjustment. This was a necessary sequel to the earlier hit-and-miss expansion of national life and to the pronounced changes that have been taking place in our economic needs and living habits. This process of readjustment was immensely accelerated during and after the World War. It has been marked by the rise of great new national industries, by a marvelous increase in wealth, and a world-wide extension of markets made possible by widely extended transportation and communication. The rapid and continuous expansion of the automobile industry, with the construction of a nation-wide network of improved highways, the sudden developments of radio and aviation, the spectacular growth of the moving picture industry, revolutionary changes in styles and in taste for wearing apparel, the wide diffusion of means to satisfy desires for luxuries, pronounced changes in methods of merchandising goods—all these factors have radically modified the relative position of New England in the industrial life of the nation. This third phase has increasingly manifested their interdependence.

THE PEOPLE OF NEW ENGLAND

The industrial position of any region is determined by two basic factors: first, by its people and, second, by its natural resources and material equipment. Its man power provides the human effort required to convert raw materials into the multitude of articles, services, and conveniences that make up the satisfactions of modern civilization. Upon the enterprise, foresight, energy, and skill of the population depends first of all the position the region will attain and continue to occupy.

New England's greatest asset lies in these human resources. Measured in percentage of the nation's population, its present man power is relatively slight, representing about one fifteenth of the total. With the country's growth the early pioneer stock of New England has become widely diffused throughout the nation and has carried with it the spirit and enterprise that have played so important a part in the development of newer regions. As an example, it is said that more people of native New England stock are to be found in Portland, Oregon, than in Portland, Maine.

The drain on the native New England stock from western migration in past decades has been met in turn by large infusions of immigrant blood from Europe and from Canada. These new elements are keeping up the vitality of pioneer New England and are absorbing in remarkable measure its ideals and standards. They are making a flexible and plastic people, perhaps somewhat less rigid and austere than the old New Englanders, and often more amenable to change and to new ideas. They are playing a vital part in maintaining the man power for New England's industries, while the descendants of the old native stock are perpetuating the leadership, enterprise, and high intelligence that guided the building of the region's enviable industrial position.

It is true, however, that conflicts between the newer social elements and the older New England stock in some sections have presented serious problems. These conflicts have their roots in political and religious cleavages on the one hand and in the control of financial and industrial power by the old Yankee stock on the other. These cleavages retard the development of harmony of interest and effort essential to the fulfillment of the region's economic possibilities. It seems, indeed, that the industrial future of some communities will depend more on their success or failure in harmonizing the conflicting racial and social elements than on economic conditions. Persistent sympathy, understanding, and mutual forbearance are required to unify these human assets for the general advancement.

The Material Equipment of New England: Location

Let us consider very briefly the material equipment of New England, the economic development that has taken place, and the resources with which the region is endowed by nature. Consider first its location. New England is in the great industrial area of the Northeastern United States, bounded roughly by the Mississippi on the west and the Ohio and Potomac rivers on the south. This area includes two thirds of all the people in the United States and by far the greater part of its industries. It provides the great consuming market of America. One third of the nation's population dwells within 500 miles of Boston. More than half the people of the United States, and most of the population of Canada, are included within a radius of 850 miles.

Added to this advantageous location is New England's frontage on the Atlantic, which provides easy access to the Southern states and Gulf ports by coastwise shipping, and to the Pacific coast through the Panama Canal. At its very threshold is the world's greatest market place and financial center, New York City, whose metropolitan area contains one tenth of the nation's population—the greatest aggregation of consumers to be found in any like area of the world. Such a favorable situation, with immense marketing capacities at its doorway and with convenient transportation facilities for reaching more distant markets, should certainly be regarded among New England's most valuable assets.

Predominance of Manufacturing

With its great diversity of commercial, agricultural, and industrial interests, the paramount concern of New England continues to lie in its mills and factories. Manufacturing[1] has for generations supplied the life blood for the New England population. A million and a quarter of its eight million men, women, and children work in these factories or find employment in business connected with them. In New England in normal times thirteen persons out of every hundred are on factory pay rolls; in the rest of the country there are only seven persons in industrial employment per hundred of population. One dollar out of every ten dollars of the nation's manufacturing income goes to the people of New England, who comprise only one fifteenth of the nation's population.[2]

The manufacturing processes brought an income to the region in 1929 of over three and a quarter billions of dollars, outside the cost of materials, containers, fuel, and power used in manufacture. This income represents only the value contributed by the industrial activities of the people in the six states: it is far less than the gross value of manufactured products. Indeed the total value of products is about twice the value added by manufacture. The manufacturing activities created a consuming market for materials and supplies costing more than three billions of dollars—a large slice of the nation's total industrial business.

The widespread popular impression that the bulk of New England's manufacture consists of textiles and shoes still persists in the face of clear evidence to the contrary. No doubt this mistaken impression has arisen from the fact that New England contributes a large part of the nation's production in these articles. While it is true that in certain specialized manufacturing centers these dominate the industrial picture, yet in New England as a whole they yield importance to a quite different type of manufacturing—one based upon the use of metals for its principal raw materials. This includes a wide variety of machinery and other articles fabricated from iron and steel, besides brass and bronze products, silver manufactures, jewelry, and metal novelties.

The metal industries taken together mean more as a source of income to New England than any other type of manufacture. They provide about one third of all the region's industrial revenue while all the textile industries together contribute only one fourth of it. The metal industries have a larger number of plants than any other single type of manufacture, and they are more widely distributed. Although they employ fewer workers than the textile industries, they pay nearly as much in wages. The expenditure for materials and supplies in the textile lines, on the other hand, is nearly twice that in the metal lines. From the higher relative revenue obtained from metals, it is apparent that the possibilities for maintaining or increasing the income of the region lie in this type of products.

DIVERSITY OF MANUFACTURES

The diversity of New England's manufacturing has been so often glorified that it seems almost trite to mention it here. To this characteristic, it should be remembered, is to be credited the fact that industrial conditions in New England are generally more stable and less subject to violent changes than in the parts of our country that have highly specialized industries. New England keeps on an even keel in boom periods, and in times of depression goes forward without the violent setbacks that disturb less diversified regions.

An idea of this diversity of industry may be gathered from the fact that nearly two thirds of the 350 distinct lines of national manufacturing are represented in New England plants. Each of the six largest single industries of New England brought manufacturing revenue to the region in 1929 exceeding $125,000,000; yet these six leaders together contributed less than one third of the income derived from all New England manufactures. Indeed, the twenty leading lines together contributed but slightly more than half of this total.

From a national viewpoint, New England retains a surprisingly important place in many lines of manufacture. There are more than a dozen outstanding lines in which its factories still contribute upwards of half of the national total for each. These include such important products as woolen and worsted goods, textile machinery, cutlery and edge tools, rubber footwear, plated ware, firearms, and abrasives. Besides these outstanding items, there are numerous other lines in which New England factories contribute more than a fourth of the national production. The list includes such items as cotton goods, hardware, brass and bronze goods, paper, clocks, typewriters, jewelry, felt hats, mechanics' tools, needles and pins, woodenware, motor cycles. The mere mention of such an array is certainly sufficient to scout the absurd notion sometimes ignorantly expressed that New England's industrial importance has become a thing of the past.

Despite the greatly increased growth of cotton manufacture in the Southern states and its recession in New England, this area is still the most highly concentrated single section of the country for making cotton textiles. In 1929 New England mills contributed 30 per cent of the total national revenue from cotton manufacturing. The Boston wool market handles over 60 per cent of all the wool consumed in the United States. The leather industries of New England provide a third of the national revenue from leather making. They brought a net revenue to the region in 1929 of two hundred million dollars. In the making of boots and shoes, New England factories contributed three eighths of the nation's output, despite the widely heralded recent growth of this industry in the Middle West and the Middle Atlantic states. In manufactures of paper and wood pulp, again, New England's factories contribute more than a fourth of the nation's total: Massachusetts alone makes more than half of all the fine rag paper of the country. Of a considerable number of other products New England factories continue to be the nation's most important single source.

RECENT TRENDS IN MANUFACTURE

What have been the recent trends in New England manufacture? Looking back over its long history, we find that at the time of the first manufacturing census in 1850 New England had an eighth of the nation's population and that its factories contributed a fourth of the national manufacturing income. In 1929 New England contained about a fifteenth of the nation's population, and the income from its manufactures was about a tenth of the national total.[3]

Although manufacturing in New England has advanced continuously from one decade to the next, and sometimes rapidly, for the last fifty years there has been a continuous and fairly regular recession in its *relative* position in the nation. This was the logical result of the development of other sections. The rate of growth of manufacturing in New England was exceeded by that of the nation as a whole in every census interval up to 1914. Industrial development in this region was so far advanced in earlier years that the later advancement of other sections has overshadowed its more moderate recent growth here. The continuous national expansion in the last fifty years has been at the relative expense of New England. This expansion appears to be gradually approaching an equilibrium. In recent years this region has maintained its relative position as well as in former intervals, despite serious setbacks in some of its larger industries.

The simple truth is that the recession suffered acutely by many New England factories in the last few years has blinded people's eyes to the fact that the region is still doing an immense volume of business quietly in its usual way at the old stand. The low spot in its industrial activity before the current depression appears to have been reached in 1925. That year marked the turning point in many lines and roused the business men to the need for effective common action. Since then there have been various ups and downs. Many concerns found that 1929 was the best year in their history. There are numerous indications that New England industry is weathering the storms of depression rather better than other parts of the country.[4] In the past it has been characteristic of New England that in periods of general recession this region has shown surprising stability.

The inactive factories and empty houses conspicuous in some communities are mute evidence of the industrial and human losses suffered in the readjustment that New England has been undergoing. The evidence is most pronounced in areas dependent on a single type of industry or perhaps a single large establishment. Communities with diversified activities have suffered far less. One of the hopeful directions taken by the new industrial planning for greater stability of income is toward diversity of manufacture in the individual city as well as in the larger areas.

The Future of New England Manufactures

What then of the future? New England manufacturers since the war have faced a competitive situation similar in many respects to that of old England, whose former world markets have been seriously impaired by industrial developments in India, China, and continental Europe. New England, in a similar way, has felt the effects of the rise of great new industries in other sections of the United States. Her industrial future depends upon the alertness with which her manufacturers adapt themselves to changed national and world conditions, which in the last few years have shown the insufficiency of some of the old standards and methods.

Since the war, industry and society as a whole have become more highly organized and more closely interrelated than ever before. Profound advances have taken place in the technical processes of manufacturing. Along with expanded markets, competition for the consumer's dollar has become increasingly keen. The choice of the consumer now dictates more relentlessly than ever before. Opportunity in manufacturing lies increasingly with those who meet the consumer's needs most efficiently and most skillfully.

However, the New England business and industrial world is more keenly alive than ever before in its history to the need for meeting these changed conditions. The most progressive companies see the importance of catering to the consumer. They are following their product through to the point of final consumption, instead of bidding it farewell at the factory door. Sharp changes in our distributive system have made this imperative. They have shown the necessity of continuous improvement in equipment and methods and of eliminating every possible waste in distribution as well as in production.

True values and genuine service now receive a more respectful hearing than they did in the decade that followed the World War. Hopeful signs are not wanting to the individual New England manufacturer who is alert to the real needs of a saner consuming public. There is encouragement in the fact that, with the exception of style fabrics, most New England products are of types essential to the well-being of the people or to the basic industries of the nation.

The great industrial advances of New England in the past were based largely on inventions and on skill and relentless effort, supported by Yankee ingenuity in developing them. New England minds gave birth to all the great American textile inventions, starting with Whitney's cotton gin. A small town in Vermont has to its credit over two hundred mechanical inventions. The beginnings of the nation's rubber industry may be traced back to experiments in Connecticut. New England initiative and experiment have made immense contributions to the industrial development of the whole nation.

This inventiveness is now being challenged again to make the necessary adjustments to new and difficult conditions. Industrial New England has been going through another pioneering experience. It is facing a new frontier, arising not from hostile Indians or unconquered forests, but from new industrial conditions that have brought fresh problems of production and marketing. These problems call for all the resourcefulness of the old pioneer life.

The fetish of mass production and mass operation, in the minds of some of our most discriminating business leaders, has reached its logical limit; perhaps it has gone far beyond this limit. These leaders see that there is no merit in mere size. The basic principles of sound management, foresight, and careful judgment continue to be the determining factors, whether the enterprise be large or small.

New England character in the past expressed itself primarily in production. Yankee shrewdness was confined mainly to the technique of manufacturing, while distribution and market promotion were left largely to shift for themselves. Out of this arose almost a scorn of trading. "Let the goods speak for themselves" was the general attitude. New conditions have made this formerly successful attitude wholly inadequate. With all due respect to the philosopher, the world today will not wear a path to the New England maker's door in search of his "mousetrap." The mousetrap must be taken to the people who have mice to catch.

Natural Resources

What of New England's natural resources? While manufacturing is the dominant source of income to its people, yet the activities that depend directly on the land and adjacent waters are of decided importance in maintaining the economic stability of New England. The region long ago passed through the pioneer stages of agriculture and forestry. In its heyday fifty years ago there were twice as many acres in farms as at present and twice as many people living on farms. Ninety years ago there were nearly 4,000,000 sheep on the farms of New England. Now there are less than one twentieth of this number. The march of national development has brought an utter change in type of farming.

New England agriculture[5] has had to face on the one hand the rivalry of near-by New England factories and, on the other, the increasing competition of products of distant agricultural regions made accessible by improved transportation and refrigeration. It has thus been forced to narrow its field of activity to specialized production of quickly perishable articles for local consumption. It has had the great advantage, however, of direct markets of large capacity afforded by the concentrated industrial population in its cities and towns. This has fostered a distinctive type of agriculture, in which dairying is the mainstay, with specialized production of potatoes, onions, apples, cranberries, garden truck, and tobacco in areas particularly adapted to these crops. Throughout the New England states thousands of acres of land and many entire farms have gone out of production. The net result, however, has been that New England agriculture today, with half the former farm population and half the land in farms, produces twice as much food for its population as at the zenith of its farm activity fifty years ago.

The forests of New England,[6] once its glory, are now largely a memory. Lumber production, which loomed large in the region up to two generations ago, was followed by the cutting of pulpwood for paper stock; and this has exhausted all but a remnant of the stand of mature timber. Now the cheaper and more abundant lumber supplies of the Pacific coast and the South, and pulpwood and paper stock from Canada and northern Europe, are holding back the exhaustion of the remaining remnant. The old type of forestry is a thing of the past. New England, with two thirds of its land surface better adapted to forest growth than to any other use, is one of the best areas in the United States for scientific forest production. While holding a prominent place in its emphasis on scientific forestry, this region has made only a slight beginning in realizing its possibilities in this direction. Adequate forest development requires not only forest planting and protection from fire and other enemies but also modification of methods of taxation in a way that will encourage the maturing of timber crops for permanent revenue rather than the premature cutting that has heretofore prevailed.

The mineral resources of New England are seldom thought of as significant either nationally or locally. This region possesses no commercial coal deposits or petroleum or natural gas and must depend altogether on outside sources for these mineral fuels. It has none of the metallic minerals. The value of New England's mineral production represents only 1 per cent of the national total. And yet New England quarries provide 45 per cent of the value of the nation's granite and 38 per cent of its marble, besides substantial percentages of feldspar, mica, talc, and other secondary minerals. Indeed its total mineral production—approaching fifty million dollars a year— makes up a substantial and stable income to the region.

Turning now from the land resources of New England to the resources of the sea, we find that the fishing ventures of the region[7]

provide a substantial revenue, having an annual production worth
some twenty million dollars and yielding a livelihood to some 25,000
persons directly engaged in these activities. Thus the earliest form of
New England industry, antedating its permanent settlements, still
makes a vitally important contribution. New England has all the
essentials of a continuously prosperous fishing industry. Here too,
it has the unique advantage of location, lying opposite the richest
fishing grounds in the world, between the Gulf of St. Lawrence and
the Carolina coast. The New England fisheries are the most important on the Atlantic seaboard. They contribute a fifth of the
national fish production and a fourth of the canned and preserved fish.

During the past generation, while the total volume of fish caught
has declined, the value of the products in this industry has increased
materially. Production of New England offshore fisheries now
appears to have reached a level on which productiveness may well
be expected to remain in coming years. The Boston fish market sends
its supplies to most of the states of the Union. With the recently
improved methods of packaging frozen fish, its sales in the interior
of the country bid fair to bring increasing profits.

Summarizing the various natural resources of New England, we
may say that its agriculture, after passing through a long, trying
process of adjustment, has reached a position of relative stability,
accomplished by concentrating its efforts on specialized production
for consumption in near-by markets. New England forestry is
waiting for the scientific development of millions of acres of land
that are now unproductive. Under proper safeguards and protection they can be made to produce regular timber crops for profitable
near-by future markets that are in prospect when the present natural
timber supplies of the nation have become exhausted. The mineral
resources of this region promise to continue to provide a very considerable revenue. And the activities of New England fisheries may
reasonably be expected to be sustained and even increased with the
widely extended market that is being developed under new methods
of preserving and distributing fish products.

Coöperative Organization on a Regional Basis

In these last few years New England has been organizing itself
for united action as a community. Through experience it has been
forced to learn the value of organized coöperative effort. This forward step is not accidental; it is the result of careful planning and
reasoned action, initiated a few years ago by a small group of men who
believe in New England and who did not hesitate to challenge the
doubters to look forward instead of backward. The movement,
given concrete form in a positive program by the New England
Council, has set an example of what can be done when a whole region
unites to organize its leadership around a worth-while program.

Speaking before a representative gathering of New England business men a few years ago, a prominent financial leader said: "In
material things New England is wholly sound; her troubles arise
mainly from her mental attitude and lack of vision." Another
sympathetic observer, when questioned as to New England's basic
problems, said: "The main trouble with New England is its attitude
of mind." For some years it has been the style to disparage the
industrial importance of this section. But the public now hears
less from the Anvil Chorus, and more often there comes to its attentive
ear the quiet, earnest humming of a region that is too busily occupied
in its work to be alarmed by outside clamor.

Observers comment on the remarkable change in point of view
that has come about in the last few years. Under the spur of necessity,
New England has gone far in setting its industrial house in order. It
has undertaken a pitiless self-analysis to find out its weak spots as
well as its sources of strength. It has probably gone farther in making
adjustments to changed industrial conditions than any other section
of the country. The past hard experiences, by laying the foundation
for restoring its industrial vitality, have proved a real advantage in
preparing the way for future regional progress and leadership.

To be sure, many glaring weaknesses still persist in New England
industry. Some of these are physical and some are mental. One of
the most serious problems is the obsoleteness of many factories, both
in equipment and in methods. The older industries have far to go in
this respect before they can keep pace with modern progress.

Much remains to be done also in harmonizing the human relationships between workers and management. Too often a local and
provincial attitude of mind persists, which refuses to see the new
problems that have grown up out of new conditions. That ominous
word "nepotism" applies with special force to old communities where
hereditary control excludes the ability that in younger communities
is selected by competition for business leadership. This inherited
authority is in exaggerated control in too many business establishments. On the other hand, New England has the great advantages
that accrue to a fully mature industrial section, with abundant financial resources, long experience in business organization, and national
prestige built up in its long industrial history.

CONCLUSION

In conclusion it may be said that the industries of New England
as a whole are as sound as ever and continue to play a vital part in the
national life. The industrial future of New England depends largely
on the courage and intelligence shown by the present generation of
business men in facing recent changes and in adjusting their methods
to new conditions. In general, New England is highly favored by its

location. It has a vitally important place in the economic unity of the industrial Northeast, where the great consuming market of America lies. In experience and technical equipment, developed through its long history, in its generally able leadership and highly developed business organization, New England has intangible assets which will go far to assure its industrial permanence.

NOTES

[1] See also Dr. J. S. Keir's paper entitled *New England's Manufactures*, in the present volume, pp. 322–343, below.

[2] See Table II, p. 328, below.

[3] See Figure 2, p. 327, below.

[4] For statistical and other data tending to show that New England has suffered less than the United States as a whole see especially E. S. French, *New England– 1930*, in *Harvard Business School Alumni Bull.*, April 1, 1931, pp. 187–194; and *New England News Letter*, 1931, No. 103, p. 4; No. 104, pp. 1 and 7; No. 107, p. 4; No. 108, p. 6.—EDIT.

[5] See also the papers on New England agriculture by Professor I. G. Davis, Professor A. E. Cance, and Dr. F. V. Waugh in the present volume.

[6] See also the papers on New England forests by Professors R. T. Fisher, H. S. Graves, and F. R. Fairchild, in the present volume.

[7] See also the papers on New England fisheries by Messrs. Lewis Radcliffe and G. A. Fitzgerald in the present volume.

ADDITIONAL NOTE
By the Editor

This note deals briefly with certain published and unpublished sources of information regarding New England's industries in general. For the sources of information concerning the several main branches of industry—manufacturing, forestry, agriculture, etc.—the chapters dealing with these subjects should be consulted.

Basic Statistics. The reports of the United States Census Bureau provide fundamental facts concerning the industries of New England. As they are well known and readily accessible they require no detailed comment. Among the state governments, that of Massachusetts has been the most active in the gathering of industrial statistics. From 1875 through 1915 the Massachusetts state census ranked high among the censuses of the world (see C. F. Gettemy, *The Massachusetts Bureau of Statistics, 1869–1915: A Sketch of Its History, Organization and Functions, Together with a List of Its Publications and Illustrative Charts*, Boston, 1915). Unfortunately the census in its comprehensive form has been given up, although the Division of Statistics of the Commonwealth's Bureau of Labor and Statistics still takes an annual census of manufactures and publishes, besides, current statistical details on labor and unemployment. These are presented in the form of mimeographed bulletins. In the Rhode Island state censuses of former years industries were covered, but here, too, the compilation of statistics of this nature by the state government has been largely abandoned. For a synoptical key and index map to census statistics by towns, 1910–1925, see J. K. Wright, *New England*, in *Geogr. Review*, Vol. 19, 1929, pp. 488–493.

The New England Council has brought out a useful pamphlet, *New England Economic Data: A Directory of Current Economic Statistics Relating to New England, Indicating Sources from Which Statistics Are Obtainable*, [1931]. Here are listed statistics published at weekly, monthly, and quarterly intervals covering general business, manufacturing, natural resources, public utilities, and wealth, both for New England as a whole and for the different states. Under "General Business," statistics are listed on employment, carloadings, business and mercantile failures, building contracts, bank debits, postal receipts, automobile sales, newspaper advertising, etc. There is need for a similar list of statistical data published at intervals of a year and longer.

The Federal Reserve Bank of Boston publishes a *Monthly Review of Industrial and Financial Conditions in the New England District*, by Frederic H. Curtiss, Chairman and Federal Reserve Agent. In each number a summary, illustrated by graphs, is given for New England, together with notes on business conditions in the United States as a whole. The New England Council has established a composite statistical index of general business activity in New England. This index is based on monthly data for bank debits to individual accounts, freight carloadings, electric power consumption, cotton consumption, wool consumption, production of boots and shoes, etc. "Each series has been adjusted to eliminate the effects of long-time growth and seasonal variation and given a weighting determined by its importance" (*N. E. News Letter*, No. 99, July, 1931, pp. 7–8). The Providence Chamber of Commerce compiles a similar index for Rhode Island, and the Manufacturers' Association of Connecticut prints one for Connecticut in its monthly, *Connecticut Industry*. A graphic "barometer" of industrial activity in New England based on energy consumption appears from time to time in *Electrical World* (McGraw Hill Co.).

Recent Surveys. Several of New England's leading industries were in a depressed condition for a good many years before the world-wide crisis that began in 1929. Adversity often provides a stimulus to the search for facts. It impels business men to look for the underlying causes of their difficulties. It leads economists to analyze the troubles affecting communities. It is also an invitation to the sensational journalist and muckraker, as well as to the booster who would ferret out "points" that make good advertising and tend to discredit the prophets of gloom. The years since the World War have been preëminently a period of fact-searching in New England, and all these motives have been represented. Space does not permit a discussion here of this growing "literature" on industrial New England, but a few outstanding surveys and studies may be mentioned. Many of these, even when the purpose has been primarily one of publicity and propaganda, have disclosed or brought together facts of importance.

On the basis partly of census material and partly of original field investigations and answers to questionnaires the Bureau of Foreign and Domestic Commerce of the U. S. Department of Commerce in coöperation with the New England Council has carried out the most elaborate study of economic conditions in New England that has yet appeared. The data were gathered under the direction of Dr. C. E. Artman mostly before 1927 and were published in 1929 and 1930 in three parts under the general title *Commercial Survey of New England*. Part I, *Industrial Structure of New England*, Washington, 1930 (*Domestic Commerce Ser. No. 28*), by Dr. Artman himself, covers agriculture, mineral resources, fisheries, transportation, power, fuel, population, manufactures, building, and construction. Parts II and III, by E. F. Gerish, entitled *Commercial Structure of New England*, 1929 (*ibid., No. 26*), and *Market Data Handbook of New England*, 1929 (*ibid., No. 24*), deal among other matters with wholesale and retail distribution, commercializing recreational facilities, food supply, income and banking, and marketing areas. In the *Market Data Handbook*, statistics are given by towns for trade outlets, wealth, standard of living, etc.

Second only to the *Commercial Survey of New England* in comprehensiveness are the recent economic surveys conducted by the two major telephone companies. Although the results of these have not been published, they have been mimeographed in two reports, one for Connecticut and the other for the five remaining states, and the telephone companies have allowed serious students to consult the reports. These studies are of interest from the geographical point of view. New England is divided into industrial regions based on the recognition of geographical factors. These regions are shown on maps, and statistics are presented for each region as a whole. (New England Telephone and Telegraph Company, *Economic Survey— Maine, Massachusetts, New Hampshire, Rhode Island, Vermont, 1925–1950* (summarized in *Boston Evening Transcript*, Nov. 21, 1930); Southern New England Telephone Company, *Regional Survey—Connecticut, 1929–1950*.)

Developmental Organizations. Elaborate programs for the study of New England's industries are being carried on by the New England Council. This body was organized in 1925 to foster the coöperation of leaders in the six states in meeting problems common to all. It was a challenge to the adverse publicity from which New England as a whole was believed to be suffering. The Council consists of 72 members, 12 from each state. Committees of the Council and a group of coöperating committees are engaged in a wide range of promotional and fact-finding activities. The Council maintains a permanent staff. Its publications include the semi-monthly *New England News Letter*, recording the activities of the Council and other news pertaining to the industrial life of the region, as well as informational pamphlets for use in advertising, committee reports also published in pamphlet form, and other miscellaneous documents, many of which are referred to elsewhere in this volume.

Another organization devoted to the promotion of the industrial prosperity not only of Boston but of New England at large is the Boston Chamber of Commerce. Shortly before the organization of the New England Council a General Committee on New England Industries was established by the Boston Chamber of Commerce to conduct a series of surveys of the status of five important New England industries in their relation to competing enterprise in other sections of the United States. These surveys embraced shoe manufacturing, agriculture, foundry and machining, cotton manufacturing, and fishing. The results were printed in pamphlet form.

Somewhat comparable in purpose to the New England Council are the Maine Development Commission, the New Hampshire Development Commission, and the Massachusetts Industrial Commission, all established during the last five years.

The power utilities companies have aimed to promote industrial expansion in the areas served by them. Partly to determine the status and prospects of industry in these areas and partly to obtain data that may be used to advantage in advertising, several of the power companies have had surveys made. The Division of Municipal and Industrial Research of the Massachusetts Institute of Technology in 1930 carried out surveys of Vermont and New Hampshire for certain companies belonging to the New England Power Association. Summary reports only of these studies have been published (in pamphlet form), but further details are on file at the offices of the several companies, the New England Power Association, and the Massachusetts Institute of Technology. Maine as a whole and especially the parts of Maine served by the New England Public Service Co. were investigated for that company by Lockwood Greene Engineers, Inc., of New York, in 1929. The results are presented in mimeograph and constitute a valuable compendium of information concerning labor, power, resources, transportation, industrial development, government, educational and recreational facilities, and other topics.

The New England Council, through its Committee on Community Development, has done much to encourage local communities, as represented by chambers of commerce and similar bodies, to carry out fact-finding surveys of their resources and conditions and to "keep books" reflecting trends of commercial and industrial enterprise. Although the quest for data that make good advertising is a large motive in this local fact-finding, in several instances sound and thorough work has been accomplished (see, for instance, the reports of the economic and industrial surveys of metropolitan Providence, 1927–1928; Pawtucket and Central Falls, R. I., 1927–1928; Norwood, Mass., 1928; and Bangor and Brewer, Me., and vicinity, 1929; and the survey of municipal and industrial conditions in Somerville, Mass., 1930, all conducted by the Division of Industrial and Municipal Research of the Massachusetts Institute of Technology). The New Haven Chamber of Commerce in 1931 undertook an industrial survey of the New Haven area in which special stress was to be laid on discovering handicaps to the progress of New Haven as an industrial community.

Industrial Research. " Progressive business has lifted a page from the experience of science, and there is a growing realization that the formulation of successful management policies must be based on the accurate and thorough collection, organization and interpretation of facts." This quotation is from a pamphlet entitled *Better Business Through Research in New England Industry: Introduction and Summary of Findings*, prepared for the Research Committee of the New England Council by the Policyholders Service Bureau of the Metropolitan Life Insurance Co. [1929], p. 7. The Boston Chamber of Commerce has also published similar studies with particular application to industrial conditions in New England.

The coöperation of the universities in the study of New England's industrial problems has likewise been enlisted. The New England Council has suggested thesis topics, many of which have been worked up by advanced students in New England institutions (especially the Massachusetts Institute of Technology). Some of these theses are kept on file at the offices of the Council and are loaned on request. The Council has also distributed a pamphlet entitled: *A Directory of the College and University Research Facilities of New England Which Are Available to New England's Agricultural, Commercial and Industrial Interests for Aid in Solving Their Problems by the Practical Application of the Research Method.* Current research projects in the field of business and social affairs are listed in *Current Social Research in Massachusetts*, published in 1931 by the Town Room Committee of the Massachusetts Civic League. Professors E. F. Gay and Allyn Young of Harvard sponsored the publication in 1927 of a volume of nine undergraduate theses under the title *The New England Economic Situation* (Chicago)—in the main, interpretations of statistics.

UNEMPLOYMENT IN NEW ENGLAND

SOME FUNDAMENTAL FACTORS

Edward A. Filene

I FIRMLY believe that in time New England will again be in the vanguard of industrial success. New England has distinctive advantages. Even in its unemployment problem New England is distinctive.

The problems of technological unemployment, of cyclical unemployment, of seasonal unemployment New England shares with the nation. All three of these need and, until they are solved, will continue to demand our best New England attention. But overshadowing them is an unemployment problem that for us in these six states of the Northeast is not merely serious but vital—a problem that existed before the beginning of the present economic crisis.

For New England the real problem of unemployment is the problem of jobs that have vanished, not through increase of efficiency, but for the lack of it; not through failure to keep men employed in "bad times" as in "good," or summer and winter alike, but for the simple reason that at present there are not as many jobs in New England as there used to be. It is this larger problem of unemployment and not the present abnormal situation that will be analyzed in this paper.

Fortunately, the problem is by no means unsolvable. The very abilities that brought New England its primacy in times past can reëstablish New England leadership on a new and sounder basis.

THE LAW OF THE SURVIVAL OF THE FITTEST AS APPLIED TO NEW ENGLAND

New England's problem is merely this: as a region it is experiencing, in business, a law that New England minds of an earlier generation helped to formulate for the world of plants and animals—the inexorable law of the survival of the fittest.

To the New England of the days of the first American college and the first printing press; of the days when its ships of home-cut timber sailed everywhere, brought home everything from West Indian rum to Chinese curios, and took out New England commodities in exchange; of the days when the first textile machinery in America was erected; of the days of whaling and packet boat and clipper ship; to the New England that made cottons and shoes for all America and a good part of the world; to the New England whose capitalist adventurers built western railroads and sank western copper mines deeper into the earth than man had ever before descended—to this New England the law of the survival of the fittest was no threat, for New England was herself the very symbol of fitness.

When was it that the change came? Someone has said that it took place when the wealthy sons of New England's greatness sold the capital stock of their inherited enterprises to the public and took bonds for themselves. Whether it was cause or effect, certainly this mutation may stand as the symbol of a changed New England, a New England which in the later years of the last century was interested more in standing secure than in forging ahead, more in stabilization than in enterprise.

But least secure of all roads is the road that proclaims itself the direct road to the preservation of what is. The virtues of one generation become the vices of the next, and a constantly new outlook is the only true preserver of prosperity and profits. This is the lesson New England is learning in a school far older than the most venerable of its institutions—the school of experience.

And with the lesson goes unemployment.

In the years of their growth the industries of New England were fitter than industries elsewhere. They had the valuable habit of meeting and beating all competition.

By shrewd management these businesses were also made profitable for their owners. They kept New England capital busy in New England or for New England.

So long as these advantages were maintained, our six states continued to be a workshop for many other localities. Less than twenty years ago (1914) our one fourteenth of the nation's population was performing one eighth, in value, of the nation's manufacturing work. But when, partly through development elsewhere and partly through stagnation and nepotism at home, the traditional advantages of New England lost their edge, New England manufacturers ceased to be the fittest for survival. According to the 1929 census our share of work was less than one ninth—still a notable share but by contrast with former days an unsatisfactory one.

Not only did fitter industries develop elsewhere, but in many cases even New England capital found it advisable to seek other regions. This has been notably true, of course, in the textile field, for many of the most active cotton mills of the Piedmont region have been built, equipped, and operated by transfer of capital formerly busy in New England. What is more, in this newer region New England capital has installed the newest of machinery, machinery which in one case I know of turns 25 per cent faster than the dear old primitive equipment that father installed and son is still using back home in the North.

ADVANTAGES OF NEW ENGLAND'S LOCATION

If New England's present industrial condition is the result of the working out of the law of survival, it is equally sure that such of its markets and its prestige as have been lost can be regained (or new markets set up in their place) only by the achievement of a superior fitness. New England must again be able to lay down its goods in other markets with an advantage in price, in quality, in style, in timeliness, in aggressiveness—or a combination of these—and at a profit that will be attractive to capital. It must again be able to meet and beat competition.

The local availability of raw materials has not for many years been a New England advantage, except in minor instances. Cotton, leather, wool, and metals, the fabrication of which has long occupied the greater part of our industrial population, have been imports.

Yet because of its unrivaled seacoast, New England may, if it wishes, enjoy a definite advantage in respect to many raw materials. Coal has recently been shipped to New England from Russia through the port of Archangel, paying a freight charge no greater than that by rail from the Pennsylvania mines. The long-staple cottonfields are nearer to New England, in terms of cost if not in mileage, than they are to the great highland manufacturing region of the South. The Gillette Safety Razor Company finds Swedish and British steels, because of certain chemical components, better suited to its needs than steels of American make. Where, from the raw materials standpoint could this company be more suitably located than in Boston?

Geographical nearness of markets has likewise not for decades been an outstanding New England asset. Most of the region lies more than a thousand miles from the center of population of the United States.

But, as in raw materials, miles are not everything in markets. The final advantage is what counts, and the final advantage is not mileage but cost of transportation. Seacoast New England can actually reach two thirds of the buying power of the United States at less cost than can, for instance, Indianapolis, within two hundred miles of the center of population. With intelligent use of motor trucks, any point in New England is nearly as well off. And, abroad, the world is at New England's door.

That we of New England are not making full use of these natural transportation advantages is a very important point in this problem of reëstablishing vanished employment. We must be fittest, not potentially by nature or inheritance alone, but in fact.

But, although we must make better use of our geographical endowment, transportation cannot give New England the superior fitness it requires. Not by where the raw materials come from, nor by where the finished products go, is going to be told the greater part of the story, but by what happens to materials while they are in New England hands.

The "Second Industrial Revolution"

"Fittest" for New England must mean fittest in all the activities of production and distribution. It must mean fittest in the application of sound principles and methods in the work life of New England. By and large it must mean fittest for what I have elsewhere chosen to call the methods and principles of the "Second Industrial Revolution."[1]

We in America have entered upon a period of business history already marked by changes as revolutionary as those that followed the introduction of machine power. The alterations in our factory system are affecting profoundly and will affect still more profoundly not only our methods of doing business but the lives of our people. A relentless overhauling of the mechanisms of both production and distribution lies just ahead of us, with results that we can at present only surmise.

New England's logical position in this Second Industrial Revolution is clear.

In the past, New England commercial leadership was due, more than to any other factor, to being first in the field.

Eli Terry of Connecticut was the first to manufacture clocks in quantities of one hundred or more, and Chauncey Jerome, also of Connecticut, first to make clocks with works of brass. Because brass could survive the dampness of many weeks in the hold of a vessel, and wood could not, and also because brass clocks could be made at astonishingly lower cost, Jerome was also first to make clocks for export. Both Connecticut's clock industry and its great brass industry, today employing together more than a tenth of its industrial population, are a heritage of this foresight and fore-action.

Adventurous New England sea captains, coasting all the oceans, found it convenient to load homeward-bound ships with hides from Spanish California. Their enterprise contributed to the development of Massachusetts' shoemaking, which still, in spite of its decline, employs more individuals than the shoe industry of any other state; and of its tanneries, which also lead the nation in employment.

It was the enterprise of such wide-awake citizens as Moses Brown of Rhode Island, with whose financial assistance Samuel Slater set up the first spinning machinery in America, that made New England for more than a century and a quarter the textile center of America.

To an even more marked extent New England must now be keenest to anticipate the changes of the industrial revolution that

[1] For notes see below, p. 95.

is upon us. It must be first to see what should be done and first to do it. If it can be first in these, not only will it solve its problem of jobs for all but, likely enough, will also find solutions for the more general problem of jobs at all times.

What the Second Industrial Revolution particularly requires of New England is the scientific use of its resources (including its population), in the making of the things it is best fitted to make for the rest of the world.

What are these things?

We must find out. In this, as in other matters, we must learn to do business on facts, not on guesses or "hunches." Is this statement in itself an opinion? A study of such companies as Ford Motor Company, General Motors Corporation, General Electric, E. I. du Pont de Nemours & Company, or Metropolitan Life Insurance Company will show that these companies have done away with opinions and spend millions to know facts. The same study in New England will disclose the seat of our troubles.

NEED OF MASS PRODUCTION

Particularly we must find out what New England is best equipped to make by mass production and market by mass distribution.

In the scientific study that our manufacturers will have to make, if they are not going to depend on miracles, it will be found that a large percentage of the goods produced in this country can be made by mass production. This means that one by one producers either in New England or elsewhere are going to undertake mass production of more and more goods, and as each new mass unit becomes well established, the smallest unit that can compete with it will be one that is at least big enough to bring overhead costs down to a negligible percentage.

This point will be clear from a moment's glance at the automobile industry. Who would undertake, today, to start a new enterprise for the manufacture of motor cars without an investment of millions of dollars? But this investment in itself sets up an immediate overhead such that a daily production of many cars must be established before the cost of the output will compare favorably with established costs.

Nor must New England manufacturers overlook the time factor in mass production.

If your competitors are still pursuing small-scale and odd-lot production, it is usually possible to undertake mass production and so to reduce your overhead that you have a definite advantage over them in costs, while actually paying your employees a higher wage because of their greater production per man. Once let other mass producers get established ahead of you, and your course is not so simple. This is what I mean by the time factor. Today New England could undertake the mass production of many items, with advantage on her side. If her industrialists wait too long, opportunities will one by one be seized by others first.

A German shoe manufacturer visited one of our New England mass producers, the Thom McAn shoe factories. Comparing notes, he found these to be the facts: that in Germany he was paying $1.50 a day in wages, and producing shoes at a cost of $4.50, whereas at the Thom McAn establishment wages were, roughly, $4.50 a day and the price of a better pair of shoes $4. The German workman had to work three days to buy one unit of what he was making, the American less than a day. When the German workman had paid for housing and food, he had no money left for shoes. Consequently he patched and patched his shoes until he was forced to forego something else in order to buy a new pair. But mass production in the American plant was not only lowering costs (with overhead 4 per cent as against 12 per cent in Germany) but was also building a market for both shoes and other manufactured products.

This particular shoe plant in New England has found the way to mass production. It has been doing a growing business while other shoe manufacturers have been failing. The cold facts are that in New York State the output per man in the shoe industry (in 1929) was $2597; Massachusetts' comparable output was $2134; Maine's, $1820; New Hampshire's, $1924 (see also Fig. 3, p. 90, below).

And not until New England's manufacturers learn the secret of mass production, based on knowledge of facts, will such comparisons be in favor of New England. Meanwhile, the shoe manufacturers of New York and perhaps of Missouri, by moving in the right direction themselves, have the time factor in their favor. If New England has lost its birthright, its mess of pottage is unscientific, nineteenth-century, low output-per-man production.

This important fact should be pondered by every manufacturer who is attempting to find other roads to current net profits: any step that in any way delays the undertaking of sound mass production in New England only makes her problem the harder—because of the time factor. Are other regions underselling us? Then we must attempt, by the development of style goods, to justify higher prices for New England merchandise, say some. As a matter of fact, in a study of style that I have been making, I have found that 25 per cent of style changes are the necessary result of social and economic changes. Another 25 per cent offer a reasonable and necessary field for experimentation and progressive betterment. The rest simply represent an attempt to escape competition, and it is the most dangerous expedient of which New England industries can avail themselves. If, instead of trying to escape competition, New Englanders would devote themselves to examining and eliminating the wastes in their production and distribution, they would find a far larger field for their efforts, and their efforts would be leading them in the direction in which in any case they must ultimately go.

Scientific Management and the New England Mind

Since the first step in scientific use of resources is a sound plan of action, and since sound planning implies full knowledge of opportunities, New England's scientific management must begin with research. It must also, for success, be accompanied by continuous supplementary research, to cover not only opportunities but methods and means.

And since both a scientific plan and the scientific operation of a plan require trained minds, the training of individuals in scientific method must be an important part of New England's way out.

Fortunately for us, we are better equipped than any other section of the country for the conception and carrying out of a program for the establishment of regional leadership through scientific management.

By people from other regions New England is frequently accused of conservatism. It is "old," it is "staid," it is "snobbish," it is "steeped in tradition." Whatever may be the truth of these matters —and it is easy to see where the rumor starts—it is unquestionably a fact that New England has a habit of mind that is characteristic of herself.

The first characteristic of the New England mind is, it seems to me, willingness to think independently.

Along with this goes a relentless logic. In his thinking a New Englander may reach entirely different conclusions from those reached by another American presented with the same raw thought material, and in many cases he starts with premises not in the consciousness of the others: this is the influence of tradition. But grant him his premises and his background, the New Englander of the type I am considering seems to think his way through—he does not jump at conclusions, he weighs, selects, pushes forward to a logical end.

Certainly nowhere else in the country does the population contain so many individuals who could successfully play parts in a program of fact-finding and a plan of action based on facts found.

Yet in recent years the "New England mind" has held New England back. If untrained, the too logical mind may expend its energy in discovering weaknesses in new ideas presented to it, where a less thorough mind would leap into action with less consideration of obstacles. An unfortunate cocksureness is also quite often with us. Not an offensive cocksureness but a dangerous one: dangerous because it leads us to proceed (or stand still) without due knowledge of the facts. Because we think we know, we do not take the trouble to find out; this is our weakness.

Fortunately, New England is the richest part of the country in institutions for the necessary training and in "follow-ups." A very important fact about its institutions for the education of young men and women is that they are constantly at the forefront of all the universities, colleges, and technical schools of America in the development of scientific method in teaching and practice. Harvard University pioneered in development of the case method in teaching law and now has applied this method to the study of business management in its Graduate School of Business Administration. In engineering education the Massachusetts Institute of Technology sets standards for the nation. Numbers of other New England universities and colleges, both for men and for women, stand in the front rank; and educational standards have made their way down through the high schools and the primary schools.

It has been said that New England has a library in every village. How nearly true this must be is shown by the amazing figures gathered a few years ago by the librarian of the University of North Carolina.[2] These show that when the forty-eight states of the American Union are ranked in order of the number of volumes per capita in their public libraries, the six New England states hold first, second, third, fifth, sixth, and seventh places. The intermediate state is California. In the amount of reading done by the people to whom these many collections of books are available, New England's showing is not so outstanding but still is remarkable. Second to California, Massachusetts citizens each read an average of nearly five books a year. Connecticut, fourth to Oregon's third, New Hampshire fifth, Vermont sixth—read nearly four books per citizen. Only nineteen states read annually more than two library books per citizen, and six of these nineteen are the states of New England.

In technical libraries and specialized scientific libraries, so close to the heart of a program of scientific training and scientific management, New England also leads the nation.

Scientific Management Must Begin with Research

Considering all these elements—a population inclined to mental activity, an unrivaled wealth in institutions for training in scientific method, outstanding resources for the supplying of needed facts— New England seems almost ideally equipped for reasserting its old habit of being first, this time by being first to apply the principles of scientific management to the solution of the business problems of which unemployment is the danger signal.

But a program of scientific development for New England must, as I have said, begin with research. Research means "finding out," in every sense of that phrase. It means finding out what needs to be done, what can be done, what others are doing, what is best to be done, how to do it, and above all how to do better what is already being done.

Take this matter of unemployment itself. How much do we really know about it, as a New England problem? We talk about it glibly enough, but what are the facts?

Strangely enough, little has been done to find out. So, partly to give the facts that are pertinent to this chapter but in greater part to show how enlightening even a simple analysis of facts may be, I am here presenting such an analysis. It was made for me by Chapin Hoskins, who as an editor and writer has for some years been particularly interested in unemployment problems from the point of view of industry.*

EMPLOYMENT AND UNEMPLOYMENT AS A WHOLE

This analysis is based on the reports of the United States Bureau of the Census. The problem of employment in all gainful occupations will be considered first; then, a more detailed examination of employment in the manufacturing industries will be made.

Concerning employment in all gainful occupations the U. S. Census statistics of occupations are the primary source of information. Particular use has been made of the figures for 1920 and 1930 showing the "number of persons ten years of age or over engaged in gainful occupations."[3] Besides these there are also available the results of a count of the *unemployed* taken by the Census Bureau for the first time in its history in April, 1930.[4] While this census of unemployment may not give an adequate idea of the total amount of unemployment, particularly in the years since the census was taken, it does, nevertheless, furnish about the only clue we have to the *relative* number of unemployed in different states, cities, and industries. The unemployed are divided into five classes. Our attention will be confined to "Class A," comprising "persons out of a job, able to work, and looking for a job"—in other words, "persons who are unemployed in the strictest sense of the word." In the following discussion figures quoted for "unemployed," "unemployment," etc., refer to Class A unemployed only and are given for purposes of comparison rather than as representing true totals or percentages. Likewise, the terms "employed," "employment," "jobs," etc., should be interpreted as referring either to "persons ten years of age or over engaged in gainful occupations," or to "wage earners" in manufacturing industries. The essential data for employment and unemployment as a whole are summarized in Tables I and II.

During the ten years from 1920 to 1930 total employment increased about 17.3 per cent in the United States. In New England the increase was only 6.1 per cent. To some degree the difference may be attributed to the fact that New England's population had gained less rapidly than that of the country at large. Yet, even when this allowance is made, employment appears to have lagged behind in New England. Throughout the whole country the part of the population ten years of age or over—or old enough to work—gained 19.3 per cent during the decade, the corresponding gain in New England being only 12.8 per cent. Comparing the two sets of figures, we see that the gains in employment fell short of the gains in potential workers by 2.0 per cent in the United States but by no less than 6.7 per cent in New England.

---

*Mr. Hoskins' analysis was prepared before the results of the Fifteenth Census of the United States were available. The editor has therefore recast some of the statistical data in the light of the later figures, without, however, affecting Mr. Hoskins' conclusions. The editor has also contributed the introductory paragraphs on employment and unemployment as a whole.—EDIT.

TABLE I—DISTRIBUTION OF EMPLOYMENT IN NEW ENGLAND AND THE
UNITED STATES IN 1920 AND 1930[a]

EMPLOYMENT[b]	N. ENG.	MAINE	N. H.	VT.	MASS.	R. I.	CONN.	U. S.
All industries, 1930 (thousands)	3,431.4	308.6	192.7	141.2	1,814.4	297.2	677.3	48,832.6
Percentage increase, 1920–1930	6.09	−0.40	−0.08	1.95	4.98	8.06	14.81	17.35
Percentage of potential workers,[c] 1920	54.4	49.9	53.3	48.7	55.6	56.8	54.2	50.3
Percentage of potential workers,[c] 1930	51.1	48.0	50.4	48.4	51.7	53.1	51.3	49.5
Difference	−3.3	−1.9	−2.9	−0.3	−3.9	−3.7	−2.9	−0.8
Manufacturing and mechanical industries, 1930 (thousands)	1,568.4	102.0	88.6	40.1	837.4	163.9	336.4	14,317.5
Percentage of all employment, 1930	45.69	33.05	45.97	28.40	46.16	55.14	49.66	29.32
Percentage increase, 1920–1930	−3.91	−15.17	−10.82	−10.16	−5.68	1.20	5.71	11.69
Trade, 1930 (thousands) . . .	561.7	39.7	22.5	16.2	325.4	45.2	112.6	7,537.0
Percentage of all employment, 1930	16.37	12.86	11.68	11.48	17.94	15.21	16.63	15.44
Percentage increase, 1920–1930	70.47	44.34	53.32	47.78	67.98	70.41	101.0	77.62
Domestic and personal service, 1930 (thousands)	336.5	28.3	17.6	13.6	188.9	26.3	61.8	4,812.1
Percentage of all employment, 1930	9.81	9.17	9.13	9.63	10.42	8.85	9.12	9.85
Percentage increase, 1920–1930	29.22	17.77	24.96	16.70	26.74	36.94	45.77	41.04
Transportation, 1930 (thousands)	274.1	29.9	15.6	13.2	148.4	18.9	48.2	4,438.6
Percentage of all employment, 1930	7.99	9.69	8.10	9.35	8.18	6.36	7.12	9.09
Percentage increase, 1920–1930	27.37	32.0	26.36	42.38	21.71	18.71	45.37	44.87

[a] Based on U. S. Census Reports for 1920 and 1930 cited in note 3, p. 95 below. The census figures for 1930 are not strictly comparable with those for 1920. The former include clerical workers among the several industry groups, whereas in the census of 1920 clerical workers were reported as a separate category. As a consequence, for each industry group except agriculture, forestry, and fishing the increases are considerably exaggerated and the decreases considerably understated. This would account for what are apparently very large proportional increases in trade, in which an unusually large fraction of all workers are engaged in clerical pursuits. This vitiates detailed comparisons of the changes as between different industry groups. It is likely, however, that within each group there is about the same ratio of clerical workers to all workers in each state. Hence comparisons of the changes within each group as between any two New England states or between New England and the United States as a whole are probably on the whole well founded.

[b] Persons ten years old and over engaged in gainful occupations.

[c] "Potential workers" are all persons ten years old and over.

TABLE I—Continued

EMPLOYMENT[b]	N. ENG.	MAINE	N. H.	VT.	MASS.	R. I.	CONN.	U. S.
Professional service, 1930 (thousands)	267.5	21.4	13.5	9.5	153.8	19.2	50.2	3,425.8
Percentage of all employment, 1930	7.80	6.93	7.004	6.73	8.48	6.46	7.41	7.02
Percentage increase, 1920–1930	52.6	28.5	43.89	24.46	55.69	58.82	62.9	59.8
Agriculture, 1930 (thousands)	213.3	51.5	22.1	38.1	56.0	8.9	36.7	10,482.3
Percentage of all employment, 1930	6.22	16.68	11.47	26.99	3.09	2.99	5.42	21.46
Percentage increase, 1920–1930	-4.84	-15.9	-13.2	-8.7	8.9	15.6	0.4	-1.9
Public service, 1930 (thousands)	88.4	7.1	3.5	3.2	51.4	8.2	15.1	1,057.9
Percentage of all employment, 1930	2.58	2.30	1.82	2.27	2.83	2.76	2.23	2.17
Percentage increase, 1920–1930	33.29	29.4	19.42	72.3	35.99	-3.45	53.35	37.3
Forestry, 1930 (thousands)	11.6	6.1	2.26	0.77	1.9	0.19	0.42	196.0
Percentage of all employment, 1930	.34	1.98	1.18	.55	.11	.06	.06	0.40
Percentage increase, 1920–1930	-47.98	-51.7	-53.8	-68.6	24.68	-8.2	-40.2	-9.9
Fishing, 1930 (thousands) . .	11.3	3.5	.06	.02	5.99	0.90	0.85	74.1
Percentage of all employment, 1930.	0.33	1.14	0.03	0.01	0.33	0.30	0.13	0.15
Percentage increase, 1920–1930.	25.2	0.6	-8.5	-4.5	31.2	89.4	97.7	28.8
Extraction of minerals, 1930 (thousands)	10.2	2.2	0.9	2.7	2.9	0.4	1.1	1,158.1
Percentage of all employment, 1930	.30	.71	.47	1.91	.16	.13	.16	2.37
Percentage increase, 1920–1930	109.3	193.5	118.7	43.12	138.2	179.4	139.6	6.22

The same comparison may also be expressed in terms of percentages of employed persons to the total number of persons ten years of age and over, or what we may call for short "employment ratios." In the United States, in 1920, 50.3 per cent of all persons ten years of age and over were employed; by 1930 this ratio had fallen to 49.5 per cent, a decline of 0.8 per cent. In New England the corresponding employment ratios were somewhat higher (54.4 per cent in 1920 and 51.1 per cent in 1930), but the decline was more pronounced (3.3 per cent). The decline, moreover, was more marked in New England than in the two other principal manufacturing sections of the country (1.5 per cent in the Middle Atlantic section and 0.8 per cent in the Eastern North-Central section). This means that throughout the country there were fewer jobs to go round in 1930 than ten years earlier. It also means that the number of jobs to go round fell off more in New England than it

Table II—Distribution of Unemployment in New England and the United States, 1920 and 1930[a]

Unemployment, Class A	N. Eng.	Maine	N. H.	Vt.	Mass.	R. I.	Conn.	U. S.
All industries, 1930 (thousands)	203.8	13.4	8.2	5.3	116.2	22.4	38.2	2,429.1
Percentage of all employed	5.9	4.3	4.2	3.7	6.4	7.6	5.6	5.0
Manufacturing and mechanical industries, 1930 (thousands)	121.1	5.3	4.5	2.1	70.2	15.7	23.5	1,122.6
Percentage of all employed, 1930	7.7	5.2	5.0	5.2	8.4	9.6	7.0	7.8
Trade, 1930 (thousands)	19.4	0.699	0.418	0.328	12.4	2.0	3.5	251.5
Percentage of all employed, 1930	3.5	1.8	1.9	2.0	3.8	4.4	3.2	3.3
Domestic and personal service, 1930 (thousands)	14.1	0.918	0.459	0.417	8.6	1.4	2.3	210.4
Percentage of all employed, 1930	4.2	3.2	2.6	3.1	4.6	5.2	3.7	4.4
Transportation, 1930 (thousands)	14.1	0.897	0.45	0.448	8.5	1.32	2.5	207.8
Percentage of all employed, 1930	5.1	3.0	2.9	3.4	5.7	7.0	5.2	4.7
Professional service, 1930 (thousands)	5.0	0.28	0.148	0.130	3.3	0.374	0.822	75.3
Percentage of all employed, 1930	1.9	1.3	1.1	1.4	2.1	1.9	1.6	2.2
Agriculture, 1930 (thousands)	5.3	1.0	0.5	0.65	1.8	0.28	1.1	111.2
Percentage of all employed, 1930	2.5	2.0	2.3	1.7	3.2	3.2	2.9	1.1
Public service, 1930 (thousands)	2.1	0.099	0.086	0.038	1.4	0.159	0.332	23.3
Percentage of all employed, 1930	2.4	1.4	2.4	1.2	2.8	1.9	2.2	2.2
Forestry, 1930 (thousands)	1.84	1.13	0.254[b]	0.089[b]	0.491[b]	0.026[b]	.027[b]	17.5
Percentage of all employed, 1930	15.8	18.7	10.9[b]	11.2[b]	6.2[b]	2.4[b]	2.1[b]	8.9
Extraction of minerals, 1930 (thousands)	0.65	0.073	0.033	0.200	0.236	0.043	0.065	90.8
Percentage of all employed, 1930	6.4	3.3	3.7	7.4	8.3	9.6	6.1	7.8

[a] Based on *Fifteenth Census of the United States, 1930: Unemployment*, Vol. 1, Washington, 1931. Totals cover persons out of work, able to work, and looking for a job. Percentages are of all gainful workers in each group.

[b] Includes fishing industry. Class A unemployed in New England fishing industry, 1930: 217; percentage of all employed: 1.9.

did in the country as a whole and more in New England than in the rest of the industrial northeast.

One might expect, therefore, that there would also be relatively more *un-employed* in New England than in the country as a whole, and the returns of the 1930 census of unemployment show that this was the case. In New England 5.9 per cent of all gainful workers were reported as Class A unemployed, as contrasted with 5.0 per cent in the whole country (Table II). But, though the loss in the number of jobs was proportionally greater in New England than in the Middle Atlantic and Eastern North-Central states, the latter sections and the Pacific states had more unemployment than New England. In the Middle Atlantic states 6.2 per cent of all gainful workers were reported as Class A unemployed, in the Eastern North-Central section 6.5 per cent, and in the Pacific states 6.3 per cent. It does not invariably follow that the most unemployment is found where employment ratios have fallen off the most during recent years. The actual number of un-employed in any one place at any given time is due to local and often temporary conditions. There is more unemployment in urban and manufacturing centers than in rural districts. As between manufacturing sections it would also seem that those where business expanded the more rapidly during the boom years have also been the sections in which the larger number of persons were thrown out of work when the crash came in the winter of 1929–1930. This would explain the high ratios of Class A unemployed to all gainful workers in the Middle Atlantic and Eastern North-Central sections as well as differences between the several New England states.

In no New England state was the employment ratio higher in 1930 than ten years earlier. In Vermont, however, there was almost no change in this ratio. While employment increased nearly 5 per cent in Massachusetts during the decade, and 8.1 per cent in Rhode Island, the declines in the employment ratios of these states, 3.9 and 3.7 per cent respectively, exceeded the corresponding decline in New England as a whole (3.3). In Connecticut employment increased 14.8 per cent, an increase approaching that of the United States (17.35 per cent), but Connecticut none the less suffered a marked decline in her employment ratio (2.9).

Vermont has a relatively larger rural and agricultural population than any other state in New England. This may account for the fact that the employment ratio decreased the least there and that there were the fewest unemployed. In marked contrast are the highly industrialized communities of Massachusetts and Rhode Island, where employment ratios fell the most and where were found the highest percentages of unemployed to all gainful workers. The decline in Connecticut's employment ratio (2.9) was about the same as that of New Hampshire (2.9) and somewhat more pronounced than that of Maine (1.9). Connecticut, however, had many more unemployed, both in absolute numbers and as expressed in percentages of all gainful workers, than did the two northern states. The crisis in the winter of 1929–1930 seems to have deprived proportionally more persons of their jobs in the urban and industrial states of Massachusetts, Rhode Island, and Connecticut than in the more rural states of the north. In this respect these states bear some-what the same relation to northern New England that the Middle Atlantic and Eastern North-Central sections bear to New England as a whole. It is also probable that many factory workers thrown out of work in northern New England have sought jobs in vain in southern New England.

Among the larger general divisions of the population as determined by occupa-tions the heaviest losses in New England between 1920 and 1930 occurred in the manufacturing and mechanical group (63,866), in agriculture (10,835), and in forestry (10,728). The proportional losses, however, were far greater in forestry (48.0 per cent) and slightly greater in agriculture (4.8 per cent) than in manufac-turing. While employment in the manufacturing and mechanical industries lost 3.9 per cent during the decade, there was a corresponding gain of 11.7 per cent in the manufacturing and mechanical group for the United States as a whole. As would be expected, there were more Class A unemployed in the manufacturing and mechanical occupations of New England (121,134) than in all other occupations put together (82,639). Forestry, however, had the highest percentage of unemployed to all gainful workers (15.8; the excess in forestry may possibly be due in some measure to the fact that the unemployment census was taken at an off-season).

The decline in agricultural employment was confined to the three northern states. Considerable gains in the number of agricultural jobs were recorded for Massachusetts and Rhode Island; but in Connecticut agricultural employment barely held its own. Despite the decline of farming in northern New England between 1920 and 1930, comparatively few agricultural workers were reported in 1930 as out of work. Such farm folk as have gone to the cities and subsequently lost their jobs there were reported as unemployed in other occupational groups.

Increases in employment occurred between 1920 and 1930 in all the other principal occupations of New England: trade, domestic and personal service, transportation, professional service, fishing, extraction of minerals, and public service. In all but the extraction of minerals, the relative increase was less than that of the same group throughout the country. Increases occurred in each group in each New England state, except in fishing in New Hampshire and Vermont and in public service in Rhode Island. In relation to the number of workers in each group there was slightly more Class A unemployment in New England than in the United States in trade, transportation, and public service and somewhat less in domestic and professional service and in the extraction of minerals.

To emphasize the essential facts which this analysis has disclosed, we may note that:

1. In the ten years before 1930 the total number of jobs *increased* both in New England and in the United States as a whole.

2. The increase was less rapid in New England.

3. In relation to the population old enough to work the number of jobs *decreased* both in New England and throughout the country.

4. This relative decrease in the number of jobs to go round was more marked in New England than throughout the nation as a whole.

5. There were slightly more unemployed in New England in 1930 in proportion to all gainful workers than there were in the country as a whole but somewhat fewer in New England than in the Middle Atlantic and Eastern North-Central sections.

6. Employment during the decade 1920–1930 fell off in New England's mechanical and manufacturing industries, in agriculture, and in forestry but increased in the other chief occupational groups.

7. The greatest proportional decrease in employment (48 per cent) occurred in forestry; agricultural employment declined 4.8 per cent, and in the manufacturing and mechanical industries employment declined 3.9 per cent.

8. In 1930 there were more unemployed manufacturing and mechanical workers than there were unemployed workers in all other occupations put together. However, in proportion to the total number of gainfully employed in the industry there was considerably more unemployment in forestry.

Manufacturing Employment in New England

As a rule it is a mistake (and an altogether too common one) to consider, in a discussion of unemployment, only the figures of employment in manufacturing industries.

A lessening of employment in manufacture is not of itself an unfavorable sign. Though technological progress may tend to reduce the numbers of men and women needed in the production of established products, it also creates many new occupations outside the manufacturing field. An example frequently given is the development of automobile service stations and filling stations, which employ thousands of mechanics and attendants. Thus it is always conceivable that a decrease in manufacturing employment may take place as a part of a transition which in fact increases the total number of individuals in gainful occupations, and manufacturing figures should always be read in terms of their context.

But in New England there does seem justification for using manufacturing figures in a study of unemployment conditions. In New England as a whole, and in each of its states except Maine and Vermont, manufacturing in 1930 supplied the livelihood of about half the male working population.

Although for women it was not so predominantly a livelihood as for men, manufacturing did employ the majority of working women in Rhode Island and about 40 per cent of those in New Hampshire, Massachusetts, and Connecticut, and was the predominant source of gainful work for women in New England as a whole.

In view of these facts, the course of employment in New England manufacturing industries would seem to be by far the most important single factor in total employment, and, in the absence of contrary indications, it would appear sound to consider the course of manufacturing employment as a key to the total employment situation.

Moreover, no comprehensive figures of employment in other fields than manufacturing are available for any intermediate years between 1920 and 1930. Manufacturing employment figures are available for all of New England at two-year intervals.[5] Hence, a study of manufacturing is in fact about the only key available to an understanding of the fluctuations that have occurred in New England within the past decade.

MANUFACTURING EMPLOYMENT AND PRODUCTIVITY

The total production and distribution of any given region determine the possible consumption of that region. In general, New England, or any other region, can consume only to the degree of its success in production and exchange. Although part of what it consumes will be brought in from outside regions, it must in general (except in so far as it is a creditor district to other districts) pay for its importations with the fruits of its own labor. This payment may be in the form of goods actually sent out of the region or partly in the form of services rendered to travelers and temporary residents coming into the region from outside. In any case a lessening of the total output of the region must mean either:

1. Lowering of the standard of living for the people of the region
2. Lowering of the standard of living of part of the people of the region
3. Emigration from the region
4. A combination of all these results.

Unemployment accompanied by a decrease of output, if more than temporary, would be marked by at least one of these unfavorable results.

If the total output of a region increases, the results would naturally be reversed. That is to say:

1. Higher standard of living for the entire population
2. Higher standard of living for part of the population
3. Immigration, or natural increase of population
4. A combination of these.

A fifth possibility is, of course, savings, with investment in business enterprise elsewhere but still leading toward higher living standards.

Because of these causal relationships, a decrease in the number of individuals employed in manufacturing, if in fact due to technological improvements, would theoretically be paralleled by the development of new non-manufacturing jobs. Thus a decrease in manufacturing employment might actually mean an improvement in the condition of the region as a whole.

It is therefore important:

1. To note what has been the actual course of manufacturing employment in New England in recent years

TABLE III—DISTRIBUTION OF MANUFACTURING EMPLOYMENT IN NEW ENGLAND
AND THE UNITED STATES, 1919–1930[a]
(Wage Earners in Thousands)

	1919	1921	1923	1925	1927	1929	GAINS	LOSSES
United States	9,000.1	6,946.6	8,778.2	8,384.3	8,349.8	8,807.5	. . . . . .	192.5
New England	1,351.4	1,071.1	1,253.9	1,122.2	1,098.7	1,100.0	. . . . . .	251.3
Maine								
All manufactures	88.7	75.7	83.3	73.8	68.1	69.6	. . . . . .	19.1
Pulp and paper	13.1	11.2	12.5	11.8	11.9	12.1	. . . . .	0.9
Woolen goods	6.9	6.1	8.3	7.3	6.1	6.5	. . . . . .	0.4
Lumber and allied products	9.8	8.1	7.3	5.3	3.9	3.4	. . . . . .	6.4
Shipbuilding	7.0	1.6	1.2	0.6	0.3	1.1	. . . . . .	5.9
Cotton goods	11.8	13.3	13.8	11.9	10.2	b		1.6[c]
Net loss other industries, 1919–1929	. . . . . .	. . . . . .	. . . . . .	. . . . . .	. . . .	. . . .	. . . .	4.0
New Hampshire								
All manufactures	83.1	67.4	75.3	66.7	65.5	65.1	. . . . . .	18.0
Boots and shoes other than rubber	12.3	8.9	13.6	12.3	12.1	14.5	2.2	. . . .
Cotton goods	21.2	22.7	18.5	14.7	14.7	13.8	. . . . . .	7.4
Lumber and allied products	5.0	3.7	3.7	3.3	2.3	2.0	. . . . . .	3.0
Net loss other industries, 1919–1929	. . . . . .	. . . . . .	. . . . . .	. . . . . .	. . . .	. . . .	. . . .	9.8
Vermont								
All manufactures	33.5	25.8	30.8	27.6	26.2	27.6	. . . . . .	5.9
Marble, granite, slate, etc.	5.4	3.8	5.0	4.7	5.2	5.3	. . . . . .	0.1
Lumber and allied products	3.0	2.6	2.8	2.2	1.7	2.4	. . . . . .	0.6
Woolen goods	3.0[d]	2.6	4.3	2.9	2.6	1.5	. . . . . .	1.5[e]
Net loss other industries, 1919–1929	. . . . . .	. . . . . .	. . . . . .	. . . . . .	. . . .	. . . .	. . . .	3.6
Massachusetts								
All manufactures	713.8	578.6	666.6	591.4	578.1	559.4	. . . . . .	154.4
Cotton goods	122.5	106.3	113.7	96.2	90.9	70.8	. . . . . .	51.7
Boots and shoes other than rubber	80.2	64.5	69.4	57.4	56.0	55.1	. . . . . .	25.1
Worsted goods	36.3	40.9	45.8	36.8	35.1	30.0	. . . . . .	6.3

[a] Based on U. S. Census of Manufactures, 1919–1929.
[b] No data.
[c] Loss 1919–1927.
[d] Includes worsted goods.
[e] Excessive because 1919 figure includes worsted goods.

TABLE III—Continued

	1919	1921	1923	1925	1927	1929	GAINS	LOSSES
Massachusetts (continued)								
Electrical machinery, apparatus, and supplies .	23.9	17.6	26.4	25.1	24.8	28.8	5.0	......
Foundries and machine shops	27.7	20.0	24.7	19.5	19.9	21.2	......	6.5
Woolen goods	17.6	15.7	19.0	18.1	15.9	15.7	......	1.9
Printing and publishing .	13.5	12.8	14.2	14.2	14.4	15.2	1.7	......
Pulp and paper	13.0	12.4	13.3	12.9	12.1	12.4	......	0.6
Rubber boots and shoes .	13.1	9.3	12.5	11.4	12.1	11.2	......	1.9
Leather	15.2	9.0	11.4	10.4	10.8	10.7	......	4.5
Textile machinery . . .	17.4	16.5	18.7	13.7	12.0	10.6	......	6.8
Knit goods	12.8	10.5	11.7	10.6	9.7	8.8	......	3.9
Rubber goods	9.4	5.0[g]	11.4	10.7	10.4	[b]	1.0[f]	......
Net loss other industries, 1919–1929	......	......	......	......	......	......	......	52.8
Connecticut								
All manufactures	292.7	210.9	263.2	242.4	240.8	253.5	......	39.2
Foundries and machine shops	20.1	12.1	19.1	17.0	16.8	19.5	......	0.7
Hardware	18.6	17.0	22.2	21.6	18.2	18.0	......	0.7
Electrical machinery, apparatus, and supplies .	11.4	8.4	14.4	14.2	14.5	15.2	3.8	......
Cotton goods	15.6	14.3	14.9	12.0	12.6	10.8	......	4.9
Silk goods	11.3	10.9	12.4	10.0	9.2	10.5[h]	......	0.8
Typewriters and supplies	6.5	6.0	7.1	7.0	8.7	8.9	2.3	......
Fur-felt hats	4.6	3.7	4.9	5.5	5.5	6.1	1.5	......
Woolen goods	5.4	4.9	6.2	6.5	5.9	5.4	0.006	......
Clocks, etc.	4.9	2.9	4.6	3.1	4.9	5.0	0.08	......
Corsets and allied garments	5.6	4.7	4.5	4.0	3.1	2.8	......	2.8
Brass and bronze . . .	29.6	15.4	23.	20.4	20.4	[b]	......	9.1[c]
Net loss other industries, 1919–1929	......	......	......	......	......	......	......	28.0
Rhode Island								
All manufactures	139.7	112.7	134.7	120.3	120.0	124.8	......	14.8
Cotton goods	31.4	29.3	34.0	29.3	26.2	21.8	......	9.6
Worsted goods	21.2	20.0	23.4	18.9	21.1	21.2	......	0.033
Dyeing and finishing . .	9.3	5.5	9.5	9.9	9.6	9.2	......	0.077
Silk goods	4.2	4.5	4.9	6.1	6.5	7.6[h]	3.4	......
Textile machinery . . .	3.8	4.2	4.5	3.8	3.4	3.7	......	0.065
Net loss other industries, 1919–1929	......	......	......	......	......	......	......	8.5

[f] Gain 1919–1927.
[g] Does not include data for two establishments manufacturing rubber tires and inner tubes.
[h] Includes rayon.

2. To learn, if possible, whether there has been a corresponding change in the total output of the region.

A comparison of rows 1 and 2 in Table III shows that manufacturing employment in the United States as a whole has increased when manufacturing employment in New England has increased, and decreased when manufacturing employment in New England decreased. These figures standing by themselves, therefore, are no indication of conditions peculiar to New England. A percentage comparison, however, seems to tell an interesting story. The percentages that New England manufacturing employment bore to the total manufacturing employment of the United States are as follows, with gains and losses indicated: 1914, 16.55 per cent; 1919, 15.02(-); 1921, 15.43(+); 1923, 14.29(-); 1925, 13.39(-); 1927, 13.16(-); 1929, 12.48(-). This was an almost unbroken decrease.

The next question is whether this indicates that New England is doing a better or a less effective job.

For an answer we may turn to an examination of the value of the manufacturing output of New England. At the census of 1919 this value was in excess of $7,000,-000,000; at the census of 1921, in sympathy with the general decline of the country, it was just under $5,000,000,000. At the censuses of 1923, 1925, 1927, and 1929 it was in each case something over $6,000,000,000, but with a slight decrease from one census to the next through 1927 in the face of a slight increase for the United States as a whole. Between 1927 and 1929 there were slight increases both in the United States and in New England.

The following are the percentages which the value of New England manufactured products bore to the value of the products manufactured in the United States: 1914, 12.28 per cent; 1919, 11.59(-); 1921, 11.24(-); 1923, 10.61(-); 1925, 9.8(-); 1927, 9.61(-); 1929, 9.14(-).

Conceivably even this general downward trend might mean nothing more than that regions outside of New England, growing in population and in ability to absorb manufactured products, were having their new needs supplied by manufacturers in other regions, while New England retained practically its normal business. There is, however, one further indication that New England has not been holding its own in comparison with the rest of the country. Value of products, just given, is not in itself an indicator of work accomplished, since in the figures for value are included the costs of materials, supplies, containers for products, fuel, and power. If, however, these costs as given by the census are subtracted from the value of the products figures, we have "value added by manufacture"—a reasonably accurate reflection of trends in the value of the work performed by labor and management forces, with the assistance of machines and power. If the total value of work performed as reported by each census (expressed, however, in terms of the purchasing power of dollars of 1913) is divided by the number of wage earners, the following result is obtained:

TABLE IV—VALUE OF OUTPUT PER WAGE EARNER IN TERMS OF
DOLLARS OF 1913

	NEW ENGLAND	UNITED STATES EXCLUDING NEW ENGLAND
1914	$1136	$1490
1919	1163	1384
1921	1508	1841
1923	1618	1955
1925	1646	2065
1927	1846	2309
1929	1986	2490

This shows that whereas the value of output per worker for the United States outside of New England increased 80 per cent from 1914 to 1929, in New England the increase was only 71 per cent.

All these figures point directly to two conclusions: (1) that manufacturing employment in New England has been decreasing and (2) that the decrease appears to have been unfavorable rather than favorable to New England and is a symptom of difficulties that must be overcome if New England's population is neither to sink to a lower standard nor be forced in part to emigrate.

MANUFACTURING EMPLOYMENT, 1919–1929

Is New England manufacturing unemployment universal or have some states and some industries suffered relatively more than others? We have pointed out that employment in the manufacturing and mechanical industries, as revealed by the statistics for occupations of the Fourteenth and Fifteenth Decennial Census reports, fell off 63,866, or 3.9 per cent between 1920 and 1930. The Census of Manufactures shows that a much greater loss took place between 1919 and 1929. During this period the average number of wage earners in the manufacturing industries of New England decreased by about 251,300 (Table III). In the United States outside of New England there was a corresponding increase of about 58,800. The net decrease for the whole country was therefore about 192,500, or 2.14 per cent.

Let us take this figure of 2.14 per cent to represent what we may call the "normal" decline (resulting perhaps from technological gains) and apply it to the states of New England (Table V).

TABLE V—DECREASE IN MANUFACTURING EMPLOYMENT, 1919–1929,
NEW ENGLAND STATES

STATE	EMPLOYMENT IN 1919	DECREASE 1919–1929			ACTUAL EMPLOYMENT, 1929, AS PERCENTAGE OF "NORMAL," 1929
		"NORMAL"	ACTUAL	EXCESS OF ACTUAL OVER "NORMAL"	
Maine .	88,651	1,897	19,058	17,161	80.2
N. H. .	83,074	1,778	17,955	16,177	80.1
Vermont	33,491	716	5,909	5,193	84.0
Mass. .	713,836	15,280	154,393	139,113	80.1
R. I. . .	139,665	2,992	14,827	11,835	91.0
Conn. .	292,672	6,266	39,204	32,938	88.0

One sees at a glance from these figures that in Massachusetts alone lay the greater part of all New England's losses in manufacturing employment, though Connecticut too had a large excess of loss. The percentage column shows clearly that the most serious decreases in relation to the "normal" occurred in Massachusetts and the three least populous states, Maine, Vermont, and New Hampshire.[6]

Table III and the graphs (Fig. 1) illustrate the same process in greater detail. They show how manufacturing employment in each state has risen and fallen during the two-year intervals between the biennial censuses of manufactures.

In Figure 1 the curve for the whole United States, indicated by a broken line, is repeated on each graph in order that the movement in each state may be compared with the "normal" movement of the country at large. Plotted on the logarithmic scale, the curves reveal equal amounts of *relative* change by lines of equal steepness. Where any two lines run parallel the same percentage of loss or gain is indicated.

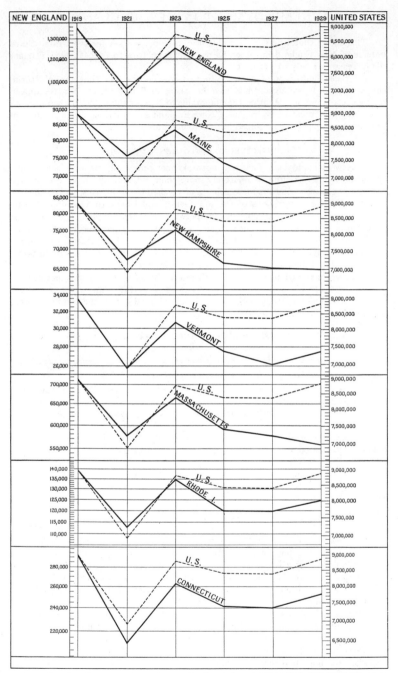

Fig. 1—Number of wage earners, 1919–1929, in all manufacturing industries, New England and the several New England states (solid lines) as compared with the United States (broken lines). Based on U. S. Census of Manufactures, 1919–1929.

84

The more the solid lines for New England and its several states rise above (or fall below) the broken lines for the United States at any given date, the greater the relative gain (or loss) in New England between 1919 and the date in question.

The year 1919 marked the crest of the post-war boom; 1921 was a year of depression and 1923 another boom year. The curves show that between 1919 and 1921 the decline in manufacturing employment was slightly less pronounced in New England than in the country at large. In every state but Connecticut the depression of 1921 seems to have affected employment somewhat less adversely than throughout the nation. It is probable that the same has been true of the much more severe recent depression, but unfortunately no figures for manufacturing employment in 1931 are yet available to confirm this opinion. At all events, in April, 1930, as we have seen, the ratio of Class A unemployed to gainful workers in the manufacturing industries was slightly lower in New England than the corresponding ratio in other manufacturing sections of the country.

If manufacturing employment in New England, excepting Connecticut, withstood the depression of 1921 somewhat better than was the case elsewhere, the recovery with the return of prosperity in 1923 was far less substantial. Nor did New England maintain the levels reached in 1923 as did the rest of the United States. During the six years of prosperity from 1923 to 1929 employment in the manufacturing industries of the United States practically held its own. There was a slight sag in 1925 and 1927 with a rise in 1929 to a peak higher than that of 1923, though not quite as high as the level reached in 1919. In New England, on the other hand, the decline between 1923 and 1927 was much more marked than in the country at large, and instead of experiencing an upturn between 1927 and 1929 employment remained almost stationary. In Connecticut and Rhode Island, to be sure, the trend from 1923 to 1929 was more nearly parallel to that of the country as a whole. Apparently in these two states employment during the years of prosperity followed about the course it followed in the greater part of the United States, but in Massachusetts and the three northern states the movement was very different. Here we note critical departures from the "normal" curves. The declines from the peak of 1923 were considerably greater than in Connecticut and Rhode Island. Indeed, during the years 1927–1929, when gains were being recorded nearly everywhere else, employment fell off materially in Massachusetts and to a slight degree in New Hampshire.

Let us examine a little more closely the losses and gains in different industries between 1919 and 1929.

The difficulties met by the cotton manufactures of New England during recent years account for over 30 per cent of the total net decrease in manufacturing employment during the decade 1919–1929. A quarter of this total loss occurred in the cotton industry of Massachusetts alone. Declines in the boot and shoe industry of Massachusetts are responsible for 10 per cent of New England's net decrease. The remaining losses were fairly widely scattered.

The thirteen industries for which curves are plotted for Massachusetts in Figure 2 suffered an aggregate decline in manufacturing employment of 99,573, or nearly two thirds the entire decline for the state. More than 51,000 persons were released by the cotton mills alone, more than 18,000 by the woolen, worsted, textile machinery, and knit goods industries, and more than 25,000 by the boot and shoe industries. The textile and boot and shoe industries suffered a shrinkage of about 32 per cent as compared with a shrinkage of 14 per cent in all the other industries of the state combined.[7] When 1919 is compared with 1929 it appears that the worsted and textile machinery industries made a somewhat better showing than the other manufactures just mentioned. Employment in these industries, however, rose to higher peaks in 1923, and the decline from then to 1929 was hardly less severe than in the other types of textile manufacture and in the shoe industry.

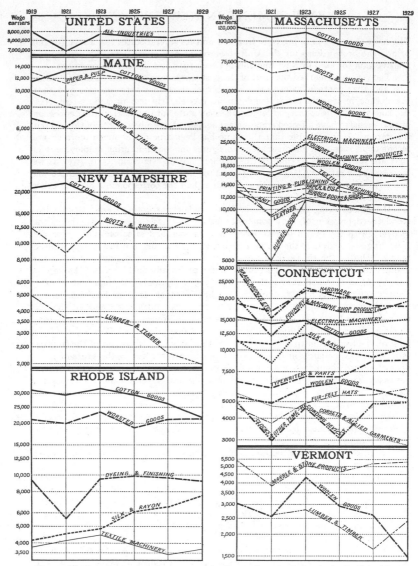

FIG. 2—Number of wage earners, 1919–1929, in all manufacturing industries in the United States and in the more important manufacturing industries in the several New England states. Based on U. S. Census of Manufactures, 1919–1929. See also Fig. 4, p. 330, below.

86

Employment in the foundry and machine shop industries of Massachusetts lost ground during the decade as a whole, though there was a slow recovery after 1925. In other industries employment was generally stable. The most striking advance occurred in the manufacture of electrical machinery and supplies, though the relative gain was not as great as that which took place in the same industry outside New England. The curves for printing and publishing show a slow, steady increase; there was a slight loss in paper and wood pulp. Most of the loss in the leather manufactures occurred before 1921, and employment in that industry after 1923 was almost stationary.

Connecticut fared better than Massachusetts. The net loss for the state between 1919 and 1929 was only slightly more than a quarter that of Massachusetts, whereas Connecticut had nearly three sevenths as many wage earners in manufactures. Employment in the cotton mills of Connecticut, as in those of its northern neighbor, showed an almost continuous downward trend: 4900 workers lost their jobs in this industry during the decade. There were only half as many wage earners in the manufacture of "corsets and allied garments" in 1929 as there had been ten years before. However, the greatest loss (9100 between 1919 and 1927) occurred in the bronze and brass industry, though most of the decline here took place between 1919 and 1921. The depression of 1921 seems to have cut more deeply into employment in the metal industries of Connecticut than in the textiles group, but the former had largely made up their losses by 1923. Gains or stability from 1923 to 1929 in the manufacture of electrical machinery and supplies, brass and bronze, foundry and machine-shop products, typewriters, and fur-felt hats indicate strength in Connecticut's specialties, some of which have been established in the state nearly as long as the textile and shoe industries in Massachusetts. The number of jobs in the making of electrical machinery, typewriters, and hats increased significantly, and the important manufactures of hardware, foundry and machine-shop products, and woolen and silk goods offered reasonably sure employment.

In relation to the total number of workers employed in 1919 employment declined less in Rhode Island than in any other New England state. The continuous decrease in the cotton mills was partly compensated by an increase in the silk mills. The worsted industry and the manufacture of textile machinery appear to have followed even courses; the same may also be said of the dyeing and finishing industry except for a severe drop in 1921.

Maine's difficulties are of another sort, traceable chiefly to declines in its forest products. Table I shows that employment in the forests of Maine was cut more than half during the ten years 1920–1930. In the manufacture of lumber and timber products employment decreased to an even more marked degree between 1919 and 1929, from 9800 to 3400; and in shipbuilding the loss was still greater, from 7000 to 1100. The 1919 figure for Maine shipbuilding, however, is not representative owing to the abnormally expanded employment during that year in shipyards in connection with war-time contracts. The relative declines in the paper and wood pulp and textile industries of Maine were not so severe.

New Hampshire's experience during the decade was partly like that of Massachusetts and partly like Maine's. Cotton goods with a loss of 7400, woolen goods with a loss of 1300, and lumber and timber products with a loss of 3000 account for nearly two thirds of the state's total net loss of 18,000. By contrast with Massachusetts the boot and shoe industry gained 2200 wage earners.

A considerable portion of Vermont's loss of 5900 may be attributed to a sharp decline in employment in the woolen industry. The exact amount of the decline from 1919 to 1929 cannot be determined, since the 1919 figures include the worsted with the woolen industry, whereas the later figures are for woolen only. The decline in the woolen industry from 1923 to 1929 amounted to 2800 wage earners. Between 1919 and 1929 the lumber and timber industries of Vermont released 600 workers,

TABLE VI—DISTRIBUTION OF UNEMPLOYMENT, CLASS A, IN MANUFACTURING AND MECHANICAL INDUSTRIES, NEW ENGLAND AND THE UNITED STATES, 1930[a]

	NEW ENGLAND		MAINE		NEW HAMPSHIRE		VERMONT	
	Number[b]	%[c]	Number[b]	%[c]	Number[b]	%[c]	Number[b]	%[c]
All manufactures .	121,134	7.7	5,262	5.2	4,458	5.0	2,077	5.2
Building industry	31,153	14.2	1,357	8.0	916	8.5	784	10.3
Textile industries	28,850	8.7	1,466	6.7	1,314	5.7	296	6.4
Cotton mills .	11,849	9.4	516	5.4	710	5.6	35	3.1
Woolen and worsted mills	10,404	11.3	811	9.3	356	6.8	185	7.8
Silk mills . .	1,787	6.2	d	d	80	9.2	d	d
Knitting mills	692	6.2	d	d	62	3.2	30	4.9
Other textile mills . . .	4,118	5.5	139	3.8	106	4.9	46	9.6
Shoe factories .	7,743	7.1	d	d	849	4.6	d	d
Electrical machinery and supply factories	3,205	6.9	d	d	d	d	d	d
Metal industries[g]	20,346	6.5	336[f]	4.3[f]	339	4.4	165[f]	2.7[f]
Clothing industries	2,810	4.7	36	1.9	22	1.9	58	4.7
Woodworking and furniture industries . . .	2,807	5.6	238	3.1	226	3.6	236	4.4
Rubber factories	2,859	8.0	d	d	d	d	d	d

TABLE VI—Continued

	MASSACHUSETTS		RHODE ISLAND		CONNECTICUT		UNITED STATES	
	Number[b]	%[c]	Number[b]	%[c]	Number[b]	%[c]	Number[b]	%[c]
All manufactures .	70,208	8.4	15,653	9.6	23,476	7.0	1,122,610	7.8
Building industry	18,666	15.8	2,809	14.9	6,621	13.8	395,090	15.4
Textile industries	16,678	9.6	6,592	9.7	2,504	5.9	72,100	6.1
Cotton mills .	7,951	10.8	2,116	11.5	521	4.9	23,373	5.5
Woolen and worsted mills	5,760	11.9	2,660	12.8	632	9.4	14,256	10.2
Silk mills . .	d	d	593	6.5	518	5.2	9,387	5.3
Knitting mills	d	d	d	d	d	d	8,984	5.2
Other textile mills . . .	2,967	5.8	1,223	6.3	833	5.6	16,100	5.9
Shoe factories . .	6,254	8.1	d	d	d	d	16,159	6.0

[a] Based on *Fifteenth Census of the United States, 1930: Unemployment*, Vol. 1, Washington, 1931.

[b] Persons out of work, able to work, and looking for a job.

[c] Percentage of all gainful workers in the industry.

[d] No data.

[e] Lumber and furniture industries.

[f] Iron and steel industries.

[g] Blast furnaces and steel rolling mills, other iron and steel industries, metal industries except iron and steel (except those marked f).

TABLE VI—Continued

	MASSACHUSETTS		RHODE ISLAND		CONNECTICUT		UNITED STATES	
	Number[b]	%[c]	Number[b]	%[c]	Number[b]	%[c]	Number[b]	%[c]
Electrical machinery and supply factories	2,250	7.1	174	8.9	736	6.3	30,358	8.0
Metal industries[g]	7,984	6.3	3,989	10.4	7,503	6.1	175,937	6.5
Clothing industries	1,553	4.9	103	3.8	1,038	4.9	46,052	5.8
Woodworking and furniture industries	d	d	d	d	290[e]	5.3[e]	53,631	6.2
Rubber factories .	1,903	8.8	327	5.1	615	8.1	11,818	7.1

paper and wood pulp lost 800, and "car and general construction and repairs, steam-railroad repair shops" released 700. The remaining decrease was scattered. While employment in the lumber and timber industry shrank during the decade, the decline was not as rapid as in Maine or New Hampshire, and there was a slight recovery between 1927 and 1929. Employment in Vermont's largest manufacturing industry, that of "marble, granite, slate, and other stone products," remained almost stationary except for a temporary shrinkage during the depression of 1921.

Broadly speaking, the manufacturing industries that threw the most workers out of employment between 1919 and 1929 were also the industries in which the most men and women were looking for jobs in April, 1930, as revealed by the Census of Unemployment (Table VI). In New England as a whole there was a total of 121,134 Class A unemployed in the manufacturing and mechanical industries. In this category the largest single group, amounting to 31,153 workers, was made up of unemployed in the building trades (not covered by the Census of Manufactures). Outside of the building trades there were 89,981 unemployed in the manufacturing and mechanical category, and of these nearly a third, or 28,850, were found in the textile manufactures. The metal industries came next, with 20,346 out of work, and were followed in order by shoe manufacturing, the manufacture of electrical machinery and supplies, and the rubber industry. As shown by the ratio of Class A unemployed to all gainful workers in the industry the building trades were in by far the worst condition of all the mechanical and manufacturing industries, with 14.2 per cent out of work in all New England and 15.8 per cent in Massachusetts. The textile group took second place, with 8.7 per cent, and was followed by the rubber industries (8.0 per cent), boots and shoes (7.1 per cent), electrical machinery and supplies (6.9 per cent), and the metal industries (6.5 per cent). 11,849 cotton mill workers, or 9.4 per cent of all the cotton mill workers of New England, were looking for jobs, and 10,404 workers in woolen and worsted mills (11.3 per cent of all wage earners in the industry). We have seen that nearly a third of the total net loss in manufacturing employment in New England between 1919 and 1929 may be ascribed to the cotton industry alone. Unemployed cotton workers, however, accounted for only about two fifteenths of all the unemployed in the manufacturing and mechanical group (excluding the building trades). This shows that a large part of the employees released by suspension of operations in the cotton and other textile mills must have found employment in other industries, often again to lose their jobs. The number of Class A unemployed attributed to

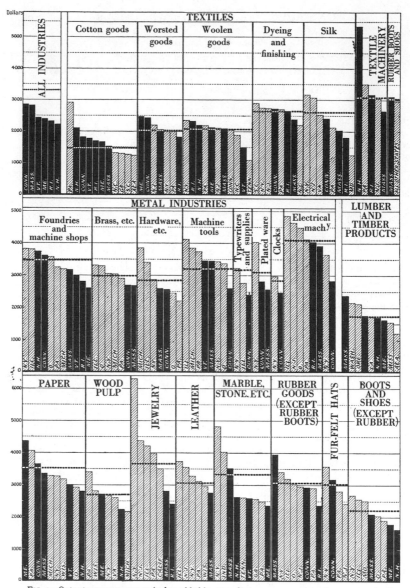

FIG. 3—Output per wage earner (value added by manufacture per wage earner), 1927, twenty-four leading manufacturing industries of New England. For each industry comparison is made with states outside New England (shaded bars) highest in reported employment for the industry. The national averages for all industries and for each separate industry are shown by the broken horizontal lines. Based on U. S. Census of Manufactures, 1927.

In the census reports "the average number of wage earners is unavoidably overstated to some extent" (for explanation see *Biennial Census of Manufactures, 1927*, Washington, 1930, p. 1255), and consequently the output per wage earner is somewhat understated upon this chart. However, the use of the census figures yields such consistent results as between different industries and different census years that the margin of error is apparently not great. The method also yields valuable results not otherwise obtainable.

the textile industries in the Census of Unemployment certainly fails to give an adequate idea of the amount of unemployment produced by the difficulties encountered by these industries.

NEW ENGLAND MANUFACTURES HAVE BEEN LOSING GROUND

From the figures just given, three facts are evident:

1. That the northern New England states have suffered from the loss of industries closely linked to their forests and that the loss has not been regained in other industries.

2. That Massachusetts in particular, but the other New England states as well, have seen tens of thousands thrown out of work by the weakness of the textile and the boot and shoe industries.

3. That not only these, but nearly every industry in New England has been losing ground, and only with rare exceptions have strong new industries been built up, or old ones strengthened, to absorb the surplus of wage earners.

Consider how important this third fact is. If, aside from its cotton and shoe industries, New England were today leading the nation in the efficiency of its manufacturing, its employment surplus would soon be absorbed when normal times return.

But the actual situation is quite the reverse.

Outside of New England, the average value of output per wage earner, in all industries, was (in 1927) about $3393 (Fig. 3).

In Massachusetts, out of 314,000 wage earners in the state's twelve leading industries, 91,000 produced less than half this amount. For 198,000 workers, the output was less than two thirds of it. And for 269,000—or by far the greater part of the 314,000—it was below the standard for the rest of the nation. Of the twelve industries only two were above the national average.

Connecticut makes a somewhat better showing. Nevertheless, in its twelve leading industries 19,000 wage earners (out of 128,000) had a per-man production less than two thirds of standard; and 111,000 of the 128,000 were below standard. Of the twelve industries only one was above standard.

Of Rhode Island's five leading industries (employing more than half her workers) not one equaled the standard of output of the rest of the nation. Of 71,000 workers in them 26,000 had less than half the standard output per man; 54,000 had less than two thirds the standard.

Of Maine's five leaders one was above standard. Of 38,000 workers 10,000 produced less than half the national standard; 26,000 less than two thirds; 30,000 less than standard.

In New Hampshire four industries employed more than half the manufacturing wage earners. In not one of these was production per man as much as two thirds the national standard.

Vermont, smallest in total employment, makes a somewhat better showing than the other two northern states. Of six industries employing the majority of workers, one was above standard, none below the halfway mark. But of 13,200 workers 5500 had less than two thirds of standard output; 11,800 less than standard.

Why is it that New England comes out on the wrong side of a comparison like this?

There are two possibilities. One is that New England people are engaged in industries whose output per man is low everywhere in the United States. The other is that in each industry New England's output is below the average for that industry.

Actually, both of these are the case, as Figure 3 rather depressingly indicates. Of 24 leading industries of New England 19 had a national average below the national average of all industries. In the 24 industries, the output of the New England states was more often below the average than above it. Only in rare cases did a New England state lead even these low-production-per-man industries.

In all this comparing of output per wage earner it must be kept in mind that the output is only in part a matter of labor efficiency. A good deal of New England's ability and energy has been distracted by fights with labor unions. From the business standpoint this is unpardonable, especially now that labor is officially on record that high production must go with high wages.

But though output per man sets a limit above which wages cannot possibly move, this output is in reality a result of management.

The choice of product; marketing arrangements and marketing effectiveness; whether the manufacturing plant is new or obsolete; the machinery available and the way in which it is used; production engineering and production management— these taken together are what determine output per man. What counts is not so much what labor does as what labor gets a chance to do.

The Need of Research

Thus this bit of research into unemployment points clearly to New England's need of research for its own good. It is plain that something besides optimism and faith in miracles is required. Which of the various factors mentioned in the previous paragraph is chiefly our difficulty? Or if all are troubling us, how are we going to meet the problem raised by each? How are we going to become better planners, better producers, better merchandisers?

Only by knowing the facts.

An investigation reported in 1928 by the National Research Council showed that of six hundred "millionaire companies" in the United States known to have appropriations for research, more than one half were supporting research for improvement of quality of products or service. Nearly one half were interested in reduction of costs of manufacture, one third in developing new uses for present products, one fourth in developing by-products or new materials, one in fifteen in the development of new products. If we add as a very important item research for the purpose of reducing marketing costs, New England business corporations must undertake research on their own account in something like these characteristic proportions. Many New England corporations already do so, and the coming to life of more than one moribund New England business has been due to just such searching for facts.

Yet, what the individual corporation can do is, in all probability, not enough. This matter of unemployment in New England, together with the background of business recession revealed by it, is to some degree a geographical phenomenon. It concerns all those who live or work or control capital in this geographical region we call New England and is partly the result of factors peculiar to the region. The problem is going to be solved rightly only by research in the general interest of New England, followed by action in the general interest.

Will this research in the general interest be undertaken by public bodies, by public institutions, by coöperative business groups, or by public-spirited individuals? Time holds the answer. But it should be possible to point out what are some of the forms this research can take, what some of the accomplishments toward which it may lead.

A PROGRAM OF RESEARCH

Most important, there must be special studies to fit New England for *mass production and mass distribution*. Are we giving our chief attention to products that cannot be expected to yield a proper return to our wage earners or to capital? What products is New England particularly suited to produce in quantities? Are we frittering away our energies in unsound attempts to raise our prices instead of our output? We should find out.

Transportation. Potentially, New England's marvelous seacoast gives us an outstanding advantage. Actually, we are scarcely beginning to use this great natural endowment. We should develop, not only better harbors, but great free ports fitted to keep great numbers of our population busy in manufacturing goods for both foreign and domestic markets. We should coördinate our rail and highway transportation with our waterways and harbors. Exactly what can be done in these directions? We should find out.

Railroads are still in the stone age of transportation of freight and passengers—their rails, stations, etc., are not busy more than a third of the time. If the railroads really seize the idea of mass production of transportation they will set out to keep their rails busy twenty-four hours of the day; and this means doing for passenger rates what Ford has done for the price of his car—setting the price where people can and will pay and then using all their brains to make that rate profitable. The question of freight rates can be handled in the same manner by fixing the prices as low as possible in advance.

City and State Planning. The difference between real wages and money (or, as I like to call them, counterfeit) wages is well known. By foresighted city and state and business planning, the *real wage* scale of New England can be raised without raising dollar wages. Such matters as housing, medical practice, distribution wastes in the community are fit subjects for investigation and action.

Education. In what way can our educational institutions best fit into a program for New England betterment? How can we be assured of the continued development of these institutions and particularly of attracting to them the most able administrators and teachers? Unless the situation is studied and met we shall see most of the best scientists and educators transferred from educational institutions to the research laboratories of business.

Finance and Credit. How can New England's wealth and its current savings be used for the common good of New England?

Effective Use of Population. Our people are our greatest resource; we need to know more about them. We need more facts about unemployment. Among other things we need to plan not only for more employment but for year-round employment. To raise our output per man to the point where we can meet and beat all competition we must patiently and persistently study man idleness as a scientific factory manager studies his machine idleness. There must be full opportunity for every worker to make his maximum contribution to the success of New England. Mass production cannot live unless the masses of workers have adequate buying power.

Research into Research. Research itself is not infallible. To avoid wasting our time and energies on profitless searches, we must constantly check our results by research into our research.

CONCLUSION

Research is of course but the beginning; but it is an important beginning, for New England in particular. Above all things we need a breakdown of our old, bad habits; and the worst of these habits is the habit of acting on guesses or "hunches" or shrewd judgments instead of on facts. We must not only acquire information, we must exchange it.

With facts known, and facts shared, we must also acquire the habit of facing the facts. Our present habit is, I fear, the opposite. What the cold truth of New England's low standards of efficiency is, the figures in this chapter have shown. Yet we in New England are constantly taking credit to ourselves because we have a few outstanding examples of scientific management and mass production (such as the Thom McAn shoe factories, the Kendall Company, the Dennison Manufacturing Company) and because here and there new industries are starting, or old ones thriving. Every bit of such efficiency is clear gain; but, so long as so many of our industries are living in the nineteenth century instead of the twentieth, it counts for little.

If New England will search for facts, share facts, face facts, act on facts; if our manufacturers will develop sound programs of mass production and mass distribution; if they can have at their service scientifically worked out transportation facilities, including great free ports; if the real wages of our people are kept at a high standard, and opportunities provided for continuous employment; if the mental and physical and financial resources of this remarkable region are intelligently used in a sound program for the betterment of New England as a whole; if all these things are done—and done before other regions have beaten the time factor and established themselves in markets which New England may claim by acting first—then not only will the unemployment problem in New England disappear, but our six states will once more assume the position of all-round leadership formerly occupied by them.

NOTES

[1] E. A. Filene and C. W. Wood, *Successful Living in This Machine Age*, New York, 1931.

[2] W. S. Gray and Ruth Munroe, *The Reading Interests and Habits of Adults*, New York, 1929, p. 19.

[3] *Fourteenth Census of the United States, 1920*, Vol. 4, *Occupations*, 1923; *Fifteenth Census of the United States, 1930: Population*, Vol. 3, 1932.

[4] *Fifteenth Census of the United States, 1930: Unemployment*, Vol. 1, 1931.

[5] *Biennial Census of Manufactures*, bound volumes for 1921, 1923, 1925, and 1927, and mimeographed press releases for 1929.

[6] See also below, Fig. 1, p. 325, and Fig. 3, p. 327.

[7] It is notable that this decrease of 14 per cent for Massachusetts industries other than textiles and boots and shoes is considerably in excess of "normal" for the United States, 2.14 per cent.

NEW ENGLAND AND THE NORTHEAST

A STATISTICAL COMPARISON

R. J. McFall

WHILE industrialism is spreading over the entire nation, the Northeastern states* are preëminently the industrial section of the country. New England is an integral part of this area. There are, however, striking differences as well as similarities between the economic status of New England and that of the remaining part of the nation north of the Potomac and Ohio rivers and east of the Ohio-Pennsylvania line. Some of these fundamental differences and similarities, as recent statistics reveal them, may be pointed out.

AREA, POPULATION, AND INCOME

The land area of all these Northeastern states is 5.8 per cent of the total land area of the United States, while that of New England alone is 2.1 per cent; thus the area of the whole section is about two and three quarters times that of New England. A much smaller proportion of the national population, however, is found in the six New England states, New England's population accounting for only 6.7 per cent of the 30 per cent contributed by the entire Northeastern area; thus the density of population is much smaller. The density of the population of the whole region is well over two hundred to the square mile, while that of New England alone is only five eighths as great. Thirty per cent of the national population lives in these Northeastern states on less than 6 per cent of our land area.[1] From the standpoint of congestion of population it may readily be concluded that the region as a whole is much more specialized in industry and commerce, much more one-sided, than is its easterly portion.

With the concentration of human beings in this region goes a still greater concentration of income. It is estimated that just over one half of the total income accruing to individuals in the whole United States appears in this small area of less than 6 per cent of the national area. The income of our corporations is even slightly more concentrated. New England, however, is not so richly endowed; its individual income is less than 10 per cent of the national total, and its corporate income only a little more than 6 per cent of it. In the case of corporate income, New England has slightly less than its

*Maine, New Hampshire, Vermont, Rhode Island, Connecticut, Massachusetts, New York, Pennsylvania, Delaware, New Jersey, Maryland, District of Columbia.

[1] For notes see below, p. 102.

share in the nation on the per capita basis. In the case of individual income, the New Englander enjoys a decided advantage over his average fellow citizen.[2]

It is also worthy of note that the Northeastern states have less than their share, on the per capita basis, of passenger automobiles. The number of persons per car for the United States is 5.7 as against 6.5 for the Northeastern states and 5.9 for New England.[3] Are the people so close together that they have less need for cars, or is the region so congested that its inhabitants have less opportunity to indulge in the great American sport of motoring? If the latter is the true situation, some cynic might wonder as to whether or not their great wealth was worth while. New England follows the rule of the region as a whole, with its subnormal share of automobiles, but its retail trade figures denote an unusual degree of use of automobiles and trucks.[4]

COMMERCIAL ACTIVITY AND MANUFACTURES

If it be assumed that the commercial activity registered by total check payments is an index of the economic status of a region, New England takes a small place, but the area as a whole takes an overwhelmingly large place in the nation. Thanks to the business activity centering in New York, with its speculative exchanges and other great financial institutions, the Northeastern states show over three quarters of the monetary activity of the nation through check payments. New England has less than 5 per cent of this national business.[5] Of course, in many of these transactions centering in New York at least one of the interested parties is located in other regions of the country.

There has been much talk to the effect that New England is losing its place in the industrial life of the nation. This pessimism has been overplayed. That group of states still stands high in industrial activity in the United States. The Northeastern region as a whole turned out over 29 billion dollars worth of manufactured goods in 1929 as compared with a national total of over 70 billions. With only 30 per cent of the national population, the Northeastern states turned out 41.3 per cent of the factory production and used 39.2 per cent of the raw materials going into factories. Thus it is evident that the actual contribution of the factories located here to national production represented in value added by manufacture is even more noteworthy than the gross output. The value added by manufacture in the factories in this region is 43.8 per cent of the national total, and the wages paid are 44.6 per cent. In the New England part of the area the gross manufacturing output per capita ($783) is somewhat less than in the area as a whole ($791). On the other hand the value added by manufacture, on the per capita basis, is slightly greater

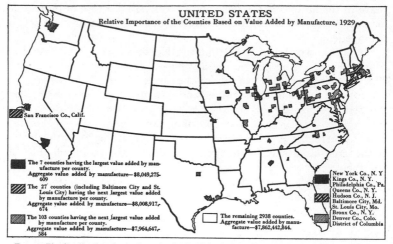

FIG. 1—The distribution of manufacturing in the United States. The relative importance of counties based on value added by manufacture in 1929. From U. S. Census of Manufactures, 1929.

in New England ($397 as against $379), and the total wage bill in New England ($165 per capita) is appreciably greater in proportion than in the whole region ($141 per capita).[6] New England's industries are peculiarly of the type in which the part played by labor in the local factories is important. The grosser type of industry in which the value of the raw material is a large part of the final value of the product is less common in New England than in the Northeast as a whole. It is small wonder that the commoner type of textile production is giving place to more highly specialized industries.

The accompanying maps show the concentration of industrial and wholesale activity by counties in the United States for 1929. In the map (Fig. 1) entitled "Relative Importance of the Counties Based on Value Added by Manufacture, 1929" the shaded counties contributed 75 per cent of the value added by manufacture for the whole country, although only 4.5 per cent of the total number of counties is so shaded. It is noteworthy that so large a proportion of these counties is in the Northeastern states, although many of the counties in northern New England and the mountainous regions of New York and Pennsylvania are unshaded. Three of the seven counties claiming a quarter of the value added by manufacture for the whole country are in the Northeastern states. One of these counties ranks highest, and the total value added by manufacture for the three is over $3,500,000,000, representing nearly one half of the first quarter. Except for northern New England and New York and for southern Maryland and Delaware the Northeastern states form the eastern half of a great manufacturing belt that extends

FIG. 2—The concentration of wholesale business in the United States by counties, 1929. From *Fifteenth Census of the United States, 1930: Wholesale Trade, United States Summary*, Washington, 1930.

from the Mississippi to the Atlantic. Outside of this belt manufacturing cities are scattered and isolated. Within it they tend to be clustered in well defined groups.[7]

The map (Fig. 2) showing the concentration of the wholesale business in the United States by counties, 1929, clearly indicates a decided concentration of the wholesale activity in the Northeastern states. Of the sixty-nine and one half billion dollars representing the total wholesale business of the country this group claims 42.74 per cent, and the New England states 6.36 per cent. In this connection, recognition must be given the influencing factor represented in the wholesaling activity of New York State, which leads all states with a percentage of 25.41. Although New England has a relatively small percentage of the total wholesale business of the United States, it is significant that this division has a large representation of counties in the 100 to 500 million and the 50 to 100 million dollar groups.

FOOD SUPPLY AND RAW MATERIALS

In relation to local requirements in both agricultural and forest production the Northeastern states are very much below the average of the nation. However, that fact is due not to any actual backwardness in farming but merely to the great demand arising from the concentration of population. In New England the farm income is somewhat greater in relation to area than the average for the country. For the Northeast as a whole the value of farm production is twice as great per unit of area as it is in the entire country.[8] Nevertheless, the region as a whole, and especially New England, is very far from being self-sufficient in farm production.

In the case of coal, the Appalachians produce a material surplus beyond the needs of the whole region, while New England is entirely dependent upon supplies from outside its borders. In other mineral production, except quarrying, the Northeast takes a relatively unimportant place.[9]

A general situation of a surplus of industrial production and commercial services with a deficiency of food and raw materials characterizes this region as a whole, just as it does old England. The products and services of a highly developed community must be traded for the products of less highly developed regions. Specialization brings with it a higher rate of money income but deprives the region of self-sufficiency. New England, in particular, is far from self-sufficiency in that she must buy her fuel as well as her food and raw materials.

EXTERNAL TRADE

Add to this lack of self-sufficiency the fact that the Northeastern states are on the most important trade routes between the interior of the nation and the outside commercial world, and we have the chief factors making up the peculiar external trade relations of this region. In this external trade the absence of coal in New England and the comparative absence of foreign trade through its ports sets it off sharply from the remainder of the Northeastern area.

Owing to the absence of coal and raw materials and the comparative lack of foreign trade moving directly through it, New England's external trade is extremely one-sided when rated in tonnage. The surplus production of coal in Pennsylvania and the heavy tonnage of exports of western products as well as local goods make the total incoming and outgoing tonnage of the whole Northeast more nearly balance.

New England brings in six tons to one it sends out. One half of the incoming tonnage is coal, and materially more than one tenth is petroleum and its products. Almost one half of the total tonnage moves by water, but only a small part of this is foreign trade, the only heavy foreign tonnage now being imported petroleum, wood pulp, and sugar. Formerly there was a substantial outward movement of Canadian wheat through Portland. There is now only a light tonnage of incoming freight to be shipped out again in foreign trade, and the external trade balance reflects an economically highly developed region depending on the outside for food, fuel, and raw materials while shipping out its concentrated finished products.[10]

When we include the whole of the Northeast in our view, we find the situation regarding foreign trade radically different. The ports of New York, Philadelphia, and Baltimore play a very important part in foreign commerce. Against exports of about $50,000,000 through New England ports in 1929, we find exports of more than $2,000,000,000 through all the Northeastern ports. The imports amounted to more than $2,850,000,000 through all the ports but to only $337,000,000 through New England ports. While formerly Boston and Portland handled a considerable amount of export trade for both the western part of the United States and for Canada, this trade no longer amounts to much. The other North Atlantic ports still handle Canadian exports in quantity as well as products from our own West.[11]

No study has been published of the outside rail traffic of the Northeast comparable to the one made by the writer for New England.[10] General knowledge of the economic situation of the regions and statistics of rail traffic published currently by the Interstate Commerce Commission coupled with census data render it possible, however, to make some observations on this trade.

A very heavy proportion of the traffic of these regions consists of coal, of which the Appalachian region has a large surplus. It is, unfortunately, impossible as yet to distinguish clearly between the movement of Pennsylvania coal and that of the Virginias. It seems certain, however, that the westward shipment of Pennsylvania coal is sufficiently heavy to make the total outbound rail movement of all freight at least equal to the total inbound movement. The next largest movement is iron ore, which comes inward via lake and rail to the amount of more than 25,000,000 tons a year. Petroleum does not move long distances by rail throughout the central part of the country. More than 5,000,000 tons of crude petroleum move in by pipe line and more than 20,000,000 tons come in by water both in foreign and domestic trade. The production of iron and steel in the Pittsburgh region is so great that there is a surplus of several million tons of such products. Offsetting this is a large inbound movement of lumber and of automobiles. Of course, there is a very heavy movement of general manufactures, with the weight not far from equal in both directions but the outbound value much greater. The movement of agricultural and animal products parallels fairly closely that of New England on a larger scale in approximate ratio to population, except that there is a fairly large export movement of grain (mostly Canadian), some pork products, and cotton through the ports; and this adds to the inward movement by rail. Roughly speaking, the inbound rail tonnage is probably three times as great as that of New England, and the outbound appears to be still greater.

The seaboard traffic of New England amounts to over 30,000,000 tons moving inward and 4,000,000 tons moving outward (1930). Of this, somewhat more than 5,500,000 tons are imports while the exports are small. For all the Atlantic ports the inbound movement is about 115,000,000 tons, and the outbound about 63,000,000 tons. Of this, nearly 18,000,000 tons are imports moved through New York, 5,400,-000 moved through Philadelphia, and 5,500,000 through Baltimore. The exports amount to about 9,000,000 tons through New York, 2,000,000 through Philadelphia, and just over 1,000,000 through Baltimore. The coastwise receipts at Boston amount to more than 10,300,000 tons, at New York nearly 31,000,000, at Philadelphia nearly 11,500,000, and at Baltimore over 3,100,000. Of this tonnage much is intercoastal traffic from the Pacific ports of the United States. The coastwise shipments from Boston are only a little more than 1,000,000 tons, from New York 8,000,000, from Philadelphia over 4,700,000, and from Baltimore considerably more than 1,000,000.[12]

New England plays a large part in the industrial life of the Northeast. Her commerce is largely for herself. The rest of the Northeast sits at the crossroads of national commerce and is a middleman for others.

NOTES

[1] U. S. Dept. of Commerce, Bur. of the Census, *Fifteenth Census of the United States, 1930*, Vol. I, *Population*, Washington, 1931.

[2] U. S. Treasury Dept., *Statistics of Income for 1929 (Preliminary Report) Compiled from Income Tax Returns for 1929 Filed to Aug. 31, 1930*, Washington, 1931.

[3] U. S. Dept. of Agriculture, Bur. of Public Roads, *Motor Vehicle Registrations and Revenues*, 1929 (mimeographed report).

[4] *Fifteenth Census of the United States, 1930: Census of Distribution, Final Series, ⁿetail Distribution*, Washington, 1932 (one bulletin for each state).

[5] U. S. Federal Reserve Board, *Debits to Individual Bank Accounts by Cities and Federal Reserve Districts, December, 1929* (mimeographed report).

[6] U. S. Dept. of Commerce, Bur. of the Census, *Census of Manufactures, 1929* (mimeographed releases).

[7] See Steñ De Gear, *The American Manufacturing Belt*, in *Geografiska Aññaler*, Vol. 9, 1927, pp. 233-359.

[8] U. S. Dept. of Agriculture, Bur. of Agricultural Economics, *Farm Value, Gross Income, and Cash Income from Farm Production*, Part III. *State Summaries of the Income Estimates 1928-1929* (mimeographed report).

[9] U. S. Dept. of Commerce, Bur. of Mines, *Mineral Resources of the United States*, 1929, Washington, 1932.

[10] R. J. McFall, *The External Trade of New England*, U. S. Dept. of Commerce, Bur. of Foreign and Domestic Commerce, Washington, 1928 (*Domestic Commerce Ser. No. 22*).

[11] U. S. Dept. of Commerce, Bur. of Foreign and Domestic Commerce, *Foreign Commerce and Navigation of the United States for the Calendar Year 1929*, Washington, 1930, pp. xiv and 500. On foreign trade of New England see below, pp. 372-392.

[12] *Report of the Chief of Engineers, U. S. Army, 1931*, Washington, 1931, Part II, *Commercial Statistics: Water-Borne Commerce of the United States for the Calendar Year 1930.* See also Tables in Professor Roorbach's article, pp. 373-376, below.

THE FOOD SUPPLY OF NEW ENGLAND[1]

Alexander E. Cance

C OMPARATIVELY few comprehensive regional studies of food consumption have been made, and it is fair to say that none covering any definite geographic areas are satisfactory. Most studies include a small selected group of commodities or cover a short period of time, or both. It is a matter of common observation that food demands are changeable and elastic. Within recent years the development of national advertising and superior salesmanship, the extensive improvement of food manufactures, the technical advance in food preservation, transportation, and retail distribution following a war-time experience that compelled changes in dietary and a post-war social psychology that welcomed them, have brought about a situation where fashions in food are becoming almost as significant as fashions in clothing.

Meager as are the details of food consumption in New England, certain characteristics stand out. New England is a dependent food area. The area is, in general, far from sources of food materials. On the whole, food costs more per person than elsewhere, the quantity consumed averages well, and the quality is high. This favorable food expenditure is in part due to natural and racial causes, in part to a high average level of wealth, income, and productive employment.

According to the U. S. Census the farm population of New England in 1930 was 573,801, or only about 7.3 per cent of the total population. There were 124,925 farms in the region, less than 2 per cent of all the farms in the country. Crop land and plowable pasture comprised slightly less than 4,979,000 acres out of a total area of about 39,664,640 acres. Of the 3,660,000 acres of crop land harvested in 1929 about 2,772,000 acres were in hay. Obviously, therefore, only a small fraction of New England is in agricultural crops. Furthermore, although yields per acre of staple food crops are higher than in any other great section of the country, the improved land has decreased continuously since 1880, and the number of farmers dependent for a livelihood on the products of the soil has declined steadily.

FOOD IN THE FAMILY BUDGET

Food occupies a comparatively large place in the family budget. Studies of the United States Department of Labor show that 35 to 45 per cent of the total income is spent for provisioning the family.[2] The expenditure of a family depends on the amount of the income

---

[1] For notes see below, p. 115.

and the amount and kind of food eaten, as well as on the price of food, which, while fairly uniform in industrial cities, varies greatly at different periods and in different regions.

New England, chiefly southern New England, has been obliged to pay more for food than the average expenditure in other sections of the country, partly because the same amount and kind of food costs more in the North Atlantic states, and partly because the number of calories eaten is greater. Calculations based on the year 1926 indicate that, roughly, the food of a New England industrial family costs 15 to 20 per cent more than that of the average household elsewhere in the United States.[3]

It is difficult to estimate the amount spent by this section in feeding itself. The National Industrial Conference Board places the figure for 1926 at about $460 a family for the 43 articles of food making up the budget of the Department of Labor.[4] Since this is approximately 70 per cent of the total estimated expenditure, the amount for a family of five persons would be something like $660 annually. If this estimate holds for New England as a whole the food bill of this region, if calculated at market prices, is more than a billion dollars a year. (On the other hand it is evident that many families are not adequately fed and that an increasing number in New England supplement their purchases by their home gardens.) Inasmuch as the total wage bill of New England manufacturers in 1927 was about one and one-third billion dollars, earned by about one-half of the working population, this figure is probably not far from the market value of the food consumed annually.

The fact that southern New England has been paying more for its food supplies than other sections has been known for a long time, and at intervals attempts have been made to analyze the causes for this fact and to propose some remedies.[5] It is important of course to the wage payer as well as to the worker. For, whatever may be the factors influencing the rate of wages, the amount necessary to maintain the worker's standard of living is certainly preëminent. The necessity for importing a large percentage of food products from a great distance is usually mentioned as an important contributing cause, with the obvious recommendation that New England produce more of her supply at home. It is also held that the high cost is due to the better quality and perhaps the greater quantity demanded by the householders in a region where education and intelligence dictate dietaries and where climate sharpens the appetite. A rather careful scrutiny of wholesale prices in New England and elsewhere shows that as a whole New England prices are very little higher and, for some products in large demand, are lower than in most other parts of the country. This leads to the conclusion that where disparity exists in retail prices the cause probably lies in the higher costs of distribution within New England.

At one time or another it is probably true that each of these factors has been effective in enhancing our food expenditure. Economists generally have agreed that increased home production of most food products would increase rather than decrease costs. Indeed our home-produced milk, cream, eggs, and poultry, which are our most important local products, are notably high priced.

A survey of prices of 35 food products in Massachusetts cities and towns, made in 1926 by the Massachusetts Department of Agriculture,[6] seems to give some support to the suggestion that higher wages and fuller employment give rise to higher prices of both local and shipped-in food. At any rate those cities mainly dependent on the textile and the depressed shoe industries enjoyed a lower food-price index than those where incomes were larger and employment more nearly maximum. It was significant that the cities of western Massachusetts and those with more difficult commercial contacts were in the higher-priced group. Boston, which, according to the reports of the United States Department of Labor for the whole United States, has a comparatively high food cost, ranks about normal or a little below the normal for Massachusetts.[7]

Kinds and Sources of Food Materials[8]

The above remarks refer only to 35 perishable food products and deal only with prices. The family food budget, of course, is made up by multiplying price by quantity. The quantities of food products unloaded in New England have never been accurately determined. Perhaps the very best typical data are those dealing with the production of raw foods and food materials as compiled by the federal census and the United States Department of Agriculture, and the records of receipts on the Boston market.[9] The latter have been compiled from various official sources for a number of years by the Massachusetts Department of Agriculture. Since the 2,000,000 inhabitants of Boston and its environs are fairly typical of consumers throughout a large part of New England, and since the Boston unloads are practically all consumed in New England, they will be freely quoted in this article.

Cereals

A comparatively large part of the budget, both for animals and men, is made up of cereal foods. In 1917–1918 Raymond Pearl estimated that cereals accounted for over 40 per cent of the weight of nutrients and supplied one third of the caloric energy of the American diet.[10] The cereal production of New England is small. In 1929 all New England produced only about 110,000 bushels of threshed wheat and rye, enough (less seed) for 18,000 people.[11] In 1924 she imported about 800,000 tons of flour and grains, including rice, for human food—nearly 99 per cent of it milled outside of New England. Locally grown grain for animals in 1924 amounted to little more than 150,000 tons, whereas imports of grains and mill feed approached 2,000,000 tons. The farm feed bill in 1929 was $67,416,362 or $539 per farm as reported by the census. Actually New England probably pays $80,000,000 annually for imported feed. It may be said, therefore, that the animal industry of New England depends on the West for considerably more than 90 per cent of its grains and mill feeds and that the human population must look to the outside for almost its entire supply of cereals.

The flour-milling industry is not extensive, but the value of bread and other cereal food products manufactured in 1927 was over $115,000,000. Receipts of flour and corn meal at Boston alone amount to around 1,600,000 barrels a year, nearly all from western mills. Although exact statistical data are lacking, it is certain that the consumption of bread and kindred cereal foods is declining.

MEATS

Few reliable data on the consumption of various kinds of meat, poultry, and fish are available for specific areas of the country and different economic and racial groups. Such as we have indicate that as a unit New England consumes materially less pork and somewhat less beef than the average for the remainder of the country but more veal and mutton. Consumption varies somewhat as between rural and urban regions, chiefly in the greater rural consumption of pork and poultry; but the country population of the North Atlantic states is credited with a veal consumption twice as great and a pork consumption only 78 per cent as great as the average for the rural population of the United States. Boston is known as a lamb-eating center, and the large Irish element consumes a great amount of beef.

New England depends largely on the West for beef, veal, mutton, lamb, and especially for pork products. It is significant that beef production, as such, has proved almost universally unprofitable in this region, and local beef is largely the product of discarded dairy animals. About 10 per cent of the beef and mutton, and about one-third of the veal, are locally produced. Sheep and lambs have been decreasing in numbers for many years. About 100,000 sheep and lambs were slaughtered locally in 1928 in all New England. During the same year the receipts at Boston alone accounted for nearly one million of these animals, local and imported.

New England is not a large consumer of cured pork, but the demand for fresh pork is such that some 800,000 hogs are slaughtered in Boston packing houses annually. Only 6 or 7 per cent of these are local hogs. The great bulk of them is shipped from western stockyards. Boston receives for consumption the edible products of a million or more hogs a year. If the census is correct, the production of hogs in this region fell off amazingly between 1920 and 1925. Since then their numbers have increased somewhat but not sufficiently to keep pace with the increase in population. Local and farm slaughter accounts for less than 300,000 hogs a year, while the food requirements call for 3,000,000.

POULTRY PRODUCTS

No accurate account of the products of the New England hen has ever been made. The census reports of her numbers and activities fall far short of her accomplishments as a supplier of food. Offhand it would seem easily possible and profitable for New England to raise sufficient poultry and eggs to supply local needs. As a matter of fact nearly two thirds of the poultry and more than one half of the egg supply are imported, mostly from a great territory west of the Mississippi extending from Texas to Minnesota and Oregon. Moreover, the number of chickens on farms has not materially changed since 1924. Connecticut has increased her farm flocks about as much as the other states have decreased theirs. It is well known that the supply of poultry products is greatly augmented by the back-yard flocks of urbanites and part-time farmers, but this contribution to New England's food has never been measured.

It is interesting to note that the Boston market usually receives as many eggs a year as all New England produces on her farms. Only 7 or 8 per cent of the eggs received and 1 per cent of the dressed poultry arriving in Boston are produced in New England. About 55,000,000 pounds of dressed poultry are unloaded in that city yearly, of which 10 per cent now comes from Illinois as compared with more than 40 per cent six or seven years ago. Next in order are Iowa, Minnesota, Texas, Kansas, and Nebraska, with rapidly increasing amounts from North and South Dakota, Oklahoma, and even Oregon and California (Fig. 1).

Despite the high prices of local poultry products the relative proportion of home-produced poultry does not seem to be increasing. Indeed, the shipments from the most distant sources in the United States tend to increase most rapidly. Poultry requires a heavy ration of good grain. New England produces only enough grain of all sorts to feed about half of her poultry. Grain shipped in from west of the Mississippi must produce more desirable eggs in Massachusetts than in Iowa if the Massachusetts feeder is to compete with the Iowa eggs that come through on the same train with the feed. The quality of the western product is improving. Oregon and California eggs sell in competition with the best "near-by" eggs on eastern markets the year round. Cold-storage eggs are carefully inspected before refrigeration and expertly handled in cold storage. More

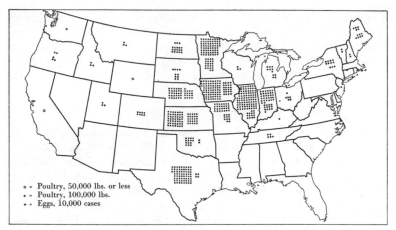

FIG. 1—Map of the United States showing the origin of poultry and eggs unloaded in Boston in 1929 from principal states. Based on *Receipts and Sources of Boston's Food Supply*, Mass. Dept. of Agric., 1929.

careful handling of western-raised products all the way from farm to consumer is improving the quality of the distant product in many cases even above that of the local article. All these improvements are likely to increase with the growth in scientific and technological knowledge. Competition will grow keener as the price margin between local and distant products decreases. To meet this competition, organization of the industry, improvement of the quality of the product and of marketing methods, reduction of distribution costs, and good salesmanship will be necessary if local poultry raising is to maintain its present standing.

DAIRY PRODUCTS

For many families this is the largest single item in the food budget. New England is a large consumer of fresh milk and cream, owing in part to the high quality of the product and the convenience of the market. In general, New England supplies its own population with all its fresh fluid milk, practically all the table cream, and most of the ice cream. About three pounds of butter and one tenth of a pound of cheese per capita are made annually on local farms and in factories, but this manufacture is steadily declining. The supply of butter now comes principally from Minnesota, with increasing amounts from Nebraska, Iowa, and Ohio. Boston received 81,000,000 pounds in 1929; nearly 35 per cent of this came from Minnesota, 15 per cent from Nebraska, and less than 1 per cent from New England. In 1924 Vermont ranked third as a source of Boston's butter supply. Now her contribution is almost negligible. Wisconsin is the main source of New England's cheese supply, but New York and Illinois furnish a significant amount. In 1929, 62 per cent of Boston's cheese came from Wisconsin and 12 per cent from New York.

While New England can supply her own milk and cream, there is a considerable interchange of dairy products between New England and outside territory. Boston received in 1931 nearly 40 per cent of her fresh cream from New York and states west, notably Wisconsin, Michigan, and Missouri. An unknown amount of sweet butter and powdered and condensed milk is shipped in from the West for ice-cream manufacture; there is an interchange of fluid milk with New York.

Recent proposed legislation in the interest of a better cream supply would have the effect of closing the markets of New England to all sweet cream except that from inspected sources within her borders. This raises the question as to whether New England should attempt to furnish her own milk and cream throughout the year at the expense of butter production and a more uniform seasonal flow of milk. If it becomes possible to freeze and store sweet cream safely and economically it is probable that the production of milk and cream will just about equal the local demands. One real difficulty encountered in the milk supply of New England is the uneven production. Owing to the large dependence on pasturage for feed, many sections, particularly in the northern part of the region, produce a large quantity of milk during the summer and a small quantity during the fall and winter. The New England Milk Producers Association is attempting to remedy this situation by a price policy that puts a premium on a larger flow of milk during the months of short production and to some extent penalizes overproduction.[12]

The demand of New England consumers and the activities of state and municipal boards of health have been instrumental in raising significantly the standards of milk, especially in Connecticut. The factors in quality are butter-fat content, freedom from harmful bacteria, absence of tuberculosis germs, and pasteurization. Attempts are being made to secure legislation that will prevent the sale of milk from herds tainted with contagious abortion. The enforcement of regulations of this sort requires a large, alert inspection service and adds materially to the cost of producing the milk. Although dairy products cost more than any other item in the budget, milk consumption increased rather rapidly from 1920 to 1930. Advertising and educational propaganda have had some influence, but chiefly the assurance of a safe, clean, wholesome product that is delivered regularly at the door every morning in good condition has been the great factor in creating and sustaining the demand for milk. Density of population has made possible this convenient delivery of bottled milk.

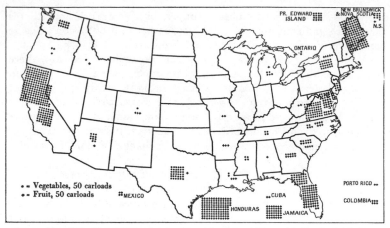

FIG. 2—Map of the United States showing the origin of vegetables and fruit unloaded in Boston in 1929 from principal states and foreign countries. Based on the same source as Figure 1.

FRUITS AND VEGETABLES

It is evident that more people in New England are eating more vegetables and fruits and that the market is supplied the year round with a larger variety of fresh vegetable food than ever before. The greater consumption is due in part to educational stimulus, but more to the greater number of retail outlets, chiefly grocery chains, which are displaying attractively a large variety in nearly every city and town in southern New England.

The trend in receipts on the Boston market can be taken as typical of the consumption of four-fifths or more of the population. Supplies come freely from every section of the country (except the northern Great Plains region), from Cuba, Mexico, Canada, and tropical sources (see Figs. 2 and 3). Shipments from the South have trebled within the last five years. In spite of the great distance, Boston receives more fresh fruits and vegetables from California than from any other state. In 1929 more than 10,400 carloads of fresh fruit and 2600 cars of fresh vegetables were shipped to Boston from the Pacific coast states. Receipts of twenty-one important vegetables rose from 23,500 cars in 1925 to 30,400 cars in 1929, an increase of 30 per cent. Twenty of the twenty-one commodities shared in this increase. Unloads in Boston of eleven important fruits increased from 25,000 to 29,000 cars in the same period. A thousand cars of bananas and 2500 cars of oranges and lemons accounted for most of the increase. These facts are all of vital importance to New England growers and dealers.

The two most important products of this group produced by New England in actual exportable quantities are potatoes and cranberries. In 1930 Maine produced about one eighth of the total potato

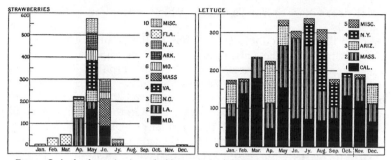

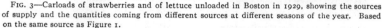

FIG. 3—Carloads of strawberries and of lettuce unloaded in Boston in 1929, showing the sources of supply and the quantities coming from different sources at different seasons of the year. Based on the same source as Figure 1.

crop of the United States. The great area of commercial potato production is Aroostook County, the most northern county in the state.[13] A short season, yields greater than in any other state and more than twice the United States average, a favorable soil, large enterprises, and production methods that reduce costs have built up a notable industry in spite of the precariousness of potato yields and prices. The short growing season which limits the choice of crops has contributed to give the potato a commercial monopoly. Yields vary, but the average is relatively high and the trend upward. The annual acreage planted has almost consistently increased for twenty-five years. Maine potatoes are shipped both as seed potatoes to Long Island and the southern states and for food purposes to all states east of the Mississippi and to several west of it, when the yield is normal. Shipments are also made to Canada, the United Kingdom, and Cuba.

New England produces about 6 bushels of potatoes per person as compared with 3 to 4 bushels for the United States average; hence the local yield is more than ample for consumption during the season of distribution, but from May to August, inclusive, heavy shipments of early white potatoes are unloaded in New England markets. Out of total receipts of 10,000 cars in 1929, Boston unloaded 6500 from Maine, 1000 from New Brunswick and Prince Edward Island, which openly compete with Maine, and imported the remainder from the southern states and New Jersey. In addition to this Boston consumed nearly a thousand carloads of sweet potatoes.

Of all vegetables and fruits, potatoes are by far the most important in American diet and supply more calories than all other vegetables combined. Among all foods they stand eighth in contributing to calories consumed, just above poultry and eggs. Notwithstanding the large consumption and exports, the land devoted to potatoes in New England had, up to 1929, averaged less than 220,000 acres.

Potatoes are New England's most notable contribution to the vegetable supply.

New England produces 60 per cent of the cranberry crop of the United States.[14] The only producing area of importance is about 14,000 acres in eastern Massachusetts, with an output which fluctuates between 325,000 and 425,000 barrels annually. This crop has long been marketed in large part by a well organized coöperative company which distributes it to practically every state in the Union. Owing to the merchandising methods of this company the season of cranberry consumption has been materially lengthened and the consuming area greatly increased. Successful attempts have recently been made to put canned berries and cranberry sauce on the market. The total value of the Massachusetts crop is only four to five million dollars a year, but it represents one largely exported New England fruit crop, handled by one of the most successful coöperatives in America.

The local vegetable supply of New England is, in general, excellent in quality, is produced by some of the most intelligent and experienced market gardeners in the country, and is of great variety. Both outdoor and greenhouse culture have been highly developed in southern New England. The natural handicaps of unfavorable climate and scarcity of well located soils, which necessitate the substitution of artificial for solar heat and the importation of great tonnages of coal and fertilizer, have been increased by rising land values, encroaching residential demands, and increasing labor costs.

The chief problem, however, is the increasing demand for fresh vegetables and fruits every day in the year, a demand answered by the competition of the trucking areas of the West and South and increasing local commercial crops. Freshness and attractiveness are qualities for which vegetable users are willing to pay a premium. Until recently freshness and, to some extent, attractive appearance were confined chiefly to near-by products. Better methods of packing and shipping and more rapid distribution now give housewives the choice of fresh-appearing vegetables from fields a thousand or more miles away. Some of these products are inherently better than the local article. Lettuce is an example. Next to potatoes the car-lot receipts of lettuce at Boston are greater than those of any other vegetable. In 1929 more than 2800 cars were unloaded, 1200 of them iceberg lettuce from California, which found a market in Boston every month of the year. Receipts of the California product have tripled during the last eight years, whereas the famous Boston head lettuce, which was produced near by and for years dominated the market, has relatively fallen to one third of the total consumption. Apparently the distant product is more desirable and often actually cheaper than the home-grown.

In season a large part of the demand for fresh vegetables and fruits in all the smaller markets of New England is supplied by home-grown products; but probably aside from potatoes this accounts for little more than half the fresh vegetables and perhaps two thirds of the fresh fruit, not including citrus fruits. The Connecticut Valley onion industry is often mentioned as a great commercial enterprise. It is important. It is a highly intensive farm enterprise, occupying excellent soil, and producing comparatively high values per acre. The total reported onion shipments from the area, however, are just about equal to the onion receipts at Boston. New England onions make up about one fourth of Boston's demand, but they amount to not more than 60 per cent of the receipts from competing regions farther west.

CITRUS FRUITS AND APPLES

The most striking feature of fruit consumption is the steadily increasing demand for citrus fruits and the stationary or declining demand for apples. One fourth of the total receipts of fruits at Boston are citrus, a ratio that probably holds for New England. Banana shipments to Boston, which is the New England distributing point for this fruit, amounted to the equivalent of nearly 9000 carloads in 1929.

New England produces a fine quality of apples,[15] but until recently the matter of careful grading and packing received too little attention to induce a wide market demand. A considerable part of the Maine shipments are exported to Europe, and an increasing number of carloads are shipped to American markets outside New England. Nevertheless the total shipments reported by the United States Department of Agriculture from New England in 1928–1929 and 1929–1930 amounted to less than 4000 carloads as compared with nearly 85,000 from Washington and Oregon. However, a very large part of the production goes into the local markets directly and does not appear in the shipment record. Boston receipts of apples are usually about half the oranges unloaded.

SUGAR

Excepting grains, meats, and dairy products, the sugars make the largest contribution of calories (more than 13 per cent) to the New England diet. Sugar is imported chiefly as raw sugar and refined in New England factories. The consumption per capita is high, probably more than 112 pounds. Part of this is maple syrup and sugar, the making of which is a considerable industry in Vermont and adds materially to the local sugar supply all over New England except the southeastern portion.

TRANSPORTATION AND STORAGE

It is obvious that a dependable and continually functioning transportation system is essential if New England is to be properly fed.[16] It is estimated that the storage facilities of distributors at any average moment hold a supply of food sufficient for a few days only. While the reserve stocks vary greatly with the commodity and the season, modern food merchandising is coming more and more to depend on a continuous flow of products from source of production to consumer. The physiography of New England is such that nearly all supplies by rail must enter through four main gateways, namely, the southern gateway along Long Island Sound, Maybrook where the Hudson is crossed at Poughkeepsie, the north Berkshire gateway through Albany and the Hoosac Tunnel, and the crossings north of Lake Champlain.[17] A comparatively small amount of traffic crosses the Canadian boundary. About 80 per cent of the food tonnage enters by rail and 20 per cent by water. The great bulk of food supplies from American sources is shipped in by rail.

The necessity of long-distance shipments of heavy perishable foods by rail should be an advantage to local production. As a matter of fact, the improvements in shipping facilities have made it possible to import almost every important food product except fresh milk in competition with home-produced supplies. Freight rates are not high enough to offset the natural advantages and, perhaps, lower labor costs of distant competition. Moreover, derivative foodstuffs are more cheaply shipped than raw materials; hence flour, animal products, and canned foods, which can be economically converted near the point of production, are likely to come to New England in finished form rather than as raw grains, fruits, and vegetables. Every scientific advance in food preservation or packaging makes it more likely that the product will be prepared, freed from waste, and put up in consumer packages as near the source of production as possible. Large savings through mass-conversion economies and utilization of wastes and culls are often possible, and distributing charges are decreased. Meantime home-grown products, unless they have superior quality or enjoy a privileged market, survive with difficulty.

The retail distribution of food presents few peculiarities. The chain-store development in southern New England is noteworthy. Almost all food products, including dairy products, fresh meats and poultry, and a great variety of excellent green fruits and vegetables are sold through a number of great grocery chains the year round. Milk is sold in many of them, and frozen meat cuts in consumer packages ready for the oven are contemplated. The Thrift Stores have not gained headway in this territory, but numerous independent "markets," handling every variety of food, are found in every large city. These chains and markets frequently run their own bakeries and often prepare cooked meats and poultry. The roadside stand has developed to a large extent along the main highways leading into

Boston and other large cities of New England. These stands under proper direction offer an opportunity to the motorist to obtain fresh supplies directly from the farm. Studies made in New Hampshire, Connecticut, and Massachusetts indicate that a very material amount of food is distributed in this manner, although the percentage is comparatively small.[18]

CONCLUSION

On the whole it appears that food supplies are convenient and of good quality. Supplies from a distance are perhaps more efficiently handled than are local products. This is, in part, the fault of the grower whose quality or quantity is insufficient. In part the local dealers find it convenient to buy, or by force of habit do buy, through the regular wholesale houses in the large centers. There is, however, an increasing demand for distinctive products, sold under brand or label in comparatively small quantities to a discriminating group of buyers.[19] By studying the wants of this upper trade stratum and satisfying them the local producer will succeed, whether. he sells in a larger city market or in a smaller one.

NOTES

[1] Detailed studies of the food supply of New England are not numerous, but some general investigations have been made and a good many research studies, chiefly under the New England Research Council on Marketing and Food Supply, have been and are being carried out. In 1910 the Commission on Cost of Living in Massachusetts published a comparatively large volume dealing with the subject (*Report of the Commission on Cost of Living, May, 1910*, Boston, 1910, [*Mass.*] *House, No. 1750*). This summed up all the general studies that had been completed up to that time and added a few new data with particular reference to Massachusetts. In 1924 *The Food Supply of New England* (New York), by A. W. Gilbert and others appeared. This book is really a compilation of material put together by the commissioners of agriculture of New England. Its chapters attempt to cover the whole field of production and distribution, but they are of unequal value. The book as a whole contains many inaccuracies but does give a picture of the New England situation.

More recently Dr. R. J. McFall has made a study of the food market in New England as a part of the commercial survey of New England of the Bureau of Foreign and Domestic Commerce of the U. S. Department of Commerce (see above, p. 62) and has contributed a chapter to the published report (see E. F. Gerish, *Commercial Structure of New England*, Washington, 1929 (*Domestic Commerce Ser. No. 26*), pp. 158–206). This chapter is, after all, the best and most recent résumé of this subject.

The New England Research Council on Marketing and Food Supply has prepared bibliographies of its studies on the food supply which it is distributing in mimeographed form. These researches cover a variety of subjects, most of them dealing with the distribution of food. A general study of the cost of living in the United States was made by the U. S. Department of Commerce in 1918–1919. This included budgets from various towns in New England and gave an opportunity to compare costs of living in these towns with those in other parts of the country. A general quantitative statistical study of food supplies of the United States was made by Raymond Pearl in *The Nation's Food*, Philadelphia, 1920. Since 1918 the National Industrial Conference Board has made and published at intervals estimates of the cost of living in the United States. The volume entitled *The Cost of Living in the United States, 1914–1927*, New York, 1928, compares food costs in 39 cities.

[2] *Cost of Living in the United States*, Washington, 1924 (*U. S. Bur. of Labor Statistics Bull. 357*), p. 5.

[3] *The Cost of Living in the United States, 1914–1927*, National Industrial Conference Board, New York, 1928, pp. 36–39.

[4] *Ibid.*, pp. 35–39.

[5] See *Report of the Commission on Cost of Living* (in Massachusetts), 1910, pp. 90–133; R. J. McFall, *Higher Cost of Food in Massachusetts*, in *Journ. Amer. Statist. Assoc.*, Vol. 19, 1924, pp. 362–377; Mass. Commission on the Necessaries of Life, annual reports.

[6] *Comparison Between Retail Prices of Selected Food Products in Thirteen Massachusetts Cities*, Mass. Dept. of Agric., 1926 (mimeographed).

[7] Monthly reports on the cost of living in various cities published in the *Monthly Labor Review* of the U. S. Bur. of Labor Statistics.

[8] See also the two papers on *Agricultural Production in New England*, by Professor I. G. Davis, in the present volume, pp. 118–167. This article does not cover fisheries, as this topic is discussed by Dr. Lewis Radcliffe and Mr. G. A. Fitzgerald in their papers on the fisheries of New England in the present volume, pp. 247–277.

[9] *Receipts and Sources of Boston's Food Supply*, Mass. Dept. of Agric. (mimeographed annually).

[10] Pearl, *op. cit.*, pp. 212 and 229.

[11] Commodity statistics noted in this and the following paragraphs were obtained chiefly from U. S. Censuses of Agriculture and Manufactures; from C. E. Artman, *Industrial Structure of New England*, U. S. Dept. of Commerce, Bur. of Foreign and Domestic Commerce, Washington, 1928 (*Domestic Commerce Ser. No. 28*); from E. F. Gerish, *op. cit.*; from *Receipts and Sources of Boston's Food Supply*, Mass. Dept. of Agric.; and from R. J. McFall, *The External Trade of New England*, Washington, 1928 (*Domestic Commerce Ser. No. 22*).

[12] See A. R. Gans, *Elasticity of Supply of Milk from Vermont Plants—Factors Affecting Deliveries per Patron, I. The Milk-Feed Ratio*, Burlington, 1927 (*Vermont Agric. Exper. Sta. Bull. 269*), and other studies carried out by the Department of Agricultural Economics, University of Vermont; also files of *The New England Dairyman*.

[13] See E. M. Wilson, *The Aroostook Valley: A Study in Potatoes*, in *Geogr. Rev.*, Vol. 16, 1926, pp. 196–205; E. A. Wixson, *An Economic Study of the Production, Destination, and Farm Price of Maine Potatoes*, Orono, Me., 1929 (*Univ. of Maine Studies*, 2nd Ser., No. 12; on cover *Maine Bull.*, Vol. 31, No. 14, June, 1929).

[14] See C. Y. Mason, *The Cranberry Industry in Massachusetts*, in *Econ. Geogr.*, Vol. 2, 1926, pp. 59–69.

[15] *The Apple Situation in New England*, published by the Connecticut and Maine Agricultural Experiment Stations and the Extension Services of New Hampshire, Rhode Island, and Massachusetts, 1927.

[16] See also the papers in the present volume by Professor W. J. Cunningham entitled *The Railroads of New England* (pp. 344–361) and by Professor G. B. Roorbach entitled *The Importance of Foreign Trade to New England* (pp. 372–392).

[17] See Figure 1, p. 345, below.

[18] M. G. Eastman, *Roadside Marketing in New Hampshire*, Durham, N. H., 1929 (*Univ. of N. H. Agric. Exper. Sta. Bull. 249*); Paul Mehl, *Roadside Marketing in*

Connecticut, Storrs, Conn., 1923 (*Conn. Agric. Coll. Extension Service Bull. 65*); *A Survey of Roadside Stand Selling*, Mass. Dept. of Agric., Division of Markets, 1930.

[19] See also paper by Dr. F. V. Waugh entitled *The Marketing of New England's Farm Products: Demand Factors*, in the present volume, pp. 168–177.

AGRICULTURAL PRODUCTION IN NEW ENGLAND

NATURAL AND SOCIAL BACKGROUND

I. G. Davis

IN this paper attention will be directed to those circumstances of the natural, social, and economic environment that condition agricultural production in New England.[1] In another chapter the writer will discuss more specifically agricultural production itself—its history, present status, and major problems.

The location of agricultural enterprises in any given region, the organization of the production and marketing processes of those enterprises, and the character of their combination in farm business units are conditioned by many and extremely complex influences. These spring in part from (1) the *natural environment:* soil, topography, climate, and the indigenous plant and animal life. They are in part determined by (2) the extent, location, and character of the *population*, both of the farms and of the surrounding urban and industrial territory, and by (3) the matrix of *social and economic institutions* that constitute the background and setting of farm life. (4) *Historical inheritances and traditions*, both technical and cultural, are also important factors. Finally, (5) *the competition of other regions* in serving the same markets exerts a powerful influence on the character of agricultural production. As a general rule every market will be supplied in the main by those producers willing and able to supply products at prices lower than those asked by other producers. The latter are excluded by the lowness of the price. Within the potential supply area of a given market, therefore, only those farmers actually produce whose advantages are such that their expenses of production taken over a considerable period of time are less than the prices received per unit of output. Consequently there will be found in every supply area numerous districts well adapted in many respects, such as soil or location, to the production of certain commodities but nevertheless unable to produce those commodities except at an economic loss. Such submarginal districts—so called because they are below the margin of economic operation for those products—comprise no small part of the farm lands of New England.

These various influences are constantly changing. No account of the natural and social background of New England agriculture given in static terms would be of value. With the development of

---

[1] For notes see below, p. 136.

transportation technique and with improving methods of production and marketing, the relative economic advantages of various regions are also undergoing ceaseless change.

In this chapter, therefore, an attempt will be made to describe the background of New England agricultural production so far as possible in terms of present tendencies and with particular reference to factors affecting the costs of production.

CLIMATE

New England, lying in the humid region of the eastern United States, has sufficient rainfall, well distributed throughout the year, to make possible the production of practically all farm crops adapted to the prevailing temperatures of temperate regions. Average annual rainfall varies from forty-five inches in certain parts of southern New England to thirty inches in the extreme north.[2] About two thirds of the total precipitation occurs during the warmer months of the year. The variation in annual rainfall is not great. Drought of a killing nature is never experienced, and extremely dry, years are few. Dry weather during the latter half of the growing season combined with early rainfall is particularly favorable to large yields of potatoes,[3] and the successful harvest of the hay crop depends on plenty of dry sunshiny weather during late June and July. In general, hot and sunny summers accompanied by plenty of rainfall early in the growing season are favorable to New England farming. Summer hailstorms constitute a major hazard in the tobacco industry of the Connecticut Valley, the cost of insurance at the time of writing running as high as forty dollars an acre. Hail also in rare cases inflicts damage on fruits and vegetables and on growing corn. The prevailing temperatures vary from an average of around sixty degrees in summer to a winter average of twenty to thirty degrees in southern New England and twenty degrees in the north.[4] Seasonal extremes are more marked. Northern New England has a long snow-bound winter, but in the coastal parts of southern New England snow is intermittent. Along the coast both summer and winter are tempered by the presence of water. The length of the growing season[5] varies from less than a hundred days in extreme northern New England to nearly two hundred days in some parts of southern New England. Most of northern New England has a growing season of about 120 days (see Fig. 3, p. 21, above).

Both the Champlain and Aroostook valleys of northern New England and the intervening hilly country lie north of the corn belt; nor can the popular commercial varieties of apples be successfully grown in these areas, although potatoes, hay, clover, oats, barley, and peas grow unusually well under favorable soil conditions. Climatically southern New England is ideally adapted to corn, fruits, vegetables and, in the Connecticut Valley, to tobacco. Hay, oats, clovers, alfalfa, and potatoes flourish under suitable culture and soil conditions. Marked variations in the length of the growing season appear as a result of topography and exposure. The interval between killing frosts may be six weeks to two months longer on the crest of a hill or ridge than at the bottom two or three miles away. Thus even in southern New England there are flats and little valleys that are climatically out of the corn belt, while high, broad hilltops two hundred miles farther north may grow good corn. Little is known in a scientific way of the effects of topography on local climate in New England and of the consequent relationship to agricultural production and farm management policy.

SOIL AND TOPOGRAPHY

Soil and topography throughout New England are varied. The entire area was glaciated, and the effects of glaciation complicate the situation, often giving rise to diverse soil and topographic types within very limited areas. Viewed from the economic standpoint, there are no fixed or unchangeable criteria of value in land. In one period land may derive economic value from possessing certain plant foods; in another period, when chemical fertilizers are available at low price, ease of cultivation and adequate moisture supply may be the prime elements affecting value. Ten acres of good arable land in one block may have great value in one generation; in a later generation, one hundred or even four hundred acres of the same kind of land may be the minimum unit for economic cultivation, and the ten-acre lot alone be valueless, although its soil is identically what it was in the previous generation. Land that was valuable in one generation may be valueless in the next because the opening up of new supply areas or changes in consumption habits have lowered the prices of the products it is adapted to produce. Under present conditions and with prevailing tendencies, the most important qualities in land for agricultural use seem to be: (1) its relationship to moisture supply, (2) the extent of compact or unbroken areas capable of being operated as single production units, and (3) the peculiar adaptabilities of the soil and climate of particular locations to the production of specific commodities. The extent to which certain essential and replaceable chemical elements are present in the soil is not as important a factor.

The following is a description of the soils of New England prepared for this chapter by Professor M. F. Morgan of the Connecticut Agricultural Experiment Station, who also prepared the accompanying map (Fig. 1):

THE SOILS OF NEW ENGLAND

Soils, in common with the topographic features on which they occur, are extremely varied in practically all parts of New England. The rocks that form the parent material of soil are everywhere of diverse character. The entire area was glaciated, and in a region with rocks of varying degrees of resistance to erosion glaciation appears to add to the complexity of the soils that arise from their deposits.

A general picture of the main features of the soils of New England is presentéd in the accompanying map (Fig. 1). No attempt is made to show the local variations that occur almost everywhere. Regions are identified on the basis of the soil types of special importance or geographical interest that are to be found in the greatest abundance.

HEAVILY FORESTED AREAS

Over much of northern New England, particularly in Maine, there are large, unbroken areas of forest land. In Maine these heavily forested areas are not always rough or mountainous, as in the case of other parts of New England. The Maine "Big Woods" are usually only moderately hilly, and extensive areas lie so level as to be of swampy character. Obviously it is both unnecessary and impracticable to present a picture of the soils of these areas. When well drained, the soils are usually stony, moderately sandy, and belong to the podsol group, with a light gray layer of varying thickness beneath the humus of the forest floor. Very extensive areas of peat of the highly acid sphagnum type occupy the swampy regions of the Maine forests and are found to a lesser extent elsewhere.

VARIOUS STONY SOILS

A very large part of New England is covered, for the most part, with stony, thin, and light-textured (fine sandy loam and loam) soils, on irregularly hilly to mountainous topography. Woodland now occupies more than 60 per cent of the area, but scattered small fields, reclaimed by the partial removal of the larger boulders for stone walls or located on the sand and gravel deposits of the lower valley slopes, have permitted some agriculture over most of the region. The typical farm rarely includes more than sixty acres of tillable land. Forest soils are slightly podsolized in northern New England; and in southern New England, under predominantly hardwood forest, these soils, except for their high degree of stoniness, may possess the characteristics of the less stony upland soil groups described below.

LIGHT-TEXTURED, ACID UPLAND SOILS

Gloucester-Brookfield Group. Much of the agricultural land of the hilly, upland sections of southern and eastern New England is made up of soils derived from loose, coarse, unstratified glacial débris, predominantly of granitic or granite-gneiss origin in case of the Gloucester soils and of ferruginous mica-schist origin in case of the Brookfield soils. The latter are somewhat redder and more micaceous. Fine sandy loams and loams predominate. Such soils are of moderate fertility under general dairy farming management, but the irregularity of topography and the small size of fields, as well as stone and rock outcrops, form serious handicaps in economic production. The porosity of the substratum tends to droughtiness and rapid deterioration of hay lands.

Coloma Group. In the Narragansett Basin and in important areas elsewhere in southeastern Massachusetts there is an area of sandstone or quartz-schist rock, of Carboniferous age, which has weathered to give a soil of somewhat lighter, sandier texture, although predominantly less stony than in case of the Gloucester-Brookfield soils. A high percentage of silica and a somewhat poorer natural fertility is thus characteristic of the Coloma group. However, under favorable conditions of topography these soils may be fairly satisfactory for truck crops or corn when heavily fertilized, limed, and manured.

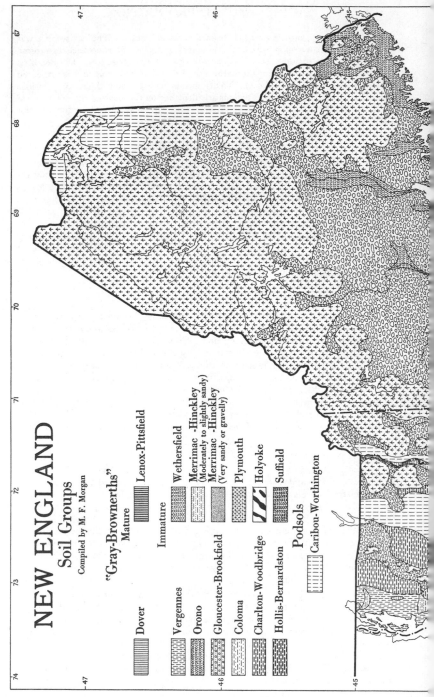

NEW ENGLAND
Soil Groups
Compiled by M. F. Morgan

"Gray-Brownerths"

Mature

▥ Lenox-Pittsfield

Immature

▥ Dover

▦ Wethersfield

▤ Vergennes

▦ Merrimac -Hinckley
(Moderately to slightly sandy)

▦ Orono

▦ Merrimac -Hinckley
(Very sandy or gravelly)

▦ Gloucester-Brookfield

▦ Plymouth

▦ Coloma

▨ Holyoke

▦ Charlton-Woodbridge

▦ Suffield

▦ Hollis-Bernardston

Podsols

▦ Caribou-Worthington

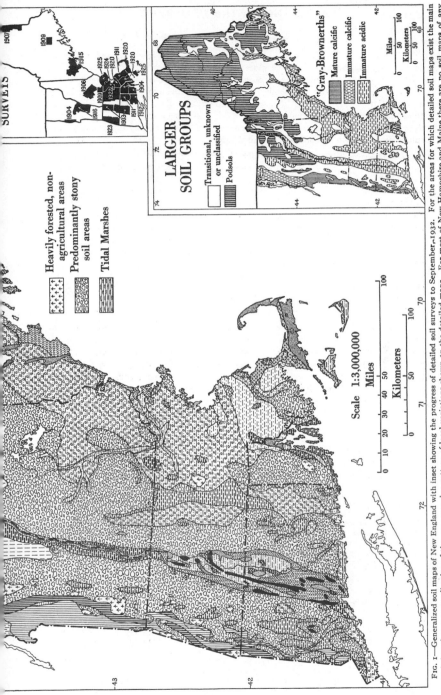

1907
1909
1915
1925
1924
1920 1911
1922 1920
1906 1925
1909
1904
1916
1904 1903 1912
1923 1911

LARGER
SOIL GROUPS

Heavily forested, non-
agricultural areas

Predominantly stony
soil areas

Tidal Marshes

Transitional, unknown
or unclassified

Podsols

"Gray-Brownerths"

Mature calcific

Immature calcific

Immature acidic

Miles
0   50   100

Kilometers
0   50   100

Scale   1:3,000,000

Miles
0   10   20   30   40   50   100

Kilometers
0   50   100

FIG. 1—Generalized soil maps of New England with inset showing the progress of detailed soil surveys to September, 1932.   For the areas for which detailed soil maps exist the main map is based on a generalization of the very complex pattern of local variations shown on the detailed maps.   For most of New Hampshire and Maine there are no soil maps of any kind available, and these areas had to be approximated from what the compiler could gather from geological surveys, correspondence, and travel.   See also footnote on p. 124.

HEAVIER, ACID UPLAND SOILS

Charlton-Woodbridge Group. Over a considerable part of the uplands of central
New England, especially on the more smoothly rounded ridges of more or less
"drumlin" shape, the soils are less stony, slightly heavier in surface texture (typically
a loam), and materially less leachy, owing to the more compact character of the
glacial till from which they are derived, than the other soils of the region. The Charlton-Woodbridge group, named from the two most important soil series, is mainly
devoted to dairy farming, although numerous successful apple orchards are to be
found on these soils in southern New England.

Hollis-Bernardston Group. The upper Connecticut Valley between New Hampshire and Vermont cuts through soft shale and phyllite formations which weather
to give somewhat heavier soils, with a less pronounced yellow color in the subsoil
than is generally to be encountered in other upland soils of New England. Soils
of the same character occur in a few other isolated areas, particularly in Woodbridge
and Orange, Conn., and east of Narragansett Bay. Such soils are usually comparatively free from large stones; they are retentive of moisture and are associated
with smoothly rolling topography except on steep valley slopes. High acidity and
low availability of mineral nutrients are common characteristics, though these
disadvantages may be overcome on fields that are exceptionally well manured.
With good management, they are excellent grassland soils, as evidenced on Aquidneck
or Newport Island, R. I.

PARTIALLY CALCAREOUS UPLAND SOILS

Dover Group. A more or less well-defined belt of massive marble and limestone
deposits extends from Ridgefield, Conn., to Lake Champlain. The occurrence of
this formation in a region surrounded by granite-gneiss and schist rocks that are
much more resistant to weathering processes has caused the development of lower-
lying areas and broad valleys wherever this belt of calcareous rock widens out to
any appreciable extent. The Dover soils are almost wholly derived from the underlying marble and limestone formation, are rarely acid to a harmful degree, and are
frequently calcareous, even in the surface horizons. They are mellow and friable
and in common with most limestone soils are favored with respect to available
chemical elements of fertility. Unfortunately, the Dover soil areas are of rather
local occurrence and in many places are cut up with rock outcrops.

Lenox-Pittsfield Group. Closely associated with the Dover group are soils only
partially influenced by the calcareous rock. These are usually derived to a con-

NOTE ON FIGURE 1—On the main map the symbols suggest the character of the soil areas. Thus
the predominantly stony soils and the heavily forested areas are indicated by symbols representing
stones and trees respectively. Very sandy soils are represented by stippling; sandy soils with many
boulders or rock outcrops by stippling in combination with small circles; loamy or other less notably
sandy soils by lines (either straight or zigzag). Where lines are employed acidic soils are shown by
horizontal lines, calcific soils by vertical lines, mature soils by solid lines, immature soils by broken
lines, heavy texture by heavy lines, and light texture by light lines. The symbols for the Orono,
Wethersfield, and Suffield soil groups conform with this scheme (i.e. they are broken zigzag lines). The
symbol for the Holyoke soils of the trap ridge of the Connecticut Valley Lowland is an exception to the
scheme, these soils being shown in solid black owing to the limited areas that they occupy.
    In the legend and on the larger inset map the soils are classified according to whether they fall into
the group of podsols or "gray-brownerths" (see L. A. Wolfanger, *The Major Soil Divisions of the United
States: A Pedologic-Geographic Study*, New York, 1930, pp. 18–23; the same, *Economic Geography of the
Gray-Brownerths of the Eastern United States*, in *Geogr. Rev.*, Vol. 21, 1931, pp. 276–296). Owing to
lack of detailed information the stony upland soils are not definitely assigned either to the podsols or
to the "gray-brownerths," nor are they classified on the basis either of maturity or of chemical characteristics (acidity or calcification). It is probable, however, that all of them are acidic. In northern
New England, moreover, these soils are probably for the most part podsolized, and in southern New
England they probably belong among the "gray-brownerths." The soils of the heavily forested areas
in northern New England are probably for the most part mature acidic podsols and are so shown on the
larger inset map.

siderable degree from schists and gneisses adjacent to the limestone belt. The Lenox-Pittsfield group constitute the predominant soils of the limestone valleys, owing to glacial mixing of rock material. These soils are somewhat heavier in texture, more compact in the substratum, and more strongly acid than those of the Dover group. They differ from the Charlton-Woodbridge soils in their less acid reaction and somewhat hilly topography, but otherwise they possess the same agronomic features.

Caribou-Worthington Group. In two important areas of New England the soils are derived from calcareous shales and schists. The first of these is the well-known Aroostook County area, where potato culture has reached a very high state of development on the broad, nearly level expanses that mark the occurrence of the Caribou and related soils. A light, open, friable loam prevails, the drainage is good, and fields are practically free from stones of sufficient size to form impediments to specialized cultural machinery. Such soils are apparently exceptionally well adapted to the crop that has made this region famous.

In east-central Vermont a similar group of rocks has given a very similar soil condition, except that the topography of the region is for the most part very hilly. The Worthington soils are the most important series mapped in a recent reconnaisance survey of Vermont. They form what may well be considered the best large area of good grazing land in New England, and dairying is consequently the chief enterprise.

SOILS OF THE CHAMPLAIN BASIN

Vergennes Group. The low-lying area in northwestern Vermont east of Lake Champlain is in reality an extension of the St. Lawrence basin and, in common with it, is generally covered with clay loam or clay soils of dark color overlying heavy clay deposits of considerable thickness. The topography is level to rolling. The fields are free from stone, but the natural drainage is poor in many places. The predominating Vergennes soils are of strong fertility and are well adapted to grassland, oats, and such early varieties of corn as the climate permits.

SOILS OF THE TRIASSIC (OR CONNECTICUT VALLEY) LOWLAND AND ASSOCIATED SOILS

From near the northern Massachusetts border southward to Long Island Sound at New Haven extends a broad trough. Except where this lowland is interrupted or split by the abrupt trap-rock ridges characteristic of these formations of Triassic geologic age, elevations are from two to five hundred feet lower than those of the gneiss and schist uplands lying to the east and west.

Wethersfield Group. The part of the Triassic Lowland that shows a smoothly sloping hilly topography is generally covered by dark reddish-brown, loamy soils developed over reddish sandstones and shales. They are well drained, moderately fertile, comparatively free from stone, and show a wider range of crop adaptation than most of the other soils of New England. Dairying, orcharding, trucking, and tobacco farming all appear to be successful in commercially important areas.

Holyoke Group. The steep, rugged, and stony ridges of the trap-rock formations are practically non-agricultural, but, except for the generally bare cliffs and talus slopes that mark their westward faces, the Holyoke stony loam soils are excellent for hardwood forest production.

Merrimac Group. A large part of the Triassic Lowland north of Rocky Hill, Conn., is covered with deposits of stratified sand and gravel, occurring as nearly level terraces at various elevations above the present flood plain of the Connecticut River. These terraces are frequently a few miles in width and may extend for longer distances to the north or south. The soils are generally sandy, entirely free from stone, and easily worked. The Merrimac sandy loam is the typical tobacco soil of the Connecticut Valley. Market gardening is also well developed. Certain terraces are excessively sandy and are of little agricultural value except for special crops, such as shade tobacco on the East Granby-Suffield sand plain.

In many other valleys of New England similar terraces occur. Their soils are usually more gravelly in the substratum and more loamy at the surface than the Merrimac soils of the Triassic Lowland, although they are mapped with them on the accompanying map. Where not excessively sandy or gravelly, the Merrimac soils occurring outside the Connecticut Valley, particularly in the Merrimac Valley and along the southern New England coast, are valuable for market-garden crops, potatoes, and vineyards. Their occurrence is usually coincident with urban and suburban development.

Widely distributed localized areas of gravel and sand deposits in the form of irregular hummocks and knolls give rise to the excessively sandy or gravelly soils of the *Hinckley group*, which are not separately shown on the generalized map because of its small scale. These soils are most widespread in the areas mapped as the Gloucester-Brookfield group, where they occupy most of the valley land adjacent to the main streams and their tributaries. The Hinckley soils are of limited agricultural value, although small plots favorable for early crops frequently occur on the lower areas between the gravelly knolls. Much of the land of this type is being developed for plantations of white or red pine.

Suffield Group. In a few areas of the Connecticut Valley temporarily impounded waters formed at the close of the glacial period gave rise to stratified silt and clay deposits. Where these lie at or near the surface, the heavy, drab-colored silty clay loam or silt loam soils of the Suffield group are found. Unless occurring as eroded slopes along recent valley cuttings, these soils are somewhat poorly drained, late, and "cold." They are more difficult to till than the sandy soils of the region. However, the occurrence of Suffield soils in the town of that name in Connecticut, in association with the lighter Merrimac soils, has given rise to an unusually good balance between dairying and tobacco growing.

SOILS OF THE MAINE COASTAL SHELF

Orono Group. The New England coast north of the mouth of the Merrimac River has been materially elevated since the close of the glacial period, although before that time extensive subsidence must have occurred. Marine clays formed over the previously submerged areas now occupy extensive lowlands near the Maine coast. These clays are frequently covered with sandy material, but the soils are predominantly silt loams and clays. Owing to the calcareous nature of the clay the Orono soils are less acid than the somewhat similar Suffield soils of the Connecticut Valley. Important areas are devoted to sweet corn for canning.

SOILS OF THE GLACIAL TERMINAL MORAINES

Plymouth Group. Belts of coarse sandy soils, with an irregular hummocky surface strewn with granitic boulders of all sizes, mark the position of the ice front at its maximum southward extension, or during long periods when the ice front was temporarily stationary during its recession. These morainal areas, identified as the Plymouth soils, occur in southwestern Rhode Island, the western Cape Cod region, and on Nantucket and Marthas Vineyard islands. The soils are extraordinarily barren and are of little value for either agriculture or forestry.

Tidal Marshes. Along the coasts of Long Island Sound and of the Atlantic south of the mouth of the Merrimac River frequent tidal marshes occur, particularly in the inlets about the mouths of streams. These areas are frequently protected by dikes or flood gates and ditched for mosquito control. This has permitted the cutting of salt-marsh hay used for animal bedding and commercial packing. Many of these areas are being filled in and converted into building sites or aviation fields.

THE NEED FOR COMPREHENSIVE SOIL SURVEYS

The extreme diversity of soils in New England and the rapid changes occurring in New England agriculture make more detailed knowledge of the character of New England soils very desirable. Detailed soil surveys have been completed in certain parts of the region. The formulation of sound public policy with relation to the use of the land and the wise guidance of the thousands of persons who need help each year in purchasing land for agricultural purposes both necessitate the early completion of adequate soil surveys. While the soils and topography can be described in a very generalized way, such descriptions are of little value in guiding a prospective farmer or a state agency in formulating policy with relation to a particular piece of land. The requisite information must be specific and available, and significant research of an economic and social character must be deferred until this fundamental information is at hand.

In Vermont and Massachusetts comprehensive programs are in operation, and when finished complete and detailed soil surveys will be available for each of these states. Connecticut has a detailed research project in soil science and in land utilization but has so far failed to inaugurate soil surveys beyond the early ones made in Hartford, Windham, and New London counties before the World War. In Maine a survey has been made in Aroostook County, and in Rhode Island and New Hampshire beginnings have been made. An inset map on the soil map (Fig. 1) shows the areas for which detailed soil survey data are available.

POPULATION

Population must be considered in relation to New England agriculture from two points of view: (1) that of the extent, location, purchasing power, and buying habits of the peoples who constitute the market for New England farm products; and (2) that of the character of the farm population and the conditions of New England's farm labor supply.

With the exception of Aroostook potatoes and the tobacco of the Connecticut Valley, the farm products of New England are produced for sale in the local markets. New England produces for these local markets perishables of high value, such as fluid milk, sweet cream, fresh eggs, and bulky perishables, such as fruits and vegetables. The prosperity of New England's farms depends on the extent and purchasing power of the local population. When this purchasing power is high the people are inclined to buy high-grade perishables, like fluid milk and the local vegetables and fruits, rather than canned milk and vegetables or substitutes of inferior quality. The reader is referred to the population map on pages 22–23 and his attention is called to the concentration of population around Boston, in the Connecticut Valley, and near New York City. More than twenty million people live within one hundred and fifty miles of Middletown, Conn., in what has been one of the most concentrated areas of high purchasing power in the world. This is the most important single fact affecting the agriculture of New England. Indeed, within the limits of a temperate climate and of certain soil and topographic factors, it may be said to be its determinant.

The population of the New England countryside up to 1800 had been almost entirely of colonial origin. Practically the entire arable area outside of northern Maine had been settled by that time. The emigration to the West had been of excess population, resulting from the high birth rate. The period between 1850 and 1870 was one of Irish and German immigration. The immigrants settled in the cities and manufacturing villages that were rapidly springing up and moved out to the farms as hired men and maids, supplanting the sons and daughters of farmers who were migrating to the West. In the period following 1870 many farms came into the possession of the sons of these immigrants. The change in ownership, however, was not by any means universal and tended to be localized. These immigrants were pretty well assimilated, and the elements of New England culture survived, modified of course by the Industrial Revolution, humanitarianism, and the reaction to the opening of the West. In this later period there was a movement of French Canadians first into the textile regions of northern New England, thence down through the textile cities of the entire area, and thence to the farms. In the early part of the twentieth century, after the period of land abandonment had nearly run its course, many local areas were entirely taken over by Poles, Russians, Italians, Portuguese, and Jews. The French Canadians were assimilated somewhat less slowly and tended in some places to settle in groups. Nuclei of Swedish and Polish settlements also appeared. It is impossible to mention the small local settlements. The larger groups are the Poles and Russians in the upper Connecticut Valley Lowland, Portuguese in southeastern Massachusetts and Rhode Island, Jews in eastern Connecticut, Italians about the minor population centers of southern New England, and French Canadians in Maine, Vermont, and to a less extent in southern New England.[6] French Canadians also appear in northern Maine, where they are near their native country or where they can combine small farming with guiding sportsmen and tourists. These groups of recent European or Canadian origin have in many places been able to continue in farming because they were satisfied with a lower standard of living and because they were reinforced by the free labor of large families of children. Where they were able to purchase good farms they have prospered. They have persisted in many areas that would otherwise have been abandoned. Their competition has in many instances constituted a serious problem to native farmers on the better farms. As succeeding generations tend to approximate an American standard of living these problems are becoming less acute—how fast we do not know.

The proximity of cities tends to be the main factor in determining the farm wage rate. This rate is influenced far more strongly by the supply and demand for industrial labor than by conditions in any market for agricultural labor. While this is less evident in northern than in southern New England, it is doubtful whether any part of the section is free from it as a dominant influence.

In general, the variations in the racial character of rural population are not factors of great importance affecting agricultural production. The more important effects have already been discussed. It is true that the older native farmers predominate in some of the poorer regions and unskilled foreign farmers in other poor regions. These conditions are not peculiar to New England and are not the cause of the backward agricultural development. It seems more reasonable to believe that they are manifestations of the general tendency for the factors of production of like efficiency to become associated.

SOCIAL AND ECONOMIC INSTITUTIONS

In southern New England the social and economic institutions that serve the farmer are urban in their general character. This is not entirely true of northern New England, and in some places it is not the case to any great extent. New England has its complement of specialized economic institutions functioning entirely in the interests of agriculture.

The operations of the middleman agencies for supplying feed, fertilizers, and seeds to New England farmers, the credit agencies which supply the capital funds, the marketing agencies which complete the production process by carrying products to the consumer— these are all of great importance in the organization of agricultural production. The experiment stations, the agricultural colleges and high schools, the college extension services, and the crop and market reporting agencies likewise form an integral part of the picture. While the numerous minor functionaries could be enumerated, the relative importance of certain of these agencies may, perhaps, best be visualized from an enumeration of the main items of expenditure made by New England farmers for productive purposes (Table I).

TABLE I—MORE IMPORTANT ITEMS OF EXPENDITURES ON
NEW ENGLAND FARMS, 1929[a]

(In dollars, ooo omitted)

EXPENDITURES	MAINE	N. H.	VT.	MASS.	R. I.	CONN.	TOTAL
Feed	11,497	7,622	11,547	20,671	3,047	13,030	67,414
Fertilizer	7,287	439	681	3,014	336	3,653	15,410
Labor	9,042	3,980	5,495	17,288	2,276	11,755	49,836
Machinery . . .	5,384	1,699	3,083	4,134	581	2,724	17,605
Electric power .	498	306	331	1,051	153	645	2,984
Mortgage at 5% .	1,127	409	1,318	1,703	132	1,178	5,867
Taxes on farm property operated by owners .	3,595	1,276	2,066	3,380	226	1,657	12,200
Total value of above items . .	38,430	15,731	24,521	51,241	6,751	34,642	171,316

[a] Based on *Fifteenth Census of the United States, 1930: Agriculture, Statistics by Counties, Second Series*, Washington, 1931.

Although lack of credit facilities may hamper agriculture, there is no reason to believe that New England farmers have suffered recently from such a lack. The opposite is more likely to be true. The too ready extension of merchants' credit to tobacco and potato growers has probably been one of the reasons for some of the difficulties facing these farmers. The Federal Land Bank of Springfield, the northeastern unit of the Federal Farm Loan system, extends first mortgage credit up to 50 per cent of the value of approved applications throughout New England. This bank extends credit on notes which may be amortized by annual payments during a period that may extend to thirty-five years. Under these conditions the bank must give careful consideration to the future trends in land values. Its policy is a most enlightened one, and it, more than any other agricultural agency in New England, is using all the facts and power at its disposal to guide New England agriculture along the lines of sound policy in regard to land utilization. This is only a matter of good business. This credit system, while under quasi-governmental control, is coöperative in its capital stock structure and payment of earnings and is one of the real forces in New England agricultural production. It has outstanding a total of nearly $24,000,000 in loans to New England farmers.[7] Second mortgage credit is extended to New England farmers for the most part by individuals and banks.

The Federal Intermediate Credit Bank of Springfield is associated with the Land Bank and like it is part of a federal and nation-wide institution organized into regional units. It rediscounts farmers' intermediate paper for banks and coöperative associations. Intermediate paper runs from nine months to four years and is secured by livestock or warehouse receipts on stored crops. The facilities of this bank are not extensively utilized by New England farmers.

An important need of New England farming is a more intelligent administration of the extension of short-time credit. Banks as a rule do not needlessly discriminate against farming. It is expensive business, however, for city and village banks to have to bother with small loans to farmers, especially as there is often no employee of the bank who knows how to judge applications for such loans. As a result, loans are usually granted solely on the basis of the applicant's net worth and liquid assets, no consideration being given to the probable profitableness and productivity of the objective of the loan. As a result many loans are granted to farmers who would suffer less loss and be better off if the loan had been withheld. On the other hand, capable and younger men without assets, as yet, often deserve and should have loans they cannot secure. The banking system, while it has made an honest effort on numerous occasions, has so far not been able to solve this problem in a way consistent with the profitable operation of its own business. The extension of fertilizer manufacturers' credit to the potato, tobacco, and other crop producers of New England has gone so far as to be almost ruinous to both manufacturers and farmers. While prices were dropping, stocks piling up in storage, and every factor in the situation pointing to the wisdom of acreage reduction, fertilizer distributors were bidding against each other for volume by extending more and more liberal credit to farmers. In time efforts were made to regulate the practice, but credit extension practices not consistent with sound agricultural policy seem to persist. These practices not only perpetuate production under submarginal conditions but create such a gap between the cash and credit price of fertilizer that they have stimulated the coöperative purchase of fertilizer by those farmers who have had the ready cash to buy outright in quantity. As dairy farmers receive their income monthly, the credit problem in this industry has not been serious.

Source of Farm Supplies

The question of the source of farm supplies is also an important consideration in New England agriculture. The poultry industry is entirely dependent on shipped-in feeds, and the dairy industry could not maintain its present status without them. According to the census New England farmers purchased sixty-seven million dollars' worth of feedstuffs and twenty million dollars' worth of fertilizer in 1929. The fertilizer industry is attempting to adjust itself to new conditions. A considerable number of concerns are struggling to expand, and some must eventually be eliminated or merged. The conditions have been somewhat chaotic and have been characterized by overextension of credit and high prices for limited quantities on a credit basis as compared with the prices that might be obtained for cash in quantity.

Farmers have as a whole been well served by the feed-distributing trade during the past decade, much better than was the case in the preceding ten years. There are a number of national and regional feed companies that have been rendering excellent and highly intelligent service in the assembly and distribution of feedstuffs to the dairymen and poultrymen of New England. The Eastern States Farmers Exchange, a farmers' coöperative purchasing association, does more than 10 per cent of the feed, fertilizer, and seed business of the area. It handles a growing percentage of the total requirements. In its service it emphasizes quality and gives attention to the carrying out of policies designed to increase the profits of its members. It constitutes a wholesome element of competition to private concerns and corporations throughout the whole region served by it.

Technical Overhead

The colleges, experiment stations, extension services, and state boards of agriculture constitute the technical, scientific, and economic overhead of New England's agriculture. Inspection of feeds, fertilizers, and spray materials, development of more efficient methods of production and instruction of the rank and file in their application, insect and disease control and methods of their application, studies of the best organization of farms and of the adjustment of management policy to changing economic conditions are among the matters in which these agencies are designed to exercise leadership, to carry on research, and to do educational and service work. The organization in New England is similar to that throughout the United States. The outstanding characteristics of the New England situation arise from the smallness of the states and the danger that conflicting policies may cause chaos and operate against the interests of a strong central policy for the section as a whole. A number of organized efforts for coördinating the activities of these agencies have thus far proved remarkably successful. Among those which deserve mention are the following:

(1) The New England Research Council on Marketing and Food Supply, an organization for coördinating the research work of the experiment stations and the endowed institutions in the field of agricultural economics.

(2) The Association of Commissioners of Agriculture. The commissioners of agriculture, by meeting regularly and coöperating in their attack on major problems, have added much to their own efficiency and have served New England agriculture in a notable way at critical periods.

(3) The New England Institute of Coöperation. This institute conducts annually a forum in which farmers and representatives of coöperative associations and the colleges discuss questions relating to marketing policy.

(4) The New England Council. This organization was brought into being by the joint action of the governors of the New England states to assist in bringing about forceful coördinated action in matters of common interest to New England. It functions in the fields of industry, transportation, agriculture, recreation, and in the promotion of the interests of New England as a whole.

(5) Various New England associations of technical specialists.

TECHNICAL AND CULTURAL INHERITANCE

Among New England's most important historical inheritances on the technical side are the small farms, small fields, and stone walls of colonial agriculture, and the tendency to perpetuate labor-wasting practices in crop production. Many farms on poor soils whose clearing in colonial times and operation up to the middle of the nineteenth century may have been justified are today unquestionably submarginal, although still in operation. In the hill regions the character of the topography and the variability of the soils both render very difficult the problem of joining these units together into farms adapted to economic operation. Some progress has been made in merging holdings. The question has not, however, been studied in any systematic way, nor have its possibilities and difficulties been thoroughly explored.

Throughout New England small crop acreage (Fig. 2, p. 143) is as important a cause of submarginality as soil. Where small crop acreage is combined with poor soil the situation is usually hopeless as far as the present and immediate future is concerned. In northern New England these small farms, except when used as summer homes of the well-to-do, have little value unless they can be amalgamated with adjacent holdings. In southern New England they tend to become the homes of part-time farmers, who supplement an urban income with agricultural operations on a small scale. On some of the sandier soils, like the Gloucester and Merrimac, they have been developed as poultry, small fruit, or vegetable farms where the operations are intensive and require little land. The supply of such farms, however, so greatly exceeds the probable extension of the market for these products that these uses may not be expected to solve the problem of the utilization of undersized farms. Since all present tendencies lead us to expect that the size of units adapted to economic operation will increase in the future, this problem is not likely to become less pressing, except as definite steps are taken for its solution. Not only are many farms too small, but in numerous instances both in northern and in southern New England the volume of products originating in one locality is not great enough to permit of efficient processing, transportation, or merchandizing. This has been shown to be true of many milk plants in small communities in Vermont,[8] and of the volume of poultry, eggs, and vegetables originating south of a line from Brattleboro, Vt., to Lewiston, Me. The problem of readjusting production to the requirements of efficient marketing is a fundamental one but is complex and difficult. The problems growing out of size of business appear more strikingly in the upland regions than in the lowlands, although they constitute a major issue in the Connecticut Valley.

Inefficiency in the utilization of labor is partly a function of size of business. On one-man or less-than-one-man farms, which are the more common upland type, the operators cannot own and utilize their proper complement of labor-saving machinery. Moreover, they seem to have inherited from the age of large families and self-sufficient farming a lack of realization of the value of labor. Many operations are performed by two men which could be performed by one with equal ease and with little or no increased expenditure. This is true of upland farms over the whole area. When inheritances of attitudes and culture, the influence of self-sufficiency in previous generations, and the failure of leaders of agricultural thought to take into consideration the facts of the New England background are considered, the conditions are easily enough explained, but they raise, none the less, difficult and pressing problems.

If New England agricultural production suffers any cultural handicaps, they are associated with the ideals of thrift, hard work, and petty saving that were necessarily a part of the régime of self-sufficient agriculture and with the period of extreme depression that prevailed in New England agriculture during the latter decades of the nineteenth century.

That the New England farmer is either an ultraconservative or a poor supporter of business coöperatives is untrue. He has been given an entirely false reputation in both respects. No farmer has readjusted his production policies so drastically, so often, or so courageously as has the New Englander in the past three quarters of a century. No farmer is keener in rejecting the half-baked advice of his would-be saviors or in responding to the real opportunities for improving his position. Coöperative marketing and purchasing have been developed consistently and far. In general the New England farmer is an intelligent and loyal coöperator. His inheritances from the town meeting and the democratic traditions of New England make him especially well adapted to the federated type of coöperative organization, and poor material for the autocratic organizations of the centralized type. The nature of the marketing opportunities make the problems of coöperative organization particularly difficult in production areas contiguous to markets. Despite these difficulties beginnings of real progress in the development of coöperative methods adapted to such conditions have been made among the egg producers of Connecticut and the vegetable and fruit growers of Rhode Island and Massachusetts.

Proximity to industrial and commercial centers and the contacts established as a consequence have for seventy-five years imbued the New England farmers on the whole with the point of view of business management. The constant intermigration between farm and city has strengthened the effect of these contacts. These factors undoubtedly operate with greater force in areas near than in those remote from the cities. Working in the other direction at all times is the tradition of the self-sufficient farm of an earlier age. Contact with cities has undoubtedly been a constant stimulant to the demand for an urban standard of living on farms. Near-by cities have competed with the farm for labor supply, and south of Brattleboro and in southern New Hampshire and Maine this has long been and still is a real force in speeding up the abandonment for farm use of farms that have ceased to return as good a living as that which the same families could attain by city employment. Many of these families while discontinuing their farming operations have continued to reside on the farms. Farther north these adjustments have in general occurred less rapidly.

The narrowing base of public support for various social agencies is an important problem in regions of declining population. This situation exists particularly in the poorer agricultural areas of northern New England where there has not been a compensating development of recreational activities or part-time farming. The falling value of taxable property and the loss of those persons of means who are the backbone of the support of social institutions in all rural communities throw a burden upon the remaining farms even though they be excellent. At the best, social services are usually inadequately or poorly performed in such communities. Schools tend to be poor, and the communities fail to attract a high quality of new citizenship.

The differences in the social and cultural inheritances of groups of different national origins have had little effect on agricultural production, except as has already been pointed out. The differences between individuals of the same race in any situation are wide. There seems to be little difference in efficiency that can be attributed to racial character. The Italians seem predisposed to fruit-growing and to vegetable gardening; the Portuguese to vegetable gardening; and the onion industry of the upper Connecticut Valley is largely carried on by Poles. Whether these tendencies are inherent or are likely to disappear, time alone will show.

The competitive factors that are of prime importance in determining the prices of New England farm products and the extent to which they can be sold are beyond the scope of this chapter. Here we have attempted to describe in a general way the outstanding facts of the local environment of New England agriculture that, in conjunction with many others not mentioned, operate together to affect the costs of production of New England farm products and to determine the survival or disappearance of types of farming and of rural life and activity in various parts of the region.

NOTES

[1] For references bearing upon the topics discussed in the present article see not only the following notes but also the notes on pp. 164–167, below.

[2] See J. H. Weber, *The Rainfall of New England*, in *Journ. New England Water Works Assoc.*, Vol. 42, 1928, pp. 137–149, 278–312, and 414–430, especially Plate I; Gragg Richards, *The Rainfall of Northern New England*, ibid., pp. 431–456; *Atlas of American Agriculture*, Part II, Sect. A, *Precipitation and Humidity*, by J. B. Kincer, U. S. Dept. of Agric., Washington, 1922.

[3] F. V. Waugh, C. D. Stevens, and G. Burmeister, *Methods of Forecasting New England Potato Yields: A Study of the Relationship of Yields to Reported Condition and Weather Data*, U. S. Dept. of Agric., Bureau of Agric. Econ., Washington, 1929 (mimeographed).

[4] *Atlas of American Agriculture*, Part II, Sect. B, *Temperature, Sunshine and Wind*, by J. B. Kincer, U. S. Dept. of Agric., Washington, 1928.

[5] *Ibid.*, Part II, Sect. I, *Frost and the Growing Season*, by W. G. Reed, Washington, 1918.

[6] See paper by Professor J. L. Hypes entitled *Recent Immigrant Stocks in New England Agriculture*, in the present volume, pp. 189–205.

[7] The following data showing the approximate amount of loans outstanding as of July 1, 1932, have been furnished by courtesy of the Federal Land Bank:

	NUMBER	AMOUNT
Maine	2759	$7,891,400
New Hampshire	507	1,166,800
Vermont	1343	4,047,200
Massachusetts	1662	5,026,200
Rhode Island	209	686,900
Connecticut	1489	5,144,400
	7969	$23,962,900

[8] W. A. Schoenfeld, *Some Economic Aspects of the Marketing of Milk and Cream in New England*, Washington, 1927 (*U. S. Dept. of Agric. Circular No. 16*).

AGRICULTURAL PRODUCTION IN NEW ENGLAND

PRESENT CONDITIONS AND MAJOR PROBLEMS[1]

I. G. Davis

HISTORICAL OUTLINE[2]

FROM the days of earliest settlement until well into the nineteenth century, agriculture in New England was organized as a form of self-sufficient domestic economy   True, there was a fringe of commercial farming about the centers of Boston and Providence, and certain portions of the interior not too far from the waterways produced meats and cheese for the West Indian trade and to a limited extent forest products of value to the shipping industry. Local and family self-sufficiency, however, prevailed throughout New England, which by this time had been completely settled excepting northern and some portions of eastern Maine.

During the second quarter of the nineteenth century, village and small-town manufacturing became spread over the whole of southern New England and had also penetrated into southern New Hampshire and southwestern Maine. The shipping industry was thriving. The settlement of the Middle West was progressing at an increasing rate, and western wool, meat, and cheese came into competition to some extent with the products of New England farms. By the middle of the century, spinning and weaving had left the farm and were being rapidly abandoned as a family activity. The self-sufficient local and family economy of the previous century began to give way to a commercial agriculture.

After the Civil War, agriculture expanded with extreme rapidity in the western United States. Railroads were extended and merged into great systems of communication; refrigeration in transit was perfected. New England agriculture gradually became more commercial in character as a result of the creation of near-by urban and industrial markets. Rural standards of living had risen, and constant immigration to the cities and to the West set up reactions in rural thought and ideals of life that definitely established the commercial character of the agriculture of New England.

Toward the end of the century the developments in the West and in the system of transportation had been such that New England farmers came into competition on their own local markets with the vigorous, extensive, and low-cost agriculture of the central part of the

[1] For notes see below, p. 164.

country. The great fresh beef industry of the northeast was unable to produce cheaply enough to survive and followed the sheep industry into oblivion. Attempts to substitute cheese and butter production for the displaced meat industry were only partially and temporarily successful. More than two decades of farm abandonment and agricultural readjustment followed, in which more than half the improved land of southern New England and nearly half in northern New England passed out of active agricultural use.

By the beginning of the World War, New England agriculture had adjusted itself to the economic situation along new lines. The specialized production of potatoes in Aroostook County in Maine; of tobacco and onions in the Connecticut Valley; of cranberries in Plymouth and Barnstable counties in Massachusetts; of butter and maple syrup in Vermont; of blueberries along the coast of Washington County in Maine, and vegetable production near all population centers had appeared. The agriculture of the inland and upland regions, which constitute by far the greater part of New England, had become a form of general farming. Its core was dairying, around which were grouped minor enterprises in fruit, vegetable, and poultry production and usually the sale of forest products of some kind.

In general it may be said that, by the time of the World War, New England farms were turning out products either so perishable or so bulky with relation to value that they were not affected by the competition of areas outside the region. In addition, they were producing along the specialized lines noted above. Much part-time farming had developed in the vicinity of industrial cities and villages.

PRESENT FORCES COMPELLING ADJUSTMENT[3]

A process of continuous adjustment to changing conditions—to market demand, to competition, to new techniques of production and transportation, and to the attractions that near-by cities offer to farm people—has characterized New England agriculture since the beginning of the period of commercial farming. Since the World War old forces have assumed new forms and new factors have appeared. The chief forces to which New England farm production is in process of adjustment at the present time may be described briefly.

Shrinkage of Market for the Farm Products of the United States. Since 1920 the market for American agricultural products has shrunk, as a result of lessening export demand, changing habits of consumption, and a slackening rate of population growth. At the same time, the displacement of horses by the tractor, increased efficiency of animals in turning forage and grain into human food, and the application of scientific methods in general have greatly reduced both the number of men and the acreage necessary to produce given quantities of products for human consumption. The result has been that American agriculture possesses a large excess capacity for meeting both the normal and the emergency needs of its markets. The situation has been particularly serious in the great meat and cereal and cotton industries. Farmers in these industries and in others where excess capacity has appeared have attempted to utilize that capacity profitably by turning their attention to supplying the eastern markets with products whose prices have remained firmer, especially in the industrial cities of New England and the East: notably fluid milk, high grade eggs, fruits, and vegetables. They have not in all cases produced commodities directly competing with the New England-grown product, but their competition, even when indirect, has been felt. Up to the time of writing this particular force has not to any important degree displaced any product except sweet cream. The displacement of sweet cream, however, and the increasing disparity between cream and fluid milk prices has created, for the first time in the decade just past, a condition that may compel drastic readjustments. The greater part of the agricultural area and the majority of the farmers of New England are involved to some extent.

Increased Mobility of Farm Labor. The rapid increase in the use of automobiles and the equally rapid extension of hard roads and the telephone have placed the farmer in closer contact with his market. More important than this, however, has been the effect on the mobility of farm labor.[4] Every farmer in New England, south of a line extending from Augusta, Me., west to Concord, N. H., and thence to Brattleboro, Vt., and Pittsfield, Mass., may be said to live in urban territory. If farming ceases to be as remunerative as industrial or commercial employment he can shift his employment without changing his place of residence. City workers have been induced to purchase or build houses in areas formerly agricultural, and part-time farming and rural residence on the part of persons formerly living in cities has become very common. In northern New England this tendency towards part-time farming has of course been less pronounced, and in more remote areas it has not appeared. In the north, as well as in parts of southern New England, numerous farms have come to be owned as summer homes. Occasionally agricultural operations are continued after their purchase for this purpose, but in most cases the farms so purchased were submarginal as units for economic agricultural production. These shifts to recreational, part-time farming, and residential uses of lands, and the increasing mobility of labor between agricultural occupation on one hand and commercial or industrial employment on the other are among the important tendencies of the past decade.

Farm Machinery and the Size of Farms. The increase in the use of farm machinery adapted to extensive farming and the application of science to the operations of farming are having a double effect on

New England agriculture. Machinery directly enlarges the unit of farm operations and tends to make small-scale farming less and less likely to provide a family with a satisfactory living. The applications of science have indirectly had the same effect. They have increased production per animal and per acre, and hence production per man, and have been one of the causes of falling prices. Falling prices necessitate a larger volume of business and the application of the most efficient methods of production if standards of living are to be maintained. Thus there has been a constant tendency for the minimum size of farm business compatible with satisfactory living to become larger. As was noted in the preceding chapter, both topography and the inheritance from a hand-labor agriculture operate to make the attainment of adequately sized businesses difficult in many parts of New England, especially in the uplands, although some slight progress has been made in combining farms to secure adequate units of operation.

The problem of the size of farms deserves careful attention. Small-scale operations involve many inefficiencies on their own account; there are many enterprises in which two- and three-man farms tend to be more efficient than one-man farms. Areas like Aroostook County and the Champlain and Connecticut valleys, where nature interposes fewer obstacles to the adjustment of size of farm and the scope of field operations to a larger scale, have had and will probably continue to have growing advantages.

Changes in Methods of Distribution. In no respect has there been greater change in the past decade than in the organization for the distribution of agricultural products. The development of chain retailing of food products, the establishment of nation-wide corporations devoted to the processing and distribution of dairy products, and the appearance of many coöperative organizations mark the more important of these changes. With the invention of new types of equipment for milk plants and the trend to fluid milk production, many of the plants of northern New England that were established to manufacture into dairy products milk not available for the fluid market have become obsolete. Data from the United States Tariff Commission shows that milk-plant costs, per 100 pounds handled, increase very rapidly as the annual volume handled goes below 7,000,000 pounds.[5] Where production is more scattered the collection costs per 100 pounds increase. Altogether, those areas where production is scattered and where the size of plant is limited by the available supply are subjected to increasing natural handicaps in economic competition. In southern New England this disadvantage is less serious because of nearness to market and because assembly and distribution occur in the same plant.

Coöperative associations selling eggs, fruits, and vegetables in eastern markets have subjected New England farmers to a new and more severe form of competition in quality of product and service. This has given rise to the so-called New England Marketing Program, which aims at the standardization and labeling under a New England label of standard-grade farm products. In general, there is a growing demand for standardized farm products available in large quantities and continuously. While much of the older procedure of direct marketing by the producer of a wide variety of products to consumers, retailers, and jobbers still continues, there is a pronounced movement towards the mass sale of standardized products to large distributors. This factor, although it has not as yet markedly affected production policy, may be expected to have an increasing effect as time passes. More general farmers will probably specialize in the production of one or a small number of products rather than in the raising of a wide variety, as the market gardener has done in the past. The older market-garden farms, located near the cities, have been and will probably continue to be subdivided for residential use. More and more there is likely to be an incentive towards the coöperative organization of vegetable and fruit growers for the grading and selling of their products to large buyers.

All these changes which have been occurring in the marketing field, as well as the rise of chain retailing, coöperative marketing among competitors, and nation-wide food distributing organizations, point to adjustments in the same direction. These adjustments are likely to take the form of greater specialization in production, more standardization of products, and further dependence on coöperative grading and distribution.

The Problem of Agricultural Land Utilization[6]

The tendencies just outlined, as well as all the circumstances of the natural and social environment discussed in the preceding chapter, have an effect on price and in many cases are affected by price. The farmer attempts to locate where he can make money and shifts the character of his farm business to enable him to keep on making money. Money to him is living, good or poor as he makes more or less. If the farmer is to make the most for himself, which means in general if he is to contribute the most to society, he must produce on land well adapted to his line of business. If a given piece of land cannot yield a living as good as the living he may expect to get elsewhere, the conclusion must be that the land is too poor to be retained in the particular use to which it is put. It represents submarginal excess capacity for that industry. The determination, therefore, of a policy of land utilization is important. It involves an attempt roughly to classify all lands within the entire production

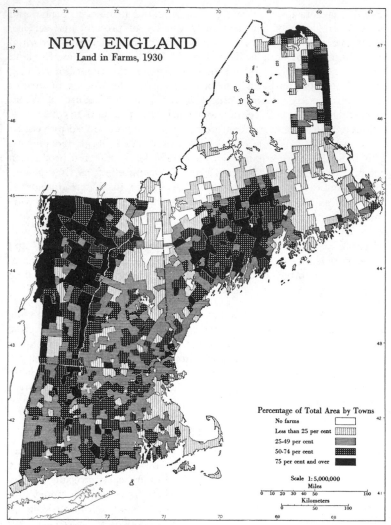

FIG. 1—Land in farms in New England, 1930. This map gives a rough picture of varying intensities of agricultural land utilization. Based on U. S. Census of Agriculture, 1930.

area for a given market, to appraise the competitive factors involved, and to forecast demand and supply factors sufficiently far ahead to permit the projection of land-use programs that are essentially long-time in character. The problem defies attempts at accuracy or refinement and can result only in approximations of the most general character. Nevertheless, these approximations are of the utmost value and, when made to constitute a part of the basic data

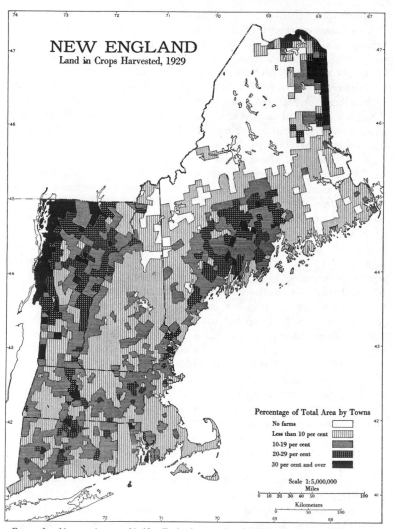

NEW ENGLAND
Land in Crops Harvested, 1929

Percentage of Total Area by Towns

No farms
Less than 10 per cent
10-19 per cent
20-29 per cent
30 per cent and over

Scale 1:5,000,000
Miles
0 10 20 30 40 50 · · · 100
Kilometers
0 · · 50 · · 100

FIG. 2—Land in crops harvested in New England, 1929. Based on U. S. Census of Agriculture, 1930.

for public as well as private policy in the use of land, may be used to forestall grave errors. In New England, particularly, there is need for careful study of the whole question of land utilization. Such a study, however, involves the entire United States and must take into consideration the land resources of all areas that might compete in our markets as well as the trends in national demand for various farm products.

The point of departure in all land-utilization work is present use. Present use represents the adjustment of present operators and managers to the forces of the past. If changes of a technical and social nature were to cease, the uses of land that would eventually come about would probably be in better adjustment to the whole background than any that could be projected by economists and technicians. A picture of the agricultural land utilization of present-day New England is furnished by Figures 1 and 2. These maps show the proportion of the total land area (1) in farms and (2) in harvested crops.

Comparison of these maps with similar maps for earlier dates would reveal the fact that in all parts of upland New England there has been during the past sixty years a steady movement of land out of farms and out of tillage. In many parts of northern New England farms have survived—scattered it is true, but nevertheless in considerable numbers in the aggregate—whose operation is not justified on economic grounds. The maintenance of roads and schools is a greater load than the communities can bear, and their aid a source of expense to society at large. These farms and the areas in which they lie are undoubtedly submarginal agriculturally. The definition of the margin for agricultural use and the adoption of measures that will discourage the continuation of agricultural operations in these submarginal areas is a pressing problem and one that calls for the exercise of great patience and tact in dealing with the many difficult social and human issues involved.

In many parts of northern New England the agricultural use of the land becomes secondary. The primary use is recreational or a combination of forest and recreational use. With few exceptions, the utilization of the entire coast line is recreational, the farmers operating various services for the benefit of tourists and summer visitors. Along the coast will be found scattered farms producing perishable foods for vacationists and numerous small or part-time farms where, as frequently as not, agriculture constitutes a secondary or quite minor element in the income of the landholder. In southern Vermont, to some extent, and in the mountain and lake regions of New Hampshire and Maine a similar situation prevails. In Maine there is also an extensive development of sporting camps. Hunters and fishermen frequent these, and agricultural development is so slight that oftentimes not more than two or three up to twenty part-time farms are found per township in the areas bordering the streams and lakes or in the great forests.

In southern New England the question assumes a somewhat different form. While farm abandonment is not found here at the present time, nevertheless many farms are submarginal for agricultural use. In most communities the residences pass into the hands of persons working in cities, and the farms are operated as part-time farms or are not operated at all.

In both northern and southern New England poor and very often submarginal farms are sold and resold to a succession of purchasers, usually from the cities or of foreign extraction, who have no realization of the impossibility of making from them a living that approximates an American standard. Any classification of farms that could give prospective purchasers some guidance in the selection of farms and any system that would bring these purchasers in touch with such information seem to be necessary parts of an effective land policy. New England is spending more than a million dollars a year in its agricultural and home economics extension work to assist farmers to produce and market their farm products more economically and to live better lives on the farms. The most important thing a farmer ever does is the act of selecting and purchasing his farm. It is practically impossible for average men to make a decent living on farms that are too small or too broken, or where the soil is poor. Yet we pour out millions every year in considerable part to help men to accomplish the impossible or the unlikely, while we spend hardly a cent to prevent these recurring cases of disappointment and of human and social loss.

Important investigations that should be conducted in this field are: (1) studies in the definition of the margin—how the line should be drawn between the areas that should be used for agricultural purposes and those that should not, in view of the present long-time outlook; (2) studies relating to the problems of taxation, and of the social, political, and economic organization of submarginal regions; (3) studies relating to the problem of part-time farming.

DESCRIPTION OF LAND UTILIZATION IN NEW ENGLAND[7]

Four important types of land utilization may be distinguished in New England outside of the cities and municipal watersheds: agricultural, residential, recreational, and forest utilization. The second and third appear seldom as large areas exhibiting one type of utilization to the exclusion of others, but rather as a mixture of agriculture and forestry with the other uses in varying proportions. These combinations often occur in the same landholding. Some kind of agricultural production is usually one of the components of the combination.

Such combinations are called part-time farming. They are very important throughout New England and should be classified among the main types of land use in the region. There are two principal classes of part-time use. The first consists of farming combined with residential use, the landholder securing a substantial portion of his income from non-farm sources and operating the farm on a scale

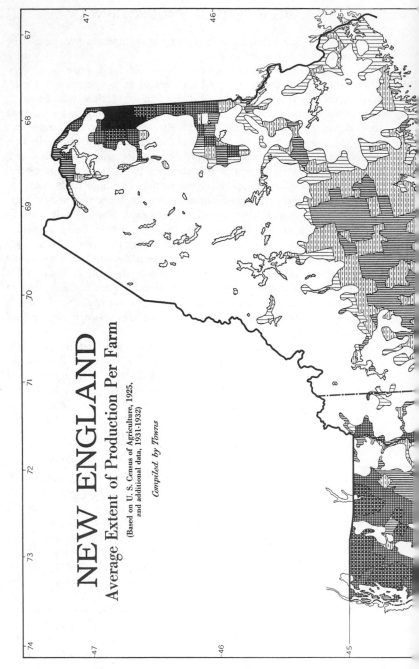

NEW ENGLAND
Average Extent of Production Per Farm

(Based on U. S. Census of Agriculture, 1925,
and additional data, 1931-1932)

Compiled by Towns

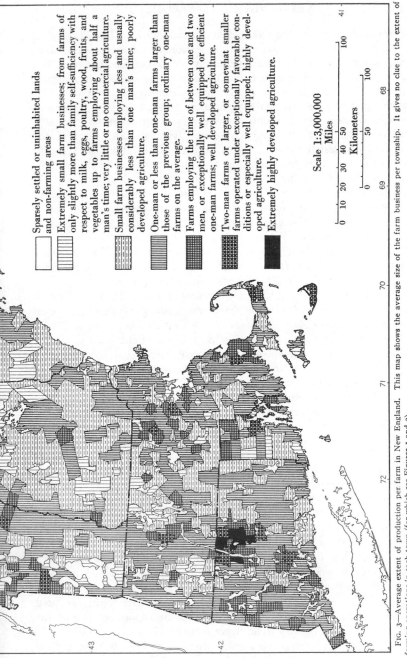

Sparsely settled or uninhabited lands and non-farming areas

Extremely small farm businesses; from farms of only slightly more than family self-sufficiency with respect to milk, eggs, poultry, wood, fruits, and vegetables up to farms employing about half a man's time; very little or no commercial agriculture.

Small farm businesses employing less and usually considerably less than one man's time; poorly developed agriculture.

One-man or less than one-man farms larger than those of the previous group; ordinary one-man farms on the average.

Farms employing the time of between one and two men, or exceptionally well equipped or efficient one-man farms; well developed agriculture.

Two-man farms or larger, or somewhat smaller farms operated under exceptionally favorable conditions or especially well equipped; highly developed agriculture.

Extremely highly developed agriculture.

Scale 1:3,000,000

Miles

0 10 20 30 40 50   100

Kilometers

0   50   100

FIG. 3.—Average extent of production per farm in New England. This map shows the average size of the farm business per township. It gives no clue to the extent of farming operations in each town (for which see Figures 1 and 2).

147

substantially smaller than that of a one-man farm. The other class is made up of a combination of recreational and agricultural uses. In this case the land is used primarily as a summer residence, but the farm is operated on a part-time basis either by neighboring farmers hired for the purpose or by the occupants during the summer. This latter type, the recreational-agricultural, is not nearly as important as the former, the residential-agricultural. Rozman has made a study of the latter in Massachusetts.[8] He estimates that of the 30,000 farms listed by the census for that state, about 50 per cent are carried on a part-time basis and that there are additional part-time farms sufficient to bring the total for the state to about 60,000. He concludes that part-time farming develops on submarginal land or on land having marked value for residential purposes and, furthermore, that one third of the agricultural output of the state comes from the part-time farms. When we consider that Massachusetts is representative of most of the area south of a line extending from Augusta west to Concord, Brattleboro, and Pittsfield, the great importance of part-time farming in New England becomes apparent.

Purely agricultural utilization occurs in the potato farming of Aroostook County in Maine, the dairy farming of the Champlain Valley, the general farming areas of the southern counties of Rhode Island, and the tobacco region of the Connecticut Valley. Even within these areas forests will occasionally be found on the farms or interspersed between them, and where the forests are of considerable extent part-time farming appears. General farming, of which dairying is the backbone, combined with volunteer forest growths occupying considerably more than half of the farm land is usual throughout the better portions of the upland. On the poorer, rougher, or smaller farms in the south there is a good deal of part-time farming, and near industrial cities there are very many holdings with small acreages on which buildings have been erected since the World War and where part-time farming is the rule. In northern New England, far from cities, small, rough or isolated farms or those with poor soil have either become summer homes or, as is perhaps fully as common, have been abandoned.

Young has studied thirteen towns in the upland areas of central Vermont.[9] He finds that from two thirds to seven eighths of the entire area is wooded. Of 1380 farms 718 were operated in 1929, 377 were partially operated, and 280 were abandoned. Of these 152 had been abandoned in 1929. Only one in eight of the operated farms had sufficient acreage, according to the report, to enable the securing of a satisfactory living from farming alone.

In twelve representative rural towns of the eastern Connecticut highland the writer has found that of 2128 farms only 995 were farms in any true sense, 613 being classified as part-time farms and 520 as residences only.[10]

In the upland areas of northern New England and in the rougher uplands everywhere throughout the region, there are extensive tracts of volunteer forest not in farms nor yet in any cultivated forest plantations. These tracts are usually privately owned, the taxes on them are paid regularly, and once in a generation it may be expected that they will be cut over. They are swampy, rocky, or simply rough areas having a poor soil. For the most part they are the relics of farms abandoned in the last quarter of the nineteenth or early twentieth century.[11]

Along the entire Atlantic shore line, along the fringes of innumerable lakes, in the White and the Green Mountains, at chosen spots of commanding elevation and fine scenery in the Berkshire and Litchfield Hills, and here and there over the whole upland area from Connecticut to central Maine lie the recreational lands of New England. Shorn of forests most of these areas would be largely devoid of recreational value. The utilization must, therefore, be regarded as forest utilization in which the values arise in part from the recreational use of the woodlands.

Purely forest utilization occurs in the great woodlands of northern Maine, in lesser areas in the mountains of New Hampshire and Vermont, and in small tracts scattered widely elsewhere. Even in these areas where the land is used solely for producing timber and pulpwood, there is gradual encroachment here and there of recreational use. The time is approaching when practically all lands in New England will have developed recreational value.

Extent of Agricultural Development

The extent of agricultural development may be measured by two criteria: the size of farm businesses and the distribution and density of farms or farm lands. These two measures are not always related, and in order to appraise the situation adequately the reader must take both criteria into consideration. This he may do by comparing Figure 3 with Figures 1 and 2.

The prevailing or average size of the farm business per township (Fig. 3) was measured by the use of the same data that were applied to the measurement of farm type, as will be explained below. Farms were classified roughly according to whether the business activity of the average farm in each township, apart from any other occupations not connected with farming, would consume little, half, nearly all, or all of the time of a man under conditions of average efficiency of production. Where production conditions are difficult, farmers may devote their entire time, on the average, to their farms and the latter still be classed as less than full one-man farms. Under particu-

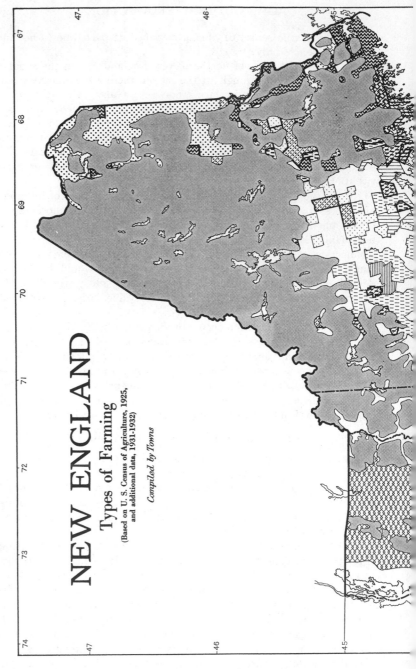

NEW ENGLAND
Types of Farming
(Based on U. S. Census of Agriculture, 1925,
and additional data, 1931-1932)

Compiled by Towns

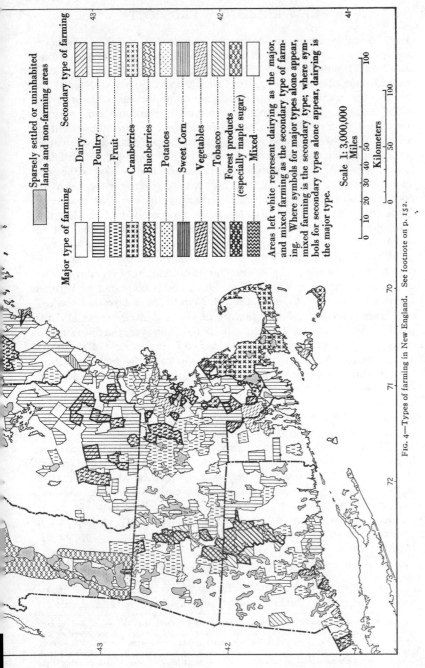

Major type of farming

	Dairy
	Poultry
	Fruit
	Cranberries
	Blueberries
	Potatoes
	Sweet Corn
	Vegetables
	Tobacco
	Forest products (especially maple sugar)
	Mixed

Sparsely settled or uninhabited lands and non-farming areas

Secondary type of farming

Areas left white represent dairying as the major, and mixed farming as the secondary type of farming. Where symbols for major types alone appear, mixed farming is the secondary type; where symbols for secondary types alone appear, dairying is the major type.

Scale 1:3,000,000

Miles
0 10 20 30 40 50   100

Kilometers
0   50   100

FIG. 4—Types of farming in New England. See footnote on p. 152.

larly favorable conditions from the standpoint of labor efficiency
the opposite may be true. In many regions, such as southern Maine
and New Hampshire, recreational enterprises may be so associated
with farming that the agriculture may appear poorly developed on
the average in the towns, yet there may be numerous excellent farms
in the towns in question. In southern New England the same may be
true either as a result of part-time farming or of recreational enterprises. While some towns may appear improperly classified because
certain special conditions are obscured by the average, nevertheless
Figure 3 is believed truthfully to represent the general situation.
The mistake, however, must not be made of regarding the towns of
poor agricultural development as generally decadent or marginal.
Some of them are, but others are quite prosperous and the low development of agriculture may be completely offset by the extent to
which farming is combined with other enterprises.

While Figure 3 reveals the size of business of the average farm,
township by township, it gives no clue to the extent of farming operations in each township as a whole. The latter is suggested by Figures
1 and 2. The percentages of the total land area in farms as marked
on Figure 1 present a rough picture of varying intensities of agricultural land utilization. It should be noted, however, that over much
of the upland a large portion of the land in farms consists of woodland
and unimproved pasture. Where this is the case, the darker shadings
on the map undoubtedly give a somewhat exaggerated impression
of the development of farming. To some degree this erroneous
impression may be corrected by study of Figure 2 showing the percentage of the total area in harvested crops; but the latter map,
in turn, fails to do full justice to areas where the cultivation of orchards
and the production of forest products, such as maple sugar, are
important farm enterprises. Although neither of these three maps,
therefore, provides a wholly satisfactory picture, the reader may
learn much by studying them in combination with one another,
with Figure 4 showing types of farming, as well as with the maps
published elsewhere in this volume showing density of population
and increases and decreases in population (Figs. 4, 5, and 6, pp. 22–23,
26, 27, above).

TYPES OF FARMING

The major products of the farms of New England are dairy
products, eggs and chickens, potatoes, tobacco, apples, and miscel-

NOTE ON FIGURE 4—This map shows both the major and the secondary type of farming for each
town. On the method employed in compiling the map, see p. 154. As shown in the legend, various
symbols represent different types of farming as of major and of secondary importance. There are no
symbols, however, for dairy farming as the major type or for mixed farming as the secondary type.
Consequently, where no symbol for a major type appears, it is to be assumed that dairying is the
major type of farming; where no symbol for a secondary type appears, that mixed farming is the
secondary type; and where no symbol whatever appears, that dairying is the major type and mixed
farming the secondary type.

laneous fruits and vegetables. There are numerous minor products, sometimes of local significance but of very limited significance from the standpoint of New England as a whole. Table I shows the relative importance of the principal products sold by New England farmers.

TABLE I—MORE IMPORTANT ITEMS OF INCOME ON
NEW ENGLAND FARMS, 1929[a]

(In dollars, 000 omitted)

VALUE OF PRODUCTS SOLD	MAINE	N. H.	VT.	MASS.	R. I.	CONN.	TOTAL
Dairy products sold . . .	12,527	9,097	29,182	23,348	4,545	18,408	97,107
Chickens and eggs sold . .	6,923	5,735	2,658	11,644	1,460	8,017	36,437
Vegetables, including potatoes, sold	58,337	2,289	2,884	9,198	1,055	4,277	78,040
Fruits and nuts sold . . .	3,458	1,327	1,649	6,765	552	2,032	15,783
Tobacco, etc., sold[b] . . .	. . . . . .	. . . . . .	. . . . .	4,805	. . . . :	12,703	17,508
Nursery and greenhouse products grown in open and under glass	849	390	339	10,179	1,345	4,795	17,897
Forest products cut on farms	7,956	3,063	4,905	3,655	330	1,688	21,597
Wool shorn—unwashed . .	173	35	100	20	3	15	346
Honey	37	18	60	18	3	31	167
Total value of above items	90,260	21,954	41,777	69,632	9,293	51,966	284,882

a Based on *Fifteenth Census of the United States, 1930: Agriculture, Statistics by Counties, Second Series*, 1931.

b The figures cited are actually those for the category "all other field crops" of the census. Tobacco, however, in Massachusetts and Connecticut, constitutes the greater part of this item.

While the character of the output of New England farming as a whole is roughly summarized in Table I, these data fail to disclose the character of the farming in the different parts of New England. The best device for this purpose is a type-of-farming map with a description of the types found in the various localities. In the immediately following paragraphs the type-of-farming concept will be described and discussed, and, in connection with the accompanying map (Fig. 4), a description will be given of the more common types of farms found in New England.

Just as the uses of the land tend in the course of time to be those that represent the best economic adjustment to a given situation, so the type of farm appearing in a given set of conditions tends to approach the best adjustment to those conditions. Type of farm is a term used to include the enterprises that constitute a farm business, the proportions in which they are combined, and the significant features of the equipment or practices of the farm. Taken together with size of business, type of farm gives us a rough picture of the farm business and its sources of income.

To get an exact picture of the type of farming prevailing under given conditions one should, of course, visit all the farms appearing under those conditions, obtain as accurate data as possible regarding their business, and arrange and classify them according to type. To do this for every town of New England, even by sampling, would be so expensive as to be prohibitive under ordinary conditions. It happens that township data were secured from the Bureau of the Census by each New England Land Grant College from the original schedules of the 1925 census.[12] These average figures were used to formulate an approximation of the type of farming and the size of farm business in each township. The results were checked by the opinions of agricultural economists in the several states.

The various census data giving the crop acreages and the numbers of various classes of livestock were taken from the different state reports and reduced to a per-farm basis. They were reduced to a common basis by multiplying each by the number of days' labor required on the average in association with the given acreage or number of livestock for one year. These, when totaled, gave the sum of "man-work units" (in days) constituting the business of a hypothetical average farm in the town. The various enterprises constituting the farm business were then expressed as percentages of the total. The total becomes a measure of the size of business. As an accurate measurement of constituents of a farm business this method is susceptible of much criticism. When, however, it is used for the classification of farms into a few groups on the basis of size and constituent enterprises it is believed that, with the checks used, it is a measure entirely consistent with the character of the results it is desired to achieve in this chapter.

The statistical average alone in some cases may furnish misleading evidence regarding the farming of a town. For instance, suppose that in a town there are one hundred dairy, fifty specialized poultry, and fifty fruit farms. The average would show that the type of farming in this town is mixed farming with dairy as the main enterprise with fruit and poultry as side lines. This is not the case. By checking the statistical results against the observations of men familiar with the situation such errors have, it is hoped, been avoided and a more accurate picture obtained than would have been possible by either method alone.

Minor changes in the enterprises that constitute farm business are always going on. Under the impact of revolutionary forces such as those operating in the last quarter of the nineteenth century in New England, existing types of farming may be entirely altered or may disappear in a comparatively short time. The agriculture of any region is usually built about some one principal enterprise. The secondary enterprises are such as give a good distribution of labor throughout the year and result in a net income definitely higher because of them. At the present moment it is impossible to say how far-reaching are the changes occurring in the dairy farming regions of New England. If New England surrenders her sweet cream market permanently, they are likely to be drastic and to involve considerable retraction of the margin. Specialized dairy farming is likely to expand and be carried on in larger operating units in the more favored areas, such as the Champlain Valley and certain other parts of Vermont, while it shrinks or disappears in the less favored areas. Specialized dairy farms and farms combining dairying with other enterprises will probably continue to be operated in more favored situations in the hills of southern New England. Vegetable production, pushed away from the cities by real estate developments, is likely, under the influence of the tendency toward larger farm units, to become associated with dairying or poultry in the former dairy farming areas, and in a few sections the entire agriculture may be turned into vegetable and fruit production. In Maine and in the hills of Vermont and New Hampshire considerably more land seems likely to be abandoned.

The great need is for intelligent guidance of the changes in the types of farming as the situation develops and the course of events becomes clearer. This sort of guidance is the function of economic research and extension forces as they operate through the Land Grant Colleges. In order that the situation may be met administrators should recognize the need for much broader and more courageous programs of research than have as yet been attempted. Farm management data and records of farm business operations should be collected continuously from areas representing every important type of farm organization in the different parts of New England. Careful studies should be made of competitive conditions and the trends of price and cost. Efforts should be made to set up adequate bases for predicting the course of prices. All these data should be associated with the annual series of farm business records for each type of farm in an effort to project the character of adjustment in farm type that must be made under each important set of environmental conditions. Plans should be formulated to meet these changes as far in advance of their occurrence as possible.

DESCRIPTION OF TYPES OF FARMING IN NEW ENGLAND[13]

In depicting land utilization we have in mind the character of the use of the land area. In describing types of farming, however, we are interested not in the use of land but in the combination of income-producing enterprises that constitute the economic basis of support of the families living on the land. Types of farming, therefore, are described in terms of the farmer's economic activities and the organization of his farm business. These are, in a rather definite but not necessarily proportional manner, related to his sources of income.

The chief activity of the farmers in practically the entire upland area of New England is dairying.[14] Various other activities are associated with it. In southern New England part-time farming is usual, as has already been pointed out. A small volume of forest products is produced on almost every farm. Occasionally heavy cuttings are made, and the family wood supply is usually furnished by the farm. In eastern Connecticut, southern New Hampshire, and south-central and western Maine, and here and there throughout the upland, poultry raising is associated with dairying and oftentimes is the major enterprise.[14a] In northern and central Vermont there is a large dairying-forest products area, with maple syrup and sugar as the predominant forest product. In the Nashoba district of northern Worcester and Middlesex counties in Massachusetts; in the hills of Oxford County in Maine; on the heights overlooking the Connecticut River in southern Vermont and New Hampshire; in northern New Haven and southern Hartford counties in Connecticut; and on the intermediate ridges of the lighter Charlton soils in the western and eastern highlands of southern New England are grown the Baldwin, the MacIntosh, and some minor commercial apples.[15] Numerous farms specialize in apples as a cash crop, but the agriculture of the towns is built, in most cases, about the usual core of dairying and general farming. There is no part of the upland not adapted to apple production, and orchards are scattered over all parts of it. On the hills of eastern and central Maine the production of sweet corn for the cannery becomes an important source of farm income. Here as elsewhere it is almost always secondary to dairying. Within a radius of fifteen miles of smaller cities and villages all sorts of fruits, vegetables, poultry products, and the retailing of farm products are combined with dairying.

The upland dairy and general farm of any of the subtypes described above is usually a one-man and in some places a two-man farm having from fifteen to sixty and, in exceptional cases, up to one hundred acres of tillable land. It carries from three to twenty-five cows, the one-man farms usually running from two or three to twelve and the two-man farms from ten to twenty-five. The tillable farm acreage ranges from ten to fifty acres but normally is about fifteen. A family garden and poultry flock is nearly always found. An acre or more of apples or potatoes or of the truck crops is usually planted as a secondary source of income. The farm furnishes the family house rent, fuel, and food, usually worth from $500 to $800 at wholesale market values of 1930.

Figure 5 gives the layout scheme of a farm in the eastern Connecticut upland, which may be taken as typical of the layout of the upland farms in that region. On the larger farms silos are frequently found, and an acreage of silage is grown proportional to the number

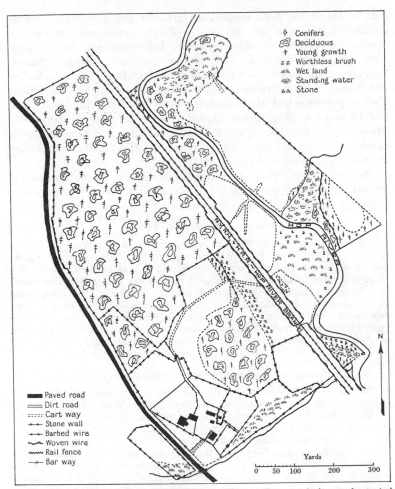

Conifers
Deciduous
Young growth
Worthless brush
Wet land
Standing water
Stone

Paved road
Dirt road
Cart way
Stone wall
Barbed wire
Woven wire
Rail fence
Bar way

Yards
0   50 100   200   300

FIG. 5—Farm of Mr. X, Tolland Co., Connecticut. This map illustrates the layout of a typical farm in the southern New England upland. Farms vary considerably in total area and in area of tillable land. The open areas within the farm are tillable land.

of cows kept. Family labor is employed freely on these farms, and on the larger ones a year-round hired man and, in exceptional cases, two or more may be employed. Incomes vary from an amount just sufficient to keep body and soul together to a return commensurate with low to good professional incomes. Probably 15 to 20 per cent of farm incomes may be rated during normal times in the latter class. The ability of the farmer, the character of the farm, and the size of business all are important factors in determining income.

Throughout the dairy and general farming regions of the upland will be found scattered specialized farms of non-dairy types. Specialized dairy farms are frequent. Farms specializing in poultry production are scattered everywhere but especially in southern New England, southern New Hampshire, and southern Maine. Specialized apple and peach farms are found in the Connecticut Valley and eastern Massachusetts. Apple farms appear in the Connecticut Valley north-central Massachusetts, southern New Hampshire, and Oxford and·Knox counties in Maine. In certain parts of the central Maine region specialized potato farming occurs, as well as in northeastern Vermont and along the east side of the Connecticut Valley between Springfield and Hartford.

In addition to the general and dairy farming of the upland the following types of specialized and localized farming deserve more extended comment.

BLUEBERRY FARMING IN MAINE[16]

The blueberry region of Maine runs along the shore from Penobscot Bay to Eastport. The land is usually burnt over every third year. The next year the green sprouts of new growth appear, and in the succeeding years, after the plants have borne fruit buds, they produce. Holdings vary in size from a few acres owned by a fisherman, shopkeeper, or general farmer, to large tracts. The burning and picking constitutes the labor of the year. The berries are picked with rakes by men, women, and children who specialize in the work year after year. They are packed in boxes and delivered to the canning factories. Blueberry growing is not usually a type of farming so much as it is the annual exploitation of a wild crop which, with a little work, has at times been made profitable to the landowner.

THE CRANBERRY INDUSTRY IN SOUTHEASTERN MASSACHUSETTS[17]

Interspersed among the barren Plymouth soils of Plymouth and Barnstable counties in Massachusetts, and on the islands of Marthas Vineyard and Nantucket are found numerous bogs and marshes which have become the site of an intensive and highly specialized cranberry industry. There are two centers of concentration, one about the towns of Carver and Wareham in Plymouth County and one at Harwich and Brewster on Cape Cod. Cranberries are produced in the intervening territory and north from Carver to Marshfield and Sharon and west to Freetown in Bristol County. There are many large plantings and numerous small bogs of one or a few acres. The cultivation of the cranberry requires intensive preparation of the soil, including sanding of the bogs and a handling of the water to permit flooding at critical frost periods. The investment per acre is about a thousand dollars. The most important labor requirement is for harvesting, for which experienced gang labor at good wage rates is used. The labor of harvesting is highly seasonal and the work difficult.

THE POTATO INDUSTRY OF AROOSTOOK COUNTY[18]

The potato industry of Aroostook County is so specialized that many of the producers buy eggs, milk, and fuel for family use. The area extends north from Houlton to Fort Kent. Its center is at Presque Isle and Caribou. It lies in the rolling hill country comprising the watersheds of the St. John, Aroostook, and Allegash rivers. Little more than a decade ago the total production of the region was about twenty-five million bushels. The estimated output for 1932 is about forty-three million bushels.

At the present time the methods of farming in the Aroostook region are in process of rapid reorganization. The tractor is rapidly coming into use, clover is fast being introduced into the rotation as a soiling crop, and the soil is receiving a light application of lime in preparation for clover. The usual practice is to mow the first cutting of clover, let the second growth come up through it, and plow it all under later in the season. New spraying devices having greater power and wider range are being developed for use with the tractor. The optimum size of the farm unit is increasing. While the ordinary family farm usually grows from thirty to fifty acres of potatoes and a considerable acreage of oats, it is not uncommon to find farms operating a thousand acres of land, of which four hundred will be in potatoes. Since annual yields are usually well in excess of three hundred bushels of marketable potatoes an acre in the absence of blight, this means that some farms frequently produce one hundred thousand bushels. Management is an important factor on these farms, and there is at present a tendency for a number of independent farms to be operated under one manager. The price of potatoes is very variable, and years of great profit and of severe losses are both common. The potato area is still being extended, both by the clearing of land in the Allegash Valley and by the extension of acreage in the older areas. This extension is the best evidence that the returns and the outlook for the industry are considered satisfactory.

Dairying in the Champlain Valley[19]

The Champlain Valley is a level tract of heavy, fertile, calcareous soil. South of Burlington the Addison and Vergennes soils predominate, and to the north those of the Woodbridge and Merrimac groups. The northern portion is underlain with limestone and grows hay and clover easily and abundantly. The tempering effect on the climate of the waters of the lake makes silage corn production possible. One of the main advantages of the valley is the absence of natural barriers to the extension of size of farm; it was formerly a sheep country and the farms were originally laid out on a generous pattern. The valley is reasonably close to the fluid milk markets of Boston and New York and is accessible to the supplies of feeding concentrates originating in the mills of the west. It is far enough from the cities to lie beyond the zones where urban influences alone determine the farm wage rate. This area is undoubtedly destined to be a region of expanding dairy production and one in which larger operating units will be possible. The Worthington soils of east-central Vermont also afford grazing of high quality and possess marked advantages for dairy production, and parts of north-central Vermont are likewise well adapted to dairy farming.

Tobacco Production in the Connecticut Valley[19]

The heart of the Connecticut Valley, comprising a row of townships on each side of the river from East Hartford north on the east side and from Windsor north on the west side, forms a specialized tobacco-producing area. In the outlying rows of townships tobacco is now combined with dairying and other enterprises but had remained the dominant enterprise until recently. North into Massachusetts general farming appears and then tobacco combined with onion-raising and general farming. On the east side of the river in Connecticut broadleaf tobacco is the main variety produced; on the west side Havana seed.

During the early part of the past decade sun-grown tobacco was produced on small farms. An acreage of ten acres of tobacco on farms of from fifteen to twenty acres in size afforded a satisfactory family income, and many farms did not exceed this acreage. Other farms on a two-man basis or employing more summer help were larger. Shade-grown tobacco was produced in larger holdings, and much of it by the larger tobacco corporations. During the World War and afterward much negro labor was imported for this crop. The drastic fall in tobacco prices after 1922 caused a reduction of nearly 40 per cent in tobacco acreage in the valley. The small farms became too small to support a family at the lower level of prices. Since that time the organization of the production of tobacco has been in process of evolution. The principal trends are toward larger farm businesses, the changing of small farms into part-time farms, and an increasing volume of dairy, poultry, and vegetable production on farms formerly producing tobacco. Leasing of farms and the operation of chains of farms under one management have appeared. This trend is not as rapid as the change in prices would seem to require, probably because of the farmer's reluctance to make radical changes. This is particularly true in the heart of the valley, where specialized tobacco production has been in operation for more than a century.

Specialized Vegetable Production[20]

The typical vegetable farm is a farm growing a succession and variety of crops from early springtime until late fall and selling them on the markets from day to day. During the winter greenhouses are operated on many of these farms, and of the early products on the market many are started under glass. Farming of this type is conducted on a very intensive basis. The larger family farms will employ two, sometimes three, men the year round and crews of extra help, often as many as fifteen or twenty boys and women, in rush seasons. A few farms are much larger and have extensive acreage and large crews during setting, weeding, and harvest. In the past these farms have been located within five to twenty miles of the market, according to the size of the market centers. Regions of specialized vegetable production are found adjacent to the larger centers of population. Production of vegetables is showing a somewhat marked rate of increase at the present time. The tendency in the business is towards extension of the areas of production and increased specialization by vegetables produced. Specialized production of asparagus, tomatoes, cauliflower, Brussels sprouts, strawberries, and other vegetables and fruits is beginning to appear in areas more remote than the former market garden areas. In the meantime the extension of urban areas is rapidly displacing the market garden farms of the age of the horse and wagon. One or more vegetables, particularly the truck crops, are appearing as cash crops on dairy farms.

Marketing[21]

Marketing must be considered as an integral part of the production process. Not only is the production process incomplete until goods are in the hands of the consumer, but if any of the so-called marketing processes fail of performance, goods pile up and low prices disturb the regular continuity of production.

No general statements can be made regarding the agencies functioning in the marketing of New England farm products as a whole. Rather, each commodity must be discussed separately.

Dairy Products.[22] In southern New England milk is sold by the producer directly to the consumer in the villages and small cities. In cities of over twenty thousand inhabitants and in thickly populated districts in the inland parts of New England the milk distributors usually receive milk from collection trucks which pick it up on the farms. They process it and sell to the consumer. Boston's supply and a considerable part of the supply of Providence come from northern New England. Vermont furnishes most of this, although a small amount arrives from Maine and more from New Hampshire. Usually the distribution facilities are owned and operated by corporations or individuals and are not under the control of farmers. In Vermont, however, a considerable part of the assembly and processing facilities is owned by farmers' coöperative organizations. Many of these coöperatives are joined together into a federation of coöperative milk plants. Others operate independently. The greater part of New England's fluid milk distributed in cities of over twenty thousand is sold through two coöperative bargaining associations, the New England Milk Producers' Association and the Connecticut Milk Producers' Association. Both of these organizations have set up price systems intended to counteract the natural tendency to heavy seasonal production in the spring and early summer and low production in the fall. The demand for milk is fairly even. By imposing penalties on excess production in one season and by paying more for production in the short season both associations have endeavored to adjust the supply to the demand. These associations also eliminate inefficiency by adjusting supply to demand as between markets and dealers. Their other primary function is to represent the farmer in collective bargaining with the representatives of milk dealers.

The coöperative creameries and milk plants of Vermont were originally organized to separate the cream from the surplus milk and to manufacture it or sell it as cream. As the price of butter has fallen, competition has made inroads into the cream market, especially since 1928, and the Vermont plants have been led to compete with southern New England producers for a larger share in the fluid milk market. Under the price systems prevailing with the coöperative bargaining associations, milk is classified according to its final use and a different price is paid for each class. Thus all the milk sold as fluid is paid for at one price. Milk used as cream nets the farmer a lower price, and that used as butter a price still lower. The dealer pays for his entire supply an average price much less than the price he pays for the portion of his milk actually sold in fluid form. Some dealers, therefore, may secure the milk for their fluid requirements at a price higher than the average price for milk for all uses and yet obtain their milk for the fluid trade at a price considerably less than that paid by their competitors. It became possible in this way for the coöperative creameries in Vermont to sell their milk for considerably more than the average price received by farmers selling through the bargaining associations, while at the same time their customers received their fluid milk at a lower price than that paid by their competitors buying through the coöperative bargaining association. This condition has brought about, in recent months (1932), what amounts to a price war in the Boston market. Some system of stabilizing production from season to season through penalizing seasonal surplus is generally agreed to be essential and to be in the interests of producer and consumer alike. It seems probable that the scope of the farmers' coöperative will be extended in such a way as to solve these new problems. Plans to this end have been formulated and may have been put in operation by the time this chapter is published.

It remains to be seen whether New England will surrender her cream market to western competitors. If this occurs to any marked degree a serious and difficult problem of readjusting land utilization and type of farming through the New England upland and dairy regions will be created. This complex problem, if it occurs, should be faced scientifically, and efforts should be made to eliminate as far as possible the human suffering and economic loss that inevitably accompany changing conditions.

Fruits, Vegetables, and Eggs.[23] In the marketing of perishable fruits, vegetables, and eggs, methods are diverse. The organization of market distribution is changing rapidly, and numerous experiments are being tried. Small local coöperative associations for standardizing the grades of the product and for supervising the grading have been organized in eastern Massachusetts. These include the asparagus growers about Concord, the vegetable growers at Dighton, and the strawberry producers on Cape Cod. These associations function in coöperation with the State Bureau of Markets inspecting the grading of farm products. In Connecticut, coöperative produce auctions have been instituted in an experimental way. In the larger cities of southern New England outside of Boston the farmers' wholesale market—sometimes a curb market and usually conducted in the market section of the city—is an important center of sale. Large amounts of produce are sold directly to consumers and retailers by the farmers, and the roadside market is a factor of real significance in the marketing of produce in southern New England. The Nashoba Apple Growers' Association in the area about Littleton, Mass., is an important farmers' coöperative organization.

The geography of vegetable production is rapidly changing. Small areas of specialized production are springing up in many places that good roads and the use of the motor truck have brought within easy range of the cities. Marketing methods are becoming adjusted to these changes as well as to developments in long-distance motor transport, in terminal rail facilities, and in the express movement of refrigerated products from competing areas of production.

The vegetable industry is expanding, and the future of its growth is partly dependent on the development of marketing facilities adequate to present conditions of demand, supply, and competition.

Cranberries. The coöperative marketing system of the cranberry growers is one of the most effective of its kind operating in the United States. The production area being extremely limited and highly localized, the association possesses certain monopolistic powers. The products satisfy a semi-luxury demand and consequently yield a return to advertising and sales expenditures. The association supervises the grading and packing, sells and advertises the product, and constitutes an important factor in the production of this commodity.

Tobacco.[19] The tobacco industry in the Connecticut Valley is engaged in producing cigar wrappers and binders. The shade-grown industry—so-called because the tobacco is produced under cheesecloth tents, sometimes tens or scores of acres in size—supplies the larger portion of the wrappers. The industry is confined to certain soil types in the valley where conditions are particularly favorable to the production of the qualities desired. The wrapper producers face severe competition from Sumatra and from the binder producers of Wisconsin and Pennsylvania. The past decade and a half has seen a constant but slow decrease in the demand for cigars, accompanied by a rapid increase in the demand for cigarettes. A comprehensive coöperative association organized in 1922 to pack, warehouse, and sell the entire output of the valley dissolved in 1927. Its dissolution was brought about by the losses following attempts to maintain prices in the face of unfavorable supply and demand factors. The charges on large quantities of tobacco being withheld in warehouses were very heavy, and members and creditors alike lost confidence in the association and forced liquidation. Farmers suffered severe losses. Since that time tobacco has been bought from the farmers by the representatives of manufacturers and by dealers and has been packed, cured, and warehoused by them. The present situation is not satisfactory to the farmers. There is no standardization of grades, and many farmers charge collusion among buyers in keeping down the prices of particular lots.

Potatoes.[24] Like the tobacco industry, the potato industry of Aroostook County has also had an unfortunate experience with coöperative marketing and has abandoned its use for the present, although the leaders of the industry are preparing for the resumption of coöperative methods of distribution. Aroostook County produces both seed and table stock. The chief market for seed stock is in the south and along the Atlantic seaboard from Long Island south. Table stock is sent forward to Boston and Philadelphia markets by country shippers and large growers who consign or sell to wholesalers in these markets. The product is, for the greater part, loosely graded. Shipping and receiving-point inspection services have been set up. It seems to be true in both the potato and tobacco industries that there are no generally applicable methods by which the products of higher quality demanded by the market may realize for the farmer prices commensurate with the prices the markets are willing to pay. The result is that the producer of quality is penalized, and the region as a whole suffers injury in competition with other areas of production.

CONCLUSION

Future changes in New England agricultural production will undoubtedly depend, as in the past, on the extent of the market for farm products of various kinds and on the competition of outside areas for these markets. Freight rates and the speed of shipments of perishables, the technologies of the preservation and care of food-stuffs, new methods of production, and the tariff—all these factors affect the competitive situation to a marked degree. The more important internal factors bearing on the future would seem to be the size and purchasing power of our city populations, the rate of development of rural roads, truck shipment, and the ability of New England producers to achieve methods of low cost production on the fertile but rough uplands of the region.

If we may assume that these conditions remain relatively un-changed, then we must expect a further increase of part-time farming in southern New England, a further intensification of dairy production in northern Vermont and in the better dairy regions elsewhere, a further recession of dairying in the areas (Fig. 3) where the size of the prevailing dairy farm business is small today, and, finally, a continuing development of many local specialized areas of the production of vegetables and fruits.

NOTES

[1] Besides the statistical publications referred to in note 12, below, the following general descriptive studies and surveys of New England agriculture deserve mention: A. W. Gilbert and others, *The Food Supply of New England*, New York, 1924; Boston Chamber of Commerce, *The New England Agricultural Industries*, Boston, 1926; chapter on agriculture in C. E. Artman, *Industrial Structure of New England*, U. S. Dept. of Commerce, Bur. of Foreign and Domestic Commerce, Washington, 1930 (*Domestic Commerce Ser. No. 28*), pp. 11–47; *The Tercentenary of New England Agri-culture, 1630–1930*, published by the Commissioners of Agriculture of the six New England States; I. G. Davis and C. I. Hendrickson, *A Description of Connecticut Agriculture*, Storrs, Conn., 1925 (*Storrs Agric. Exper. Sta. Bull. No. 127*); S. A. Anderson and F. M. Woodard, *Agricultural Vermont*, in *Econ. Geogr.*, Vol. 8, 1932, pp. 12–42; *Rural Vermont: A Program for the Future, by Two Hundred Vermonters*, The Vermont Commission on Country Life, Burlington, 1931; J. L. Tennant, *A Study of the Organization and Management of Rhode Island Farms*, Kingston, R. I., 1931 (*R. I. Agric. Exper. Sta. Bull. No. 230*).

The following bibliographical publications cover New England agriculture: New England Research Council on Marketing and Food Supply, *Tentative Bibliography of Published and Unpublished Research in Agricultural Economics, Farm Management* and *Rural Sociology* (mimeographed), Boston, 1928; *Research in Agricultural Economics in the Northeastern States: A Classified List of Active and Completed Projects Conducted in Agricultural Economics by the Agricultural Experiment Stations of the Northeastern States During the Years 1910–1930 Together with the Titles of Publications on the Same*, New Hampshire Agricultural Experiment Station, Durham, N. H. [1931]; R. B. Handy and M. A. Cannon, *List by Titles of Publications of the United States Department of Agriculture from 1840 to June 1901 Inclusive*, Washington, 1902 (*U. S. Dept. of Agric. Bull. No. 6*); M. G. Hunt, *List of Publications of the United States Department of Agriculture from January, 1901, to December, 1925, Inclusive*, Washington, 1927 (*U. S. Dept. of Agric. Misc. Publ. No. 9*); *List of Bulletins of the Agricultural Experiment Stations in the United States from their Establishment to the End of 1920*, Washington, 1924 (*U. S. Dept. of Agric. Bull. No. 1199;* supplements are published biennially); *List of State Official Publications Containing Material on Agricultural Economics*, Washington, 1932 (*U. S. Dept. of Agric., Bur. of Agric. Economics, Agric. Economics Bibliography No. 38*); various bibliographical publications of the library of the U. S. Department of Agriculture, notably the mimeographed series *Agricultural Economics Literature;* for current literature especially see *The Agricultural Index* published by H. W. Wilson Co., New York, since 1916.

The most important source on marketing and credit matters is the *Proceedings of the New England Institute of Coöperation*, mimeographed by the Connecticut Agricultural College (1927), the Massachusetts Agricultural College (1928), the University of Vermont (1929), the Rhode Island State College (1930), the University of Maine (1931). See also the files of the *New England Homestead*, of *Bureau Farmer*, and of the *New England Magazine*.

² On the history of New England agriculture see: E. E. Edwards, *A Bibliography of the History of Agriculture in the United States*, Washington, 1930 (*U. S. Dept. of Agric. Misc. Publ. No. 84);* P. W. Bidwell and J. I. Falconer, *History of Agriculture in the Northern United States, 1620–1860*, Washington, 1925 (*Carnegie Instn. of Washington Publ. No. 358);* P. W. Bidwell, *Rural Economy in New England at the Beginning of the Nineteenth Century*, in *Trans. Conn. Acad. of Arts and Sci.*, Vol. 20, 1920, pp. 241–399; L. H. Bailey, *Cyclopedia of American Agriculture*, 4 vols., New York, 1908–1909 (Vol. 4 contains data on the history of New England agriculture).

³ See notably O. E. Baker, *A Graphic Summary of American Agriculture Based Largely on the Census*, Washington, 1931 (*U. S. Dept. of Agric. Misc. Publ. No. 105);* the same, *National and World Trends of Significance to Connecticut Agriculture*, in *Conn. Agric. College Bull.*, Vol. 25, 1929, pp. 16–30.

⁴ See J. C. Folsom, *Farm Labor in Massachusetts, 1921*, Washington, 1924 (*U. S. Dept. of Agric. Bull. No. 1220*).

⁵ W. A. Schoenfeld, *Some Economic Aspects in the Marketing of Milk and Cream in New England*, Washington, 1927 (*U. S. Dept. of Agric. Circular No. 16*), pp. 26–29.

⁶ See J. D. Black, edit., *Research in Agricultural Land Utilization: Scope and Method*, New York, 1931 (*Social Sci. Research Council Bull. No. 2*).

⁷ Among recent detailed studies of land utilization in New England there may be mentioned: J. H. Burgy, *Land Utilization in the Greenfield, Massachusetts, Region as Affected by Geographic Conditions*, in *Bull. Geogr. Soc. of Philadelphia*, Vol. 29, 1931, pp. 211–214; C. E. Walker, *Land Survey of the Town of Durham, New Hampshire*, Durham, N. H., 1931 (*N. H. Agric. Exper. Sta. Bull. No. 255*); C. E. Walker and P. M. Hodgkins, *Survey of Land Holdings in Towns of Fremont and Boscawen, N. H.*, Durham, N. H., 1932 (*ibid., 264*); R. J. McFall and R. E. Sherburne, *Tendencies in Milk Production in Massachusetts: A Study in Land Utilization*, in *Annals Amer. Acad. of Polit. and Soc. Sci.*, Vol. 142, 1929, pp. 58–69; I. G. Davis and C. I. Hendrickson, *Soil Type as a Factor in Farm Economy: I. The Town of Lebanon*, Storrs, Conn., 1926 (*Storrs Agric. Exper. Sta. Bull. No. 139*). Several unpublished studies of land utilization in limited areas in New England have been made by graduate

students at Clark University, Worcester, Mass., as part of the requirements for the master's and doctor's degrees.

[8] David Rozman, *Part-Time Farming in Massachusetts*, Amherst, Mass., 1930 (*Mass. Agric. Exper. Sta. Bull. No. 266*); the same, *Part-Time Farming in Massachusetts*, in *Journ. of Farm Economics*, Vol. 12, 1930, pp. 326–328.

[9] See *Rural Vermont* (cited in note 1, above), pp. 142–148.

[10] Conclusions based on as yet unpublished studies.

[11] See A. O. Craven, *The Abandoned Farms of New England*, in *Annual Report of the Amer. Historical Assoc. for the Year 1922*, Washington, 1926, Vol. 1, pp. 353–354.

[*12] The statistics for 1925 on which the map showing type-of-farming areas was based have been published for Maine, New Hampshire, Connecticut, and Rhode Island in the following documents: C. H. Merchant, *Maine Agriculture; A Statistical Presentation*, Orono, Me., 1927 (*Me. Agric. Exper. Sta. Bull. No. 338*); *Agricultural Census Report of the State of New Hampshire by Towns*, N. H. Dept. of Agric., Division of Statistics, 1926; I. G. Davis and J. R. Jacoby, *Five-Year Trends in Connecticut Agriculture*, Storrs, Conn., 1927 (*Storrs Agric. Exper. Sta. Bull. No. 145*); R. B. Corbett, *Rhode Island Agriculture: A Statistical Description*, Kingston, R. I., 1926 (*R. I. Agric. Exper. Sta. Bull. No. 206*). The statistics for Massachusetts and Vermont are on file in photostatic form at the American Geographical Society and in the offices of the Economics Departments of the agricultural colleges in these two states.

[13] See also R. L. Mighell and Marian Brown, *Type-of-farming Areas in Massachusetts*, Amherst, Mass., 1928 (*Mass. Agric. Exper. Sta. Bull. No. 244*).

[14] See especially: J. A. Hitchcock, *A Study in Vermont Dairy Farming*, Burlington, Vt., 1925 (*Vt. Agric. Exper. Sta. Bull. 250*); A. R. Gans, *Elasticity of Supply of Milk from Vermont Plants, I. The Milk-Feed Price Ratio*, 1927 (*ibid., 269*); *Studies in Vermont Dairy Farming, IV.* (also *V.*) *Cabot-Marshfield Area*, 1928, 1929, by E. W. Bell (*ibid., 283, 304*); *Studies in Vermont Dairy Farming, VI. Charlotte, Ferrisburg and Panton Area*, 1931, by H. P. Young (*ibid., 329*); J. E. Carrington, *The Effect of Extension Education on the Seasonal Surplus Milk Problem in Addison County, Vermont*, 1931 (*ibid., 330*); M. G. Eastman, *An Economic Study of Dairy Farming in Grafton County, New Hampshire, 1930*, Durham, N. H., 1931 (*N. H. Agric. Exper. Sta. Bull. No. 260*); R. J. McFall: *The Milk Supply of Massachusetts*, Amherst, Mass., 1927 (*Mass. Agric. Exper. Sta. Bull. No. 236*); also the files of the *New England Dairyman*.

[14a] H. C. Woodworth and F. D. Reed, *Economic Study of New Hampshire Poultry Farms*, Durham, N. H., 1932 (*N. H. Agric. Exper. Sta. Bull. No. 265*).

[15] See C. H. Merchant, *An Economic Survey of the Apple Industry in Maine*, Orono, Me., 1927 (*Me. Agric. Exper. Sta. Bull. No. 339*); G. F. Potter and H. A. Rollins, *Commercial Apple Industry of New Hampshire*, Durham, N. H., 1926 (*N. H. Agric. Exper. Sta. Bull. No. 223*); H. W. Yount and L. P. Jefferson, *An Economic Study of the Massachusetts Apple Industry*, Amherst, Mass., 1926 (*Mass. Agric. Exper. Sta. Bull. No. 228*); I. G. Davis, F. V. Waugh, and H. McCarthy, *The Connecticut Apple Industry*, Storrs, Conn., 1927 (*Storrs Agric. Exper. Sta. Bull. No. 145*); *The New Ten Year Program for Massachusetts Fruitmen*, Amherst, Mass., 1931 (*Mass. Agric. Coll. Extension Leaflet 114*, revised); H. C. Woodworth and G. F. Potter, *Studies in Economics of Apple Orcharding, 1. An Apple Enterprise Study—Costs and Management*, Durham, N. H., 1931 (*N. H. Agric. Exper. Sta. Bull. No. 257*); A. E. Stene, *Some Phases of Apple Growing in Rhode Island*, Kingston, R. I., 1930 (*R. I. Agric. Exper. Sta. Bull. No. 226*).

[16] C. H. Merchant, *An Economic Study of 239 Blueberry Farms in Washington and Hancock Counties, Maine*, Orono, Me., 1929 (*Me. Agric. Exper. Sta. Bull. No. 351*).

[17] See C. Y. Mason, *The Cranberry Industry in Massachusetts*, in *Econ. Geogr.*, Vol. 2, 1926, pp. 59–69.

[18] E. A. Wixson, *An Economic Study of the Production, Destination, and Farm Price of Maine Potatoes*, Orono, Me., 1929 (*Univ. of Me. Studies, 2nd Ser., No. 12;* on cover: *Maine Bull.,* Vol. 31, No. 14, June, 1929); E. M. Wilson, *The Aroostook Valley: A Study in Potatoes*, in *Geogr. Rev.*, Vol. 16, 1926, pp. 196–205.

[19] *An Economic Study of the Agriculture of the Connecticut Valley: 1. Production, Supply and Consumption of Connecticut Valley Tobacco*, by F. V. Waugh, Storrs, Conn., 1925 (*Storrs Agric. Exper. Sta. Bull. No. 134*); *3. Tobacco Farm Organization*, by C. I. Hendrickson (*ibid., 165*); *4. A History of Tobacco Production in New England*, by C. I. Hendrickson, 1931 (*ibid., 174*); S. H. De Vault, *The Supply and Distribution of Connecticut Valley Cigar Leaf Tobacco*, Amherst, Mass., 1919 (*Mass. Agric. Exper. Sta. Bull., No. 193*).

[20] A. E. Wilkinson, *The Vegetable Industry of Connecticut*, Storrs, Conn., 1922 (*Conn. Agric. College Extension Service Bull. 51*).

[21] See the paper by F. V. Waugh entitled *The Marketing of New England's Farm Products: Demand Factors* in the present volume, pp. 168–177, below; also files of the *Proceedings of the New England Institute of Coöperation* (see above, note 1).

[22] See W. A. Schoenfeld, *Some Economic Aspects of the Marketing of Milk and Cream in New England*, Washington, 1927 (*U. S. Dept. of Agric. Circular No. 16*); F. V. Waugh, *The Consumption of Milk and Dairy Products in Metropolitan Boston in December, 1930*, Mass. Agric. Exper. Sta., N. H. Agric. Exper. Sta., Mass. Dept. of Agric., coöperating with New England Dairy and Food Council, New England Research Council on Marketing and Food Supply, and U. S. Bur. of Agricultural Economics, 1931; J. E. Carrington and E. H. Loveland, *Meeting the Market Demand for Milk*, Burlington, Vt., 1929 (*Vt. Agric. Exper. Sta. Extension Service Circular No. 58*).

[23] L. P. Jefferson, *The Market Outlet for Massachusetts Apples*, Amherst, Mass., 1927 (*Mass. Agric. Exper. Sta. Bull. No. 231*); the same, *The Consumer Demand for Apples*, 1929 (*ibid., 250*); M. S. Parsons, *Some Economic Phases of the Marketing of Maine Apples*, Orono, Me., 1930 (*Me. Agric. Exper. Sta. Bull. No. 359*); *An Economic Study of the Agriculture of the Connecticut Valley. 2. Connecticut Market Demand for Vegetables*, by I. G. Davis and F. V. Waugh, Storrs, Conn., 1926 (*Conn. Agric. Exper. Sta. Bull. No. 138*); R. B. Corbett, *Preferences and Practices in Buying Vegetables in Providence, Rhode Island*, Kingston, R. I., 1929 (*R. I. Agric. Exper. Sta. Bull. No. 220*). See also note 20.

[24] F. V. Waugh, C. M. White, and M. R. Hersey, *Market Preferences and Premiums for Maine Potatoes*, Maine Development Commission in Coöperation with the U. S. Dept. of Agric. and the Maine Dept. of Agric., 1930 (*Bull. No. 2*); the same authors, *Maine Potato Quality Related to Market Prices*, 1931 (*ibid., Bull. No. 3*).

THE MARKETING OF NEW ENGLAND'S FARM PRODUCTS: DEMAND FACTORS

Frederick V. Waugh

NEW ENGLAND has the smallest per capita acreage of improved farm land of all the major geographic divisions of the United States. With the rest of the northern Atlantic coast it constitutes a deficit region in the production of food and other agricultural products. In other words, the locally produced supply is insufficient to satisfy the demand of the local markets, making necessary the importation from other regions of a large part of the agricultural products consumed. It has been estimated that the state of Massachusetts annually "raises enough hogs to feed herself for about one week, enough sheep for only one day, poultry and poultry products for six to ten weeks, beef for only one or two meals, vegetables for eight to twelve weeks, potatoes for three to six weeks, and only enough butter to spread her bread for one meal or so."[1] If the food production of Rhode Island and Connecticut is compared with consumption, similar conclusions are reached.[2] When we consider New England as a whole, while the difference between production and consumption is less, it is still clear that the region produces much less than enough to feed its population.

SOURCES OF FOOD SUPPLY[3]

Except for a few commodities such as fluid milk, cranberries, cigar binder tobacco, maple sugar, onions, and potatoes, which New England farms produce in excess of the local market requirements, New England markets must rely on outside areas for a large part of their supply of agricultural products. In many cases the source of supply is far distant. Thus, the state shipping the greatest amount of butter to Boston in 1929 was Minnesota; the most important source of cheese was Wisconsin; of eggs, Kansas; of poultry and meats, Illinois; of fruits and vegetables, California.[4] Data concerning the sources of the food supply of other New England markets show much the same results. Particularly in the case of fresh fruits and vegetables a large part of the supply is being brought to the market from producing regions as far away as California, Florida, and Mexico.

The Boston market must pay prices high enough to attract to it these products from long distances. The price must average high enough to cover the charges of transportation and the costs of handling

[1]For notes see below, p. 176.

and selling and still leave something to the iceberg lettuce grower in California or to the egg producer in Kansas or Iowa. As a result of the deficient production in New England and the consequent reliance on distantly produced supplies, the local New England producer has a market which is "protected." That is, he has the same kind of protection that a tariff gives to the manufacturer: that of increasing the cost of competing supplies. The market price of shipped-in products cannot for any long period go below the costs of transportation and marketing. This establishes a minimum price for many commodities and insures the local producer a moderate return even in the years of heaviest supply. It costs the apple grower on the Pacific coast about a dollar and a half in transportation charges and dealers' costs to put a bushel box of apples on the northeastern markets of the country.[5] The New England apple grower is assured that the price of high quality apples in the Boston market will not stay long below that price so long as it is still necessary for the Boston market to get a part of its supply from the Pacific coast. In a similar way the New England producers of vegetables, milk, eggs, and potatoes are protected by the marketing costs which producers in distant regions must pay to put their commodities on the eastern markets.

TYPES AND QUALITIES OF PRODUCTS RECEIVED

The high cost of transporting food products from distant points and selling them in northeastern markets not only has the effect of maintaining a relatively high market price, but it makes it necessary for the distant producer to send to the market products of the highest quality. Only the best of the crop can be sold at prices high enough to pay marketing costs and leave a profit to the grower. For that reason, the more distant producers have built up agencies for grading and inspecting these products at the shipping point. They have carefully and effectively standardized not only the quality of their products but their packs and containers. This careful standardization and grading and the elimination of inferior grades from the market has a decided influence on the "trade"—that is on the dealers who handle food products. The dealer can buy fruits and vegetables from the far west or south by car lots and be assured that they will be of uniformly good quality. Moreover, he knows that he can buy the same grade in the same container tomorrow or next week and get the same quality he gets today. The food dealers are demanding well-graded products, and they can get products of this kind most satisfactorily from the large, well-organized, commercial producing regions of the country.

Not only are the dealers demanding graded and standardized products; the sale of these products to consumers has brought about a demand on their part for a fancy, "dressed-up" commodity. As yet, the consumer has learned little about grades and not much more about the brands and trade-marks that identify farm products. Nevertheless, the housewife is attracted by the use of fancy wrappers, by the diagonal layer pack of apples, by high and uniform color, by uniformity in size, by freedom from disease and insect injury, and by other qualities she finds in the case of many shipped-in products. Consumers are becoming more and more particular. While they may not be able to name a single variety of apple, they may refuse to buy an apple that is undercolored or has a slight blemish. The margin between the price of the higher grades and the lower grades of food products is large and probably is growing larger as consumers become accustomed to demand superior quality.[6]

The constant improvement in the quality and appearance of many of these distant products on the northeastern markets un- doubtedly accounts for at least part of the remarkable increase in their consumption during the last ten years. Unfortunately, there are practically no data available on consumption of food products. Nevertheless the statistics of acreage, production, shipments, and receipts on the market all indicate clearly that consumption of such commodities as spinach, lettuce, and carrots has been increasing rapidly. The total receipts of vegetables in the Boston market increased steadily from 12,000 car lots in 1921 to 22,000 car lots in 1929. A part of this increase may be due not to an increase in per capita consumption but to the widening of the Boston market area, which now reaches a larger population, since new facilities have been built. But the increase in receipts was apparent many years before these terminal facilities were completed; and, while no definite measure of consumption trends is possible, it is certain that the total consump- tion of vegetables as a group has risen. The consumption of fruits also appears to be increasing but at a rate slower than that of vege- tables. Board of Health data indicate a slow, gradual rise in per capita milk consumption. Milk consumption appears to be well maintained in the Boston market up to the present time (May, 1932) in spite of the business depression.[7]

The increase in the consumption of vegetables may be accounted for largely by two factors: (1) the gradual recognition by consumers of the health value of these foods; and (2), the improvement in the quality and appearance of vegetables on the market. The writer believes that the second of these factors has had an important influ- ence. The greatest increases in consumption have been largely in the case of commodities produced in distant commercial regions and graded and packed in a superior way.

The increased supplies of shipped-in products have sometimes been considered a menace to New England agriculture. It is worthy of note, however, that, while the receipts of shipped-in products have been mounting rapidly, the receipts of locally grown vegetables have also increased slightly.[8] The distant producer does not appear to be crowding the local producer off his local market. Rather, he is developing in the local market a new or increased demand for a superior product.

THE NEED FOR DATA ON MARKET PREFERENCES

The improvements in quality, grading, and packing, which have been developed so successfully in many distant producing regions, illustrate the attempt of growers and of growers' organizations to meet the preferences of the markets. It is probable that improvements along this line will continue. There is, however, a need for more definite and accurate data on market preferences than are now available, in order that growers may be able to make these improvements most rapidly and effectively. There has been little organized research directed at discovering the facts about market preferences. Growers have learned through experience and through contact with dealers on the market that an honest pack, uniformity of size and quality, freedom from blemishes, and similar qualities improve prices. But this kind of information, valuable as it is, should be put in more specific and precise terms.

The qualities preferred vary a great deal from commodity to commodity and from market to market. If the producer is to take best advantage of the preferences of New England markets, he needs to know, for example, that the Boston market pays a large premium for asparagus with from six to nine inches of green color, while Worcester and Springfield pay a premium for large stalks but practically none for green color and Providence prefers short stalks packed loose (unbunched) in a bushel box. He needs similar facts about the other commodities. Few such facts are available.

Most of the published information on market preferences for food products is the result of surveys of dealers or consumers. A few examples will show the type of information now at hand.

CONSUMER DEMAND SURVEYS

A recent bulletin of the Rhode Island Agricultural Experiment Station[9] gives the results of a consumer survey of demand for vegetables in Providence. The results are based on questionnaires answered by 182 housewives and a few interviews with housewives. The qualities most frequently mentioned as being desirable were: in the case of lettuce, firm heads; spinach, clear, dark green color; tomatoes, firmness; asparagus, freshness and tenderness; sweet corn, yellow color; celery, good bleach; beets, small to medium size; carrots, small to medium size; potatoes, medium size; squash, dryness and mealiness;

string beans, freshness and tenderness; peppers, green color; and cabbage, whiteness.

A discussion of the complete results of the Providence survey is impossible here. The factors listed above are only those mentioned most frequently. Many other factors of quality are covered in the bulletin. This survey is the only one that has been made in a New England market covering a variety of commodities. The results are both interesting and valuable to the market garden industry in showing possible methods of improving the quality of vegetables sold in order to meet market demand.

Similar surveys have been made for individual commodities. A recent Massachusetts bulletin[10] indicates that the McIntosh apple is the most popular variety for eating and the Baldwin the most desirable for cooking. Two and three quarter inches in diameter is the favorite size for the McIntosh, and three inches the favorite for the Baldwin. The qualities that consumers indicated as influencing their purchases are, in order of their importance: flavor, condition, appearance, juiciness, and size. Color is named by only a small percentage of consumers, although it is noted that dealers say the demand is almost entirely for red apples.

In a similar survey in Connecticut,[11] 97 per cent of the consumers stated a preference for red apples; consumers were divided as to the desirability of grading to uniform sizes; and the other qualities mentioned were firmness, juiciness, size, soundness, and flavor. Baldwin was given as the first choice both for eating and cooking. For eating, McIntosh was a close second, while for cooking, greening was the second choice.

A recent survey in New Hampshire[12] shows the preferences of White Mountain hotels for vegetables and poultry products. The hotel buyers stated that they preferred dark red, oval-shaped beets from two to three inches in diameter. They wanted compact cauliflower with heads at least six inches in diameter; dark-green cucumbers from six to nine inches long; firm-headed lettuce; green string beans; dark-red tomatoes from 2¼ to 2½ inches in diameter; eggs with uniform color of yolk; and they preferred poultry that was milk-fed, light-colored, and of heavy breeds.

Such demand surveys as these give a much more definite picture of market preferences than can be obtained from conversations with a few dealers. More surveys of the same sort are desirable and are being made. The various divisions of the United States Bureau of Agricultural Economics have completed during the past few years a number of surveys of this type covering many agricultural commodities in several of the important markets of the country. They have been of considerable value in determining the requirements for official grades.

Only a small amount of published material is yet available, however, to indicate the preferences for different types of food products in individual New England markets. From observation in some of these markets it is possible to arrive at some general conclusions. For example, Worcester prefers a pink tomato while Springfield, Hartford, and most other markets pay premiums for dark red color. Rhode Island markets, Fall River, and New Bedford like greening apples, while there is a strong preference for red varieties in Boston and generally in northern New England. The large markets like Boston also usually pay higher premiums for large sizes of apples than do smaller markets. White sweet corn sells fairly readily in Hartford, while many other markets have a strong preference for yellow varieties. Worcester and Fall River prefer green beans, while wax beans are considered more desirable in Springfield and Hartford. The Boston market pays a premium for long carrots, while shorter types are preferred in Springfield and many other markets. The demand for hot peppers, broccoli, kale, okra, chicory, and juice grapes varies with the size of the Italian population.

STATISTICAL MEASUREMENT OF MARKET PREFERENCES

While the demand surveys have given some useful information concerning market demand and consumer demand in New England markets, the results are not entirely satisfactory. The most important defect of such surveys is the difficulty in getting an estimate of the premiums paid for desirable qualities. If the survey shows, for example, that the market prefers a dark-green cucumber from six to nine inches long, we immediately wish to know how strong this preference is. Will the market pay more for an eight-inch cucumber than for a five-inch cucumber? and if so, how much more will it pay? How desirable is dark-green color? The cucumber grower could make good use of quantitative statements of this kind when he decides on the variety to grow, the production technique to follow, and the grading and packing policies to adopt.

A series of studies is now in progress on the Boston market, which attempts to measure in quantitative, statistical terms the influence of various physical characteristics on prices of fruits and vegetables. By physical characteristics is meant such qualities as size, shape, degree of firmness, color, and degree of injury from insects and diseases. Such characteristics go to make up what is vaguely called "quality." Quality is not something intangible, unmeasurable, or "qualitative"; it is made up of definite characteristics, most of which are fairly easily measured in terms of inches, pounds, percentages, and similar standards. Only a few qualities of food products have not as yet been subjected to satisfactory physical measurement. The most important of these factors are taste and smell. Some day, satisfactory measures of these factors will be devised. The method of the Boston studies has been to correlate sales prices of individual lots of certain commodities with definite measurements of various qualities of the same lots. Such an analysis determines the net relationship of prices to each of the qualities studied. It shows in dollars and cents how much each quality added to or subtracted from prices, and it also shows the relative amount of price variation attributable to the various qualities.

The Boston studies have included analyses of asparagus,[13] tomatoes, hothouse cucumbers, McIntosh apples,[14] early celery, late celery, onions, and potatoes.[15] The detailed findings of a number of these studies have been published and can be found by referring to the publications given in the notes. It will be possible here to point out only a few examples that show the type of results obtained.

The study of asparagus mentioned above revealed a high degree of correlation in Boston between asparagus and three qualities; the length of green color, the diameter of the stalk, and the uniformity in size of stalks. The first of these factors was by far the most important. Asparagus received on the Boston market varies in the amount of green color from about three inches to nine and one half inches. Each additional inch of green color tended in 1928 to increase the price by an average amount of 38½ cents a dozen bunches. This fact has interested many New England growers in the possibility of producing "long green" asparagus. The Massachusetts Agricultural College has published a bulletin that describes a method of producing this type of asparagus economically.[16] This change in production practice appears to be profitable to farmers who market their asparagus in Boston. Similar studies in Worcester and Springfield, however, indicate that practically no premium is paid for green color but that in these markets the size of the stalk is the most important quality determining prices.

One of the striking results of the study of the McIntosh apple quality was the importance of container and pack. It was found that apples of average quality when jumble-packed in the Boston box sold for an average price of $1.95 a bushel as compared with $2.58 for the same quality of apple when wrapped in paper and layer-packed in a Northwestern apple box. In order of importance the other factors found to be related to McIntosh apple prices were insect injury, size, scab, uniformity of size, deformity, color, bruises, skin punctures, and codling moth injury.

The study of potato quality mentioned above is still in progress. Preliminary analysis indicates that the most important qualities related to Maine potato prices are: the amount of bruises and mechanical injury, size, color of skin, and shape. Bruises and cuts are particularly important; and as a direct result of the market study, a field investigation is now being conducted under the direction of the University of Maine to discover what processes in digging, picking up, storing, grading, and transporting are responsible for most of the bruises and also to discover economical methods of controlling the amount of this defect.

Such are the known facts about market preferences in New England. They are made up from general observation, from surveys, and from detailed statistical analyses. They are not by any means complete. They never can be entirely complete, because market preferences change from year to year. Yet a good deal of progress has been made of late in discovering these facts, and it is likely that the next few years will see greater progress in this direction.

THE SITUATION OF THE NEW ENGLAND PRODUCER

The market situation described above may appear quite advantageous to local producers. The market absorbs a much greater quantity of farm products than can be produced locally. Prices are protected by the high cost of transporting these products from distant regions and selling them in New England markets. The markets of New England have definite preferences for certain qualities of food for which they pay substantial premiums.

But the New England farmer, because of his very nearness to the market, is faced with a difficulty that confronts the near-by producer around all large consuming centers. He has a market for his entire crop—good, bad, and indifferent. Scabby, wormy apples are salable at some price. Someone will buy overripe tomatoes or dirty, undersized potatoes and be glad to get them at a low price. However low the price of these low-quality products may be, they are sold; because the cost of marketing is practically nothing. Often they are sold to consumers at a roadside stand right on the farm. Or they may be brought to market along with something else.

It would be disastrous for many of the poorer consumers if a supply of this low-grade produce were not available at low prices. The local producer is the only one who can afford to supply such produce. He can supply it, does supply it, and will continue to supply it because it will bring enough in the market to pay for transporting and selling it. On the other hand, mainly because of freshness, a large part of the local supply of such products as milk, eggs, sweet corn, asparagus, and apples is of better quality than that of any similar products that could possibly be brought into the local markets from distant sections. The New England farmer, then, produces and sells some of the finest and some of the poorest of the food products sold in New England and can be expected to continue to do so. But products of poor quality placed on the market are in many cases injuring the reputation of local products in general and tending to decrease their sale.

The way out of this difficulty appears to be the adoption of a program of grading and labeling New England-grown products. Such a program is being developed by the state departments of agriculture with the coöperation of the New England Council. Under this program commodities meeting certain quality standards may be identified by the New England Quality label. The purpose of such a program is to protect for the local grower the market for the higher qualities of his products without interfering with the sale of the lower qualities at lower prices. The success of such an undertaking will depend largely on the ability and willingness of local growers to adopt the program and on the ability of the state officials to make sure that products sold under the quality label do in fact come up to proper requirements. So far, at least, the greatest progress in grading and labeling has been made by coöperative marketing associations. One of the principal functions of such associations is the standardization of quality.

NOTES

[1] A. W. Gilbert, edit., *The Food Supply of New England: Prepared Under the Auspices of the Executive Committee of the New England Agricultural Conference*, New York, 1924.

[2] Data on the food supply of Connecticut and Rhode Island will be found in the following publications: R. B. Corbett, *Receipts of Food by Rail and Water in Providence, Rhode Island*, Kingston, R. I., 1927 (*R. I. Agric. Exper. Sta. Bull. No. 211*); the same, *Sources of Carload Receipts of Food in Providence, Rhode Island, 1921–1925*, Kingston, R. I., 1928 (*ibid., No. 215*); E. H. Hodge and G. R. Parsons, *Connecticut Market Demand for Certain Agricultural Products, 1929*, Hartford, Conn., 1930 (*Conn. Dept. of Agric. Bull. 5*).

[3] See also Professor A. E. Cance's paper entitled *The Food Supply of New England* in the present volume, pp. 103–117, above.

[4] E. W. Bateman, *Receipts and Sources of Boston's Food Supply*, 1929 (one of a series of annual mimeographed bulletins of the Massachusetts Department of Agriculture).

[5] W. P. Hedden, *Some Facts About Margins and Costs in Marketing Fruits and Vegetables in the Port of New York District*, Port of New York Authority coöperating with U. S. Dept. of Agric., Bur. of Agricultural Economics, New York, 1925.

[6] In some cases the poor demand conditions of 1930–1932 have lowered premiums for superior quality. It is likely, however, that improved demand conditions will bring a return of high premiums.

[7] Milk consumption in Boston during the early part of the depression is discussed by F. V. Waugh, *The Consumption of Milk and Dairy Products in Metropolitan Boston in December 1930*, Mass. Agric. Exper. Sta., N. H. Agric. Exper. Sta., Mass. Dept. of Agric., coöperating with New England Dairy and Food Council, New England Research Council on Marketing and Food Supply, and U. S. Bur. of Agricultural Economics, 1931.

[8] Supporting data will be found in F. V. Waugh, *Problems of the New England Market on Fresh Fruits and Vegetables*, in *Proc. New England Inst. of Cooperation*, Amherst, Mass., 1928.

[9] R. B. Corbett, *Preferences and Practices in Buying Vegetables in Providence, Rhode Island*, Kingston, R. I., 1929 (*R. I. Agric. Exper. Sta. Bull. No. 220*).

[10] L. P. Jefferson, *The Consumer Demand for Apples*, Amherst, Mass., 1929 (*Mass. Agric. Exper. Sta. Bull. No. 250*).

[11] I. G. Davis, F. V. Waugh, and Harold McCarthy, *The Connecticut Apple Industry*, Storrs, Conn., 1927 (*Storrs Agric. Exper. Sta. Bull. No. 145*).

[12] E. H. Rinear, *White Mountain Demand for Vegetables and Poultry Products*, Durham, N. H., 1929 (*N. H. Agric. Exper. Sta. Bull. No. 241*).

[13] The first three of these studies are described in F. V. Waugh, *Quality as a Determinant of Vegetable Prices: A Statistical Study of Quality Factors Influencing Vegetable Prices in the Boston Wholesale Market*, New York, 1929 (*Columbia Univ. Studies in History, Economics, and Public Law No. 312*).

[14] Julius Kroeck, *McIntosh Apple Study*, Mass. Dept. of Agric., Boston, 1928.

[15] F. V. Waugh, C. M. White, and M. R. Hersey, *Market Preferences and Premiums for Maine Potatoes*, Augusta, Me., 1930 (*Maine Development Commission Bull. No. 2*); the same, *Maine Potato Quality Related to Market Prices*, 1931 (*ibid., No. 3*).

[16] V. A. Tiedjens, W. D. Whitcome, and R. M. Koon, *Asparagus and Its Culture*, Amherst, Mass., 1929 (*Mass. Agric. Coll. Extension Leaflet No. 49*).

THE YANKEE COMMUNITY IN RURAL NEW ENGLAND

H. C. Woodworth

THE many Yankee communities that were in existence in New England at the beginning of the last century have passed through varying experiences. A considerable number have ceased to be, and little remains except some irregular stone walls to indicate former habitation. A few have grown into industrial centers. Of the rural communities now existing many have retained the spirit of the pioneer, directing their thought and energy toward better agriculture. But in others farming has long been on the wane. Let us compare these last two types of agricultural community.

THE PROGRESSIVE COMMUNITY

The individual in the progressive community is likely to have a long-time program. He will tell you that he intends to set out apple trees in one of his small fields now and in a second field next year; that he is now making improvements in his home and expects to take out a stone wall and to lime and seed down the larger field a year hence There is a forward look. The community has faith in itself.

Usually the people have developed a specialized skill in some larger enterprise. If the community is chiefly interested in apples, one will find knowledge of apple production and skill in coping with pests and diseases. If it is a dairy community, one will find a sound practical understanding of the breeding, feeding, and management of livestock and a thirst for new and pertinent information. If it is a poultry section, one soon learns that individual farmers can use scientific names and discuss detailed problems of disease control as readily as a trained veterinarian. There is not only an optimistic forward look but a constant and vigilant focusing of the mental and physical powers on the problems involved. Quite naturally the physical plant or business unit is constantly made better, the herd improved, the soil enriched, the home modernized.

The cumulative effect of this improvement in production, this amassing of special skill and interest and enthusiasm, is an important factor in the success of the community; for each generation begins its work a step higher up the ladder. Each generation inherits a going business, not only an efficient physical plant but a spirit or psychology of progress. Ambition to achieve has been carefully nurtured and developed by the example of the elder generation. The gradually increasing assets in good land, in fine herds and productive orchards, and in community progressiveness are great enough to tempt back children who have made their way into other occupations. If the farm must be sold, a neighbor's boy may buy and carry on.

THE DECLINING COMMUNITY

At the other extreme are the Yankee communities where agriculture is declining and the people drifting hopelessly. The individual has no plans for the future. He is no longer a pioneer. He cuts the hay, milks a few cows, brings in the winter supply of wood, and raises a few bushels of potatoes and beans in an absent-minded way. Neither his mind nor his heart is in the job.

A vision of future abandonment hangs over such communities and paralyzes any new step toward progress. The people have accepted defeat and seem to be awaiting the summons to surrender. Even with the young folk there is little aggressive desire or ambition to farm. Energy is used to protect the retreat. It is more like a rear-guard action than an attack.

With constant deterioration in buildings and equipment, a decline in production, a slowing up of enthusiasm and interest, and a lack of faith in the future each generation is poorer than the generation before. An individual may inherit a few acres of run-out hay land, some cut-over timberland, a few inferior cows and possibly a score of veteran apple trees that partially survived the gypsy moth, and, along with all this, a community sense of failure and a community psychology that is both depressing and enervating. These assets are hardly enough to tempt children back to the farm if hitherto they have been able to exist elsewhere. The cumulative effect is to leave both the individual and the community impotent in the task of farming.

WHY COMMUNITIES DIFFER

In many cases it is difficult to account for this difference between communities. Of course, if the declining community has rough and rocky fields some distance from market or railroad and the progressive community has good level land near a market outlet, the reason is evident; but when the declining community has outwardly in soil, in layout, and in location more to its advantage than another community that is progressing, what can be the explanation?

Do differences in personnel account for it? It is to be assumed that by the year 1800 inherited ability was pretty well distributed over New England. In the process of settling and developing the country the population had multiplied rapidly, and the surplus had to overflow into the wilderness to clear land and build new homes. No particular selective process was at work. There was no alternative to farming. Each family was obliged to put forth tremendous energy in order to have a home, food, and clothing. It may be that certain very virile and vigorous families multiplied rapidly and that in clinging to a given town such a family would affect in one way or another the whole community, but in general the distribution of ability was probably similar in the various settlements.

By 1830 most of New England except for the forest areas of the north had been settled. Some farming communities near the coast had been in existence for two hundred years; others in the north were even then in the pioneer stage. Yet for all of them the preceding period had generally been one of self-sufficing agriculture, with little change in the habits of the people; and it is doubtful if the age of a settlement made much difference in the relative capacity of its inhabitants. The two-hundred-year-old community seems to have shared most of the handicaps of the newer places.

After 1830, with the building of railroads, the westward movement, and the growth of manufactures, selective influences began to change the character of the several communities.

Thus, wherever a new industry made its beginning, farm people were directly associated with it, and their sons and daughters tended to follow its development rather than to cling to agriculture. It is probably a good thing for New England and for the country at large that many New ˌEnglanders were switched over to manufacturing at this early period, but the important point as far as present-day rural life is concerned is that the starting of these various industries was a selective force acting quite differently in different places. Some districts were remote and little affected, while others were immediately involved. The communities in southern New England responded more directly to the call to man the shops and mills than those of northern New England. Some communities became industrially-minded, while others remained farm-minded.

Two Typical Declining Communities

Nute Ridge in southern New Hampshire is an example of a small farming community that became industrially-minded—to its detriment agriculturally.[1] The ridge was first settled in 1800, and the pioneers pushed the clearing and building of homes with enthusiasm and vigor for about thirty-five years. Then a trader began putting out shoe material—uppers, soles, linings, etc. The farmers took these supplies to their homes and brought back the finished shoes. From that moment farming was secondary. The individual continued to live on the farm. He still had a cow and a pig and a garden, but little new land was cleared. The making of shoes in the farmer's home continued for several decades, until, with the invention of machinery,

---

[1] H. C. Woodworth, *Nute Ridge: The Problem of a Typical Back-Town Community*, Durham, N. H., 1927 (*Univ. of N. H. Extension Service, Extension Circular 68*).

village factories supplanted piecework. After that the individual
chose to commute from his farm to the factory rather than to depend
on farming. Without aggressive farming there was no accumulation
of skill and no improvement in land or stock. Finally the people on
the ridge could take up farming only with great handicaps, and the
longer the return was delayed the more difficult it became. Here, then,
is an instance where another option appealed to the people and switched
them from farming to industry. And when this option flitted away
at the end of several generations, it was not easy to meet the competition from communities that had remained dependent on agriculture
and had given it their chief attention.

Although Nute Ridge may well have the inherent physical properties and advantages of location requisite for a prosperous farming
community, to become such a community it would have to start all
over again. It would have to build up its agriculture and its marketing
facilities, a far more difficult thing to do now than a century ago.

Another New Hampshire town, Deerfield in Rockingham County,
once had many prosperous farms. Its ridges are broad and its soil is
a good loam, typical of the better hill lands of the state. Its future at
the beginning of the last century seemed so secure that its widest and
most attractive ridge was considered as a possible location of the
state capitol. However, its agriculture declined and its population
fell from 1,768 in 1870[2] to 635 in 1930.

When the railroads came, in the period 1840 to 1850, the town was
left at some disadvantage; but this alone does not explain its decline,
for other farming communities as far from a railroad as southern
Deerfield have prospered. Indeed, it is hard to say with assurance
why it has declined. Town histories in general ignore economic influences, and the memories of the older people usually fail to weigh
seemingly minor economic factors that may ultimately affect the
destiny of a town. The older men state that the community declined
"because the young people left," but there is little agreement as to
why they left. With a note of sarcasm one man insists that they did
not like to work; another, that they craved excitement.

For a hundred years the young people of Deerfield have had the
choice of remaining on the farm or going out into other occupations,
and for the most part they have chosen to go out. A few have reached
high places, but most of them have worked in mills and remained in the
lower ranks of life. The emigration has been a product of the individual decisions of hundreds of young people. Lack of opportunity in

---

[2] Even as late as 1870 the town was evidently putting considerable energy on its farms as the
following figures will show: at that time there were 1947 cattle, 336 horses, 727 sheep, 223 swine. The
production for the year was 10,151 bushels of corn, 2803 bushels wheat, 495 bushels rye, 3056 bushels
oats and barley, 980 bushels peas and beans, 3063 pounds clipped wool, 25,975 bushels of potatoes,
$12,102 worth of fruit, 125,750 pounds butter, 5600 pounds cheese, 2500 pounds maple sugar and
$14,135 worth of lumber. The total value of farm products was $178,518 (E. C. Cogswell, *History of
Nottingham, Deerfield, and Northwood*, Manchester, N. H., 1878, p. 321).

comparison with other options has been the underlying factor, but we do not know to what extent the failure of opportunity at home has been due to the drifting and aimless farming of previous generations.

In Deerfield the farms remained of the small general type. No one branch of farming was expanded to any extent. During the period 1870–1910, the total production of all the small orchards was considerable, perhaps as much as 10,000 barrels a year. Apples were bringing in an income, but orcharding as a specialized industry never grew to any extent. Probably, in spite of the income, no particular skill was developed. When later the gypsy moth invasion came, there was little interest in learning how to save the trees, and eventually the trees were lost.

At present there are at least three orchards in Deerfield that have been well cared for and maintained by new settings and have had good yields of high-quality fruit. These are small orchards, each of one hundred trees or so; but they are mute demonstrations of what Deerfield might now have had, if its people had been somewhat more skilled in apple production and somewhat more interested in apples when the crisis came.

A TYPICAL PROGRESSIVE COMMUNITY

In contrast, other communities under similar conditions have evolved from the small general farm stage toward specialization, as, for example, in apples. With this trend has gone interest in apple production, faith on the farmer's part in his ability to control pests and disease, and an enthusiasm to raise apples on an ever larger scale. When the gypsy moth came, instead of taking a fatalistic attitude and abandoning the trees, the farmers put up a fight and won and, moreover, kept right on planting.

One community in Wilton and Lyndeborough (Hillsboro County, New Hampshire) had small general farms and was in a somewhat comparable position to Deerfield. The individual was having a difficult struggle. Like Deerfield, the region was in a good apple section but had a layout somewhat inferior. The returns from small orchards were good, however, and the men became interested in fruit and began setting out more trees. At a critical stage, when dairying on a small scale could no longer give the people a satisfactory living, they pinned their faith on fruit and put forth all their energy and Yankee ingenuity in developing orchards.

Just why one community should develop an interest to the extent of specializing in an enterprise, and another, equally or better fitted to survive, should fail to do so, is difficult to ascertain. It often happens that some minor influence, some insignificant incident, may be responsible.

One incident that may well have widened the differences between the community in Wilton and Lyndeborough and other less progressive communities was the arrival of Ben Richardson in Hillsboro County. Richardson, an enthusiastic and practical fruit man trained in the theory and practice of horticulture, was located in the county as a representative of the state college of agriculture. One day the leaders in the Wilton community came to him and stated that they wanted to have a winter fruit school and called on him to lead. Richardson outlined a winter's course for them, each farmer purchased a text on apple production, and the work began. They met once a week and discussed the chapters far into the night.

No doubt they gained much in subject matter from the text, from their instructor, and from their own discussion; but the important fact is that an enthusiasm and faith in the future of apples was developed. Not just an individual here and there but a group of individuals began to plant trees and to care for them with sprays and fertilizers. The community had insured itself against abandonment.

THE PSYCHOLOGICAL FACTOR IN A COMMUNITY'S GROWTH

While economic influences determine to a considerable extent the course of a community's life, the human element, often influenced by a minor event in the beginning, may roll up a different complex with resulting changes in interests, skills, and capacities. Men in different communities may react with a different crowd psychology to the same sort of economic pressure.

The psychology of a community is an important factor in its life and one that very little is known about. Many of the farm fields in New England are hidden from public view. Neighbors do not know what other neighbors are doing. There is little stimulus from competition or comparison. Consequently, there is little outside the individual's own initiative to push him to do his best throughout the season. Now and then he has an objective so definite that he can go through depressions and discouragements with unslackened enthusiasm and undiminished energy, but most of us are dependent on and subject to outside influences.

There are some Yankee communities in New England where men in full vigor of life have apparently never been subjected to competitive influences like those that compel most business and professional men to develop their capacities to the full. There is a young man in a back town on a rough and rocky soil in the midst of a partially abandoned neighborhood who seemingly is not affected by the decline about him. He inherited a rocky farm but also a herd of cattle that represented the life goal of his father. Today he has more cows and better cows than he inherited. This man has found an incentive within himself and has striven through the years to reach his goal.

But many farmers are met, seemingly just as capable as this young man, who have never felt the inner urge to quicken their pace or do their best. They have been reared in an atmosphere that called forth only a small part of their ability, and as they grew older and inherited farms they have continued in the same way. In one instance a family with two grown boys had two acres of corn, twenty-five acres of hay, and six cows. They merely drifted along. They had all summer to put up hay, and so they took all summer. If this family had been placed in a community where there was a competitive spirit of accomplishment it would have been considered shiftless and either would have stepped up its pace and caught the spirit of doing things or would have had to accept a minor place in the community's life. In this particular community there was no standard of accomplishment, and the family held its position in the respect of its neighbors. In such communities there are men who may hold high places as officers of the town or local grange or farm bureau or even as representatives in the legislature and who may perform these duties well and yet never accomplish much on the farm.

I have sometimes thought that the brighter men, finding that the farm as operated takes only part of their mental capacity, let their minds drift into other channels. While living on farms and going through the motions of farming, they are not thinking about what they are doing.

Indeed, there are whole communities in which the people have more ability than they are using. Here the farming that is done is not a measure of inherited capacity. If placed in situations demanding their best, such communities could hold their own. When the lack of some force impelling men to achievement results in the decline and abandonment of one farm after another, a cloud hangs over the community. Any individual who does attempt to accomplish something seems to be carrying the whole community on his back. Without encouragement and with the combined criticism of all his neighbors, he tires easily and succumbs to the dead weight. One county worker in New England had a declining agricultural community in one end of the county. To do effective work there he had to sandwich in two days a week in a progressive area in order to overcome his depression and regain his courage and enthusiasm.

In a general way therefore, there is a community psychology which may either stimulate the individual to better farming or dull his interest. It may direct his energies into fruitful channels, or it may confuse and bemuddle his objective. It is an endless circle. Enthusiasm and interest make for success, and success stimulates interest. Lack of interest contributes to failure, and failure dulls interest. Where failure is due to basic economic conditions, it is the starting point, and lack of enthusiasm is to be expected; but in other cases the starting point may be merely the psychological complex of the community.

One of the great needs of New England is a study of these various psychological attitudes. Wherever they result from other than economic or physical facts, perhaps something can be done to help the communities find themselves.

DIFFERENCES OF PERSONNEL WITHIN THE COMMUNITY

So far we have been discussing general trends only. The community, however, is made up of individuals; and close scrutiny of its personnel will nearly always reveal a highly complicated situation. There are a few communities where all the families are of a capable, energetic, Yankee type; but more often there is a mixture of the young and the old, the vigorous and the feeble, the capable and the weak, the intelligent and the slow. The study of any community should take full account of the distribution of these various classes. The mere statement of an average will not suffice.

In some sections of the country, especially where land is high in price and considerable skill is required to manipulate high-value factors of production, selective processes are at work. Where this is true, the farmers that remain are usually capable. The incapable cannot survive except as workers for the others. There are such sections in New England; but on the whole our farms are low in capital value, and an old or a shiftless man without any large cash expense can somehow sell a few things from the farm and in addition grow some potatoes, beans, fruit, poultry, and milk for himself. Often side by side on two farms of equal intrinsic value one may find a mentally and physically vigorous man, fitting into situations and using his energy to the utmost in developing his opportunities, and an old man who has given up active farming, or a somewhat shiftless family that "gets by," earning little and spending less. Then again, good farms and small rocky farms are intermingled. If the abilities of the personnel were all similar, economic pressure would cause the poor farm to be given up and only the good farms would be left; but, since there are all types of people in a community, the poor farm may be the abode of a family that is well able at least partially to support itself. Furthermore, in some instances, the selectmen permit families to occupy small farms for years after default of taxes, realizing that if the family were deprived of this means of partial support, the town might be called upon to maintain it wholly.

Even the best farm in town may run down as the farmer grows older. While continuing to live on the farm he may gradually give up active operations. He may sell off the cattle and for a period of years sell hay standing. In ten to twenty years the yield of hay is no longer worth the expense of cutting. The longer the old man lives, the less valuable is the farm as a business enterprise. So, occasionally, the best farm becomes the poorest. If such a farm is put up for sale there is usually no improvement in farming. The lack of capital, of experience, and perhaps of ambition will usually mean a year or two of abortive attempts at operation, followed by a long period of declining usefulness. Lack of funds means not even a pretense at repairs of paint or reshingling, and the next time the farm is up for sale, the new personnel is quite likely to be of little ambition and undesirable as a part of a rural community. This is the usual thing in a declining community, but it may happen to a good farm in the midst of a good community. In most forward-looking sections, however, neighbors anxious to expand their business may buy the farm and incorporate it with their other farm holdings.

As farms are abandoned or depreciate in value, the tax burden for roads and schools is shifted to the few remaining farms. In districts that have been on the decline for a long time, there is a tendency for many of the abler people to leave, and after a while the educational disadvantages and the general backwardness force out the remaining better elements. Yet this can be stated only as a trend, a tendency. Many a man is bound by strong ties of sentiment or of obligation to his parents and will linger on.

FAMILY TRADITION AS A TIE TO THE SOIL

In some families there seems to be a tradition handed down from generation to generation that one member of the family must carry on the farm. It is not uncommon to have a man state that he is of the seventh generation of Smiths, Wiggins, or Chesleys to occupy the place and that his son will be of the eighth. This continuity of family effort has an appeal to most of us, but close examination shows that the tradition may become a great handicap. If the eighth Wiggin inherits a splendid herd of cows on a good farm in a thriving community with a good school and a strong community church, such tradition may have merit. But the original Wiggin in 1750 could never know how the railroads would run or how competition with the world would affect his particular farm. Is it practical or sensible for the Wiggins a century later to be bound by sentiment to maintain the unwitting mistake of their ancestor? The original mistake was not so bad; it is the upkeep that is costly. It uses up men's and women's lives in ineffective and purposeless struggle.

A Yankee farmer recently requested me to visit his farm in the hills. He stated rather proudly that it had been in the family for two hundred years. On the way up I pictured to myself what great progress might be made by two hundred years of family effort toward an ideal. What could not be accomplished in two centuries of intelligent herd building or farm planning? Here might be something comparable to the achievement of the Bates or Cruickshank families in England. What I found was evidence of a tremendous amount of work done long ago in clearing fields of timber and piling rocks in stone fences. A great house and a large barn were monuments to the skill and energy of another generation; but, as to the descendants, the only evidence available was eight inferior scrub cows and thirty acres of run-out hay land.

It is neither logical nor fair nor economic to expect people to remain on a farm through sentiment. Men should not be bound by family traditions, and ability should be free to seek opportunity wherever it may be.

Farm Abandonment and Community Progress

Our concern is the welfare of the people, and from this point of view we can regard the physical community as the temporary abode of a people in the march of progress.

If the people of a rough and rocky region in Vermont, Maine, or New Hampshire realize that there is little opportunity in that particular area and put the major emphasis of their lives in training and educating the children to take responsible places in industry and the professions, they may achieve greater success than others who hold back their young folk in a futile attempt to save the physical community. Some communities that were abandoned quickly have been more successful than others that have merely delayed the ordeal and after using up several generations of youth in an unhappy energy-sapping battle have failed to accomplish anything worth while.

Thus, if we think of the decline of certain communities in terms of the welfare of the people, we soon appreciate that in many instances retreat is the logical economic step, especially if the retreat brings the people into situations more abundant in opportunities.

That the New England Yankee has usually been able to make this adjustment, to retreat from the settlement and aggressively enter into the stream of progress on a better basis, does credit to his native ability. Suppose even that he cleared some land and built a home at great cost in time and energy and then finally left it all and moved on; if by moving out he was able to better himself and give his family a larger opportunity, there is nothing much to regret. The cleared fields may grow up to pine, the weather-beaten old house may gradually fall to pieces, and in a score of years there may remain nothing but an old cellar hole and the crumbling brick of an old chimney. What of it, if the man's family and descendants are better off?

It is our nature to feel depressed in traveling through a region that has been abandoned. We instinctively associate the dilapidated house with the breaking up of a home and the decline of a whole community of people, forgetting that the people have quite likely found a better home. We are deeply rooted to the soil, tied to it by sentiments as profound and deep as religious tenets. It is difficult to regard an abandoned home in the country as we do an abandoned Ford. Somehow we have a realization that people cling to their homes, that they endure hardship and extreme privation before the change can be made. There is indeed something pathetic in viewing a community still in the process of certain decay. Yet we need not regret abandonment itself so much as the painful process involved before all the people are out.

Our main concern, however, is not with the abandoned community but with the communities that remain. And since most of these are now prosperous, our supreme problem is to keep them healthy and sound.

RECENT IMMIGRANT STOCKS IN
NEW ENGLAND AGRICULTURE[1]

J. L. Hypes

NUMBERS AND NATIONALITIES[2]

AN immigrant tide has flowed into the farming communities as well as into the mill towns of New England. About one eighth of the persons now living on New England farms were born in foreign countries; another eighth sprang from foreign-born parents, and one eleventh from marriages of foreign-born with native-born (Table I and Fig. 1). In other words, more than a third of all the farm folk of New England are of foreign stock. This is a large proportion, large enough to give rise to critical problems of social assimilation and economic adjustment in the agricultural communities of the region. New England, in fact, has a higher percentage of foreign-born in the rural population than any other major section of the country, with the exception of the Pacific states.[3]

For many years the farm population of New England has been decreasing in numbers. According to the United States Census between 1920 and 1930 the rural-farm population fell from 535,422 to 499,083. It is probable that the foreign element in the farm population has likewise decreased, although at a somewhat less rapid rate. It appears to have fallen off slightly from 1920 to 1930 in Maine and Vermont and to have gained somewhat in Connecticut; in all three of these states the percentages of foreign white stock (i.e. foreign-born and native-born of foreign and mixed parentage) in the total rural-farm population increased. Unfortunately the census figures for rural-farm population for 1920 and for 1930 are not strictly comparable, and the trends during the decade cannot be accurately determined (see notes to Table I). In any case, no great changes occurred in the ratio of foreign-born and foreign stock to the total rural-farm population.

While only about an eighth of all the people of foreign stock in New England dwell in the three northern states of Maine, New Hampshire, and Vermont, nearly half of the New England farm population of foreign origin are found in these three states. The reason for the more even distribution of the foreign farm population than of the total foreign population is clear. Agriculture is a major industry of northern New England, and the northern region has attracted immigrant farmers to a proportionately greater degree than it has attracted immigrant factory workers. Nevertheless, even in

[1] For notes see below, p. 203.

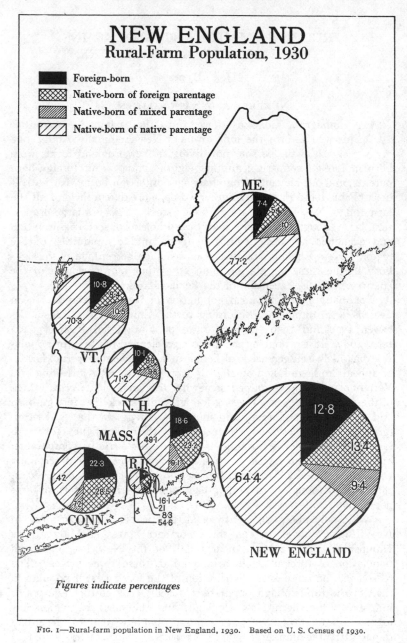

NEW ENGLAND
Rural-Farm Population, 1930

Foreign-born
Native-born of foreign parentage
Native-born of mixed parentage
Native-born of native parentage

Figures indicate percentages

FIG. I—Rural-farm population in New England, 1930.   Based on U. S. Census of 1930.

northern New England there are far more immigrants in other walks of life than on the farms.

About thirty different nationalities are represented among the foreign-born farm population (Table II). The largest group is made up of Canadians of other than French extraction (14,225), who comprise nearly a quarter of the total. Almost half of the non-French Canadians are settled in Maine, although there are important colonies in Vermont, Massachusetts, and New Hampshire. These states also have a substantial French-Canadian element on their farms, and the French Canadians (12,150), over half of whom have come to Vermont, rank second among the groups of foreign origin. Besides the Canadians there are in northern New England a good many Scandinavian, Finnish, and British farmers and a scattering from other countries. It is to be noted, however, that the foreign-born farming stocks of Massachusetts, Connecticut, and Rhode Island are more heterogeneous. Out of a total of 7216 Poles, the majority (6467) are found in Massachusetts and Connecticut; and the Irish, British, Scandinavians, Germans, Italians, Finns, Lithuanians, Portuguese, Russians, and Czechoslovaks are all represented by fairly large groups in these three states.

The preponderance of European agricultural elements in Massachusetts and Connecticut is probably due largely to the fact that these two states are highly urbanized; here recent immigrants, of farm origin in their native lands, after lingering for a time in the cities upon their arrival in America, have tended to reëstablish themselves on farms in the near-by open country.[4] When we take into account the restrictions of our recent immigration laws and current trends in the utilization of land for residential and recreational purposes, a rapid increase in the number of immigrant farm operators in New England in the near future does not seem probable.

IMMIGRANT FARMERS AND TYPES OF FARMING

For an analysis of the nativity of the immigrant farmers of New England in relation to the types of farming in which they are engaged, there does not seem to be at hand as complete information as one might desire. In Connecticut, to be sure, a recent investigation has yielded a somewhat detailed cross section, but a more extended investigation along these lines is needed.[5]

Table III, based on a study of 525 farmers distributed among six selected Connecticut towns,[6] shows in terms of chance expectancy the relationship of these two factors.[7] We note, for example, that the percentage of German farmers following dairying is considerably less than the ratio of dairy farmers to all farmers, i.e. 50 per cent of chance expectancy; whereas the number of Germans in poultry production, general farming, and on small farms considerably exceeds

TABLE I—NEW ENGLAND STATES: TOTAL POPULATION AND RURAL-FARM POPULATION, 1930 AND 1920, CLASSIFIED BY NATIVITY[a]

| | TOTAL POPULATION | | RURAL-FARM POPULATION[b] | | | | | |
| | | | ALL CLASSES | | FOREIGN WHITE STOCK | | | |
	Total	Foreign White Stock (Foreign or mixed parentage and foreign-born)	Total	All Classes	Per-centage of All Rural-Farm	Foreign-Born Number	Foreign-Born Percentage of All Rural-Farm	Native-Born of Foreign Parents, Number
New England . . . 1930	8,166,341	4,898,031	499,083	177,996	35.6	64,066	12.8	66,746
1920	7,400,909	4,512,930	535,422	161,157	30.0	59,933	11.1	56,591
Maine 1930	797,423	279,940	161,429	36,851	22.8	11,939	7.3	8,780
1920	768,014	269,915	189,026	39,769	21.0	13,243	7.0	9,743
New Hampshire[c] . 1930	465,293	224,912	54,911	15,815	28.8	5,571	10.1	4,882
1920	443,083	216,819	64,607	16,096	24.9	5,975	9.1	4,809
Vermont 1930	359,611	124,875	111,898	33,190	29.6	12,050	10.7	9,455
1920	352,428	123,492	124,445	33,756	27.2	12,297	9.8	9,838
Massachusetts[c] . 1930	4,249,614	2,763,142	80,309	40,950	50.9	14,972	18.6	18,635
1920	3,852,356	2,572,751	61,732	24,262	39.3	9,320	15.0	10,118
Rhode Island[c] . 1930	687,497	466,053	10,289	4,665	45.3	1,654	16.0	2,159
1920	604,397	420,427	5,315	1,392	26.1	516	9.7	659
Connecticut[d] . . 1930	1,606,903	1,039,109	80,247	46,525	57.9	17,880	22.2	22,835
1920	1,380,631	909,526	90,297	45,882	50.8	18,582	20.5	21,424

[a] Based on Fifteenth Census of the United States, 1930: Population, Vol. 3, Washington, 1932.
[b], [c], [d] See footnotes on p. 193.

chance expectancy. The Italians do not follow dairying or tobacco growing to any appreciable extent, but in relatively large numbers go into vegetable gardening and combinations thereof, the ratios for these two types of farming being, respectively, 600 per cent and 200 per cent of chance expectancy. Likewise, the Swiss are found to follow dairying in the ratio of 200 per cent of chance expectancy and tobacco growing in the ratio of 75 per cent of chance expectancy. The native-born farmers, while engaging in all the important types of farming found in the state, do not pursue any type far beyond chance expectancy. It would be both interesting and valuable to discover the various economic and cultural factors that combine to secure the distribution of the nationality elements of the farm population among the important types of farming as shown in Table III.

IMMIGRANT FARMERS AND SOIL TYPES

It has been generally assumed that in New England immigrants, as a class, settle largely upon the poorer farm land. However, this is a subject that merits more scientific and extended treatment than heretofore has been given it. No doubt an investigation of certain localities might show that the immigrants have settled upon the rougher and less productive land, but this would not prove conclusively that they have done so throughout the whole region. The Connecticut investigation showed[8] that the native-born farmers are found on some of the poorest soil types as well as on the best. For example, on a very stony, poor soil for extractive farming, 60 per cent

---

NOTES ON TABLE I, *continued.*

b The figures for rural-farm population for 1920 and 1930 are not comparable.

"The farm population as shown for 1930 comprises all persons living on farms, without regard to occupation. The farm population figures for 1920 include, in addition, those farm laborers (and their families) who, while not living on farms, nevertheless lived in strictly rural territory outside the limits of any city or other incorporated place. Though the number of additional persons thus included is believed not to have been very great, some allowance should be made for this difference in definition when comparing the figures. Further allowance should be made for the fact that the 1920 census was taken in January, when considerable numbers of farm laborers and others usually living on farms were temporarily absent, while the 1930 census was taken in April, when by reason of the advancing season the number of persons on the farms was appreciably larger. Since these two factors operate in opposite directions, it may well be that one largely offsets the other. It seems probable, however, that the change in the date added more to the 1930 returns than were omitted through the use of the narrower definition"—*ibid.*, p. 6. In the case of New Hampshire, Massachusetts, Rhode Island, and Connecticut there are additional differences of definition (see the following notes).

c "Rural-farm" population is farm population residing in areas that the Bureau of the Census defines as "rural." In the 1920 census all cities as well as all towns in Massachusetts, Rhode Island, and New Hampshire with a population of over 2500 were classified as "urban." In the 1930 census 76 of these towns, with an aggregate population of 288,621, "were in effect transferred to the rural classification" (*ibid.*, p. 6, note 2). As a consequence, decreases may have been greater than one would gather from the totals for 1920 and 1930 or may even have occurred where comparison of the totals shows apparent increases. The census, unfortunately, gives no data on the nativity of the "urban-farm" population.

d Four towns in Connecticut with an aggregate population of 87,086 in 1930 were transferred from the "rural" to the "urban" classification for the purposes of the 1930 census (*ibid.*, p. 6, note 3). Had these towns been retained in the "rural" classification in which they stood in 1920 the decreases in the total rural-farm population and the foreign-born rural-farm population of Connecticut would not have appeared so great as the figures suggest; the increase in the foreign white stock among the rural-farm population would have appeared somewhat greater.

TABLE II—NEW ENGLAND STATES: FOREIGN-BORN RURAL FARM
POPULATION, 1930, CLASSIFIED BY COUNTRY OF ORIGIN[a]

	CANADA (EXCEPT FRENCH)	CANADA (FRENCH)	POLAND	IRELAND	ENGLAND, SCOTLAND, WALES
New England	14,225	12,150	7,216	2,933	4,178
Maine	6,805	2,124	113	183	600
New Hampshire . . .	1,929	1,260	343	242	525
Vermont	2,888	6,714	225	298	685
Massachusetts	2,072	1,272	2,661	1,020	1,166
Rhode Island	88	176	68	89	217
Connecticut	443	604	3,806	1,101	985

TABLE II, Continued

	NORWAY, SWEDEN, DENMARK	GERMANY	ITALY	FINLAND	ALL OTHER
New England	4,001	2,549	2,797	3,094	10,923
Maine	689	115	66	859	385
New Hampshire . . .	282	107	56	382	445
Vermont	233	185	152	302	368
Massachusetts	1,180	403	694	1,026	3,478
Rhode Island	70	49	49	111	737
Connecticut	1,547	1,690	1,780	414	5,510

[a] Based on *Fifteenth Census of the United States, 1930: Population*, Vol. 3, Washington, 1932.

of the farmers were native-born; on certain soils excellent for tobacco
growing and market gardening, 66 and 57 per cent, respectively, of
the farmers were native-born; and on soils suited to general farming
and fruit growing 68 per cent were native-born.   In general, one is
impressed by the great degree of variation and the lack of consistency
in the association of soil type and nationality.   Although native-
born farmers seem to be found on the better soils in slightly greater
numbers than mere chance distribution would lead one to expect,[9]
it would be risky to attribute this tendency to a broad unanalyzed
nationality factor.   Length of residence in the locality, financial status,
experience with given types of farming, the use of land for residential
and recreational purposes, and like factors probably account for
whatever association there may be.

In the further consideration of the relationships between soil
type and nationality, we should not overlook the fact that in southern
New England there is a strong movement of city people toward the

TABLE III—TYPES OF FARMING AND THE NATIONALITY OF FARMERS[a]
(Percentage Which the Actual Numbers of Coöperators Are of Chance Expectancy)

TYPES OF FARMING	Native-Born	FOREIGN-BORN					
		German	Italian	Swiss	Polish	Lithuanian	Russian
Dairy	107	50	20	200	100	33	. . .
Dairy combinations . . .	110	100	. . .	200	. . .	100	. . .
Tobacco	88	67	40	75	167	400	350
Tobacco combinations . .	93	100	33	200	200	100	500
Vegetable	65	. . .	600	. . .	200	50	100
Vegetable combinations .	111	. . .	200	100	. . .	. . .	. . .
Poultry	106	300	. . .	. . .	. . .	. . .	. . .
Poultry combinations . .	100	. . .	b	. . .	. . .	. . .	. . .
Fruit	140	. . .	100	. . .	. . .	. . .	. . .
Fruit combinations . . .	133	. . .	200	. . .	. . .	. . .	. . .
General	95	225	50	. . .	250	. . .	. . .
Small farm	100	250	50	100	100	. . .	. . .
Miscellaneous	129	50	. . .	100	. . .	100	. . .

TABLE III, Continued

TYPES OF FARMING	FOREIGN-BORN						
	Swedish	Austrian	Czechoslov.	Irish	Danish	English	Miscellaneous
Dairy	200	150	200	. . .	b	. . .	167
Dairy combinations . . .	100	100	. . .	100	. . .	100	50
Tobacco	100	50	200	200	. . .	200	. . .
Tobacco combinations . .	. . .	. . .	100	100	. . .	. . .	. . .
Vegetable	100	100	. . .	100	b	. . .	200
Vegetable combinations . .	. . .	. . .	. . .	. . .	. . .	. . .	b
Poultry	. . .	200	. . .	. . .	. . .	b	. . .
Poultry combinations . . .	. . .	. . .	. . .	. . .	. . .	. . .	b
Fruit	. . .	. . .	. . .	. . .	. . .	. . .	. . .
Fruit combinations	. . .	. . .	. .	. . .	. . .	. . .	. . .
General	100	200	200	100	. . .	. . .	150
Small farm	. . .	. . .	. . .	. . .	b	b	100
Miscellaneous	. . .	. . .	. . .	. . .	. . .	b	200

[a] Data taken from Storrs Agric. Exper. Sta. Bull. No. 161, 1929, p. 404.
[b] Contained one case with a chance of less than 0.5.

country for residential and recreational purposes. In fact, the rise of a rural non-farm population is becoming one of the significant phenomena of recent population movements in America. In 1930 the farm population of the United States was approximately 30,157,000 and the rural non-farm population 23,662,000. In the decade ending 1930 Connecticut lost about one tenth of her rural-farm population but gained notably in her rural non-farm population; and in 1930 her rural non-farm population was about five times as great as her rural-farm population.[10] The rapid extension of hard roads and the wide ownership of automobiles, no doubt, have accelerated this movement. Thus in New England much of the rough land that is submarginal for farm purposes under present economic conditions is being taken over for non-agricultural uses and is therefore being automatically removed from farming for both native and foreign-born farmers alike. At best, the agricultural use of much of this land extends only to a little part-time farming. As a guide to the development of educational programs in vocational agriculture and as the basis for the formulation of plans for reforestation and tax adjustment, further investigations should be made of the long-term trends in the residential, the recreational, and the part-time and full-time agricultural use of the land in this section of country.[11]

STANDARDS OF LABOR

To some extent the immigrant farmers are repeating the pioneer type of life characteristic of early New England. In making their adjustment to economic conditions many have worked long hours, combined agricultural and non-agricultural pursuits, and followed such types of farming as require considerable hand labor. Thus they may have kept alive agricultural enterprises that probably long since would have become extinct because of the competition of the neighboring cities for the labor supply and because of more favorable farm conditions outside of New England. This method of adjustment, moreover, has given the immigrants an economic advantage over the native farmers, who on the whole do not care to maintain standards of work and living adopted by many newly-arrived immigrant families.[12] Herein, no doubt, lies a partial explanation of why the immigrants constitute such a large percentage of the rural population.

PROBLEMS OF SOCIAL CONFLICT

The intermingling of different ethnic groups having different standards of living, different religious faiths, and different standards of social participation almost inevitably leads to social conflict. This conflict sometimes takes the form of overt acts, such as organized efforts to keep immigrant groups out of the older communities or out of existing socio-political organizations. Sometimes it takes the form of voluntary non-participation on the part of the newly-arrived immigrant stocks in such primary social groups of the community as the church, the Grange, and the recreational club. Moreover, certain immigrant groups constituting the larger part of the population of some communities at times fail to join in the activities of the Farm Bureau and the Agricultural College Extension Service and thus effectively shut themselves off from a source of help in adjusting themselves to the farming of the locality. It may be, too, that the Farm Bureau and the Agricultural College Extension Service have an inadequate knowledge of the socio-economic problems and the cultural backgrounds of immigrant farm families and thus place themselves at a disadvantage in helping these families.

Social conflict is also shown, sometimes, by the mutual difference of attitudes between immigrant parents and their American-born children on questions of social control and ethical behavior. Familism of a patriarchal nature is rather strong among certain immigrant groups, and, when their growing sons and daughters catch the spirit of youthful freedom that seems to pervade modern America, conflict often arises between parents and children. Occasionally this conflict is aggressive and violent; but more often it is a conflict of acquiescence, wherein the parents sorrowfully and quietly resign themselves to the new order.[13]

The intermingling of groups having social cultures widely unlike and the various forms of social conflict arising therefrom may also lead to a condition of social impersonality not greatly unlike that of the city. This tendency, which has already been observed in rural sections in southern New England,[14] works toward the weakening of the social solidarity of rural communities and possibly facilitates changes in the values placed upon standards of social conduct previously established by the ancestors of the native stock. The great residential mobility which results in a frequent turnover of the population also augments this condition. Thus, in rural communities we find public opinion playing a rôle of diminishing importance as a deterrent to law breaking and moral laxity.[15] This places a greater personal responsibility upon the individual and demands constructive effort on the part of those agencies engaged in education and other forms of social control.

PROBLEMS IN THE PURCHASE OF FARMS

The settlement of immigrants upon the farms of New England, on the whole, seems to be a social asset rather than a liability. While many immigrants have failed to make adequate adjustments to farm life, others have adapted themselves happily to a situation that had previously eliminated the native farmers. People who are industrious and thrifty thus have been brought to the rural areas.

There are, however, certain problems which the settling of immigrants in the rural communities brings to the foreground. For example, to find a farm suited to a desired type of farming in respect to topography, soil type, size, water supply, and nearness to markets is a big problem for the average native farmer; for the average immigrant it is a much bigger problem, particularly since most recent immigrant farmers in New England are of urban origin. Much of the land of this section of the country has not been scientifically classified in sufficient detail to show effectively the agronomic factors that should be observed in the purchase of a given farm. This problem is particularly acute in New England, because, as the result of the glacial ice sheet, there is a great variety of soils in most localities and even on most farms. Moreover, the immigrant living for a period of years in our great cities and occupied with urban employment can hardly be expected to know what has already been done in the classification of soils or what agencies can give him trustworthy advice regarding the purchase of his farm and how to orient himself to rural community conditions.

If it is a serious problem for immigrants to become acquainted with the limitations of location and soil type for the kind of farming they wish to conduct, it is fully as important that they should learn to estimate as well their own personal and economic limitations as future farmers. As yet, the Farm Bureau does not seem to be adequately equipped to help them very effectively in the purchase of farms, for farms are usually purchased and residences of families transferred to them before the county agricultural agent has had an opportunity to make contacts with them. Thus the immigrant, who as a youth became acquainted with special types of farming in his native land, and later worked in our great cities where land values are high, may easily make serious mistakes. He may buy his farm in a poor location, pay too much for it, underestimate the capital required to run it, adopt an unsuitable type of farming, and fail in the organization of the farm business. At best, modern commercial farming is a complex and exacting vocation, poorly suited to those without adequate business ability and special training. In short, a number of cultural factors and a general lack of vocational information on modern American farming combine to make the purchase of farms by immigrants hazardous indeed. The situation surely constitutes a challenge to the various agencies that have for their purpose the transplanting of city people to farms and the vocational education of farmers.

PROBLEMS OF SOCIAL PARTICIPATION

Problems of social participation have already been mentioned. This subject needs more extended investigation than has been given

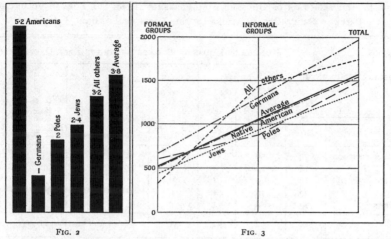

FIG. 2   FIG. 3

FIG. 2—The number of primary group organizations represented in the average household, Lebanon, Conn.; 144 households. From J. L. Hypes, *Social Participation in a Rural New England Town*, New York, 1927. For "Americans" read "Native Americans."

FIG. 3—Primary group attendance participation, Lebanon, Conn., average individual hours per household, 144 households. From same source as Figure 2.

it thus far, but such information as we have leads us to conclude that immigrants very often do not at first fit well into the organized community life of our rural New England towns. Table IV and Figure 2 taken from the writer's study of the town of Lebanon, Conn., furnish evidence in support of this statement. It will be observed that the native American households are represented in all the voluntary primary group organizations to which they are eligible. The immigrants, however, outside of the church and the high school, do not engage to any appreciable extent in any of the voluntary formal primary group activities of the locality, except the League of Jewish Women, which has both a socio-religious and a sex limitation to membership.[16] Computing from the original data on which the table is based, it is found that while the native stock constitutes about half the population of this particular town, it comprises three quarters of the organizational memberships.

Table V and Figure 3 likewise indicate that the immigrants in Lebanon participate much less in the *formal* community affairs than does the native stock, but far more in the *informal* affairs.[17] This is probably because the average native New Englander is schooled in the formal deliberative group action illustrated by the traditional town meeting. This sort of experience has not been had by many immigrants, who, consequently, are at a disadvantage in maintaining their interests in local government. Thus it appears that familism, characteristic of households of central and southern Europe, is so

TABLE IV—DISTRIBUTION OF HOUSEHOLD MEMBERSHIP AMONG THE FORMAL VOLUNTARY PRIMARY GROUP ORGANIZATIONS OF THE TOWN OF LEBANON, CONN.[a]

HOUSEHOLDS SURVEYED		NUMBER OF HOUSEHOLDS REPRESENTED IN EACH ORGANIZATION[b]						
Nationality	No.	Church and Its Subsidiary Organizations	Grange	American Men Lodge	D. A. R.	K. of P. Lodge	League of Jewish Women	Community Club
Native Americans	70	50	27	29	5	11	0	12
Poles	14	13	1	0	0	0	0	0
Germans	10	9	1	0	0	0	0	0
Jews	37	12	1	0	0	2	21	1
All others	13	8	1	2	0	0	0	3
Total	144	92	31	31	5	13	21	16

TABLE IV, Continued

HOUSEHOLDS SURVEYED		NUMBER OF HOUSEHOLDS REPRESENTED IN EACH ORGANIZATION							
Nationality	No.	Get-together Club	Dancing School	Athletic and Other Recreational Clubs	Economic Associations	High School	Town Meeting[b]	Out-of-Town Organizations	Average Percentage for All Organizations
Native Americans	70	7	16	7	7	10	59	16	26
Poles	14	0	1	0	2	2	0	13	16
Germans	10	0	0	0	0	0	1	9	14
Jews	37	1	2	1	1	10	7	6	13
All others	13	1	1	1	1	4	4	4	16
Total	144	9	20	9	11	26	71	48	20

[a] From J. L. Hypes, *Social Participation in a Rural New England Town*, p. 23.
[b] Households represented on the list of legal voters of the town are: native American, 66; Pole, 1; German, 2; Jew, 8; all others, 6. Note the amount of non-participation among the foreign households.

strong as to lead immigrants to seek the satisfaction of their social life largely at home and among other kinship groups.

Church membership and church attendance mean a great deal to most immigrants,[18] but since many of them are Jews and Catholics they seldom find efficient organizations of their own faith already set up in rural New England. Until fairly recently the rural areas of these states have been largely Protestant. Thus arises a problem of social organization; for Jews, Catholics, and Protestants generally

TABLE V—DISTRIBUTION OF HOUSEHOLD PARTICIPATION AMONG THE INFORMAL VOLUNTARY PRIMARY GROUP ACTIVITIES OF THE TOWN OF LEBANON, CONNECTICUT[a]

HOUSEHOLDS SURVEYED		NUMBER OF HOUSEHOLDS PARTICIPATING IN EACH ACTIVITY							
Nationality	Number	Holiday Events	Regular Vacations	Agricultural Fairs	Moving Pictures and Circuses	Out-of-town Business and Recreational Trips	At-Home Parties	Visiting Neighbors	Average Percentage
Native Americans .	70	65	21	57	56	53	46	64	74
Poles	14	10	3	2	5	12	8	13	54
Germans	10	6	2	3	7	8	4	10	57
Jews	37	22	13	6	21	32	17	32	55
All others	13	5	2	7	10	13	9	10	62
Total	144	108	41	75	99	118	84	129	64

NOTE: Compared with Table IV, this table shows that all nationalities participate more uniformly in the informal primary group activities than in the formal.

[a] J. L. Hypes, *Social Participation*, etc., p. 24.

do not seem inclined to come together for worship in the Protestant churches, and often an active resident religious leadership of the Jewish and the Catholic faiths is entirely wanting. As the result, many immigrants lack local church facilities, and no doubt there exists in their lives a longing for spiritual consolation and an ungratified desire for participation in church activities. The excitement, fears, worries, and loneliness that often accompany the moving of a family to a strange community and the financial hazards of relocating one's business call for adequate pastoral service and the guidance and the continued help of other social and educational agencies.

PROBLEMS OF SOCIALIZATION AND EDUCATION

The most important problems facing rural communities made up of both native and immigrant stocks are those of socialization. Dr. E. A. Ross defines socialization as "the development of the *we*-feeling in associates and their growth in capacity and will to act together."[19] It also involves the discovering and saving of valuable cultural contributions that may be brought into the total social complex by practically every immigrant group. If the native stock contributes experience in local government and the ability to carry on other socio-civic activities characteristic of our modern civilization, immigrant stocks may also contribute elements of art, music, industry, religious zeal, thrift, and other fine qualities characteristic of the good life in the open country. All of these contributions, both actual and potential, must be recognized mutually by the several social groups making up the population of rural New England and effectively integrated into a new and stronger society.

From the standpoint of social organization, the challenge for wise leadership and a socialized program of action is very great. The rural church of New England should make a critical inventory of its present status and the type of service it is rendering. Educational institutions of all kinds should secure a firmer grasp of the social composition and conditions of the rural population they serve and in the light of this information should reëxamine the objectives and the fruits of their organizational activities. The press, the civil government, philanthropic organizations, bankers, and business men generally, who have either a direct or an indirect interest in rural areas, should assume the responsibility of understanding something of the great dynamic forces that are bringing thither immigrants to become farmers and citizens. After they have obtained this information, it is their inescapable duty, both as vocational workers and as citizens, to contribute in every way possible toward a more complete socialization of these communities than now exists.

Researches Needed

From the foregoing it becomes clear that there are certain deep gaps in our knowledge of the rôle being played by immigrant stocks in rural New England. Obviously, fundamental changes are under way in the ecological distribution and the character of the rural population. The extent and the nature of these changes need to be described periodically, and the dynamic forces responsible for them need to be investigated. Current trends in the utilization of land for full-time and part-time farming, recreation, residence, forestation, and the like, need to be studied in the light of local, state, national, and world conditions, especially in relation to problems of regional planning, social organization, and tax reform. The heterogeneous folkways and mores brought about in the rural communities of New England through immigration and the intermixture of many social and cultural groups also need scientific description and comparison; until we understand these folkways and mores in the light of the total sociological matrix, we can never expect to cope with the conflicts to which the presence of heterogeneous cultural groups has given rise.

Sociological research must be directed toward the solution of problems such as these if rural social organization is to succeed in all its multifarious forms. More specifically, we may list a few matters that demand immediate attention:

1. The development of suitable means for advising immigrants on the purchase of farms.

2. Devising suitable means of discovering the educational needs of specific immigrant groups.

3. Devising adequate means of assembling and holding homogeneous adult immigrant groups for specfic units of education.

4. More especially, the development of suitable means for extending to specific socio-vocational classes of immigrant farm families the vocational education in agriculture and home economics offered by the Agricultural College Extension Service, the Farm Bureau, and other agencies.

5. Determining to what extent and in what ways the primary group association of the different ethnic groups in rural communities is possible and desirable.

6. The organization or reorganization of specific institutions in the community so as to make them serve more adequately the major social groups or the whole rural population.

7. Devising suitable methods of selection and the educational preparation of a specific type of rural leadership.

8. Ascertaining the changes in rural recreational or other cultural habits introduced by immigrants of urban origin.

9. The discovery of the social significance to rural New England of the immigrant summer boarder or other immigrant groups.

10. Determining the effect of the immigration laws and other selective agencies upon the type of immigrant coming into New England rural towns.

11. Determining the contribution of the newspaper, or any other specific agency, toward the socialization of rural communities.

12. Devising suitable research agencies for the guidance of specific forms and projects of rural social organization.

NOTES

[1] Besides the publications elsewhere cited in the notes the following works bear directly or indirectly upon the question of immigrant stocks in New England agriculture: D. C. Brewer, *Conquest of New England by the Immigrant*, New York, 1926; J. R. Commons, *Races and Immigrants in America* (new edit.), New York, 1920; M. R. Davie, *Constructive Immigration Policy*, New Haven, 1923; I. G. Davis and C. I. Hendrickson, *A Description of Connecticut Agriculture*, Storrs, Conn., 1925 (*Storrs Agric. Exper. Sta. Bull. No. 127*); H. P. Fairchild, *Immigration* (revised), New York, 1925; the same, *Immigrant Backgrounds*, New York, 1927; the same, *The Melting Pot Mistake*, Boston, 1926; G. W. Jenks, *The Character and Influence of Recent Immigration*, in *Questions of Public Policy: Addresses Delivered in the Page Lecture Series, 1913* . . . , New Haven, 1913, pp. 1–40; National Industrial Conference Board, *The Immigration Problem in the United States*, New York, 1923 (*Research Report 58*); John Phelan, *Readings in Rural Sociology*, New York, 1920, Chap. 4, *The Immigrant in Agriculture*; *Reports of the Immigration Commission*, Washington, 1911 (*61st Cong., 2nd Sess.*), which include (1) *Recent Immigrants in Agriculture*, prepared under the direction of A. E. Cance, 2 vols., constituting *Immigrants in Industries*, Part 24 (*Senate Doc. 633* [Vols. 83 and 84]), and (2) *Immigrants in Cities*, 2 vols. (*Senate Doc.*

338 [Vols. 66 and 67]); *Report of the Commission on Immigration on the Problems of Immigration in Massachusetts*, Boston, 1914 ([*Mass.*] *House* [*Doc.*] *2300*); E. A. Ross, *The Old World in the New*, New York, 1914; the same, *Standing Room Only?* New York, 1927.

[2] The statistical data presented in this section refer solely to the white population, whether native-born, native-born of foreign or mixed parentage, or immigrant. There are relatively few non-whites (negroes, Indians, Mexicans, etc.) in the rural districts of New England. The data are derived from *Fifteenth Census of the United States, 1930: Population*, Vol. 3, Washington, 1932. Most of the essential figures are tabulated in Tables I and II.

According to the 1930 census the total farm population of New England was 573,801. Of this number 74,718 were classified as "urban-farm" population because they happened to live in areas that the census designates as "urban." Though the urban-farm population has grown to considerable size, for practical reasons it has not been emphasized in this analysis (see p. 193, notes on Table I). Consequently, the references to foreign farming stock, foreign-born farmers, etc., should be interpreted as applying only to the census category of "rural-farm" population unless otherwise specifically designated. The terms "rural-farm," "urban-farm," "foreign-born," "foreign farming stock," etc., should be noted with care in order that the analysis may be followed clearly.

[3] Percentages of foreign-born in rural-farm population by sections, 1930: Pacific 13.6, New England 12.8, Middle Atlantic 7.4, West North Central 6.9, Mountain 6.3, East North Central 5.8, West South Central 0.9, South Atlantic 0.3, East South Central 0.1.

[4] Statistical support of this hypothesis is found in a recent intensive investigation in the town of Lebanon, Conn.—J. L. Hypes, *Social Participation in a Rural New England Town*, Bur. of Publications, Teachers College, Columbia University, New York, 1927. See also A. E. Cance, *Immigrant Rural Communities*, in *Country Life Annals*, Vol. 40, 1912.

[5] J. L. Hypes and J. F. Markey, *The Genesis to Farming Occupations in Connecticut*, Storrs, Conn., 1929 (*Storrs Agric. Exper. Sta. Bull. No. 161*), Table 7, p. 404. For a general description of the types of farming, the same, Chap. 2.

[6] Cheshire, East Windsor, Orange, Goshen, Ellington, and Killingworth.

[7] The chance expectancy of Germans in the group of dairy farmers was thus computed: there were 525 farmers altogether; 85 of these were dairy farmers. Thus 85/525 of all farmers were dairy farmers. There were 34 Germans in the 525 farmers; therefore, we should expect 85/525 of the 34 Germans, or 6 of them, to be dairy farmers. Since, in reality, only 3 were dairy farmers, the number of German farmers in dairying was 50 per cent of chance expectancy.

[8] Hypes and Markey, *op. cit.*, pp. 438–440.

[9] *Ibid.*, pp. 406–412, for a detailed classification of the soils included in this study.

[10] The census gives the following figures for Connecticut:

	1920	1930
Rural-farm population	90,297	80,247
Rural non-farm population	353,995	394,886

The 1920 figures include in the "rural" classification four towns that are included in the "urban" classification of the 1930 census (see p. 193, Table I, note d). The aggregate population of these four towns in 1920 was about 48,500. Of this number about 1800 constituted farm population, and the remaining 46,700 non-farm population. These figures must be deducted from the 1920 totals for Connecticut to render the latter comparable with the 1930 totals. When they have been so deducted the decrease in rural-farm population between 1920 and 1930 becomes about 8300, and the corresponding increase in the rural non-farm population becomes about 87,600. The farm population of 1920 in the four towns was estimated on the assumption that in these towns the ratio of farm population to number of farms was the same as in the state as a whole.

[11] Investigations bearing upon certain phases of this subject are now being con-ducted by the experiment stations in the states of Massachusetts and Connecticut.

[12] The statements are based largely on opinion; they need to be tested through extended research.

[13] J. L. Hypes, *Family Case Analyses*, Storrs, Conn., (Dept. of Sociology, Conn. Agric. College, mimeographed reports), Vol. 4, No. 1, 1931, Vol. 5, No. 1, 1932.

[14] Hypes, *Social Participation*, etc., p. 67.

[15] This is another statement of opinion that needs testing through research.

[16] Hypes, *Social Participation*, etc., p. 21. See also E. DeS. Brunner, *Immigrant Farmers and Their Children*, New York, 1929, Chap. 5. Membership in the public elementary schools was omitted in Table IV owing to the fact that it comes under the provisions of the compulsory attendance law, in which case membership is not wholly voluntary.

[17] Hypes, *Social Participation*, etc., pp. 21–32. For our purposes here primary social groups are termed *formal* if they have a tangible membership personnel and program, specifications for membership eligibility, and rules for participation, and if they designate a time and place for assembly. *Primary groups* are those char-acterized by intimate face-to-face association and coöperation—C. H. Cooley, *Social Organization*, New York, 1909, p. 23.

[18] Hypes, *Social Participation*, etc., pp. 25–27.

[19] E. A. Ross, *Principles of Sociology*, New York, 1920, p. 395.

THE COMPREHENSIVE SURVEY OF
RURAL VERMONT*

CONDUCTED BY THE VERMONT COMMISSION ON COUNTRY LIFE

Henry F. Perkins

THE ORIGIN OF THE COMPREHENSIVE SURVEY

FOR more than a century Vermont has been one of the most reliable seed beds of our national life. In the present generation as in the past an extraordinary number of her sons and daughters have risen to positions of distinguished service. How the fertility of this seed bed may be maintained and how the quality of the human stock may be conserved are questions that command the attention of the leaders of today in the Green Mountain State. To make a careful investigation of this problem the Eugenics Survey of Vermont was organized in 1925 under the leadership of the writer. After a two years' study of dependent and leading families of the state this work in eugenics led to the conviction that a comprehensive survey of the factors influencing life in Vermont was essential to the understanding of the human forces that make for progress in the state. As a result, in 1928 the Vermont Commission on Country Life was organized, with Dr. H. C. Taylor, agricultural economist, as director, to make a study of the environing factors influencing the life of the people of Vermont and to plan a program for their future guidance in improving rural living.

The plan of the enterprise was formed by long and careful consideration and with the advice of many wise counsellors. The Social Science Research Council worked over the project and gave it its formal approval as worthy of execution and of receiving financial

*Grateful acknowledgment is due to Dr. H. C. Taylor for his collaboration in the preparation of this paper.

There have been many surveys in New England of late. The reasons for selecting this one for special discussion in this volume are as follows:

1. The survey attempted to strike at the base of some of the most serious problems in New England life.

2. These problems are common to most of the rural sections of New England.

3. The Vermont survey was much more comprehensive in its scope than any other recent survey in New England. It was an attempt to study and plan for a region as a whole, to cut across the boundary lines between many special fields of investigation. In this respect it was in line with a widespread movement in the social sciences and illustrates a practical application of a type of study about which there is much discussion at the present time.

4. It is unique in that it is based on close coöperation between scientific specialists and the people concerned, as represented by their community leaders. Vermont people to the remarkable number of two hundred were grouped into committees chosen for their previous intelligent interest in special problems connected with rural life. They planned the study and directed the field investigators.

5. The survey was deliberately and consistently subordinated to its aim and object—the planning of better conditions of living. Only potentially useful facts were sought.—EDIT.

support. Administrative expenses were granted by a foundation and were received and administered by the University of Vermont. Substantial contributions in the way of coöperation were made by federal and state departments and bureaus and by several nation-wide

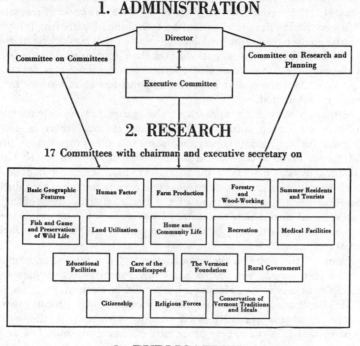

1. ADMINISTRATION

Director

Committee on Committees

Committee on Research and Planning

Executive Committee

2. RESEARCH

17 Committees with chairman and executive secretary on

Basic Geographic Features	Human Factor	Farm Production	Forestry and Wood-Working	Summer Residents and Tourists
Fish and Game and Preservation of Wild Life	Land Utilization	Home and Community Life	Recreation	Medical Facilities
Educational Facilities	Care of the Handicapped	The Vermont Foundation	Rural Government	
Citizenship	Religious Forces	Conservation of Vermont Traditions and Ideals		

3. PUBLICATION

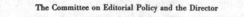

The Committee on Editorial Policy and the Director

FIG. 1—The Vermont Commission on Country Life, organization chart.

research committees, institutes, and societies. Of the fifty or more field workers engaged upon the enterprise, a majority were placed in the field by these participating bodies to assist the committees. They coöperated admirably with this unofficial, non-political, voluntary Commission of about three hundred Vermonters.

RESULTS AND FINDINGS

The ambitious range of subjects covered made of this survey a well-nigh comprehensive project (Fig. 1). Only such aspects of rural life were omitted from the program as were dangerous politically or were already well taken care of by existing agencies. These omissions were dictated by policy and economy. Wasteful and prejudicial controversies were conspicuously lacking.

The Country Life Commission held what was advertised as its "final meeting" in June, 1931. Within a few weeks the report of the Commission was published in book form under the title *Rural Vermont: A Program for the Future, by Two Hundred Vermonters.* With very little effort to describe the technique of gathering information the committees submitted for inclusion in this book their findings on the basis of the investigations and their recommendations based on the findings and on seasoned opinion. Each committee presented a plan for the future, and both courage and foresight are evident in the plans submitted.

Although very little appears in the report that is calculated in any way to arouse animosity for political reasons, there is plenty of basis for argument concerning some of the proposed policies, and this is perhaps one of the most promising aspects of the Commission's work. So many questions are touched upon concerning which Vermonters have positive ideas one way or the other that during the time since the publication of the book no little discussion has been aroused throughout the state. This discussion is bound to result in more careful perusing of the report and more exacting scrutiny of the recommendations.

Some of the detailed recommendations of the several committees will be mentioned, but first a surprising repetition of fundamental principles in one report after another should be noticed.

At least one of these has an important geographical bearing. A number of the committees expressed belief that, if the present town system in Vermont could be rather drastically modified or entirely superseded, the state would be benefited in regard to the special problems considered. The committees pointed out that Vermonters are already doing their trading at the nearest or most advantageous points irrespective of town boundaries and that in the school system a considerable amount of readjustment has already taken place. The school districts, each presided over by a superintendent, have broken over the old limits of the town and have to a considerable extent followed the "larger parish" plan that has been tried by the churches.

A greater participation in the administration of state affairs by volunteer boards is another recommendation which received considerable emphasis. The Fish and Game Committee feel that a Commission or Board supervising or advising the Commissioner would guarantee more uniform state-wide policies and administration. Other committees have made similar recommendations, and if one may judge by the generous and earnest application of thought to the problems of the state by the members of Commission groups there is every reason to believe that a much larger proportion of the citizens

of Vermont than heretofore might readily be brought into the planning
and administering of her affairs. This would mean more "government
by the people."

Land utilization is another topic touched upon by several committees. The committees on Fish and Game, on Recreation, on
Summer Residents and Tourists, and on Agriculture and Forestry
have found this an unusually fertile field for investigation and experiment. The mountainous character of the state, its beauty of landscape,
its accessibility to the great cities of the East suggest to many minds
the feasibility of using Vermont as a great vacation playground.
Many of the submarginal areas of no great value agriculturally or
industrially can be used for camps, summer homes, state forests
and otherwise turned to account for recreation.

The definitely human problems of rural life studied by the several
committees are closely bound up with the proper utilization of land.
One of these problems is that of relocating a good many Vermont
homes now situated within areas where it is difficult or impossible
to maintain an adequate standard of living.

A copy of *Rural Vermont* marked for passages advocating better
roads and planning and zoning gives forceful proof that these matters
were felt to be of outstanding importance in the future development
of the state. The recommendations, if carried out, would greatly
facilitate many more specialized betterment measures.

Consideration of geographic factors is introduced in many of the
committee reports. The topography of Vermont, the state's relation
to neighboring states and cities, its contiguity to Canada, and various
other aspects of descriptive and physical geography are recognized
as having a direct and constant effect upon the lives of Vermonters,
no matter what their occupations or social status may be. The committees point out that existing physical conditions are not sufficiently
considered by the people themselves or in matters of government.
A splendid relief model of Vermont was produced by the Committee
on Basic Geographic Features and has been an object of great interest
in the Fleming Museum at Burlington. This is one of the visible
and permanent contributions of the Commission, and replicas and
process copies will probably be available for study in many places
in Vermont and elsewhere.

The recommendations made by a single committee, chosen almost
at random as an example, show how some of the proposals apply
particularly to the interests of the special committee itself, whereas
others impinge on the provinces of various other groups. The Committee on Medical Facilities presents and discusses the following
suggestions: (1) group practice of physicians, (2) subsidy of physicians
by towns, (3) use of medical students as assistants to physicians,
(4) organization of physicians in specified areas, (5) employment of

resident nurses by towns, (6) increased use of attendant nurses, (7) public health training of nurses as part of the hospital curriculum, (8) some method of utilizing larger health units, (9) instruction of local health officers at state expense, (10) increased resources for inspecting and controlling camps, recreation places, and tourist lodging houses, (11) increased efforts to secure immunizing of school children against communicable diseases.

It will be noted that (8) brings up the question of larger health units just as the Committee on Educational Facilities argues for the need for larger local educational units.

It may not be out of place to call special attention to the Vermont Foundation. This is the first state-wide independently organized body having for its purpose the receiving of bequests and gifts of money to be administered for the benefit of the people of the state and in conformity with the spirit of the gift. This Foundation was not only recommended by a committee of the Commission but has actually been set up and is functioning. A considerable sum, known to be allocated in wills for certain specified purposes, has already been bequeathed to the Vermont Foundation for administration. Adjustments to changing conditions rather than adherence to the circumscribed limitations formerly believed to be necessary are wisely provided. Education of young people for careers in such fields as letters or music, all nonsectarian charities, and all other worthy objects now provided for inadequately, if at all, by existing agencies will be encouraged by this means.

At this time when the financial depression is focusing attention on the need of greater economy in state as well as private expenditures, it is worthy of particular note that in general the recommendations of the Commission have been made with due caution, to avoid heavy inroads on public funds. This is decidedly different from the recommendations of some surveys. Perhaps it is the native Vermont thrift again coming to the front. Many of the recommendations definitely contemplate a saving of money as, for example, one of those made by the Committee on the Care of the Handicapped. This has to do with the administration of poor relief and advocates the abolition of the present system of town poor farms, which is regarded as wasteful and inefficient. Wherever improvements can be effected without any or considerable increase in appropriations, surely there ought to be little question of the adoption of the plan.

PROGRESS SINCE THE SURVEY

After the "final meeting" in June, 1931, the funds of the subsidy lapsed, and the Comprehensive Survey submitted its reports and came to an end. Since then, contrary to the predictions of some skeptics, interest in the work of the Commission has increased rather than lessened. Promotion of the program has gone on by means of education, in the definite adoption of policies, and in plans for a permanent organization. One cannot predict the form that will be assumed by the Commission or its successor, but several of the committees as well as the central organization have emphatically refused to go out of existence. A meeting of the Commission is soon to be held for the purpose of making plans and effecting a reorganization.

Rural Vermont has been used and will be used during the coming season as a textbook for a large number of study clubs, and those who were active in the Commission have addressed many audiences on the program as a whole and on its various single aspects. By these means hundreds of people have for the first time been made directly aware of the importance of this whole enterprise to their local problems. A spirit of state-wide coöperation in the program of improvement, built up and fostered during the three years of the survey, is being crystallized and energized.

The Committee on Traditions and Ideals had ready before the close of the survey the *Green Mountain Series*, a set of four fascinating books on Vermont biography, prose, folk-songs, and ballads and verse. Even more important has been the stimulus given by the Committee to the acquisition of greater familiarity with the traditions and ideals of the state—a stimulus that is bound to increase in strength as time goes on. A series of *Green Mountain Pamphlets* is now in prospect to accompany the four books. These pamphlets will deal with various subjects of general interest not to be found in any works now available. The *Green Mountain Series* has had a splendid sale already and constitutes another tangible monument to the work of the Commission.

Conclusion

In plan, scope, methods, and accomplishments the survey has had certain unusual features. It was emphatically only a means to an end. Fact finding was from the beginning subordinated to the purpose of bringing about real, specific, and lasting benefits. The survey was set up merely as necessary machinery through which the Commission hoped and expected, by means of its own continuing organization or through other agencies, present or future, to initiate such improvements and benefits.

The many committees shown on the chart actually operated and made their several contributions to investigations and recommendations covering a remarkably large part of the total complex of environmental forces. It was an attempt to study and plan for a region as a whole, cutting across the boundary lines between the fields of economics, sociology, and the natural sciences.

The survey accomplished the notable achievement of enlisting a large body of leading citizens in a common enterprise irrespective of individual bias towards special problems. A new habit of thinking in regard to a whole region was thereby set in motion and, along with it, the determination to continue.

The subordination of trained technique to the planning of the committees of Vermonters was perhaps unusual. The survey attempted to strike at the base of some of the most serious problems in country life—problems that are common to most of the rural sections of New England. The attack upon these problems was, so far as possible, scientific.

As to accomplishments, the phase of the situation most gratifying to contemplate at this writing is the activity since the conclusion of the survey, the actual adoption of not a few committee recommendations, the increasing and serious use of the report of the Commission and of the other publications resulting from the survey, and the cheering prospect of a continued organization.

REFERENCES

There follows a list of references to the outstanding publications resulting from the Comprehensive Survey of Rural Vermont. They may be obtained from the Office of the Vermont Commission on Country Life, 162 College St., Burlington, Vt.

Rural Vermont: A Program for the Future, by Two Hundred Vermonters, The Vermont Commission on Country Life, Burlington, Vt., 1931. Contains the reports of the committees of the Commission. Several of these reports were also reprinted in 1931 as Circulars of the Vermont Agricultural Extension Service, Burlington, as follows: Rural Home and Community Life in Vermont (Circular No. 68; reports of the Committees on Rural Home and Community Life and on Recreation); The Agriculture and Forestry of Vermont (Circular No. 66; reports of the Committees on Agriculture, on Climate, on Soils, and on Forestry and Woodworking Industries); Summer Residents and Tourists in Vermont (Circular No. 67; reports of the Committees on Land Utilization and on Summer Residents and Tourists). The report of the Committee on Educational Facilities for Rural People has also been reprinted.

The Green Mountain Series, consisting of the following books, all published at Brattleboro, Vt., 1931: W. H. Crockett, edit., Vermonters: A Book of Biographies; A. W. Peach and H. G. Rugg, edits., Vermont Prose: A Miscellany; H. H. Flanders and George Brown, edits., Vermont Folk Songs and Ballads; W. J. Coates and Frederick Tupper, edits., Vermont Verse: An Anthology.

Genieve Lamson, A Study of Agricultural Populations in Selected Vermont Towns: A Report Prepared for the Committee on the Human Factor of the Vermont Commission on Country Life, Burlington, 1931.

Allan Peebles, A Survey of Medical Facilities of the State of Vermont, Univ. of Chicago Press, Chicago, 1930 (Publs. of the Committee on the Costs of Medical Care No. 13).

Selective Migration from Three Rural Vermont Towns, Burlington, 1931 (Fifth Annual Report, Eugenics Survey of Vermont).

The Vermont Foundation, The Vermont Commission on Country Life, Burlington, 1931.

NEW ENGLAND FORESTS: BIOLOGICAL FACTORS[1]

R. T. Fisher

The Original Climax Forest

WHEN settlements were first established on our coast, early in the seventeenth century, New England was almost entirely forested. The accompanying map indicates the general composition and the distribution of the tree species originally characteristic of the district. Broadly speaking, the occurrence of these regional units of forest is governed by the climate, physiography, and soils. Thus northern New England was in the main covered with spruce and fir and the so-called northern hardwoods: beech, yellow and white birch, and sugar maple. Southern New England was mainly dominated by a large variety of hardwood species more characteristic of the Middle States, in which a number of species of oak and hickory predominated. Between these two extremes was a large more or less transitional area, roughly described as "Central New England," where white pine and hemlock mingled in varying proportions both with species characteristic of the adjacent regions to the north and south, and with certain others, such as red oak and white ash, not originally so abundant in either. None of these regional units was sharply distinct, but each exhibited extensions due to the effect of elevation or of fundamental soil composition upon climate and moisture. Thus the northern forest extended well down into Berkshire and Hampshire counties into Massachusetts, along the higher elevations of the Berkshire Hills, and in a few elevated spots in Worcester County. Similarly the oak forests of southern New England came north for a considerable distance into the lowlands of southeastern Massachusetts and up the Connecticut River valley. Cape Cod, almost a climatic and geological unit by itself, bore a forest principally of pine and oak.

In size and outward appearance these so-called original forests were in marked contrast to most of the woods of today. In the main the stands were mixed, often containing a great variety of species of many sizes and ages. If we disregard extremes of situation—such as mountain summits, sand plains, or swamps—and consider only the preponderance of area where temperature and moisture were not subject to wide variations, the life history of these forests, whether in the north or south, was much the same. Over central New England, for example, one may picture a forest in which broad-leaved trees

---

[1] For notes see below, p. 222.

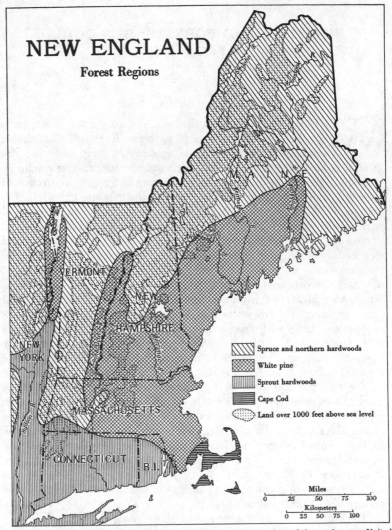

FIG. 1—Forest regions of New England. Based on map of forest regions of the northeastern United States, by P. W. Stickel, Northeastern Forest Experiment Station, Jan., 1927. Altitudes generalized from U. S. Geol. Survey's map of the United States, 1 : 2,500,000, 1914.

and hemlock formed a dense stand from eighty to one hundred feet high, above which, either by small groups or single trees and varying greatly in abundance, white pines reached a height of 150 feet or more. It is generally believed that such a forest was self-maintaining, in other words that the losses through old age or injury were recruited from younger and smaller trees gradually developing underneath, so that over periods of centuries and on the average the representation of species remained about the same and the general size and appearance of the forest was unchanged. This condition of equilibrium is what is generally called a "climax forest." It means that if the stand is truly self-maintaining, all of the species represented are long-lived and more or less capable of reproducing and surviving for long periods under the heavy shade and prolonged suppression of the larger trees.

CHANGES IN THE CLIMAX FOREST

It is a popular if not a scientific idea that the primeval forest was almost as changeless as the hills. If the ordinary physical factors of temperature, rainfall, and the other manifestations of climate were regular in their operation and not complicated either by exceptional changes or by the influence of man, as on sheltered sites with deep soils, some forests might indeed remain unchanged for indefinite centuries. If, however, we study—as has recently been done[2]—the detailed records of life history in such original forests as still remain, we find evidence, even with no human factors in operation but the aboriginal Indian, that there must have been over long periods important changes in the distribution of species and the character of the forests within each of our climatic regions. Undoubtedly forest fires are more prevalent and destructive today than when the Pilgrims landed; but there is convincing evidence that everywhere fires were of periodic occurrence both from the practice of the Indians and occasionally from lightning. The principal difference between the aboriginal forest fires and those of today is that the earlier fires were probably less destructive in the larger woods and less prone to cover big tracts in a single burn. In addition to fires it is only necessary to consider longer stretches of time, such as centuries or more, to find unmistakable signs of other destructive agencies: windthrow, generally occurring on uplands or exposed ridges and often prostrating large areas of trees; lightning, which sometimes kills a dozen or fifteen trees with one bolt; ice storms, shattering many acres of tree tops; and, probably in the wake of these, fluctuating attacks from injurious forest insects or disease. It is likely, especially on drier and more exposed sites, that such periodic calamities as these, upsetting for a time and sometimes over large areas the equilibrium between local climate and soils and the natural requirements of tree species, were collectively the most powerful influence governing pre-Colonial forest history. Without the recurrence of fires we should not have had the heavy forests of pine in central New England reported in some localities by the early settlers. It is likely also that, without these periodic upsets providing breaks and exposures in the ancient forests, many of our short-lived, light-seeded species such as gray birch, pin cherry, and aspen would have been even more rare and restricted in distribution than they actually were in the original forest. Thus, while areas of big timber certainly predominated in the early forests as traversed by the pioneers, there must also have occurred many areas where reversions to younger woods or shorter-lived species were in progress. As a background for the study and understanding of forest succession and growth, and for interpreting the many and varied forms of degeneration that have followed settlement and development, the original or climax forest is invaluable. It is unfortunate for scientific as well as economic reasons that today less than 5 per cent of existing forests date back to the settlement of New England.

To understand what has happened to the remaining 95 per cent of our original forest area, it is necessary to trace the progress of the use of land down to the present day.[3] In such a complicated development only the principal tendencies can be touched upon. As regards ultimate effect upon the forest, we may almost disregard the century from 1600 to 1700. This was in the main a period of pioneering. For the most part the settlements and clearings, at first mainly for agricultural purposes, were confined to coastal strips of a few leagues in width or to the bottom lands of important rivers, like the Connecticut. Aside from the initial clearing, such timber as was used and the little that was exported was culled at convenient distances from the sea or along the principal rivers. Furthermore, much of the land thus cut or cleared has continued to be devoted to agricultural, industrial, or residential uses and may be omitted from consideration of forest history in general. The bulk of the forest area, however, did not begin to be seriously altered until the early eighteenth century with the settlement and gradual development of the interior.

In the forest history of the last two hundred years we may distinguish two main types of land use: farming and lumbering. Although at the start and in the typical small community of the eighteenth century the two forms of use were combined, the lumber business as it became better organized spread into the wilder portions of Maine, New Hampshire, and Vermont, where farming was difficult or impossible. We may thus for simplicity consider southern New England, including roughly the area south of northern New Hampshire, central Maine, and northern Vermont, as a region primarily affected by agricultural settlement and the rest of the region, in general the wilder, colder, and more mountainous parts, as a district affected largely if not exclusively by lumbering. Each of these two main types of land use has had a profound effect upon the character and productiveness of the forests of today.

FOREST HISTORY OF THE FARMING DISTRICT

In the farming district practically the entire area came to be covered by organized towns, most of them settled and incorporated

during the first half of the eighteenth century. A steadily increasing
area was cleared for crops or grazing, and the remainder of the original
forest was utilized little by little for lumber and building material,
generally used locally and manufactured in the small water mills
which were common in every town. Early census figures for Worcester
County, Massachusetts,[4] whose history is typical of most of the region,
show that the percentage of cleared land rose steadily until about
1830 and at its maximum included from 55 to 65 per cent of the total
land area, exclusive of ponds, swamps, etc.

About 1850, with the opening of the West, the development of
the principal railroads, and soon afterward with the drain of the Civil
War, land abandonment set in in earnest. For a time the effect
upon the area in farms was partly neutralized by the clearing of new
land hitherto in forest; but the decline has continued down to the
present day so that nearly seven million acres were thus left to revert
to nature between 1880 and 1925. From 1850 on, while New England
farming and farming populations were rapidly declining, the old fields
and pastures were seeding up to new forest, much of it pure stands of
white pine. Meanwhile, as the local supplies of original forest disappeared, wood-working industries, originating in the early towns and
gradually developing with the improvement of markets and transportation, began to use these second-growth forests, many of which by 1890
had reached merchantable size. From that date to 1925, for wooden
boxes and woodenware alone, fifteen billion feet of pine lumber have
been cut, over 80 per cent of which originated on old farms abandoned
since 1845.[5] At a fair average yield per acre of 10,000 feet, taking
good stands with poor, this is equivalent to one and one-half million
acres and represents a manufactured value of not less than four
hundred million dollars. More than half of this generous sum went
to the populations of the towns where the timber grew, an unearned
income which in many communities has gone far to keep the remaining
farms alive.[6]

Now that the use of old-field timber has been in progress for more
than a generation, still a third phase of land use, or, perhaps more
properly, disuse, is well advanced, and is represented by an immense
and increasing extent of cut-over area, much of it covered with comparatively worthless stands of inferior hardwoods or underbrush, and
much of it a frequent prey to forest fire. At the same time, especially
in southern New England where hardwood forests predominated, great
areas that had not been cleared for farms but were periodically cut for
local wood supplies became more and more degenerate in composition
and vigor through the drain of repeated sprouting from the same
stumps with less and less renewal by new seedlings. Today in the upland farming districts of New England the amount of area to be classed
only as woodland is at least 60 per cent, or a little more than what it

was a hundred years ago. Nature has produced a second crop of timber; but, according to any present or foreseeable use, the third crop is a liability rather than an asset.

FOREST HISTORY OF THE LUMBERING DISTRICT

If we now consider the history of forests in the northern or lumbering district, we find a similar but less rapid decline in value and productiveness. In the earlier days of lumbering, especially in the state of Maine, only the larger, better trees were cut, at first white pine and later, as pine became exhausted about 1870, spruce, which was for a long time the principal building material in New England. Later, with the development of modern sawmills and more efficient logging methods, the forests were cut more heavily. Always there has been a steady reduction in the better species of timber trees; and, though the earlier partial cuttings had a tendency to allow replacements in the forest and thus keep it moderately productive, the lumber areas of the north as a whole showed a gradual increase in the relatively inferior hardwood element as compared with spruce and pine. Here also, as in the farming district, cut-over lands were apt to burn destructively and over large areas and thus occasion a serious deterioration in the quality and quantity of forest production.

DEPLETION OF THE FORESTS

Thus in two centuries the people of New England have used up all but a scant two million acres of an original forest covering thirty-nine of the forty million acres included in the six states. Not less than fifteen million of these acres became farm and pasture, of which at least ten million have been abandoned to revert to forest and thus accidentally to produce a supplementary crop of timber, the best of which has now also been cut down. There are still about twenty-seven million acres in woodland, but of this more than half is covered with comparatively valueless trees or undesirable species. For a region two fifths of which is probably unfit for anything but the growing of timber this situation is economically discouraging. But even less favorable as related to the problem of restoring forests for the future are the less obvious indirect effects produced by this period of destructive or neglectful use upon the physical and biological factors of the forest—for example, the condition and distribution of tree species, the prevalence of pests, the fertility of soils, the fluctuations of wild life.

EFFECTS OF FOREST WEEDS

Today perhaps the greatest natural obstacle of all to successful forestry, at least in central New England, is the extent to which forest weeds, both trees and underbrush, have multiplied as compared with the species of greatest use and value. As long as most of the land was occupied either with tillage or pasture or by the still uncut areas of original forest in which only the long-lived and better timber trees survived, the weed element remained in abeyance. Thus, during the earlier abandonment of farm lands it was still white pine as the species most adapted to prompt reseeding that took possession of the fields and pastures; but, as time went on and more land was abandoned, the light-seeded, fast-growing species—gray birch, pin cherry, poplar, red maple, alder, to say nothing of many kinds of shrubs—were able to rival the pine and outstrip the larger, heavier-seeded hardwoods in spreading over vacant lands. Still further impetus was added to the spread and development of forest weeds after the pine wood lots began to be cut and left, as they almost invariably were, to come up to a thicket of hardwoods. In such thickets the stock of valuable seedlings that originated under the pine stand is gradually suppressed by the faster-growing shrubs and forest weeds. Less rapidly but nevertheless steadily a similar process has been going on in the wilder regions where lumbering has been the only treatment of land. Fires also, which only provide further areas more adapted to poor than to good species of trees, have aggravated the process. The increase in forest weeds as compared with desirable timber trees during the last two hundred years is beyond estimate. In central New England it is probable that there are at least five hundred acres of forest weeds to one of good timber, actual or prospective.

DETERIORATION OF SOIL

That our present woodland is so much of it intrinsically of little use is not the end of the trouble. Since the present associations of species occur almost wholly as results of farm abandonment, lumbering, or fire, they are often physiologically unsuited to the sites they occupy and therefore, in the absence of fire, tend gradually to revert to some other mixtures more adapted to the local factors of soil and climate. Conversely, these temporary or transitional forests may often have an injurious effect upon the current fertility of the soil, so that, even where a given kind of timber may be commercially valuable, it does not follow that it may be safely reckoned upon as a permanent forest crop for the land. A case in point is the large area of old-field pine already referred to, which has proved so valuable a raw material for local woodworking industries during the last generation. These stands, originating on medium to better soils often improved over their primitive condition by a century of farming or grazing, exhibited in early life a rapid growth. Experience and research at the Harvard Forest[7] have shown that such pine stands gradually arrest most of the organic decomposition that in a healthy forest tends to maintain soil fertility and at the same time exhaust the original top soil, so that at fifty to sixty years of age their growth suddenly falls off. On the other hand, the replacement of such pine stands with certain associations of deciduous trees has proved beneficial by restoring under the more active influence of temperature, moisture, and light, the metabolism of organic materials that is indispensable to the productiveness of a forest soil. It is axiomatic that cultivation and fertilization as applied to agriculture will always be impracticable in forestry. The only way in which these processes can be kept up in forests is by the use of such species as will maintain the necessary decomposition of forest débris and favor the biological influences—earthworms, fungi, etc.—that supplement the action of physical factors. Not all natural forests accomplish this, since in all cases the general regional climate is the deciding factor; but many associations are beneficial, especially if properly managed. To build up a favorable forest soil may be the work of years. With our present inferior second-growth forests, soils have widely deteriorated: first, by the transition to unfavorable mixtures of species or stands of inadequate density; and second, and often repeatedly, because forest fires have consumed the organic element in the soil.

INSECT PESTS AND DISEASES

This general transition from mixed forests of older woods into smaller stands of short-lived or enfeebled trees has brought with it increasingly favorable conditions for insect pests and disease. In the original forests the absence of large areas of any one type of vegetation of uniform age or condition prevented the undue development of pests peculiar to any given species. In the woods of today we find immense tracts of relatively unhealthy forest running strongly to one type of mixture or often to pure stands and, in consequence of their life history, less vigorous than the forests they have replaced. How this has affected insects is indicated by the history of the white pine weevil, a native insect and now one of the most destructive pests of white pine plantations. Relatively harmless in the original forests, where pine did not often grow in continuous bodies and where the percentage of younger stands at any one time was low, this insect found in the period of farm abandonment and the widespread reversion of these lands to pure pine a favorable environment on an immense scale. Today the white pine weevil is so abundant and widespread as to destroy a large part of the value of most pine stands within its range.

RELATION OF WILD LIFE TO FOREST ENVIRONMENT

Among biologists the essential control of wild life by the character of the environment is admitted, if not yet understood in detail. A significant example may be found in the way in which the known fluctuations of the partridge and the woodcock in central New England have followed the progress of land abandonment, reversion to pine wood, and subsequently to various mixtures of hardwood. Neither of these species was naturally abundant in the heavy forests of early New England; but from 1870 to 1900, during the period of most rapid reversion of old fields to forest, both species reached the greatest abundance recorded by sportsmen. That the partridge has since steadily declined in abundance and the woodcock, at least recently and locally, increased may well be accounted for by the changes that have taken place in the character of the cover and attendant food supply.[8]

The pine wood developed on old fields and pastures, together with more or less hawthorn, running blackberry, viburnum, blueberry, apple trees, and birches. The process of change from shrubby field to forest was gradual, and during the first twenty to thirty years the combination of vegetation was ideal for the partridge—increasing shelter, varied food plants, and open dusting places. From then on the pine rapidly closed up; and most of the food plants, even the old apple trees, were killed out. Since the bulk of the pine woodlands reached this condition twenty to thirty years ago, the favorable cover was reduced to the margins where the pine gave way to brushy openings or birch thickets more characteristic of recently abandoned fields. Thus there was going on a progressive reduction in good cover even before the logging activities of the last generation.

But if the maturing and removal of the old-field pine has deprived the partridge of more and more of his best habitat, the process has, in many cases, accomplished the opposite for the woodcock. This came about through the soil changes referred to above. In the soil under a pine wood there are no earthworms. With the change to certain species of hardwood, if the situation is not too wet or too dry, the original bed of leaf litter disappears in from fifteen to twenty years, the current fall of hardwood leaves decays almost annually, and the resulting fine humus merges with the mineral soil, sometimes to a depth of ten inches or more. There results a rich brown loam in which earthworms are characteristically abundant. On many such areas, once the new forest has begun to close up, breeding woodcock have appeared in numbers. This transformation is not universal but is apparently confined to certain combinations of sites and tree species. In sum total, however, the change has taken place in favorable spots over wide areas. Thus, there would seem to be reason for the recent abundance of woodcock in northeastern covers.

THE FUTURE OF NEW ENGLAND FORESTS

Looking to the future it is plain that, even though rapid changes in utilization and the recent decline in the demand for native timber make it difficult to predict what kinds of forest should be the objective of forestry in the several regions, nevertheless, it is safe to expect that from one fourth to one third of New England's area must be used, if at all, as forest. If it is to be used as forest, its permanence and productiveness, whether for wood, safeguarding of stream flow, protection of wild life, or recreation, will have to be secured by a proper understanding and control of the biological and physical factors that have hitherto been so seriously upset. Much of the knowledge necessary for this kind of management is still lacking. The required principles, however, are evident. In many ways the conditions obtaining in the original virgin forests were favorable, but reproducing the complexities of their life history will not make a productive forest. Their very stability involved also an undue slowness of growth, a high percentage of defect, and, as compared with ideal conditions, relatively inactive soils. On the other hand, although much of our second-growth timber has had periods of excellent commercial value and has exhibited very rapid growth—as in the case of the white pine wood lot—such types do not offer a safe model for sound forestry. Being in nearly every case the product of human interference with natural conditions, these types are almost invariably unstable, both as to composition of species and soil conditions. The silviculture of the future will copy the virgin forest by selecting the most valuable, fast-growing, or hardy species so mingled as to secure the greatest possible mutual protection from insects and disease, and the best influence upon soil metabolism and upon the quality of wood. It will follow to some extent also the more uniform density and concentrated production shown by the best of the second-growth forests, in which, for brief periods at least and for certain types, timely exposures of the soil and the predominance of certain beneficial species have produced high yields of wood as well as active fertility. Whatever may prove to be the economic or social objectives of New England forest policy, it will be necessary in the long run to understand and control an essential equilibrium of biological factors, on the one hand to avoid the wasteful complications of the natural process and, on the other, to restore and maintain the resources in good timber and productive soil that human occupation has by now so greatly reduced.

NOTES

[1] For additional bibliographical data see the notes to Dean H. S. Graves's paper entitled *Forest Economics and Policy in New England*, in the present volume, pp. 224–236, below. For a general description of New England forests see R. C. Hawley and A. F. Hawes, *Forestry in New England: A Handbook of Eastern Forest Management*, New York, 1912; the same, *Manual of Forestry for the Northeastern United States, Being Vol. 1 of "Forestry in New England,"* Revised, New York, 1918, 1925.—EDIT.

[2] *Life History of the Climax Forest on the Pisgah Tract, Winchester, New Hampshire*, Harvard Forest Study (unpublished manuscript).

[3] A. C. Cline and C. R. Lockard, *Mixed White Pine and Hardwood*, Petersham, Mass., 1925 (*Harvard Forest Bull. No. 8*). [See also R. M. Harper, *Changes in the Forest Area of New England in Three Centuries*, in *Journ. of Forestry*, Vol. 16, 1918, pp. 442–451.—EDIT.]

[4] Early decadal census of Worcester County, Massachusetts (original in possession of the American Antiquarian Society, Worcester, Mass.).

[5] *Analysis of the Wooden Box Industry in New England: A Study Made for the New Hampshire Lumbermen's Association by the Harvard Forest, Distributed Among Members of the Industry by the New England Council*, 1926.

[6] R. W. Averill, W. B. Averill, and W. I. Stevens, *A Statistical Forest Survey of Seven Towns in Central Massachusetts*, Petersham, Mass., 1923 (*Harvard Forest Bull. No. 6*).

[7] B. G. Griffith, E. W. Hartwell, and T. E. Shaw, *The Evolution of Soils as Affected by the Old Field White Pine-Mixed Hardwood Succession in Central New England*, Petersham, Mass., 1930 (*Harvard Forest Bull. No. 15*).

[8] R. T. Fisher, *Our Wild Life and the Changing Forest*, in *The Sportsman*, Vol. 5, March, 1929, p. 65.

FOREST ECONOMICS AND POLICY IN NEW ENGLAND

Henry S. Graves

THE forests of New England are an asset of far-reaching economic importance. In the past they have played a significant part in the development of the region, especially in maintaining the industrial vitality of the rural sections. For three centuries the forests have been subject to the cutting of timber for industrial and domestic use; thousands of acres have been devastated or gravely injured by fire; waves of infestations by insects and fungi have swept over portions of the forest; and windstorms and other destructive agencies have taken their toll through the years. In spite of the long continued attrition of past abuse, there still remains a surprisingly large amount of timber, particularly in the three northern states; and elsewhere volunteer stands of younger growth, struggling against continued maltreatment and neglect, await the corrective measures of forestry to rehabilitate them for productive service.

Forests render varied services in the economic life of a region. These include: supplying a basic raw material of great importance; sustaining industrial establishments dependent on forests; contributory support of local communities through taxation; auxiliary aid to agriculture; contribution of substantial tonnage to railroads; conservation of the sources of water; checking of torrents and regulation of the regimen of streams; prevention of erosion; provision of favorable conditions for the perpetuation of wild life; protection of scenic values of public importance; and creation of facilities for public recreation in manifold forms. The value of forests to the people of a region is measured by the extent to which these services are obtained. The forest is a renewable land resource. Its various benefits may be made permanent and continuous, if the forest is properly handled. Forest lands are of little advantage in the long run to a region like New England, if periodically they are wholly or largely stripped of timber and reduced in productiveness. This necessitates a long process of restoration, with great industrial loss. In order to obtain from the forest the best economic service, there are required: a sustained timber capital yielding annually material for the industries, prompt replacement after the removal of the mature trees, and the maintenance of a forest cover most advantageous for the general protective benefits that may be derived from well-managed forests. Such a condition does not exist in New England at the present time, owing to overexploitation and abuse.

The Forests of New England

The forests of New England cover about 27,250,000 acres. This represents about 68 per cent of the land surface of the region. In Maine 78 per cent of the land is classed as forest, which is a larger ratio than in any other state in the Union. Even in Massachusetts, Connecticut, and Rhode Island, which in density of population rank among the first four states, more than 45 per cent of the land is in forest. The dominant position of New England in industry has tended to obscure the fact that there is a forest land resource of such magnitude. The economic value of forests, however, is not measured by area alone. The character and condition of the forests, the quantity and quality of the timber, the potentialities for future production, the location of the forests with reference to transportation and markets, the character of ownership, the utility of the forests for purposes other than the production of raw materials, and various other factors must be considered in measuring their value to the community.

For the purposes of the present discussion, the forests may be divided into two broad categories; first, the upland portions of the northern tier of states, where there are extensive areas of continuous forests; and second, the forests in the agricultural zone, which intermingle with land cleared for agricultural, industrial, and other purposes. The forests of the first class contain the bulk of the old timber of merchantable character; they produce the greater part of the lumber and pulpwood credited to New England; they support many important industrial establishments; portions of them are in large ownership; and in many other ways the economic problems are very different from those prevailing in the forests of the agricultural region. These forests are chiefly within the zone of spruce, balsam fir, and the northern hardwoods. Most of the forests were cut over in the early days for the high-grade pine and the larger spruce. The best trees were selected here and there, while the bulk of the forest was left untouched. The gaps were quickly closed, the stumps rotted away, and the forest assumed the character of an original stand. Many of these areas were cut over later, often several times, under the same system of selecting the larger specimens of softwood; and each cutting removed the trees to a smaller diameter; while the more recent lumbering for pulpwood removes the softwoods to a small size. The hardwoods have been left standing upon extensive areas, especially in Maine, maintaining an excellent forest cover, though tending to develop stands predominantly composed of deciduous trees. On the upper mountain slopes and the ridges and on certain land characterized by meager or poorly drained soils, where the spruce and fir predominate or occur to the exclusion of other species, the cutting has been very heavy, often practically clearing the land. Many of the old fires occurred on these lands, burning in the slashings, consuming the surface layer of duff, and causing widespread devastation.

In the agricultural region the forest occurs in blocks of limited size, separated by lands cleared for agriculture and other purposes. Generally speaking, the hardwood species predominate, with white pine and other softwoods as a conspicuous element in certain sections. The greater part of the woodland is owned by farmers. The forests occupy the poorer soils, including lands that were never cleared for field or pasture and those that were found unprofitable for cultivation or grazing and have reverted or are in the process of reverting to tree growth. These are the forests most accessible to population. They have provided raw materials through the years for local industries and for the miscellaneous uses of the farm. For the most part the forests have been cut without special effort to maintain their productiveness. Fire has frequently run through them, sometimes killing all the growth and sometimes killing or injuring a portion of the trees. The effect of this treatment has been the progressive deterioration of the forest. Increase in the proportion of inferior species, predominance in many places of sprout growth in place of seeding growth, prevalence of a large amount of defect due to fungi and insects, and reduced growth and yield, especially of material of good quality and potential value, are the conspicuous results of unintelligent handling of the forests. The old timber has been largely removed. Here and there are patches of old trees that have been carefully protected, but most of the land is covered with trees less than fifty years of age, with a large part from ten to thirty years old. The outstanding features of the forests in the agricultural regions are the limited amount of timber capital, the scattered character of such merchantable timber as exists, and the impaired productiveness of the forests expressed in quantity and quality of growth. Such are the forests of Massachusetts, Connecticut, and Rhode Island and the southern parts and the valleys of the three northern states.[1]

Recent estimates by the United States Forest Service place the total amount of saw timber in New England at slightly less than 58 billion feet, board measure. About 57 per cent of this is composed of softwood species; the rest of hardwoods. In addition, the New England forests contain about 150 million cords of wood too small or too rough for the saw. It is estimated that the material suited for wood pulp aggregates about 206 million cords. This estimate necessarily overlaps that for saw timber and cordwood, because some material in each of these categories may be used for wood pulp.

The rate of growth of the forests in New England is far below what could be obtained under forestry methods of management. The government estimates indicate a total increment of about 390 million cubic feet a year. This is less than half of what might ultimately be produced even if a crude practice of forestry were in effect over the whole area. If intensive forestry were practiced the growth could probably in the long run be more than trebled.[2]

FORESTS AND THE INDUSTRIES

New England is an industrial center requiring a large amount of wood products of very diversified character. The annual consumption of lumber is in excess of that produced in the region and in excess also of that represented by growth in the forest. At the present time a large amount of lumber of high grade enters the New England market from the South and the West at prices within the reach of the consuming industries. Our country has been accustomed to wood products of the highest quality, such as is obtained only from first-growth timber. When the old timber in a given region has been depleted there is a natural tendency to look to other sources of virgin supplies. This is exactly what has occurred in New England. As long as the product of the virgin forests of the South and West is offered at reasonable cost, it will be used in preference to the local product for purposes requiring material of high quality.

Increasingly, therefore, New England has been looking away from local sources of lumber supply. This is reflected in reduced production of lumber and also in the decline of the industries concerned with exploitation and manufacture of lumber and its products. Census reports indicate that lumber production declined between 1919 and 1929 slightly more than 50 per cent; that the number of active establishments (reporting to the census) decreased 65 per cent; that the average number of wage earners was less by 56 per cent; and that the total value of products declined 44 per cent.[3] This recession has been due to the depletion of good quality timber, to the competition of western and southern lumber, to the use of substitutes for wood, to the shifting of the use of spruce for lumber to its use for pulpwood, and to other less clearly defined causes.

The foregoing refers only to the lumber industry and those wood-using industries engaged in further fabrication of the products of the sawmill. The data do not include facts regarding the paper and pulp industry. For many years the northeastern region has constituted one of our most important centers of manufacture of paper and pulp. Only a portion of the requirements of the mills has been supplied from local forests. While a certain amount of pulpwood is brought in from other states and Canada, a large amount of material in the form of pulp is imported from other parts of the United States, from Canada, and from northern Europe.

In recent years there has been a marked expansion of the paper and pulp industry in the South and West and in Canada. New England has about held its own, but not much more. The advance in the knowledge of the chemistry of wood and of methods of manufacture has made available for pulp products species formerly not used for this purpose and has introduced a new element in the competition between other sections of the country and New England.

Serious inroads have already been made on the wood capital of New England for current demands. Continued overexploitation of forest supplies will in the long run react against the paper and pulp industry, as has been the case with lumber. Every consideration points to the necessity first of establishing a proper balance between the utilization of pulpwood cut from the forest and production by growth, and second of managing the forests on the principles of forestry in order to secure the highest possible continuous yield of material of desired quality.

A highly industrial region like New England may not be expected to meet more than a part of its requirements for timber products from the local forests. It is a serious matter, however, if the unwise depletion of its forests results in the decline of industry. There is a loss to the community where the manufacturing plants had been located. There is a loss when a renewable natural resource no longer renders a service to industry. The forests of New England have heretofore provided materials for a large number of widely distributed manufacturing plants that have been a vital factor in the industrial life of the region, especially in the country districts.[4] The progressive depletion of the merchantable timber has been one of the primary causes of the reduction in the number of these plants. Of special significance has been the closing down of small factories and shops in the rural sections. The closing of a planing mill in Boston, Providence, or Bridgeport would have relatively little influence on the industrial life of the community. In a rural district the small sawmill or woodworking plant is frequently the only local manufacturing enterprise and is a chief factor in the local industrial life. It furnishes a market for the products of the forests and, where farming is on a small scale, has a relatively large importance in the local market for agricultural products. While the number of men employed, the money handled by the local bank, the increase to the tax list, and the tonnage furnished to the railroad may be actually small, the influence in a small town may be relatively very important.

RELATION OF FORESTS TO AGRICULTURE

There is a close interrelation between forests and agriculture. In many parts of New England the agricultural and forest lands constitute the principal local resources. Where the land is dominantly agricultural, as in the rich valleys, the forest plays a minor part in the general economic support of the region. In less fertile sections the cultivable areas are in smaller units, less adapted to modern methods of farming, relatively more costly in effort and money to operate, and capable of yielding smaller net returns. In such regions supplemental resources are essential to maintain the agricultural lands in productive use. In the past the farmer in these sections has obtained a substantial part of his income from the sale of material from his woodland, through labor in near-by forests owned by others, through work at the local mill, and through the use of his teams and other equipment in connection with some forest enterprise. It used to be said that many farmers earned as much as 20 per cent of their annual income from such sources. Frequently the ratio was much higher. Doubtless the opportunities for earnings afforded by the forest have been an element in sustaining many farms in active operation; and the depletion of the forests and the closing of the local forest industries have caused the final abandonment of many farm undertakings. One of the first effects of liquidating the forest capital in a region is the reduction in the tax assessments against the land. When a considerable part of the land is forest that has been made unproductive by overexploitation or fire, the burden of taxes on the farms and other property is correspondingly increased if roads, schools, and other public undertakings are to be maintained. Forest destruction may result in the impoverishment of rural districts and hasten the abandonment of farms and the decline of the village communities.[5]

GENERAL BENEFITS OF FORESTS

There are public benefits derived from the very existence of well managed forests, even where the products are not used at all. Of first importance is the influence of the forest on water conservation.[6] The forests exercise an important influence on the regularity of stream flow. They do not always prevent torrents and floods, but they retard them. By increasing seepage water they aid in maintaining springs, raising the summer stages of the streams, and purifying sources of potable water. The influence of forests on water resources is conspicuous and has been closely studied on the larger rivers of the country, where regularity of flow is important in the use of water for power and for manufacturing purposes. Less attention has been given to the effect of forests on water supplies in the industrial states of Massachusetts, Connecticut, and Rhode Island. The increased demand for water for domestic purposes, not only in the large urban centers but in the suburban districts and small towns, presents a problem of water resources which in the near future may be comparable to that in the semiarid sections of the West. Every drop of water that can be conserved for use will be needed. The forests must be brought into a condition to exert their maximum influence in preventing water wastage.

A second public benefit of forests is their service in outdoor recreation. The development of the recreation movement has introduced a new factor in the earning power and prosperity of rural communities. The mountains, forests, lakes, streams, and the countryside generally are attracting thousands of persons to the rural districts for temporary vacation visits and for the establishment of summer or permanent homes. New local markets for the produce of the farm, new taxable values of property, new sources of patronage for the merchant, the hotel, the boarding house, and the garage in town, and new opportunities for skilled and general labor are created. The forest plays a large part in this movement. The forest gives special character to a highway; it creates a setting for mountain or lake and in itself is often the most pleasing element of a landscape. Forests harbor wild life, which frequently is the feature that attracts visitors to the wilderness. Many forests have greater economic value for their recreational service than for the production of wood materials.

PUBLIC RESPONSIBILITIES IN FORESTRY

New England has already recognized the need of constructive measures of forestry. Under the leadership of foresters and other forward-looking citizens the first steps toward a better handling of the forests have been taken. The aim is to check the processes of destruction, to bring into practice effective methods of forest replacement after logging, to restock idle lands, and progressively to improve the poorly stocked second-growth forests that now cover much of the woodland areas.

These objectives will not be achieved by the unaided efforts of private landowners. The public must share in the undertaking. By direct control or ownership the public must insure the proper protection and management of the forests needed for water conservation and other general benefits. It must aid in removing the chief economic obstacles that discourage or actually prevent the adoption of forestry measures by private owners. It must coöperate sympathetically and liberally with private owners in inaugurating methods of land management which to many are still little appreciated or understood. And finally the public must carry most of the burden of research and experimentation which will lay the foundations for applied forestry practice. The chief accomplishments in forestry in New England as elsewhere in the country have been due to the efforts of the public. Further progress will be in proportion to the extent to which the public redeems its responsibilities through appropriate legislative and administrative action.[7]

PUBLIC FORESTS

The primary purposes of public forests are the protection of watersheds, control of areas of special scenic interest, provision for public recreation, conservation of wild life, and the productive utilization of lands of such a character and so located that they would not be well handled under private ownership. Incidentally public forests serve as demonstration grounds for the practice of forestry and as centers of activity in fire protection and marketing of products in coöperation with the private owners in the vicinity.

The public interests in some areas extend beyond the boundaries of single states and justify the federal government in establishing national forest reservations. This is the case in the White Mountains, where the government has already acquired nearly 500,000 acres in building up the White Mountain National Forest (see Fig. 2, pp. 16–17, above). A second national forest unit has been established in the Green Mountains of Vermont. The national park system is represented in New England by the Lafayette National Park on Mount Desert Island.

Four New England states have adopted a policy of establishing state forests. The forestry leaders in Massachusetts, Connecticut, New Hampshire, and Vermont have projected a program of forest acquisition calling for an aggregate area of about 1,500,000 acres. An excellent start has been made toward this program, with more than 225,000 acres already acquired and incorporated in organized state forests. In Maine and Rhode Island, however, there is a lack of progressive sentiment in regard to this important feature of forestry.

The town forest is a form of public reservation that has gained favorable recognition in recent years in several of the states. Massachusetts, in particular, has developed a wide interest in this policy among the towns. These reservations have a high value locally, though they will not by any means fulfill the functions of the state forests.

It is impossible to forecast at present the total area of forests that ultimately will be included in some form of public ownership. It is the writer's belief that from 12 to 15 per cent of the forest area of New England should be publicly owned. This means that the bulk of the forests will remain in private hands. The chief supply of timber supporting the industries will be derived from private sources. It is imperative, therefore, that every effort should be made to bring these forests into a productive condition.[8]

PRIVATE FORESTRY

The number of private owners in New England who are endeavoring to do something in the way of forestry is large. It is small, however, compared with the total number of owners, and the greater part of the private lands are still handled without special effort to maintain and increase their productivity. The best examples of private forestry are on lands that are under a stable form of ownership. Hydraulic companies, quasi-public institutions, large private estates, wood-using industries with large capital investment in plants that are largely dependent on local supplies, recreation organizations, and a limited number of farmers are among the owners who are undertaking to use the principles of forestry in handling their properties. Some of the large paper companies are using conservative methods of cutting, seeking to maintain a forest capital for continued use. The Brown Company of Berlin, N. H., has set aside an experimental tract and is conducting research on this area and on various parts of its holdings. A number of other industrial concerns also have made distinct progress in applied forestry. Generally speaking, however, it is believed that the large owners could, to their own advantage, utilize more intensive methods than at present in their woods operations, even under present conditions. The farm wood lots as a whole are not well handled. The present system of contracting the cutting to small sawmill operators is detrimental to good field practice, and the wood lots are deteriorating under this process. Some headway is being made in farm forestry through the educational and coöperative work of the state officers and extension foresters of the agricultural colleges and experiment stations. The distribution of planting stock has greatly stimulated the establishment of forest stands on open lands. There is, however, a large area of abandoned farm and pasture land that would render its highest service if planted with forest trees. Only a small beginning has as yet been made in rehabilitating lands that require artificial methods of restocking.

OBSTACLES TO PRIVATE FORESTRY

Fire is the first obstacle to the successful practice of forestry by private owners. Experience has shown that efficient fire protection requires centralized direction and organization, such as can be provided only by the state. It is recognized also that the public should share in the expense of fire protection. No real progress was made in protecting the forests of New England until the organization of state-wide protective systems administered by state agencies. The private owners participate in this undertaking and pay their share. It has been proved that fires can be prevented or at least that the risk can be enormously reduced. Fires still occur in alarming numbers, but this is due to the failure of the legislatures to provide adequate funds for the protective work.

A second obstacle to private forestry is the existence of an unsound and uncertain system of taxation. As the present general property tax is often applied, the possible profits of raising trees as a business venture are absorbed before the timber is mature. The very uncertainties of future taxation prevent many owners from managing their land for timber production. The establishment of a sound system of forest taxation will not in itself bring about the practice of forestry, for other economic factors equally important bear on the problem; but a reform in the tax system is essential to make feasible the general practice of forestry by private owners. Here again it is necessary for the public to take definite action to lay the foundations on which private forestry may be built. Several states have enacted laws designed to encourage the growing of timber. They are not, however, generally applied. The root of the trouble has not yet been reached. It is hoped that the tax investigation of the government now in progress will aid the states in working out this problem.[9]

A third problem which troubles private owners is that of marketing of products. The marketing of timber is a question of ordinary business enterprise where, as in northern New England, there is still a quantity of merchantable material, and need not be discussed here. The chief interest of the public lies in the necessity of maintaining the needed forest capital to support the forest industries. This can be accomplished if the principles of forestry are used in the management of the lands. The situation on the cut-over forests in the agricultural and industrial zone is much more difficult and calls for special coöperation by the public. The blocks of merchantable timber are scattered, small in area, and held by many owners. Prevailing methods of small-unit manufacturing are often defective and inefficient. The buyer must deal with many different persons, and the element of dependability upon the local woodlands for a continuous supply is lacking. Manufacturers naturally prefer to deal with centralized concerns where material of uniform quality can be obtained in desired amounts and where transactions are conducted with one or a few individuals. It is clear that a new system of merchandising of products from small forests must be devised, which introduces the principle of organized handling of timber in quantity through central agencies. The solution of the problem of marketing is the key to the practice of forestry on the small tract.[10] Public agencies can make a very important contribution to it through practical investigations and measures of coöperation.

The practice of forestry involves procedures unfamiliar to most private owners. The study of land utilization and timber growth must form a part of the management of forest property.[11] The natural tendency of owners is to cut off everything from a given area that is salable and to pay no attention to forest production. It is incumbent on the public, through its executive representatives, to coöperate with private owners in demonstrating the methods of applied forestry. In some states public nurseries are maintained for the distribution at cost of planting materials, especially among small owners. These, together with extension work, demonstrations on public and other forests, and other measures of coöperation now used should be enlarged.

RESEARCH

The federal government has inaugurated research work in forestry on a large scale throughout the country. A field experiment station, known as the Northeastern Forest Experiment Station,[12] is located at New Haven, Conn., and is conducting researches in New England and New York. In addition, several forest schools in the region constitute centers of activity and contribute not only through their training of foresters but also through their research and practical demonstration work. Of special importance is the work of Yale and Harvard Universities, both of which operate important demonstration forests. These agencies, supplemented by the investigative work of the state foresters and a number of private companies, are undertaking to develop the knowledge essential to the successful practice of forestry. Specially pertinent to the subject of this paper are the economic studies of the government which aim to·determine the extent and character of the timber and its relation to industry, the taxation study which will be completed in a year or so, and market investigations conducted by a number of agencies. Less attention has been devoted to the study of the influence of forests on the conservation of water. This should constitute a project of special study, supported by liberal appropriations. It is important also that the investigations, initiated by several agencies, to determine the relation of the forests to agriculture and rural industrial life generally should be granted larger financial support.[13]

CONCLUSIONS

The service of the forests in the industrial economy of New England has been steadily declining. Commendable efforts have been made to correct this situation. The work so far accomplished has demonstrated that the problem of forestry in New England is susceptible of solution. Actual trial of forestry in the field, experiments, and research indicate the policies that must be adopted by the public and by private owners to secure the greatest benefits in the long run from the forest lands. It is recognized that any program of forestry must be progressive in application and that achievements must be measured by decades and not by years. Public support, far more liberal than at present, is essential. The very fact that considerable time is required to rehabilitate our forests is a most cogent reason to press forward now with the greatest possible vigor. Private owners are expected to do their part in this undertaking and to adopt such measures of forestry as are feasible in practice. The public increasingly will insist upon the replacement of destructive methods by sound forestry, especially if the public redeems its own responsibilities in organized fire protection, sound taxation, and other appropriate measures of coöperation.

NOTES

[1] A. F. Hawes, *New England Forests in Retrospect*, in *Journ. of Forestry*, Vol. 21, 1923, pp. 209–224. See also reports and bulletins of the State Foresters of the New England states.

[2] The data in this section are based on recent estimates prepared by the U. S. Forest Service for the use of the Timber Conservation Board.

[3] See *Fourteenth Census of the United States, 1920: Forest Products, 1919, Lumber, Lath, and Shingles;* also *Fifteenth Census of the United States, 1930: Manufacturers, 1929, The Principal Lumber Industries.*

[4] J. B. Downs and C. B. Gutchess, *The Wood-Using Industries of Massachusetts*, Petersham, Mass., 1928 (*Harvard Forest Bull. 12*); E. D. Fletcher and A. F. Hawes, *The Use of Lumber and Wood in Connecticut*, Hartford, Conn., 1928 (*Bull. of the Conn. Forest and Park Commission*); A. H. Pierson, *Wood-Using Industries of Connecticut*, New Haven, Conn., 1913 (*Conn. Agric. Exper. Sta. Bull. 174*); J. C. Nellis, *The Wood-Using Industries of Maine*, in [9th Biennial Report of] *Maine Forest Commissioner*, 1912, pp. 83–188; H. Maxwell, *A Study of the Massachusetts Wood-Using Industries*, Massachusetts State Forester, Boston, 1910; R. E. Simmons, *Wood-Using Industries of New Hampshire*, New Hampshire State Forestry Commission in Coöperation with the Forest Service, U. S. Dept. of Agric., Concord, N. H., 1912; H. Maxwell, *The Wood-Using Industries of Vermont*, Rutland, Vt., 1913 (*Vermont Forest Service Publ. No. 11*).

[5] H. S. Graves, *How to Bring Back Factories and Farms to the Towns*, Society for the Protection of New Hampshire Forests, Boston, 1921; the same, *What State Forests Will Mean to Rural Connecticut*, Connecticut Forestry Association, New Haven, Conn., 1924.

[6] P. W. Ayres, *Reforestation on Water-Sheds*, in *Journ. New England Water-Works Assoc.*, Vol. 37, 1923, pp. 127–141; *New England Flood Control, Preliminary Report of a Special Committee of the New England Section, Society of American Foresters*, in *Journ. of Forestry*, Vol. 28, 1930, pp. 103–107.

[7] H. S. Graves, *Federal and State Responsibilities in Forestry*, in *American Forests and Forest Life*, Vol. 31, 1925, pp. 675–677 and 686.

[8] Philip Ayres, *Our Eastern National Forests*, in *American Forests and Forest Life*, Vol. 36, 1930, pp. 438, 439, and 483; *Recreation Resources of Federal Lands*, National Conference on Outdoor Recreation, Washington, 1928; B. M. W. Nelson, *State Recreation, Parks, Forests and Game Preserves*, National Conference on State Parks; H. H. Chapman, *National and State Forests*, in *Journ. of Forestry*, Vol. 27, 1929, pp. 622–655; H. A. Reynolds, *Inventory of New England's Public Forests and Parks, ibid.*, pp. 923–926; the same, *Town Forests; Their Recreational and Economic Value*, American Tree Association, Washington, 1925.

[9] See the paper by Professor F. R. Fairchild entitled *Taxation of Forests and Farm Woodlots in New England* in the present volume, below, pp. 237–246; also J. W. Toumey, *The Destructive Nature of Forest Taxation in New Hampshire*, Society for the Protection of New Hampshire Forests, Concord, 1930.

[10] Reports of the New England Section of Society of American Foresters, Committees on Markets and on Stabilization of the Lumber Industry (mimeographed), 1931 and 1932; A. F. Hawes, *Utilizing Southern New England's Low Grade Forest Products*, in *Journ. of Forestry*, Vol. 27, 1929, pp. 917–922; H. O. Cook, *Sustained Yield in Certain Forest Localities in Massachusetts, ibid.*, Vol. 21, 1923, pp. 48–53; A. F. Hawes, *An Industrial Community at Forestdale, Vermont*, in *American Forestry*, Vol. 28, 1922, pp. 477–478.

[11] For general studies pertaining to New England forestry, see A. F. Hawes, *Forestry in New England: A Handbook of Eastern Forest Management*, 1st edit., New York, 1912; the same, *Manual of Forestry for the Northeastern United States*,

Being Vol. 1 of "Forestry in New England," Revised, New York, 1918, 1925; S. T. Dana, *Timber Growing and Logging Practice in the Northeast*, Washington, 1930 (*U. S. Dept. of Agric. Technical Bull. No. 166*).

[12] The Northeastern Forest Experiment Station (established in 1923) publishes annually in mimeograph an *Investigative Program*, summarizing the research being carried on by the station, and also a mimeographed summary of *Forest Investigations Under Way in New England and New York*, in which are reported current investigations both by the staff of the station and by other institutions. The topics covered by these reports include dendrology, forestation, forest ecology, soils and physiography, forest economics, management, mensuration, protection, products and utilization, fish and game, and recreation.

[13] E. H. Clapp, *A National Program of Forest Research*, published by the American Tree Association for the Society of American Foresters, Washington, 1926.

TAXATION OF FORESTS AND FARM WOODLOTS IN NEW ENGLAND

Fred Rogers Fairchild

FOREST· taxation is a national problem, with regional variations.[1] Owing to the relatively large area of land in forests and farm wood lots in New England, the problem is particularly acute in that region. We start with these premises: (1) the American public has a vital interest in the preservation and conservative utilization of the existing forests and in the devotion to forest growing of waste land best suited to such use; (2) the greater part of the forest land is in private ownership and will long continue so; (3) the fate of the forests is therefore bound up with the practice of forestry and the growing of trees as a private business enterprise; (4) any artificial obstacle in the way of private forestry is a matter of public concern.

AMERICAN FORESTS UNDER THE GENERAL PROPERTY TAX

Taxation under the time-honored American general property tax has proved to be such an obstacle. Even a theoretically perfect property tax discriminates unfairly against property whose value is rising because its principal income is long deferred. In addition there arises still more serious difficulty from the prevailing laxity of assessment, through which the American property tax has become the most arbitrary and uncertain of all modern taxes. To the ordinary business, with an annual cycle of income and expenditure, this situation is tolerable. To the one who contemplates investment in forest growing, for a return that may not appear for forty or fifty years or more, the impossibility of making even an approximate calculation of future tax liability is generally enough to call a halt. It can be shown that the property tax, as currently administered, could easily absorb the entire net income of a forest-growing enterprise.

These are the general principles. The application varies in relation to the forest conditions of the different parts of the country. Three principal types are readily recognized.

The Pacific Northwest represents the last great reservoir of virgin timber. Although the principal attention is here naturally devoted to the exploitation of the mature timber, there already arises the question of what is to become of the cut-over lands. In most cases their obvious destiny is the growing of a new crop of timber. But the investor looks askance.

---

[1] For notes see below, p. 245.

In the Lake states we have a later stage of development. Here the original forest cover has been practically removed. At the time of removal there still remained in other parts of the country vast stores of virgin timber. The lumber industry naturally moved on to these other regions, and there was little interest in the future of cut-over lands apart from the hope that they might prove valuable for agriculture. This hope has generally proved illusory, and there remains a heritage of waste land, producing nothing and suffering deterioration through fire and neglect. If these lands are ever to be an asset to their states, instead of a liability, they must be utilized for forest growing. But the investor, even were he otherwise interested, is frightened away by the property tax.

New England has had a still longer history and represents a third type. Here the forests were originally a liability—they had to be cleared to make room for agriculture. Along with agriculture, there was for a long time a flourishing lumbering business, until the virgin forests were largely cut off. Lumbering has now declined to a small fraction of its former importance, and, though the pulp industry has in part taken its place, the latter industry is now dependent in a substantial degree on imported wood. Always there have been the wood lots associated with the farms. But agriculture has suffered a decline. In many parts of New England farms have been abandoned or their cultivated areas reduced, and the forests are returning to take possession.

Now it appears that forest growing is the most advantageous use for much of the abandoned agricultural land as well as for those lands that have always had a forest cover. Apparently the progress of the forest, in winning back the lands originally wrested from it for agriculture, should not be opposed but rather aided by recognized silvicultural measures.

The property tax, though it may not yet have had far-reaching effects, stands as a danger signal to the landowner or investor who may be considering a program of land utilization which would otherwise be most profitable to him and most beneficial to the community.

RECENT FOREST TAX LAWS IN NEW ENGLAND

Public interest in tree growing has led to much tax legislation. The earlier ventures in this field took the line of attempts to encourage the planting of trees by means of special favors in the way of tax exemptions, bounties, and rebates of taxes. In this phase of forest tax history all the New England states were represented. These laws obviously had little relation to the real problem of forest taxation as here outlined, and their total result has been negligible.

In addition to these inconsequential plantation-promoting laws, all of the New England states, with the single exception of Rhode

Island, have forest tax laws of the modern type. A glance at the principal features of these laws will be worth our while.[2]

The Maine law was originally enacted in 1921 and has been amended in 1923 and 1929. On properties specially classified as "auxiliary state forests" the trees are exempt from the property tax, while the land is assessed at the same valuation as stripped forest land in the vicinity, with a limit of two dollars an acre. A yield tax is imposed upon the stumpage value of all trees cut for sale or manufacture from such properties, with liberal exceptions for trees cut for the owner's use or to clear the land for agricultural purposes. To enjoy the advantages of this law, the land must be covered with trees, either natural or planted, capable of producing 15,000 board feet of softwoods or[3] 8000 board feet of hardwoods per acre. Application for classification must be made by the owner.

The Massachusetts law (enacted in 1922) is short and simple. It provides that on "classified forest lands" all forest trees are exempt from taxation. The land is subject to the ordinary property tax. A yield tax at the rate of 6 per cent is imposed on wood and timber cut from such lands. The owner or tenant may cut not to exceed twenty-five dollars' worth in a year for his own use free of tax. To qualify under this law, the property must not have been assessed in the next preceding year for more than twenty-five dollars an acre. The forest must not average more than twenty cords per acre but must promise to yield per acre at least 20,000 board feet of softwoods or[3] 8000 board feet of hardwoods or a proportionate mixture. Application for classification must be made by the owner.

New Hampshire in 1923 copied practically the Massachusetts law of 1922, except that constitutional limitations precluded the yield tax. In its place the law provides that timber when cut shall be subject to the property tax of that year, though the owner or tenant may in any year cut for his own use not more than fifty dollars' worth free of tax. The "classified forest lands" must be forest land; the trees, exclusive of fuel wood, must not be worth more than twenty-five dollars per acre, but the forest must be so stocked with young trees as to promise an average yield of 25,000 board feet of merchantable timber per acre. There is the further limitation that the property must not exceed one hundred acres in any one town. On such properties, the land is subject to the property tax, while the standing forest trees are exempt. Application for classification must be made by the owner.

The Vermont law (first enacted in 1913 and amended in 1919) is a bit more complicated in that its special classification distinguishes: (1) "young timber lands," which must be fully stocked with forest trees not more than fifteen years old (except for scattered older trees without taxable value), and (2) "waste, partially denuded, and wild forest lands," occupied wholly or in part by trees more than fifteen years old. On properties classified in the first group the trees are exempt from the property tax. The land is assessed at the time of classification, with a limit of three dollars per acre; this valuation remains fixed till 1950; in that year it is again to be assessed, without the three-dollar limit, and this valuation is to stand for another fifty years. A yield tax of 10 per cent is imposed upon all products cut from the land except that cut for domestic use and thinnings with no net value above cost of cutting.

In the case of properties classified in the second group, the assessed value, including land and trees, as of the last quadrennial appraisal before the date of classification, is fixed as the assessed value till 1950. In that year the property is again to be assessed, and this valuation is to stand for another fifty years. A yield tax is imposed on live trees cut, except those cut for domestic use. The rate is graduated: one tenth of 1 per cent if the land has been classified one year, with an increase of one tenth of 1 per cent for each year of classification, to a maximum of 7 per cent. In either group, classification is initiated by the owner's application and depends on certain qualifications, which for the first class are complicated.

Connecticut has two laws of interest in this connection. The law of 1913 permits classification of "forest lands" in either of two classes: (1) "land bearing timber of more than ten years growth, said timber having a taxable value," and (2) land stocked with forest trees not more than ten years old, except scattered older trees not adding to the assessed value. Properties in the first class are assessed at the time of classification at the actual value of land and trees separately. This assessment stands for fifty years. At that time land and trees are again to be separately assessed, which assessment is to stand for another fifty years. During the first one hundred years of continuous classification the rate of the property tax may not exceed ten mills. Where the trees are entirely removed and the land reforested, the property may be reclassified in Class 2 and thereafter taxed accordingly. On properties in Class 2, the trees are exempt from the property tax. The land alone is assessed, revalued, and taxed in the same manner as provided for Class 1.

For all classified properties there is a yield tax, from which materials cut for domestic use are generally exempt. On trees cut from properties in Class 1, the rate of the yield tax is 2 per cent if they are cut not more than ten years after classification; this rate is increased by 1 per cent for each additional ten years to a maximum of 7 per cent when they are cut fifty years or more after classification. The rate of the yield tax in Class 2 is 10 per cent. To qualify under the law the property must contain at least five acres, the land must be woodland or land suitable for forest planting and must not be worth more than twenty-five dollars an acre. In Class 2 there are rather complicated qualifications as to stocking. Application for classification must be made by the owner.

In 1929 Connecticut adopted a law with certain novel features. Specially classified properties are assessed as of the last assessment prior to the owner's application for classification. This assessment cannot then be changed until the next general revaluation of all the taxable property in the town. At that time and thereafter the land is assessed in the same manner as other land in the town, while the trees are exempt from the property tax. There is no yield tax. Application for classification must be made by the owner. In order to qualify, the property must include trees and be of such character that in the opinion of the state forester it would be advantageous to the community and the owner to permit the trees to remain standing until they become suitable to be cut for lumber. This law is peculiar in the absence of a yield tax or anything in its place, the liberal qualifications for classification, and the wide discretion given the state forester.

CHARACTER OF RECENT LEGISLATION

Here we have an interesting group of special tax laws intended to promote private forest growing. Certain general principles can be readily discerned. The more obvious defects of the general property tax are evidently recognized, and there is groping for escape. Hence, the provisions for fixed assessments and maximum limits to assessed values and tax rates. The superiority, from the forestry viewpoint, of the yield-tax principle over the tax on capital value has come to be generally recognized. On the other hand there is the fear lest whole-hearted change should deprive the local communities of revenue or substitute an uncertain and irregular flow of revenue. Thus, while all the states have granted, with more or less liberality, exemption to growing trees, none has seen fit to exempt forest land. When limits are placed on the taxation of the land, care is usually taken, as in Vermont and Connecticut, to see that present income at least shall not be reduced.

It is remarkable that, although the tax menace to forestry arises chiefly from the slipshod assessment of the general property tax, our New England forest tax reformers have not seen fit to attempt reform of property tax assessment. Beyond imposing certain specific limits upon the freedom of the assessor, the reformers have declined to concern themselves with the fundamental weaknesses of the property tax, from which all kinds of property are suffering to a greater or less degree.[4] This attitude has doubtless been the result partly of ignorance and partly of the feeling that the property tax is hopeless and the only escape is to get the forests out from under.

Yet before he gets under way on this path, the reformer is thrown into reverse by the stubborn fact that the local governments cannot sacrifice any substantial amount of their current tax revenues. Without stopping to think out this aspect of the problem the forest tax reformer immediately surrenders and subjects his reform measure to such restrictions as to permit of no real departure from the property tax after all. The land, generally the chief or only element of present value, is left taxable. A yield tax is imposed, which interests nobody very much since its effect is so far in the future. And finally the whole plan is hamstrung by making the application of the law optional with the owner and hedged about with qualifications, applications, hearings, official interference, and a mass of red tape.

RESULTS OF RECENT LEGISLATION

Why should anyone suppose that a tax thus entangled would work? At the expense of leading this essay into a pitiful anticlimax, let us see what results are to be credited to these modern attempts at forest tax reform.[5]

In the state of Maine there are, according to the best estimates, about 15,000,000 acres of privately owned forest land. The Maine yield-tax law is so worded as to be applicable (according to rough estimates) to only 5,000,000 acres, or one third of this land. At the present time the land actually under the law consists of 20,000 acres, listed by 25 owners, and equal to four tenths of 1 per cent of the eligible land, or thirteen hundredths of 1 per cent of the privately owned forest land.

In Massachusetts it is estimated (also roughly) that about 1,000,-000 acres, 44 per cent of the 2,290,906 acres of privately owned forest land, would be eligible to classification. To the present time 95 owners have listed 25,000 acres. This is 2.5 per cent of the eligible land and 1.1 per cent of all privately owned forest land.

Under New Hampshire's exemption law only about 250,000 acres are estimated to be eligible to classification out of 4,211,688 acres of private forest land, being 6 per cent of the total. The law has been taken advantage of by 198 owners, who have registered 8431 acres, being 3.4 per cent of the eligible land and one fifth of 1 per cent of all private forest land.

Vermont has 3,300,064 acres of privately owned forest land, of which a rough estimate places about 1,015,000 acres, or 31 per cent, eligible under her yield-tax law. Twenty owners have listed 37,472 acres, which is 3.7 per cent of the land that is eligible and 1.1 per cent, of all private forest land.

In Connecticut there are 1,516,480 acres of privately owned forest land, of which it is estimated that about 1,000,000 acres could be listed under either of the state's special forest tax laws. The eligible land is thus 66 per cent of the total. Thirty-four owners have thus far listed 4565 acres under the older yield-tax law, being half of 1 per cent of the eligible land and three tenths of 1 per cent of all private forest lands. In addition, under Connecticut's new exemption law, eighteen owners have listed 2281 acres or about one quarter of 1 per cent of the eligible land. Only forty-five hundredths of 1 per cent of Connecticut's private forest land is now listed altogether under these forest tax laws.

This completes the statistical summary of accomplishment under New England's special forest tax laws. It is indeed a meager result. Only in Massachusetts and Connecticut is more than a third of the private forest land eligible. In only one state have as many as 100 owners taken advantage of the law, and the amount of land classified has in no state exceeded 1.1 per cent of the total private forest land; of the eligible land, 3.7 per cent has been classified in Vermont, 3.4 per cent in New Hampshire, 2.5 per cent in Massachusetts, and less than 1 per cent in the other states.

Of course we must not assume that the effectiveness of a voluntary forest tax law is to be measured merely by the part of the total area of privately owned forest land that has been brought under its operation. As has been pointed out, taxation is a problem to those who contemplate forestry as a business enterprise. Other forest owners will not be particularly concerned over taxation. They may be getting on pretty well under the existing tax methods and will naturally choose rather to bear those ills they have than fly to others they know not of. In Massachusetts, for example, it would appear that most of the large forest owners who are interested in the practice of forestry have registered their lands. The effect of forest tax reform is negative only. It may remove an obstacle, but it cannot promote forestry when the will is lacking.

Nevertheless, these insignificant results must mean something. The rock-ribbed mountains of New England have labored and brought forth this puny litter of mice. We have sought to remove the trees from the property tax while not decreasing property tax revenue. We have feared to impose our laws upon unwilling owners, as is elsewhere the universal rule of taxation, and by restrictions and interference we have frightened away owners who might have been interested. Worst of all, while leaving the property tax in almost complete possession of the field, we have refused to take any interest in its improvement or in the broad problems of state and local finance, of which forest taxation ought by now to be recognized as an integral part.

THE "WILD LANDS" OF MAINE

What is possibly the most interesting contribution that New England has to offer to forest tax discussion is entirely distinct from special forest tax legislation. Because of peculiar historical and economic development there is an area of ten million acres in the state of Maine which has been definitely set aside by legislative enactment as a "wild lands" zone.[6] This area, representing roughly one half the area of Maine and one quarter of the area of New England, is in practice dedicated by the owners to forest use and has thus not generally been open to agricultural settlement. Within this area there is no local town organization, and school and road taxes have been largely eliminated.

As a result the two thirds of Maine's 15,000,000 acres of forest lands that are within this zone pay a tax of about 11 mills on the dollar of valuation fixed by the Board of State Assessors. In contrast, the five million acres of scattering forest lands in the state outside of the "wild lands" zone pay an average tax of 49⅓ mills on the dollar of valuation fixed by 519 local town assessing boards.

The minimum and maximum tax rates in the unorganized territory in 1930 were as follows:[7]

	MINIMUM	MAXIMUM
State tax	.0075	.0075
Forestry district tax	.00225	.00225
County tax . . . . ?	.00106	.0035
Road tax . . . . :	none	.0200
Total	.01081	.03325

Of the 7½ mill state tax, 3⅓ mills, or $217,936.98 collected in unorganized territory, went into the general school fund of the state, which is distributed among all organized towns as directed by the Legislature. An additional school tax of three dollars is collected from each male person over 21 years of age residing in unorganized territory. The 1930 budget for schools in this territory amounted to $44,433.52. One mill of the state tax is appropriated to aid in the construction by the state of second class or graveled roads and third class or dirt roads.

The forestry district tax is spent entirely for fire protection which costs, on an average, two cents per acre.

The county tax rates vary according to the county in which the land is situated.

The road tax is assessed by County Commissioners but is limited to a maximum of 2 per cent of assessed valuation and is levied only on those townships crossed by roads, and only the part of road tax that is to be spent in each township is levied in that township. About 87 per cent of the area in the unorganized territory bears no local road tax.

It should be noted that this novel situation was not the result of conscious design or legislative action by the people of Maine. It has resulted from natural causes in the economic history of the state, enforced by wise action on the part of the large landowners of the region. Nevertheless, here is a very suggestive example of what may be accomplished by the geographic segregation of forests and forest industries in the regions approaching wilderness conditions.

THOROUGHGOING FINANCIAL REVISION NEEDED

Forest tax reform in New England, as in the United States generally, has gone through two phases. The results thus far accomplished have been negligible. This, as regards the modern type of laws, is doubtless due in part to the prevailing lack of interest of owners in the practice of forestry. Were this the sole cause, we might well say that there is no immediate problem of forest taxation in New England, since forest tax reform (not involving special favors) can have no effect when there is not otherwise the will to practice forestry. Even so, there is reason to believe that sooner or later economic forces are destined to make forestry profitable, given a fair field and no favors; and so the emergence of the tax problem is only postponed. As a matter of fact, there is evidence that owners are even now taking an interest in forest investment and that the taxation problem is present and pressing.

Before this problem is solved, I am convinced that our experiments in legislation must enter a third phase, different from anything in the past. In the perfecting of our forest tax legislation, we shall, first of all, have to give careful thought to the entire system of state and local finance. We shall, for example, have to reopen the whole question of whether the state, the county, or the town shall provide our public highways and of how their cost shall be met. We shall likewise have to overhaul the control and financing of public education. We shall have to screw up our courage to face the chaotic state of the general property tax, instead of dodging it. Forest tax reformers will have to surrender their attitude of aloofness and join hands with other interests working for an honest reform of the tax system. Forests will not be properly taxed until either the property tax is reformed or the forests are removed entirely—land as well as trees—from its jurisdiction. Either result is to be obtained only at the cost of careful study and long labor, enlisting the coöperation of all interests concerned and looking toward a fundamental overhauling of the whole system of state and local finance.

NOTES

[1] The Forest Taxation Inquiry, of which the author of this article is Director, was organized in 1926 as an independent bureau of the United States Forest Service to carry out the intent of Congress, as expressed in the Clarke-McNary Law of 1924. It is making a study of the whole subject of forest taxation in America and abroad, for the purpose of presenting facts and conclusions that may aid the people of the

several states in revising their tax laws to the end that taxation may not in future be an obstacle in the way of private forest growing. The Inquiry has a technical staff of twelve economists and foresters, and statistical and clerical assistants, bringing the total personnel up to about twenty-five. Its investigations are now nearly completed, and the final report will be published by the United States Government. In the meantime, the Inquiry publishes frequent *Progress Reports*, copies of which may be obtained on application to the Director, 360 Prospect Street, New Haven, Conn.

Besides those that deal with forest taxation in particular parts of the United States, *Progress Reports* have appeared entitled *Forest Taxation and the Forest Taxation Inquiry, Principles of Forest Taxation*, and *Methods of Research in Forest Taxation*. Digests of state forest tax laws are also from time to time published as *Progress Reports*.

In New England the Inquiry has made an intensive study of the situation in New Hampshire, the results of which are to be published in a *Progress Report*. Special studies have been made also in Maine, Massachusetts, and Connecticut. The results will be incorporated in the final report.

² Abstracts of the forest tax laws of all the states in effect January 1, 1932, are contained in Forest Taxation Inquiry, *Progress Report No. 16*, where will be found citations for the several statutes here discussed.

³ The word in the statute is "and," but it seems impossible to believe that the Legislature did not intend "or."

⁴ For a brief account of the American general property tax, indicating its fundamental weaknesses, see F. R. Fairchild, E. S. Furniss, and N. S. Buck, *Elementary Economics*, revised edit., New York, 1930, Vol. 2, Chap. 43.

⁵ See Forest Taxation Inquiry, *Progress Report No. 16*, and reports by State Foresters.

⁶ See map accompanying Professor J. F. Sly's paper on *State and Local Government in New England*, Fig. 1, pp. 416–417, below.

⁷ Data regarding Maine cover the year 1930 and are from an unpublished report of the Forest Taxation Inquiry based on official state publications and interviews with state officials.

THE FISHERIES OF NEW ENGLAND

PRODUCTION AND ADMINISTRATION

Lewis Radcliffe

NEW England lies near the center of the richest fishing area of the world. Numerous rivers, a broken coast line with many havens of retreat from storms, a gently sloping ocean floor, a broad continental shelf of relatively shallow water (mostly of a depth less than sixty fathoms) on which there are more than twenty offshore "fishing banks,"[1] and a wealth of lakes and streams suited to the finest of fresh-water game fishes—these natural factors help us appreciate the significant part played by the fisheries in New England's history. For 150 years the fisheries were "the corner stone of New England's prosperity," and, if their importance was lost sight of for a period, they are again looming large as one of the most valuable resources of the region. Urgent, therefore, is the need for a continuing program of husbandry to insure a maximum yield from this great resource.

LARGER PROBLEMS OF THE FISHING INDUSTRY

As might be expected, so important a resource has been coveted by other nations. Despite the frequent and prolonged attempts to settle the international complications that have arisen between the United States and Great Britain upon the intent and meaning of the several treaties that have been made regulating the fishing interests of the two countries, "the provisions of the convention of 1818 have been the basis of our fishing rights in Canadian and Newfoundland waters much of the time since 1818, and, with certain modifications, are still in force."[2] With the recent rapid expansion of the fisheries on the high seas, new problems of control have arisen which must await settlement by international agreement. These problems include the prevention of the exhaustion of the fish supply on the fishing banks off our North Atlantic coast and the menace to the eastern North Pacific salmon fisheries through possible exploitation in extra-territorial waters.

At the present time in New England about 17,000 persons are engaged in fishing as well as thousands of others in the manufacturing, distributing, and merchandising of fishery products and by-products. The need for staunch, speedy, seaworthy fishing vessels, moreover, was long a great stimulant to shipbuilding in New England; and other industries have benefited in providing equipment used in the fisheries,

---

[1] For notes see below, p. 259.

such as cordage, nets, lines, small boats, salt, ice, paint, rubber clothing, gasoline and oil, and sundry other articles. New England's small production of farm crops in comparison with that of other similar areas and its dependence on outside sources of supply of foodstuffs have greatly enhanced the importance of the fisheries as a source of food for home consumption and trade. During the last half-century the annual yield has ranged between 200,000 and 450,000 tons, and during the last twenty-seven years the value of the yearly harvest to the fishermen has increased from $12,500,000 to $29,000,000.[3]

The principal grounds harvested by New England fishermen lie between Newfoundland and Long Island. They include inshore rivers, bays, and near-by shoals, and offshore grounds—the numberless submerged islands or "banks" comprising an area greater than that of the New England states.

Of the 1928 catch of about 604,000,000 pounds of fish and shellfish accredited to New England, ten products accounted for 90 per cent of the total. The catch of each of these in millions of pounds was: haddock, 238; cod, 90; sea herring, 71; flounders, 50; mackerel, 43; hake, 18; lobsters, 12; pollock, 11; squid, 8; and clams, 8. These may be grouped as follows: (1) ground fish, or species chiefly found on the bottom, such as the haddock, cod, hake, pollock, and flounders; (2) pelagic fish, or species occurring for the most part at the surface and usually in schools, such as mackerel and herring; and (3) shore forms, or species common to the inshore areas, such as the shellfish and some of the flounders.

OTTER TRAWLING

Before 1905 American fishing vessels operating on the western North Atlantic fishing banks used hand lines or trawl lines. In 1905 the steamer *Spray* was built for Boston owners, constructed on the general plans of British fishing steamers and equipped for using the otter trawl.[4] Steam replaced sail, and for the hand line and trawl lines was substituted a huge, flattened, conical bag, or otter trawl, towed along the bottom. Not until 1910, however, did the fishing industry appear to awaken to the full possibilities of the otter trawl when used in vessels of greater speed and superior seagoing qualities, capable of operating on a larger scale and at all seasons, winter included, and of bringing in fares of fresh fish at regular intervals. In that year two more steam trawlers were built, and one in each of the three succeeding years. The World War gave a considerable impetus to the acquiring of vessels of this type. In fact, many more vessels were acquired than were needed, with the result that some of them did not actually enter the fishery until nearly ten years after the end of the war.

The stimulant to the New England fisheries resulting from the rapid development of the packaged fresh-fish trade initiated in 1921 has not only created a demand for these vessel$ during recent years but has brought about the construction of many new trawlers. In 1931 the fleet of trawler vessels landing at the three principal New England fishing ports was as follows: 67 vessels of over 90 tons net; 91 vessels (draggers) of 21 to 90 tons; 62 vessels (flounder draggers) of 5 to 20 tons. The catch of these vessels exceeded 153,000,000 pounds or 58 per cent of the total vessel landings.

In the period of less than a quarter-century since the otter trawl was introduced in the New England fisheries its use has been extended until the present vessel landings by this type of gear approximate total landings at the time it was introduced. It is a most efficient type of gear. With further improvements in vessel equipment to include provision for freezing the fish as caught and for caring for the waste and trash fish for manufacture into fish meal and oil, the cruising radius and the days of absence from port may be materially increased and a more complete utilization of the catch may be effected. Yet the future of the otter trawl may not be as secure as this picture would indicate.

In comparison with hand lines and trawl lines, the otter trawl takes a much larger proportion of small fish of marketable and unmarketable classes. As the fish are massed in the cod end of the bag while it is being towed and landed, inevitably they cannot escape bruising and cannot equal individually caught fish in quality. Should depletion of the fishing banks occur or should the demand increase greatly beyond the available supply, warranting the utmost care in bringing to the consumer a product of the highest possible quality, the interests of both conservation and of business may dictate a return to the former types of fishing. Such a change may be long delayed or avoided by improvements in the otter trawl itself with a view to reducing the volume of the catch of the smaller-sized fish and lessening the injuries to the fish as landed aboard the vessel. In fact, recent investigations indicate that the construction of the otter trawl may be so modified as greatly to reduce the number of immature undersized fish taken.

THE COD FISHERY

The most important fishery of the western North Atlantic is for cod. On the great fishing banks and on some of the inshore grounds along the mainland this fishery is shared by the nationals of five countries—Newfoundland, France, Canada, the United States, and Portugal—who for thirty years have taken a catch averaging more than 1,100,000,000 pounds annually. While the productivity of this fishery during the thirty years ending with 1925 was subject to fluctuations, in the long run it has neither increased nor declined.[5] The share of the United States averaged 130,000,000 pounds, or 12 per cent, and on the whole has shown a distinctly downward trend. Since 1916 there have been fairly consistent increases, and with recent innovations in the merchandising of fresh fish a rather sharp rise may be expected in the total annual catch, which if long continued may soon become an important factor affecting the abundance of supply.

In recognition of the importance of this fishery and of the need for knowledge as to the changes in abundance of this and other bank fisheries, for some years the United States Bureau of Fisheries has been conducting scientific investigations of the cod.[6] Since migrations promised to be an important factor, thousands of cod have been tagged both on inshore and offshore grounds. The results of tagging to date indicate that in some localities, such as those around Mount Desert, the cod population is resident the year around. In other localities seasonal migrations occur. For example most of the cod that spend their summers on Nantucket Shoals migrate southward to the coast of New Jersey and even as far as the Chesapeake Capes in winter, returning to Nantucket Shoals in the spring. On the other hand, preliminary studies of the cod population on the offshore banks indicate that, while they do not make regular seasonal migrations, they do move about considerably more than those in the Mount Desert region. These studies demonstrate well-marked differences in the habits of cod of different regions, clearly showing the necessity for full knowledge of the separate populations composing the cod stock in studying fluctuations of the fishery. Furthermore, oceanographic studies lead one to believe that few codfish grounds are self-perpetuating.

An investigation of the situation in Massachusetts Bay has shown that practically all the eggs there spawned are carried out by ocean currents, some to Nantucket Shoals, others to the banks to the east and north.[7] These data show the need for detailed scientific investigations not only of the habits of the adult population but of the distribution of eggs and young as well. For, although the adult population of a given ground may be fairly stationary, its increment of young cod depends on the success of spawning on other grounds; and the wiping out of the stock of adults on one ground may result in the depletion of the stock on a fairly remote ground. To insure full knowledge of what is happening on these fishing banks, it is of the highest importance that the studies of the cod be carried to completion and that similar investigations be made of every other important commercial species of ground fish. Not only that, but suitable machinery for scientific investigations must be maintained after the completion of these preliminary researches in order that at all times the condition and trend of the population of each important species may be known.

The Haddock Fishery; Fish Packaging

The haddock, a species common to both sides of the North Atlantic, is one of the most abundant fishes in this great fishing-bank area. Until recently the fishery was much less important. The catch to a considerable degree was incidental to that of the more highly prized cod. Before 1905, the year in which the otter trawl was introduced, the United States catch was usually less than 50 million pounds—on a parity with the Canadian catch.[8] As about 80 per cent of the catch by otter trawls consisted of haddock, it became increasingly desirable to create a greater demand for this excellent but little-known and little-prized species. In 1920 concerted effort was made by the trade with the help of the Bureau of Fisheries to popularize the haddock. As a result there came a slowly increasing demand for this species, one of the lowest-priced food fishes in our markets. In the late fall of 1921 a Boston dealer began the shipment of fresh had-dock fillets wrapped in parchment paper. This was the beginning of a new feature of fresh-fish merchandising which was bound not only to revolutionize the merchandising of haddock but the fresh-fish business as a whole. Improvements followed one another in rapid succession: packing of fillets in tin containers surrounded by ice, the development of quick-freezing methods to aid in wider distribution or in the accumulation of stocks when fish are plentiful, packing the fish in cartons, trade-marking, advertising individual brands, and many other innovations in line with modern methods of mer-chandising food products.[9]

Initiated in 1921, the production of packaged fresh and frozen fish in 1925 amounted to 8,000,000 pounds; to 30,000,000 pounds in 1927; and to 85,000,000 pounds in 1929; declining to less than 66,000,000 pounds in 1931. The 1929 production employed about 210,000,000 pounds of fish in the round, packed in 112 plants in twelve states, and haddock constituted 85 per cent of the total.

Mention has been made of three factors bearing on the develop-ment of the fishery for haddock: the otter trawl, popularization of the species with government aid, and fish packaging. With this in mind let us review the growth of the fishery and its effects.

The following was the average catch in millions of pounds per annum for five-year periods: 1905–1909, 64.4; 1910–1914, 69.1; 1915–1919, 73.2; and 1920–1924, 92.6. By 1924 the development of fish packaging had reached important proportions and the demand for haddock had been greatly augmented. The result was a rapidly increasing intensity of fishing effort, as the catch for succeeding years indicates: 1925, 119; 1926, 126.5; 1927, 174; 1928, 230; and 1929, 340 millions of pounds. At the height of the fishery on the South Channel grounds the catch amounted to 114 pounds per acre per annum. That this rate of growth could continue for more than a very few years appeared doubtful. In fact, the catch of 1931 approximated only 190,400,000 pounds. Signs of a lessened stock in heavily fished areas are in evidence. Efforts are being made to develop new fishing areas. Moreover a great fishing industry has been established without the corresponding studies of the condition and the trend of the fishery. We lack data to guide us in husbanding the supply and capital and as to the extent to which further exploitation may be safely indulged in. This is another illustration of the need for detailed biological studies of each important commercial fishery, and it also shows the rapidity with which demand may be built up to a dangerously high level through new merchandising methods.

The Mackerel Fishery

The common mackerel is one of New England's most valued fishes. In habits it is markedly different from ground fish such as cod and haddock, the abundance of which does not appear to be subject to violent fluctuations. The mackerel is a pelagic species, schooling and feeding at or near the surface and subject to extremely wide fluctuations in abundance. In most years the additions to the mackerel stock are not large. Occasionally, under more favorable conditions for the development of the eggs and young, the number of survivals and growth to maturity are so great that the sea is full of mackerel for the next few years.

Studies of the U. S. Bureau of Fisheries on the composition of the catch reveal that the additions to the stock of mackerel from the spawnings of 1922, 1924, 1925, and 1926 were negligible.[10] There was a fair survival in 1921 and 1927, and large additions in 1923 and 1928. As a result of the additions of 1921 and 1923, when the fish of these year-classes reached market size, there was a rapid rise in the market catch from less than 10,000,000 pounds in 1921 to nearly 50,000,000 pounds in 1926. Then, with the lessening in abundance of these groups, the catch declined during 1927 and 1928; but by 1929 the rich year-class of 1928 began entering the market catch, bringing about an upward trend to a new high level of production of 68,400,000 pounds in 1930.

There are two significant facts connected with this fishery. In the first place, there is as yet no definite evidence that man's fishing activities have any marked effect on the abundance of mackerel. Whatever effect there may be is certainly much less than that due to natural fluctuations. Secondly, the biologists have demonstrated the practicability of determining the abundance of new stocks of mackerel before they reach a commercial size. By analysis of the several year-classes they could predict in advance of the fishing season the probable abundance of the different sizes of mackerel and thus render a distinct economic service to the industry. Provision should be made for the regular collection of data to make such a service possible. Even though man's fishing activities may have little influence on the population of mackerel and as yet no definite method of building up the stock in lean years has been developed, the fishermen should carefully consider the desirability of limiting the catches of the smaller fish, purely for economic reasons. In the spring of 1931 the Bureau of Fisheries predicted a catch of 35,300,000 pounds[11] exclusive of 1930 tinker mackerel (i.e. small-sized mackerel). There was an error of 8.5 per cent in this prediction, the actual yield of the sizes of fish considered being 32,164,000 pounds with a total catch of 36,472,000 pounds.

THE LOBSTER PROBLEM

The American lobster of our North Atlantic waters is the most highly prized marine food common to the region. The New England fishery appears to have reached its maximum in 1889 with a catch of nearly 30,450,000 pounds valued at $833,736, or 2.7 cents a pound to the fishermen. Thereafter there was continued decline to less than 10,000,000 pounds in 1924, for which the fishermen received $3,000,000, or more than 30 cents a pound. At 1924 prices the 1889 catch would have had a value of more than $9,000,000. Thus the favorite and highest-priced fishery product has been permitted to decline to a dangerously low level. In 1929 the catch amounted to 10,300,000 pounds and in 1930 to 12,350,000 pounds.

As Dr. Herrick (1909) fittingly expressed it twenty years ago:

"More lobsters have been taken from the sea than nature has been able to replace by the slow process of reproduction and growth. In other words, man has been continually gathering in the wild crop, but has bestowed no effective care upon the seed. The demands of a continent steadily increasing in wealth and in population have stimulated the efforts of the dealers and fishermen, who must work harder each year for what they receive in order to keep up the waning supply. The natural result has followed, namely, a scarcity of numbers and a decrease in the size of the animals caught, with steadily advancing prices paid for the product. This is precisely what we should have been led to expect, had we based our judgment upon any sound principles of common sense and human economy, not to speak of a knowledge of the mode of life and general natural history of the animal in question.

"The problem before us is how to aid nature in restoring and maintaining an equilibrium of numbers in the species, or how to increase the number of adult animals raised from the eggs. It concerns not only the fisherman who earns a livelihood through the fishery, or the dealer who has capital at stake, but the public of many lands; in fact, everyone in the Western Hemisphere at least who likes the lobster for food. When the decline of the already depleted fisheries became a serious menace protection was sought in legislation, but since the lobster supply of this country is drawn from several states and from Canada and the maritime provinces as well, no uniformity of laws or methods was to be expected. Each state enacted its own laws, which were often widely at variance, unscientific, and subject to continuous change. Up to the present time every effort to check the constant and ever-increasing drain upon this fishery has signally failed, which shows that either the laws are defective or that the means of enforcing them are insufficient."[12]

In spite of the fact that Dr. Herrick in his report made many specific recommendations, measures hitherto adopted by the New England states have not served to bring back the lobster to its former abundance. As the difficulties are enhanced by lack of uniformity in adjoining states in regard to legal sizes and other factors, it appears important to establish a commission of representatives from the several states to control so valuable a fishery by interstate treaties or agreements.

OYSTER FARMING

Next to lobsters, oysters are perhaps the most universally liked sea food produced in New England waters. Together with other shellfish, such as lobsters, clams, and scallops, they are unusually rich in elements of importance in the diet.

Production of oysters in New England is confined almost wholly to the area south of Cape Cod. As long ago as 1898 New England's production of oysters amounted to 2,650,000 bushels. It reached its maximum about 1912 with a production in excess of 3,700,000 bushels, followed by a decline to 648,000 bushels in 1928 and an increase to 1,220,000 bushels in 1930. As a result of the rapid industrialization of southern New England, with the outpourings of sewage and trade wastes, many of the shore areas were rendered unsuitable for habitation by oysters. The one thing that has kept the oyster industry alive has been the development of oyster farming. In spite of the oyster farmers' efforts, production in Rhode Island declined from 2,268,000 bushels in 1910 to 894,537 bushels in 1919, and the decline in oyster grounds leased by the state to individuals for the same relative period was from 21,000 acres to 7000 acres. Since the war, however, the oyster farmers have extended their producing areas into deeper waters; and, with a realization of the damages of pollution and a betterment of conditions, the outlook for the oyster industry of the future appears to be greatly improved. Much of this improvement has come about through the aid of scientific research in solving the oyster farmers' problems.

For example, one of the great problems has been to get a "set," or annual crop of growing oysters. Research has shown that in those years when water temperatures were above normal spawning and setting of the young oysters was successful and when temperatures were below normal setting was a failure. By the use of continued observations the scientist can predict favorable setting conditions and the approximate time of their occurrence and thus guide the oystermen as to when and how many shells they should put out to secure a successful set of young oysters. The scientist has also contributed much in the development of improved types of set collectors, which will enable the oyster farmer to obtain a much higher production of seed than was formerly possible.[13]

The result of the work done has been to demonstrate the practicability of oyster farming as a commercial enterprise and to reveal that where oyster farming is practiced the oyster industry is being saved from exhaustion. Scientific research should be continued. The state authorities should encourage capital to enter the industry and should provide such safeguards as will insure to the investor the products of his own labors. The field of scientific research needs to be broadened to demonstrate the practicability of cultivating clams and possibly other shellfish.

Game Fishes

One of New England's greatest natural resources is her wealth of lakes and streams capable, if properly administered, of providing some of the finest sport fishing for trout and salmon in the country. One of her great needs is to provide out-of-doors recreation for her countless thousands of workers in factory, shop, mill, and office, and one of her great opportunities for bringing wealth to her communities is to provide good fishing and other recreational facilities in attractive form to non-residents.

With the development of thousands of miles of excellent roads, the increased ownership of automobiles, more hours of leisure, and the growing need for relaxation from modern business demands in office and factory, greater numbers are seeking healthful out-of-doors recreation. States with an abundance of streams and lakes well stocked with game fish are finding their wealth augmented by the expenditures of these recreation seekers for lodging, supplies, boats, bait, guides, and other needs. They are finding that fish translated into the sportsman's dollar command many times the value of the same fish sold in the market or caught for home consumption.

Many factors have contributed to the difficulties of keeping the streams amply stocked with game fish. These include deforestation with changed stream flow, the construction of dams and other barriers, pollution, inadequate legislation and lax enforcement, much heavier fishing resulting from good roads, more automobiles, and shorter hours of labor, and, finally, political control of departments of fish

and game, with attendant difficulties in establishing a sound conservation policy and in acquiring the services of officials especially
trained for the work. The problem is fast becoming more complicated
through the acquisition of the good fishing streams by private individuals and by the posting of streams by persons with little interest
in angling but desirous of protecting their property from destruction
through the carelessness or maliciousness of the angler. On the
other hand, the reversion of many abandoned farms to a wild state
has benefited many streams.

The principal contribution to maintaining the supply has been
through fish-cultural activities by the federal and state governments.
In the early stages of fish propagation too much dependence was
placed on the development of mechanical means for hatching out
more and more millions of fish. Instead of planting the newly hatched
fry, the modern aim is to rear a greater number of the game fish to
legal size before planting them in the streams. The need for this is
especially emphasized in the more thickly populated sections where
the streams are very heavily fished. The posting of the streams
and the acquirement of fishing privileges in the best streams by private
wealth necessitate still further action on the part of the state if the
great mass of its population is to enjoy sport fishing in the future.
For one thing, the sportsman must expect to pay a larger fee for his
angling license, and the state must take such action as is necessary to
keep open the streams for fishing to the general public.

Connecticut has assumed a position of leadership in her efforts to
save the game and fish for the use of the common people. "The
Connecticut Plan" may be summed up as follows.[14] The General
Assembly of 1925 authorized the State Board of Fisheries and Game to
acquire by gift, lease, or purchase the fishing rights in streams, ponds,
and lakes and to make regulations as to their administration. The
board has leased the fishing rights on sixteen of the larger trout
streams, comprising an aggregate length of 160 miles, and, in addition, on numerous spring-fed tributaries, which serve as sanctuaries.
The leased waters are stocked annually with six- to nine-inch trout. The
streams are patroled throughout the fishing season. Stiles are constructed over fences between adjoining properties, and the rights of
the landowner are properly safeguarded. On the opening day of the
trout season in 1929 some 10,000 trout were caught in these leased
streams, representing a replacement value of at least $25,000 on the
basis of commercial breeders' prices. All persons, men and women,
over fifteen years of age are required to have a license, and youths
under sixteen years must have a permit, forfeitable on violation of
the regulations. This will serve as an illustration of the needs for a
well-defined stocking policy in all the New England states and of one
way in which real progress is being made. Consideration should

also be given to providing good fishing for the youngsters and adults who with less expensive fishing tackle are satisfied with a creel filled with sunfish, catfish, or other common pond fishes.

IMPORTANCE OF MARINE FOODS

No evaluation of the importance of New England's fishery resources is complete without consideration of the place of marine products in the diet. "Modern researches on foods and nutrition," according to Professor E. V. McCollum, "have brought to light many surprises, both as regards the nutritive needs of the body and the dietary properties of individual foodstuffs, among which the most marked contrasts have been found. In no case have any foods gained more recognition as having unique dietary values than have the principal fish and shellfish."[15] It is now a well known fact that there are a number of chemical substances indispensable for normal nutrition in man and animals, the absence of which in the diet results in deficiency diseases. These deficiency diseases can be prevented or cured only by the inclusion of proper vitamins. Fish fats and oils are rich in vitamins A and D. Oysters contain both vitamins B and C.

Sea products are rich in minerals, and there is much less danger of our encountering deficiencies in such elements by eating products of the sea than if our diet is confined to land foods. It has been shown that marine fish and shellfish contain a higher percentage of iodine than any other common foods. Oysters, clams, and lobsters contain about 200 times as much iodine as milk or eggs; shrimp, 100 times as much; and crabs and most ocean fishes, 50 times as much. These facts should be of interest to persons living in the so-called goitre belts and particularly to those planning the diet of young people living in areas where disorders of the thyroid gland are common. The proteins of salmon, mackerel, and butterfish are easily and almost completely digested, as are also the proteins of oysters, clams, scallops, and mussels. According to Tressler, "Very few experiments have been carried out to determine the digestibility of crabs, lobsters, shrimp, and other crustaceans, but by analogy we may conclude that the proteins of these shellfish are readily digested."[16]

A study of all phases of the dietary properties of marine foods reveals that they are highly important for man and his domestic animals. This is an added reason for conserving New England's aquatic resources in order to make them widely available to the American people.

FISHERIES ADMINISTRATION

We have been afforded glimpses of some of the important fisheries, such as those for cod, mackerel, lobsters, oysters, and the game fishes. These vary greatly in character. The problems of their administration are equally varied and complex. In the high-seas fisheries outside the three-mile limit fishermen from the nations of the world may engage, and for many years Europeans have fished the banks off our coasts. If the fish supply becomes endangered, regulation must come through international agreement, a most difficult procedure.

Control over the fisheries inside the three-mile limit and within state boundaries is vested in the state, except such control as is exercised by the Army Engineers in keeping navigable waters free from obstructions to navigation. In the case of migratory fishes, such as the shad and mackerel, the state is limited in its control to the fishes within its boundaries and cannot control fishing operations for such species once they have passed beyond its jurisdiction. For the most part state administration activities are confined to the enforcement of the laws and to the propagation of fish, chiefly the game species.

Any successful program of fish husbandry must be based on a thorough knowledge of the life histories and habits of each species, the condition and trend of each fishery, the effects of fishing gear and other equipment, and the wise application of this knowledge through channels of legislation, supplemented by the assistance of man where practicable, as in the case of oyster farming and the propagation of food and game fishes. The individual states have depended largely upon the U. S. Bureau of Fisheries for biological investigations and statistical inventories—that is, for the acquirement of the basic knowledge upon which good administration must be founded. The Bureau's facilities have been inadequate to cover satisfactorily all of the important fisheries along our Atlantic, Gulf, and Pacific coasts, the Great Lakes, the Mississippi Valley, and Alaska. Valuable investigations, however, are being made of cod, haddock, mackerel, oysters, and other species of importance.

It remains to be demonstrated whether man can exercise any appreciably helpful measures of control over the abundance of cod, haddock, and other ground fish except by preventing unnecessary destructiveness of fishing operations. This at least, should be done. While man may not be able to exercise appreciable control over such species as mackerel, investigations may be extremely helpful to him in predicting in advance the abundance of the supply he is about to draw upon. The greatest opportunity for wise administration lies in the coastal and river fisheries and particularly in such fields as the development of shellfish farming and the stocking of streams with game fish.

Properly to husband New England's fishery resources the following matters should receive serious consideration:

1. Provision for—(a) annual fishery statistics in sufficient detail to enable the biologist to follow the condition and trend of each im-

portant fishery; and (b) an extension of the program of biological research to each of these species.

2. Coöperation between federal and state agencies to insure the collection of statistics that are comparable throughout the range of a species and for the coördination of research.

3. Setting up of interstate agencies for control of such fisheries as present problems common to more than one state, as for example, lobsters and shad.

4. Increasing the authority of state executives to make changes in regulations as fast as the need arises and the taking of the appointment of state conservation officers out of politics.

5. Development of a broader, more effective program of stream stocking with game fish and the fullest development of the state's recreational facilities.

6. Centralization of control of the fisheries in the state government.

NOTES

For a general bibliography consult Bashford Dean, *Bibliography of Fishes*, 3 vols., American Museum of Natural History, New York, 1923. Statistical and other data on the fisheries of New England are given in the section *Fisheries* (prepared for the most part by O. E. Sette) in C. E. Artman, *Industrial Structure of New England*, U. S. Dept. of Commerce, Bur. of Foreign and Domestic Commerce, Washington, 1930 (*Domestic Commerce Ser. No. 28*). Essential material concerning the fisheries of New England will be found in the publications of the U. S. Bureau of Fisheries. For these through 1920 see R. M. E. MacDonald, *An Analytical Subject Bibliography of the Publications of the Bureau of Fisheries, 1871–1920*, Appendix V to *Report of the U. S. Commissioner of Fisheries, 1920*, Washington, 1921 (*Bur. of Fisheries Doc. No. 899*), pp. 1–306. More recent publications of the Bureau are listed in the annual *List of Publications of the Department of Commerce* and its monthly *Supplement* and in mimeographed bibliographical memoranda issued from time to time by the Bureau. The Bureau publishes periodically as an appendix to the *Annual Report of the Commissioner* a pamphlet entitled *Fishery Industries of the United States* containing a review of the progress of the industry region by region with statistics by months on landings of different kinds of fish at the principal fishing ports (especially Boston, Gloucester, and Portland in New England). Another appendix to the *Annual Report* covers *Progress in Biological Inquiries*. The "results of research in applied science in the fields of biology, technology, economics, and statistics of the fisheries" are published in a series of *Investigational Reports, Economic Circulars*, and *Fishery Circulars*, and in the *Bulletin of the U. S. Bureau of Fisheries.*— EDIT.

[1] See H. B. Bigelow, *Physical Oceanography of the Gulf of Maine*, from *Bull. U. S. Bur. of Fisheries*, Vol. 40, 1924, Part II (with bibliography) (*Bur. of Fisheries Doc. No. 969*), pp. 511–1027; the same, *Exploration of the Waters of the Gulf of Maine*, in *Geogr. Rev.*, Vol. 18, 1928, pp. 232–260; W. H. Rich, *Fishing Grounds of the Gulf of Maine*, Appendix III to the *Report of the U. S. Commissioner of Fisheries, 1929*, Washington, 1929 (*Bur. of Fisheries Doc. No. 1059*), pp. 51–117; H. B. Bigelow and W. W. Welsh, *Fishes of the Gulf of Maine*, in *Bull. U. S. Bur. of Fisheries*, Vol. 40, 1924, Part I (with bibliography) (*Bur. of Fisheries Doc. No. 965*), pp. 1–567; H. B. Bigelow, *Plankton of the Offshore Waters of the Gulf of Maine*, from *Bull. U. S. Bur.*

of Fisheries, Vol. 40, 1924, Part II (with bibliography) (*Bur. of Fisheries Doc. No. 968*), pp. 1–509.

[2] Raymond McFarland, *A History of the New England Fisheries*, New York, 1911, p. 322 (bibliography, pp. 338–363). The statement quoted is equally true today.

[3] These figures, based on statistics collected by the U. S. Bureau of Fisheries (see Table IV, p. 272, below), should not be confused with the total catch of the nations on the fishing banks.

[4] See paper by Mr. G. A. Fitzgerald entitled *The Fisheries of New England: Economic Factors*, in the present volume, pp. 261–277, below, especially pp. 269–270.

[5] O. E. Sette, *Statistics of the Catch of Cod off the East Coast of North America to 1926*, Appendix IX to the *Report of the U. S. Commissioner of Fisheries for 1927*, Washington, 1928 (*Bur. of Fisheries Doc. No. 1034*), pp. 737–748.

[6] See especially W. C. Schroeder, *Migrations and Other Phases in the Life History of the Cod off Southern New England*, from *Bull. U. S. Bur. of Fisheries*, Vol. 46, 1930 (with bibliography) (*Bur. of Fisheries Doc. No. 1081*), pp. 1–136; and other publications of the Bureau of Fisheries.

[7] C. J. Fish, *Production and Distribution of Cod Eggs in Massachusetts Bay in 1924 and 1925*, from *Bull. U. S. Bur. of Fisheries*, Vol. 43, 1927, Part II (*Bur. of Fisheries Doc. No. 1032*), pp. 253–296.

[8] See Fig. 1, p. 273, below; also A. W. H. Needles, *Statistics of the Haddock Fishery in North American Waters*, Appendix II to *Report of the U. S. Commissioner of Fisheries, 1930;* Washington, 1930 (*Bur. of Fisheries Doc. No. 1074*), pp. 27–40.

[9] These innovations are described in greater detail by Mr. Fitzgerald, pp. 264–267, below.

[10] See the annual reports of the Division of Scientific Inquiry, U. S. Bureau of Fisheries, entitled *Progress in Biological Inquiries* for the years 1927–1930.

[11] O. E. Sette, *Outlook for the Mackerel Fishery in 1931*, U. S. Bur. of Fisheries, August, 1931 (*Fishery Circular No. 4*).

[12] F. H. Herrick, *Natural History of the American Lobster*, in *Bull. U. S. Bur. of Fisheries*, Vol. 29, 1909 (*Bur. of Fisheries Doc. No. 747*), pp. 149–408.

[13] See various publications of the U. S. Bureau of Fisheries, especially H. F. Prytherch, *Investigation of the Physical Conditions Controlling Spawning of Oysters and the Occurrence, Distribution, and Setting of Oyster Larvae in Milford Harbor, Connecticut*, from *Bull. U. S. Bur. of Fisheries*, Vol. 44, 1928 (with bibliography) (*Bur. of Fisheries Doc. No. 1054*, 1929), pp. 429–503.

[14] F. C. Walcott, *The Connecticut Plan*, in *Field and Stream*, April, 1930, pp. 26–27 and 74.

[15] *Nutritive Value of Fish and Shellfish*, Appendix X to the *Report of the U. S. Commissioner of Fisheries, 1925*, Washington, 1926 (with bibliography) (*Bur. of Fisheries Doc. No. 1000*), pp. 502–552, reference on p. 548.

[16] *Ibid.*, p. 528.

THE FISHERIES OF NEW ENGLAND*

ECONOMIC FACTORS

Gerald A. Fitzgerald

HISTORICAL OUTLINE

THE fisheries of New England have always played an exceedingly important rôle in the economic life of the region.[1] The early settlers gained their living largely from fish caught in Massachusetts Bay. It is interesting to note that the first free public school in the United States was organized at Provincetown, Mass., from the proceeds of license money obtained from fishermen using the town waters. Boston University was founded on a gift from Isaac Rich, the man who first recognized and took advantage of the fact that swordfish makes a delicious and thoroughly salable product. In fact, the early fisheries formed the principal industry of Massachusetts and may well have helped prevent the disruption of the colony.

Cape Cod was an important fishing center in the first part of the nineteenth century. Here the men who fished in the summer months worked in the salt factories during the winter. However, when foreign salt began to flood our markets the industry became seriously affected. The 616 salt works of 1837 had dwindled to 181 in 1850 and disappeared altogether with the reduction of the protective tariff in 1876. Meanwhile fishing was rapidly pushing to the fore on Cape Ann. The fishermen of the summer became shoemakers and netmakers in the winter. Gloucester long has been famous for its large vessels and hardy, courageous fishermen. Although in point of production Boston is now in the lead, Gloucester has by no means retrogressed. The curing, packing, canning, and freezing industries, together with netmaking and shipbuilding, swell to nearly ten thousand the number of Gloucester's inhabitants directly identified with the fisheries.

From 1835 onward the vessels out of Boston began to multiply rapidly as the dealers on old Commercial Wharf developed facilities for handling the increased catches. In 1884 a union of fish dealers leased the entire property at T Wharf, and some 250 schooners landed their catches regularly. This was the first step toward unification. Although both Boston and Gloucester rose practically simultaneously

---

*This paper was prepared by Mr. Fitzgerald with the coöperation of Messrs. Gardner Poole and W. H. Raye of the Birdseye Packing Co., Boston, Mass. Acknowledgment is also made to Mr. Wetmore Hodges for helpful suggestions.—EDIT.

[1] For notes see below, p. 276.

as fishing centers, a far greater number of fishing vessels were registered at Gloucester than at Boston; however, the location of Boston gave it a decided advantage from an economic point of view, and many Gloucester vessels landed catches there. In the meantime Eastport, Rockland, and Portland in Maine had developed as important fishing centers. Eastport still retains a prominent place, thanks to its proximity to the Passamaquoddy herring fisheries. Its business is canning "sardines." Portland gradually developed into the chief center for fresh fish, because of its superior inland transportation facilities. However, owing to remoteness from markets, the development of the Maine fisheries as a whole has had to await certain innovations in the field of refrigeration. Boston and Gloucester are still the chief fishing centers of New England.

THE MODERN ERA

Basically, the modern era of the New England fisheries began in 1858 when fish was first shipped from Boston to New York with excellent success. Ice was used to preserve the fish in transit.[2] In 1858 the center of distribution of fresh Boston fish was in Boston itself. Shipments were seldom made any farther west than Worcester, a distance of fifty miles. Today, the center of distribution of Boston fish lies a thousand miles away. The use of ice has been only partly responsible. There are but two or possibly three main causes for this gradual business growth. Coöperation in the fishing industry and progress in allied industries, such as refrigeration and transportation, are the chief causes; but the advent of new methods such as filleting has also played an important part.

THE NEW ENGLAND FISH EXCHANGE

The first concrete result of the new coöperative spirit was the opening of the New England Fish Exchange at T Wharf in 1908.[3] The value of the New England Fish Exchange is not appreciated until one realizes the conditions that existed before it was organized. At a very early hour each business day the captains of vessels with a fresh catch would be greeted by representatives of all the wholesalers and commission merchants on the wharf. These representatives would start bidding before the captain could leave his vessel and often they would have formed in advance a buyer's pool. After the captain had announced the kinds and quantities of fish making up his fare he would sell to the highest bidder, who in turn would sell that part of the catch he could not handle to other buyers, usually at the same price. This method of doing business was very inefficient and led to bitter enmities among dealers and captains. Prices bore no relation to public demand. If a large number of vessels reported simultaneously, prices would be lowered automatically. The newer method, instituted by the Exchange and agreed to by captains and dealers, is to have all fish that has been brought in sold in a room provided by the Exchange, the only exception being fish for salting which could be sold on the wharf. The auction takes place at a definite hour in order that all interested buyers who are members of the Exchange may be present. Since this privilege can be obtained for a merely nominal sum, all fish buyers in New England have an equal advantage. The privilege is exercised for the most part by Boston wholesalers, although outsiders having a sufficient volume of purchases also make use of the Exchange. The Exchange looks out for the business end of all transactions; but, equally important, it brings the fishermen and buyers together in a common market where prices are stablized. Thus are corrected many of the abuses that had previously existed in the trade.

THE BOSTON FISH MARKET CORPORATION[3]

Through further coöperative effort the Boston Fish Market Corporation was formed in 1910. Its goal was the acquisition from the Commonwealth of Massachusetts of a new location in South Boston for the industry. With the natural growth of business the situation at T Wharf had become unbearable. The dealers and captains were crowded for space; opportunity for development was lacking; unsanitary conditions and general inefficiency existed throughout the T Wharf market. After a quarter of a century T Wharf had been outgrown. The outcome of the overtures to the state was the new Boston Fish Pier (erected at a cost of over $2,000,000) into which the industry moved on March 28, 1915.

THE BOSTON FISH PIER, 1932[3]

By 1924 it was evident that the industry had again outgrown its quarters, this time in but a decade. Since then and up to very recently the industry has been undecided as to its future course. After trying a number of methods to increase the efficiency and capacity of the present pier, the pier owners now (1932) are contemplating building the nucleus of a thoroughly remodeled pier. The remodeled pier will undoubtedly have a complete modern handling and conveying system—probably the largest if not the first to be installed by the fishing industry. It is expected that the capacity of the present quarters will be more than doubled because of the increased efficiency of the facilities to be provided. The same spirit of coöperation that resulted in the new Fish Pier in 1914 is responsible for the present attempt to improve conditions.

EARLY IMPROVEMENTS IN HANDLING AND MARKETING[4]

After the first successful long-distance shipment of fish packed in ice in 1858 the age-old inhibitions of the industry were broken down.

Naturally the fish business expanded rapidly as shipments in ice became a universal practice. Fish had now been taken out of the ultra-perishable class. Yet, except in the winter months, shipments beyond three or four hundred miles were rare. When transportation facilities improved and express companies provided a re-icing service, the distance a shipment could be made was doubled. However, the markets near at hand absorbed the greater part of the New England production. That part not sold fresh was salted. Sales efforts were meager and unorganized. The advent of the commercial telegraph and telephone broadened the market considerably. Still, even in the winter a shipment as far west as St. Louis was rare up to very recent years. Although the progress of the industry followed closely the progress of other industries that provided improved services, the first really rapid strides in the history of the fish business have been due to radical improvements in methods of merchandising the fish itself.

The Development of Mechanical Refrigeration[5]

One of the most important contributions of science to the New England fisheries has been the remarkable advance made since the latter part of the last century in the application of mechanical refrigeration. With artificial low temperatures came the realization that the gluts of the fish business could be absorbed by freezing the fish and storing it until the market improved. Of course many abuses crept in, and much fish was frozen that had been kept too long and really should have been thrown away. This means of preservation, however, was used to the fullest extent in the mackerel fishery, and through the subsequent stabilization of prices it has been the savior of that fishery. Production grew as the market for fresh fish expanded, but with the inroads of industrialism it became more difficult to obtain sufficient quantities of natural ice for the vessels. Artificial ice manufacture then began to play an ever more important part in the development of the fisheries. Except at a few small places along the Maine coast, practically all the ice now used in the New England fisheries is artificial. The ice plants are located on or near the fish wharves, and this in itself has increased efficiency.

The Introduction of Quick Freezing

The fishing industry took the lead in the freezing of perishable food products. As far back as 1861 Enoch Piper received a United States patent for freezing fish by means of salt and ice. Such methods were used on a small scale between then and 1892, when the first ammonia refrigerating machine was introduced for freezing fish. Subsequently, and particularly since the beginning of the present century, the method of freezing in cold rooms has come into widespread use. More than a hundred million pounds of fish are so frozen annually in the United States today.

In 1869 William Davis was granted a patent for freezing fish packed tightly in covered metal pans completely surrounded by ice and salt. This method was capable of producing frozen fish of excellent quality and is still in use on the Great Lakes. In 1916 Plank[6] and others set forth the scientific reasons why the rapid freezing of fish produces a commodity of superior quality, and since about 1919 more serious and widespread attention has been given to the development of rapid freezing processes.

THE INTRODUCTION OF FILLETING[7]

Further advance was made upon the introduction of a new method of preparation of the fish itself, when about the year 1919 Kenneth Fowler of New York conceived the idea of dressing fish ready-to-cook (as fillets, steaks, and pan fish), wrapping them separately or in small bundles, chilling them to just above the freezing point, and shipping them in insulated (balsawood) boxes direct to the retailer. This was probably the first sanitary trade-marked package of dressed fresh fish ever used.

In 1921, Dana Ward, a Boston fish merchant, developed a more economical package which was rapidly adopted by the industry. The fish were filleted—that is all bones were removed—and the clear-flesh sides of the fish brined, wrapped in parchment, packed in a wooden box, and shipped by express direct to the retailer.   John C. Wheeler, one of Ward's Boston competitors, improved on this method by packing the parchment-wrapped fillets in a tin box which was then placed in a wooden box large enough to admit plenty of ice. Other dealers followed in quick succession. By 1924 there were 40 filleting plants; this number was swelled to 85 in 1928, to 112 in 1929, and to 128 in 1930. In the latter year 33 species of fish were produced as fillets in about 25 cities in 15 different states. By far the greater part of this business is concentrated in New England.

THE COMBINATION OF QUICK FREEZING AND FILLETING[8]

A further advance was made by Clarence Birdseye, a New Yorker, when in 1923 he developed an apparatus for quick-freezing blocks of fish fillets, steaks, and pan fish. Several other quick-freezing apparatus for fillets were evolved shortly afterwards. By 1927 three important processes for freezing fillets were being employed in New England. Clarence Birdseye, who by this time had transferred the scene of his experiments to Gloucester, Mass., had now developed a newer method of far-reaching importance. The fillets were packaged, hermetically sealed, and then subjected to temperatures as low as fifty degrees below zero Fahrenheit. The packages were placed in a cold tunnel between two very cold heat-conducting surfaces—such as continuous metal belts—and the contents frozen in a remarkably short time without direct contact with the refrigerant. The patents on which the process is based were recently sold to a large food corporation, and the system is now quick-freezing meats, fruits and vegetables, and is well on the way to revolutionizing the whole perishable-food industry.

The Advent of Brands and Trade-Marks

For the first time in its history, the industry has a product easily adapted to branding and trade-marking. Both fresh and frozen fillets are merchandised wholly under special brands and trade-marks, and this business is growing at a very surprising rate. With particular brands of fish to advertise, mammoth programs of association and individual advertising are being undertaken. The year 1930 was marked by the first use of radio for advertising nationally a private brand of fillets.

Some Advantages of Quick-Freezing Fillets[8]

The older method of freezing in cold rooms, called slow or sharp freezing, appears simple enough but causes a great deal of irremediable damage to the fish. Quick freezing, on the other hand, introduces a perfect product. On defrosting, the cells retain their natural fluids, while the tender juiciness and natural flavor are returned unharmed. Fresh fish, fresher than one ordinarily obtains even in the Boston market, is the result, because it is quick-frozen within only a few hours after leaving its habitat, the sea.

Quick-frozen fillets, which can be frozen so much faster than whole fish, enhance the quality of the resulting product. They can be packaged economically and so protected from desiccation and oxidation during storage. The final step appears to have been already achieved. It is the method developed by Clarence Birdseye, wherein the fillets are packed and hermetically sealed before freezing in neat trade-marked packages which go directly to the consumer without ever being exposed to contamination, desiccation, or oxidation at any place or any time while en route. Because of its pliability fish conforms nicely to the shape of the package, assuring excellent contact with the freezing surface.

The outstanding economy of filleting is the reduction of shipping weight by elimination of the waste portions of the fish at the point of production. This amounts in all cases to more than 50 per cent and in the case of flat fish to as much as 75 per cent. The outstanding economy of freezing is in the adaptability of the preserved product to storage, whereby the peaks and valleys of production and demand may be leveled to stabilize the industry. The result is price stabilization in an industry that has heretofore had tremendous price fluctuations even from day to day. Moreover, a quick-frozen fillet is not

TABLE I—PACKAGED FISH PRODUCTION IN THE UNITED STATES[a]

YEARS	HADDOCK Pounds	COD Pounds	HAKE Pounds
1921	....	....	....
1922	....	....	....
1923	....	....	....
1924	....	....	....
1925	....	....	....
1926	14,600,000	1,400,000	800,000
1927	....	....	....
1928	56,600,000	1,950,000	1,300,000
1929	71,400,000	3,500,000	2,600,000
1930	62,146,000	6,602,000	2,418,000

TABLE I, Continued

YEARS	SQUETEAGUE Pounds	MISC. Pounds	TOTAL Pounds	VALUE Dollars
1921	....	....	50,000	....
1922	....	....	250,000	....
1923	....	....	1,750,000	....
1924	....	....	4,000,000	....
1925	....	....	8,000,000	....
1926	200,000	1,300,000	18,300,000	....
1927	....	....	30,000,000	....
1928	1,300,000	3,900,000	65,050,000	$9,790,024
1929	1,325,000	3,875,000	82,700,000	14,541,000
1930	1,036,000	7,811,000	80,013,000	12,579,664

[a] Based on *Fishery Industries of the United States, 1921–1930*, U.S. Dept. of Commerce, Bur. of Fisheries, Washington. The figures include data for a very small amount "of steaks," "sticks," and "pan-dressed" fish besides fillets. The figures previous to 1926 have been estimated. For 1929 there was an additional amount of 1,685,355 pounds of smoked packaged fish produced, valued at $272,479. Total fillet production for 1928, 1929, and 1930 was 58,217,881, 78,413,938, and 73,753,000 pounds respectively. Of these amounts, 21,632,000 pounds were frozen in 1929 and 20,319,000 in 1930.

perishable while protected at a properly low temperature. So protected it can be shipped anywhere. New markets are being opened that never before sold a pound of New England's fish except salted, canned, or pickled. The demand is now greater than the supply. New England fisheries are in the midst of revolutionary changes, an economic development all-embracing and without precedent in the fishing industry.

ECONOMIES OF THE NEW SYSTEM

The quick-frozen fillet has placed the New England fishing industry on a high business plane. Packing-house methods are now employed.

The business is gradually becoming amalgamated into larger units, where all the economies of large-scale production can be enjoyed. Even the relatively small producers have increased their efficiency by improving their production layout and by including labor-saving equipment, such as mechanical hoists, conveyors, and packaging machinery. For those who cannot afford to own their own quick-freezing equipment, public cold storages have provided this facility at a reasonable tariff. Stocks are now prepared ahead in times of plenty to be sold in times of scarcity. Market gluts are a thing of the past, and the business is on an even keel and forging ahead rapidly.

TABLE II—PRODUCTION OF FROZEN FISHERY PRODUCTS[a]

Illustrating the increases in New England due mainly to the addition of quick-frozen products

YEARS	UNITED STATES Pounds	NEW ENGLAND Pounds
1920	92,259,671	....
1921	80,737,000	....
1922	75,154,028	18,618,000
1923	91,548,643	....
1924	97,324,144	21,686,000
1925	91,165,000	24,561,000
1928	113,638,000	30,802,000
1929	121,543,000	39,511,000
1930	139,297,000	52,624,000

[a] Based on *Fishery Industries of the United States, 1921–1930*, especially 1929 issue, pp. 760–772, and 1930 issue, pp. 174–184.

It was mentioned above that in filleting more than 50 per cent of the round weight of fish consists of inedible parts. With the reduction of this amount in weight comes a corresponding saving in cost of transportation that can be handed on to the consumer. This is borne out by the fact that in 1929 the cost of transportation, icing, etc., was paid on but 84,000,000 pounds of finished product, representing over 200,000,000 pounds of whole fish which would have been handled under the old system. With car-lot transportation of quick-frozen fillets to storage in market areas comes an additional saving over the old single-order express shipments of the past. Here is a further economic advantage for the consumer. The result is that the housewife gets her fish at no greater cost than formerly and is relieved of the unpleasant necessity of cleaning it and preparing it for cooking. She now receives it in a neat package or waterproof wrapping on which are printed several recipes for tempting dishes.

The retailer is no longer a loser because of fish spoiling from overbuying or poor trading conditions. He keeps the product frozen in his mechanically refrigerated show case, where it remains in excellent condition for two weeks or more if necessary. His profit on a given quantity of fish is now a certainty. He is able to handle fish on the same margin of profit as is common for less perishable merchandise. Again the consumer is benefited.

Tracing the evolution of new economies in the fish business from the sea to the consumer, we perceive that they have been brought about through the elimination of waste and the increase in efficiency at all stages. A further economy which may be seriously considered for the first time is the utilization of the waste of filleting plants. Table III shows the great increase in waste utilization since the advent of filleting. This has been possible only through the accumulation of waste at central points. The outlet for the dry fish meal is for animal feeding.

TABLE III—PRODUCTION OF FISH MEAL IN NEW ENGLAND[a]

YEAR	TONS PRODUCED	FACTORY VALUE	PRODUCTION INCREASE (PERCENTAGE)
1924	1,600	$80,000	...
1925	2,800	145,000	75.0
1926	3,100	165,000	10.7
1927	4,500	290,000	45.2
1928	8,800	580,000	95.6
1929	13,000	880,000	47.7
1930	11,500	701,000	−11.5

[a] Based on private communications from U. S. Bur. of Fisheries for years 1924–1928. See also *Fishery Industries of the United States, 1929*, p. 755; *1930*, p. 161.

The figures in Table III indicate an increase of 618.7 per cent in production and 776 per cent in value of fish meal made from filleting plant waste in seven years. Thus the New England fishing industry is now operated like our large meat-packing establishments. The present outlook indicates that the industry may go still further and put its packing plants afloat to operate on the fishing banks several hundred miles from land.

THE FISHING FLEET CATCHES THE NEW TEMPO[9]

Until early in the second decade of the present century the evolution in fishing vessels was slow and for the most part had consisted of changes in design to produce a fast sailing craft of the schooner type. Very few of the sailing vessels had installed auxiliary gasoline engines at this time. However, a type radically new to American waters was introduced in 1905 by the Bay State Fishing Company of Boston with the steam trawler *Spray*. Although built at Quincy,

Mass., the *Spray* was patterned after the English trawlers, some 1400 of which were plying their trade in the North Sea at that time. At once a great hue and cry was heard from fishermen along the New England coast. Heretofore only baited hooks had been used to catch haddock and cod on Georges Bank, New England's own fishing grounds. These fishermen claimed that the large otter trawls, or bag-shaped nets which the steam vessels dragged along the sandy bottom scared away the fish so they would not bite and that their tremendous catches would soon deplete the Georges Bank fisheries and deprive the fishermen of their livelihood. Such sentiment waxed so strong that in 1914 the Bureau of Fisheries took a hand in the matter. Investigators went along with the steam trawlers and studied their catches to determine if they were killing off a large proportion of undersized fish, as this would certainly deplete the fisheries if allowed to continue. After receiving a clean bill of health from the Bureau of Fisheries, the trawling industry obtained a new lease of life. By 1918 there were fourteen steam trawlers out of New England ports and one from Canada, but until the introduction of filleting their value was not fully realized. A steam trawler represents an investment of at least $150,-000, which precludes its use by the ordinary fishermen.

The latter were not slow in adapting the new gear to their smaller boats. After several abortive attempts to adapt ordinary fishing vessels to otter-trawling, the first success was obtained in 1919, when Captain Daniel F. Mullins of New Bedford built the *Mary* especially for trawling gear. The *Mary* towed a net having a hundred-foot sweep, about three fourths the size of that towed by the larger steel steam trawler. This vessel was really a large flounder dragger with certain improvements in mechanical equipment to fit her for dragging in deeper waters. The *Mary* was the first vessel of this type to fish successfully on the Georges Bank. She was also the first of the smaller vessels to make the gasoline engine the main driving power and sail the auxiliary. Today this class of vessels is the fastest-growing group on the Atlantic seaboard. As a class they are called draggers. Although many improvements have been made, they were successful from the start, and their numbers have increased from the single dragger of 1919 to 198 in 1929. The reasons for this really phenomenal development are clear when we consider that a dragger costs about one third as much as a steam trawler, operating expenses are about one fourth as great, the crew only one half as large, the catch fully two thirds as much, and, finally, as a consequence, the net profit is considerably more.

The larger interests have not been slow to grasp the significance of this. Until about 1928 investments in steam trawlers and other large steel-hulled fishing vessels were few. These vessels, to be sure, had many points in their favor. The most important was seaworthiness, the ability to fish in all kinds of weather throughout the whole year. It was only natural that strong efforts should be made to increase their efficiency. In 1928 there were 41 trawlers of over 100 net tons fishing out of New England ports. Only a year later 19 more had been added, and during 1930 there was a similar gain. The adoption of the Diesel engine is the outstanding reason for this rapid growth. It was suddenly realized that 6000 gallons of fuel oil can be made to take far less space and give far greater cruising radius than the bulky coal that occupies so much room in the usual steam trawler. The vessel could be made much smaller and still have the same fish-carrying capacity. The ordinary steam trawler, however, rarely catches more than 50 per cent of the hold capacity, since it must return to port after a few days' fishing to assure a product of high quality. Hence, by reducing the capacity of the hold one third or more, an additional reduction in the size of the whole vessel is made possible. In the building of the last few steel trawlers, therefore, this has been taken into consideration. From 125- to 165-foot vessels, this class is gradually assuming a 110- to 125-foot length with corresponding reductions in other dimensions. Accordingly, their original and operating costs have been greatly reduced and their net profits increased to such an extent as to make them even more desired than the dragger class of vessels.

Although the older forms of fishing still exist, the strictly sailing vessel is a thing of the past. Vessels are still built with sails, but all are now powered with auxiliary engines. During the last few years there has been a tendency greatly to increase the power by using larger engines and thus to insure greater speed in returning to market with the catch. As power increases, sails become useless. However, in certain forms of fishing where dories are used the mother boat usually tacks back and forth along the line of dories during fishing. The use of sails in this case is economical, and this type of fishing will probably be the last in which they are given up.

Modern comforts unknown even ten years ago are now built into fishing vessels. Electric lighting, radio for entertainment, housed-in steering wheel, and well-designed sanitary sleeping quarters are regarded as necessities. The larger vessels carry an experienced radio operator who informs the owners of their position, of the amount of fish caught, and of the approximate arrival time. The owners can also control the vessels' movements by this means. If the market is glutted at one point they can order the vessel to another port where they will find more favorable market conditions. In the case of sickness or accident to vessel or crew, medical or other advice can be received over the radio while assistance is being sent from shore or near-by vessels. A fisherman's life today is much safer and infinitely more comfortable than a few years ago.

PRODUCTION COMPARISONS

In Table IV a comparison of the fisheries production is made for the five New England states covering the period from 1880 to 1930. Although production did not greatly increase during these fifty years, the value has steadily increased. Massachusetts, however, shows a remarkable increase in production during the final four-year period

TABLE IV—FISHERIES OF THE NEW ENGLAND STATES,[a] VARIOUS YEARS, 1880 TO 1930

(In thousands of pounds and thousands of dollars)

YEARS	MAINE		NEW HAMPSHIRE		MASSACHUSETTS	
	Quantity	Value	Quantity	Value	Quantity	Value
1880	......	2,742	....	171	......	7,960
1887	131,380	2,365	4,255	99	299,544	6,464
1888	132,930	2,292	3,843	90	302,046	6,356
1889	129,560	2,111	4,355	89	299,218	5,858
1898	123,405	2,655	3,021	49	202,258	4,464
1902	242,390	2,919	1,593	50	230,646	6,482
1905	124,724	2,386	1,036	52	255,655	7,025
1908	173,843	3,257	677	53	244,313	7,095
1919	147,956	3,889	529	93	246,951	10,860
1924	116,707	4,137	447	56	243,363	10,799
1928	123,326	4,231	239	45	380,169	15,649
1929	162,940	4,897	378	52	447,689	18,052
1930	143,824	4,329	1,069	69	442,474	16,289

TABLE IV, Continued

YEARS	RHODE ISLAND		CONNECTICUT		TOTAL	
	Quantity	Value	Quantity	Value	Quantity	Value
1880	......	697	......	933	......	12,503
1887	45,285	684	39,750	301	520,214	9,913
1888	91,687	825	42,402	297	572,908	9,860
1889	127,365	935	92,672	1,558	653,170	10,551
1898	32,854	955	31,920	1,559	393,458	9,682
1902	21,614	1,156	37,832	1,799	534,075	12,406
1905	23,896	1,547	74,973	3,174	480,284	14,184
1908	44,254	1,752	66,942	2,982	530,029	15,139
1919	48,251	3,296	23,653	1,701	467,340	19,839
1924	20,535	1,819	25,770	2,007	406,822	18,818
1928	27,666	2,398	72,198	3,297	603,598	25,620
1929	28,401	2,435	54,878	3,636	694,286	29,072
1930	25,972	2,287	88,012	4,519	701,351	27,493

[a] From U. S. Bur. of Fisheries, *Statistical Bull. No. 971*, Washington, 1932. p. 3.

tabulated. This is mainly due to the increased intensity and efficiency of fishing operations brought about by the new filleting business. The increases for Maine, Rhode Island, and Connecticut in this period are undoubtedly due to the same cause. Shellfish and crustacea account

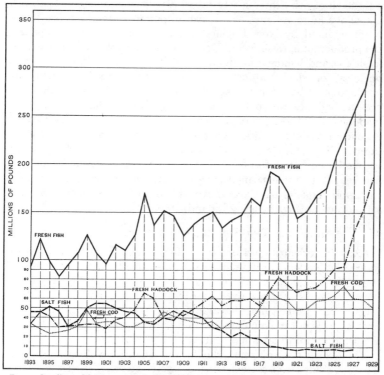

FIG. I—Landings of fish by vessels at New England ports, 1893–1929, showing trends in fresh and salt fish production and in fresh cod and haddock. Based on *Fishery Industries of the United States, 1929*, U. S. Bureau of Fisheries, Washington, 1931 (*Fisheries Doc. No. 1095*), pp. 834–837.

for an important part of the totals, with approximately 10 per cent of the total production and 25 per cent of the total value. In these articles Maine leads in the production of lobsters and soft clams; Massachusetts leads in that of hard crabs, hard clams (quahogs), scallops, and squid for bait; and Connecticut leads in the production of oysters.

Production Trends

The accompanying diagram (Fig. 1) shows the comparative growth of the cod and haddock fisheries since 1893. Until 1919 the catch of cod was greater than that of haddock. However, from 1893 as a rule until 1912 the greater part of the cod catch was usually landed as salt fish. From 1909 onward the amount of salt cod landed shows a steady decline owing to the fact that improved transportation and refrigeration extended the marketing area and increased the demand for fresh fish. The condition of the salt fish industry is not indicated by these curves, because in preparing them no consideration was taken of fish subsequently salted after being landed as fresh fish, nor of the large volumes of salt fish imported from Nova Scotia and Newfoundland by New England firms. From 1919 to the present the production of fresh fish in New England has followed the trends of fresh cod and haddock production. With the growth of the filleting business, for which haddock has always been in greatest demand, the production of haddock has steadily increased, and from 1926 to the present haddock production for filleting purposes has increased tremendously. The future of the filleting business, in so far as haddock is concerned, depends upon whether the yearly increase can be maintained. Efforts are already being made to popularize other excellent species in the filleted form to relieve the constant drain on the haddock fishery. With the ever-increasing consumption of fish resulting from the improvements described above, this problem has become the most serious one now confronting the industry.

THE SHELLFISH INDUSTRY[10]

Any historical discussion of the fisheries of New England would indeed be inadequate if shellfish were not mentioned. Not only did they play a notable part in the early history and development of the New England states, but the oyster industry alone until comparatively recent years ranked first in value among the fisheries of the United States. It is not too much to say that our shellfish products taken as a whole still retain that important place.

The early settlers found shellfish in quantities along our shores. There is evidence of the existence of oyster beds as far east as Mount Desert Island, while the soft clam and scallop abounded along the coast of Maine. Large heaps of oyster shells are found at Damariscotta, in the Sheepscott River, and also at Kittery, Me. Some of these contain several million bushels of shells, although at present no oysters are produced north of Wellfleet on Cape Cod. Free fishing with lack of protection is probably responsible in a large measure for the extinction of this product. The states of Rhode Island and Connecticut very early recognized the importance of their oyster industry, but Massachusetts and Maine have failed to protect their shellfish against depletion through over-fishing.

Connecticut was the first state to grant vested rights in oyster ground, and the growth of the Connecticut oyster fisheries shows how sound a policy it has been. In 1842 it first became lawful for the owner of land wherein there were salt water creeks to protect such property for the growing of oysters. In 1845 the cultivation of oysters in the harbors of Connecticut began. In 1855 a law known as the Two Acre Law was passed which provided that land might be leased to any resident in area not greater than two acres per person. In 1865 the deep-water cultivation of oysters in Long Island Sound was begun. In 1881 the State Commission was formed and intrusted with the administration of the shellfish laws. In 1889 radical changes were made in the laws regulating offshore fisheries. Today nearly all the legally available land for oyster planting in the rivers, harbors, or bays has been designated or deeded to private ownership, and there is now a great system of deep-water oyster farming stretching for miles along the shores of Connecticut. The first steamer for the oyster trade was built in 1877 at South Norwalk, and in a few years a large number of such boats were engaged in the cultivation of oyster lands. In 1910, 70,855 acres of land under water were under franchise in the state of Connecticut, and 24,708 acres of this land were said to be under cultivation; in 1928 there were 52,835 acres under franchise and probably 10,000 additional acres under lease, of which about 35,000 acres may be said to be under cultivation. In this state large private interests are protected and encouraged, and they give employment to nearly two thousand men in the various branches of the industry.

In Rhode Island the cultivation of oysters began in 1864 with the granting of vested rights in oyster grounds. Starting in that year with a revenue of sixty-one dollars received by the Shellfish Commission for leases, the growth was gradual until 1906, when an income of fifty-nine thousand dollars was received from this source. The growth was rapid till 1912 when the income to the state from the 20,846 acres of leased land under water amounted to $133,341. Since that time, unfortunately, the industry has greatly declined in Rhode Island owing to the pollution of the waters of Narragansett Bay by industrial wastes. However, steps have been taken to correct this situation. As the result of the work done by the Rhode Island Purification Board, the waters of Narragansett Bay have been largely rid of pollution, and the oyster industry appears to be regaining its former prominence there.

Massachusetts has been more backward than the other states in encouraging private culture, largely because of the character of the laws which make it difficult for private capital to acquire sufficiently good title to areas in quantity suitable for private culture. Without such protection, private interests cannot be induced to make the large expenditures necessary for profitable operation of this industry.

One of the greatest assets of the New England states remains undeveloped in the tremendous clam flats of Maine, Massachusetts, and Rhode Island. These are still controlled by the local towns, which throw them open to private fishing under limited restriction. No great attempt has ever been made to encourage private culture in these areas, and yet many of these lands are capable of producing average crops substantially in excess in value per acre of any known land crops. There are records of lands under water in Connecticut producing annual crops to a value of $1000 an acre, and it is probable that the soft clam industry of New England could be developed equally well. However, in spite of the failure of some states to follow more progressive methods, it is a safe assertion that the value of the shellfish—including oysters, soft clams, quahogs, and scallops—is probably greater than that of any other single branch of the fisheries and accounts for not less than 25 per cent of the total value of the New England fisheries.

THE PROSPECT

In retrospect, it is safe to assume that the New England fisheries have successfully emerged from their formative period and embarked upon a career of progress based on sound business principles. In perspective, the application of the newer methods of processing and merchandising, which are yet in their infancy in many respects, will place a larger volume and a greater variety of New England fish products in homes in every one of our United States. These products will be served in Arizona or any other place in just as fresh condition as in Boston. With the rapid development now in progress of refrigerated railroad transportation providing sub-freezing temperatures and with the equally rapid development and dissemination of sub-freezing display cabinets for retail stores, also in progress, the nearly $30,000,000 which the New England fisheries contribute annually to the national income is certain to be greatly increased. What New England industry does 1933 find in a more enviable position?

NOTES

[1] For bibliographical data see also the notes to Mr. Lewis Radcliffe's paper entitled *The Fisheries of New England: Production and Administration* in the present volume, pp. 259–260, above. For the early history of the fisheries see Lorenzo Sabine, *Report on the Principal Fisheries of the American Seas, Prepared for the Treasury Department of the United States*, Washington, 1853; also Raymond McFarland, *A History of the New England Fisheries*, New York, 1911.

[2] For early history of refrigeration of fish see C. H. Stevenson, *The Preservation of Fishery Products for Food*, in *Bull. of the U. S. Fish Commission*, Vol. 18, 1898 (1899), pp. 358–388; also H. F. Taylor, *Refrigeration of Fish*, Appendix VIII to the *Report of the U. S. Commissioner of Fisheries for 1926*, Washington, 1927 (*Bur. of Fisheries Doc. No. 1016*).

[3] An excellent description of the Boston Fish Pier appeared in an article *Boston as a Fishing Port—Past and Present*, in *The Fishing Gazette*, New York, Vol. 32, 1915, pp. 545–552. (This article includes descriptions of the New England Fish Exchange and the Boston Fish Market Corporation.)

[4] See Stevenson, *op. cit.*

[5] *Historical Review of the Rise of Mechanical Refrigeration*, in *Ice and Refrigeration*, Vol. 21, July–Dec., 1901, *passim*.

⁶ R. Plank, E. Ehrenbaum, and K. Reuter, *Die Konservierung von Fischen durch das Gefrierverfahren*, Berlin, 1916.

⁷ See H. F. Taylor, *Improvements in Methods of Merchandising Fish*, Paterson Parchment Paper Company, Passaic, N. J., 1925.

⁸ Clarence Birdseye, ¡*Some Scientific Aspects of Packaging and Quick-Freezing Perishable Flesh Products*, in *Industrial and Engineering Chemistry*, Vol. 21, 1929: I. *More Rapid Freezing Means Better Preservation*, pp. 414–417 (May, 1929); II. *Packaging Flesh Products for Quick-Freezing*, pp. 573–576 (June, 1929); III. *Sanitary Measures in a Fish Dressing Plant*, pp. 854–857 (Sept., 1929).

⁹ For historical sketches of the evolution of fishing craft see article cited in note 3 above, and also F. H. Wood, *Trawling and Dragging in New England Waters* (in two parts), in *Atlantic Fisherman*, Goffstown, N. H., Vol. 6, No. 12, Jan., 1926, pp. 7 and 11–23; Vol. 7, No. 1, Feb., 1926, pp. 11–24, 28, and 30; *Otter Trawling in the Atlantic Fisheries*, in *The Fishing Gazette*, Annual Review Number, New York, 1925, pp. 61–64; J. C. Allen, *Fishing Boats of Marthas Vineyard: Their Origin and Development*, in *Atlantic Fisherman*, Vol. 8, No. 1, Feb., 1927, pp. 13–15 and 24; *Publications Containing Information on Apparatus, Methods, Vessels and Boats Used in the Fisheries of the United States and Some Foreign Countries*, compiled by Gerald Fitzgerald (mimeographed list of references), Bureau of Fisheries, Washington, 1930 ([*Memorandum*] *S-46*).

¹⁰ See especially the following publications of the Dept. of Fisheries and Game, Massachusetts: D. L. Belding and F. C. Lane, *A Report upon the Mollusk Fisheries of Massachusetts*, 1909; D. L. Belding, *The Quohaug and Oyster Fisheries of Massachusetts*, 1912; the same, *The Soft-Shell Clam Fishery of Massachusetts*, Nov., 1930; the same, *The Scallop Fishery of Massachusetts*, March, 1931; the same, *The Quahaug Fishery of Massachusetts*, April, 1931. See also State Board of Fisheries and Game, Connecticut, *Report of the Investigation of Oyster Properties*, Board of Equalization, 1910; Connecticut Shellfish Commission, *Biennial Report*, 1927–1928. For Rhode Island, see Commissioners of Shell-Fisheries, *Annual Report for the Year Ending December 31, 1911.*

SOME PROBLEMS OF POWER IN NEW ENGLAND*

POWER RESOURCES, INTERCONNECTION, AND MERGERS
OF PUBLIC UTILITIES

E. W. Morehouse

ON October 1, 1930, President Hoover in Washington pressed a button to start turning seven hundred miles away the water wheels of New England's largest single hydro-electric development, and the fourth largest in the country. A few moments later electrical energy was sent singing along gracefully dipping wires to a point 126 miles away where it was broken into "packages" for ultimate distribution to homes, factories, and shops in and around Boston. Mere size and distance do not measure the significance of this event. Rather, the first unit of the New England Power Association's Fifteen Mile Falls development, as thus dramatically inaugurated, stands as a symbol of what hydro-electric power now means and will come to mean to the people of New England.

In the planning and execution of this great undertaking most of the problems that surround all power resources have had to be met. These problems are intricate; they involve technical and economic complexities; they blend with problems in other fields of thought; they take different forms and differ in degree of importance in various sections of the country and even within New England; and their evaluation will change with the observer and his experience. Consequently, the most one can hope to do in a short space is to name a few peaks, raise questions, and run the risk of inaccuracy by generalizing.

Properly understood, the word "integration" unifies the threefold division of this paper's subtitle as well as sums up two decades—even a century—of activity in the development and use of power resources. The word has come to mean "tying together," but it is broader than mere interconnection of electric plants. In this wider sense the knitting together of sources and supplies of power, of facilities supplying power, and of owners of those facilities constitutes a single process viewed from different angles.

Yet integration from its Latin root also means renewing and restoring, and this sense of the word summarizes New England's

*The writer wishes to acknowledge gratefully the assistance or coöperation, in furnishing information, of the following: members of the staff of the Institute of Economic Research, especially Mary Louise Ramsey in the work of tabulation and Hanina Zinder; O. S. Wessel, of the Rate and Research Department, Public Service Commission of Wisconsin; the secretaries and staff members of the several public service commissions in New England, including Barker & Wheeler, Engineers, of New York City, consulting engineers for the Vermont Commission; officials of several public utility companies, especially the Edison Electric Illuminating Company of Boston, the New England Power Association, and the Middle West Utilities Company; and the Rorrison Investment Company.

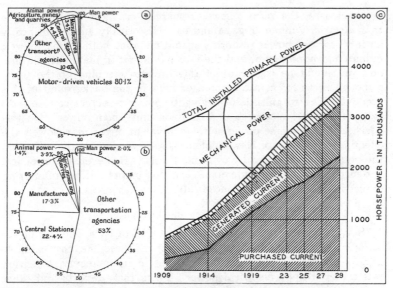

FIG. 1—(a and b) Distribution of power resources in New England: (a) including motor-driven vehicles, (b) excluding motor-driven vehicles. Based on U. S. Geol. Survey, *Water-Supply Paper No. 579*, corrected by latest figures available from other sources, such as U. S. Census reports on manufactures and occupations and *Yearbook* of the U. S. Department of Agriculture. (c) Mechanical and electrical power in New England factories, 1909–1929, installed prime-mover and electric-motor capacity. Based on U. S. Census of Manufactures. Since prime movers driving electric motors are about 91.5 per cent of the capacity of the motors connected to them, the total electric horse power used in industry exceeds the total prime-mover capacity devoted to generating electricity for these motors.

power history. For more than a century the region's power resources have been expanded, renewed, and restored. Falling water gave the Yankees an industrial head start when they turned from maritime merchandising to fabricating along New England streams. Primitive water wheels were improved, and streams were made to do more work by the use of canals (as in Holyoke, Massachusetts, even today). Then steam engines overshadowed water wheels as means of producing mechanical power; now these prime movers, supplemented or displaced by the steam turbine and internal combustion engine, are turning generators of electricity, and electricity is gradually superseding a large part of both mechanical power and human labor in factory, shop, and home and on farms.

This synthesizing process is not complete, but it is far advanced—landmarked, for the moment, by the Fifteen Mile Falls development. The goal is the orderly, hand-in-hand development of power supplies from various sources at the least cost, in order that the beneficent uses of power facilities may be spread most widely and most bountifully.[1]

---

[1] For notes see below, p. 302.

Obviously, the term "power resources" is more comprehensive than electricity alone (Fig. 1a and b). Historically and scientifically an inventory of power resources should embrace both animal power, human and non-human, and the forces inherent in inanimate nature, and we should be cognizant of this broader meaning of the term, although these forces are ignored or kept in the background of this account. The magnitude of aggregate power resources can be indicated if they are measured in a common unit—man power. On this basis, using one horse power as the equivalent of ten man power, the effective population of New England is somewhat more than fiftyfold the population disclosed by counting heads.[2] However, the electrical and mechanical power made in public utility plants and manufacturing industries is the orthodox concept of "power resources."

Power Supplies and Demands

Several more or less comprehensive studies of New England power resources have been published since 1920.[3] Of these, the most valuable is now more than seven years old,[4] and in it, moreover, attention was centered upon electrical power. From these reports and other sources[5] have been tabulated twenty-four "indicators" of the supply, movement, and marketing of power in the public utility field and in the manufacturing industries, emphasizing differences among states (Table I). These indicators show some of the chief features of a cross-section view. While they do not disclose historical trends, they help to reveal the localization of certain problems.

Before considering these problems a few characteristics of mechanical and electric power may be recalled. (1) Most forms of mechanical and electrical power are practically or commercially non-storable, except indirectly as energy is stored in coal or water in a pond. (2) Power has to be brought from the place of manufacture to the point of application. This is mentioned because of the frequently overlooked heavy expense of delivering power from manufacturer to user and because of the importance of having the right amount of power at the right place at the right time. (3) Applications of power are intermittent and do not coincide in time, either through the day, month, or year. This "diversity of demand" from different users, both in amount and in time, is extremely important. (4) Power-supply equipment represents a large fixed investment which, because of the character and timing of power demands, is idle generally half the time or more. The significance of this "load factor" will be made more apparent later.

The demands for power in New England come chiefly from eastern Massachusetts, Rhode Island, and southern and western Connecticut. In these states we find four fifths of the folk of New England living and working; 82 per cent of the total number of central station customers in New England; 80 per cent of the total consumption of electricity; 73 per cent of the installed capacity of prime movers in manufacturing establishments; and 75 per cent of the power production in central stations. The power requirements of New England as a whole are increasing roughly at an annual rate of 1.5 to 2 per cent, while electrical power demands have increased four or five times more rapidly than this average rate.[6]

In view of previous surveys and the table of "indicators" here shown, only a few main features of the power supplies to meet these growing needs will be mentioned here for their bearing on later points. New England's power system is founded upon *domestic* water power, chiefly in Maine, New Hampshire, and Vermont, and on *imported* coal.[7] Somewhat more than half of the total potential water powers remain to be developed,[8] the bulk of which are in three drainage basins in Maine. Oil, which likewise has to be imported, is a very minor source of electric power at present.[9]

The greater part of these power supplies is made available by two largely competitive methods: (1) self service, where a manufacturing enterprise owns its own prime movers and generators; and (2) pooled service, where the loads of many classes of users are concentrated in a central (public utility) station. More than three fourths of New England industry's power capacity is applied electrically, and of this "electrical horse power" less than 38 per cent is now supplied by industrially owned plants (Fig. 1c and Indicators 23 and 20). Self-supplying industries north of Massachusetts have increasingly relied on water power, while the reverse trend is noticeable in the concentrated industrial area (Indicator 24, and historical data not shown). As a group, however, New England manufacturers supplying their own power requirements have come to rely during the past twenty years slightly more on fuel-burning prime movers than on water-driven equipment.

In the central-station industry, which has expanded in a spectacular manner, there is a slight tendency also to rely more on fuel-burning prime movers than on water powers.[10] Central stations in the three southern states, with more convenient and cheaper access to coal imports, generate more than four fifths of their electricity from coal.

Fig. 1c summarizes twenty years' growth of the industrial power market. That central stations have captured the bulk of the loads is not surprising. Closer examination will reveal that utilities have been most successful in attaching the loads of newly established industries. The superseding of mechanical power has not gone as far as in other areas,[11] and private generating plants have stoutly resisted the call to the scrap heap. The latter circumstance is partly explained by the importance of steam-using industries in New Eng-

TABLE I—NEW ENGLAND: TWENTY-FOUR INDICATORS OF POWER SUPPLY AND DEMAND CHARACTERISTICS [a]

	NEW ENGLAND	MAINE	NEW HAMPSHIRE	VERMONT	MASSACHUSETTS	RHODE ISLAND	CONNECTICUT
I. Central station (public) power resource data							
A. Supply							
a. General							
(1) Distribution of New England central station power produced in each state (1930)							
1. Amount—millions of kilowatt-hours	6400	731	367	480	2908	547	1367
2. Percentage distribution	100%	11.4	5.7	7.5	45.5	8.5	21.4
(2) Percentage of central station power in each state generated by fuel (1930)	66.6	8.9	19.6	.4	82.7	99.5	85.9
(3) KVA rating of electric systems operating with purchased energy exclusively (1929) (thousands)							
1. Amount	317	3	6	10	239	9	49
2. Percentage distribution	100%	.9	1.9	3.2	75.7	2.8	15.5
(4) Kilowatt capacity of generators, public power supply (1931) thousands							
1. Amount—thousands of kilowatts	2938	261	286	180	1344	243	624
2. Percentage	100%	8.9	9.7	6.1	45.8	8.3	21.2
(5) Proportions of generator capacity in each state driven by steam power and water power (1931)							
1. Steam power	68.6%	19.0	14.7	6.2	85.5	99.3	83.5
2. Water power	26.8%	80.0	76.2	90.6	8.7	.7	12.4

[a] See below, p. 285.

TABLE I, Continued

	NEW ENGLAND	MAINE	NEW HAMPSHIRE	VERMONT	MASSACHUSETTS	RHODE ISLAND	CONNECTICUT
b. *Water power*							
(6) Distribution of developed water power capacity among states (Jan. 1, 1932)							
1. Total—amount	1939	613	559	202	362	30	172
Total—percentage	100%	31.6	28.8	10.4	18.7	1.5	9.0
2. Public—percentage	100%	26.6	36.3	13.6	13 6	.3	9.6
3. Manufacturing—percentage	100%	39.3	17.4	5.6	26.3	3.5	7.9
(7) Proportion of developed water power capacity in each state owned by public utilities or municipalities (1929)	53.2%	44.7	51.8	83.4	43.9	10.0	64.9
(8) Distribution of potential water power resources of New England states (thousands of h.p.)							
1. Available 90 per cent of the time—amount	998	536	186	80	106	25	65
Percentage	100%	53.7	18.7	8.0	10.6	2.5	6.5
2. Available 50 per cent of the time—amount	1978	1074	350	169	235	40	110
Percentage	100%	54.3	17.7	8.5	11.9	2.0	5.6
B. *Movement*							
(9) Circuit miles of transmission lines (1927)							
1. Amount	8604	1889	908	1084	3470	465	788
2. Percentage	100%	21.9	10.5	12.6	40.4	5.4	9.2
(10) Percentage of central station power generated in each state that is exported (1930)	19.0%	..	25.4	67.4	13.4	42.3	7.4
(11) Percentage of total consumption of central station power of each state from *imported* power (1930)	19.0%	.1	7.0	7.3	25.2	43.4	8.2

TABLE I—NEW ENGLAND: TWENTY-FOUR INDICATORS OF POWER SUPPLY AND DEMAND CHARACTERISTICS, cont'd.

	NEW ENGLAND	MAINE	NEW HAMPSHIRE	VERMONT	MASSACHUSETTS	RHODE ISLAND	CONNECTICUT
(12) Percentage distribution of aggregate New England power *exports* (1930)	100%	..	8.7	30.8	31.4	21.1	8.0
(13) Percentage distribution of aggregate New England power *imports* (1930)	100%	..	1.9	1.2	66.4	21.5	9.0
(14) Net imports or exports from each state (millions of kilowatt-hours) (1928–1930)							
1. Net imports							
1930	..	..	..	..	406	10	13
1929	..	..	..	..	332	..	75
1928	..	..	..	..	234	148	81
2. Net exports							
1930	..	..	75	326	..	..	..
1929	..	..	36	285	..	41	..
1928	..	..	68	304	..	..	..
C. *Marketing*							
(15) Distribution of consumption of electricity by states (1930) (millions of kilowatt-hours)							
1. Amount	5933	702	302	178	2980	558	1213
2. Percentage	100%	11.8	5.1	3.0	50.3	9.4	20.4
(16) Number of central station customers—thousands (1931)							
1. Total	2258	205	126	82	1227	191	427
2. Domestic lighting	1881	157	108	64	1044	163	344
3. Commercial lighting	337	41	14	15	165	24	77
4. Power and miscellaneous	41	7	4	3	18	4	5

TABLE I, Continued

	NEW ENGLAND	MAINE	NEW HAMPSHIRE	VERMONT	MASSACHUSETTS	RHODE ISLAND	CONNECTICUT
(17) Percentage distribution of central station customers (1930) . . .	100%	9.1	5.6	3.6	54.3	8.5	18.9
(18) Number of homes receiving electric service—thousands (1930)							
1. Amount	1859	153	104	63	1036	162	340
2. Percentage	100%	8.2	5.6	3.4	55.8	8.7	18.3
(19) Percentage of number of farms in each state electrified (1930) .	35.6%	40.9	46.7	12.9	50.5	25.4	26.7
(20) Percentage of electrically driven equipment in each state driven by central station power (1929)	62.5%	45.4	41.6	67.1	63.0	75.1	70.2
II. Industrial power resource data							
(21) Percentage of factory requirements in each state met by purchased current (1929)	47.5%	24.8	25.2	50.9	52.4	56.7	58.0
(22) Distribution among states of total industrial prime mover capacity in New England (1929) (thousands of h.p.)							
1. Amount	4687	679	402	164	2069	464	909
2. Percentage	100%	14.5	8.6	3.5	44.1	9.9	19.4
(23) Percentage of industrial power capacity[b] in each state that is mechanical (1929)	23.9%	45.3	39.4	24.1	16.7	24.5	17.2
(24) Percentage of industrially owned equipment in each state driven by water power (1929) . . .	30.2%	66.1	47.7	48.3	14.6	12.7	13.8

[a] Based on data from U. S. Geological Survey, Indicators 1, 2, 4, 5, 6, 7, 8; U. S. Bureau of the Census, *Central Electric Light and Power Stations*, 1927, Indicator 9; *Census of Manufactures*, 1929, Indicators 20, 21, 22, 23, 24; National Electric Light Association, *Statistical Supplement to the Electric Light and Power Industry in the United States, Revised to Jan. 1, 1931*, Indicators 6, 7; *Statistical Bulletin*, No. 7, Indicators 10, 11, 12, 13, 14, 15, 18, 19; *Electrical World*, Annual Statistical Number, 1929, Indicator 3; Annual Statistical Number, 1932, Indicators 16, 17.

[b] Power capacity obtained by subtracting horse power of motors driven by electricity from total installed prime mover capacity. Since prime movers driving electric motors have a rated capacity less than that of motors connected to them, these percentages, in terms of prime mover capacity, should be several points higher.

land's industrial structure.[12]   In many of these establishments, steam made for industrial processes can also be applied to generators, making electricity a relatively cheap by-product.

In examining the data on which the above sketch is based, three problems, or rather groups of interrelated problems, stand out:[13] (1) building up load factors; (2) power costs and prices; (3) modernizing equipment.

Problems of Building Up Load Factors

One form of unemployment too little appreciated by the general public is the idleness of dollars invested in power capacity.   To illustrate, if the load factor[14] of a generating station could be raised from 30 to 55 per cent, the probable reduction of generating costs per kilowatt-hour would be nearly 4 mills (practically a one third decrease in a modern steam generating station).[15]   Attaining this reduction is the chief purpose and justification of central stations, which were conceived with the idea that a concentration of the diverse and intermittent power loads of the community permits a more intensive and regular use of the investment than is possible if each user sets up his own equipment.   If this aim is not realized, something is wrong.

Public utilities are well aware of the outstanding importance of a more intensive use of present power capacity.   They are continually examining their load factor data as a guide to policies of merchandising, extension, and pricing—policies designed to increase the use of existing investments without creating a need for added generating capacity.   Recently, their efforts along this line have been redoubled because revenues per dollar invested have tended to decline while total investment per kilowatt of installed generating capacity has tended to increase.   Some companies have made notable progress and reached load factors of 50 per cent or more; others lag.[16]

The task of building up load factors ramifies into a host of special problems.   Cultivating greater use of off-peak power in the home by selling household appliances, extending service to farms, electrifying railroads, persuading more industries to buy power from a central station and scrap their own prime movers, and extending transmission lines so as to concentrate the load in the more economical stations— all these activities, and many more, involve the building up or dragging down of load factors.

In hydro-electric developments load factor is of special significance because the first cost is high relatively to running cost.   The flows of New England rivers vary considerably; hence, to regularize flow, water storage is necessary, and when natural storage in lakes and ponds is not available expenditures for this purpose[17] have to be weighed against investments in existing or proposed steam plants, all in the light of uncontrollable prospective power demands. Under these circumstances an intelligent scheme requires comprehensive planning for all sites in each stream's drainage area, instead of the piecemeal planning and development of particular sites.[18]

Likewise is it not a mistake to divorce the improvement of load factor in central stations from similar betterments in industrially owned plants, particularly in view of the large generating capacity owned by manufacturers?[19] (Indicators 22, 20, 24).

How to increase the *use* of existing power capacity is, indeed, fundamental to most problems of power resources. We placidly assume that any new development of water powers or added generators is a sign of progress. This may or may not be true, for added capacity reduces for the time being at least the average intensity of use. The newspaper which headlines on the front page a 10 or 15 per cent increase of load factor shows a keener sense of values than one that features the installation of a new generator.

PROBLEMS OF COSTS AND PRICING

Three problems in this field are particularly noteworthy.[20] Whether or not a given industry should scrap its self-serving plant and buy power from central stations depends largely on the cost of power in the industry's plant compared with the price of purchased power. This choice could be made more easily and wisely if the industries concerned could determine their power costs accurately from a proper, standardized power-cost accounting scheme. Especially in steam-using industries such standardized cost analyses might facilitate reduction in the cost of both steam and by-product electricity, reveal the desirability of selling surplus industrial power to central stations, and give the data for establishing a proper balance between industrially-owned and utility-owned power capacity.

A major expense item in electric service is the cost of delivery.[21] At present these delivery costs to the average consumer are several times the cost of generation. The situation is aggravated in highly urbanized sections, such as eastern Massachusetts, Rhode Island, and parts of Connecticut, by underground construction[22] and the higher costs of transmission lines,[23] as well as by the distance from this market to the major water powers of the northern states. Whether these delivery costs can be appreciably lowered is not clear; we need to know more about them in particular areas.[24]

A third group of problems in this field revolves around the pricing policies of the utilities. Proper pricing may have an enormous influence upon intensive utilization of existing power capacity. Yet lack of uniformity among the rate schedules of different or even the same distributing companies is well known, as is also the possibility of unjustifiable discrimination in the spread between rates to large consumers, who may be potential competitors of the central stations, and the great bulk of domestic and other small users. On the other hand, uniformity of prices over a wide area to a given class of customers may not be altogether a blessing if it results in a feeling of undue discrimination against communities located near generating centers, or against particular classes of customers. Greater uniformity may be expected from the tendency, noted later, toward unified control of utilities; but, so far as the writer is aware, in New England little attention has been given to this field of inquiry, except by those engaged in the utility industries or in their regulation.

Problems of Modernizing Equipment

Figure 1c reveals certain points of interest in regard to the modernization of power-supplying and power-using equipment. To the extent that the New England states, or particular sections of them, lag behind other areas in installing the most up-to-date equipment, the power resources of the region do not yield the utmost benefits. Striving to build up the load factor on antiquated machinery seems a waste of effort and retards reduction of power costs.

To illustrate, Figure 1c shows that about 30 per cent of the installed power capacity in industry is applied mechanically, i.e. by shafts and belts rather than by wires carrying electric power to motors. Yet in near-by states (New York, New Jersey, and Pennsylvania), which are of comparable industrial age to New England, the corresponding percentage is less than 20 per cent.

What is the reason for the reluctance of New England industries to shift from mechanical to the more flexible electrical power? Superior efficiency of shafts and belts? Industrial ownership of water-power sites and self-serving plants (compare Indicators 23, 24, and 20, 21)? Need for retaining equipment supplying industrial steam and heat?[25] Cost of scrapping still serviceable equipment in the light of the financial condition of particular enterprises? Whatever influences are at work, here is an important problem and one concerning which more data by industry and location are needed.

In the central-station field, modernization of equipment is somewhat less of a problem but still challenging. The utility companies themselves have made great strides in scrapping equipment with high operating costs or in utilizing it only for stand-by purposes. The extent to which the movement toward concentrating loads in modern, low-cost generating stations can be accelerated depends very largely upon the facilities for interchanging power, a subject to which we now turn.[26]

Interconnection

The extent of interconnection[27] may be visualized from the transmission line map of 1930 (Fig. 2) which almost shames a railroad map in its complexity.[28] The transmission system in Massachusetts in 1914 (shown in the inset) affords a striking contrast. These maps, however, are inadequate in at least two respects: (1) there are a number of true interconnecting lines of lower voltage than the minimum of 11,000-volts pressure shown on the 1930 map, but inclusion of these would still further complicate the picture; (2) the maps show the existence only of facilities for interchanging electricity; they do not show the use of those facilities, i.e., actual movements of energy along these lines.

ELECTRIC TRAFFIC

Some available data on the volume of "electric traffic" between central station systems are given in Table II. The figures on interstate

TABLE II—NEW ENGLAND: MOVEMENTS OF ELECTRICITY ALONG INTERCONNECTING LINES

	INTERSTATE TRANSFER OF ELECTRICITY[a]						
	Kilowatt-hours Exported (Millions)				Kilowatt-hours Imported (Millions)		
	1931	1930	1929	1928	1930	1929	1928
New England .	1,229	1100	839	697	1128	884	789
Maine	1	1	1	. . .	1	1	1
New Hampshire	300	96	53	77	21	17	9
Vermont . . .	306	339	305	320	13	20	16
Massachusetts .	398	344	254	261	750	586	495
Rhode Island .	121	232	200	10	242	159	158
Connecticut . .	102	88	26	29	101	101	110

TABLE II—Continued

	INTRASTATE TRANSFER OF ELECTRICITY[b]		
	Kilowatt-hours Sold (Millions)	Kilowatt-hours Bought (Millions)	Bought from Private Manufacturing Plants (Millions)
Maine . . . . . (1926)	74	90	15
New Hampshire . (1930)	407	161	c
Vermont	c	c	c
Massachusetts . . (1928)	1074	917	18
Rhode Island . .	c	c	c
Connecticut . . . (1930)	322	460	c

  [a] Based on: National Electric Light Association, *Statistical Bulletin*, Nos. 4, 5, 7, and 8 (1929, 1930, 1931, and 1932).
  [b] Compiled from the State Public Utilities Commissions' Reports.
  [c] Not available.

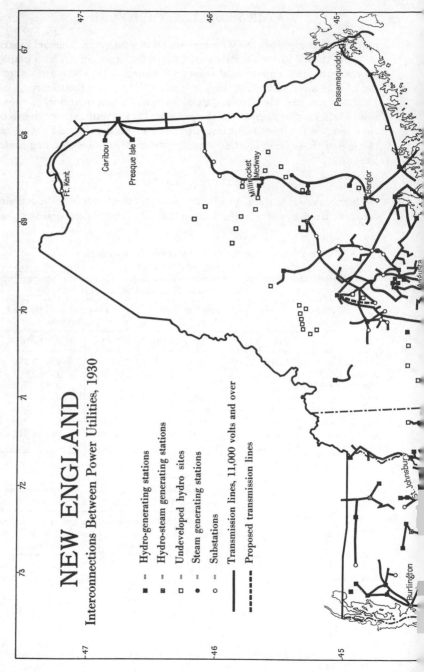

NEW ENGLAND

Interconnections Between Power Utilities, 1930

■ = Hydro-generating stations
▣ = Hydro-steam generating stations
□ = Undeveloped hydro sites
● = Steam generating stations
○ = Substations

Transmission lines, 11,000 volts and over

Proposed transmission lines

Ft. Kent

Caribou

Presque Isle

Millinocket
Medway

Passamaquoddy

Bangor

Augusta

St. Johnsbury

Burlington

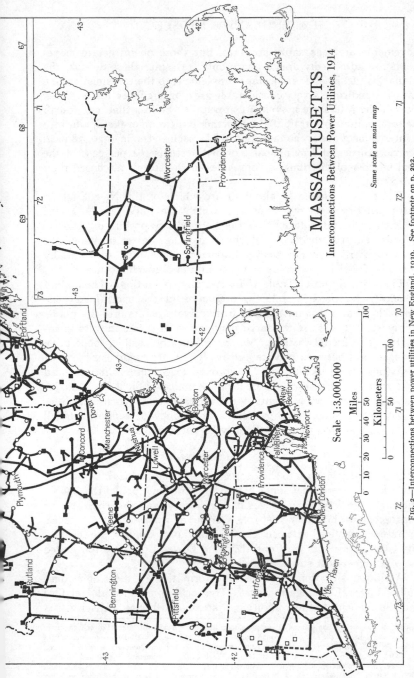

MASSACHUSETTS

Interconnections Between Power Utilities, 1914

Same scale as main map

See footnote on p. 292.

Scale 1:3,000,000

FIG. 2—Interconnections between power utilities in New England, 1930.

movements are reasonably accurate, but those on intrastate movements are admittedly approximate only. Despite these defects, the tabulation furnishes an important supplement to the transmission-line map, as it indicates a very considerable use of interconnection facilities. Indeed, the interstate movement appears to be less than one fourth the total volume of "traffic."[29] A further indication of the significance of interconnections is the fact that in Massachusetts, in 1929, 78 local electric utilities and municipally owned systems (64 per cent of the total number of distributing companies in the state) purchased their entire supply.[30]

The data in Table II also indicate which of the New England states are exporters of power and which are importers.[31] Maine is forced to be self-sufficient by the Fernald law prohibiting exports of hydro-electric energy.[32] Of the remaining states, normally the three southern ones are clearly importers, depending substantially on the hydro-electric surplus of Vermont and New Hampshire.[33]

The last column of Table II invites an explanation. The bulk of the electricity used in industry originates in the central stations; relatively small amounts are sent from private plants into the public supply system, despite the large installation of prime movers in industry. This seems wasteful. Where technically feasible, coöperative arrangements between private and utility plants might easily result in savings on reserve capacity, improved load factors, and reduced costs to both agencies.[34] Aside from technical difficulties, a major obstacle to such arrangements is the apparent reluctance of utilities to buy from seeming competitors. The policy of economizing all resources, however, should ordinarily be paramount.

ADVANTAGES OF INTERCONNECTION

Of what significance to the people of New England is this extensive network of interconnections? Two illustrations point the moral. The high and low-water stages of the Saco River and those of the Androscoggin and Kennebec rivers occur at different times; hence, an interconnection between the Cumberland County Power and Light Company and the Central Maine Power Company forestalled use of a higher-cost steam plant.[35]

A similar situation prompted the formation of the Connecticut Valley Power Exchange in 1924. The local companies at Hartford and Springfield needed additional steam-generating capacity. A

NOTE ON FIGURE 2—The sources of the main map are: New England Council Power Committee map, corrected to March 1, 1930, through courtesy of Edison Electric Illuminating Company of Boston; New England Power Association; New England Public Service Company, map to Dec. 31, 1929, with supplemental information from Middle West Utilities Company; Barker and Wheeler, Engineers, for Vermont Public Service Commission, map corrected to June 1, 1930; Connecticut Public Utilities Commission, map as of January 1, 1925, corrected by later information from other sources; Massachusetts Department of Public Utilities; Rorrison Investment Company. Inset based ·on map accompanying Massachusetts Board of Gas and Electric Commissioners, *Annual Report*, 1914.

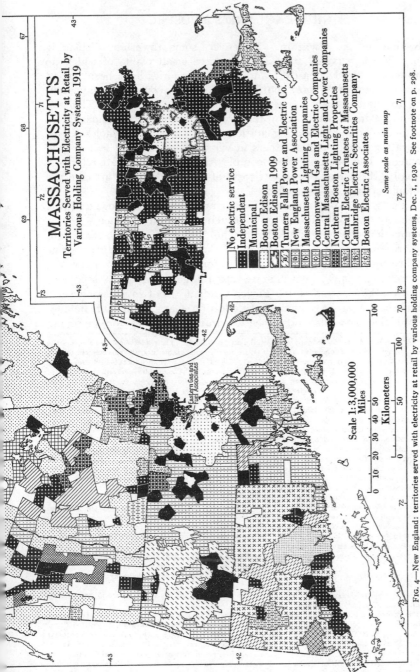

MASSACHUSETTS

Territories Served with Electricity at Retail by
Various Holding Company Systems, 1919

☐ No electric service
■ Independent
▨ Municipal
▨ Boston Edison
▨ Boston Edison, 1909
▨ Turners Falls Power and Electric Co.
▨ New England Power Association
▨ [a] Massachusetts Lighting Companies
▨ [b] Commonwealth Gas and Electric Companies
▨ [c] Central Massachusetts Light and Power Companies
▨ [d] Northern Boston Lighting Properties
▨ [a] Central Electric Trustees of Massachusetts
▨ [b] Cambridge Electric Securities Company
▨ [c] Boston Electric Associates

Same scale as main map

Scale 1:3,000,000

Miles
0 10 20 30 40 50   100

Kilometers
0   50   100

Eastern Gas and
Fuel Associates

See footnote on p. 298.

FIG. 4.—New England: territories served with electricity at retail by various holding company systems, Dec. 1, 1930.

dwelling in the township. Moreover, some townships displaying "no electric service" may actually have small plants of which no authentic record is easily found. The territories have been named according to the topmost controlling interest or company, not according to the corporate name of the distributing company. This top company may merely own the stock of subsidiary companies or actually operate generating stations whose output is wholesaled to operating subsidiaries or others in whose name bills are sent to customers. This obscures many complexities of intercorporate relations. Finally, the extent of the territory, of course, does not indicate the volume of business controlled.[44]

The general procedure of concentrating control and ownership is probably too well known now to require much comment. After acquisition of voting stock by the holding company or association, practice varies. The New England Public Service Company (controlled by the Middle West Utilities), for example, usually merges the acquired companies in each state into a large operating organization, such as the Central Maine Power Company; but in Massachusetts state regulations prevent this. In addition, many of the large holding companies have also organized separate companies for supplying

NOTE ON FIGURE 4—These maps show retail distribution only. The reader should be aware of the fact that some retailing companies buy their entire supply from a large company at wholesale, though the local corporate entity remains independently owned. It was found impossible on these maps to indicate these wholesale transactions with the ownership of the companies involved.

The sources of information were: *McGraw Hill Central Station Directory*, 1930; *Moody's Public Utility Manual*, 1930; *Poor's Public Utility Manual*, 1930; *Report of Connecticut Public Utilities Commission*, 1929; *Report of New Hampshire Public Service Commission*, 1929; *Report of Maine Public Utilities Commission*, 1927–1928; *Report of Vermont Public Service Commission*, 1925–1926; Massachusetts Department of Public Utilities; U. S. Department of Commerce Market Survey, 1928; records of Middle West Utilities Company as to communities served by its subsidiary companies; answers to questionnaires sent to certain companies and postmasters.

Questionnaires were sent to postmasters of all communities listed in Rand-McNally road maps as having 500 population or over for which the writer did not have information from other sources, to learn whether they had electric service and, if so, from what company. No questionnaires were sent to communities having less than 500 population, although information was available about many of them from other sources. Blank spaces on the maps indicate territories for which no record of electric service was found.

For the inset map the sources were: reports of Massachusetts Department of Public Utilities; *Moody's* and *Poor's Public Utility Manuals;* reports to stockholders of some of the companies served.

In shading the maps, if one town or village in a township was known as having service, the entire township was shaded. If two or more companies served different villages, the township was divided. In towns or villages served by more than one company, only the dominant company was shown. In a few instances where the information did not class either company as dominant, the territory was divided.

The classification of companies as "independent" means that no holding company affiliations were discovered.

The inset map of Massachusetts for 1919 also marks out the territory served by the Edison Electric Illuminating Company of Boston in 1909.

The controlling interest in the following companies in 1930 is given in parentheses: (2) Middle West Utilities (Insull), (5) Central Public Service (Pierce), (6) Public Utilities Consolidated Corp. of Arizona (W. B. Foshay Co.), (9) Eastern States Public Service Corp. (Fitkin), (10) International Hydro-Electric Co., New England Power Association, Massachusetts Utilities Associates (International Paper), (11) Eastern Utilities Associates (Stone and Webster), (13) Colonial Utilities, Inc. (Glidden-Morris), (14) Cities Service Co. (Doherty), (15) Tenney properties (C. H. Tenney), (16) Utilities Power and Light Corp. (Harley L. Clarke), (17) Tri-Utilities Corp. (G. L. Ohrstrom), (18) Eastern Gas and Fuel Associates (Mellon and Morgan), (20) United Gas and Improvement Co. (Mellon and Morgan).

certain services to operating organizations regardless of state lines. These "servicing" companies perform such functions as general management, consulting engineering, construction of properties, financing, purchase of materials and supplies, purchase of real estate, etc.

The era of consolidation has roughly coincided with the spread of interconnections, though two Massachusetts holding associations have existed for three decades. That the pace of consolidation was enormously accelerated after the war may be inferred from the map of Massachusetts in 1919 (Fig. 4, inset). The most noteworthy recent acquisitions were the purchase by the New England Power Association (controlled by the International Paper Company) of C. D. Parker & Company's interest[45] in Massachusetts Utilities Associates, in 1930, and of the North Boston Lighting Properties (formerly controlled by Tenney Properties) and the Green Mountain Power Corporation (formerly controlled by Tri-Utilities Corporation), in 1931.[46] The last two purchases occurred since the map was prepared.

Looking to the future, the map for New England indicates that consolidation has not attained its farthest reach. Here and there in all the states, especially perhaps in New Hampshire and Vermont, anomalies appear, and it is not unlikely that these are destined to be wiped out when, as, and if circumstances are propitious. Indeed some holding companies are in the business only to pick up properties for resale to other, larger companies. Opinions differ as to whether the holding company era is only a temporary stepping-stone to state-wide or regional corporate organizations, in which case New England might have to consider something similar to the present proposed railroad consolidation; or whether smaller operating units, grounded in local interests, do not have merits too blithely ignored at present.[47]

The final outcome of these tendencies toward consolidation will be considerably affected by the answer to certain merger problems. At the moment the difficulties of regulating interstate holding company systems by state commissions have captured the center of the stage, but in the background is a deeper problem, one which in a sense covers all merger problems. Are the benefits of consolidation, as practiced now, worth what they cost? As thus phrased, the issue cuts deeper than the mere impotence of regulating commissions, the task of making interconnection most valuable, or the difficulties of up-building load factors. In reality, private property in power resources is on trial.

ADVANTAGES AND DISADVANTAGES

The benefits of integrated control of utilities are numerous and many of them are not to be denied; but there are offsetting disadvantages from the standpoint of consumers. To balance or to appraise the two sets of considerations is not easy in a short space.[48]

Among the benefits claimed for holding companies, aiding inter-connection is frequently stressed; standards of management are alleged to have been raised, largely as a result of higher-grade personnel and the pooling of experience from a wide territory in specialized management, engineering, and other service companies; purchases of materials have been combined into large orders warranting large discounts, along with savings in the standardization of specifications for materials; research by technical staffs in central offices has brought improvements in operating technique.

Especially emphasized are the financial economies obtained through holding companies in an era of rapid expansion. During prosperous times holding companies pooled weak and strong proper-ties and combined demands for capital with the result, it was said, of raising funds more cheaply than could have been done by most of the companies acting singly. Surplus funds in one part of a system can be easily transferred to another subsidiary. A line of credit can be established with large metropolitan banks, enabling temporary borrowing at lower cost than if operating companies were independent and had to rely on local banking resources. In short, accumulation of all kinds of capital has been cheapened, it is said, because holding companies have popularized the electric industry in investment markets.

Finally, from the consumers' point of view, service has been expanded and its quality bettered. And these benefits have been provided at constantly lower costs and prices.

But there are offsets to these advantages very plausibly attributed to holding companies. While consolidated ownership has unques-tionably aided interconnection, that it has not been indispensable is attested by the considerable number of connections between unaffiliated companies. To be sure, of the interconnections across state lines in New England in the last few years, only two are said to involve unrelated companies.[49] That is not all, however. The savings from interconnected as compared with isolated self-sufficient systems may not be clear gain, for the interconnected system requires larger expenditures for transmission and creates some new difficulties for regulatory agencies.

A second disadvantage of holding companies is that in many ways they have unduly complicated regulation by state commissions. Not only are interstate connections under some circumstances immune from state regulation and not at present regulated by the federal government, but also transactions wholly within one state may create difficulties for state commissions seeking to control delivery or gateway prices. These demerits, discussed in another chapter, are most serious, for, if holding company organizations contain abuses that cannot be checked by existing regulatory agencies, consumers' interests are harmed and new controls may be needed.

The most serious objections to holding companies are financial. Accusations and evidence of stock-jobbing abound; the charge is even made by some within the industry.[50] Holding companies piled on top of one another, with satellite servicing companies, are said to inflate capitalization, if not in the sense of issuing more securities than the assets of operating subsidiaries are worth, at least in the sense of creating more capital obligations than earnings of operating subsidiaries warrant.[51] A small group of dominant owners of the topmost holding company, so the indictment runs, have so arranged the entire financial structure that there is insistent pressure to get all the profits possible from operating companies. This pressure is exerted in many ways, not easily discoverable. It may take the form of concealed profit-taking through management, engineering, or construction contracts, through inter-company borrowing, through purchase or exchange of materials, through buying and selling securities among related companies, or through writing up the values of assets used as a basis for determining reasonable rates to consumers. Again it may take the form of inflating dividends or postponing provision for maintenance and depreciation in years of poor business in order to maintain dividends that constitute part of the holding company's income. The receivership of several holding companies and the weakness of others, so strikingly evidenced during the past year, furnish strong evidence supporting these criticisms. Many holding companies have turned out to be "fair weather" helpers and liabilities in a time of prolonged and severe adversity.

The meat of these objections is that holding companies take the lion's share of the economies of mass production instead of dividing those economies equitably with customers in the form of more rapidly reduced rates. From the standpoint of consumers, this is the most serious count in the indictment.[52]

Do the alleged abuses outweigh the asserted advantages of holding companies? Unquestionably some holding companies have yielded some of the advantages claimed; unquestionably some abuses exist. Some of the practices are sanctioned by business ethics; others are debatable. Certainly not all holding companies indulge in all the undesirable practices; holding companies, like individuals, differ in their ethical principles. Moreover, some holding-company officials have expressed perplexity in deciding what is a fair division of economies between customers and investors. Should it be fifty-fifty or some other ratio?[53]

So far as holding companies owning property in New England are concerned, an elaborate investigation would be necessary to assess the balance of meritorious and blameworthy practices.[54] The present writer feels that the answer lies in the future because holding-company regulation has scarcely begun. In New England, as elsewhere, some unreasonable practices have offset the benefits of holding companies. These organizations are at the bar of public opinion, and they must sustain the burden of proving their good faith and permit regulatory bodies, state or federal, to correct inequitable practices. If this is not done, outlawing the holding company device and substituting some other system of organization or ownership would be justifiable.

As to the outlook for the future, one observer's picture of a New England served by a complete union of power utilities arouses partial approval and dissent.[55] "It seems improbable that the cost at the switchboard of steam generated power at a given load factor can be reduced by any substantial amount from the figure now reached by the more efficient stations." The same conclusion is drawn regarding hydro-electric power, because the best sites are now used and higher development and transmission costs will result from developing remaining sites. The remedy, in his opinion, is to improve load factor by interconnections. "Before really low production cost can be reached the whole New England market must be combined at some central point, in the office of a load dispatcher, or rather a power broker, where all the power produced in the area will be bought and sold." For illustration the Connecticut Valley Exchange is cited. To accomplish this centralized dispatching, a single holding company and the abolition of Massachusetts and Maine laws, respectively limiting consolidation and prohibiting power exports, are thought necessary.

So far as interconnection is concerned, the proposal is in the right direction. But in the present writer's view, combined ownership under a *single* holding company is neither essential in centralizing power resources nor altogether desirable. The Connecticut Valley Exchange operated before the Western Massachusetts Companies were formed. Massachusetts laws regarding consolidation may need change but not weakening. Before altering Maine laws on power exports, adequate guaranties safeguarding and satisfying consumer's interests in that state are probably essential. Finally, with a weather eye for possible economies in modern oil-burning plants, interconnections may well embrace not merely public utility systems but also, wherever technically feasible, industrially owned power plants.

NOTES

[1] Stuart Chase, in *Men and Machines* (New York, 1929), challenges the assumed beneficence of our machine civilization. He even questions the real labor-saving qualities of power machinery. Into such questions we cannot enter, though they may well make us ponder.

[2] As Figure 1a shows, the great bulk of this multiplied man power is in motor-driven vehicles. We are prone to overlook the fact that our public ways are the scene of a far greater utilization of power than are factories, stores, homes, farms, and electric generating stations added together. The problems arising from motor

traffic, while not commonly regarded as power problems, have some features in common with and certainly affect other power facilities. Think, if you will, of the plight of electric and steam railroads in the face of motor competition. For data on horse power of prime movers in motor vehicles in 1923, brought up to 1928 by estimates for use in Figure 1a, see C. R. Daugherty, A. H. Horton, and R. W. Davenport, *Power Capacity and Production in the United States*, Washington, 1928 (*U. S. Geol. Survey Water-Supply Paper 579*).

[3] *Super Power Studies, Northeast Section of United States*, Northeastern Super Power Committee, Herbert Hoover, Chairman, [Washington], 1924; *Report to Associated Industries of Massachusetts, Power Investigating Committee*, 1924; F. M. Gunby, *Power Supply for New England Industry*, in *Trans. Amer. Soc. of Mechanical Engineers*, Part I, Vol. 51, 1929, F. S P. 26, pp. 133–144; C. E. Artman, *Industrial Structure of New England*, Dept. of Commerce, Bur. of Foreign and Domestic Commerce, Washington, 1930 (*Domestic Commerce Ser. No. 28*), pp. 101–115.

[4] *Report, Power Investigating Committee*, cited above.

[5] U. S. Census of Manufactures, U. S. Geological Survey, National Electric Light Association statistical bulletins, *Electrical World*.

[6] *Report, Power Investigating Committee*, cited above; Gunby, *op. cit.;* and U. S. Geological Survey data on electricity generated.

[7] Bituminous coal comes in equal amounts from northern and southern fields. More than half the coal imports are water-borne on some part of the journey. Transportation charges form such a large proportion of coal costs to New England buyers that tidewater locations for industries or central stations ordinarily afford opportunities for economizing.

[8] The inexactness of most estimates of water powers is seen from the fact that the New England figures used by the Northeastern superpower survey in 1923 are repeated unchanged under a 1929 date line (Artman, *op. cit.*, and *National Electric Light Association Publication No. 182*, 1930). Examination of engineers' estimates, based on varying storage developments, should confirm one's scepticism of general estimates

[9] Natural gas does not enter New England, but manufactured gas companies offer facilities for considerable heat energy, primarily for special industrial processes.

[10] About two thirds of the electricity generated in central stations normally comes from fuel, although 68.6 per cent of the generator capacity is driven by steam power (Indicators 2 and 5, Table I).

[11] See p. 288.

[12] Such industries—woolen, paper, dyeing and finishing textiles, and rubber, for example—are found especially in Massachusetts and Rhode Island and to a lesser extent in New Hampshire and Maine. In these enterprises industrial ownership and operation of prime movers is likely to persist. (See *Report, Power Investigating Committee*, cited above; Artman, *op. cit.*, and Gunby, *op. cit.*)

[13] Excluding interconnection and merger problems outlined later. A fourth group of problems, focused by the concept of balance, arise chiefly from interconnections among power plants. As seen by the writer, these problems are (1) balancing the sources of power—coal, falling water, oil, or gas—so as to achieve high load factors and low costs; (2) balancing ownership of power capacity between self-suppliers and central stations; (3) balancing the geographical distribution of power capacity to minimize transmission costs and reliance on unstable supplies of high-cost fuels.

[14] "Load factor" is the ratio of the average power load to the maximum or "peak" power load of a station during a certain period of time—a day, a month, or a year. Thus a 50 per cent load factor indicates that, excluding reserve capacity, on the average only half the plant is used.

[15] G. H. Jones, *Effect of Load Factor on the Cost of Production and Methods of Improving Load Factor*, in *Transactions, Second World Power Conference, 1930*, Vol. 15, pp. 3–37.

[16] The Power Investigating Committee in its *Report* (pp. 141–142) gives some scanty data on load factors, now considerably out of date.

[17] Such expenditures have grown as river bottoms have been settled and roads built. Redevelopment of old sites has been handicapped in this way.

[18] Haphazard development, by manufacturers as well as central stations, along some streams has put obstacles in the way of broad-gauged planning, and the high cost of redevelopment prevents correction of mistakes.

[19] Common ownership of steam and /or electric plants by industries, leasing private plants to utilities for operation, sale of surplus industrial power to central stations are some of the schemes that seem worth exploring.

[20] Reference is made later to the handicap of being able to secure only average costs, which obscure the range of costs, instead of precise, actual costs of particular undertakings.

[21] Delivery lines are here interpreted to include: (1) distribution lines between substations and customers' premises; (2) transmission and primary distribution lines (a) among generating stations and distributing systems and (b) from load centers to substations.

[22] Notably in the case of the Edison Electric Illuminating Company of Boston.

[23] The Massachusetts Department of Public Utilities has received cost data on 6½ miles of double tower line leading to Tewksbury, Mass., part of the line from Fifteen Mile Falls, which average $55,000 a mile.

[24] In the rural territory where customers are widely spaced the incidence of delivery costs is particularly acute. Some standardization of practice may be expected from efforts of the power committee of the New England Council. See *A United New England—Four Years of Progress*, New England Council, 1930.

[25] Compare the above indicators with material in Artman, *op. cit.*, and Gunby, *op. cit.*

[26] The writer's experience in gathering data supporting the above statements suggests the desirability of a central agency, with at least two responsibilities: (1) making and keeping up-to-date a *continuous inventory* of New England power resources, with data on their utilization and the problems involved; (2) standardizing the data to be collected, as, for example, stimulating standardized power-cost accounting in industries serving themselves. The New England Council seems the best existing vehicle for this coördinating work, as it has already taken steps along this line in the rural electric service field, in interstate power movements, and in keeping a map of interconnection facilities abreast of the times. See *A United New England*, etc., cited above.

[27] The writer prefers "interconnection" to "superpower" because of the many visionary ideas that have been infused into the latter word. By "interconnection" is meant the tying together of generating plants or distributing systems, not the distributing lines between customers and substations.

[28] Though there are noticeable gaps, the generating plants of New England, especially in Massachusetts, are interconnected more completely than in New York and Pennsylvania and are about on a par with those of Indiana and Ohio (C. L. Edgar, *Interconnections Between Central Power Stations in New England*, New England Council, 1927).

The first recorded instance in New England of a "true interconnection" was in 1890 when the Edison Electric Illuminating Company of Boston connected three of its stations (*ibid.*). The progress from that day to the present is dramatically evidenced by the relay interconnection of companies between Boston and Chicago in 1926. Transmission line development began in earnest after 1909 when the Vernon plant in New Hampshire was connected with Worcester, Mass. A great spurt of activity occurred after 1922.

[29] The "traffic," to apply a railroad term, may be divided into three classes: (1) regular supplies of energy to distribution systems, usually at from 11,000 to 66,000 volts; (2) breakdown or dump power by interchange or relay among separate distribution-transmission systems, mostly above 66,000 volts; (3) block power over long distances, without dropping off power along the line, generally at high pressure up to 220,000 volts. See *Electric Power Survey*, National Electric Light Association, Great Lakes Division, 1925.

[30] *Annual Returns of Gas, Electric and Water Companies*, Mass. Dept. of Public Utilities, 1929.

[31] See also Indicators 10, 11, and 14, Table I. The figures for 1928 represent the more normal situation, because 1929 was an exceptionally dry year. The influence of drought and the value of interconnection are indicated in the Rhode Island export figures for 1929 and 1930, when that state's steam generating stations picked up part of the load relinquished by northern stations on dried-up streams.

[32] An amendment relaxing this law was submitted to the voters in 1929 and defeated. While the wisdom of Maine's policy, considered from the standpoint of New England as a whole, may be debatable, particularly since the bulk of undeveloped water powers are located there, its local interests are entitled to respect. See also Professor Hormell's paper entitled *Governmental Control of Power Utilities in the New England States*, in the present volume, pp. 307–321, below.

[33] Massachusetts is something of a way station for northern power destined for Rhode Island or Connecticut, but the possible duplications in the data on this account have been minimized by the compilers in Table II.

[34] A concrete illustration, outside New England, is discussed and cost data are presented in B. F. Wood, *Power Interchange with Industrial Plants*, in *Electrical World*, Vol. 96, 1930, pp. 1039–1040.

[35] *Electrical World*, Vol. 95, 1930, p. 380.

[36] Payments to the Exchange are based on the savings in fuel cost to the buying company, and the accumulated payments are periodically prorated to the companies in the scheme. See also W. R. Peabody, *Why Bay State Favors Local Company Grouping*, in *Electrical World*, Vol. 95, 1930, pp. 739–740.

[37] The possibilities and probable costs of hydro-electric power from the St. Lawrence and its tributaries delivered near Boston are discussed in *Super Power Studies* (cited above, note 3) and *Report, Power Investigating Committee* (cited above, note 3).

[38] Some of the larger public utility companies have some information but are reluctant to give it publicity, partly because they fear that the general public will overlook transmission and distribution costs.

[39] Whether the proposed tidal power project in Passamaquoddy Bay "way down East" in Maine would come within this range is doubtful.

[40] *Super Power Studies* and *Report, Power Investigating Committee* (cited above, note 3). Conservative assumptions, judged by 1930 standards, and the age of the data chiefly account for these estimates being higher.

[41] It is interesting to note that the Hudson, Mass., municipal plant reported in 1929 a generation cost of about 8 mills from its new Diesel engine.

[42] The Fifteen Mile Falls project was designed for a "comparatively *low* load factor" distinguishing it from high load factor plants like some of those in Canada. The price is in the form of an annual payment for 2000-hour power (primarily to meet peak demands), price adjustments being made periodically for such factors as the cost of steam power. (Letter from Frank D. Comerford, President, New England Power Association, to the writer.)

[43] For example, Hartford's experimental mercury vapor installation in a recent test generated a kw. hr. with only 9140 B. t. u., equivalent to about 7/10 of a pound

of coal, less than half the average coal consumption of all utility plants in the United States (*Electrical World*, Vol. 94, 1929, p. 970). But between February 4 and December 14, 1930, the average B. t. u. consumption per kw. hr. was 10,310 (*ibid.*, Vol. 96, 1930, p. 1114).

44 Thus in Massachusetts, in 1928, 93.9 per cent of the electricity generated came from seven systems; the balance was generated by municipal plants or independent local companies. Of these seven systems, three controlled over 70 per cent of the output. On the other hand, these seven systems controlled only 90.5 per cent of the electricity sold at retail, almost two-thirds of the sales being made by three systems.

45 The New England Power Association had previously owned a minority interest.

46 *Annual Report*, New England Power Association, 1931.

47 See *Electrical World*, Vol. 92, 1928, p. 1079.

48 Consult *Report of the Special Commission on Control and Conduct of Public Utilities*, Boston, 1930 ([*Mass.*], House [*Doc.*] *No. 1200*).

49 *A United New England*, (cited above, note 24).

50 T. T. Whitney, Jr., *Relation of the Banker to the Public Utility*, in *Stone & Webster Journal*, Vol. 44, 1929, pp. 26–33.

51 Professor W. Z. Ripley's description in *Main Street and Wall Street* (Boston, 1927) of the bewildering mazes of financial pyramiding gives a fuller account than can be attempted here.

52 See article by the present writer in *Christian Science Monitor*, Dec. 2, 1930, and his *Some Problems of State Control of Public Utility Holding Companies*, in *Journ. of Land & Public Utility Economics*, Vol. 5, 1929, pp. 19–28; also general literature on the subject, especially J. C. Bonbright and G. C. Means, *The Holding Company: Its Public Significance and Its Regulation*, New York, 1932.

53 Peabody, work cited above, note 36.

54 An inconclusive investigation was made in Massachusetts last year (*Report* cited in note 48, above), and one is under way in New Hampshire at the time of writing.

55 Discussion of Gunby's paper by Professor Cabot of Harvard (Gunby, work cited above, note 3).

GOVERNMENTAL CONTROL OF POWER
UTILITIES IN THE NEW ENGLAND STATES

Orren Chalmer Hormell

ELECTRIC POWER, within two decades, has assumed a dominant position among the economic and governmental factors in
the New England states, and undoubtedly during the next two
decades no more insistent problem will face the governments of those
states than that of just and effective control of the electric power
utilities.

Twenty-two years ago (1911) a large majority of the electric
utilities in New England were owned by local capital and operated by
local companies. They were still largely in the ownership and control
of the original local promotors, who through thrift had accumulated
capital sufficient to begin the development of local resources. Today
more than 90 per cent of the electric current in New England is
generated and distributed under the control of holding companies
whose interests are not limited by state boundaries.

The *laissez-faire* period of control, featured by intermittent,
ineffective regulation through legislative acts granting, amending,
altering, and repealing charters, was brought to an end and a policy
of positive regulation was inaugurated in the period 1911 to 1915.
Such regulation was instituted by the enactment of laws in each of the
New England states setting up public utilities (or public service)
commissions.[1]

AUTHORITY OF PUBLIC UTILITIES COMMISSIONS

Such public utilities commissions have in common the function
of acting as agents of the legislature, to regulate and control the
services and charges of the electric utilities. Their function is to
secure for the public adequate service at reasonable rates and to permit
the utility to earn, if economically possible, a fair return upon the fair
value of its property used in the service.

The extent of the regulatory authority in the commissions varies
greatly among the several states. Massachusetts, New Hampshire,
and Maine, both through the granting of authority and through providing a working staff, have developed a comparatively extensive
regulatory authority, while the authority exercised by the commissions
in Connecticut and Rhode Island is comparatively narrow. The
Vermont commission has quite extensive powers on paper (statutory
authority), but such powers are extremely limited on account of
meager appropriations and an inadequate working staff.

---

[1] For notes see below, p. 320.

In general the commissions have authority to prescribe to the utilities forms for keeping accounts and to require of utilities annual reports on forms provided by the commission. Since the rate to the consumer must be sufficient to meet all the legitimate expense items of the operating utility, the form of the reports and the care with which they are inspected and checked up by the commission are of first importance. To date, the exercise of this authority has been of slight advantage to the consumers in most instances, because meager appropriations have necessitated inadequate or incompetent accounting staffs.

Each commission is authorized to hear complaints made by consumers or municipalities with regard to the quality of service and the fairness of rates.

The authority of the commission to investigate service and rates on its own initiative is much more limited. Such authority is vested in the commissions of New Hampshire, Maine, and Massachusetts, but to date has been exercised very little on account of insufficient appropriations and an inadequate staff.[5] The law of 1927 for the first time vested in the Massachusetts Department of Utilities the power to act on its own initiative relative to the reasonableness of electric rates.[2]

The law and practice concerning the approval by the commission of securities issued by utilities companies lack uniformity and effectiveness. For example, the Vermont commission is given authority to approve stock and bond issues and for that purpose to make an appraisal of the entire properties of both domestic and foreign corporations. Such policy puts an undue burden upon the Vermont consumers, since in some cases they bear the burden of evaluating assets, the greater part of which is in other states. The law of New Hampshire extends such authority only to issues of securities made for expenditures within the state, whether by foreign or domestic utilities. It has had little success in adequately checking the assets of interstate companies. Furthermore, the commission has no jurisdiction over the issue of securities for properties outside of the state, even though they constitute a lien on New Hampshire properties. Massachusetts provides a third type by giving the Department of Utilities jurisdiction over the issues of domestic utilities for both local and outside-of-state purposes but gives it no jurisdiction over foreign corporations operating utilities within the state.[3] Maine requires the approval of the commission for the issuing of securities by domestic corporations based upon assets in Maine but specifically exempts issues based upon property outside of the state.[4] The Connecticut commission is given no authority over the issues of securities; and the Rhode Island commission has no jurisdiction over securities, except where the special charter, granted to a utility by the legislature, vests such authority

in the commission. The chaotic condition in New England relative
to issuing of public utilities securities can be removed only by uniform
securities laws among the several states.

Mergers are regulated in each of the New England states, but the
significance of such regulation is rapidly decreasing by reason of the
centralization of control through the ownership of common stock by
holding companies, which policy is rapidly displacing centralization
of control through mergers.

Effective regulation by the commissions requires that the position
of the commissioner should carry with it the dignity and prestige equal
to that of a judge of the supreme court of the state, so that a man of
first-rate ability might be willing to serve until retired on account of
age.   In no New England state is the salary of a public utilities
commissioner large enough to give him such a position.   Moreover, the
staff of the commission is generally greatly undermanned and under-
paid.[5]

Municipal Ownership

Massachusetts and New Hampshire are the only New England
states to provide by general law for municipal ownership of electric
utilities.   In each of the remaining states a municipality, to own and
operate a public utility, must apply to the legislature for a charter
which, if granted, is in the form of a special legislative act.

Rate Regulation

Since the celebrated case of *Smyth* v. *Ames* (169 U.S. 466, 1897[6])
the outstanding problem of public control of electrical utilities has
been the determination of an adequate rate base. It has been generally
conceded that reasonable rates, in the interest of the utilities and the
investors on the one hand and of the consumers on the other, must be
a "fair return upon a fair value" of the property used and usable in
providing the service to the public.

The above principle is embodied in the public utility laws of each
of the New England states. The commissions in each of the states
have accepted "fair return upon a fair value" as a just basis for rate
regulation.   There has been no unanimity, however, with regard to
what is a fair return and what is a fair value. Each commission has
undertaken to decide the elements of fair value in each individual
case by giving what it considers to be due recognition to the several
elements of value enumerated in the *Smyth* v. *Ames* decision. The
relative weight given to each of the elements of value has varied greatly
among the several commissions and even in the decisions over a period
of time handed down by a single commission. The chief disturbing
factor has been the controversy between the "prudent investment or
actual cost theory" and the "cost of reproduction less depreciation
theory."

Prior to the chain of U. S. Supreme Court decisions, beginning about 1921[7] and culminating in the Indianapolis Water Co. case (1926) and the O'Fallon case (1928),[8] a majority of the New England commissions gave important (if not dominant) weight to the "prudent investment" or actual cost theory of valuation.

As late as 1926 the New Hampshire commission emphatically expressed its approval of the prudent investment theory as follows: "The prudent investment, which means original cost wisely and economically made, is considered by this commission as evidence of fair value and as much weight is given to it as is permissible under the law. *Cost of reproducing the property at current prices has no stability for a rate base*"[9] (italics ours). The commission believes the rate of return should be sufficient "to enable the company to maintain its credit, in order that it may borrow money at a reasonable rate and sell its stocks at par."[10]

The Maine commission in its second report, 1916, expressed its preference for the "original cost or actual cost" over "cost new, or cost of reproduction less depreciation," in determining fair value for purposes of rate making.[11] As late as 1920 the commission in its report still favored the prudent investment theory to that of the reproduction cost less depreciation theory.[12] The decisions of the commission since 1920 seem to indicate that the prudent investment theory has been abandoned for the reproduction cost less depreciation theory as an element of value deserving greatest weight.

At present the commissions of all of the New England states except Massachusetts seem to be guided in their decisions by the emphasis recently placed by the Supreme Court of the United States upon the necessity of arriving at the reproduction cost on the basis of present prices.[13]

Massachusetts alone among the New England states still clings tenaciously to the so-called prudent investment theory. The commission believes that "regulation should be certain, definite, and capable of speedy application in the determination of rates which will do justice both to the public and to owners of the utility; that a rate base which takes as the controlling factor capital honestly invested possesses these qualifications, while "a rate based upon reproduction value less observed depreciation is not only unsound legally and historically but also economically."[14] By "investment" is meant the money paid by the stockholders into the treasury of the company, which includes premium as well as principal. Such investment becomes the *fixed rate base*. The utilities are then allowed to earn sufficient dividends to attract fresh capital. The commission believes that the *rate of return* should be elastic. It has never undertaken to determine what a fair rate of return on that fixed rate base should be for all utilities. It recognizes that a number of factors enter into a determination as to what the rate of return should be for the specific utility. "The efficiency or inefficiency of the management, the value of the dollar, the going rate of return in other sound and stable business enterprises, the question whether a utility has paid out all its earnings in dividends or has plowed some of its earnings back into capitalizable improvements which have not been capitalized, the credit of the company, the question whether the business of the specific utility is growing rapidly, slowly, or is at a standstill, and other similar factors—all enter into the question as to what the rate of return should be for the specific utility at the time when the rate is being determined."[15]

The above principle was clearly embodied in the recent (1930) Edison Electric Illuminating Company rate case as follows: "rates ought not to be so regulated as to impair the incentive upon the part of the company for efficient and progressive management" and ought to "enable the company to pay dividends, after proper allowances for depreciation, which will maintain the market value of its stock at the highest price at which, acting under our statutes, we or our predecessors have required it to be offered to stockholders."[16]

It appears that the utilities in Massachusetts generally have been satisfied with the above policy, as no case has ever been carried from the commission to the U. S. Supreme Court even though the commission has apparently derived its rate base "from the liabilities side of the balance sheet" rather than from "an inventory and appraisal of assets."[17]

The successful working of the Massachusetts rate plan is conditioned largely on the power of the commission to fix or review the price at which securities shall be sold.

The application of the prudent investment theory, it is alleged, has continued without a break from the enactment of the turnpike law of 1804 to the present day.[18]

Standardization of Rates

Comparatively little has been done to date in any of the New England states to bring about equitable standardization of rates or a fair adjustment of the rates charged to the several classes of consumers. The highest rate is everywhere charged to the domestic lighting consumers, and the lowest to the industrial consumers of power. In general, rural consumers pay a higher rate than is paid by consumers in large urban centers.

The commission in each state, however, is beginning to consider the problem of standardization and equalization of rates; and two states, Vermont and New Hampshire, through special appropriations, have provided for and recently completed investigations of rate schedules.

Commissions are looking with favor on "promotional" rate schedules devised to encourage more diversified use of energy by domestic consumers.

There is a growing opposition to the policy of permitting the utilities to grant to industrial power users energy at rates lower than the actual cost of producing the energy. No state to date, however, has required utilities to raise such rates. Power rates are subject still to competitive conditions, since a great industry may generate its own electricity if the rate granted by the utility is not sufficiently favorable.

If the electric utilities continue to enter the field of industrial ownership and operation, greater supervision of minimum charges for power to such industries seems desirable.

THE HOLDING COMPANY

There has appeared within the last three or four years in four of the New England states, Vermont, New Hampshire, Maine, and Massachusetts, a growing public opinion in favor of some form of regulation over holding companies. In 1929 an act was introduced into the Vermont Legislature conferring upon the Public Service Commission jurisdiction over holding companies. The bill, although it failed to pass during the closing days of the session, was supported by rather extensive public opinion in the state.[19]

The New Hampshire Public Service Commission attempted to extend its authority over holding companies, nonresident in New Hampshire, owning the stock of New Hampshire companies, and having intercorporate relations with operating companies in New Hampshire. The Public Service Commission ordered the New England Gas & Electric Association, a holding company in the form of a Massachusetts voluntary trust company, and the New York Associated Gas & Electric Company, a holding company affiliated with the New England Gas & Electric Association, to appear before the commission with all books and papers that would show the intercorporate relations existing between the local companies and the two parent concerns. They were directed to submit all contracts, correspondence, and other evidence of intercorporate relations to the commission for its inspection, so that it might decide what effect, if any, such affiliations had on the rates and service of the operating utilities.[20] The preliminary injunction asked for by the above-named holding companies was granted by the federal court, in so far as the order of the commission related to evidence situated outside of the state. The court restricted the commission's inquiry to "those companies which operate public utilities within the state." The court held that the utilities cannot be required to go beyond the jurisdiction of the commonwealth to acquire evidence not in their possession or control. Accordingly, it appears that it is most difficult, if not impossible, for the state of New Hampshire to discover fully the financial operations and the inter-utility contracts between the operating companies in New Hampshire and the nonresident holding companies, which actually control the operating companies through the ownership of underlying securities.

The relation between holding companies and operating companies in Massachusetts has not been considered of any great importance by the Public Utilities Department in Massachusetts. It has considered the effective control of the operating companies, including the control of actual mergers and of issuing of securities, to be sufficient for its purpose. However, after the recommendation of a special commission on the control and conduct of public utilities, the legislature made a slight beginning in the regulation of holding companies.[21] The extent to which the 1930 legislation will permit the Massachusetts Department of Public Utilities to investigate the relations between the operating companies and various holding companies is somewhat doubtful in the light of the New Hampshire injunction case outlined above.

INTERSTATE TRANSMISSION OF ELECTRIC ENERGY

Interstate transmission of electric energy in New England is associated with the policy of state control in two important aspects: (1) the authority of the states to regulate or control the rates for the sale of electric energy generated in one state and transmitted across state lines for consumption in a second state, and (2) the law and practice relative to the limitation or prohibition of the exportation of electric energy beyond the boundaries of the state.

The first aspect—rate regulation of electricity transmitted across state boundaries—is of interest to each of the New England states. A number of court decisions culminating in the Attleboro Steam and Electric Company case[22] establishes the principles that (a) the state in which the energy is ultimately sold to consumers has jurisdiction over the rates charged to such consumers, (b) neither the exporting state nor the receiving state has any jurisdiction over prices fixed in interstate wholesale contracts, and (c) the state in which energy is generated and from which it is transmitted across the state boundary has no control over either the wholesale rate or the ultimate rate charged to the consumers.[23] The above-mentioned chain of decisions makes it impossible for the New England states to continue the policy of requiring a company to secure the approval of a public utilities commission for wholesale contracts, a notable example of which may be found in the decision of the Vermont Public Service Commission in 1919.[24]

The law and practice relative to the limitation or prohibition of the exportation of electric energy are of first importance economically and politically in New England. New England comprises six states not separated by geographical barriers. These states constitute what engineers point out to be one of the eight hydro-electric regional districts into which the country may be divided. Industrially New England may be considered a unit which logically or economically cannot be divided into six arbitrary divisions along lines of state boundaries. Nevertheless, about 60 per cent of the developed water power capacity in the New England states is in New Hampshire (28.8 per cent) and Maine (31.6 per cent), that is in states either restricting or prohibiting the exportation of hydro-electric energy, and about 72 per cent of the potential water power resources of New England is in these two states (New Hampshire 18.7 per cent, Maine 53.7 per cent).[25]

New Hampshire and Maine have adopted the policy of giving preference to, or retaining for, their own inhabitants the use of hydro-electric energy produced in their states. This policy comes into distinct conflict with "the new engineering and economic tendency to pool the power resources of given areas into interconnected systems with full and free exchange." Such restrictive or prohibitive policy is especially important in New England, since the dominant demand for power is from the great industrialized sections of Massachusetts, Connecticut, and Rhode Island.

New Hampshire's restrictive policy dates from the original public utilities law of 1911, which provided that "no corporation engaged in the generation of electrical energy by water power shall engage in the business of transmitting or conveying the same beyond the confines of the state unless it shall first file notice of its intention so to do with the public service commission and obtain an order of said commission permitting it to engage in such business."[26]

The original law, while requiring permission of the commission before exportation, made no provision for revoking such permission. An amendment to the law was enacted in 1929 providing for the discontinuance of such exportation "in whole or in part, to such extent and under such conditions as the commission may order . . . whenever . . . the commission shall find that such electrical energy . . . is reasonably required for use within this state, and that the public good requires that it be delivered for such use."[27]

Permission was given in December, 1929, to the Grafton Power Company, a subsidiary of the New England Power Association, to export to Massachusetts consumers power generated at the power plant at Fifteen Mile Falls on condition that such exportation be limited to the ability of the company to meet all legitimate demands for the purchase of power by New Hampshire users.[28] The policy of New Hampshire is clearly to permit the exportation of surplus energy only and to curtail or prohibit such exportation whenever it appears that the energy is needed in the state.

Maine Policy on Exportation of Power

The policy of the State of Maine with regard to the exportation of power had its inception in the so-called Fernald Law of 1909.[29] This law expressly prohibits the exportation from the state of hydro-electric power except with the permission of the legislature. Maine is the only state in the Union that goes to such drastic length in the prohibition of the exportation of electric energy.

In accordance with the recommendation of Governor Fernald in his message to the Legislature in 1909 an act to prohibit corporations from transporting electric power beyond the confines of the state was introduced into the Senate by Senator Percival P. Baxter. The act, it was argued, would preserve the great natural resource, water power, for the people of the state of Maine and prevent it from falling into the hands of "trusts, monopolies and speculators from other states." Such a policy it was believed would draw industry into the state.[30]

The chief argument in opposition may be summarized as follows: Such restrictive legislation is economically unsound and politically inexpedient and unjust. Potential power goes to waste unless it is put to work. "The only reason," it was argued, "for confining it here to the State of Maine is the thought that if we do not wire it out of the State, manufacturers will come to the State of Maine and use it. It would be equally true that if we objected to the shipment of lumber beyond our State, people might come here to build their houses, and, if we did not ship our potatoes, they might come here to eat them, and, if we did not ship our Poland Spring water . . . , they might come here to drink it."[31]

The Fernald Law has come up for discussion and criticism many times. The most vigorous and continuous opposition has developed within the last few years. The movement for its repeal culminated in a bill before the Legislature in 1927, which was vetoed by Governor Brewster. A somewhat similar bill was enacted by the Legislature in 1929 and submitted to a vote of the people. The title of the bill was "An Act to provide for the Exportation of Surplus Power." The act provided in part for the organization, under the general laws of the state, of companies authorized only to buy surplus power for the purpose of exportation. Such surplus power could be sold by the generating companies to the transmission companies only after permission had been granted by the Maine Public Utility Commission. The utilities selling the surplus power were to pay to the state, as an excise tax, 4 per cent of the gross operating revenue received from such sales. It was further provided that the statute was to be incorporated as a part of the contracts between the companies and the state and that a violation of the statute would automatically revoke the permit.

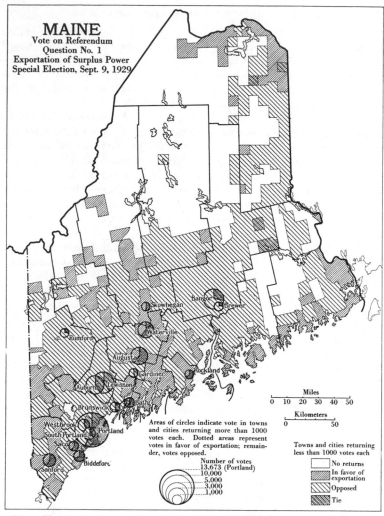

FIG. 1—Map showing the vote in the referendum held in Maine in 1929 on the repeal of the Fernald law forbidding the exportation of surplus hydro-electric power.

The arguments for the adoption of the act and the modification of the Fernald Law were substantially as follows:

At present under the Fernald Law about two thirds of the potential hydro-electric energy of the Maine rivers runs to waste.

Under the present state of development there is a considerable surplus power that can find no market in Maine. Maine consumers now pay, in higher rates, for the wasted surplus power. Hence exportation of surplus power will take such burden off Maine consumers and result in lower rates in Maine.

In addition to the 4 per cent excise tax the state will receive increased taxes from the capital invested in the now idle resources.

The export law will stimulate development of power resources. *Developed power* will attract new industries.

The development of power sites will provide abundant labor to Maine workmen and markets at home for millions of dollars of Maine products.[32]

The arguments in favor of the retention and strengthening of the Fernald Law may be summarized as follows:

Economically, it is held, Maine stands to lose by the transmission of water power. Scientific development of the distribution and transmission of electricity which makes it possible to market electric current in neighboring states makes possible also the transmission and distribution of electricity to Maine homes and Maine farms.

If Maine keeps her factories and manufacturing plants and secures electric current for out-of-the-way rural communities, no surplus exists now or will exist in the near future.

There is danger, it is said, that many of our factories now suffering severe competition from the south would be lured away if a ready market in neighboring states could be found for the water power now owned by such factories. Maine, it is feared, is in danger of becoming merely a power station for out-of-the-state industrial centers or merely a summer resort.

Again, it is argued that the holding companies now in control have come into Maine so recently, and their policies are as yet so uncertain, that it would be wise to go slowly in the matter of granting them further privileges. Why not, it is asked, leave them on their good behavior a few years at least, before giving them a privilege the consequence of which cannot be foretold?

Furthermore, it is claimed that when the power once leaves the state it immediately escapes all control by the state and the state becomes powerless to enforce any agreements that have been made when the privilege was granted.

After a vigorous campaign, in which the power people accused the opponents of the bill of being demagogues and the leaders favoring the retention of the Fernald Law accused the power interests of using an unjustifiably large amount of money, the proposed export law was defeated by a vote of 54,072 to 64,044. Nine of the sixteen counties gave a majority against repeal. The returns by counties are listed in Table I, and the vote by towns and cities is shown on Figure 1. The coastal counties and the counties bordering the Kennebec River voted in favor of exportation, while the interior counties, led by Androscoggin and Penobscot, rolled up the largest majorities in opposition.

TABLE I—MAINE: VOTE BY COUNTIES ON REFERENDUM, QUESTION NO. 1, EXPORTATION OF SURPLUS POWER, AT SPECIAL ELECTION, SEPTEMBER 9, 1929

COUNTY	YES	No
Androscoggin	4,423	8,134
Aroostook	3,009	3,476
Cumberland	12,089	11,409
Franklin	1,045	1,629
Hancock	1,971	2,200
Kennebec	7,367	5,923
Knox	1,959	1,276
Lincoln	1,766	948
Oxford	1,782	3,659
Penobscot	3,313	10,542
Piscataquis	1,038	1,862
Sagadahoc	1,622	1,330
Somerset	2,960	3,350
Waldo	1,402	1,818
Washington	2,384	1,693
York	5,942	4,795
Total	54,072	64,044

Here the opposition, led by Governor Brewster and the Grange, was better organized and more skillfully managed. The strictly rural population, it appears, furnished the backbone of the opposition. This may be inferred from the fact that the vote in all municipalities that returned less than 1000 votes apiece was Yes 27,502, No 37,793, whereas the combined vote of all the larger places was Yes 26,570, No 26,251. With the exception of Bangor and Brewer in Penobscot County, Lewiston and Auburn in Androscoggin County, Rumford in Oxford County, and Brunswick and Westbrook in Cumberland County, majorities in favor of repeal were returned in every municipality where more than 1000 votes were cast. It is also significant that the four college presidents, the industrial leaders, and all the newspapers, with the exception of the Portland *Evening News*, supported the measure, while the opposition was headed by Governor Brewster and leaders of the Grange. Factional party politics and hostility to an outside holding company probably were among the chief elements in bringing about the result.

It is still a mooted question whether the Fernald Law is constitutional. There is wide difference of opinion among the best legal authorities in the country with regard to the question. Eminent legal authorities and Supreme Court decisions may be cited on both sides of the question. Those who favor the constitutionality of the Fernald Law cite the case of *Geer* v. *Connecticut* (161 U. S. 519, 1895), which held that common ownership of wild game carried with it the right to keep the property always within the jurisdiction of the state and to prevent it from being exported from the state or becoming an article of interstate commerce. The next important case bearing on the same subject was the *Ohio Oil Co.* v. *Indiana* (177 U. S. 190, 1899). In this case the court held that "once natural gas is reduced to possession the state cannot prevent the owners from transporting it from the state." In the *Kansas Natural Gas Co.* v. *Haskell* (172 Fed. 545, 1909[33]) the court held that when gas is reduced to possession it becomes a subject of interstate commerce and that, while the state may regulate it with regard to health and safety, it cannot prohibit its exportation. This decision was upheld by the Supreme Court (224 U. S. 217, 1911). Somewhat later the Supreme Court was called upon to decide the case of *Pennsylvania* v. *West Virginia* (262 U. S. 553, 1922). The state of West Virginia attempted to prevent the exportation of gas into Pennsylvania in order that the consumers in West Virginia might have an adequate supply. The court held that West Virginia had no right to regulate the interstate business to the advantage of local consumers, even though the supply of natural gas was no longer adequate for the needs of all. Justice Holmes, in a dissenting opinion, argued somewhat convincingly in favor of the principle that "the constitution does not prohibit a state from securing a reasonable preference for its own inhabitants in the enjoyment of its own products, even when the effect of its law is to keep property within its boundaries that otherwise would have passed outside." An interesting case, which presented an additional legal element, is that of the *Hudson County Water Co.* v. *McCarter* (209 U. S. 349, 1907). This case is of interest because there is a relation between the generation of hydro-electric power and the utilization of flowing streams. The U. S. Supreme Court has held that a state may prevent the diversion of its water from the state. The question then arises, can a state prevent exportation of electric energy generated by the use of water power? The decision in the New Jersey case was given by Justice Holmes, and in this case he supported the right of the state to prevent the diversion of its water on the ground of police power which gave the state rights over its natural resources. In considering all the cases concerning exportation of natural resources, the two cases, one having to do with wild game and the other with water, are generally regarded as exceptions to the rule that the state cannot prohibit or restrict the exportation of its natural resources. The final decision with regard to the validity of the Fernald Law probably will depend upon whether the majority of the court will follow Justice Holmes's liberal views on the police power of the state or the more conservative views of the majority of the court as expressed in the West Virginia and Kansas cases.

NOTES

[1] Positive regulation to a limited extent in Massachusetts dates from 1887, when the duties of the Board of Gas Commissioners were extended to include jurisdiction over electric lighting companies (but not over power companies). A Board of Gas and Electric Light Commissioners with more extensive and clearly defined powers was created in 1895. In 1919 it was consolidated with the Public Service Commission to form the Department of Public Utilities.

[2] Massachusetts, *Acts and Resolves*, 1927, Chap. 316.

[3] H. L. Elsbree, *Interstate Transmission of Electric Power: A Study in the Conflict of State and Federal Jurisdictions*, Cambridge, Mass., 1931, Chap. 5.

[4] Maine, *Revised Statutes*, 1930, Chap. 62, Sect. 41.

[5] Financial support of utilities regulation, however, varies to a marked degree among the states, as is illustrated by the following table.

STATE	TOTAL APPRO-PRIATION, 1930	NUMBER ON STAFF
Maine	$123,250	20
New Hampshire	60,700	13
Vermont	16,000	2
Massachusetts	160,600	70 (about)
Connecticut	70,232	17
Rhode Island	33,000	5

Vermont supplements the activities of its commission and staff by calling in expert accountants and engineers from outside to collect data on rate and security cases. The cost of such outside experts is charged to the companies being investigated and is passed on by the companies to the ultimate consumer in rates paid for current.

A 1931 law (New Hampshire, *Laws*, 1931, Chap. 127) enacted by the New Hampshire Legislature authorized the commission to charge to the utilities involved the cost of rate investigations. Such expense is charged to operating expenses and allowed for in rates charged to the consumer. The same legislature increased the salaries of the commissioners to $5000 a year (*ibid.*, Chap. 149).

[6] References in the text and notes given in this form are to volume, page, and year of U. S. Supreme Court, *United States Reports*.

[7] *Galveston Electric Company* v. *City of Galveston* (258 U. S., 388, 1921).

[8] *McCardle et. al.* v. *Indianapolis Water Company* (272 U. S. 400, 1926); *St. Louis & O'Fallon Railway Company et. al.* v. *United States* (279 U. S., 516, 1928).

[9] New Hampshire, *Public Service Commission Reports*, Vol. 10, p. 306 (No. D-964 [Mar., 1926], p. 964).

[10] *Ibid.*, p. 307.

[11] Maine, *Public Utilities Commission Report*, 1916, p. 100.

[12] *Ibid.*, 1920, p. 14.

[13] *Ibid.*, 1929–1930, p. 10.

[14] *Massachusetts Dept. of Public Utilities*, No. 2609, June 3, 1927.

[15] Louis Goldberg, letter, Oct. 9, 1930.

[16] *Massachusetts Dept. of Public Utilities*, Nos. 3642, 3737, 3763, July 31, 1930.

[17] E. W. Morehouse, *The "Regulatory Rebellion" in the Bay State*, in *Public Utilities Fortnightly*, Vol. 5, 1930, pp. 814–826.

[18] New York (State), *Commission on Revision of the Public Service Commissions Law Report*, Albany, 1930, 4 vols. (paged consecutively), p. 1583.

[19] Vermont, *Senate Documents*, 1929, pp. 205–206; *Amer. Polit. Sci. Rev.*, Vol. 25, 1931, pp. 103–114, reference on p. 114.

[20] *The New Hampshire Holding Company Dispute*, in *Public Utilities Fortnightly*, Vol. 6, 1930, pp. 252–253.

[21] Massachusetts, *Acts and Resolves*, 1930; Chapter 395 authorizes the department "to examine the books, contracts, records, documents, and memoranda or the physical property of any company . . . and of any affiliated company with respect to any relations, transactions, or dealings, direct or indirect," between the company and an affiliated company. Chapter 342 provides that no electric company may enter into a contract for the purchase of electricity covering a period in excess of two years without the approval of the Department of Public Utilities unless such contract contains a provision subjecting the price to be paid to review and determination by the department. Chapter 396 provides that no contract may be entered into by an electric company for a period exceeding two years, relative to services to be rendered by an affiliated company without the consent of the Department of Public Utilities. unless such contract contains a provision subjecting the amount of compensation to review and determination by the department. "Affiliated company" was defined so as to include "holding company."

[22] *Public Utilities Commission of Rhode Island et.al.* v. *Attleboro Steam and Electric Company* (273 U. S., 83, 1926).

[23] The most thorough and satisfactory treatment to date of the subject of interstate transmission of electricity is Dr. H. L. Elsbree's book cited in note 3, above.

[24] Vermont, *Biennial Report, Public Service Commission*, 1919, p. 24.

[25] Data from U. S. Geological Survey; see above, p. 283, Table I, Indicators 6 and 8.

[26] New Hampshire, *Laws*, 1911, Chap. 164, Sect. 7, e.

[27] *Ibid.*, Chap. 106.

[28] *Manchester Union*, Jan. 4, 1930.

[29] Maine, *Acts and Resolves*, 1909, Chap. 244.

[30] Maine, *Legislative Record*, 1909, p. 1114.

[31] *Ibid.*, p. 1116.

[32] See *Surplus Power Export Law*, a pamphlet issued in 1930 by the Central Maine Power Company.

[33] *Federal Reporter*, Vol. 172, 1909, p. 545.

NEW ENGLAND'S MANUFACTURES[1]

John S. Keir

OST of the soils of New England are rocky, much of the land surface is hilly and rough, and the climate is severe. The cold winters strictly limit agricultural enterprise. In southern New England the growing season ranges from 140 to 190 days annually, but in the north only 90 to 130 days may be counted upon.[2] As a result, not only is it impossible to raise many kinds of crops, but for many months each year farms are unproductive and farmers idle. Manufacturing, on the other hand, may proceed the year round. The comparatively poor opportunity offered by agriculture is, surely, at least a negative explanation for the rise of New England's manufactures.

THE RISE OF MANUFACTURES[3]

New England has also afforded notable positive advantages to the development of manufacturing. Foremost among these have been her position on the seacoast and her water power.

Nearness to the sea has benefited the many lines of industry that manufacture for export or make use of imported raw materials. Long before the invention of artificial humidifiers the damp air of the seaboard in part fulfilled their function by rendering certain textile fibers workable. In colonial days fish was the main staple of a wide oversea trade from New England ports. The development of fishing in colonial times was favored by rich offshore fisheries, by a plentiful supply of pine timber for ships, and by an indented coast line. Out of the fishing trade grew the much larger carrying trade of the first half of the nineteenth century, when New England vessels roamed the oceans of the world. Early New England manufacturers thus had the choice of world markets for their products. Ocean freighting furnished the initial capital with which the manufacturers built their enterprises. The New England merchants preferred to invest their surplus in local businesses rather than to risk it farther afield. Manufacturing in New England was developed largely by local capital under the close and watchful eyes of New England investors.

The abundance and quality of New England's water-power resources also fostered the growth of her manufactures. To be utilizable, water power must possess evenness of flow; otherwise spring freshets may tear down the walls of the mills, or, when low

---

[1] For notes see p. 341, below.

water comes in summer, the wheels may stand idle for months at a time. Most New England rivers are of fairly even flow. Floods like those of 1927 are exceptional. Lakes and ponds, the products of glaciation, regulate the streams, checking the freshets and doling out the water in dry seasons. A hilly topography provides suitable sites for artificial reservoirs. Although coal has now taken first place as the source of energy in manufacturing, more water power is used today than ever before.[4]

Obviously these and other geographical circumstances favorable to manufacturing would have meant nothing had not the people of New England been endowed by natural aptitude and by training for this form of endeavor. Among the early settlers a large proportion had been townsmen in old England, accustomed to use their hands and to work with tools. They came of an intelligent, ingenious, and thrifty stock, and their Puritan beliefs emphasized the dignity of hard work and the worthiness of wealth.

Furthermore, the very fact that manufacturing had an early start in New England gave the region two great cumulative advantages as time progressed.

In the first place, channels of trade, like habits once set, are hard to change. A town becomes known as a center for the production and sale of a certain commodity. Each year buyers gather there. The manufacturer is afraid to leave, lest he miss the trade and new concerns come to share in a trade already established. Thus a static condition tends to persist, and an industry may long remain where it does not seem strictly to belong.

The second cumulative advantage has been the development of skill. A manufacturer who requires such talent must choose his location carefully. He must go where skilled artisans live, or he will fail because his product is of inferior grade. Skilled workers are generally more highly paid, more intelligent, more attached to the community, and considerably less mobile than the unskilled. Skill, moreover, tends to accumulate in those centers where an industry is oldest and biggest. Here it may be passed from father to son. Recognizing that their continued success depends upon the maintenance of a supply of skilled workers, communities may establish specialized trade schools, as, for example, the schools of spinning and of weaving in Worcester, Lawrence, Lowell, and New Bedford.

Every invention of machinery that replaces skilled labor theoretically lessens New England's advantage in this respect. Jobs formerly done by three or four trained artisans may now be performed by a highly complicated automatic machine attended by a single unskilled laborer. The automatic machine—the iron man—acts as a leveler of sectional advantages. Nevertheless, despite the hue and cry recently raised about "mechanization," skill remains a large factor in many tasks, and it must be remembered that the intricate, automatic machine itself requires skilled nursing and may not, perhaps, in the long run appreciably diminish the total demand for skill.

DISTRIBUTION OF MANUFACTURES

Just over half of all New England's wage earners in manufacturing establishments were found in Massachusetts alone in 1929, and more than 85 per cent in the three southern states of Massachusetts, Rhode Island, and Connecticut. The distribution of manufacturing corresponds closely to the distribution of population.[5] More than half of all New England's people live in Massachusetts, and about 80 per cent of them in the three southern states. It is a mistake

TABLE I—NEW ENGLAND: EMPLOYMENT IN MANUFACTURES AND
AGRICULTURE, 1929 AND 1930

	WAGE EARNERS IN MANUFACTURES, 1929[a]		PERCENTAGE OF TOTAL POPULATION ENGAGED IN	
	NUMBER	PER CENT	MANUFACTURING AND MECHANICAL INDUSTRIES, 1930[b]	AGRICULTURE, 1930[b]
New England .	1,100,043	100.0	19.2	2.6
Maine	69,593	6.3	12.8	6.4
New Hampshire	65,119	5.9	19.0	4.8
Vermont . . .	27,582	2.5	11.0	10.6
Massachusetts .	559,443	50.9	19.7	1.3
Rhode Island .	124,838	11.3	23.7	1.3
Connecticut . .	253,468	23.0	20.9	2.3

[a] U. S. Census of Manufactures, 1929 (mimeographed press releases).
[b] Based on Bureau of the Census, *Fifteenth Census of the United States*, 1930: *Population Bulletin (Second Series)*, *United States Summary*, *Composition and Characteristics of the Population*, Washington, 1931.

to think of Maine, New Hampshire, and even of Vermont as primarily agricultural. New Hampshire has almost as large a proportion of its population working in factories as Massachusetts or Connecticut. While the corresponding ratio is somewhat lower in Maine, even in that state twice as many people are at work in mills and mechanical occupations as on the farms. In Vermont alone is there an approach to a balance between agriculture and manufacturing. Nevertheless, the census shows that manufacturing is slightly in the lead in Vermont also.

Table I shows some essential figures concerning the distribution of manufacturing in New England as revealed by census statistics for the number of wage earners. Figure 1 gives a more detailed picture.

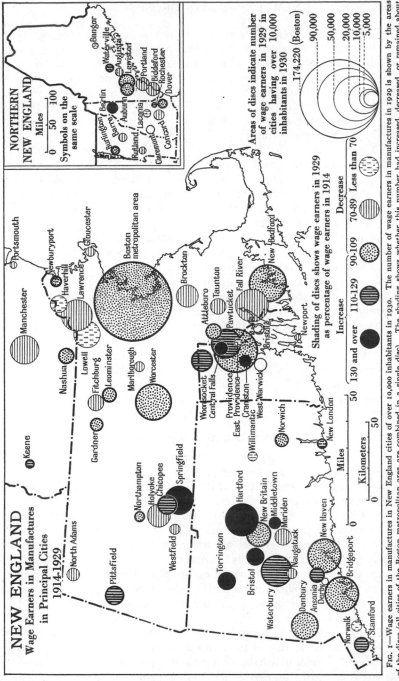

FIG. 1—Wage earners in manufactures in New England cities of over 10,000 inhabitants in 1930. The number of wage earners in manufactures in 1929 is shown by the areas of the discs (all cities of the Boston metropolitan area are combined in a single disc). The shading shows whether this number had increased, decreased, or remained about stationary between 1914 and 1929. The data cover establishments with an annual value of output of over $5,000. For the places represented by unshaded discs no data are available for 1914. Based on U. S. Census of Manufactures for 1914 and 1929.

Within the map:

NEW ENGLAND
Wage Earners in Manufactures
in Principal Cities
1914-1929

NORTHERN
NEW ENGLAND
Miles
0   50   100
Symbols on the
same scale

Areas of discs indicate number
of wage earners in 1929 in
cities having over 10,000
inhabitants in 1930

174,220 (Boston)
90,000
50,000
20,000
10,000
5,000

Shading of discs shows wage earners in 1929
as percentage of wage earners in 1914

Increase   Decrease
130 and over   110-129   90-109   70-89   Less than 70

Miles
0   50
Kilometers
0   50

325

Here the discs represent cities of over 10,000 population, except in the metropolitan area of Boston where all cities of over 10,000 are combined in a single disc. The area of each disc is in proportion to the number of wage earners in the manufacturing industries of each place. Taken all together the discs account for nearly three quarters of the manufacturing wage earners of New England. Two thirds of the remainder are scattered among the smaller towns and villages of the three southern states.

The discs are shaded in such a way as to show whether the number of wage earners increased, decreased, or remained about stationary between 1914 and 1929. Of the 64 places so marked, 19 held their own during the fifteen years; in 19 the number of wage earners increased over 10 per cent, and in 8 it increased over 30 per cent. In 26 places there was a loss of more than 10 per cent, and in 7 a loss of more than 30 per cent. Thus we see that the places in which there were marked losses considerably outnumber those where there were marked gains. It is also evident at a glance that most of the losses took place in eastern Massachusetts and in the states north of Massachusetts. The most serious decrease of all occurred in Lowell, where manufacturing employment fell off nearly 43 per cent. Most of the Connecticut towns either gained or held their own. The largest proportional gain in New England was that of Middletown, Connecticut, 69 per cent. In general the most pronounced decreases occurred in the centers of textile, shoe, paper, and lumber manufacture; and the most notable gains in the cities of diversified manufactures. Several of the cities that suffered the greatest losses in manufacturing employment also suffered losses in the total population during the period.[6]

PRESENT SITUATION AND TRENDS[7]

About five years ago a thorough investigation of New England's manufacturing industries was carried out by the U. S. Department of Commerce under the direction of Dr. C. E. Artman. The results were published in an important volume, "The Industrial Structure of New England,"[8] which sets forth the essential facts in detail and analyzes them in clean-cut terms. The present writer can hardly do better than quote extensively from Dr. Artman's book in setting forth the view of present-day manufacturing in New England that forms the subject of the following paragraphs. However, later figures based upon the preliminary reports of the U. S. Census of Manufactures for 1929 have in many instances been added to or substituted for Artman's data.

Table II shows the general relation of the manufacturing activity of New England to that of the entire country.

The advance of industrial activity and population in New England as compared with the rest of the United States is illustrated in the

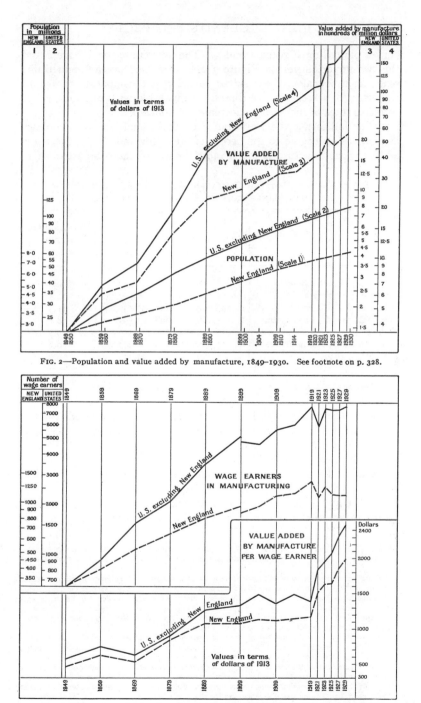

FIG. 2—Population and value added by manufacture, 1849–1930.   See footnote on p. 328.

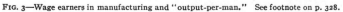

FIG. 3—Wage earners in manufacturing and "output-per-man."   See footnote on p. 328.

curves plotted on Figures 2 and 3. The four curves on Figure 2 and the two upper curves on Figure 3 are all plotted on the logarithmic scale, as this scale is best suited to bring out comparative *rates* of change. All six curves are directly comparable with one another in so far as rates of increase or decrease are concerned.

"For indicating the importance of the manufacturing processes as a source of income to the people of New England . . . the value added by manufacture is much more accurate" than the gross value

TABLE II—NEW ENGLAND COMPARED WITH ENTIRE UNITED STATES
IN TOTAL MANUFACTURING ACTIVITY DURING 1929[a]

ITEM	NEW ENGLAND	UNITED STATES	NEW ENGLAND PERCENTAGE OF TOTAL
No. of Mfg. Establishments . .	18,318	210,710	8.7
No. of Wage Earners	1,100,043	8,807,536	12.5
Wages Paid	$1,345,092,011	$11,649,536,855	11.5
Cost of Materials, Power, etc. .	$3,165,680,771	$38,293,533,500	8.2
Value of Products	$6,419,619,789	$70,137,459,352	9.5
Value Added by Manufacture .	$3,253,939,018	$31,843,925,852	10.2
Population, 1930	8,166,341	122,775,046	6.6

[a] Based on U. S. Census of Manufactures, 1929 (mimeographed press releases).

of the products made. The total worth of goods produced "is not a satisfactory measure, because only a part of this value is created within the industry. A large part of it is contributed by the value of the materials used. Moreover, the cost of materials contains a great deal of duplication on account of repetition in the different stages of manufacture."[9]

In the curves for value added by manufacture (Fig. 2) the misleading effect of changes in price levels has been eliminated by stand-

NOTES ON FIGURES 2 AND 3

FIG. 2—Rates of change of population, 1850–1930, and of value added by manufacture, 1849–1929, New England compared with the United States excluding New England. Based on U. S. Census reports.

The effect of changes in commodity price levels has been eliminated by reducing all values to those of dollars of 1913 (on the basis of the index numbers of wholesale prices in *Report of the Commission of Gold and Silver Inquiry*, U. S. Senate, European Currency and Finance, Serial 9, Vol. 1, p. 436, and *Index Numbers of Wholesale Prices on Pre-War Base*, 1890–1927, U. S. Bureau of Labor Statistics, Washington, 1928; the index number for 1929 represents a conversion of the U. S. Bureau of Labor Statistics' index number for that year to the 1913 base).

FIG. 3—Rates of change in number of wage earners and in value added by manufacture per wage earner ("output-per-man"), 1849–1929, New England compared with the United States excluding New England. Based on U. S. Census reports. See also above, Fig. 3, p. 90.

In both Figures 2 and 3 the breaks at 1899 in the curves for value added and number of wage earners are due to the fact that after that date establishments whose output was valued at less than $500 were not included in the census tabulations. After 1919 establishments with an output of less than $5000 were excluded, but the resulting differences are too slight to affect the curves.

ardizing all values in such a way that they are expressed in terms of the purchasing power of dollars of 1913.

When the two sets of curves of Figure 2 are compared it is evident that both in New England and the rest of the United States the increase in value added by manufacture since 1849 has been much more rapid than that of the population. These curves show, furthermore, that both in population and in value added New England's growth has been somewhat slower than that of the rest of the country. It was hardly to be expected that with a diminishing part of the nation's man power New England could continue to contribute the same part

TABLE III—IMPORTANCE OF THE LARGER GROUPS OF
NEW ENGLAND MANUFACTURES, 1929[a]

NATURE OF MATERIAL	WAGE EARNERS, 1929		VALUE ADDED BY MANUFACTURE, 1929	
	THOUSAND EMPLOYEES	PERCENTAGE OF TOTAL	MILLIONS OF DOLLARS	PERCENTAGE OF TOTAL
1. Textiles	342	31.1	720	22.2
2. Metals, Stone, Transportation Equipment, and Related Industries[b]	308	28.0	1,039	32.1
3. Leather and Rubber .	118	10.7	267	8.3
4. Paper and Printing .	74	6.7	322	9.9
5. Forest Products . . .	45	4.1	115	3.5
6. Foodstuffs	41	3.8	163	5.1
7. Chemicals	14	1.3	83	2.6
All Others	157	14.3	531	16.3
Total	1,099	100.0	3,240	100.0

[a] Based on U. S. Census of Manufactures, 1929 (mimeographed press releases).
[b] Includes manufactures of transportation equipment and of materials made out of stone and clay.

of the nation's income from manufactures that it did eighty years ago. But even relatively to the growth of population, manufacturing enterprise in New England has tended somewhat to lag. As Dr. Artman observes elsewhere in the present volume, the "industrial development of this region was so far advanced in earlier years that the later advancement of other sections has overshadowed its more moderate recent growth. The continuous national expansion in the last fifty years has been at the relative expense of New England."

The two upper curves of Figure 3 show the progress of manufacturing enterprise as measured by the number of wage earners.[10] Whereas both value added by manufacture and population have shown a fairly consistent advance since 1849, the curves for wage earners have flattened out since 1899 and especially since 1919. In New England there was actually a decline in number of wage earners between 1919 and 1929, and a greater decline would doubtless appear were the figures available for the depression years of 1930–1932.[11]

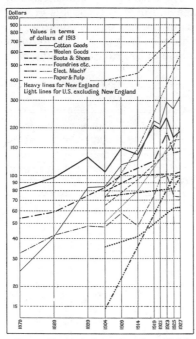

That value added by manufacture should increase at a fairly constant rate and at a rate more rapid than that of the number of persons engaged in manufacturing has been due largely to improvements in machinery and to other technical factors. In New England value added has continued to increase at the same time that there has been an actual decline in the manufacturing personnel. Here of course, lie the roots of the problem of "technological unemployment." Technical improvements have made it possible for each worker to produce manufactured articles in greater quantity and of greater value than formerly. The lower curves of Figure 3 show the trend in the value of output per worker since 1849 and reveal strikingly the rapid jump since 1919. But they also show that the value of output per worker has been, throughout, somewhat lower in New England than in the rest of the country as a whole.

FIG. 4—Rates of change in value added by manufacture in New England and in the United States excluding New England for manufactures of cotton goods and woolen and worsted goods, 1879–1927, and for certain other manufactures, 1904–1927. Based on U. S. Census reports.

"The diversity and the broad range of manufacturing activity in New England are indicated by the fact that there were 221 lines of its manufactures which were of sufficient size to be included in the census tabulations for 1927, comprising nearly two thirds of the 348 separate classifications for the whole United States . . . "

Table III shows the relative importance of the larger groups of manufactures in 1929. The textile industry leads in number of wage earners, the metal industry in value added by manufacture.

The progress, as indicated by value added by manufacture, of the cotton and the woolen and worsted industries from 1879 through 1927, and of certain other fundamental New England manufacturing industries from 1904 through 1907, is shown on Figure 4. For purposes of comparison the progress of the same industries elsewhere in the United States is also shown.

THE TEXTILE INDUSTRIES

The textile industries employ about a third of the employees in all the manufactures of New England, pay them about a third of the total wages paid, and put out a product having about a third of the gross value of all products. On the other hand, the outlay for raw materials is considerably more than a third, leaving a value added by manufacture of only 22.2 per cent of the total (1929).

The great majority of the textile firms are located south of a line drawn from Augusta, Me., to Bennington, in the southwestern corner of Vermont.[12] Concentration of textile plants within definite centers and areas is characteristic. At the outset, advantage was ordinarily taken of some local circumstance, such as water power at Lawrence or cheap tidewater transportation of coal at Fall River. Other concerns were tempted to come to a town where favorable local conditions had helped one concern to succeed. Once a city was recognized as a textile center, further advantages arose, as we have seen, from this very circumstance. Capital was relatively easy to get, a supply of skilled labor accumulated, and freight rates to an established center were lower than to a remote mill village among the hills. There were also advantages in selling, as buyers recognized the wide choice of materials to be obtained. The manufacture and repair of machinery, the utilization of by-products, and the opportunity to specialize in one field offered additional inducements to the *entrepreneur*. But there were also disadvantages. In a one-resource community anything that harms the dominant industry hurts the whole town. Trade depressions, changes in styles influencing demand, and labor troubles have been particularly disastrous in Fall River, Lowell, and New Bedford. Labor unions are stronger and competition keener in the larger centers; there are also problems of urban congestion and of higher rents and taxes.

THE COTTON INDUSTRY

"Cotton manufacturing,[13] the most important single textile industry of New England, provided 9.3 per cent of the region's entire income from all manufactures in 1925" but only about 6.2[14] per cent in 1929. "Although some cotton manufacture is scattered about many parts of [the region], the greater portion of the industry is localized in a few highly specialized areas."

"While there have been no radical changes in the processes of cotton manufacture in recent years . . . a number of new elements have entered into the situation . . . " An excessive competition

UNITED STATES
Cotton Spindles, 1926

• = Under 5000 Spindles
• = 5000 to 25,000
• = 25,000 to 100,000
● = 100,000 to 250,000
● = 250,000 to 500,000
● = 500,000 to 1,000,000
● = 1,000,000 to 5,000,000
● = Over 5,000,000

FIG. 5—Distribution of cotton manufacturing in the eastern United States, 1926.   From C. O. Paullin, *Atlas of the Historical Geography of the United States*, New York, 1932, Pl. 137 A.

has grown up, resulting from a "capacity to produce beyond the consumption requirements of the market. . . . During this period of adjustment many New England spindles and looms have gone out of production, some of them temporarily, and many of them permanently. . . . In general, the mills which have fared best are: (a) those favorably situated in respect to power, either from local water power, purchased electric power, or cheap tidewater coal; (b) those with well-arranged plants and the most efficient equipment; (c) those under the most intelligent and most skillful management; and (d) those which have given special study and attention to the market for their product."

"In contrast to relatively slight changes in the factors of production, pronounced changes in marketing and distribution of the product of cotton mills" have occurred. "In place of the staple cotton fabrics . . . the market has turned largely to novelty goods and specialties, in which style, beauty, and design are the primary requisites, rather than durability and quality."

Shifts have also occurred "in the outlets through which cotton goods are distributed. In earlier years these goods found a market mainly for sale as piece goods through the wholesale and retail trade. The pronounced change in the market from piece goods to ready-to-wear garments has meant that an increasing volume of the output of the mills goes to garment manufacturers and others in the cutting-up trade for further manufacture into ready-made apparel, while a diminishing amount is sold through wholesale and retail channels as piece goods."

Supremacy in the manufacture of the cheaper-grade goods seems to be gradually passing to the Southern states. Between 1914 and 1919 the value added by manufacture by the cotton mills of other parts of the country first came to exceed that added by the New England mills (Fig. 4). The accompanying map (Fig. 5), showing the distribution of cotton spindles in the United States in 1926, makes clear the magnitude of the industry in the South as compared with New England. Although New England apparently still occupies a strong position in the preparation of the finer fabrics and the further processing into the articles to which the consumer demand has now largely shifted, time alone will show whether this position can be maintained in the face of Southern competition.

The Wool Manufacturing Industry

Wool manufacturing[15] is somewhat less concentrated than the manufacture of cotton, although in this field also there are a few large centers, Lawrence, Mass., outstanding among them. Providence and Woonsocket in Rhode Island and Holyoke and Lowell in Massachusetts are also prominent. Through Boston, the leading wool market of the western hemisphere, flows over 60 per cent of the wool consumed in the United States.

"New England contains approximately one-half of all the wool manufacturing establishments of the United States." Their output represented in 1925 "about 8.5 per cent[16] of the total New England income derived from all manufacturing activity." This compares with the 9.3 per cent previously mentioned for cotton manufacture. As between the two main branches of the industry, woolens and worsteds, Maine, New Hampshire, Vermont, and Connecticut are stronger in the woolens, while Massachusetts and Rhode Island are more active in worsted manufacture.

During late years "New England woolen and worsted manufactures have shared the general fortunes of these industries throughout the country." There has been a "curtailed consumption of wool fabrics . . . , especially in women's wearing apparel . . . Changes in the market situation resulting from the increased importance of the style factor, changes in demand from piece goods to ready-to-wear garments, and the general institution of small-scale buying for current needs have affected this industry in much the same way as they have affected cotton and the other textiles."

However, throughout the forty-seven-year period from 1880 to 1927 New England maintained its national preëminence in the making of woolens and worsteds (Fig. 4). The census shows that New England's share in the United States' totals for the number of wage earners increased slightly from 1880 to 1925, shifting gradually from 56.7 to 63.7 per cent; that it remained practically constant for the value of the product manufactured, 62.6 to 64.2 per cent, and decreased slightly for the value added by manufacture, 62.6 to 58.4 per cent. In other words, while New England may not have lost ground as measured by the percentage of the total work performed, other parts of the country appear to have been relatively somewhat more successful in terms of the profitable conduct of the enterprise.

THE METAL INDUSTRIES

Although they do not employ so many wage earners as the textile industries, "the industries which depend primarily upon metals for their raw materials[17] comprise the most important group of all New England manufactures when regarded as a source of revenue to the region." In 1925 the metal industries accounted for 28.2 per cent of the total number of wage earners (28.0 per cent in 1929), paid 31.9 of all the wages, and contributed 31.9 per cent of the value added by manufacture (as contrasted with 27.2 per cent for textiles). Wages in the metal industries were considerably higher than in other types of manufacturing, an average of $1347 per worker as against $1133 for all other classes of manufacture.

The metal industries turn out a very wide range of products, whose sale depends, with a few exceptions (such as jewelry and silverware), on utility and service rather than on preference and style. Herein they present a significant contrast to the textile industries. From 1925 till the beginning of the economic depression in 1929 there was on the whole an upward trend in these industries.[18]

About 85 per cent of the reported manufacturing income from the metal and related industries in 1929 ($1,039,000,000) was derived from the following eight classes of enterprise, in order of importance:

1. Hardware, cutlery, and mechanics' tools (18.1 per cent)
2. Electrical equipment (16.9 per cent)
3. Foundries and machine shops (16.7 per cent)
4. Manufactures of brass, bronze, and other non-ferrous materials (11.3 per cent)

5. Jewelry, silverware, and plated ware (6.4 per cent)
6. Textile machinery, machine tools, and other types of machinery (6 per cent)
7. Automotive equipment, motor cycles, bicycles, and parts (4.6 per cent)
8. Stone, clay, and glass products (4 per cent)

As part of the survey carried out by the Department of Commerce an attempt was made to ascertain by means of a questionnaire "the factors which in the minds of manufacturers have been of importance in determining their location in New England. From this inquiry it was found that "the large numbers of highly skilled New England workmen stand out as a very important asset in the metal industries. . . . With the heavier and less highly fabricated metal industries, location of markets was given as the principal reason for plant location." In the case of textile machinery, of which nearly two thirds of the national output is made in New England, proximity of markets was also the determining factor. Repair and replacement work may also be done more efficiently when the equipment company is not too far from the mills.

The Leather and Rubber Industries

As measured by the number of wage earners, the group comprising the leather and rubber industries[19] takes third place, although the value added by manufacture (8.3 per cent of the total in 1929) in this case is much less than that added by either the textiles or the metal industries. The factories of New England "provided about thirty per cent of the national revenue from all leather manufactures and gave employment to nearly one third of the wage earners employed in the country's leather industries" (1925). The making of boots and shoes yielded about 85 per cent of the total revenue of the leather manufactures, the primary tanning of hides and skins about 12 per cent, and the manufacture of miscellaneous leather goods the remainder. The industry is concentrated for the most part in eastern Massachusetts—boot and shoe manufacture more particularly in Essex, Plymouth, Suffolk, and Middlesex counties.

During 1928 New England produced 44.8 per cent of the national total of women's shoes, 37.5 per cent of the men's shoes, and about 25 per cent of the total in children's, boys', and infants' shoes and moccasins.

In shoe manufacturing, as in the metal industries, the presence of a readily available supply of skilled labor appears to be the main reason why manufacturers have established themselves in New England and have continued their operations there. Accessibility of leather and other materials and nearness to markets are important although secondary reasons.

New England will probably be unable to maintain the predominance possessed in the past in respect to shoe manufacture. Other sections nearer large local markets and in certain cases nearer the sources of raw material are making their own shoes on an increasing scale. This is notably true of New York, Missouri, and Illinois. While there may be some small increase in New England in the number of pairs produced, the rate of growth for this section will presumably be less than that for the country as a whole (Fig. 4). The fortunes of the leather tanneries will probably be closely associated with that of the shoe business.

The Paper Industry and Lesser Industries

The paper and printing industries[20] together constitute the fourth most important group judged by the number of employees and the third most important on the basis of value added by manufacture. These industries employed 6.7 per cent of the wage earners of the region during 1929 and contributed 9.9 per cent of the value added by manufacture.

Paper manufactures are found in three principal areas: (1) on the fringes of the northern forests of Maine and New Hampshire, where local supplies of pulpwood are used; (2) in the Connecticut Valley, with Holyoke, Mass., as a center; (3) in the Thames Valley of Connecticut just north of New London. The Holyoke region produces for the most part high-grade bond and other rag papers; the Thames Valley specializes in box boards made from wood pulp and other materials shipped in for the purpose. Approximately two thirds of the total activity in the New England paper industries is represented by paper mills engaged in the primary manufacture of paper from wood pulp, rags, and minor materials. From 1914 to 1925 the increase in primary paper manufactures in New England was notable, 145 per cent, although considerably less than the corresponding increase in the United States as a whole, 207 per cent (Fig. 4).

Other important New England manufactures are those of lumber and other forest products, foodstuffs, and chemicals and drugs.

These seven main industries—textiles, metals, leather and rubber, paper and printing, forest products, foodstuffs, and chemicals—accounted in 1929 for about 86 per cent of the manufacturing activity of the region. The remaining 14 per cent may be ascribed to a group of sundry minor industries.

Prospects for the Future

Much has been said of late years about the relative decline of New England manufactures as compared with those of other parts of the country. Certain statements have been warranted, but there has also been much unjustifiable pessimism.

From the curves plotted on Figures 2 and 3 we see that New England down to 1929 not only failed to keep pace with the rest of the nation in value added by manufacture but suffered a positive decline in the number of wage earners.

What accounts for this falling off? To some extent it may have been due to the removal of individual manufacturing concerns, as in the case of certain cotton firms which have transferred their activities and even their machinery to the South. This factor, however, should not be exaggerated. In the opinion of Willard L. Thorp, who has analyzed recent shifts in the geographical distribution of American industry as a whole,[21] changes are "more often the result of the closing down of some concern in one place, and the opening of a new concern elsewhere. Furthermore, there has been a marked tendency recently toward the establishment of branch plants to feed certain areas. Finally, new industries develop, which do not necessarily settle in the old areas. All these changes result in a net migration of industry."[22] And even in the cases where a particular firm does move, machinery and equipment are but rarely transported. As equipment becomes obsolete or worn out at the old site it is generally discarded there and replaced by new equipment at the new site.

Other regions are now attaining the stage of industrial maturity which New England reached several decades ago.[23] A far greater area has become the workshop of the nation. In the words of N. E. Peterson of the First National Bank of Boston, "to hold that [New England] could continue for an indefinite period to maintain the same relative position is to shut one's eyes to the pronounced increase in the country's population, to the development of the West, as well as to the industrial progress of the South since the Civil War."[24]

The future for New England lies in the adjustments she will make to these changed and ever-changing conditions. The success of every manufacturing community depends ultimately on (1) nearness to supplies of power; (2) nearness to sources of raw materials; (3) nearness to supplies of suitable labor; and (4) nearness to markets.

As a whole, New England is weak in respect to the first two of these essentials, strong in respect to the last two. Aside from her water power, she has no native supplies of power, no coal nor oil. After transport charges have been met, there is an excess cost of steam power in Worcester or Pittsfield as compared with Philadelphia or Pittsburg. The same may be said of the iron and steel, the cotton, most of the lumber, and the grain that enter into New England's major manufactures, although the seacoast position still gives a comparative advantage in the case of certain raw materials shipped from beyond the seas. The strength of New England's manufactures lies in the supplies of highly skilled labor at their command and in proximity to great markets within the borders of the region and close at hand to the south and southwest.[25] Here again, moreover, the sea-coast position gives the New England manufacturer a measurable advantage in reaching oversea markets.

It would seem that New England can hardly hope to compete with other sections in manufactures—such as those of steel and of automobiles—that make large use of bulky raw materials. The industries of this sort already established are gradually diminishing in number, and this tendency may be expected to continue. On the other hand, industries that specialize in the manufacture of high-grade goods from non-bulky or imported raw materials, and those that employ superior types of labor, will undoubtedly remain and prosper. The manufacture of small metal goods, for example, seems particularly well adapted to New England conditions. This industry depends on skilled labor, it benefits from an established market and reputation, it does not require much coal, and the necessary raw materials may be brought to it at comparatively low cost.

There is also bound to be a selective sorting of manufacturing enterprise not only by industries but by firms and companies, a testing of managerial ability and of the degree to which owners, managers, and wage earners can coöperate for the welfare and continued existence of the individual concerns.

In the long run New England firms cannot hope to escape the disadvantages under which they labor in the matter of freight rates and basic raw materials. Over the course of years they must win through the employment of skilled labor and through the application of the highest quality of management. Managerial ability must exceed the average sufficiently to offset adverse geographical differentials. The concerns that avail themselves of the least efficient management will be the ones to bear the brunt of intersectional competition most heavily; those with the keener management will be the ones best able to hold their own. The industries and firms in New England that will compete most successfully in the national and international markets of tomorrow will be those marked by originality of product and design; by alert contact with trends in consumer preferences and demand; by ingenuity in methods of production, of distribution, and of cost reduction; by skill of workmanship; and by the use of a wide range of far-drawn materials.

In 1929 twenty editors of McGraw-Hill publications made a survey of New England's manufacturing activities. Their findings are so important that they may well be quoted at length:

Major Favorable Factors	*Major Unfavorable Factors*
1. There is evidence of a progressive mental flexibility in New England industrial management in the presence of many younger executives, who sense	1. New England industry is carrying a staggering burden of old buildings. Many date back more than fifty years and were constructed long and narrow

the growing importance of mechanization, of advanced personnel policies, of accurate market knowledge for the guidance of production, and of the value of new ideas from other fields.

2. The use of specialized equipment has reached a forward position in New England, much of it the product of your inherent Yankee ingenuity and much of it of western manufacture.

Many plants are outstanding for the extent to which they have developed automatic machinery and efficient methods of handling materials through the flow of parts and a progressive assembly.

3. We found several cases of conspicuous progress in the application of research to the utilization of by-products and the development of markets, that rate well with the best practice in the use of this important new resource of industry.

4. We found some examples of the most advanced personnel work in the form of well organized trade schools, shop councils, sanitary and hospital facilities, and recreational provisions.

5. The prosperity of the workers was attested at many plants by the presence of hundreds of private automobiles parked within the grounds and the fact that from 25 to 30 per cent of the personnel there were riding to and from work in their own cars. There is further evidence, of course, in the recently published fact that New England savings bank deposits show increase per capita against a general record of reduction.

to provide daylight. They are not adapted to the efficient arrangement of modern machinery nor to present ideas of materials handling. There is too much in and out and up and down. Too many are crowded into the center of congested districts where the value of land is high. It would pay better to erect new buildings on the fringe of town than to suffer longer the costs entailed by using ill-adapted structures.

2. Many of the older industries are clinging to obsolete equipment because it has been written off and represents no book investment. They are denying themselves the practical economies of new equipment that are worth infinitely more. We saw, in many cases, forests of overhead belting, heavy friction load, labor-wasting old machinery and ancient power plants that are an inescapable drag on profits.

3. The lighting of New England factories appeared to us to be distressingly bad, despite a few examples of the most advanced industrial illumination. Great floors of machinery spotted only with dirty lamps in inefficient or improvised reflectors at the tool, supported by no adequate general illumination, is a common condition. With this, dark halls and stairways come as a matter of course. It all takes an inevitable toll in accidents, slow speed and spoilage of materials.

4. As a natural attendant of poor lighting, we saw many cases of bad housekeeping—poorly arranged machinery, cluttered aisles, neglect of ventilation, painting, cleaning and modern sanitary facilities, and poor provision for the care of employees' clothing.

5. This kind of an atmosphere naturally reacts against vigilance in safety work. Many alert plants are conducting safety competitions. Many apparently do no more than expose safety signs. There is a noticeable lack, however, of the practical safeguards applied to machines, belts and tools that must be the backbone of all accident prevention work.

6. Figures presented at this meeting show that despite the troubles of the textile industry you have a net gain in number of industries and employees and unemployment is no worse than in other areas. This indicates a high capacity to absorb released labor and denotes a splendid recuperative power.

7. Most New England industries are constructing their new buildings according to modern practice and applying the economic advantages of well arranged machinery, good lighting, ventilation and sanitation, and the mechanical conveyance of materials.

8. Railway transportation receives almost universal commendation throughout the area. There are, of course, some situations where further relief is considered necessary, but the reorganization of New England freight service that has been effected in recent years provides a resource for industrial development that is locally acknowledged and appreciated to a striking degree.

9. Electric power has kept pace with the growth of New England industries and by the development of both hydro and steam generation and the interconnection of systems affords as progressive a service as is available in any section of the country and at favorable rates.

6. Much hand work still lingers that can be eliminated by mechanization. The use of modern methods for materials handling while ingeniously developed in some plants is in general in a backward state through lack of equipment and planning.

7. Opportunity also exists in the majority of the plants visited for the development of more continuous flow of work and progressive assembly by the use of conveyors and other devices. This feature is highly perfected in some plants but neglected in many more.

8. There appears to be a tendency toward excessive inventory, in some lines of manufacture, because of lack of more vision in production scheduling, and there is considerable opportunity for simplification through the elimination of excess and duplicating varieties of product.

9. Because of the age of many of your industrial institutions and the traditions that have grown up both with the management and the workers some of whom have followed their fathers into the plant, human relations are in places way behind the times. Working conditions, personnel policies, and an inherited attitude of paternalism are apparently taken as a matter of course by both labor and management. This reflects itself in many ways—long hours of work, poor provision for the safety and comfort of workers, crude methods of hiring and firing and other sources of industrial unhappiness that write themselves plain in terms of bad morale and low return on the payroll.[26]

While this picture in all truth cannot be called over rose-tinted, neither does it present a condition of desperation that has sometimes been ascribed to New England. Most encouraging is a growing willingness among New Englanders—particularly as represented by the New England Council[27]—to search for the facts, to face them courageously and intelligently, and to seek a way out.

Diversification of manufacturing processes and intelligent management are the prime essentials. Provided they are maintained and augmented, the total volume of business will develop satisfactorily, even though the relative importance of the staple industries continues slowly to decline. In the light of the most intensive studies made of this region during the last few years, it does not appear unreasonable to expect a rate of growth in proper proportion with the increase in population. While there will be no return to the heyday of former times, New England may feel confident of her ability to maintain in the years to come a balanced share in the country's manufacturing activity.

NOTES

[1] The editor has supplied the illustrations accompanying this paper and also certain statistical and bibliographical details. The references in the notes to the paper by Dr. Charles E. Artman entitled *New England's Industrial Prospects*, in the present volume, pp. 61–64, above, should be consulted.

[2] See Fig. 3, p. 21, above.

[3] The history of New England manufacturing to 1928 is treated as part of a larger theme but nevertheless in considerable detail by V. S. Clark, *History of Manufactures in the United States*, *1607–1860, 1860–1893, 1893–1928*, published for the Carnegie Institution of Washington by the McGraw Hill Book Co., 3 vols., New York, 1929 (useful bibliographies). See also O. L. Stone, *History of Massachusetts Industries: Their Inception, Growth, and Success*, 4 vols., Chicago, 1930; J. W. Hammond, *Twentieth Century Manufactures* (1890–1930), in *Commonwealth History of Massachusetts*, edited by A. B. Hart, Vol. 5, New York, 1930, pp. 370–398; G. B. Chandler, *Industrial History*, in *History of Connecticut*, edited by N. G. Osborn, Vol. 4, New York, 1925, pp. 1–451. In 1928–1929 a series of articles on the rise of manufactures and industries in the several leading manufacturing cities of Massachusetts appeared in *Industry: A Weekly Journal of Industrial Information*, published by the Associated Industries of Massachusetts.

On geographical conditions in New England in relation to the rise of manufacturing see J. Russell Smith, *North America*, New York, 1925, pp. 70–91; also Malcolm Keir, *Some Influences of the Sea Upon the Industries of New England*, in *Geogr. Rev.*, Vol. 5, 1918, pp. 399–404.—EDIT.

[4] See above, p. 281.

[5] See Fig. 4, pp. 22–23, above. E. F. Gerish, *Commercial Structure of New England*, U. S. Dept. of Commerce, Bur. of Foreign and Domestic Commerce, Washington, 1929 (*Domestic Commerce Ser. No. 26*), pp. 9–66, gives a useful summary account of the principal manufacturing cities and towns of New England.

[6] See Fig. 6, p. 27, above.

[7] The federal government has taken a census of manufactures in connection with the decennial census of the United States since 1850 as well as in 1914 and biennially since 1919. For the 1929 census certain "industrial areas" were established (not to be confused with the "metropolitan areas" of the census of population; see below, p. 422). Each industrial area comprises the county in which an important manufacturing city is located, together with any adjoining county or counties in which there is a large development of manufacturing. Six out of thirty-three industrial areas so marked out in the United States are included in New England, viz.: Boston (Essex, Middlesex, Norfolk, and Suffolk counties, Mass.), Hartford (Hartford Co., Conn.), Bridgeport-New Haven-Waterbury (Fairfield and New Haven counties, Conn.), Worcester (Worcester Co., Mass.), Springfield-Holyoke (Hampden Co., Mass.), Providence-Fall River-New Bedford (Providence Co., R. I., and Bristol Co., Mass.).

"Massachusetts . . . is the only state in the United States which conducts . . . a complete annual census of manufactures and the only state delegated by the United States Census Bureau to obtain such information for use in the United States Biennial Census of Manufactures" (*New England News Letter*, No. 111, Jan. 1932, p. 5). From 1886 through 1921 the results of this census were published as *Annual Reports on the Statistics of Manufactures*, Commonwealth of Massachusetts, Department of Labor and Industries; for the period since 1921 the reports are available either in the form of press releases or in manuscript. In the report for 1930 data by principal industries are tabulated for the state as a whole and for 39 cities. Summary figures are also given by towns and for metropolitan Boston.—EDIT.

[8] C. E. Artman, *Industrial Structure of New England*, U. S. Dept. of Commerce, Bur. of Foreign and Domestic Commerce, Washington, 1930 (*Domestic Commerce Ser. No. 28*).

[9] Except where otherwise indicated quotations are from Artman, *op. cit.*

[10] The following changes in the percentages of employees in certain New England states to total employees in certain industries throughout the United States are significant (figures for 1904 and 1925 from R. H. Lansburgh, *Recent Migrations of Industries in the United States*, in *Annals Amer. Acad. of Polit. and Soc. Sci.*, Vol. 142, 1929, pp. 296–301, reference on p. 300; figures for 1929 from Bur. of the Census, *Biennial Census of Manufactures*, 1929): cotton goods: Mass., R. I., and N. H., 1904 40%, 1925 31%, 1929 25%; foundry and machine shops: Mass. and Conn., 1904 13%, 1925 9%, 1929 9%; boots and shoes: Mass., 1904 43%, 1925 29%, 1929 27%; paper and pulp: Mass. and Me., 1904 28%, 1925 21%, 1929 19%.—EDIT.

[11] See the more detailed discussion of this subject in Mr. E. A. Filene's paper entitled *Unemployment in New England*, in the present volume, pp. 65–95, above.

[12] Dot maps illustrating the distribution of the textile industry as well as other industries in New England will be found in Artman, *op. cit.*

[13] See Artman, *op. cit.*, pp. 281–332. For a study of cotton manufacturing in New England from the geographical point of view see J. H. Burgy, *The New England Cotton Textile Industry: A Study in Industrial Geography*, Baltimore, 1932 (useful maps and bibliographical references). A fundamental work is M. T. Copeland, *The Cotton Manufacturing Industry of the United States*, Cambridge, Mass., 1912 (*Harvard Economic Studies, Vol. 8*). The difficulties through which the cotton manufactures of New England have been passing of late years have been the subject of much discussion in both the technical and popular press. To dispel undue pessimism believed to be as injurious to healthy progress as the positive difficulties under which the industry was laboring, the New England Council carried out as one of its first tasks a series of surveys of the textile situation. The files of such business periodicals as *Textile World*, *Bankers' Magazine*, *Commerce and Finance*, and *Transactions of the National Association of Cotton Manufacturers* should be consulted for editorial estimates of the situation as a whole and for discussions of particular problems.

On Southern competition with New England cotton mills and the migration of New England cotton manufacturers to the South see *Report of a Special Investigation into Conditions in the Textile Industry in Massachusetts and the Southern States*, Commonwealth of Massachusetts, Dept. of Labor and Industries, 1923 (reprinted in *Amer. Wool and Cotton Reporter*, Vol. 38, 1924, pp. 1237–1278); R. M. Brown, *Cotton Manufacturing, North and South*, in *Econ. Geogr.*, Vol. 4, 1928, pp. 74–87; R. W. Edmonds, *Yankee Thrift and Southern Progress: Some Yankee Views of the South's Industrial Awakening and Its Bearing on the Future Prosperity of New England*, in his *Cotton Mill Labor Conditions in the South and New England*, Baltimore, 1925. Two scholarly studies by Europeans, of interest for their detached point of view are: D. Pasquet, *L'industrie du coton dans le sud-est des Etats-Unis*, in *Annales de Géographie*, Vol. 38, 1929, pp. 366–383 (deals with New England as well as the South), and Andreas Predöhl, *Die Südwanderung der amerikanischen Baumwollindustrie*, in *Weltwirtschaftliches Archiv.*, Vol. 29, 1929, pp. 106–159, 66*–80* (contains useful references).—EDIT.

[14] New England, excluding Maine and Vermont.

[15] Artman, *op. cit.*, pp. 333–364. See also A. H. Cole, *The American Wool Manufacture*, 2 vols., Cambridge, Mass., 1926, and *Bulletin of the National Association of Wool Manufacturers*.

[16] Incomplete data (statistics for worsted goods are lacking for Vermont and New Hampshire) would seem to show that this ratio had dropped to about 6.5% in 1929.—EDIT.

[17] Artman, *op. cit.*, pp. 197–278.

[18] See curves for electrical machinery and appliances and machine shop products, Fig. 4, p. 330, above, and also Fig. 2, p. 86, above.

[19] Artman, *op. cit.*, pp. 406–446.

[20] *Ibid.*, pp. 447–480.

[21] *Recent Economic Changes in the United States: Report of the Committee on Recent Economic Changes of the President's Conference on Unemployment, Herbert Hoover, Chairman*, 2 vols., New York, 1929, reference in Vol. 1, pp. 206–216. Mr. Thorp points out that three main types of geographical change are in progress: (1) a transfer from the cities to the smaller towns, facilitated by the wider distribution of readily available electric power; (2) a tendency away from the excessive concentration of particular industries in particular centers; (3) movements from one part of the country to another. All three of these changes are affecting New England.

[22] *Ibid.*, pp. 207–208.

[23] See J. S. Lawrence, *New England, A Case of Industrial Maturity*, in *Independent*, Vol. 116, 1926, pp. 440–441.

[24] N. E. Peterson, *American Industries by Geographical Sections*, First National Bank, Boston, 1928, p. 4.

[25] See Dr. C. E. Artman's paper in the present volume, p. 52, above.

[26] Earl Whitehorne, *Some Impressions of Industrial New England: Being the Report of a Survey of New England Manufacturing Activities by a Party of Twenty McGraw Hill Editors* (pamphlet), New York, 1929, pp. 6–8 and 10–12.

[27] See also pp. 63–64, above.

THE RAILROADS OF NEW ENGLAND

William J. Cunningham

T HE railroad mileage in New England is 3 per cent of the total in
the United States. This is more than New England's proportion
of the total area, 2.2 per cent, but less than New England's
proportion of the total population, 6.7 per cent. For each 100 square
miles of territory in New England the railroad miles are 11.4; for the
country as a whole they are 8.2. For each 100,000 population there
are 93 miles of railroad in New England. The comparable figure for
the United States is 203. In each case the difference between New
England and the other regions is the reflex of the concentration of
industries and population in southern New England, with their
demand upon transportation agencies.

This discussion of New England railroads should, at the outset,
note the important fact that as a group they are not homogeneous.
Between southern and northern New England there are wide differences—geographic, economic, and social. The two sections may not
clearly be defined. The distinction is more in economic than in geographic factors. One section, the south, is primarily industrial; the
other, the north, is largely agricultural. The industrial section embraces
an area from 50 to 75 miles from seaboard, Stamford, Conn., to Portland, Me. The map of that section is thickly dotted with industrial
cities and towns.[1] The population is dense; and the territory is well
served by railroads, waterways, and highways with dense traffic.
The northerly area of Vermont, New Hampshire, and Maine, with
some exceptions, has relatively few manufacturing sections. For its
economic existence it depends in large part on the products of farms,
forests, and quarries. The population is relatively sparse, the transportation facilities limited in extent, and the volume of traffic light.

DESCRIPTION OF THE INDIVIDUAL ROADS

The railroads in New England, with their mileage and operating
revenues, are listed in Table I (p. 348, below). The New York, New
Haven & Hartford R. R., hereinafter referred to by its shorter name,
the New Haven road, is the most important, having the greatest mileage and the heaviest traffic. With the exception of a few branch lines
the New Haven's network of rails serves a distinctively industrial
region and by reason of that fact has peculiarities in its physical, traffic,
and operating characteristics. It has a practical monopoly of rail
transportation in a wide industrial area and controls also practically

---

[1] For notes see below, p. 360.

344

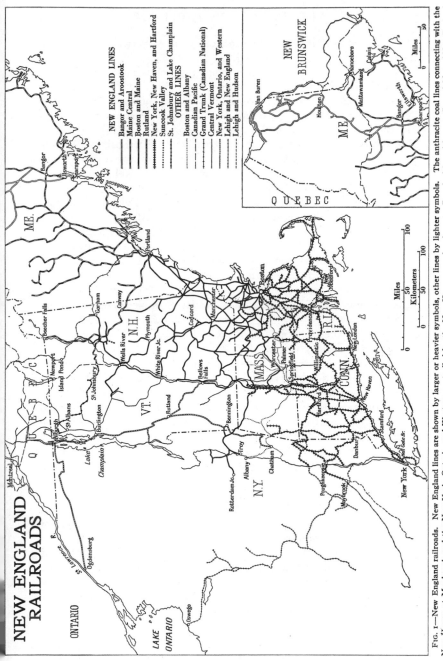
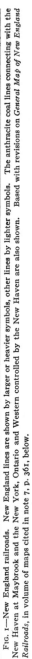

NEW ENGLAND RAILROADS

NEW ENGLAND LINES

Bangor and Aroostook
Maine Central
Boston and Maine
Rutland
New York, New Haven, and Hartford
Suncook Valley
St. Johnsbury and Lake Champlain

OTHER LINES

Boston and Albany
Canadian Pacific
Grand Trunk (Canadian National)
Central Vermont
New York, Ontario, and Western
Lehigh and New England
Lehigh and Hudson

Fig. 1.—New England railroads. New England lines are shown by larger or heavier symbols, other lines by lighter symbols. The anthracite coal lines connecting with the New Haven at Maybrook and the New York, Ontario and Western controlled by the New Haven are also shown. Based with revisions on *General Map of New England Railroads,* in volume of maps cited in note 7, p. 361, below.

345

all of the important water transportation lines between New York and ports as far east as New Bedford.

The nucleus of the New Haven system, which is made up of nearly two hundred once independent railroads, was the line from New York to New Haven. The present company was organized in 1872 by the consolidation of the Hartford and New Haven (incorporated in 1833) and the New York & New Haven (incorporated in 1844). Between 1890 and 1900 it pursued a policy of expansion by purchasing or leasing other companies, so that it finally controlled all railroads, except the Central Vermont, south of the Boston & Albany, as well as the entire network in the southeastern section of Massachusetts.

There are three through routes between New York and Boston, with a fourth via Springfield and the Boston & Albany, and an important through freight route via Danbury and the Poughkeepsie Bridge to Maybrook, N. Y., where connection is made with the trunk lines. The New Haven controls also the New York, Ontario & Western Ry. with its lines into the anthracite regions and to Oswego on Lake Ontario. Jointly with the Pennsylvania R. R. the New Haven road owns the Hell Gate Bridge over the East River in New York City and operates the through Washington trains over that bridge and through the tunnel of the Long Island R. R. into the New York passenger station of the Pennsylvania.

The Boston & Maine R. R. is dominant in New Hampshire and in the industrial sections of Massachusetts north and northeast of Boston. Like the New Haven road the Boston & Maine has a virtual monopoly of rail transportation in a wide area. The company was incorporated in 1835. Its history until 1900 is one of constant expansion by the purchase and lease of other small railroads. The system as now constituted extends from Rotterdam Junction and Troy, N. Y., to Portland, Me., with north and south lines from Springfield and Boston to Wells River, Vt., and numerous crisscross branches throughout New Hampshire. The system is made up of what were once about 130 separate and independent railroad properties.

The Boston & Albany R. R. was incorporated in 1867, a merger of the Boston & Worcester (incorporated in 1831) and the Western (incorporated in 1835). Between 1867 and 1890 the company acquired by lease several short branches, now of little traffic importance. The properties were leased by the New York Central R. R. in 1900. The Boston & Albany is essentially a through line between the two cities and carries an exceptionally heavy passenger traffic as well as a large volume of through freight.

The Maine Central R. R. was organized in 1862 to take over some bankrupt companies whose original charters in some cases were dated in the thirties. Its lines now extend from Portland via Bangor to the New Brunswick border at Vanceboro, with a branch from Bangor via Ellsworth to Calais. The Mountain branch runs northward from Portland to Conway, N. H., and through the Crawford Notch in the White Mountains. There one line continues westward to St. Johnsbury, connecting with the St. Johnsbury & Lake Champlain R. R., and another line runs northward to the Quebec border at Beecher Falls. The area in the vicinity of Portland has industrial characteristics, but in other sections the railroad relies for its traffic mainly on farming, lumbering, and fishing.

The extreme northeastern section of Maine is served principally by the Bangor & Aroostook R. R. (chartered in 1891). The main line extends from Searsport, on Penobscot Bay, through Bangor and Houlton to Van Buren on the extreme northern boundary of New Brunswick, and there are several branches. The road handles the bulk of the potato crop of Aroostook County and carries a substantial tonnage in products of forests.

The Central Vermont Ry. (originally chartered in 1843) has had a somewhat checkered financial career and has gone through several reorganizations, the last in 1929 after a receivership resulting from the disastrous floods of November, 1927. It is now a part of the Canadian National System but is operated as a separate unit. Its line extends from New London through Willimantic, Palmer, White River Junction and St. Albans to Montreal, forming the southern section of one of the through Canadian differential freight routes from New England to Chicago. The company operates also a line of freight boats between New London and New York City. The Central Vermont forms the northern part of a through passenger train route between Boston and Montreal, using Boston & Maine rails between Boston and White River Junction. The road's local traffic is relatively light. It relies principally for revenue on through freight traffic to and from the Canadian National.

The Rutland R. R. (chartered in 1867) grew out of the reorganization of companies of earlier date. Its rails extend from Chatham, N. Y., through Bennington, Rutland, and Burlington along the eastern shore of and on the islands in Lake Champlain to Alburgh on the Quebec boundary, where it connects with the Canadian National to form a through route to Montreal. It connects also with the Boston & Maine at Bellows Falls by a branch from Rutland to make a through route from Montreal to Boston. A branch of the Rutland runs from Alburgh to Ogdensburg on the St. Lawrence River, where connection is made with freight-carrying boats through the Great Lakes. The traffic on the road is relatively light.

In addition to the Central Vermont the Canadian National System controls also the old Atlantic & St. Lawrence R. R., usually designated as the Grand Trunk in Maine. It extends from Portland through Gorham, N. H., to Island Pond, Vt., where it connects with the

Canadian National's line to Montreal, forming a through freight route between Montreal and Portland, where the railroad has a modern water terminal intended to handle export Canadian grain when the ports of Montreal and Quebec are closed by ice. The volume of such traffic has been diminishing, as the Canadian National finds it more expedient to use the Canadian winter ports of St. John and Halifax.

The through line of the Canadian Pacific Railway to St. John, N. B., cuts through northeastern Maine and has trackage rights over the Maine Central between Mattawamkeag and Vanceboro. Within the past three years the Canadian Pacific has extended its line from Newport, Vt., to Wells River by leasing that section of the Boston & Maine, forming a through freight and passenger route from Montreal to Boston via Plymouth and Concord.

The remaining railroads listed in Table I are of minor importance and need not here be described.

TABLE I—RAILROADS IN NEW ENGLAND[a]

RAILROAD	MILES OPERATED 1930	OPERATING REVENUES[b] (*thousands*)	
		1929	1930
New Haven	2,128	$142,459	$118,886
Boston & Maine	2,090	78,481	69,278
Boston & Albany	405	32,454	25,762
Maine Central	1,121	20,312	18,992
Central Vermont	469	8,854	7,585
Bangor & Aroostook	614	8,136	8,366
Rutland	413	6,277	5,286
Grand Trunk in Maine	172	2,346	1,938
Canadian Pacific in Maine	234	2,763	2,506
Canadian Pacific in Vermont	85	2,090	1,791
St. Johnsbury & Lake Champlain . .	96	570	546
Narragansett Pier	8	108	94
Suncook Valley	23	72	57
Wiscasset, Waterville & Farmington	44	67	44
Woodstock	14	61	42
Hoosac Tunnel & Wilmington . . .	24	55	48
Moshassuck Valley	2	39	38
Sandy River & Rangeley Lakes . .	74	193	132
Bridgton & Harrison	17	52	37

[a] From annual statistical reports of Interstate Commerce Commission.

[b] The operating revenues of 1929 were generally higher than in any previous year. The figures for 1930 show the effect of the first full year of the depression.

PHYSICAL CHARACTERISTICS

The topography of the country in southern New England is, on the whole, favorable from the viewpoint of railroad location. The

Shore Line of the New Haven road, Boston to New York, is, with the exception of easy grades between Boston and Providence, a water-level route. The same is true of the line from New Haven to Springfield. On the most direct connection between Boston and New York—the Air Line and the route of the old New England R. R. through Connecticut—the grades are fairly heavy in surmounting the ranges of hills.

The Boston & Albany has a good deal of rise and fall and curvature, especially in the western section (Springfield to Albany) with heavy grades over the main chain of the Berkshires. The maximum elevation east of Springfield is 960 feet. West of Springfield it reaches 1440 feet.

The Fitchburg division of the Boston & Maine roughly parallels the Boston & Albany about twenty miles to the north and has similar topographical conditions. The Hoosac Tunnel, however, gives the line west of the Connecticut River a lower maximum elevation (820 feet) than the Boston & Albany. East of the Connecticut River, however, the Boston & Maine has the greater maximum elevation, 1220 feet. The network of Boston & Maine lines within a radius of fifty miles of Boston, and the main stems to Portland, run through a flat or rolling country and have no heavy grades. The northern lines, on the other hand, are located in mountainous territory and have more than the usual amount of rise and fall and curvature. This is true also of the Central Vermont, the Rutland, the Grand Trunk, and the Bangor & Aroostook. The Maine Central, on the whole, has favorable topography.

OPERATING CHARACTERISTICS

For rate making and other purposes the New England railroads are considered as a collective unit having peculiar traffic and operating characteristics. While, as has already been noted, there are distinct differences between the individual carriers in the region, it has so happened that in the establishment of scales of freight rates and in the determination of the proportion which the New England carriers should receive of the revenue on interregional freight the Interstate Commerce Commission has considered the New England rail carriers as a group. A notable instance is found in the New England Divisions case[2] in which the New England railroads appealed to the Commission to compel the trunk lines to increase the New England proportion of revenue on through freight shipments. In its decision, which was favorable to New England, the Commission recognized the changed conditions that had accentuated the peculiar traffic and operating factors in the region as a whole, and in an earlier decision,[3] authorizing rate increases in New England, it had this to say:

The transportation problem of New England is in many respects distinctive. This grows in part out of geographic conditions and to a still greater extent out of industrial and economic conditions. The New England lines serve directly almost none of the territory outside of New England, and they must depend in considerable part, so far as freight traffic is concerned, upon the tonnage interchanged with their rail connections to the west and north and with steamship lines serving the New England ports. For these reasons, and because they participate in only a part of the haul on through freight traffic into and out of New England, the New England lines have sometimes been referred to as mere terminal or switching railroads, a statement that is misleading if strictly interpreted, but not wholly without value as suggesting a reason for some of the difficulties encountered by these carriers.

Another unusual feature of the New England situation is the character of the freight traffic. In no other section of the country does so large a percentage of the tonnage consist of high-grade manufactured products. Barring products of the forest and of the quarries the outbound movement of raw materials from New England is almost negligible. New England's industrial life depends largely upon importing large quantities of iron, cotton, wool, and other raw materials from the west and south and converting them into finished products. Power used in New England for these manufacturing processes is mainly derived from coal originating outside of New England and transported substantial distances by rail or water. It is estimated that for every three carloads of manufactured products moving west from New England five carloads of raw materials move eastbound into New England. Consequently there is a heavy movement of empty cars from New England to the west.

The peculiarities referred to in the Commission's decision are found in greatest degree on the New Haven and the Boston & Maine. In the Divisions case they were summarized under the headings of (a) diversity of routes and diffusion of traffic, (b) low freight-traffic density, (c) short haul, and (d) heavy terminal burdens. The four groups of factors are interrelated and overlapping. The short haul and low traffic density flow naturally from the frequency of shipping points, terminals, and yards and from the diversity of routes and diffusion of traffic. An excerpt from the Commission's decision[4] will serve to illustrate these characteristics:

The large number of junction points on the New Haven and the Boston & Maine has been referred to. In further reference to the diffusion of traffic it is shown that 70% of the tonnage of the New Haven originates or terminates at 53 stations out of about 550 stations on that road. Of the 53 stations, 16 are located on the main line, 10 on three branch lines, 8 on a group of branch lines in Massachusetts between Fitchburg and Lowell and between Fall River and New Bedford, and 19 are widely scattered. A study of the car movement through Harlem River, N. Y., and Maybrook, N. Y., for one month shows that of 54,000 cars from eastern trunk line territory, 36,000 moved via the first and 18,000 via the second gateway. Of the cars which moved by way of Harlem River and the New Haven, 5.1% were delivered between Harlem River and Bridgeport, 20.8% were delivered at or diverted from the main line at Bridgeport, Conn., 51 miles from Harlem River for movement to Waterbury, Conn., and to 10 other districts in that territory; 35.5% were delivered at New Haven or diverted from the main line to Hartford, Springfield, and 14 other stations; 5.9% were delivered at New London, Conn., or diverted north to Worcester, Mass., and to branch-line points; 8.8% were delivered at Providence, R. I., or diverted by way of a large number of branches to 15 different sections; 7.7% were delivered at Attleboro, Mass., or diverted to Taunton and South Braintree and thence; and 1.6% were delivered at Mansfield, Mass., or diverted. Only 12.9%

moved through to Boston. The above statement does not comprise cars moving less than 50 miles. Analysis of the movement through Maybrook developed a similar result, only 6.4% of the cars moving through to Boston.

PASSENGER TRAFFIC

The passenger traffic on New England railroads, especially on the New Haven and the Boston & Albany, is relatively heavy. While the railroad mileage in New England is but 3 per cent of the total in the United States, the New England rail carriers produce about 9 per cent of the total passenger miles, in contrast to but slightly more than 2 per cent of the total ton miles. The New Haven road in 1930 ran 22 trains daily in each direction between Boston and New York (including the two Washington trains), and the Boston & Albany had 19 daily trains in each direction between Boston and Albany or Springfield. The suburban passenger traffic handled by the New Haven and the Boston & Maine is large in volume. Of the total suburban (commutation) passengers carried by all railroads in the country, about 15 per cent are in New England.

The passenger traffic in New England, in common with that on railroads elsewhere, has suffered severe shrinkage since 1920. The passenger miles of all railroads in 1930 were 43 per cent less than in 1920. In New England the loss was 37 per cent. The falling off in rail passenger traffic, almost entirely in local traffic between adjacent cities and towns and in the rural sections, is attributable in larger part to the greater use of the private automobile and in smaller part to the growth in motor coach and airplane services.

The past five or six years have been a period of readjustment in rail passenger service to meet changed conditions. In an effort to hold the through business the railroads in New England, and elsewhere throughout the country, have been shortening their running time and improving the character of equipment. There were indications in 1929 that the effect of highway competition has reached its maximum and that further substantial losses by rail would not occur. It is difficult to determine to what extent the further declines in 1930 and 1931 are attributable respectively to the depression and to highway competition. The passenger miles by rail in New England in 1929 were 2791 millions. In 1930 they were 2520 millions, and in 1931 there was a further reduction to 2114 millions. The growing degree of congestion on the highways in the industrial sections and parking difficulties in cities, are slowing up the steady growth in the use of the motor car as a substitute for the journey by rail.

In Table II are shown a comparison of passenger traffic density and other related statistics for New England, the Eastern district, and the United States. The striking features are in the density and in the average journey per passenger per railroad.

TABLE II—PASSENGER TRAFFIC, 1930[a]

ITEM	UNITED STATES	EASTERN DISTRICT	NEW ENGLAND	PERCENTAGE N.E. OF	
				U. S.	E. D.
Passengers carried (millions)	704	521	89	12.6	17.1
Passenger miles (millions) .	26,823	15,376	2,520	9.1	16.4
Passenger revenue (millions)	$729	$404	$70	9.6	17.3
Miles per passenger per road	38.1	29.5	28.4		
Revenue per passenger mile	2.72c.	2.62c.	2.79c.		
Passenger miles per mile of road per day	326	805	993	304.6	123.4

From monthly statistical reports of Interstate Commerce Commission.

CHARACTER OF FREIGHT TRAFFIC

The rail freight traffic of New England is peculiar in its low proportion of products of mines and its high proportions of manufactured products and less-than-carload shipments of miscellaneous freight. The details are given in Table III.

TABLE III—REVENUE FREIGHT CARRIED IN 1930[a]
(IN MILLIONS OF TONS)

	UNITED STATES		NEW ENGLAND		PERCENTAGE NEW ENGLAND OF TOTAL
	TONS	PERCENTAGE	TONS	PERCENTAGE	
Products of:					
Agriculture . . .	211.0	10.23	11.8	14.99	5.59
Animals	41.1	1.99	2.3	2.96	5.60
Mines	1,098.6	53.25	23.4	29.81	2.13
Forests	130.7	6.33	6.0	7.58	4.59
Manufacture and Misc.	530.4	25.71	29.8	37.91	5.62
Less-than-carload	51.3	2.49	5.3	6.75	10.33
Total	2,063.1	100.0	78.5	100.0	3.80

[a] Interstate Commerce Commission, annual statistical report.

The last column of percentages in Table III is of greater significance than the second and fourth columns. It may be noted that the New England tonnage was 3.80 per cent[5] of the total, but in products of mines it carried only 2.13 per cent of the total. On the other hand, New England carried 5.62 per cent of the total manufactured products and 10.33 per cent of the total less-than-carload freight.

While the average volume of freight traffic moved over the main lines of the New Haven, the Boston & Maine, and the Boston & Albany is higher than the average for the country as a whole, a large amount of branch line mileage in those systems has very light traffic, and the freight business of northern New England is relatively thin. This brings down the total for New England. In 1930 the ton miles per mile of road per day were: New England, 3536; Eastern district, 7919; United States, 4817.

The average haul—the distance the average ton of freight moves over a single railroad—is a significant index of the frequency of terminal service and the burden of terminal cost. For the country as a whole in 1930 the average haul per ton per railroad was 186 miles. The comparable figure for New England was 119 miles. Ordinarily the terminal cost per ton is much greater than the line cost, and the former is independent of distance. The terminal cost in New England is spread over a line haul of 119 miles while for all railroads it is distributed over 186 miles. For a given amount of traffic the New England railroads, as a whole, therefore, must assume a terminal burden 56 per cent greater than is assumed by the carriers as a whole

FREIGHT CAR PERFORMANCE

The terminal characteristics just discussed work against efficient utilization of equipment. They retard car movement, restrict train loading, and hold down the daily mileage of locomotives. For freight car performance the inclusive unit reflecting the degree of utilization is ton miles per car day—the resultant of the carload, the load factor, and the miles the car moves daily. The performance in 1930 is shown in Table IV.

TABLE IV—FREIGHT CAR PERFORMANCE, 1930[a]

ITEM	UNITED STATES	EASTERN DIST.	NEW ENGLAND
Tons per loaded car	26.7	27.5	20.4
Per cent loaded of total car miles	61.4	61.5	65.8
Car miles per car day	28.7	24.5	26.4
Ton miles per car day	469	415	414

[a] From monthly statistical reports of Interstate Commerce Commission.

The light carload in New England reflects the low proportion of coal and other products of mines as well as the high proportion of manufactured products. The former move in heavy, the latter in light carload lots. The relatively high proportion of loaded to total car miles in New England may be explained by the relatively low coal tonnage. Coal cars ordinarily must return empty to the mines, and they increase the percentage of empty mileage.

The Freight Train Load

As a result of efforts throughout the country generally to achieve better train loading efficiency, and thereby to bring down ton mile costs, the average tons per train have more than doubled in the last twenty years. To that progress New England has contributed, but the operating handicaps in short hauls, frequent dropping and picking up of cars, and light carloads are holding the New England average far below that of railroads as a whole. In 1930 the train load for the United States was 785 tons; for the Eastern district, including New England, it was 884 tons; and for New England alone it was 599 tons. New England, therefore, is obliged to run 131 train miles to produce as many ton miles as the railroads as a whole produce in 100 train miles.

Operating Costs and Net Return

In consequence of all these operating handicaps and high ton mile cost the freight rates in New England are relatively high. At the time the Divisions case[6] was under consideration the rates and divisions in New England were relatively not as much in excess of the rates and divisions in adjacent territories as were the New England operating costs in excess of costs outside of New England. The New England carriers were then unable to earn as much net income and return on property investment as the railroads in the remainder of the Eastern district were able to earn under lower rates. This disparity was partially corrected when the Interstate Commerce Commission awarded to New England an increase of 15 per cent in its proportion of the revenue on interchanged traffic, and during the past six years the operating efficiency of the New England roads has been improved by substantial additional investments in terminals and equipment. Under conditions in 1930 the excess in freight revenue per ton mile in New England (1.724 cents, compared with 1.082 cents in the Eastern district and 1.063 cents for railroads as a whole) was slightly more than in proportion to the excess in New England costs, and the return on property investment in New England railroads was somewhat higher than that earned in other regions. Prior to 1926 the reverse was true.

In 1929, a year of heavy traffic, the railroads as a whole earned net railway operating income equivalent to 4.95 per cent on their investment in road and equipment, working cash, and material and supplies. For the railroads in trunk line territory the rate of return was 4.85 per cent. The lines in the Central Eastern Region earned 5.47 per cent, and those in New England earned 5.89 per cent. The comparable figures for 1930, the first full year of the depression, were: United States, 3.36 per cent; trunk line territory, 2.83 per cent; Central Eastern, 3.68 per cent; New England, 4.64 per cent.

The outstanding items in the income account of 1930 are condensed in Table V. The figures indicate that under present conditions the relationship between operating expenses and revenues in New England is slightly more favorable than in other sections of the country. New England earned 4.44 per cent of the total revenues, spent 4.23 per cent of the total operating expenses, and had 5.05 per cent of the total net railway operating revenue. The net railway operating income, however, was but 4.97 per cent of the total. The reason for the disparity is found in the relatively heavy charges in New England for debit balances in the joint use of freight cars, included in the item "Debit balance in rents of equipment and joint facilities."

The details of the operating ratio (the part of each dollar of operating revenues taken by expenses) in Table V show that New England is relatively low in the cost of maintaining equipment and in transportation expenses. The relatively high cost of New England's maintenance of way in 1930 is explained in part by heavy charges to maintenance expenses occasioned by enlargement and revision of yards and terminals on both the Boston & Maine and the New Haven systems.

TABLE V—OPERATING REVENUES, OPERATING EXPENSES, AND
NET RAILWAY OPERATING INCOME (1930)[a]
(IN MILLIONS)

ITEM	UNITED STATES	EASTERN DISTRICT	NEW ENGLAND	PERCENTAGE N. E. OF	
				U. S.	E. D.
Operating revenues	$5,343	$2,395	$237	4.44	9.90
Operating expenses	3,976	1,820	168	4.23	9.23
Net railway operating revenue	1,367	575	69	5.05	12.00
Taxes	354	145	13	3.67	8.97
Debit balance in rents of equipment and joint facilities	128	66	12	9.37	18.18
Net railway operating income	885	364	44	4.97	12.09
Operating ratio (percentage of revenues taken by expenses):					
Maintenance of way . .	13.3	12.7	15.3	. . . .	. . . . .
Maintenance of equipment	19.1	20.0	15.7	. . . .	. . . . .
Transportation	35.1	36.8	34.3	. . . .	. . . . .
Other operating expenses	6.8	6.5	5.7	. . . .	. . . . .
Total operating expenses	74.4	76.0	71.0	. . . .	. . . . .

[a] From monthly bulletins of Interstate Commerce Commission.

PROBLEMS OF 1932

The New England railroad problems of 1932 are serious but no more serious than those of 1923. Since then, except for the effects of the current depression, the situation has been improved in remarkable degree. Yet the margin of financial safety is not large; the effect of recent rate changes is uncertain; the competitive bearing of other forms of transportation on railroad earning power is problematic; and there is divergence of view on consolidations.

The net income of the New England carriers in 1929 was gratifying to those who had had part in their rehabilitation, but the bright promise for the future was dimmed by the business recession in the fall of 1929. The prolongation of the depression throughout 1930 and 1931 has required drastic retrenchment in maintenance and other expenses. The dividends of 1929 were earned, but the net income of 1930, even though bolstered by deferred maintenance, did not warrant a continuation of 1928 and 1929 dividends. There is a limit to the economies that may be relied upon to offset substantial depletion in gross revenues. Especially is this true of maintenance. Economies there, if in any degree a form of deferred expenditures, must later be made up with interest. The imperative need of conserving net income in 1930 and 1931 has led to the most minute scrutiny of every item of expenses, and the degree of curtailment of labor expenditures has been severe and disturbing.

The hope of continuation of earning power sufficient to maintain railroad credit and insure adequate transportation service lies in a revival and continued growth of traffic. The full fruits of the large additions to investment since the war period may not be realized until the additional capacity is utilized. To the restoration of traffic volume and its further growth the railroad managers can do little except in so far as intelligent rate making and good rail service may aid in fostering commerce and industry.

The present deficiency in railroad net income may not be rectified by increasing rates. Freight charges in New England are now, as a whole, as high as the traffic will stand. The New England manufacturer and merchant is competitively at a disadvantage in distance from raw materials and markets. That disadvantage is offset in the typical case by the traditional advantages of skilled labor and management, but any further addition to the freight rate handicap may destroy the equilibrium.

There is a basis for serious concern over recent rate-making policies of the Interstate Commerce Commission. The railroads of New England under their policy of fostering the industries of the section have built up a rate structure in which competition outside of New England has been the controlling factor and distance has been given but little weight. The Commission's policy is to give greater weight to distance and to place smaller emphasis on regional competition. During the past five years the Commission has been revising the scale of class rates, endeavoring to iron out the many inconsistencies, and in the new scales the rates vary indirectly with distance. The new Eastern Class Rate Scale (1931) places heavy additional burdens upon the New England shipper of merchandise moving under class rates, and there is fear that the distance principle may be given greater weight when the process of revision is carried into the commodity rates, in which the New England manufacturer has an even more vital interest.

Another problem of major importance is that of rates on export and import traffic through the New England ports, especially Boston, where the modern facilities are used only in part. Export traffic through Boston has shrunk to but a fraction of its former volume, while that of Baltimore, Philadelphia, and New York has grown steadily. The loss in Boston is the result of substituting port differentials for former equal rates to all north Atlantic ports. The rates to Boston and New York are equalized, but those to Baltimore are 2 cents per 100 pounds lower, and those to Philadelphia are 3 cents less than to Boston and New York. The same principle applies to import rates except that the differentials are greater on the higher classes of freight.

Boston has fought hard and continuously for nearly thirty years to restore the former parity, but while a few minor concessions have been made the efforts have accomplished little to restore Boston's former prestige as a port. The controversy was before the Interstate Commerce Commission in 1898, 1905, 1912, 1913, 1927, and 1929; but in each decision the differentials have been upheld. Boston is more distant than Baltimore and Philadelphia from the producing areas, and the Commission is unwilling to waive the distance principle merely to redistribute traffic among the ports.

While the rail haul to Boston is longer than to the other ports, Boston is nearer to Europe. The shorter water distance from Boston justifies a reduction in ocean rates equal to the rail differential and thus an equalization of the through rates, rail and water combined. The Interstate Commerce Commission, however, has no jurisdiction over ocean carriers, and thus far the ocean carriers have turned deaf ears to Boston's plea.

The competitive effect of motor competition in rail passenger service has already been mentioned. It has made serious inroads on local rail travel. To meet this competition the railroads have gone into the motor coach business themselves, and, especially on the New Haven and the Boston & Maine, the railroad-operated coaches on the highways are supplementing or duplicating the rail service. The principal railroad loss, however, is not to the motor coach but to the private automobile. That loss appears to be permanent. It is, however, almost entirely in local traffic over relatively short distances.

In freight service the railroad loss to motor trucks is not as serious as in passenger service, but the trucks have taken away a substantial part of the railroad's short-haul tonnage, especially that in less-than-carload lots. The zone in which the truck can effectively compete differs in localities but is roughly 75 to 100 miles. Within that zone from producing points the truck has undoubted advantages, but beyond that zone the advantages are uncertain or negative. It is probable that the period of development is about over and that further railroad losses will be small. Moreover, there is consolation to the railroads in the fact that the short-haul freight in congested areas is the least remunerative from the point of view of net revenue. The operating costs are high, and the utilization of equipment is low. The railroads would be much better off if the facilities and equipment used unprofitably for the short-haul freight could be released and the capacity utilized by the more profitable long-haul tonnage.

The last problem to be discussed is that of consolidation. The problem grows out of the mandate to the Interstate Commerce Commission in the Transportation Act of 1920 to prepare a plan for consolidating the many separate railroads in the United States into a limited number of systems. The principal reason for consolidation was to simplify and make easier the task of rate regulation by eliminating the problem of the weak railroad.

For New England the Commission, in its tentative report of 1922, suggested two plans but expressed no preference. The first, known as the Trunk Line plan, would have left the Canadian-controlled lines and the Boston & Albany (leased to the New York Central) undisturbed but would have allotted the other New England railroads to two of the trunk line systems to be created. The second, known as the New England Regional plan, would have made no change in the status of the Boston & Albany, the Central Vermont, and the Grand Trunk but would have joined the remaining roads into one regional system. At the time the tentative report was published the New Haven and the Boston & Maine were in hard straits financially, and the other New England roads were not in much better condition.

To assist the governors of the several New England states to determine the policy of New England in the matter of consolidation a Joint New England Railroad Committee was appointed in June, 1922, with the late James J. Storrow of Boston as chairman; and in June, 1923, the committee made an exhaustive report entitled "Rehabilitation by Co-operation—a Railroad Policy for New England."[7] The majority of the committee concluded that rehabilitation should first be accomplished and then, if consolidation were to be effected, the New England Regional plan would be preferable.

The discussion brought out the affirmative and negative points for each of the two plans. Favoring trunk line affiliation the two principal arguments were: (1) New England railroads were in precarious financial condition and badly in need of capital. Without financial help public service could not be bettered. The trunk lines were much stronger, could give of their substance, and share in the future earnings. (2) An affiliation of the southern New England railroads with one trunk line system and the northern New England lines with another trunk line would afford effective competition and act as a beneficial tonic on service. The principal negative argument was that outside control would be injurious to the best interests of New England as the trunk lines would be more likely to protect the regions they now serve than to assist New England in its competitive efforts.

The report of the committee was submitted to the Interstate Commerce Commission as the recommendation of the New England governors, but the Trunk Line plan was not without advocates. The Commission, however, waited until December, 1929, before publishing its final report. For New England the Commission recommended two regional systems, one based upon the New Haven and the other based upon the Boston & Maine, the Canadian lines and the Boston & Albany to remain undisturbed.

The Commission's proposal, which is "final" in name only[8] has not met with public approval. If the New England railroads are to be consolidated regionally the weight of opinion favors one rather than two systems, and there is much to support the proposal that the single system should include the Boston & Albany so that the New York Central, one of the trunk lines, should not have a competitive advantage over other trunk lines.

Shortly after the Commission's report was published a committee, similar to the so-called Storrow Committee of 1922, was appointed by the governors of the several New England states, to make a survey of all angles of the consolidation problem and to recommend a policy. The general chairman of the new committee, organized January 3, 1930, was the Hon. Rolland H. Spaulding, former governor of New Hampshire. The committee, with the assistance of staff experts, made a careful and comprehensive study, held hearings, and in May, 1931, submitted a majority report recommending a regional form of consolidation.[9] The representatives of the state of Rhode Island dissented, filing a minority report[10] supporting a plan that would have allotted the New England railroads among the four trunk line systems proposed by a plan submitted to the Commission in 1931 by the Pennsylvania, New York Central, Baltimore & Ohio, and Chesapeake & Ohio-Erie managements. That plan for trunk line consolidation specifically excluded consideration of New England's separate problem, but at the hearings in Washington in January, 1932, New England intervened, asking that its problem be considered conjointly with that of the trunk lines.[11]

The principal reason for intervention was the recent activities of the Pennsylvania Railroad, in adding substantially to its ownership of New Haven stock, and that of the Pennroad Corporation, in acquiring large interests in the Boston & Maine. Inasmuch as these acquisitions potentially placed Pennsylvania interests in a dominating position in New England, the plan for regional consolidation in New England was placed in jeopardy. The representatives of the Governors' Committee asked the Commission to require the Pennsylvania Railroad to relinquish its holdings in New England railroads in excess of 10 per cent of the voting stock so as to keep the way clear for regional consolidation within New England when the time comes for determining the best course to be followed. The views of the Rhode Island representatives favoring trunk line extension within New England were also presented to the Commission, as well as other suggestions from committees and individuals advocating various plans for New England.

At this writing (June, 1932) the Commission has concluded its hearing and has listened to oral arguments, but has not yet reached its decision on the pending Trunk Line plan or its bearing upon the railroad situation in New England.

The general feeling toward consolidation has undergone change since 1920. At that time railroad service was inferior and the railroad problem was acute. Since 1923 the service has improved progressively until it has reached a standard higher than ever before. The number of weak railroads has substantially diminished; and the financial problems, outside of those attributable solely to the current depression, are much less serious. The possibility that consolidation would do much to improve the situation in 1920–1923 led to the general acceptance of the principle; but now (1932), with adequate and dependable service, the disposition is to let well enough alone and refrain from experimenting. The alternative is to abandon the principle of pre-arranged, large-scale consolidation and, instead, allow the restoration of the former practice of voluntary consolidations in piecemeal and natural fashion as the desirability develops, subject to greater powers of scrutiny and prior approval by the Interstate Commerce Commission.

NOTES

[1] See Figure 1, p. 325, above.

[2] *Interstate Commerce Commission Reports*, Vol. 62, 1921, p. 528; U. S. Supreme Court, *United States Reports*, Vol. 261, 1923, p. 184.

[3] *I. C. C. Reports*, Vol. 49, 1918, p. 421.

[4] *Ibid.*, Vol. 62, 1921, p. 528.

[5] The ton miles in New England in 1930 were but 2.2 per cent of the total. The haul in New England is relatively short. Ton mile statistics by commodities are not available.

[6] *I. C. C. Reports*, Vol. 62, 1921, p. 528.

[7] *Report of the Joint New England Railroad Committee to the Governors of the New England States: Rehabilitation by Co-operation, a Railroad Policy for New England,* [n. p.], June, 1923. [This report includes brief discussions of the New England railroads as a group, of the importance of New England's water transportation, and of the topography of New England railroads, followed by chapters on the several systems, on passenger and motor truck transportation, on port development, and on plans for consolidation and rehabilitation. A separate volume of maps accompanies the report.—EDIT.]

[8] *I. C. C. Reports,* Vol. 159, 1929, p. 522. Commissioner Eastman referred to it as "merely a procedural step."

[9] *Report of the New England Railroad Committee to the Governors of the New England States: The New England Railroads, Recommendations for a Policy with Respect to Consolidation and Ownership* [n. p.], May, 1931. [This report gives a general description of the railroads of New England. It includes a discussion of the geography and recent growth of New England in relation to railroads, a historical sketch of the development of railroad transportation, an analysis of the present situation, a forecast of the future, and an extended discussion of problems of consolidation. By means of a questionnaire the New England Council endeavored to ascertain the opinions of business organizations of New England in regard to the report of the Committee and the minority report. Prior to December, 1931, 38 organizations had replied in support of the consolidation of the Boston & Maine and the New Haven provided Pennsylvania holdings are reduced, 7 supported such consolidation without stipulation as to stock ownership, 38 (of which 15 were Rhode Island organizations) supported the Rhode Island minority on some trunk line plan, 7 would leave the roads as they are, and 3 favored an all New England system controlled in New England (*New England News Letter,* No. 108, Dec., 1931, p. 7).—EDIT.]

[10] *Report of the New England Railroad Committee,* pp. 259–284.

[11] For the text of the Petition of Intervention see *New England News Letter,* Suppl., Dec. 11, 1931.

THE HIGHWAYS OF NEW ENGLAND

Arthur W. Dean

HISTORICAL DEVELOPMENT

THREE hundred years ago the settlements located along the New England coast maintained communication largely by water, though occasionally by horse or pack train over Indian trails. Up to 1700 there were few roads, and these were hardly more than narrow paths. The pioneers, eager to go inland, blazed forest trails, later widened for pack trains and still later converted into wagon roads; but not until about 1800 were there any well-built roads in rural communities.

In the early colonial days the building of roads was done by volunteer labor following action taken at town meetings. This procedure was so unsatisfactory that ultimately the towns were obliged to pass ordinances compelling able-bodied men to work on the roads or to pay tax money instead. However, even this did not suffice to keep the roads in good condition.

The road-building process consisted for the most part in clearing the right of way and then dumping stone, upon which was spread earth or gravel. The road was then declared finished. For a part of the year such roads were passable.

The growing demand for better carriage roads between the farms and the larger centers of population, coupled with the inability of the towns to keep such roads in satisfactory condition, led to the so-called "turnpike era," which began about 1795.[1] The maintenance of all roads previously had been an obligation or responsibility of the towns and other local communities, but the unwillingness of many local communities to support through roads for the benefit of those outside the community brought about a change in policy. Those who expected to use these roads were now required to pay tolls for their construction and maintenance. The cure for the road conditions of the time was thought to be the new method of private financing and control, whereby the special roads were built by private companies incorporated under acts passed by the legislatures. For à period this principle was carried out, until objections to paying tolls and dissatisfaction with the poor upkeep of the turnpikes led to its abandonment. In most cases the pikes reverted to the control of the local authorities.

The next step was the entrance of the state governments in the matter of aid for roads. And again in the present day appears the principle of collecting revenue for roads from those who use them

[1] For notes see below, p. 371.

in the form of the fees for motor vehicles and taxes on the use of gasoline.

Road-building in the early days was not in general considered an important undertaking, nor did it require especially trained constructors. Local experience was thought to be satisfactory for the purpose. In most cases road construction consisted of a little grading and surfacing with the most readily available local material. The roads thus built were known as natural roads. When surfacing materials from outside the locality were used, the road was called an artificial road.

The natural roads served their period of usefulness and were even improved somewhat in a few instances during the turnpike era, but these roads eventually proved incapable of meeting the growing demand for better transportation facilities, a demand which became marked in the New England states in the 1880's. Other sections of the country, particularly the eastern states, were confronted with the same problem, and it is interesting to note that not only in the United States but also in Europe the problem of better roads was also becoming vexatious at about the same time.

The lack of good roads was in part due to the fact that road construction and maintenance were carried out in the main by the cities and towns and the mileage constructed was more or less limited to local needs, as there was neither sufficient interest on the part of the authorities nor the means requisite for the construction of through routes. The whole road-building activity was a decentralized affair.

The modern conception of a good road has been evolved from several decades of study, design, and experimentation. The hard-surfaced road of today would, in the parlance of earlier days, have been called an artificial road. Although we think of it as the "real" road, it is a highly specialized product created for modern traffic conditions.

State aid in the construction and maintenance of highways in New England was provided by legislative enactment first in Massachusetts in 1892; then in Connecticut in 1895, Vermont in 1898, Maine in 1901, Rhode Island in 1902, and New Hampshire in 1903. In each state there were organized in accordance with this legislation certain commissions or other agencies. At the outset the intent was to provide some supervision of road construction as well as to afford financial assistance, and the work of the early years was largely demonstrative of types and methods thought to be the most desirable. The Massachusetts Highway Commission in 1893 was authorized under certain conditions to take over, lay out, and maintain roads to be designated state highways. Other states gradually came to acquire the same power, so that today all these states are actively engaged in the construction, maintenance, and control of certain mileages of highways.

The mileage of rural highways, including state highways, in the six New England states at the end of 1930 is shown in Table I.

TABLE I—NEW ENGLAND: MILEAGE OF RURAL HIGHWAYS, END OF 1930; FEDERAL AID ROAD CONSTRUCTION, 1932

	RURAL ROAD MILEAGE[a]			MILES SURFACED ROADS[a]			
STATES	TOTAL	STATE HIGHWAYS	LOCAL ROADS	TOTAL	STATE HIGHWAYS	LOCAL ROADS	FEDERAL AID ROAD CONSTRUCTION, MILEAGE COMPLETED JUNE 30, 1932[b]
Me. . .	20,882	2,039	18,843	6,227	1,886	4,341	720
N. H. .	12,034	2,548	9,486	3,060	2,434	626	421
Vt. . .	15,031	4,204	10,827	5,075	3,552	1,523	339
Mass. .	18,802	1,624	17,178	9,682	1,624	8,058	817
R. I. .	2,739	1,009	1,730	973	571	402	255
Conn. .	14,256	2,234	12,022	3,712	2,139	1,573	281
Totals .	83,744	13,658	70,086	28,729	12,206	16,523	2,833

[a] Data from U. S. Bureau of Public Roads.
[b] From *Public Roads*, published by U. S. Bureau of Public Roads, July, 1932.

Highways for which the United States government contributes under the Federal Aid highway acts are selected jointly by the Bureau of Public Roads and the several state highway departments in accordance with the provisions of those acts, and the type of construction and location must meet with the approval of the Bureau.

Table II shows the types and mileage of state highways.

TABLE II—NEW ENGLAND: STATE HIGHWAYS, TYPES AND MILEAGE, END OF 1930[a]

STATES	TOTAL MILEAGE, STATE HIGHWAY SYSTEM	TOTAL SURFACED MILEAGE	SAND, CLAY	GRAVEL	WATER-BOUND MACADAM, TREATED AND UN-TREATED	BITU-MINOUS MACAD-AM	BITU-MINOUS CON-CRETE	PORT-LAND CEMENT CON-CRETE
Me.	2,039	1,886	4	1,508	8	237	. . . .	129
N. H.	2,548	2,434	. . . . . .	1,920	118	173	56	167
Vt.	4,204	3,552	1,000	2,168	49	73	3	259
Mass.	1,624	1,624	. . . . . .	60	194	852	230	285
R. I.	1,009	571	. . . . . .	26	106	204	124	111
Conn.	2,234	2,139	. . . . . .	302	892	304	154	485
Totals	13,658	12,206	1,004	5,984	1,367	1,843	567	1,436

[a] Data from U. S. Bureau of Public Roads.

CLIMATIC FACTORS AFFECTING HIGHWAYS

The factors entering into the routing, construction, and maintenance of our roads are myriad. Aside from geological considerations in construction, the factor of climate limits the length of the construction season to about eight months. Freezing weather halts concrete construction, and a certain minimum temperature stops the laying of bituminous macadam by the penetration method.

The period of snowfall determines the winter use of the highways, necessitating the employment of great fleets of snowplows and other units for keeping open to travel the main through routes, particularly in the parts of New England that are becoming more and more dependent on motor vehicles for commutation and for the transportation of goods. Many sections of New England, however, are not dependent on highway transport, local activities in the main not being hampered by snow conditions. This is particularly true of the rural districts that now derive a large portion of their income from summer tourist traffic.

The main routes that are kept open for travel are plowed in part by the state highway departments or in coöperation with the cities and towns. For the heavily traveled routes the first objective is to clear off all the snow, putting the plows to work as soon as the storm starts. Ice is a considerable problem, and the endeavor is made to sand as soon as possible all dangerous surfaces.

Snow removal from the principal routes of travel in New England is an important modern development of the states' activities.[2] Cities and towns have always been responsible for keeping their highways passable in winter, but the methods formerly used were neither speedy nor extensive enough to go far beyond the more important built-up centers.

In order that the investment of industries and transportation agencies in motor equipment may be utilized during the whole year, owners of such equipment, private as well as commercial, have realized that snow removal is one of the first needs in highway operation. For motor vehicles the ideal condition is that all the snow be removed from the surface, but this does not satisfy traffic on runners. The tendency, however, is toward an increasing use of the motor vehicle, and no doubt the completely cleared road will give general satisfaction in the near future.

Freezing conditions have also given rise to restrictions on the weight of vehicles and loads that may be transported over the highways during the thawing season in spring. This control is an important factor in conserving the road surface and the investment, preventing the destruction of innumerable miles of highways. It applies particularly to the routes, which, though not constructed

TABLE III—NEW ENGLAND

STATE	TOTAL MILEAGE IN STATE SYSTEM (INCLUDING FEDERAL AID ROADS) SURFACED WITH SAND-CLAY OR HIGHER TYPES OF PAVEMENT ON JAN. 1, 1930	AVERAGE ANNUAL SNOWFALL OVER PERIOD OF YEARS IN LOCALITY OF MINIMUM SNOWFALL AND IN LOCALITY OF MAXIMUM SNOWFALL (INCHES)	CONTROL OF SNOW REMOVAL 1929–30	TRUCK P DISPLACEMENT TYPE
Maine	1,833	74.4 to 131.9	State and townships	96
New Hampshire[b] .	2,289	65.1 to 94.0	State and townships	40
Vermont . . .	3,485	63.3 to 110.6	State and townships	40
Massachusetts . .	1,625	45.4 to 61.5	State	300
Rhode Island . .	533	24.1 to 47.0	State and townships	86
Connecticut . . .	2,017	40.3 to 75.6	State and local	207

aFrom *American Highways*, Vol. 11, 1932.
bData estimated from report of previous winter.

with the heavy types of surface, are nevertheless when stabilized quite serviceable for a great amount of traffic.

HIGHWAY CONSTRUCTION

Highway building today has become a very important activity from the points of view not only of transportation but also of the construction industry. Of course, one important consideration is the method of financing and the production of as great a mileage of serviceable roadway as possible by the funds available.

Expenditures by the New England states on roads now amount annually to about $75,000,000. Contracts for construction call for the employment of probably 30,000 men in the height of the season.

Furthermore, the building of highways is not only an industry but an engineering undertaking of great magnitude. Modern procedure in any large enterprise or industry is based in great degree on research and experimentation. The magnitude of the road-building industry and the amount of money expended justify reasonable expenditures for research.

The engineering organizations of the several highway departments, therefore, not only ascertain the facts on which decisions are based

AL DATA, WINTER 1929–30ᵃ

| AL EQUIPMENT, WINTER 1929–30 | | | | SNOW REMOVAL WINTER 1929–30 | | |
ROTAR TYPE	TRUCKS AND TRACTORS	GRADERS	SNOW FENCE 1929–30 (MILES)	MILEAGE OF ROADS WITH SNOW REMOVED	AVERAGE SEASONAL SNOWFALL FROM RECORDS IN DIFFERENT SECTIONS OF STATE (INCHES)	TOTAL COST OF SNOW REMOVAL
2	96 trucks 168 tractors	..	105	5,526	70.8	$241,548
4	40 trucks 155 tractors	4	200	1,750	60.9	90,000
..	40 trucks 90 tractors	25	230	2,625	67.5	35,000
..	300 trucks 23 tractors	..	30	1,468	31.1	229,414
9	86 trucks 19 tractors	..	7	740	23.6	70,446
..	207 trucks 7 tractors	..	19	2,080	22.1	216,770

as to the location of highway improvements; they not only make plans and prepare contracts; but they also include an engineer and assistants with laboratory and equipment for testing materials and processes and for the physical and chemical control of materials used. Research to determine the adaptability of new products or methods or admixtures for various purposes is indispensable if waste of public money is to be avoided.

One of the fundamental needs of highway building is information as to the geological formations across which the roads are to pass and the sources of suitable material. The state of Maine has authorized a three-year geological survey in which the State Highway Commission is coöperating with the University of Maine to ascertain the location, quantity, and character of sand, gravel, and rock deposits suitable for highways.

Important laboratory tests are also being made of the strength of the concrete in completed roads. Sample cores are taken to determine whether the concrete conforms to the strength requirements of the specifications, and observations are made of the experimental roads and of different types of surface with a view to devising improvements.

One great advantage accrues to these states in the frequent

meetings of the testing engineers for the discussion of common problems and for the standardizing of specifications for materials and methods.

The locations of acceptable road-building materials, such as sand, gravel, and broken stone, are ascertained and many tests made of samples submitted for approval by contractors. The availability of such materials is sometimes, though not always, a deciding factor in the types of roads to be built.

In Maine on the primary state highway routes most of the surfaces have been built of cement concrete. On the secondary and tertiary roads gravel is largely used, and much of the mileage has been treated with oil.

In New Hampshire the tendency is to construct more mileage of cement concrete than of other types for the trunk-line highways. Many sections of the state are not supplied with rock that would produce a high quality of broken stone for macadam.

The situation in Vermont is much the same as in New Hampshire; more mileage is built of cement concrete than of other materials for trunk lines.

Rhode Island has a wealth of good local sand and gravel and consequently has constructed an even greater proportion of cement concrete highways. Trap rock for bituminous macadam must be largely imported.

Connecticut has generally constructed the main highways of cement concrete. She has used broken stone for this purpose, because most of the gravel deposits are not of satisfactory grade. Sand for concrete is mainly obtained from Long Island sources.

Massachusetts has an abundance of stone materials for road-building. Gravel and sand aggregates of good quality are found in the southeastern part of the state in Plymouth and Norfolk counties, where some mileage of cement concrete roads has been built. On Cape Cod the sand resources have generally controlled the type of surface, and there has been developed the high type oil mix roads of reasonable cost. Although these have not been considered adaptable for heaviest traffic, they have afforded an excellent surface for a great volume of seasonal traffic. Other parts of the state, particularly in the west, have excellent sources of trap rock. The consequence of this is that many miles, in fact nearly 80 per cent of the annual highway construction, is now being built of the so-called high type bituminous macadam.

The design of highways as an engineering undertaking is dependent not only on the type of pavement, which must be adequate for the traffic both in volume and weight, but also on suitable foundations and proper drainage of the underlying strata. The existence of free-draining gravel deposits makes possible the use of any suitable surface; but districts in which the soil is largely mixed with clay, or presents layers of peat, have a bearing on the type of surface. Excavation of clayey material and replacement with gravel may permit the use of a cement concrete pavement, but where there is underlying peat or unstable soil the use of concrete is precluded, and bituminous macadam is employed, as this type of pavement adjusts itself to settlement and is much more readily repaired.

For the primary routes in New England reinforced concrete is generally employed and undoubtedly is the best of the types of road surface in use. Its cost is somewhat higher than that of other types except in a few localities.

Bituminous macadam is used extensively in Massachusetts where there are ample resources in stone suitable for this type. In hilly country, as on the Mohawk Trail, this type has also been selected because of its non-skid surface. Furthermore, on account of its lower cost it has been used for the middle lane on heavily traveled routes with outer lanes of cement concrete. The contrast in color and texture of surface also has a psychological value in tending to keep the usual flow of traffic on the outer or concrete lanes and permit the faster moving traffic to pass on the center lanes. This black road has been used not only on three-lane routes but has been selected for a center strip of twenty feet on certain four-lane routes.

Three-lane roads have been constructed in the belief that they not only provide flexibility of traffic flow but are relatively inexpensive. Undoubtedly there may be some difference of opinion in regard to the value of the three-lane route as compared with the four-lane route. Yet as an intermediate step it would appear that the former has some advantage, particularly in cases where the movement of traffic is predominantly in one direction at one period and in the opposite direction at another.

The design of pavements for strength and adaptability to physical conditions, the location of the highway with reference to topographical peculiarities, and the adoption of standards for gradient, curvature, and visibility at curves and summits are determined by judgment based on experience.

Highway Traffic

Traffic volume is one of the factors in the determination of the routes that should be improved and in the selection of types of surface. In four of the New England states—Maine, New Hampshire, Vermont, and Connecticut—comprehensive surveys of transportation on the state highway systems have been made in coöperation with the Bureau of Public Roads of the United States Department of Agriculture.[3] These have proved of value in that they have developed actual facts and have furnished some means of predicting future use and demands. In Massachusetts a less detailed survey has been made by the state each third year, beginning in 1909, recording the numbers of vehicles passing selected points on the state highways.

The control of traffic movement is becoming one of the important phases of highway development. In the past, and to a great extent at present, the procedure has been to construct a road, then open it wide for traffic to use at its pleasure, provided certain laws of the road are observed. Police enforcement of regulations for safety, however, has become increasingly necessary, and with it further regulation of the use of highways with a view to the greatest efficiency. Such regulations may take the form of education of the driving public in an endeavor to maintain traffic lanes so that one vehicle shall not cut down the capacity of a road. This is attempted by the use of traffic markings to separate lanes of travel, important on the wider pavements particularly, and by the use of signs instructing motorists to keep in the right-hand lane except when passing a vehicle.

The capacity of highways is limited to the full use made of each lane. For a three-lane highway to carry only two lines of travel is an economic waste, because it then has no greater capacity than a two-lane road; and similarly a four-lane road or wider pavement carrying merely the equivalent of three-lane traffic in scattered flow is uneconomic. Hence the necessity of traffic lines on pavements and the advantage of the dual type of surface, concrete for outer lanes and bituminous macadam for inner lanes, a feature of construction that almost automatically preserves the high value of road capacity.

Essentially the ideal function of the highway is to provide for the maximum volume of traffic flow, or greatest number of vehicles per hour. The theoretical maximum capacity varies with the speed and may be between 1500 and 2000 vehicles per hour per lane if no cross traffic be given its opportunity to pass. For some of the most important traffic routes this problem will require attention. In fact, in Massachusetts there is under construction a new type of highway, spoken of as the new Boston-Worcester turnpike, about thirty miles long, which in effect will be an express route, providing two parallel roadways separated by a ten-foot grassplot. The present plans provide for two ten-foot lanes of reinforced cement concrete in each of the parallel roadways and outside of these a ten-foot lane of bituminous macadam or of concrete. Another important feature of this turnpike is the construction of highway grade separations for fifteen important crossroads, with approach driveways or ramps to permit traffic movement between the main highway and the crossroad and thus provide continuous traffic flow with no tie-up at intersections.

Another feature of traffic control is in the designation of certain main arteries as through ways, requiring vehicles entering from the side streets or roads to stop before entering. This is intended as a safety regulation but does not give exclusive right of way to vehicles on the through way except only under certain conditions.

Uniformity in highway numbering and designation in accordance with federal regulations has been an accomplished fact for New England state highways for several years; but the traffic regulations and traffic signals and control on local ways not parts of the state highways have lacked uniformity. The confusion arising from such conditions has been remedied in Massachusetts by legislation passed in 1928, which placed the control of such matters under the jurisdiction of the Department of Public Works. A Standard Signal Code has been promulgated, which conforms to national standards, and this code is now followed by all cities and towns of the state in the establishment of traffic regulations and the installation and operation of traffic control signals. From the point of view of safety and also for the convenience and training of the motorist these regulations require that such devices be designed and set up at certain definite positions so that the individual may know where and under what conditions he can find the instructions to proceed or stop at an intersection.

CONCLUSION

The common interest of the six New England states in many matters is demonstrated by the continued and growing attention given to the activities carried on under the leadership of the New England Council. Extensive study has been made of the particular features of New England products and resources that have distinct advantages or appeals and of the most advantageous method of gaining general recognition of them. In its diversity of products and of community development, New England presents many and varied opportunities; and these are impelling reasons for the construction of even more adequate routes for transportation than those of the present day.

NOTES

[1] See F. J. Wood, *The Turnpikes of New England and Evolution of the Same Through England, Virginia, and Maryland*, Boston, 1919. Several papers by Professor J. W. Goldthwait on early roads in New Hampshire have appeared in *New Hampshire Highways*, Vols. 8 and 9, 1930–1931.

[2] See the annual *Snow Removal Reports*, Bur. of Public Roads, U. S. Dept. of Agric.

[3] *The Maine Highway Transportation Survey*, in *Public Roads*, Vol. 6, 1925, pp. 45–58; *The New Hampshire Traffic Survey* (1931), in the same, Vol. 13, 1932, pp. 131–136; The Bureau of Public Roads (U. S. Dept. of Agric.) and The Connecticut State Highway Department, *Report of a Survey of Transportation on the State Highway System of Connecticut*, 1926; similar reports for New Hampshire and Vermont, 1927; *A Survey of Motor Vehicle Traffic in Connecticut in 1931 by the Department of Motor Vehicles*, Hartford, 1932.

THE IMPORTANCE OF FOREIGN TRADE TO NEW ENGLAND

G. B. Roorbach

IN a discussion of New England's foreign trade, distinction must be made between the foreign trade *of* New England and the foreign trade *through* New England; between the actual amount of goods produced in New England for export and the amount of those products that are marketed and shipped through New England ports; between the amount of imported goods consumed in New England and the volume of United States imports that enter the country through New England. Measured by the amount of foreign cargo moving through New England ports, New England's foreign trade is of relatively small importance. Measured, however, by the amounts of New England-made goods that enter into foreign trade, by the consumption in New England of goods imported, and by the significance of these imports and exports to the present prosperity and future expansion of her productive industries, New England's foreign trade is of very great importance.

Exports From and Through New England

Export shipments through New England ports are not only relatively small as compared to those through the ports of other sections of the United States, but for a quarter of a century they have been declining in both value and volume, except for a temporary rise during the war years (Tables I and II). The once important foreign trade of the smaller New England ports—Salem, Portsmouth, New Bedford, Providence, and the others—practically has disappeared. Only Portland and Boston remain exporting ports of any consequence.[1] Boston's exports continued to increase as the smaller ports declined until they reached their banner year in 1901, with a value of $143,-708,000. Since then exports have declined until in 1930 Boston's exports were valued at only $33,633,000, or less than one quarter of the value of thirty years ago. Boston among the North Atlantic ports long had been second only to New York in value of exports, but in 1905 Baltimore took the leadership, and in 1908 Philadelphia forged ahead. In 1930 the value of exports through Boston was only one fortieth of the exports of New York City, about one third those of Philadelphia, and less than two thirds of Baltimore's.

In volume, even more than in value, the exports of New England ports have declined. In the case of Boston, the tonnage fell from nearly

---

[1] For notes see below, p. 389.

TABLE I—EXPORTS AND IMPORTS BY PRINCIPAL NORTH ATLANTIC
CUSTOMS DISTRICTS[a]

(Millions of Dollars)

YEAR OR FIVE-YEAR AVERAGE	BOSTON		NEW YORK		PHILADELPHIA		BALTIMORE	
	EXPORTS	IMPORTS	EXPORTS	IMPORTS	EXPORTS	IMPORTS	EXPORTS	IMPORTS
1860	13	39	80	231	6	15	9	10
1871–1875 .	25	59	258	383	25	23	22	28
1876–1880 .	48	46	322	331	46	24	50	19
1881–1885 .	65	65	358	454	39	33	51	14
1886–1890 .	62	63	322	467	33	44	52	13
1891–1895 .	84	69	361	503	43	58	75	15
1896–1900 .	111	69	434	477	56	43	99	12
1901–1905 .	102	80	511	597	74	54	89	22
1906–1910 .	88	113	639	798	89	74	92	30
1911–1915 .	77	141	913	975	74	86	107	30
1915–1920 .	217	273	2,913	1,703	415	145	320	42
1921–1925 .	56	257	1,611	1,676	118	183	114	78
1926	41	306	1,663	2,225	97	196	129	106
1927	42	288	1,726	2,043	91	204	101	109
1928	45	277	1,770	1,950	88	216	99	110
1929	41	290	1,903	2,153	124	244	84	117
1930	34	176	1,384	1,469	102	166	54	104

[a] From U. S. Dept. of Commerce, Bur. of Foreign and Domestic Commerce, *Statistical Abstract of the United States, 1931*, Washington, 1931, p. 517.

1,500,000 tons at the beginning of the century to 403,486 tons in 1928 and 263,461 tons in 1930—one thirty-fourth of the export tonnage of New York, about one fourth that of Baltimore, and one eighth that of Philadelphia (Table IV). Moreover, a large part—over one half— of the small tonnage exported through the port of Boston consisted, not of New England products, but of western products, chiefly grain, flour, and animal foods forwarded to Boston for shipment. Of Portland's exports of 80,000 tons in 1930, 71,000 tons were grain and meat products from central Canada and the interior of the United States. Local products, principally apples, wood manufactures, and scrap iron accounted for the remainder. The decline in both the value and volume of exports is to be explained in large measure by the decline in shipments of these western products through New England. Since New England itself has few bulk materials to contribute to its export trade, and since New England manufacturers, as later will be pointed out, use other than New England ports, a decline in export cargo forwarded from the West has meant a decline in the export tonnage of New England ports.

In addition to oversea exports, New England has a rapidly growing trade with Canada, the largest market for the United States. As

TABLE II—IMPORTS AND EXPORTS OF NEW ENGLAND BY
CUSTOMS DISTRICTS, 1914, 1928, AND 1930[a]
(Thousands of Dollars)

	EXPORTS			IMPORTS		
PORT	1914	1928	1930	1914	1928	1930
Massachusetts (Boston)[b] . .	71,969	45,470	33,633	162,820	276,512	176,199
Maine & New Hampshire (Portland)[b]	8,188	8,141	9,571	8,403	28,584	30,893
Rhode Island (Providence)[b] . .	2,717	108	97	2,161	4,896	7,886
Connecticut (Bridgeport)[b] . .	. . . . . .	. . . . . .	1	5,384	6,890	4,344
Total by Ports	82,874	53,719	43,302	178,768	316,882	219,322
OVERLAND						
Vermont (rail)	27,551	61,060	46,390	20,209	54,905	48,112
Total	110,425	114,779	89,692	198,977	371,787	267,434

[a] From: *Statistical Abstract of the United States, 1920*, pp. 426, 432, and *1931*, p. 520.

[b] The ports in parentheses are the chief ports in each district and account for a large share of the total in each case. The figures are for merchandise entered or cleared through the customhouse. The exports include all products without reference to their source of origin, i.e. New England products, products from the interior of the country, and reëxports. The figures do not include transshipment cargoes, that is, foreign goods shipped from New England ports that have not entered the United States for consumption but are shipped in bond through New England. In 1928 and 1930 transshipments through New England customs districts were valued as follows (U. S. Dept. of Commerce, Bur. of Foreign and Domestic Commerce, *Foreign Commerce and Navigation of the United States for the Calendar Year 1928*, Washington, 1929, p. 465; the same, *1930*, Washington, 1931, p. 500):

	1928	1930
Maine and New Hampshire	$5,372,000	$2,326,000
Massachusetts	11,671,000	5,891,000
Vermont	10,882,000	6,548,000

indicated in Table II, the exports through the Vermont customs district, mostly rail shipments to Canada, amounted to $46,000,000 in 1930, more than half the value of the total exports recorded for all New England. While oversea shipments in 1930 were much less than in 1914, shipments to Canada by rail were over 60 per cent greater in value than those of 1914. Taking into account the fact that some of the shipments through the port districts also were destined for Canada, it is apparent that Canada is the most important market for shipments from New England. Some of these shipments doubtless were for reshipment to oversea markets via Montreal. Imports across the land frontier are also of growing importance, accounting for 22 per cent of the total in 1930.

IMPORTS TO AND THROUGH NEW ENGLAND

In the import trade, New England's ports stand much higher than in export. Furthermore, imports have been increasing in both volume and value. In 1930 there were nineteen New England ports record-

TABLE III—DIRECT IMPORTS AND EXPORTS OF NEW ENGLAND PORTS
BY WATER IN SHORT TONS OF CARGO—1930[a]

PORT	FOREIGN		DOMESTIC	
	IMPORTS	EXPORTS	RECEIPTS	SHIPMENTS
NEW ENGLAND	5,559,464	347,753	24,534,522	3,720,762
Boston Harbor	2,915,152	263,461	10,374,812	1,226,499
Bar Harbor, Me.	....	....	27,579	935
Searsport, Me.	34,175	....	496,285	4,800
Rockland, Me.	7,865	....	118,518	76,790
Boothbay, Me.	....	....	12,140	1,608
Portland, Me.	819,989	80,230	2,189,806	190,096
Belfast, Me.	....	....	18,000	18,992
Camden, Me.	....	....	14,392	1,688
Thomaston Harbor, Me.	....	....	3,910	95
York Harbor, Me.	....	....	1,079	....
Portsmouth, N. H.	52,237	....	240,140	190
Burlington, Vt.	375	....	....	....
Newburyport, Mass.	....	....	47,858	....
Provincetown, Mass.	....	....	300	50
Gloucester, Mass.	7,013	12	57,846	....
Beverly, Mass.	55,539	1,433	535,183	64,971
Salem, Mass.	21,178	....	471,310	....
Lynn, Mass.	2,451	....	349,971	....
Plymouth, Mass.	1,622	....	28,269	....
Scituate, Mass.	277	....	7	....
Nantucket, Mass.	....	....	51,472	9,660
New Bedford and Fair Haven, Mass.	36	220	704,984	90,927
Fall River, Mass.	820,200	2,023	739,298	695,404
Duxbury, Mass.	....	....	838	....
Rockport, Mass.	....	....	1,000	17,137
Manchester, Mass.	....	....	7,590	....
Edgartown, Mass.	....	....	6,362	1,374
Wickford Harbor, R. I.	....	....	4,081	2,829
Bristol, R. I.	....	....	11,475	712
Tiverton, R. I.	....	....	109,994	16,373
Newport, R. I.	1	187	110,822	7,265
Providence, R. I.	770,651	176	3,555,651	601,553
Great Salt Pond, R. I.	....	....	4,459	1,882
Block Island, R. I. (Harb. of Refuge)	....	....	5,091	1,242
New London, Conn.	18,900	....	513,032	109,745
Branford, Conn.	....	....	11,011	....
New Haven, Conn.	12,428	11	2,059,985	405,512
Milford, Conn.	....	....	3,404	2,500
Bridgeport, Conn.	19,375	....	980,251	125,907
Norwalk, Conn.	....	....	119,822	7,712
Fivemile River Harbor, Conn.	....	....	189	27
Stamford, Conn.	....	....	391,552	34,048
Greenwich, Conn.	....	....	135,611	1,865
Stonington, Conn.	....	....	5,115	352
Westport (Saugatuck River), Conn.	....	....	10,258	....
Cos Cob Harbor, Conn.	....	....	3,770	22

[a] From: *Report of the Chief of Engineers, U. S. Army, 1931; Part 2, Commercial Statistics,* Washington, 1931, pp. 6–7.

TABLE IV—IMPORTS AND EXPORTS OF THE PORT OF BOSTON[a]
(Expressed in Short Tons)

YEAR	IMPORTS	EXPORTS	TOTAL
1905	974,712	1,294,815	2,269,527
1906	1,229,623	1,365,786	2,595,409
1907	1,107,764	1,337,019	2,444,783
1908	979,976	1,064,445	2,044,421
1909	1,165,349	823,519	1,988,868
1910	1,256,892	765,500	2,022,392
1911	816,186	774,088	1,590,274
1912	1,330,871	659,117	1,989,988
1913	1,264,642	1,100,390	2,365,032
1914	1,352,542	726,957	2,079,499
1915	535,180	638,118	1,173,298
1916	409,180	1,013,674	1,422,854
1917	305,159	693,942	999,101
1918	407,476	458,166	865,642
1919	1,465,251	1,366,708	2,831,959
1920	1,675,092	573,489	2,248,581
1921	2,149,392	512,967	2,662,359
1922	4,608,732	588,449	5,197,181
1923	3,031,479	481,961	3,513,440
1924	2,355,094	339,215	2,694,309
1925	2,586,065	338,779	2,924,844
1926	2,904,579	314,990	3,219,569
1927	2,662,184	292,452	2,954,636
1928	2,964,876	403,486	3,368,362
1929	3,261,301	303,120	3,564,421
1930	2,915,152	263,461	3,178,613

[a] These tonnage figures are furnished by the Maritime Association of the Boston Chamber of Commerce. They are based on the data of actual cargo exported and imported as determined by the Board of Engineers for Rivers and Harbors of the U. S. Army. See publication cited in note to Table III and earlier numbers; also current issues of *Report on Volume of Water Borne Foreign Commerce of the United States*, U. S. Shipping Board, Bureau of Research.

ing imports, as against only nine with any export shipments (Table III). The value of imports recorded as entered through all New England ports in 1930 was $219,000,000, or five times the value of exports, while the volume was approximately 5,559,000 tons, or sixteen times the export tonnage (Tables II and III). Boston continues to maintain its position as second only to New York in the import trade of the United States. Nevertheless, Boston's imports are only about one eighth those of New York. While New York, which now receives nearly 50 per cent of all, the vastly increased imports of the United States, is being strengthened in its position as the dominating import port of the United States, Boston's relative position is declining. In 1914 Boston imported 8.5 per cent of United States total imports; in 1925, 7.6 per cent; in 1928, 6.8 per cent, and in 1930, 5.8 per cent.

The large volume of imports into New England is explained principally by the demands of New England's manufacturing industry. Coal and petroleum for power and fuel; wool, jute, cotton, hemp, sisal, and silk among the textile raw materials; timber, pulpwood and cabinet woods; hides, skins, and rubber; iron, steel, and metal products; cement, gypsum, chalk, abrasives, nitrates, and chemical raw materials and supplies; sugar, molasses, fruits and nuts, coffee, tea, spices, and cocoa—such are the raw materials and foods brought in for industrial New England. Relatively few of these imports are for reshipment inland. Only in the case of hides and skins and wool and certain other minor products does Boston figure largely as a distributor of imported materials beyond the borders of New England, either within the United States or to foreign countries. That Boston continues to be the national market for these products is largely because their principal market is in New England and they are goods of high value and small bulk in which transportation charges for redistribution are relatively unimportant. Boston remains the largest wool market in the United States partly as a result of the early development and continued maintenance of a highly technical and specialized commodity market in response to New England's wool manufacturing industry and partly because wool can absorb the transportation costs of reshipment to other wool-consuming markets. For the same reasons, hides and skins are imported into Boston for distribution by rail to tanneries as far away as West Virginia, Kentucky, and Wisconsin.

Other than Boston, there were in 1930 eighteen New England ports with records of foreign imports, most of them, however, of small volume (Table III). The foreign commodities imported into these ports were almost exclusively bulky fuels and raw materials to supply the local industries—goods that came in large part in single cargo or tramp shipments and much of them, like lumber, pulpwood, and wood pulp, on coastal vessels from near-by maritime Canada. Of Fall River's imports of 820,000 tons in 1930, for example, nearly the entire amount was gasoline and fuel and gas oils, coming, of course, in tankers and not in cargo steamers. Very little in the way of general import cargo or cargo of high value enters the smaller ports. Such goods are imported through the large market centers, Boston or New York; and even among Boston's imports only a small amount, relatively, of high-class general cargo is found. The facility by which the many ports of New England can obtain bulky cargo by steamship, however, is an important advantage to its industries, most of which are located at or near the coast.

In domestic coastwise trade, New England ports are very much more important than in direct foreign trade (Table III). This coastwise shipping, however, also serves efficiently New England's foreign as well as its domestic trade, in that it provides cheap and, for most of industrial New England, overnight access to the great port of New York to which coastwise vessels carry New England products for ultimate export and from which imported goods are distributed to New England.

THE PORT OF NEW YORK AND NEW ENGLAND'S FOREIGN TRADE

That the relatively small amounts of exported and imported merchandise moving through New England customs districts are not a measure of the importance of foreign trade to New England is a matter of common knowledge to those familiar with the recent development of the region's commerce. It is well known that many New England producers export through New York and import through the same port; that New England manufacturers are among the leaders in export trade; and that a large number of them maintain their export departments in New York. Statistical measure of the actual importance of that trade, however, has been impossible since the government figures of exports and imports do not show the sources of origin of exports, nor the destinations of imports.

A recent survey of New England's foreign trade,[2] however, gives some basis for estimating the value of foreign trade to its manufacturers, although it does not give the facts for all exports. In answer to a questionnaire, believed to have covered practically all the manufactures of New England, more than 2000 firms reported an aggregate of $196,000,000 as the value of their exports for 1928. The significance of this large total is more fully understood when it is compared with the $114,000,000 recorded in the official statistics as the exports through all New England customs districts in 1928. The latter included not only local New England industrial products but also raw materials and foodstuffs, as well as manufactured goods and products produced outside of New England but shipped through New England. Doubtless the $196,000,000 reported understates the total of the exports of New England manufactured goods, since many New England products are sent to other sections of the United States for assembly or remanufacture and are exported as constituent parts of other goods; and doubtless for this reason the questionnaire failed to get a complete return. The survey shows, however, that the exports alone of manufactured goods made in New England are much larger than the exports of all kinds recorded as going through New England ports.

The survey also attempted to obtain the facts as to the port of exit of the manufactured exports. In spite of the limitations of making such estimates on the part of many of the firms who replied, the replies are, nevertheless, extremely significant as indicating the extent to which the port of New York serves New England's manufacturers. They show that 65 per cent of the total of the exports

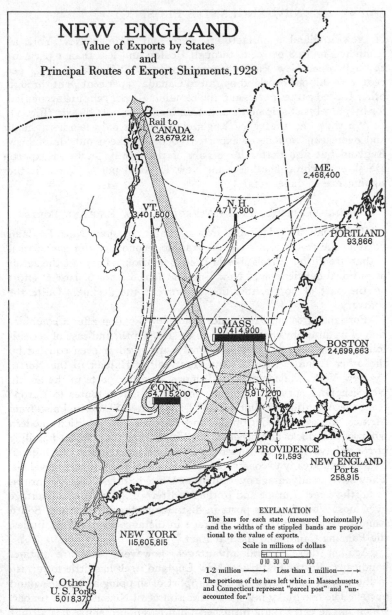

NEW ENGLAND

Value of Exports by States
and
Principal Routes of Export Shipments, 1928

Rail to
CANADA
23,679,212

ME.
2,468,400

VT.
3,401,500

N.H.
4,717,800

PORTLAND
93,866

MASS.
107,414,900

BOSTON
24,699,663

CONN.
54,715,200

R.I.
5,917,200

PROVIDENCE
121,593

Other
NEW ENGLAND
Ports
258,915

EXPLANATION

The bars for each state (measured horizontally)
and the widths of the stippled bands are proportional to the value of exports.

Scale in millions of dollars

0 10 30 50   100

1-2 million ⟶   Less than 1 million ⟶

The portions of the bars left white in Massachusetts
and Connecticut represent "parcel post" and "unaccounted for."

NEW YORK
115,605,815

Other
U. S. Ports
5,018,370

FIG. 1—Routes of exports of manufactures, 1928. The bar for each state shows the value of export
shipments, the white ends of the bars for Connecticut and Massachusetts representing shipments by
parcel post and "unaccounted for." The stippled bands, black lines, and broken lines indicate dia-
grammatically the routes of export shipments. In the case of the bands and solid lines the widths
show values; the broken lines represent values of less than $1,000,000. Based on Artman and Reed,
Foreign Trade Survey of New England, 1931, Table 18, pp. 35–36.

of New England manufacturers were sent through New York as compared to 13.8 per cent through Boston and less than 1 per cent through other New England ports (principally Portland); 13.2 per cent were shipped overland by rail to Canada; 3 per cent went through other United States ports, and the remaining 4 per cent are accounted for by parcel post shipments undetermined as to port of exit (Fig. 1).

We thus find that New England ports not only handle a small and decreasing volume of exported goods produced outside of New England but also that a large part of the locally produced exports are shipped through other than New England ports. What is the significance of these facts?

Foreign Trade Shipments· through New England Ports

The small and declining export traffic through New England ports is the result of forces—geographic, economic, and commercial —that are all but irresistible in their operation. It is not the result of physical deficiencies of New England harbors nor of lack of effort on the part of port authorities to prevent the decline. Quite the contrary.

Portland, Boston, Providence, and New London offer a combination of natural physical facilities as to size, depth, and ease of accessibility to the open sea that are hardly surpassed or even equaled by the other Atlantic harbors—by Montreal or Halifax to the North, by New York, Philadelphia, Baltimore, or other ports to the South. New England ports also lie near the Great Circle routes to Europe from the Atlantic and Gulf coasts of the United States and also from Mexico, the western Caribbean, and Panama. In addition, modern wharves and docks and other improvements for the efficient handling of cargo have been constructed at these ports, and states and municipalities stand ready to construct further facilities as the need develops. They have an advantage over all other United States ports in nearness to northwestern Europe and to the Mediterranean, a slight advantage over most United States ports in distance to the east coast of South America, and but little disadvantage in distance to the West Indies, the Panama Canal, and the Far East.

Against these natural advantages, however, there are distinct handicaps. In the first place, New England itself has little to furnish in the way of bulk cargo for the support of shipping at New England ports. The one bulky raw material resource of New England, timber, which in the early trade furnished both cargo and ships, has all but disappeared. To secure bulk export cargo, therefore, New England must rely on serving the export needs of the interior of the continent —on export grain and flour or some other product that can be attracted to New England for shipment.

This suggests the second great handicap to obtaining shipments via New England ports as compared with the rival ports of the North Atlantic. New England ports are distant from the most rapidly growing centers of production and population. Situation in a far-removed corner of the country is a handicap not only in respect to inland transport cost but also and chiefly in respect to marketing New England products. New England cities are not well situated to develop as marketing centers either for domestic or for foreign trade. The disadvantage of location, moreover, is accentuated by the poor natural connections of New England's ports to the richest productive areas of the continent. No Hudson-Mohawk lowland forms a natural highway from Boston or Portland or New London to the Great Lakes and the Mississippi Valley such as gives New York sea-level connections with the interior by highway, canal, and railroad. Boston does not, like New York and Philadelphia, hold a position at the narrow northern end of the Atlantic Coastal Plain, toward which are focused the railroads connecting with the rich agricultural and industrial regions of the Coastal Plain, the Piedmont, and the great Appalachian Valley. The handicap of the mountain barrier lying back of New England and impeding transportation to the interior is not relieved, as in the case of the Appalachian highlands back of Philadelphia and Baltimore, by the presence of rich natural resources. The deposits of coal and iron and other resources in the Appalachian uplands not only furnish power and bulk commodities for the railroads and steamships but are the foundations of industries that pour into the near-by ports bulky manufactures such as iron and steel, cement, and other products offering the volume cargo attractive to shipping. New York, Philadelphia, and Baltimore are favored as ports because of central situation on the seaboard and the availability of an abundance of bulk cargo both in the local hinterlands and the remoter interior of the country. New England ports are largely confined to a local hinterland productive of few bulky resources for export.

A third factor militating against the development of exports from the continental interior via New England ports is a political one—the United States-Canadian boundary line. Portland and Boston are well situated naturally to obtain a part of Canadian export grain and other bulk cargo especially during the winter months when the St. Lawrence is closed to navigation by ice. In the past, Portland's cargo export has depended largely upon its railroad connection with the Canadian National Railways over the Grand Trunk Railway. The development of this export outlet, however, is now being restricted by Canadian aspirations that seek to keep the trade outlets of the Dominion within Canadian territory—a situation that is further encouraged by American tariff policies in reference to our northern neighbor. Hence the rise in recent years of Halifax and St. John as winter ports serving Canada at the expense of Portland and Boston. It is conceivable, though not likely, that if the St. Lawrence ship canal were constructed there might be diverted so large a grain shipment to Montreal and other St. Lawrence ports that in winter greater shipments would come through Portland and Boston as an overflow from the all-Canadian route. On the import side, the restrictions being placed by Canada on trade through United States ports diverts import trade that formerly flowed through New England directly to Canada. For example, Canadian tariff preferences on goods imported directly into Canada through Canadian ports have compelled the United Fruit Company to establish direct shipment of bananas from Central America to St. John, thus diverting shipments that formerly came through Boston or New York for distribution by rail and coastwise ships to Canada.

FREIGHT RATES AND NEW ENGLAND'S FOREIGN TRADE

The adjustments of railroad rates on export and import commodities have partly lessened, partly augmented, some of the disadvantages of New England ports just mentioned. As far as shipments from and to Central Freight Association territory is concerned—that is the territory of the "Middle West"—domestic railroad freight rates to Boston or Portland are from 1 to 2 cents a hundred pounds higher than to New York. For export freight, however, most commodity and lower class rates to New England ports have been fixed by the Interstate Commerce Commission on an equality with those to New York; while to Philadelphia, export rates, for the most part, are two cents a hundred pounds less and to Baltimore three cents less. On export grain the all-rail differentials are less, and for combined lake and rail hauls on flour from Buffalo, Boston is now on an equality with all the North Atlantic ports. Montreal also has a favorable differential of two cents over New England ports for class rates.[3]

On the other hand, steamship rates to the United Kingdom and the Continent, once favorable to Boston, have been made the same from all North Atlantic ports so that on through rail and ocean shipments from the interior of the country Boston has higher rates than Philadelphia, Baltimore, and Montreal and equal rates with New York. Equalization of rates with New York, however, is not sufficient to induce cargo in large amounts to move by way of New England ports in competition with New York, and the lower rates via other ports are, of course, a direct handicap to securing bulk cargo from the interior for New England ports. In addition, bulk cargo, especially grain, reaches New York from the Great Lakes by way of the New

York State Barge Canal at rates much lower than railroad rates, and this traffic is increasing with the improvements in canal services. A still further handicap is created by the large number of ships, both cargo and passenger, sailing from New York and bidding for ballast cargo, especially for grain cargoes which are ideal for ballast; hence more favorable steamship rates, as well as more frequent sailings, are usually available at that port. The advantages of time in rail shipments from many parts of the country to New York, of lower rates by canal, of the certainty of obtaining frequent sailings on the fastest boats at the most favorable rates—all these combined with the marketing and financing advantages at New York and the rate advantages held by Philadelphia, Baltimore, and Montreal conspire to keep western bulk freight from moving in larger quantities to Boston. For higher class freight from the West, the disadvantages for Boston are even more insurmountable, since both time and frequency of services are more important for high cost merchandise.

Furthermore, the railway trunk lines, largely because of the location and importance of New York and partly because of the barrier that has been offered by the lower Hudson River to trunk line railway construction to points farther east, have established their eastern terminals on New York harbor. New England's railroads were constructed to serve local New England primarily. They do not penetrate the interior of the United States; in only one instance do they cross the Hudson. The result has been that the trunk lines— the New York Central, the Pennsylvania, the Baltimore and Ohio, the Erie, the Lackawanna—have been more concerned with developing freight to their own terminals in New York or Philadelphia or Baltimore than in effecting connections for shipments through to New England railway and port terminals. The acquisition of the Boston & Albany by the New York Central and the through freight arrangements of the Boston & Maine with the New York Central lines do not greatly affect this situation. Since export rates to Boston are the same as to New York, no direct gain to the railroads accrues through the encouragement of routing via New England. Even the New York Central's interest in attracting traffic on its own New England line, the Boston & Albany, to relieve congestion at its New York terminals, is not sufficient to overcome the factors pulling to New York harbor cargo for export shipment and import cargo for distribution in the United States and Canada.

The acquisition of the New York, Ontario & Western Railway by the New York, New Haven & Hartford Railroad, together with the completion of an enlarged Welland Canal capable of taking the largest lake steamers, has been hailed as a possible means of helping to solve New England's bulk export cargo problem. The New Haven,

connecting with the Ontario & Western at Saybrook via the Poughkeepsie Bridge, gives New England a direct transportation route to
Oswego on Lake Ontario. Here, it is hoped by New England port
interests, will develop a grain transit trade between the grain boats
from the upper lakes and the railway. Railroad rates to Providence
and Boston on ex-lake grain from Oswego give the New England
ports an advantage in grain rates over Philadelphia and Baltimore
sufficient, it is hoped, to attract at least a certain part of the trade,
although New York shares equally this advantage with New England
ports.[4] The realization of these hopes depends upon many unpre-
dictable factors—among them the maintenance of present rail rate
structures, the development of Oswego as a grain transit point in
competition with Buffalo and Montreal, the competition of the New
York State Barge Canal which also has a terminus at Oswego, and the
possible development of the port of Albany.

A further possible means of increasing traffic through New England
ports is by the development of fast express, mail, and passenger
services to and from Europe by way of New England. The advantage
of Boston over New York in distance to Europe combined with the
ease of access of this port to the open sea, and the freedom of the port
from congestion of traffic, would make possible a saving in time of
about a day for the North Atlantic crossing if fast passenger and
mail trains from New York, Chicago, Montreal, and other interior
cities were made to connect with fast steamships at Boston. Like
Portsmouth or Southampton in England or Cherbourg in France,
Boston's position seaward invites such traffic. The same advantages
that in 1837 made Boston the first American terminus of steamship
lines across the Atlantic may conceivably again give the port greater
importance for fast passenger and express services. This might also
stimulate the routing of grain for ballast cargo to New England
ports. While a further development of fast passenger steamship
services through Boston is well within the range of accomplishment,
it can hardly be expected that this will greatly affect the importance
of New York as the great terminal port of the Atlantic seaboard. It
would, however, give added service to New England exporters and
stimulate the development of the port of Boston.

ADVANTAGES OF NEW YORK AS A PORT OF EXPORT FOR NEW ENGLAND PRODUCTS

All of the above possibilities, however, even if accomplished,
would not alter New England's fundamental handicaps. New England
cannot expect to develop export cargo shipments sufficient in variety
and volume to give its ports the shipping and marketing services
needed for the exporting of its own characteristic commodities.

And here lies the reason why 65 per cent of New England's most important exports, its manufactured products, flow through the port of New York, and less than 14 per cent through Boston (Fig. 1).

New England products are in large measure quality manufactured goods and specialities of high value.[5] Such commodities inevitably seek the large marketing and distributing center where merchandising, warehousing, and banking facilities combine to favor their marketing and where frequent and rapid transportation services assure quick, frequent, and certain deliveries. This is a principle of trade the world around—concentration of marketing and shipping in favored centers. Such services New York can furnish in abundance. To New York come in a steady stream the ships of the world bringing cargo and sure to find cargo, both bulk and high-class merchandise. Buyers and sellers, ship operators and forwarders, bankers and brokers—all the agencies of foreign commerce from all countries are here centered to facilitate trade, making New York the greatest foreign trade mart of the world. To such a market and shipping center the quality manufactured goods characteristic of New England are attracted as steel to a magnet.

Furthermore, this great merchandising and shipping center lies at the very door of New England. The industrial regions of Connecticut and western Massachusetts especially are within the immediate zone of influence of New York; but Rhode Island, central and eastern Massachusetts, and even Vermont, New Hampshire, and Maine are not distant. In terms of transport, practically all industrial New England is overnight from New York by rail, coastwise steamship, or motor truck. Loaded tonight on trucks in Boston, goods for export are delivered tomorrow morning on the docks in New York. Shipments from a factory in the New York zone itself can hardly do better. For New Hampshire no less than 78 per cent of manufactured exports are reported as going by way of New York; in the case of Massachusetts 57 per cent of manufactured exports used New York as compared to 21 per cent which went through the port of Boston.[6] Because of its nearness to New England's industrial centers and the marketing and shipping advantages it offers for the high-grade exports of New England, New York commercially is a New England port. Its nearness is one of the great assets to industrial New England. New England exporters have their own ports and, in addition, the port of New York.

New England's Manufactures in Relation to Foreign Trade

The importance of foreign trade to New England, then, is not to be measured by the trade that passes through New England's ports. Rather, its value rests on its relation to New England's chief source of wealth, its manufacturing industries.

Historically, it was foreign trade that laid the foundation of New England's manufacturing during those early years of the republic when shipping and the carrying trade were the dominant economic activities of New Englanders. Later, when the industrial revolution had set in, especially at the end of the first quarter of the nineteenth century, it was the abundant capital produced by trade and shipping that made it possible for modern factories to spring up like magic beside New England's waterfalls and at the old New England ports. The men who before 1830–1850 had become rich and powerful through oversea trade became the leaders in establishing the cotton and woolen mills, the hardware, cutlery, and jewelry factories, the machine shops and metal-working industries, and the other industries that have made New England famous throughout the world. Even foreigners with whom New England traders carried on their business contributed to the foundation of new industries. Houqua, the wealthiest and most influential of the old hong merchants in Canton, sent the Massachusetts trader, J. Murray Forbes, a half million dollars to invest in cotton mills. Chinese capital helped start New England water wheels.[7]

The old foreign trading merchants and sea captains not only furnished capital; they gave the daring, the vision, the initiative necessary for new and untried enterprises. They were accustomed to adventure and willing to take risks. They were shrewd in business, able to manage men, energetic to the last degree. These qualities were important elements in laying the foundations of industrial New England. Francis Lowell is typical of these early leaders. Having "in youth acquired a fortune by foreign commerce under conditions that required unusual business foresight and intrepidity," he became the "leader of a group of Boston capitalists of similar temperament and experience . . . who from 1815 to 1850 controlled the manufacturing development of New England and less directly by their example guided that of the whole country."[8] The industrialization of New England has always been closely tied to foreign trade.

The industrial structure in present-day New England, growing out of and supplanting the shipping and trading activities of the earlier years, is dependent upon and conditioned by foreign trade as in no other industrial area in the United States. No longer the center of New England economic life, foreign trade nevertheless is one of the fundamental supports of manufacturing, and its importance to industry appears to be increasing.

In the first place, industrial New England is largely dependent, as has been seen, on outside materials. This is so partly because

New England's local resources are limited; partly because so many of the most characteristic industries of New England, originally founded on imports, still depend on foreign materials; partly because any highly organized industrial region, such as New England, must increasingly draw on a widening circle of imports to meet the complex and exacting needs of modern manufacturing. Not just "cotton" is needed by the textile mill, but cotton of the exact quality, be it from Egypt, or China, or Peru, or Georgia; not any hide or skin will meet the requirements of the modern tannery, but Brazil, India, and Central Europe must add their contribution to domestic products. Importing is thus acquiring a wholly new industrial significance. With its industries already organized to so large a degree on imported raw materials, New England because of her location enjoys for many types of industry advantages inferior to those of no other industrial district in the United States. Her maritime position and many excellent harbors allow direct importation of bulk materials often to the very doors of the factory. The great import market at New York in addition serves New England as fully as if that port were geographically within her territory. Nearness by rail and coastwise steamships give New England unsurpassed connections to the raw material resources of eastern Canada. More than 1100 New England manufacturers reported, in the Department of Commerce survey already referred to, a consumption in 1928 of imported products to the value of $218,000,-000, a sum greater than the value of New England manufactured exports.

Furthermore, for the many industries characteristic of New England that depend in whole or in large part on imported products, her location is on the whole of no disadvantage even when the distribution of the finished products is within the United States; and it is of decided advantage if they are for export. Imported raw materials, even when destined for ultimate consumption in the interior of the country, stop at New England factories to be converted into finished products for reshipment inland. Hides and skins go forward as shoes, wool as cloth; wood pulp and rags as paper; Swedish steel as safety-razor blades; cocoa beans and sugar as confectionery; sisal and hemp as binder twine. In raw material costs, the New England manufacturer has an advantage over the interior manufacturer at least equal to the cost of rail shipment inland; his finished products of high value may readily absorb the shipment costs. In distributing his products by coast steamship to the Atlantic, Gulf, and Pacific coast markets and in the export trade the New England manufacturer is distinctly in a more favorable position than the interior manufacturer and, on the whole, at no disadvantage as compared with his competitors in other eastern seaboard states.

Even in the case of many industries in which the raw materials come from the interior to supplement, or to be supplemented by, imported materials, the superiority of New England's location in relation to imports and ultimate reëxports may be sufficient to neutralize the handicap of transport costs from the interior. For the characteristic New England industry the raw material itself is often of low bulk and high value, in which transport cost is of relatively small importance. This is true, for example, in the case of refined silver, or copper, or aluminum; of wool and, to less degree, of hides and skins. Many of the domestic raw materials, such as raw cotton, naval stores, and lumber, can be assembled by coastwise transport at no disadvantage, and in some cases at an advantage, to New England as compared with interior or other Atlantic coast industrial regions; or even to some of the cotton mill localities in the South.

Still another though perhaps an intangible benefit enjoyed by New England manufacturing industry is the greater independence in respect to raw materials and fuel supplies that results from her maritime position. The New England manufacturer because of foreign trade facilities is less dependent on single sources of supply than the manufacturer in the interior. He has the choice of the markets of the world. He can readily take advantage of favorable opportunities for securing supplies abroad and thus minimize the handicaps of domestic shortages or high domestic prices. If a coal strike in the domestic fields shuts off his supplies, he can find quick relief by importing coal from Wales or Nova Scotia. In fact, the possibility of importing coal acts constantly as an influence to stabilize coal prices at New England ports. The New England manufacturer readily can choose between Pittsburgh or Belgium or India in the purchase of pig iron or iron bars; between Lehigh Valley or Belgium for cement; between Chicago or Buenos Aires for hides; between Puget Sound or Newfoundland or the Baltic for timber; between southern California or the Mediterranean for fruits and nuts.

While importing advantages are fundamental to New England's industrial life, exporting has been perhaps of even greater significance as an aid to industrial expansion. As in purchasing, so in selling, the whole world lies at the door of New England manufacturers. The export trade of the United States as a whole has expanded most rapidly in manufactured goods. In 1890, only 21 per cent of United States exports were manufactured exports; in 1910, it was 45 per cent; in 1920, 48 per cent; in 1930, 64 per cent. Furthermore, the most important commodities among these growing exports of manufactures, and the ones most rapidly growing, are those described as specialties— goods reflecting the peculiar genius of American manufacturers, such as labor-saving machinery, automobiles, office equipment, electric household appliances, rubber goods, paper products, clocks and watches, tools, and the thousand-and-one products that characterize the widely diversified New England industries. As the most intensely developed industrial region of the United States, the widening of foreign markets means more to New England than to any other section of the country.

That New England manufacturers have taken advantage of these conditions is indicated by the large place that New England occupies in the export of American manufactured goods. According to the Foreign Trade Survey of New England[9], in 1928 50 per cent of the hardware, cutlery, and mechanics' tools exported from the United States were made in New England; 43 per cent of textile machinery; 6 per cent of electrical machinery; 23 per cent of office appliances; 33 per cent of firearms and ammunition; 66 per cent of jewelry; 29 per cent of clocks and watches; 36 per cent of leather; 69 per cent of leather footwear; 24 per cent of other leather manufactures; 19 per cent of rubber manufactures; 17 per cent of paper manufactures; 17 per cent of industrial chemical specialties; 14 per cent of soap and toilet preparations; 17 per cent of silk manufactures. In addition there were large, but not determinable, percentages of the exports of cotton goods and other textile products, industrial machinery, and metal manufactures of many kinds.

These facts reveal the relation between foreign trade and industrial progress in New England. Today, and apparently for the future, her economic prosperity rests primarily upon manufacturing; manufacturing, however, that is being carefully adjusted to conditions peculiar to New England. More and more her industrial development appears to depend on the industries in which skill, experience, and managerial ability are combined in the production of high-grade staples and specialties—goods of high value relative to bulk, fabricated from raw materials of superior qualities, and in the production and marketing of which New England has undoubted advantages. In relation to these manufactures, foreign trade—importing as well as exporting—has been in the past, and is today, of vital importance.

NOTES

[1] Reliable figures for the volume of exports and imports by ports are not available for the pre-war years. In 1930, aside from Boston and Portland, only seven ports show exports—Gloucester, Beverly, Fall River, New Bedford, Newport, Providence, and New Haven—and the amounts from these ports are nominal only. See Table III.

[For details concerning the principal ports of New England consult the following numbers of the *Port Series*, published by the Corps of Engineers (U. S. Army) and the United States Shipping Board: No. 1 (revised 1927), *The Port of Portland, Maine*, Washington, 1928; No. 2 (revised, 1929) *The Port of Boston, Massachusetts*, Washington, 1930; No. 18, *The Ports of Southern New England*, Washington, 1928 (deals with Providence, Newport, New Bedford, Fall River, New Haven, New London, Bridgeport, Norwalk, and Stamford). See also No. 20, *The Port of New York*, 3 parts, Washington, 1926. These publications cover port and harbor conditions; port customs, regulations, services, and charges; fuel, supplies, facilities, communications, freight rates, commerce, and territory tributary to each port.—EDIT.]

[2] C. E. Artman and S. H. Reed, *Foreign Trade Survey of New England*, Bur. of Foreign and Domestic Commerce, Washington, 1931 (*Domestic Commerce Ser. No. 40*).

[3] *Export Differentials.* The following table shows the export freight differentials between Atlantic coast ports and Central Freight Association territory. The figures indicate, in cents per 100 lbs., how much less the export rates are from C.F.A. territory to the ports indicated compared with Standard all-rail export rates to New York. For example, the rate to Baltimore on export grain, all rail, is 1½ cents less than to New York or Boston. A dash indicates no rates quoted. This table and the table below showing import differentials were prepared by the writer from all available data, including information secured from individual transportation experts in New England.

To:	ROUTE	CLASS AND COMMODITY RATES VIA STANDARD ALL-RAIL ROUTES	EXPORT GRAIN, ALL-RAIL	EXPORT FLOUR, ALL-RAIL	EX-LAKE GRAIN FROM BUFFALO	EX-LAKE FLOUR FROM BUFFALO	EX-LAKE GRAIN FROM OSWEGO
Boston . . .	Standard all-rail	0	0	0	0	0	0
Providence .	"	0	0	0	0	0	0
Portland . .	"	0	0	0	0	0	–
Portland . .	Canadian all-rail differential	0	0	0	–	–	–
Montreal . .	"	–2	–1	–	–	–	–
Philadelphia	"	–2	–1	–1	–½	0	a
Baltimore . .	"	–3	–1½	–2	–½	0	a
New London	Central Vermont-Canadian National	0	0[b]	0	–	–	
Albany . . .					–½		

a Rates from Oswego to New York, Boston, and Providence are 1½ cents less than the ex-lake rates from Buffalo. Since no rates apply from Oswego to Philadelphia and Baltimore, a net advantage of 1 cent is enjoyed by both New York and Boston over Philadelphia and Baltimore on ex-lake grain via Oswego.

b Applies only on grain in sacks

Import Differentials. The import freight differentials to Central Freight Association territory are given in the following table. The figures are in cents per 100 pounds as compared to rates from New York via Standard all-rail routes.

FROM:	ROUTE	CLASS 1	CLASS 2	CLASS 3	CLASS 4	CLASS 5	CLASS 6	COMMODITY
Boston . . .	Standard all-rail	0	0	0	0	0	0	0
Boston . . .	Standard lake-rail	0	0	0	0	0	0	0
Boston . . .	Canadian all-rail differential	−5	−4	−3	−3	−2	−1	0
Providence .	Standard all-rail	0	0	0	0	0	0	0
Portland . .	Standard all-rail	0	0	0	0	0	0	
Portland . .	Canadian rail differential	−8	−8	−3	−3	−3	−3	−3
·Montreal . .	Standard all-rail	−8	−8	−3	−3	−3	−3	−3
Philadelphia .	Standard all-rail	−6	−6	−2	−2	−2	−2	−2
Baltimore . .	Standard all-rail	−8	−8	−3	−3	−3	−3	−3
New York . .	Via New London and C.V.R.R.-Canadian National	−8	−6	−5	−4	−4	−3	−3

[4] The fact that the railroads serving New York absorb lighterage charges for delivery of freight to all parts of the harbor has been said by some Boston port interests to give New York an undue and unfair advantage over Boston, where no such free lighterage services are given and where railroad switching charges from one part of the port to another are high. However, New England manufacturers shipping to New York are among the important beneficiaries of the advantages free lighterage gives to shippers using the port of New York.

[5] "The total value of exports reported by the 2,055 New England manufacturing concerns which gave figures of their 1928 foreign sales was $196,229,000.

"In the official classification of exports from the United States, manufactured goods are grouped in 11 major classes according to the principal material entering into their manufacture. . . .

"Among these 11 major classes, machinery and vehicles are found to be the most important [exports from New England], with reported values exceeding $48,-000,000, representing approximately 25 per cent of all reported exports. This is followed very closely by the general class of metal manufactures. These two major classes comprise nearly one-half (48 per cent) of the total. Leather and leather products, with a value of $29,230,000, represent about 15 per cent. Textile products, valued at $24,145,000, comprised 12.3 per cent of the reported value of exports.

"The next six classes, which include manufactures of rubber, wood and paper, chemicals, meat and fish, stone and other nonmetallic minerals, and confectionery and preserved fruits, had an aggregate value of $33,748,000, comprising 17.4 per cent of the total. Together they exceeded somewhat the value of the leather group. Reported exports in the class of stone and mineral products and of confectionery and food products are relatively small, together comprising less than 1 per cent of the total value. The class of miscellaneous products not included in any of the foregoing makes up a total of about $14,200,000 and represents 7.2 per cent of the total reported." Artman and Reed, *Foreign Trade Survey of New England*, pp. 7–8.

[6] By states the shipments of New England manufactured goods as reported in the *Foreign Trade Survey of New England*, pp. 35–36, were as follows, by percentages.

	THROUGH NEW YORK	THROUGH BOSTON	THROUGH OTHER U. S. PORTS
Connecticut	78.7%	.91%	.88%
New Hampshire	78.3%	7.10%	4.90%
Vermont	72.7%	12.20%	1.40%
Massachusetts	56.7%	21.56%	3.93%
Rhode Island	67.2%	.60%	.40%
Maine	59.5%	10.50%	.10%

[7] S. E. Morison, *The Maritime History of Massachusetts, 1783–1860*, Boston, 1921, p. 274.

[8] V. S. Clark, *History of Manufactures in the United States*, New York, 1929, Vol. 1, p. 451.

[9] Artman and Reed, *op. cit.*, pp. 10–11.

THE TRADING AREAS OF NEW ENGLAND

E. F. Gerish

THE areal pattern of New England's commerce is determined directly by the distribution and density of the population, the network of highways and railways, the freight rate structure, and inherited trading traditions. Indirectly, physiographic features have been guiding factors in the past and, it is reasonable to believe, will continue in the future at least to set limitations upon those commercial groupings of population known as trading areas. Mankind is not always aware of the significance of topography in such functional groupings, because human adjustments to topographic phenomena are made over long periods of time and the benefits or hindrances of topography are taken for granted in the daily effort to win a living. The complexity of the ever-increasing division of human labor has also tended to take the consideration of such adjustments from those most directly concerned and to place them in the hands of the scholar. Furthermore, the lack of authentic information regarding trading areas has often left the economic geographer without the facts upon which to work. The problems involved are new and many; but, as a more complete and reliable body of information is built up, physiographic features will doubtless acquire new significance in the consideration of the problems of trading areas and of future trade growth.

We may conceive of many different types of trading area. The sales territory of a single manufacturer or of a single wholesale or retail firm is the simplest. The area over which a single commodity or class of commodities is distributed is another. The type with which we are here concerned is measured, rather, by the collective operations of all the wholesale or retail firms of a given center.[1] It is the territory over which such a center exerts a preponderant commercial influence.[2]

The exact limits of such areas could be accurately determined only from far more complete statistics of distribution than have been available in the past. The immediate environs of a wholesale or retail center generally fall within its tributary area, but as we approach a neighboring center we enter a transitional zone. Some communities may even lie in transitional zones between three or more centers. Where should the boundary lines be drawn? Where does the dominant influence of one center end and that of another begin?

We could answer these questions if statistics of distribution were in existence giving a complete picture of the trading relations of

---

[1] For notes see below, p. 403.

every city, town, village, and open country community. The purpose of the U. S. Census of Distribution taken in 1930 was in some measure to provide such a picture, and when its results are published in full we shall know a great deal more than we now do not only about the limits of trading areas but about the entire functioning of the mechanism of distribution.[3]

TRADING AREAS ACCORDING TO THE COMMERCIAL SURVEY OF NEW ENGLAND

However, as a result of the work done in 1927 by the Commercial Survey of New England under the U. S. Department of Commerce, much was learned. Certain trading areas were delineated on the basis of interviews with "about 2000 . . . business men in 168 cities and towns throughout New England."[4] In the absence of comprehensive statistics, of the sort being furnished by the Distribution Census, this method was probably the best that could have been adopted. The areas as marked out at least "portray composites of the experience of a significant number of representative retailers and wholesalers . . . [and] are based upon current practice—not on any theoretical measure of what should be."

Areas of three kinds were differentiated: (1) 13 major marketing areas; (2) 32 wholesale areas; and (3) 114 retail areas. Their boundaries are shown on maps,[5] and in the "Market Data Handbook of New England" certain statistics are tabulated by townships for each area.[6]

The boundaries of the 13 major marketing areas (Fig. 1) were defined by county lines "in order to meet the needs of the distributor who is not interested in a detailed split of territories . . . These major areas, as determined by field interviews, correspond, with one exception, to the areas ascertained upon the basis of the dominant newspaper circulation in the several areas.

"The 32 wholesale areas are composites of local wholesale areas for such items as groceries, drugs, dry goods, hardware, mill supplies, tobacco, confectionery, and paper."

The 114 retail marketing areas "represent a composite of 'shopping lines' [and] were determined by the trade of such outlets as department stores, women's specialty shops, men's clothing, furniture, and other retail stores."

CHARACTERISTICS OF TRADING AREAS

Before we turn to a somewhat detailed description of the areal organization of New England's internal trade as thus revealed, two points should be stressed:

(1) The various trading areas are not in any sense water-tight compartments with no seepage of trade from one to another; and

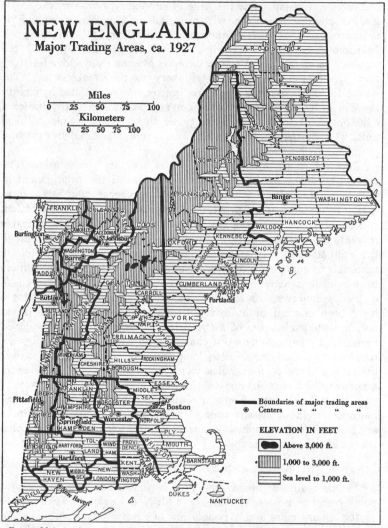

NEW ENGLAND
Major Trading Areas, ca. 1927

Miles

Kilometers

ELEVATION IN FEET

Above 3,000 ft.

1,000 to 3,000 ft.

Sea level to 1,000 ft.

Boundaries of major trading areas
Centers   "   "   "   "

FIG. 1—Major trading areas of New England, about 1927. Boundaries of major trading areas from map in E. F. Gerish, *Commercial Structure of New England*, 1929; elevations generalized from U. S. Geol. Survey map of the United States, 1:2,500,000, 1914.

(2) they are constantly changing in size and character as the years go by.

Recognizing the indeterminate character of the boundaries between the several areas and the fact that there is much interchange of trade, the *wholesale* and *retail* areas as marked out on the maps published by the Department of Commerce[5] were shown in many instances to overlap. For the sake of simplicity, however, the *major trading areas* were shown with contiguous boundaries, though it is understood that such boundaries are arbitrary to a high degree. In some cases (such as Burlington, Vt., and Portland, Me.) the wholesale area of a given center extends over an even wider territory than the major trading area tributary to the same center. The reason for this is that the major trading areas were confined by county lines in order to fit in with the current practice of many national distributors of treating the county as the smallest usable political unit, whereas the wholesale trade areas were delineated from actual practices of wholesalers.

Like all things human, these areas are far from static. The general tendency at the present time is toward the enlargement of certain wholesale and retail areas at the expense of others. This is the inevitable result of progressive improvements in transportation. Indeed, with the coming of the automobile there has been a veritable revolution in transportation during the last thirty years, though the railroads still play an important part in the movement of bulk materials to and from industrial centers and in carrying commodities to wholesale centers for further redistribution. The influence of highways, however, can hardly be overemphasized.[7] Great changes have been effected in industrial distribution by the motor truck, and the wholesale areas of distribution in many lines have widened thereby. Perhaps the greatest change of all has been wrought by the passenger automobile. Not so long ago a retail shopping area was limited to three or four miles from an urban center; today retail areas may be from thirty to one hundred and fifty miles in diameter and are still growing. Consumer buying habits and merchandising methods are in a constant state of flux, and it is becoming evermore apparent that the automobile has given free play to the emotional whims of the average shopper.

THE BOSTON AND PROVIDENCE TRADING AREAS

Let us begin our broad survey of New England[8] with the major trading area of Boston, the largest in all New England. It comprises 14,100 square miles and a population of nearly 3,700,000, or 23 per cent and 45 per cent respectively of the total area and population of the six states. Its shape is peculiar; the boundaries of the adjoining major trading areas of Worcester and Providence confine it in Massachusetts to the eastern part of the state, but northward it spreads over the whole of New Hampshire and even sends two projections (Orange and Windham counties, Vermont) westward as far as the Green Mountains. From the northernmost part of the area, Coos County, New Hampshire, trade tends to flow by railroad and highway around the western flanks of the White Mountains .through Bethlehem,[9]

Littleton, Haverhill, and Wentworth to Plymouth and on down the Merrimac Valley by way of Franklin, Concord, Manchester, and Lowell to Boston. The mountains and forests along the northern two thirds of the boundary between Maine and New Hampshire effectively block the traffic between the two states except for the passages from Gorham through Bethel, South Paris, and Poland Springs to Portland and farther south by way of Conway, East Brownfield, and Standish to Portland. The course of trade from Windham County, Vermont, is not difficult to understand when it is realized that Bellows Falls and Brattleboro, the two principal centers, are directly connected with Boston by rail and highway through Fitchburg, although there is also some trade down the Connecticut Valley with Springfield. Orange County, Vermont, is tied into Boston largely by important rail connections at Wells River, Vt., and White River Junction, Vt. The trading relations of the southern part of the Boston area are somewhat complicated by the presence of a number of large cities. Although Providence draws some trade from both Taunton and Fall River, long established commercial and political traditions bind the latter cities to Boston.

The Providence trading area, which for all practical purposes is confined to the state of Rhode Island, may be divided into three sections: a northern, a southwestern, and a southeastern. In the northern section Pawtucket, Central Falls, Woonsocket, and more than a dozen smaller manufacturing centers to the north and northwest of Providence are based on water power supplied by the falls of the Blackstone and other streams. These cities and towns give a supporting population to the trade of Providence. Through the center of the state west of Narragansett Bay runs a line of low hills that divide the cities and towns of the southeastern or coastal section from the industrial centers of the north. The coastal towns, Westerly on the west and Narragansett Pier on the east, enjoy the local trade of numerous small places, mostly summer resorts whose fortunes fluctuate with the seasons. The southeastern area consists of the shore line of Narragansett Bay with the many islands in the Bay, of which Aquidneck, or Rhode Island (upon which are located Newport and Portsmouth), is the largest. Though the greatest length of the state of Rhode Island is but forty-eight miles and its greatest width but thirty-seven, there are no less than four hundred miles of shore line bordering on sea and bay. Part of the trade from the bay region follows the shore line highway from Narragansett Pier northward to Providence. The general current of trade from Newport and Portsmouth used to be by way of Tiverton to Fall River, Mass., and thence about twenty miles into Providence. A bridge, however, has recently been constructed over Mount Hope Bay, giving Newport much more direct communications with Bristol and Providence.

The Trading Areas of Southern and Western New England

The New Haven major trading area is unusual in that it consists of two separate counties, New Haven and New London, bound together in their trading relations merely by a strip of highway and railroad along the shore line. In the western sector of this area is the Naugatuck Valley, with Waterbury to the north and Ansonia, Derby, and Shelton to the south. The trade of the valley finds its outlet at New Haven. In the eastern sector the Thames Valley in New London County, with Norwich to the north and New London at the river mouth, like the Naugatuck constitutes a fairly uniform trading subterritory whose trade flows towards New London and thence about fifty-three miles over the Shore Line division of the N.Y., N.H. & H. R.R. to New Haven.

In the Hartford and Springfield major trading areas trade is drawn from each side of the valley toward the Connecticut River. There is considerable interchange between Springfield and Hartford. The many highways radiating out of Hartford to the east and west attract the trade, in general, from Litchfield and Tolland counties in Connecticut. In Massachusetts the Berkshires tend to cut off Springfield on the west, although there are connections by rail with Pittsfield and considerable trade flows between the two points by highway: over Jacobs Ladder to the south and by the Northampton-Pittsfield road to the north. In many wholesale lines upon which there is a general New England coverage out of Boston the Connecticut River in Connecticut marks the dividing line between New England and New York territory. Many New York firms are selling in Hartford and New Haven, while Bridgeport, only eighteen miles west of New Haven, is regarded as the doorway to New York City. Farther north the Connecticut River as a boundary line between the states of New Hampshire and Vermont marks the western boundary of the wholesale areas of Manchester and Concord. It also unifies the retail trade of various towns located in its valley, such as Brattleboro, Vt., Bellows Falls, Vt., Claremont, N. H., Windsor, Vt., White River Junction, Vt., Wells River, Vt., Littleton, N. H., and Lancaster, N. H.

The easy access afforded to New York City by the Hudson Valley tends to unite Pittsfield, Rutland, and Burlington with that city rather than with Boston.

Pittsfield, drawing from Williamstown, Adams, and North Adams to the north and from Great Barrington to the south, centers the trade of Berkshire County. From Pittsfield, cut off to some degree by the mountains on the east, it is much easier to traverse the fifty miles to Albany by automobile over the modern improved highways than to go east to Springfield. Similarly Williamstown and North Adams are separated by the steep ascent over the Mohawk Trail from Greenfield and Springfield, and the retail shopper of northern Berkshire turns, rather, towards Pittsfield or Albany.

Worcester, whence many rail lines and improved highways radiate out in all directions like the spokes of a wheel, dominates the trade of Worcester County, Massachusetts, and reaches down into Windham County in Connecticut. Worcester lies about halfway between Boston and Springfield, and its eastern and western trade boundaries are rather definitely limited by these two cities. In the days before the commercial use of the automobile rail connections between Putnam and Worcester were better than rail connections between Providence and Putnam. Although a new and modern highway has been constructed between Putnam and Providence, the trade of the former, by force of habit and tradition, goes for the most part to Worcester rather than to Providence, although the distance is about equal either way. Worcester is ideally situated with reference to a great number of populous cities and towns and in many respects offers advantages as a wholesale center superior to those of Providence. Fitchburg, the most important wholesale and retail nucleus in northern Worcester County, is the center of a wholesale trading area that overlaps into southern New Hampshire.[2]

THE TRADING AREAS OF NORTHERN NEW ENGLAND

The trading areas of the more rugged regions of northern New England present many points of interest. For example, one does not find the adjustment of the wholesale areas of Rutland, Vt., and Burlington, Vt., to the line of the Green Mountains that might be expected. The population of the three northern states is relatively sparse, and it is necessary for wholesale houses to reach out farther in northern than in southern New England to get enough accounts and enough business to make their existence possible.[10] Rutland, for example, has access across the mountains via the Rutland Railroad to Bellows Falls. From Burlington two railroads cross the mountains, a southern route through the Winooski River valley to Barre and Woodsville and a northern route following the Lamoille to Hyde Park and Hardwick. Trucking plays an important part in the wholesaling of today, and the highways cutting the mountains are interconnected with a convenient network of roads.

The retail areas of Rutland and Burlington are much smaller. The retail trade of these centers is drawn almost exclusively from west of the mountains, whereas the trade on the east slope and beyond turns towards such Connecticut Valley towns as Claremont and White River and in the Burlington wholesale area toward Montpelier, Barre, and St. Johnsbury. Climatic conditions influence the flow of trade in these areas. For example, in winter when the roads are icy and bad, trade from West Bridgewater and Woodstock moves towards White River, a distance of some twenty-five miles, but in good weather this trade will cross the twenty-two hundred foot elevation to Rutland, about eleven miles away.

Lake Champlain was long a unifying factor in the Burlington area. Over a ferry across the lake Burlington used to draw trade from about forty cities and towns in New York State, including such places as Plattsburg, Ticonderoga, and Crown Point. Plattsburg gained some trading impetus during the late war and attracted some of this New York State trade away from Burlington. The inconvenience of the ferry has recently been eliminated by a bridge, and there are indications that Burlington will recapture much of its former trade from New York territory.

The St. Johnsbury major trading area covers the counties of Caledonia, Orleans, and Essex in northeastern Vermont. Shut off in some measure by the Green Mountains to the west, the White Mountains to the east and southeast, and Canada to the north, this area is most readily approached by the highways and railroads leading down the Connecticut Valley. The region is primarily agricultural. In comparatively recent years its very distance from such centers as Portland and Boston has favored the development of certain types of wholesale trade in convenience goods, such as groceries, candies, and tobaccos, and there is every prospect that the region will continue to develop in a somewhat distinctive manner. At one time trade connections with Portland, Me., were stronger than they are now; of late the tendency has been toward closer relations with Boston.

In Maine the eastern margin of the Kennebec Valley roughly marks the division between the major trading areas of Bangor and Portland. The Bangor area, which comprises all eastern and northern Maine, is knit together by railroads radiating from Bangor.

Except for that of Bangor, which reaches up to Moosehead Lake and extends over a wide tract, the retail areas of eastern and northern Maine are small and are confined to a narrow band along the coast (with centers at Belfast, Ellsworth, Machias, Lubec, and Eastport) and along the New Brunswick border as far as northern Aroostook County. This band partly encircles the forested "wild lands" of northern Hancock, southeastern Penobscot, western Washington, and the greater part of Aroostook counties.

The wholesale area of Portland covers all western Maine, Carroll and Coos counties in New Hampshire, and Caledonia, Orleans, and Essex counties in Vermont. Augusta, the nucleus of a network of railroads and highways, cuts into the wholesale business of the Portland area, though Augusta in turn is somewhat restricted by its location at the center of a triangle marked by Waterville on the north, Lewiston on the west, and Rockland on the east. The southern part of the

Portland area is the most densely populated part of Maine, a circumstance that helps explain the existence here of no less than fourteen retail shopping centers. Sea and river transportation means much to some of the Maine towns scattered along the coast. Direct boat connections make it possible for Rockland to receive overnight shipments from both Boston and Portland. Steamer service to the larger islands on the east coast brings most of the trade from that region to Rockland.

Each one of these areas has individual characteristics the understanding of which is of immediate practical value to the distributor engaged in carrying on an effective marketing program. Regardless of its type each trade area is a unit in itself and, as such, raises a host of problems.

FURTHER STUDIES NEEDED

There is a need for the accurate determination of trade areas for different commodity lines. It is highly desirable that statistics for measuring the potentialities of any one area or combination of areas be further compiled and improved. Considerable progress has been made in the development of series to measure the potentialities of a given market for consumers' goods, but little or nothing has been done in working out effective measures for the industrial goods market.

In this era of intensive competition there is likewise a growing need that trade promotional bodies and the merchants of any given trade center think in terms of trade promotion and development for the trading area they logically serve rather than in terms of the urban center in which they are located and from which they operate. Such thinking ought certainly to influence the merchant or distributor who is wont to go beyond his logical trading area and "buy out" the competition of his fellow merchants or distributors in neighboring territories. Such thinking ought to promote definite merchandise planning and selling that, for one thing, would distinguish between the portion of a given trade area in which there is no competition from neighboring centers and the portion which overlaps with one or more competing centers.

There are also problems that have an interest for the economist and economic geographer as well as for the business man. What factors influence the zone of trade activities between any two or more centers? For example, Bridgeport and New Haven, Conn., have about 147,000 and 163,000 inhabitants respectively; they are only eighteen miles apart and both draw trade from a considerable distance, yet, according to the U. S. Census of Distribution,[11] in 1930 Bridgeport had 14.9 and New Haven 19.8 retail outlets per thousand population. To the north, approximately thirty-eight miles from New

Haven, is Hartford, a city slightly larger than New Haven and a little over 17,000 larger than Bridgeport, yet with 14.09 retail outlets per thousand population. The differences in the ratio of retail outlets may be due to differences in the racial make-up of population, or in the types of residential neighborhoods, or in the scale of wages, or in the ease with which credit is granted to retail merchants by wholesalers; but no one has definitely determined the relative importance of these several elements. In the character of industries New Haven and Bridgeport are much the same. Both have trade areas cut off on one side by Long Island Sound. Hartford, on the other hand, can draw trade from a complete circle. Here is a triangle of cities, each with definite possibilities for trade expansion in a common territory. Which one, if any, will forge ahead at the expense of the others? What advantage in a trade triangle of this kind has the city with a great number of small cities close by, over either of the other competing cities? This question is not easy to answer.

Selective selling rests on the idea that a manufacturer or wholesale distributor can select from a given territory a number of outlets of a given type and class that will feature merchandise of rather definite standards. The whole assumption, however, presupposes detailed knowledge of trading areas. Such detailed studies, laid out in reference to the highway systems, show that there are certain areas that are little more than transit points or doorways leading to other trading centers beyond; still others are strategically located and have all the potentialities of dominating the whole region. What are the guiding factors in determining the relative advantages of certain areas, and just how would one or two changes in the layout of a highway system affect them?

Decentralization of industry vitally affects the entire social order and the whole business structure. That decentralization has been going on for some time in New England is shown by the removal of certain plants to Maine and, to a lesser degree, to the other northern New England states. There are a host of unsolved problems surrounding the relationship between decentralization and the evolution of trading areas.

Finally, there remains the problem of determining how far principles can be stated that are applicable to trading areas in general. This depends largely upon demarcation of the trading areas for various commodities and groups of commodities more accurately and on a much wider scale than has been attempted up to the present. A rather thorough job has been accomplished for New England, but further experience is needed from other sections of the country.

NOTES

By the Editor

[1] Several attempts have been made of late years to delimit the trading areas of the United States on the basis of different criteria. The following maps of such areas accompany P. W. Stewart, *Market Data Handbook of United States*, U. S. Dept. of Commerce, Bur. of Foreign and Domestic Commerce, Washington, 1929 (*Domestic Commerce Ser. No. 30*):

Wholesale Grocery Territories (prepared by the Bureau of Foreign and Domestic Commerce). 183 areas are outlined in the United States, and 10 in New England. These areas are based on replies to questionnaires sent out to wholesale grocers. "In most instances a study of the data on number of accounts per county compared with railway facilities presented a clear demarcation of territories, since freight rates represent the controlling factor in the distribution of nationally advertised goods." The map discloses the principal wholesale grocery centers and the areas that are reached more economically with nationally advertised merchandise by the wholesalers of these centers than by wholesalers elsewhere. The map is based on 16 separate colored maps in J. W. Millard, *Atlas of Wholesale Grocery Territories*, Bur. of Foreign and Domestic Commerce, Washington, 1927 (*Domestic Commerce Ser. No. 7*). This atlas contains statistics showing for each area and for the principal towns: population, total outlets, general stores, grocery stores, etc.

Trade Areas for Budgetary Control Purposes (prepared by Batten, Barton, Durstine, & Osborn, Inc., New York). 187 areas are marked out in the whole country, and 17 in New England. "In an effort to obtain flexibility of distribution effort to control costs, and to eliminate waste in distribution, this company in 1923 decided to segregate counties into groups that would fit the various distribution efforts that are usually employed. Newspaper circulation was taken as the basis for defining the areas," and a further effort was made "to draw a boundary around the activities of local jobbers, retailers, and chains . . . " In New England, with certain notable exceptions, the major trading areas shown on Figure 1, p. 395, above, correspond very closely to these trade areas for budgetary control purposes.

Consumer Trading Areas (prepared by International Magazine Co., Inc., Marketing Division). 632 areas are shown in the United States, and 34 in New England. They are based on a study of "population, geographical characteristics, sources of wealth, transportation, and trade outlets. . . . The map as originally made up also contains 1000 split counties, the lines purporting to show the way in which trade is actually divided within the county." As reproduced in the *Market Data Handbook of United States* the map shows the boundaries of the trading areas following county lines.

Retail Shopping Areas (by J. Walter Thompson Co.). 683 areas are shown in the United States and 29 in New England. "The existence of three department stores with a rating of $200,000 each or over was [with certain exceptions] the basis for establishing retail shopping centers. . . . [To each center] was assigned the surrounding territory (usually entire counties and multiples thereof) more accessible to this center than to any other."

[2] That trading areas are more than statistical abstractions, that they are coming to be recognized by business men, is suggested by the following quotations: "While group banking is so recent that it is difficult at this time to draw conclusions as to its ultimate success or desirability, I must confess that I am much impressed with the soundness of that movement, especially in what might be called trade areas and where such areas overlap different states" (from address delivered before the New England Bankers' Association in 1930, by Mr. F. H. Curtiss, Chairman of the Federal Reserve Bank of Boston; *New England News Letter*, No. 75, 1st July issue, 1930, p. 3). "Preliminary plans have been made for the formation of

a regional conference at Fitchburg, Mass. The area embraces towns and cities in an area roughly conforming to the Fitchburg wholesale trading area as delineated by the United States Department of Commerce in the *Market Data Handbook of New England. . . .* As another indication of the truism that economic areas bear little resemblance to political subdivisions is the fact that the towns and cities interested in the Fitchburg regional conference are about equally divided as between New Hampshire and Massachusetts" (*ibid.*, No. 55, Sept. 1, 1929, p. 6).

³ The Census of Distribution covers such topics as number of establishments, employment, wages, stocks on hand, sales, credit, kinds of business, commodities sold, types of establishments, methods of operation, etc.

The data for wholesale trade are presented in considerable detail by states and by cities and towns of over 5000 inhabitants, and in less detail by counties. Certain basic data for retail trade are presented by counties and towns; for towns and incorporated places of over 1000 inhabitants additional information is given and for states and larger cities the tabulation is extremely detailed.

⁴ This quotation and the quotations in the immediately following paragraphs are taken from E. F. Gerish, *Market Data Handbook of New England, Part III of the Commercial Survey of New England, Charles E. Artman, in Charge*, Bur. of Foreign and Domestic Commerce, Washington, 1929 (*Domestic Commerce Ser. No. 24*), pp. 1 and 2.

⁵ The maps of the wholesale and retail marketing areas accompanying the *Market Data Handbook of New England* are on a scale of about 1 : 800,000, or 13 miles to the inch, and show the boundaries of the trading areas in relation to town boundaries.

⁶ The statistics tabulated by towns in the *Market Data Handbook of New England* cover: population, number of families, wealth (bank deposits, 1920; income tax returns, 1925), standard of living (homes owned and rented, residence telephones, homes using electricity and gas, average new car sales, magazine circulation), and wholesale and retail trade outlets, classified by kinds of business.

⁷ See the pamphlet entitled *Place of Train, Trolley, Truck and Bus in New England*, New York [1925?] (*Natl. Automobile Chamber of Commerce* [*Publ.*] *No. 205*).

⁸ For a more detailed description of the major distributing areas of New England see E. F. Gerish, *Commercial Structure of New England, Part II of the Commercial Survey of New England, Charles E. Artman, in Charge*, Bur. of Foreign and Domestic Commerce, Washington, 1929 (*Domestic Commerce Ser. No. 26*), pp. 9–66.

⁹ For the location of most of the places mentioned in this paper see Figure 2, pp. 16–17, above; for railroad map see Figure 1, p. 345, above.

¹⁰ This is brought out for Vermont more clearly on the map showing wholesale marketing areas cited in note 5, above, than on Figure 1 showing the major trading areas.

¹¹ *Fifteenth Census of the United States, 1930: Census of Distribution, Final Series, Retail Distribution in Connecticut*, 1932.

REGIONAL AND CITY PLANNING IN NEW ENGLAND[1]

William Roger Greeley

THERE is a kind of foresight that aims to guide the physical growth of a community in ways that will make that community a better place to live in. The effective application of this type of foresight constitutes an art that may be called the "art of environmental planning." Its corner stones are order and beauty, and its chief field of application in the past has been the city. Pericles in Athens, Napoleon in Paris, Washington in Washington, Burnham in Chicago were great planners of environment.

PURPOSES AND SCOPE OF REGIONAL PLANNING

In past ages the city was actually a self-contained unit, capable of being planned within its own walls. Now all this is changed. The city has overflowed its walls. Every day thousands enter it by train and motor and plane and every night depart. It is fed by a broad countryside which pours varied products daily and hourly into its markets. The crowded streets send forth on Saturday and Sunday a flood of pale-faced pleasure seekers, bound for seashore and mountain and stream. The city today is merely the center of a great social organism. The complete organism requires more than a municipality to support it in all its functions. It requires a region, and the planning and development of that region constitute a new branch of the old art of environmental planning, namely, regional planning.

However, not every kind of planning that seeks to guide the development of a region is regional planning in the special sense in which this term has come to be used during the last ten or twelve years. It has been well said that city planning "deals actually with those elements of city life which can be expressed on *maps*—with streets and buildings and parks, with railroads and docks. While city planning must take into consideration many intangible facts, its recommendations must be concrete. They must be capable of being shown on a map, and they must be accompanied by a program of regulation, legislation, and finance that will make the map gradually come true on the ground."[2]

Much the same may be said of regional planning.[3] An outgrowth of city planning, it too deals mainly with material, *mappable* facts. It aims to determine and to enforce by law rational, ordered policies in the use of specific tracts of land—whether for farm or forest, park or

[1] For notes see below, p. 412.

reservoir or settlement, airport or highway or railroad. "Actually the problems and difficulties of regional planning are not so very different from those of city planning except in magnitude and in responsibility. The principal technical difference lies in the fact that regional planning deals with the interrelation of communities rather than with the problems of individual cities."[4]

Regional planning has hitherto been applied in this country almost exclusively to certain great metropolitan districts,[5] and the term "region" in the practice of regional planning has come to mean a metropolitan area. Indeed, a region has even been defined as "an area included within commutation and easy one-day shopping distance of the central cities, or city."[6] This concept is too narrow. Planning is desperately needed today for many a rural area not centering about a metropolis and is no less needed for tracts far wider than those that lie within a day's shopping distance from a city. Professor and Mrs. Hubbard have suggested a better definition: "a region is an area unified by common economic and social purposes, large enough to permit a reasonable adjustment of necessary activities to sub-areas and small enough to develop a consciousness of community aims."[7]

NEED OF REGIONAL PLANNING IN NEW ENGLAND

Surely New England as a whole may be regarded as such a region. It is more than the six northeastern states. It is the geographical region east of the Hudson Valley. It is the historical region of the Yankee. It is the ethical region of the New England conscience and of Puritanism. It is an industrial region separate from all other industrial regions, a recreational region of rugged coast, tumbled mountains, crystal streams and lakes, sloping orchards, and white pine forests. Movements such as the one that culminated in the organization of the New England Council show that New England is not too large to have "consciousness of community aims."

And yet, whatever value this regional unity may have for mankind has been almost lost as a result of the lack of any coördination among states and cities. There has developed, not one smooth, effective highway system, but many fragments ill fitted together. Lawsuits have been instituted by one state against another because of insufficient planning with regard to water supply. Great scenic highways, through negligence, have fallen prey to commercial interests that have converted them into automobile slums, defeating the purpose for which they were originally constructed. Industries have been developed in the wrong locations; poor agricultural lands have been tilled in vain for crops ill suited to the soil; waste has become a giant specter. Forests have been burned annually by the hundred thousand acres. Traffic has found such difficulties that the death toll is appalling.

Regional planning has indeed a vital work to perform in bettering these conditions and bringing order out of chaos.

New England, however, in company with other sections of the country, is awakening to the need of regional planning on a broad base. In 1929 a conference of representatives of the six New England states, appointed by the several governors, was held in Boston. At this meeting the New England Regional Planning League was formed to foster the study and practice of planning as applied to New England as a whole. The League has in view first of all the collation and completion of the surveys which must provide foundations for sound comprehensive planning. There exist already many such surveys— topographical, aerial, industrial, traffic, sociological—but none are complete.[8] Along with their promotion will go the fostering in the individual states of public interest with a view to furthering regional planning and giving it increasing support. Third, and overlapping the first two objectives wherever possible, will come the actual work of planning and of executing the plans.

The organization of the League is the outgrowth of a long period of activity in New England during which very creditable results have been achieved.[9] Boston, and in fact all Massachusetts, have for years been organized to promote city, town, and regional planning, and "Massachusetts today is one of the acknowledged leaders in planning experience."[10]

Concerted Action in Massachusetts

The Homestead Commission of Massachusetts was created in 1913 to foster housing and town planning. It carried forward a vigorous program, going even so far as to purchase land and erect houses with state funds, as a demonstration of what could be done to house mill workers and as an encouragement to private capital. The Homestead Commission introduced into the Legislature a bill providing for the appointment by each city, and the election by each town of 10,000 or more people, of a planning board. Although some few municipalities neglected to comply, the general adoption of planning as one of the functions of local government followed the enactment of the law, and at present there are about 120 planning boards in the Commonwealth. The Homestead Commission sought to stimulate and encourage the work of these boards by every means at its disposal, including the holding of an annual conference of the boards at some place in the state where, during the year, an interest in planning had been shown.

The Massachusetts Federation of Planning Boards,[11] an unofficial association of official boards resulting from these conferences, was formed in 1915 and, upon the absorption of the Homestead Commission by the Department of Public Welfare in 1920, became the active force in promoting planning in Massachusetts. Through its efforts new legislation dealing with the many phases of planning has been placed upon the statute books. As outstanding among these laws may be cited the Tenement Law for towns; the Board of Survey Act, which established boards of survey with powers in respect to the laying out, construction, etc., of streets and directed such boards to make plans to cover future growth and development; the Excess Condemnation Acts, which provide for the acquisition of more land than is necessary for actual physical improvements and for the sale of the surplus after the improvement is made; an act authorizing the levying of assessments to recover from the owners properly benefited part of the cost of the laying out and construction of streets, parks, and other improvements. This is known as the Betterment Law. Another law authorizes cities and towns to acquire land for play-grounds by gift, purchase, eminent domain, or lease. A law provides for the taking of land as a public domain for the cultivation of forest trees and the protection of water supplies. A law permits cities and towns to restrict land for industrial, commercial, and other uses according to a zoning plan. There is also a law authorizing the Division of Highways of the Department of Public Welfare to regulate billboards and enabling cities and towns further to restrict them.

The Federation has for some years taken an active part in securing a court decision on the validity of the principle of billboard regulation. The case is now (August, 1932) pending before the Supreme Court, where it has been since June, 1925.

The Federation was also instrumental in the establishment within the Department of Public Welfare in 1919 of a Division of Housing and Town Planning, with a State Consultant on Town and City Planning. This officer has for some years served the communities of the Commonwealth in the capacity of adviser and promoter of planning activities.

Just here it is well to note that planning must include more than the framing and enactment of wise laws. Like all other forms of governmental regulation, it must be wisely and patiently administered. There are many places where laws adequate on the statute books have been allowed to lapse. In 1929 the State Consultant on Planning in Massachusetts reported 90 active as against 19 dormant boards.[12] The Consultant aims to see that the planning law is observed. This officer requires each planning board to report to its own municipality annually and to send a copy of its report to him. His work is largely of a consulting nature to aid towns in the administration of their planning laws and regulations.

REGIONAL PLANNING IN MASSACHUSETTS

While the Homestead Commission and its heirs and assigns, so to speak, have carried on as above outlined, there have been other quite independent forces at work in New England in the realm of civic foresight.

Under the leadership of Charles Eliot and Frederick Law Olmsted, the great park system of Metropolitan Boston was planned and laid out over thirty years ago, financed by the public with funds that were vast indeed for those days.[13]

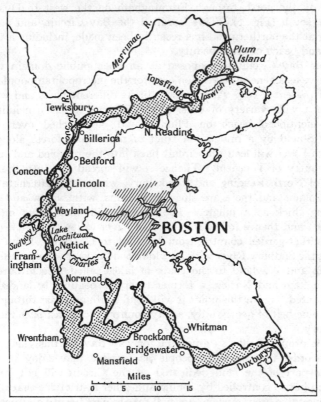

FIG. 1—The Bay Circuit, a proposed system of public reservations encircling Boston. Based on map published by the Trustees of Public Reservations, Boston.

Meanwhile Eliot's father, the President of Harvard, was presiding over a body known as the Trustees of Public Reservations—a private corporation authorized by law to acquire lands and historic places and to hold them in perpetuity for the public use and benefit. This corporation was picking up here a mountain, there a waterfall or a stretch of beach, here again a picturesque section of the Charles River, or a glacial drumlin of rare beauty. Today the Trustees hold and manage reservations from one end of the Commonwealth to the other.

In 1928 the Governor of Massachusetts appointed a Committee on the Needs and Uses of Open Spaces, which has surveyed existing public domains and published a map showing every such property in the Commonwealth together with proposed new takings.[14] Among the latter is a plan for a circumferential band of open area surrounding the Metropolitan territory in a great half circle from Plum Island beach on the north through Framingham on the west to Duxbury on the south (Fig. 1). This is called the Bay Circuit, and a large taking at the northern end has recently been made, including a three-mile sand beach of great beauty.

This Bay Circuit is proposed as an open public domain which will serve as a general recreation area for the metropolitan population. It will present a very varied aspect in its different parts and will be put to a wide variety of uses. Its northern stretches include the above-mentioned beach on Plum Island, approached over Plum Island Sound by a bridge. A tract of marsh and forest along the Ipswich River will lead the Circuit back into the tumbled and rugged hill country of Topsfield. Thence it will spread out into the peat lands of North Reading and Tewksbury, where bogs alternate with sandy plains and there are sluggish streams, with willow and alder growing thick as a jungle. The Circuit will next swing on into Billerica and thence follow the Concord River valley through orchard and market-garden country from Bedford to Concord. From here, taking the Sudbury River with its wide flood lands, it will pass through Lincoln and Wayland to the chain of lakes called "Cochituate" in Framingham and Natick, a former reservoir beautifully landscaped and planted. From this point it will bend south and east through the white pine belt of gently hilly, sandy country to the sea once more at Duxbury.

It is proposed that an ample motor way traverse this giant green belt in order that as many people as possible may enjoy it. The greater part of the land dedicated to the Circuit will not be condemned but so controlled by zoning and other restrictions that it may continue to be used in ways that will preserve its beauty and peaceful appeal. Orchards, farms, forests will make up most of the area. Encroachments and intrusions of business and industry and despoliation will be prevented.

Outside this Massachusetts Bay region a movement is on foot for the planning of the Merrimac Valley region, including Lowell, Lawrence, Haverhill, Amesbury, Merrimac, Newburyport, and the intermediate towns. A super-highway has been projected, by-passing the city centers and following generally the north bank of the river.

In the so-called Montachusetts Region, including Monadnock in New Hampshire, Watatic and Wachusett in Massachusetts, and the uplands surrounding these mountains, a careful plan for the future has been worked out and presented to representative groups throughout the region. In its general lines this plan resembles the Philadelphia Tri-State Plan in looking toward the establishment of by-pass trunk highways, freed from motor-slum development, with towns and villages intact on lateral connecting roads, each settlement to be self-contained with appropriately defined limits beyond which open spaces will be maintained, separating one community from the next.

Another region that has become organized for regional planning is the group of communities on Cape Cod. Here meetings have been held and programs developed for coöperation along various lines. A forestry fire-prevention experiment, showing amazing results, has been carried on for some years in the territory between the Cape Cod Canal and Bass River. By a midwinter educational campaign, by the "brushing out" of ninety miles of old road that had become choked with young forest growth so as to prohibit the passage of fire apparatus, and by motor patrols during the fire seasons, the loss in acreage has been cut to about 20 per cent of normal at an expense actually less than the normal cost of fighting fires! The eradication of the mosquito and the regulation of boat, rail, and auto traffic are other regional problems to which particular attention is being devoted in this area.

The planning boards of Norwood, Walpole, and Westwood through a joint voluntary Regional Planning Committee are considering plans for the development of 1000 acres of land into a residential village community, with park system, recreation areas, golf links, and many other attractive features. This study involves the determination of the routes of through automobile arteries as well as the laying out of a purely local street system of all one-way streets. Coöperation of this kind among planning boards is springing up throughout the state and promises a great advance in the near future.

Boston itself has been very active in its different capacities.[15] First it has had a strong and active board working for the city proper on every kind of city-planning work, including not only the inevitable studies of street systems, parks, traffic regulation, housing, airports, zoning, and planting but also the establishment of a system of splendidly equipped health centers in different localities throughout the city. As a metropolis Boston has been subjected (by the Legislature) to extensive planning under a District Commission, which has laid out major arteries and made comprehensive studies and plans for the improvement of the conditions that could not be handled by any of the forty municipalities acting alone. Meanwhile certain administrative functions of metropolitan government have been in the hands of another District Commission controlling the Metropolitan water, sewer, and park systems and the Metropolitan police.

Comprehensive planning, as distinguished from piecemeal or portion planning (such as zoning) has been instituted in Springfield,

Worcester, Gardner, Brockton, Brookline, Falmouth, Norwood, Attleboro, Lexington, Winchester, and perhaps a few other places.[16] The popular cry, however, has usually been for zoning, without regard to the other essentials of a city plan. Today the greater part of the population of Massachusetts is living under zoning regulations, which means that a veritable revolution has taken place in a brief period of years.[17]

CITY PLANNING IN OTHER NEW ENGLAND STATES

While Massachusetts has been developing along the lines noted above, planning has taken a strong hold in other states.

In Connecticut planning commissions have been established in a large number of cities and some towns. Hartford was among the pioneers, with a comprehensive city plan, many features of which have been carried out during the last fifteen years. The state officials have been developing a system of state parks and highways,[18] which reflects great credit upon the state, and have devised a system of highway signs and signals far ahead of anything else in New England.

In Maine, Auburn, Belfast, Mount Desert, and Waterville have planning boards, and Portland has a park commission with certain planning responsibilities.

New Hampshire's chief city, Manchester, has an official planning board, and the town of Derry "an unofficial advisory board appointed by the selectmen." The University of New Hampshire has made a notable contribution to regional planning in a state-wide survey.

Vermont, like New Hampshire, reports one city with a planning board, Burlington. Swanton has an unofficial board.

Rhode Island has official boards in Newport, Providence, Tiverton, Warwick, and Westerly, and an unofficial board in Portsmouth.[19]

In general, the progress of planning in New England has been steady and, when contemplated from the historical point of view, very rapid. The changes in the mode of living and in community growth due to the planning laws are nothing less than revolutionary. They would give cause for congratulation but for the fact that so much remains to be done.[20]

NOTES

[1] For bibliographical references on city and regional planning consult: Theodora Kimball [Hubbard], *Manual of Information on City Planning and Zoning, Including References on Regional, Rural, and National Planning*, Cambridge, 1923; T. K. Hubbard and Katherine McNamara, *Planning Information Up-to-date: A Supplement, 1923–1928, to Kimball's Manual of Information on City Planning and Zoning*, Cambridge, 1928. See also the surveys of progress in city and regional planning in the United States contributed by Mrs. Hubbard to *Landscape Architecture*, 1912–1924, and to *City Planning*, 1925 ff. Plan reports for cities and regions in the United States are also listed from time to time in *City Planning*. The results of a comparative study of "experiments [that] are being made in the cities of the United

States and [the] results [that] have come from specific lines of action in dealing with specific situations" are presented by T. K. Hubbard and H. V. Hubbard in *Our Cities To-day and To-morrow: A Survey of Planning and Zoning Progress in the United States*, Cambridge, 1929. The Division of Building and Housing of the Bureau of Standards, U. S. Dept. of Commerce, distributes from time to time mimeographed lists of city planning commissions in the United States and data concerning the progress of zoning and zoning legislation.—EDIT.

[2] Kimball, *op. cit.*, p. 4.

[3] See especially Benton MacKaye, *The New Exploration: A Philosophy of Regional Planning*, New York, 1928. The author of this stimulating and original book, while dealing with nation-wide conditions and problems, draws widely for examples upon his intimate knowledge of New England.

[4] Quoted from remarks of R. V. Black in discussion of paper by Thomas Adams on *The Goals and Snags in Regional Planning*, in *Planning Problems of Town, City, and Region, Papers and Discussions at the Twenty-First National Conference on City Planning Held at Buffalo and Niagara Falls, New York, May 20 to 23, 1929*, Philadelphia, 1929, pp. 40–41.

[5] Thomas Adams, *Regional Planning in the United States*, in *American Civic Association, Inc.*, Ser. 4, No. 1, April, 1929, pp. 5–12.

[6] Hubbard and Hubbard, *op. cit.*, p. 46.

[7] *Ibid.*, p. 47.

[8] On the important question of surveys, see H. M. Lewis, *Basic Information Needed for a Regional Plan*, in *Trans. Amer. Soc. of Civil Engineers*, Vol. 92, 1928, pp. 1056–1064, with discussion, pp. 1065–1097.

[9] The survey carried out by Professor and Mrs. Hubbard, however, appears to show that northern New England as a whole and Maine in particular have been ultraconservative in their attitude toward town planning (Hubbard and Hubbard, *op. cit.*, pp. 16 and 289).

[10] *Ibid.*, p. 74.

[11] The Federation since 1916 has published from time to time *Bulletins* dealing with fundamental planning problems. These *Bulletins* cover a large field and represent "the most consecutive and substantial contribution to the educational literature of planning which we have from any state organization" (*ibid.*, p. 67). *Bulletin* No. 8, April, 1921, contains a complete tabular statement of the field covered by town planning and the items that may come before a planning board. No. 13, January, 1924, has a clear and concise statement of the need of planning boards and the work that they can accomplish. No. 16, November, 1924, sets forth in detail the Nichols method for protecting the city plan. No. 20, October, 1926, is a "compilation of planning laws for the convenience of planning commissions." The Federation now publishes, in addition to the *Bulletins*, a monthly news sheet, keeping all member boards in close touch with current progress in planning.

[12] T. K. Hubbard, *Brief Survey of City and Regional Planning in the United States, 1929*, in *City Planning*, Vol. 6, 1930, p. 204.

[13] The *Report of the Board of Metropolitan Park Commissioners*, January, 1893 ([*Mass.*] *House, No. 150*) includes a report of Charles Eliot, landscape architect of the Commission, in which the physical and historical geography of the metropolitan district is discussed in connection with the problem of planning.

[14] See *Report by the Committee on Needs and Uses of Open Spaces in Massachusetts as Rendered to His Excellency the Governor of Massachusetts*, Boston, 1929. The accompanying map, 1 : 250,000, shows existing parks, state and municipal forests, water-supply lands, properties of state, municipal, and semipublic institutions, and through foot trails, as well as proposed open spaces. See also P. L. Buttrick, *Public and Semi Public Lands of Connecticut*, Hartford, 1930 (*State of Conn., State Geol. and Nat. Hist. Survey Bull. No. 49*) with map, 1 : 250,000, showing similar data.

[15] See E. M. Herlihy, *Planning for Boston—1630–1930*, in *City Planning*, Vol. 6, 1930, pp. 1–14; A. A. Shurtleff, *Boston Metropolitan Planning*, *ibid.*, pp. 15–19; H. I. Harriman, *The Division of Metropolitan Planning, Boston*, *ibid.*, pp. 20–22; E. M. Herlihy, *Boston's Master Highway Plan*, in *Planning Problems of Town, City and Region, Papers and Discussions at the Time of the Twenty-Third National Conference on City Planning Held at Rochester, New York, June 22 to 24, 1931*, Philadelphia, 1931, pp. 81–84. Abstracts of reports dealing in large part with city planning and related problems will be found in *A Compendium of Reports and Studies Relating to the Commerce and Industries of Boston*, compiled by William A. Leahy under the direction of the City Planning Board, Boston, Mass., 1924. See also *Zoning for Boston: A Survey and a Comprehensive Plan, Report of the City Planning Board*, Boston, Mass., 1924.

"The traffic analysis and forecast furnishes the chief factual basis for thorofare planning." An important study has been made of traffic conditions in the metropolitan region by the Boston City Planning Board, the Mayor's Street Traffic Survey, and the Division of Metropolitan Planning. The results of this study are summarized by Robert Whitten, *The Traffic Analysis and Forecast in its Relation to Thorofare Planning*, in *Planning Problems of Town, City, and Region*, 1929, pp. 179–196.

[16] For comments on some of these activities and for references consult Mrs. Hubbard's annual surveys cited above, note 1.

[17] The following table compiled from L. G. Chase, *A Tabulation of City Planning Commissions in the United States* (mimeographed), Division of Building and Housing, U. S. Bureau of Standards, April, 1932, reflects the progress of zoning and city planning in New England and the United States.

UNITED STATES AND NEW ENGLAND: PROGRESS OF
ZONING AND CITY PLANNING, END OF 1931

	NUMBER OF MUNICIPALITIES			
	WITH COMPREHENSIVE ZONING ORDINANCES	WITH ZONING ORDINANCES NOT COMPREHENSIVE	WITH OFFICIAL CITY PLANNING COMMISSIONS	WITH UNOFFICIAL CITY PLANNING COMMISSIONS
United States . . .	..	..	828	51
New England . . .	68	20	151	2
Maine	1	1	5	0
New Hampshire . .	1	0	1	1
Vermont	0	0	2	0
Massachusetts . . .	48	18	121	0
Rhode Island . . .	3	1	5	1
Connecticut	15	0	17	0

[18] See Buttrick, *op. cit.*

[19] "In Rhode Island there is a proposal afoot which recalls the joint regional committees of England—the Middletown Town Council having voted to ask coöperation with its insular neighbors, Portsmouth and Newport, in a joint planning board" (T. K. Hubbard, *Brief Survey*, etc., p. 208).

[20] There is need for village planning as well as for city and regional planning (see below, p. 475, note 16).

STATE AND LOCAL GOVERNMENT IN NEW ENGLAND

John F. Sly

N EW ENGLAND is perhaps the most diverse area of local government in America. The principal territorial units of government within the state are of four main types: counties, towns,[1] cities, and other minor civil subdivisions.[2] Table I shows how these are distributed by states (see also Fig. 1):

TABLE I—UNITS OF LOCAL GOVERNMENT AND CIVIL
SUBDIVISIONS IN NEW ENGLAND, 1931[a]

STATES	COUNTIES	TOWNS[b]	CITIES	OTHER MINOR CIVIL SUBDIVISIONS
Maine	16	435	20	295[c]
New Hampshire .	10	222	11	23[d]
Vermont	14	240	8	70[e]
Massachusetts . .	14	316	39	0
Rhode Island . . .	5	33	6	0
Connecticut . . .	8	169	21	23[f]
Totals	67	1,415	105	411

[a] Because of wide diversity, shifting status, and lack of systematic records accuracy in such data is difficult. These figures, however, are based upon Bureau of the Census, *Fifteenth Census of the United States, 1930: Population,* Vol. 1. Supplementary material has been taken from *Maine Register,* 1930–31, Portland, F. L. Tower Co., compiler, 1930, pp. 1357–1372; State of New Hampshire, *Manual for the General Court,* 1927, pp. 79–87; State of Vermont, *Vermont Legislative Directory,* 1929, pp. 249–261; Commonwealth of Massachusetts, *A Manual for the Use of the General Court,* 1929–1930, Boston, 1929, pp. 208–223; State of Rhode Island, *Manual . . . of the State of Rhode Island,* 1929–30, p. 378; and State of Connecticut, *Register and Manual,* 1930, Hartford, 1930, pp. 746–751.

[b] Places designated "town" in *Fifteenth Census of the United States.*

[c] Includes some 29 villages, 65 plantations, 211 "unorganized" areas (*loc. cit.*; also *Maine Register,* 1930–1931, pp. 1357–1372).

[d] Unincorporated places (*Manual for the General Court,* 1927, p. 88).

[e] Incorporated villages (*Vermont Legislative Directory,* 1929, pp. 249–261).

[f] Incorporated boroughs (*Register and Manual,* 1930, p. 478).

Within this broad classification there are three distinct types of town-meeting government, four of city government, a medley of special districts and civil subdivisions, marked variations in county organization, and regional and metropolitan problems of all degrees of complexity. Many of the units are in a perpetual and often rapid state of social flux, urban, semiurban, and rural areas changing at times imperceptibly, at times violently, from one condition to another. Some governmental forms represent more or less distinct periods of

---

[1] For notes see below, p. 426.

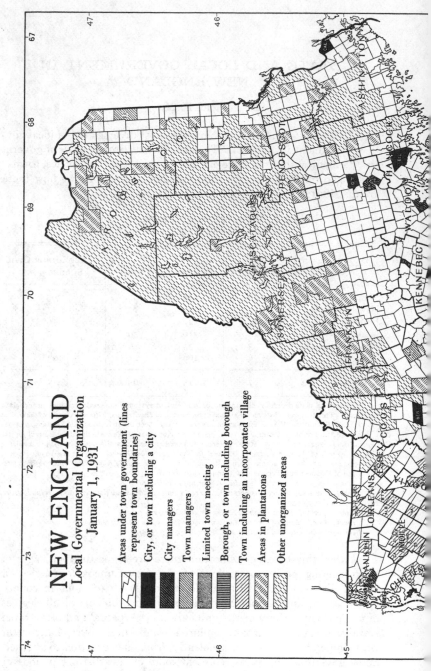

NEW ENGLAND
Local Governmental Organization
January 1, 1931

Areas under town government (lines represent town boundaries)

City, or town including a city

City managers

Town managers

Limited town meeting

Borough, or town including borough

Town including an incorporated village

Areas in plantations

Other unorganized areas

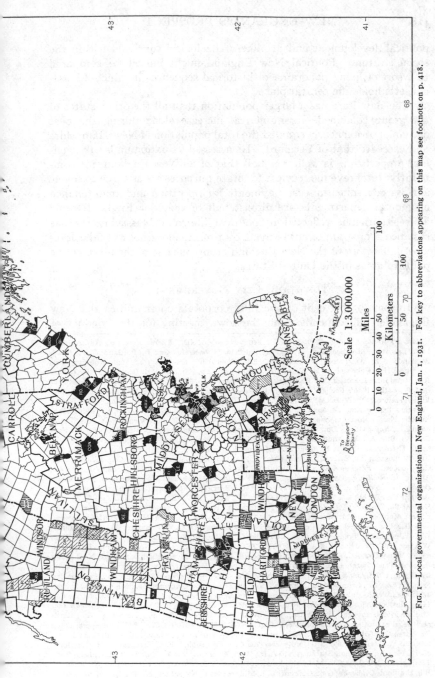

FIG. 1—Local governmental organization in New England, Jan. 1, 1931. For key to abbreviations appearing on this map see footnote on p. 418.

political development and are like archeological survivals within the social stratum. Political New England might indeed be compared to a sort of living panorama of historical sequences in which Massachusetts holds the central place.

The Bay State has a larger population than all the other states of the group combined—its numerical increase alone during the past decennial period nearly equaled the total population of New Hampshire and exceeded that of Vermont. Its assessed valuation under the general property tax is well over half that of all New England, its comparative total revenue receipts for state purposes are as three to seven, and its governmental-cost payments for operation and maintenance of general departments are almost half of the New England total.[3] This situation is reflected in political life, and Massachusetts has assumed a program of adjustment that has made it not only the foremost laboratory of the New England group but one of the most active political areas in the United States.

TOWN AND CITY GOVERNMENT

In some 93 per cent of the fully corporate communities the New Englander still depends upon the town meeting for the conduct of

KEY TO ABBREVIATIONS APPEARING ON FIGURE 1—MAINE. *Androscoggin Co.:* Au., Auburn; Lew., Lewiston. *Aroostook Co.:* F. F., Fort Fairfield. *Cumberland Co.:* P., Portland; S. P., South Portland; W'k, Westbrook. *Hancock Co.:* Ell., Ellsworth. *Kennebec Co.:* Aug., Augusta; Ga., Gardiner; Ha., Hallowell; W'le, Waterville. *Knox Co.:* C'n, Camden; R'd, Rockland. *Oxford Co.:* Ru., Rumford. *Penobscot Co.:* Ba., Bangor; Br., Brewer; O. T., Old Town; V., Veazie. *Sagadahoc Co.:* B., Bath. *Waldo Co.:* Be't, Belfast. *Washington Co.:* Cal., Calais; E., Eastport. *York Co.:* Bi., Biddeford. NEW HAMPSHIRE. *Belknap Co.:* La., Laconia. *Cheshire Co.:* Ke., Keene. *Coos Co.:* Ber., Berlin. *Grafton Co.:* Han., Hanover; L., Littleton. *Hillsborough Co.:* Man., Manchester; Na., Nashua. *Merrimack Co.:* Con., Concord; Fr., Franklin. *Rockingham Co.:* Po., Portsmouth. *Strafford Co.:* Do., Dover; Ro., Rochester; So., Somersworth. VERMONT. *Addison Co.:* B'l, Bristol; Mid., Middlebury. *Bennington Co.:* B., Bennington; Ma., Manchester; Re., Readsboro. *Caledonia Co.:* Ha., Hardwick; L., Lyndon; R., Ryegate; S. J., St. Johnsbury. *Chittenden Co.:* Bu., Burlington; Es., Essex; Hi., Hinesburg; Je., Jericho; Ri., Richmond. *Essex Co.:* Br., Brighton; Co., Concord. *Franklin Co.:* En., Enosburg; S. A., St. Albans; Sw., Swanton. *Grand Isle Co.:* Al., Alburg. *Lamoille Co.:* Ca., Cambridge; H. P., Hyde Park; J., Johnson; Mo., Morristown; St., Stowe. *Orange Co.:* B'd, Bradford; N'y, Newbury; Ran., Randolph. *Orleans Co.:* Alb., Albany; B't'n, Barton; De., Derby; Gl., Glover; N't, Newport; Tr., Troy. *Rutland Co.:* Bra., Brandon; F. H., Fair Haven; Pi., Pittsford; Po., Poultney; P., Proctor; Ru., Rutland. *Washington Co.:* B'e, Barre; Cab., Cabot; Ma., Marshfield; M., Montpelier; No., Northfield; Pl., Plainfield; Wat., Waterbury. *Windham Co.:* Bra., Brattleboro; N'f'e, Newfane; R., Rockingham; We., Westminster; Wh., Whitingham; Wi., Wilmington. *Windsor Co.:* Cav., Cavendish; Ch., Chester; Lu., Ludlow; Spr., Springfield; Win., Windsor; W., Woodstock. MASSACHUSETTS. *Berkshire Co.:* N. A., North Adams; Pit., Pittsfield. *Bristol Co.:* At., Attleboro; Da., Dartmouth; F. R., Fall River; Ma'd, Mansfield; N. B., New Bedford; Tau., Taunton. *Essex Co.:* B'y, Beverly; Gl., Gloucester; Hav., Haverhill; L., Lawrence; Ly., Lynn; L'd, Lynnfield; M'n, Methuen; New., Newbury; Pe., Peabody; S., Salem; Sw., Swampscott. *Franklin Co.:* Gr., Greenfield; Or., Orange. *Hampden Co.:* Chi., Chicopee; Ho., Holyoke; Sp., Springfield; We., Westfield; W. S., West Springfield. *Hampshire Co.:* N. H., Northampton. *Middlesex Co.:* Ma., Marlborough. *Norfolk Co.:* N'd, Norwood; S'n, Sharon; W'h, Weymouth. *Plymouth Co.:* Mid'b', Middleborough. *Suffolk Co.:* W'p, Winthrop. *Worcester Co.:* Fi., Fitchburg; Ga., Gardner; Le., Leominster; Wor., Worcester. CONNECTICUT. *Fairfield Co.:* Br., Bridgeport; Dan., Danbury; Gr., Greenwich; N. C., New Canaan; N'n, Newtown; No., Norwalk; Rid., Ridgefield; Sh., Shelton; St., Stamford; S'd, Stratford. *Hartford Co.:* Bri., Bristol; Far., Farmington; H., Hartford; N. B., New Britain; Sou., Southington; W. H., West Hartford. *Litchfield Co.:* Lit., Litchfield; Tor., Torrington. *Middlesex Co.:* Mid., Middletown; O. S., Old Saybrook. *New Haven Co.:* A., Ansonia; B'd, Branford; D., Derby; Gui., Guilford; Mil., Milford; Nau., Naugatuck; N. H'n, New Haven; Wal., Wallingford; Wat., Waterbury. *New London Co.:* C'r, Colchester; Gri., Griswold; Gro., Groton; N. L., New London; Nor., Norwich; Sto., Stonington. *Tolland Co.:* Sta., Stafford; Ve., Vernon. *Windham Co.:* Kil., Killingly; Pu., Putnam; Wi., Windham. RHODE ISLAND. *Newport Co.:* N., Newport. *Providence Co.:* Cra., Cranston; Paw., Pawtucket; Pr., Providence; Wo., Woonsocket.

local affairs, while about 49 per cent of all the inhabitants of New England live under the old system. It is true that only in a few respects does town government operate as it did a century ago, owing largely to the constantly extending influence of state government in local administration. "Centralization" as well as many other circumstances has affected the political aspects of every town, but it is likewise true that many elements are perpetuated that formed the basis of local self-government in the days of the colonies.

In structure, for instance, the system remains substantially unchanged: a town meeting composed of all qualified voters of the community, a group of selectmen, and a long list of administrative officers. In personnel, also, much the same group takes the dominating interest—a sort of untitled squirarchy recognized as the solid, permanent, and benevolent element of the community, though now increasingly composed in the larger places of energetic citizens from less distinguished ranks.

In spirit, important phases are unaltered; extreme publicity of policy and public accountability of local officers continue. But local difficulties have arisen; the personnel of the town meeting has grown too numerous, the population has become in many places both heterogeneous and transient, and extreme complexity in local policy and administration has required technical facilities that the old system could not supply. The result has been, on the one hand, a sort of encouragement, guidance, or even directory program on the part of the state well known to students as "centralization," and, on the other, local expedients and legislative enabling acts permitting harrassed communities to meet the new conditions more or less in their own way.

The forms taken by this adjustment are of interest. The first and perhaps the most obvious expedient was to turn to representative government under the well known types of city charters. But the New Englander has always been exceedingly skeptical of such a solution. Only one hundred and five of his present fully corporate areas (a bare 7 per cent) operate under such devices,[4] and to abandon the old town meeting for what seems from experience to be a somewhat doubtful adventure is widely regarded as a grave undertaking.[5]

THE LIMITED TOWN MEETING

Some of the large towns accordingly have attempted what might be regarded as either a modification of the open town meeting or as a compromise with city government. It is called the limited town meeting. In brief, the plan is this: a community is divided into a certain number of precincts—practice has established from four to nine—and from each precinct an equal number of delegates (usually from thirty to forty) known as "town meeting members" are chosen by popular vote. These, with certain *ex officio* officers, comprise the town meeting and exercise practically all powers vested in the town as a corporate body. Aside from this, warrants are issued, elections conducted, and appointive positions filled much as before. Electors, indeed, may speak at any meeting, but voting is reserved for the members composing the new assembly.

The plan was first tried (1906) in Newport, R. I.,[6] and next (1915) in Brookline, Mass. Since then, it has spread to fourteen other towns in Massachusetts; but, except for its somewhat modified use in Newport and for a partial application of the plan in the form of "limited financial councils" in a few Rhode Island communities, it has received no further recognition in New England.[7] The matter has been discussed in Maine as a possible solution for some of the local difficulties, but there seems little enthusiasm for the plan. Vermont and New Hampshire have shown no interest, and Connecticut in place of it has attempted in some cases to solve the problems of its more congested areas by a rather unsatisfactory combination of borough and town government.

So far as Massachusetts is concerned, the limited town meeting has proved both practicable and acceptable. It fits well with local traditions, it provides for popular participation in local policy, and through *ex officio* membership introduces the administrative officer into the representative assembly. When urban pressures affect other New England areas, it may, perhaps, serve as an expedient compromise with representative government but hardly, it would seem, as an enduring solution of the local problem. It appears doubtful that a governmental form can endure that is neither wholly representative nor wholly direct. The limited town meeting very narrowly misses classification as a city council of unwieldy size and offers opportunities for partisan organization that the old town meeting lacked. It is, nevertheless, a device that may well interest the student if for no other reason than as a significant transitional step in local institutional development and as an emphasis on popular elements that in the modern quest for efficiency and economy have received scant consideration in more widely advertised "reforms."[8]

Town Managers and Finance Committees

More attention, however, has been given to the improvement of administrative services in the interest of increased efficiency and economy, and both towns and cities in New England have turned to the adoption of the "manager" idea in local government. While there has yet been no attempt to combine the limited town meeting and the town manager, it may well be done before the experiment is over. The manager device is well known. It is simply the hiring of a full-time manager (in cities, by the council; in towns, by the selectmen) to become the administrative head of the community, in much the same manner that a superintendent of schools exercises his authority through responsibility to a school committee. The method has not received wide acceptance—only some twenty-five communities are at present operating under the plan by legislative sanction—but in one form or another the arrangement seems necessary to every local government whose managerial and financial problems are out of the domestic stage.

So far as the city manager is concerned,[4] his status in New England is much the same as anywhere else, but the town manager presents special problems.[9] It is the town meeting—unaltered under the manager form—that, among other things, introduces irregular features. As explained elsewhere, here is "an appointive executive who is at the same time part of a constituent assembly to which he is not directly responsible."[10] The New Englander, moreover, has for many generations, looked for leadership to his selectmen and more recently as well to finance committees. Both groups exist unimpaired with the town manager. In some respects, therefore, the manager is in a more exacting position than his city counterpart: he must often face a popular test without the prestige of elective office, he is responsible to an executive board (the selectmen) lacking legislative authority, and his immediate administrative superiors and colleagues have behind them generations of tradition that make his own leadership difficult.

There remain miscellaneous features of town government in New England that indicate significant transitions as well as practical administrative devices. Aside from the adoption of boards of survey, planning, and public works, the generous use of "permissive statutes,"[11] the advice and guidance of state officers,[12] and the more or less informal adjustments undertaken in all communities to meet local problems, finance committees have become important devices. In smaller communities the selectmen are the sole budgetary authorities, and under simple conditions where no heavy expenditures are involved the system works well enough. The embarrassments, however, that have accompanied urban development have made impossible so informal a procedure; and committees have come into existence, first by local agreement and later by legislative sanction. Beginning as devices to scrutinize all items in the warrant carrying appropriations, they have become in many places approving authorities for all articles before the voter. Indeed, in large places, their frequent public hearings, the wide publicity given their opinions, and their position as "steering committees" in the town meetings have given them a place of first importance. It is perhaps not too much to say that from exercising the limited functions of advising and supplementing the work of the selectmen, the finance committee has in some places become the decisive factor in the framing of town policies.[13]

Counties and Metropolitan Areas

Aside from city, town, and minor administrative areas, there are two units of local government that would properly engage the attention of research workers in New England institutions—the county and the metropolitan area. The former has been in a position of comparative unimportance throughout the history of New England, but probably not to the extent commonly believed. It is true that the element of "between lands" that gives the county its real jurisdiction has not often existed in New England in a significant way. All of Massachusetts, Connecticut, and Rhode Island are at present "incorporated," and it is, therefore, politically impossible to "get out of town" in the usual sense. The same is true of Maine, New Hampshire, and Vermont except for sparsely populated areas. This circumstance, of course, has tended to emphasize the importance of the city, town, and village at the expense of the county. It is also true that the judicial function—one of the important *raisons d'être* of most counties—has in some places been so centralized as to weaken even this main service. But the county persists, and, while lack of systematic investigations pertaining to its position in the political scheme make it impossible to treat the subject adequately, there is evidence that even in New England it may become increasingly useful.[14]

The metropolitan area, however, has attracted much attention in congested sections. The census of 1930 defined it as including: "in addition to the central city or cities, all adjacent and contiguous civil divisions having a density of not less than 150 inhabitants per square mile, and usually any civil divisions of less density that are directly adjacent to the central cities, or are entirely or nearly surrounded by minor civil divisions that have the required density . . . No metropolitan district was established [in which the central city had less than 50,000 inhabitants or] for those cities which did not have in the central city and surrounding area a population of at least 100,000." This admitted the following metropolitan districts in New England: (1) Boston (2,307,897 inhabitants[27]); (2) Providence-Fall River-New Bedford (963,686); (3) Hartford (471,185); (4) Springfield-Holyoke (398,991); (5) Lowell-Lawrence (332,028); (6) Worcester (305,293); (7) New Haven (293,724); (8) Bridgeport (203,969); (9) Waterbury (140,575); and (10) the southwestern tip of Connecticut, included in the New York metropolitan district. Important agitation, however, in favor of further governmental organization of metropolitan areas seems to have been pretty well confined to four cities—Hartford, New Haven, Providence, and Boston.[15]

At the General Assembly of the State of Connecticut (1929) an act was passed granting a charter for a metropolitan district in Hartford County. The act was to go into effect when the city of Hartford and one or more of the towns of West Hartford, Bloomfield, Windsor, Wethersfield, and Newington should approve its provisions.[16] These communities form a homogeneous unit, and the geographical and political lines that separate them are largely imaginary. Subsequently, all except West Hartford accepted the plan, and the legislation came into force.[17] The area was accordingly placed under the control of a continuing board of commissioners known as the "district board" elected by popular vote from each town and from the district at large. The jurisdiction of the commission extends to public highways, sewers, and water and to the necessary supplementary powers of regional planning, finance, and eminent domain.[18] The adoption of this legislation raised many issues of interest—particularly in connection with the defection of West Hartford and the subsequent relation of this town to the project.[19] The whole makes an interesting incident in the annals of New England metropolitanism.[20]

Although Providence has not extended its metropolitan activities to the point of a solution, in some respects they offer features of exceptional significance. In 1905 the General Assembly of Rhode Island defined an area adjacent to and including Providence as the "Metropolitan Park District of Providence Plantations."[21] Even at that time the homogenity of the area in economic, social, and residential matters was widely realized; but 1920 found the situation much as it had been fifteen years before. The federal census of that year placed the city in the midst of twelve minor civil subdivisions overlapping three counties and two states, a central city area of 17.8 square miles as opposed to a metropolitan territory of 197.6 square miles. In 1930 the population of the city proper was about 253,000, and that of the metropolitan area (as defined in 1920[22]) was close to 636,000.[23] On the basis of these returns Providence could be described as the "most thoroughly occupied" of the so-called "Metropolitan Cities" in the United States.[24] Time after time during the past decade the City Plan Commission has urged consideration of the problem of further metropolitan administrative amalgamation.[25] Committees composed of representatives from the city of Cranston, the towns of North Providence and Johnston, and a joint special committee of the city council of Providence have worked on the matter, but no action has yet resulted.[26]

There is no metropolitan area in New England that has been so long or so consistently faced by the many aspects of this problem as Boston. Many proposals have been made designed to bring into closer coöperation the forty-three cities and towns with a total population of nearly 2,000,000 that are commonly included in the metropolitan district.[27] The movement began in its contemporary aspects with the introduction of a bill into the General Court of 1873 providing for the amalgamation of Boston with some fifteen adjacent communities, the whole to be controlled by fifteen aldermen and ninety common councilors. In 1896, 1905, 1911, and 1924 various proposals were vigorously brought forth, the movement culminating in its most recent phases by the appointment of Mayor James M. Curley's "Greater Boston" Committee in 1929.

The net results of this activity have been a state-appointed police commissioner (1906) now in charge of the peace of Boston; a metropolitan fire district (1914); a metropolitan district commission (1919) embracing the consolidated services of water, sewer, and parks; a metropolitan planning division (1923); and a Metropolitan Water Supply Board (1926). The recent agitation personified in Mayor Curley's committee aroused the usual opposition from the surrounding towns and cities; and, in spite of over three years' existence, the committee is apparently but little closer to a solution of the problem.[28]

STATE GOVERNMENT

While it is not possible to enlarge upon the significant features of state government, the principal problems can be briefly suggested. Four of the New England states have joined the nation-wide movement for the reorganization of their administrative services. Massachusetts was the first. Serious agitation began in 1912 with the creation of an efficiency and economy commission, but the results were not of first importance. In 1916 the commission was abolished, and in 1917 a second investigation was undertaken. The constitutional convention of 1918 provided for the reorganization of the state government into not more than twenty departments; and, upon ratification by the people, a plan of consolidation was proposed and submitted to the 1919 legislature, resulting in the "administrative consolidation act." Under this legislation a reorganization was accordingly undertaken but was only a partial success. The result was another report and the creation by the General Court (1922) of the now famous Commission on Administration and Finance.[29]

In 1921 the New York Bureau of Municipal Research was engaged to make an analysis of the administrative services of Vermont. No action resulted, but two years later a rather extensive reorganization was attempted through the abolition of some twenty offices, boards, and commissions and the consolidation of their functions into some seven departments.[30] In 1919 Connecticut authorized a special commission to prepare proposals for a civil administrative code. The legislature, however, failed to act on the subsequent recommendations and, although a second commission was appointed in 1921, made no report. The legislature of 1927 did, however, put into effect some minor changes, involving the creation of a department of finance and control with six *ex officio* and four appointed members at its head.[31]

The most recent survey of state government within New England is that of Maine. In his message to the 1929 legislature, Governor William Tudor Gardiner pointed to defects in the structure and methods of the state government and subsequently succeeded in raising some $20,000 from private sources for survey purposes.[32] He then engaged the National Institute of Public Administration[33] to make a thorough investigation; and an extensive report was published in November, 1930, the gist of which was "that nothing short of complete administrative reorganization should be undertaken."[34] It is an impressive pamphlet that sweeps somewhat ruthlessly through a hundred years of political adjustment with a formula for every ill; indeed, an analysis of this report as viewed by the local press offers interesting commentaries on the expert away from home.[35]

In addition there are many special problems of a political character that have received recent attention in New England. New Hampshire has held (June 4–13, 1930) a constitutional convention; and, although five amendments to the state constitution were proposed and submitted to the voters, all were rejected at the November election. The questions involved the desirability of absent voting for biennial elections, a state estate tax, an item veto for the governor over appropriation bills, special provision for an income tax law, and a proposal for reapportionment of state representatives—the latter question having been, perhaps, the principal reason for the convention session.[36]

Vermont has recently been interested in a survey of its planning problems, the critical results of which, as summarized in the *Burlington Free Press*, revealed:

"No State owned system of State highways. No really wide highways developed in parkway fashion. No satisfactory highway approach to the State. No State landscape architect. No up-to-date State legislation for city planning and zoning. No State plan and no modern comprehensive plan for any town or city."[37]

New Hampshire and Maine seem deeply troubled over their respective tax systems; the inadequacy of the general property tax appears to be the real difficulty. Rhode Island and Connecticut are puzzled over new problems of representation growing out of urban and rural alignments. More happily, Massachusetts can show one of the best-organized legislatures, one of the most effective personnel commissions, and one of the most successful state budgetary, purchasing, and control devices among the American commonwealths. Difficulties and achievements of this sort are not confined to New England. There is hardly a state that is not considering or developing some of them. For a "conservative" region they are being faced fairly enough in New England.

CONCLUSION

From such a medley of political practices, experiments, and adjustments, it is difficult to draw conclusions at once specific and fundamental. If it is a truism to say that the town meeting form of government is passing, it is illuminating to examine in its wider significance the manner of its passing. There are some thirty-eight city managers in Michigan, thirty in Florida, twenty-seven in Texas, and twenty-two in California. In Massachusetts there is only one, and in all New England there are only twenty-five in both towns and cities. "New England conservatism" is hardly a complete explanation of this reluctance to throw over the experience of the past. Other and less extreme solutions are being found. If, with the exception of Hartford, metropolitan areas in New England are still unorganized as such or are in the "special commission" stage, it must be remembered that local identity is the palladium of self-government and the solidity of long heritage is among the most unbendable elements in politics.

It is characteristic of New England that administrative reform has not been given the prominence demanded in more "progressive" parts of the country. A descriptive chart of town meeting government is the despair of the expert; but as a "going" concern there is a long record of sustained accomplishment that newer devices of democracy have too often failed to equal. Even in the state, complete administrative reorganization has not been carried as far as in other commonwealths; but important steps have been taken in fundamental positions that will in the process of a slow but well-tried adjustment ultimately include the whole structure. There is little doubt that as a laboratory for the political scientist New England ranks high in historical perspective, in living experiment, and in variety of problems.

NOTES

[1] In an opinion of the Supreme Judicial Court of Massachusetts appears the following: "The fundamental and real distinction between the town and the city organization is that in the former all the qualified inhabitants meet together to deliberate and vote as individuals, each in his own right, while in the latter all municipal functions are performed by deputies. The one is direct, the other is representative"—*Opinion of the Justices to the Senate*, 1918 (229 *Mass.*, 609).

[2] The minor civil divisions of New England would make an interesting field of investigation, especially the relation of such units to the central government. New England (particularly the northern section) has many areas classed as "locations," "grants," "townships," "plantations," "villages," "gores," "purchases," etc. In many cases there is no political significance attached to them. They are frequently sparsely settled or uninhabited tracts that were left out of corporate limits but have nevertheless maintained a historic title for descriptive purposes and remain useful to census enumerators. In some places (notably Maine and Vermont) villages are incorporated for limited purposes—sewer, water, fire, etc.—and in some cases when a town has reached its debt limit villages may organize to build a high school or library. On the contrary, villages (as in Massachusetts) may have a distinct social unity—that is, they may be important "centers" in incorporated towns—but have no separate political status. Or similar units may have a separate status, as in Connecticut, and be known as fire, sewer, lighting, or sanitary districts (State of

Connecticut, *Register and Manual*, Hartford, 1930, pp. 475–477). For a discussion of the matter see F. G. Bates, *Village Government in New England*, in *Amer. Polit. Sci. Rev.*, Vol. 6, 1912, pp. 367–385; for the different use of local terms throughout the United States see J. A. Fairlie and C. M. Kneier, *County Government and Administration*, New York, 1930, Chap. 23, *Villages, Boroughs and Towns;* and for actual lists of such areas see *Fifteenth Census of the United States, 1930: Population*, Vol. 1. The lists in the census report are incomplete because divisions that had no population in 1910, 1920, and 1930 are not included.

[3] TABLE III—NEW ENGLAND: POPULATION 1930; ASSESSED VALUATION, REVENUE RECEIPTS, OPERATION AND MAINTENANCE CHARGES FOR STATE GOVERNMENTS, 1929

STATE	POPULATION (1930)	INCREASE 1920–1930		ASSESSED VALUATION OF PROPERTY SUBJECT TO GENERAL PROPERTY TAXES, 1929 (THOUSANDS)	TOTAL STATE REVENUE RECEIPTS, 1929 (THOUSANDS)	OPERATION AND MAINTENANCE OF GENERAL DEPARTMENTS, 1929 (THOUSANDS)
		No.	%			
Maine . .	797,423	29,409	3.8	$743,688	$18,014	$12,083
N. H. . .	465,293	22,210	5.	673,176	9,693	7,836
Vt. . . .	359,611	7,183	2.	326,838	10,506	9,526
Mass. . .	4,249,614	397,258	10.3	7,124,237	65,069	44,111
R. I. . .	687,497	83,100	13.7	1,393,742	15,471	6,978
Conn. . .	1,606,903	226,272	16.4	2,803,670	36,950	19,563
New Eng.	8,166,341	765,432	10.3	13,065,351	155,704	100,096

This table is based on: Bureau of the Census, *Financial Statistics of State Governments, 1929*, Washington, 1931, pp. 56, 58, and 122, and *Fifteenth Census of the United States, 1930: Population*, Vol. 1.

[4] New England has tried all of the standard charters but, like the remainder of the country, has given preference to various types of the mayor-council plan. There are at present (June, 1932) nine city managers (exclusive of town managers), as follows: *Maine*, Auburn, Bangor, Belfast, Brewer, and Portland; *Vermont*, St. Albans and Bellows Falls; *Massachusetts*, Fall River; and *Connecticut*, New London. New Hampshire has recently provided enabling acts for both towns and cities to adopt the manager form (*N. H. Public Acts*, 1929, Chaps. 69 and 186), but no communities have taken favorable action. Milford, Hooker, and Tilton rejected the town manager at their meetings in March, 1930; Newport "deferred action"; and Haverhill appointed a committee to investigate (*The Manchester Union*, March 12, 1930, p. 1). In Massachusetts Boston and Quincy are "strong-mayor" cities; Lawrence, a commission city; and the remainder fall under some aspect of the mayor-council plan.

[5] See below, pp. 468–469.

[6] F. E. Chadwick, *The Newport Charter*, in *Proc. Amer. Polit. Sci. Assoc.*, Vol. 3, 1906, pp. 58–66.

[7] J. F. Sly, *Town Government in Massachusetts*, Cambridge, Mass., 1930, Chap. 7. The Massachusetts towns now operating under the limited town meeting are: Brookline, Watertown, Arlington, Winthrop, Weymouth, Methuen, Greenfield, West Springfield, Belmont, Dedham, Dartmouth, Swampscott, Milton, Saugus, and Winchester.

[8] *Ibid.*, p. 230

[9] A list of the communities now operating under the town manager plan in New England follows: *Maine*, Camden, Fort Fairfield, and Rumford; *Vermont*, St. Johnsbury, Springfield, Windsor, and Bellows Falls (in Brattleboro the system was discarded Mar. 31, 1931, after three years' trial); *Massachusetts*, Mansfield, Middleboro, Norwood, Orange, and Stoughton; *Connecticut*, Stratford and West Hartford. For further information consult International City Managers Association, 923 E. 60th St., Chicago, Ill.

[10] Sly, *loc. cit.*

[11] Massachusetts has made extensive use of permissive statutes similar to the "adoptive acts" of the English system. Lists of such acts are published annually in the report of the Secretary of the Commonwealth. The subject demands further investigation.

[12] The function of advice and guidance to state officers is becoming very significant. Bureaus for government research (as the Bureau for Municipal Research, Bowdoin College, Brunswick, Me.; the Bureau for Research in Municipal Government, Harvard University; the Division of Industrial and Municipal Research, Massachusetts Institute of Technology, Cambridge, Mass.; and the Bureau of Municipal Affairs, Norwich University, Northfield, Vt.) have aided in many ways, but so successful have state officials been that a state bureau of municipal information for service to city and town officials was recently recommended to the General Court of Massachusetts (*Final Report of the Special Commission Established to Investigate Municipal Expenditures and Undertakings and the Appropriation of Money Under Municipal Authority*, Boston, 1929, pp. 14–18). There has, however, developed some tendency to criticize the advice of state officers as being so conservative as at times to restrict the use of well established practices.

[13] A profitable study could be made of the development ot finance committees. See Sly, *op. cit.*, pp. 138–139, 149–150, and 208–211. In Maine, however, some complaint is expressed that "degeneracy of finance committees" has had a serious effect on town meeting government (O. C. Hormell, in *Portland Press Herald*, Oct. 25, 1930), but they are almost universal in towns of over three thousand inhabitants. "Town Budget Commissions" are receiving serious consideration in Rhode Island (*Town Budget Commissions*, editorial in *Providence Journal*, July 5, 1929).

[14] The New England county is an almost untouched field as a subject of scholarly research. In view of a reviving interest in this long neglected local unit, investigation of its functioning would be well worth while. There is great diversity: "In the five New England states which have county boards," write Fairlie and Kneier (*op. cit.*, p. 111), "they usually consist of three members, who are elected at large in each county, except in Connecticut, where they are chosen by the state legislature. In four of these states the board is known as the board of county commissioners; but in Vermont the duties of commissioners are performed by assistant judges of the county court. In New Hampshire and Connecticut the commissioners do not exercise the power of taxation or of making appropriations. These are entrusted to biennial conventions of the members of the state legislature from each county. This arrangement reduces the importance of the county board, but avoids placing in the same body the authority to levy taxes, to make appropriations and to disburse the proceeds. In Massachusetts, county appropriations and tax levies are made by the legislature; but the estimates of the county commissioners are regularly adopted; and there have been some cases of extravagance if not of corruption." The importance of certain phases of the problem is well shown in the *Report of the Special Commission on County Salaries* (Massachusetts General Court, *Senate, No. 270*, January, 1930), in the interest that Vermont has recently expressed in possible new uses of the county (*County Government Systems*, editorial in *Burlington Free Press*, June 7, 1930), and in a proposal in Maine to lengthen the term of the sheriff from two to four years.

[15] National Municipal League, Committee on Metropolitan Government, *The Government of Metropolitan Areas in the United States*, New York, 1930.

[16] Metropolitan District Commission, *Charter of the Metropolitan District, Hartford County, Connecticut*, Hartford, 1930, Sect. 96; see L. W. Lancaster, *Hartford Adopts a Metropolitan Charter*, in *Amer. Polit. Sci. Rev.*, Vol. 24, 1930, pp. 693–698.

[17] *Establish the Metropolitan District*, editorial in *Hartford Courant*, Oct. 9, 1929; *The Metropolitan Act*, editorial, *ibid.*, Sept. 17, 1929.

[18] *Charter of the Metropolitan District* (cited above), Sects. 2–3. Within six months of the time the act became operative the governor was to appoint the first commission—one member from each town in the "first form" for two years and five at-large in each of three divisions in the "second form" for two, three, and six year terms, respectively (*ibid.*, Sect. 3). At the expiration of the appointed terms biennial elections were to fill the vacancies (*ibid.*, Sect. 4).

[19] See particularly *West Hartford's Opportunity*, editorial in *Hartford Courant*, Sept. 19, 1929; *It Depends on West Hartford*, editorial, *ibid.*, Sept. 25, 1929; *Hartford and the Metropolitan District*, editorial, *ibid.*, Oct. 26, 1929.

[20] New Haven felt the stimulus of the Hartford action, and the General Assembly in 1929 arranged for the appointment of a commission to consider the establishment of a metropolitan district in New Haven county. (*An Act Creating a Commission to Investigate the Advisability of Establishing a Metropolitan District Within the Territorial Limits of the County of New Haven*, State of Conn., *Senate, No. 374*, April 24, 1929). The plan embraced New Haven, West Haven, Orange, Woodbridge, Hamden, North Haven, and East Haven. As yet (November, 1932) no further progress has been made toward the amalgamation of these towns.

[21] Providence, R. I., City Plan Commission, *Annual Reports*, 1922–1928, Providence, 1929, p. 72.

[22] In 1930 the Bureau of the Census included Fall River and New Bedford with Providence in a single metropolitan district.

[23] *Fifteenth Census of the United States, 1930*; *Population*, Vol. 1, chapters on Massachusetts and Rhode Island.

[24] Providence, R. I., City Plan Commission, *op. cit.*, p. 70.

[25] *Ibid.*, pp. 21 ff. 45 ff., 67 ff., and 72 ff.

[26] *The Providence Journal*, April 22, 1930, editorially under *For a Greater Providence*, states the situation simply:

"Following the movement in Providence and Johnston toward a union of towns and cities at the headwaters of Narragansett Bay, a committee of seven members of the City Council in Cranston has been appointed to confer on the matter.

"No community, of course, is pledged by such preliminary steps. All that is intended is that all concerned shall get together and see what may or ought to be done. The present situation is uneconomic and unwise. The interests of all of us would be served if, with a fair regard for everybody, some of the boundary lines now existing could be altered or done away with.

"Most of the territory in this neighborhood used to be Providence; most of it will probably be Providence at some future time. We are, in many ways, a single community already, divided by official border lines that are largely obsolete and that seriously hamper us in our civic development.

"Let us recognize these facts and apply ourselves reasonably and with mutual good will to the solution of the problems to which they have given rise."

[27] The population of metropolitan Boston in 1930 was 1,955,168, as compiled from the *Fifteenth Census of the United States* by F. W. Cook and W. N. Hardy in *The Population of Massachusetts, 1930*, Boston, 1931 ([*Mass.*], *House, No. 1740*), pp. 9–11. The district as established by the Census Bureau is somewhat larger (population 2,307,897).

[28] For a brief outline of the situation see J. F. Sly, *What Metropolitan Boston Can*

Learn from London's Experience, in *Boston Evening Transcript*, June 19, 1929; and, more completely, National Municipal League, *op. cit.*, index, p. 392. [In 1931 and 1932 Mayor Curley's committee introduced into the Massachusetts legislature bills calling for the creation of a city of metropolitan Boston, but action upon them has as yet been postponed (Oct., 1932).—EDIT.]

²⁹ A. E. Buck, *Administrative Consolidation in State Governments*, 5th edit., National Municipal League, New York, 1930, pp. 14 ff. and 58. The Commission on Administration and Finance, C. P. Howard, Chairman (*Manual of the General Court (1929–30)*, p. 297) is one of the most effective devices in state government. A thorough study of its work and methods during the past eight years would be a suggestive undertaking. Mr. Howard comes, perhaps, very near to being a "state manager."

³⁰ Buck, *op. cit.*, pp. 30 ff. and 59.

³¹ *Ibid.*, pp. 49 and 57.

³² *Ibid.*, p. 56. A previous report known as the *Cole Committee Report* had been issued in 1923, but no action followed.

³³ Luther Gulick, Director, 261 Broadway, New York City.

³⁴ National Institute of Public Administration, *State Administrative Consolidation in Maine*, New York, 1930, p. 8; O. C. Hormell, *Administrative Reorganization in Maine*, in *Natl. Municipal Review*, Vol. 20, 1931, pp. 131–133.

³⁵ *Survey of Government*, editorial in *Bangor Daily Commercial*, Oct. 21, 1930; *Our Highways*, editorial, *ibid.*, Oct. 30, 1930; *Maine's Road Construction and Maintenance Program Attacked in Survey Report*, editorial, *ibid.*, Oct. 29, 1930; *Survey of State Government*, editorial in *Portland Press Herald*, Oct. 28, 1930; *State Prison Conditions Are Condemned in Survey Report*, editorial, *ibid.*, Oct. 29, 1930; *Abolition of Portland Harbor Commission Is Urged in Survey*, editorial, *ibid.*, Nov. 1, 1930.

³⁶ New Hampshire, *Public Acts and Joint Resolutions*, 1929, Chap. 190; New Hampshire, *Questions Submitted to the Qualified Voters by the Convention to Revise the Constitution, In Session June 4th to 13th, 1930* (single sheet); New Hampshire, *Articles of the Constitution as They Now Read, Which Would Be Altered or Amended, by Amendments Proposed and Adopted in the Convention to Revise the Constitution, In Session June 4th to 13th, 1930; The Representation Problem*, editorials in *The Manchester Union*, June 11 and 19, 1930.

³⁷ *Practical Ways to Plan in City and State*, editorial in *The Burlington Free Press*, June 13, 1930.

SOCIAL SERVICE IN BOSTON

Roy M. Cushman

HISTORICAL BACKGROUND

IN the history of social welfare, Boston is the oldest community in America. Located on the seacoast of one of the earliest settled colonies, she had to bear the brunt of all the varied problems attending the care of dependent persons that became manifest almost from the very beginning. Reluctantly, perhaps somewhat resentfully, in their own self-defense the colonists must needs shoulder the burden of providing for the lame, the halt, and the blind, as well as vagabonds and rogues, when they would rather have expended all their energy on the more positive side of the huge task they had set themselves— that of establishing Old World culture in the North American wilderness. Whatever may have been the case in later years, in the early days of the Massachusetts Bay Colony there was a numerous immigration of paupers and criminals from the mother country, aided and abetted by the authorities there. Much of the burden of caring for this grossly disproportionate number of idle and necessitous persons fell upon the town of Boston, the gateway of the province. Against this injustice, as they saw it, the citizens of Boston rebelled. There followed the plan of divided responsibility under which the town took care of its own paupers and vagrants and the colony took care of the "unsettled poor." Here is found the genesis of the so-called Massachusetts system of charities, under which today the towns administer relief and the state, through the instrumentality of its Department of Public Welfare, supervises and determines policy. At the same time the state has assumed direct responsibility for the care of certain groups, notably neglected, dependent, and delinquent children, and the insane.

Side by side with the development of governmental policy and facilities in the field of public welfare has gone that of private charity. Each has supplemented the other; and through both in the course of the years have come those understandings and skills that enter into the practice of modern social work, which not only ministers to the afflicted but also is one of the positive forces at work to make the world a better place to live in. It is charity in a modern world— charity utilizing all the tools made available by science for better understanding and better performance. In this movement Boston has played a distinguished part.

It would seem futile in a limited space to attempt a descriptive statement of Boston's numerous social agencies. Hence, except for a brief outline to indicate their growth and range, consideration will be given rather to certain outstanding present-day problems and trends in the field of social work as exemplified in Boston's experience.

FIFTY YEARS' GROWTH, 1880–1930

In the first directory of charitable and beneficent organizations of Boston, published in 1880 by the Associated Charities (since become the Family Welfare Society), there are listed about 225 organizations for numerous and varied purposes, including public departments and institutions, private agencies of all kinds, and established funds. The eighth edition of the directory, published in 1932 by the Boston Council of Social Agencies, shows a total of 350.

A comparison of the earlier and the later directories reveals interesting and significant changes in Boston's social welfare activity. The growth of social work in Boston is shown in another way by its cost. In 1929 the city spent for the maintenance of the Departments of Health, Public Welfare, Hospitals, Institutions, and Soldiers' Relief a total of about $8,000,000. During the same year 150-odd private agencies of all kinds, including hospitals, which appeal to the public for some part of their support, required between $17,000,000 and $18,000,000, of which amount about 30 per cent, more than $5,000,000, came from donations, 13 per cent from endowments, and 57 per cent from earnings.

The agencies described in the earlier volume concerned themselves almost entirely with the relief of distress in its various forms; institutions occupied, relatively, a much greater portion of the field; the churches as such were much more active in works of charity than they are today; except for paid employees in institutions and a small number of visitors among the poor, Boston's benevolences were carried on by volunteers; many terms, such as pauper, asylum, and fallen women, which occur frequently in the earlier volume are now in the discard; such titles as the Penitent Females' Refuge look strange to us today, and we do not wonder that those in charge of that organization prefer to carry on under the name Bethesda Society. Settlements and all neighborhood and club work as we know them today were unheard of in 1880; it was not until 1892 that Robert A. Woods, after his visit to Toynbee Hall in London two years earlier, opened South End House. Recreation as a need of the people was just beginning to be recognized. The Massachusetts probation system—the first in the world—had been established in 1878 with one officer for the County of Suffolk as compared with the sixty-nine of today. "Homes" were the chief reliance for the care of dependent children in 1880, whereas today placing out is the rule, institutions either being abandoned altogether or used as adjuncts of the placement service and notably in some instances as study centers. Not until 1905 did medical social service make its appearance, when Dr. Richard C. Cabot placed one worker in the Massachusetts General Hospital; now there are social service departments in three city hospitals and thirteen private hospitals.

The science of public health as we know it today had not been born in 1880. In the war on disease, reliance was chiefly on general sanitary measures. Just at that time—1880 to 1883—the discovery of the organisms causing three of the greatest scourges of the human race—typhoid, tuberculosis, and diphtheria—made possible a scientific attack on the causes of disease, which was soon to show results in lowered death rates. In the 1880 directory we find the term "public health" just once, and that in the title of the "Massachusetts Public Health Association," which is noted as "not yet in active operation." None of the unofficial organizations that later came to play an important part in the public health work of the city was in existence in 1880 with the exception of the Boston Dispensary, established in 1796. This institution for many years had carried the public service of providing medical aid to the sick poor in their own homes and in clinics. The year 1886 witnessed the organization of one of the most important privately supported health agencies in Boston, the Instructive District Nursing Association (now the Community Health Association), which engaged one nurse to work with the district physician of the Boston Dispensary.

A truly modern note, however, is struck in the preface of the first directory in the following sentences:

"This book shows what a multitude of noble charities Boston contains, and may bring into view some of the gaps existing between them. Many of these gaps may be closed without new institutions, by the judicious enlargement of the field of work of existing agencies, which now do not quite touch.

"The science of charity insists on a thorough study of the causes of want, and of the means of its removal and prevention, as well as its relief—and especially on thorough organization in large cities where many agencies are at work."

Two Present-Day Problems

The two big problems suggested here may well be considered the most immediately important of all the problems facing social work as a whole in Boston today: first, how to marshal the many and diverse units in the structure so that they will best serve the great fundamental purpose of the improvement of the conditions of life and the quality of the human race; and second, how better to employ the scientific method to discover the character and extent of the problems at hand and guide the agencies toward the solution of them—in a word coördination and research.

Coördination

The necessity of coördinating works of charity was recognized in Boston no less than a century ago. In 1830 Joseph Tuckerman, a Unitarian minister, advocated a central coördinating committee and a registry to facilitate the exchange of information about the recipients of charity and thus prevent fraud and avoid duplication of effort. Tuckerman did not live to develop his ideas, and not till nearly fifty years later did they begin to bear fruit. In 1875 Mrs. James T. Fields and Mrs. James Lodge started the Coöperative Society of Visitors Among the Poor, and in the following year Miss Frances R. Morse and others opened the Registration Bureau, giving practical expression to Tuckerman's ideas.

A union of the two ideas was effected with the establishment in 1879 of the Associated Charities. This organization, recently become the Family Welfare Society, was for many years the chief coördinating factor among Boston's charitable enterprises. Following the methods of the Charity Organization Society of London, it placed emphasis on service rather than on relief-giving and was the chief medium in Boston through which the technique and principles of modern social case work were developed. The practice of case work is in its nature one of the primary influences for coördination in a social work program. "It calls for the personal following of a family's fortunes, helping them to plan and work their way out of their difficulty, bringing to their aid all available resources of the community—material, medical, recreational, and spiritual." This process inevitably brings the workers of different agencies together in their daily activity.

The Registration Bureau, which soon came to be called the Confidential Exchange and later the Social Service Exchange, became at once a most important adjunct in case-work practice. It was developed and perfected by the Family Welfare Society over a period of fifty years until it became the most extensive service of its kind in the United States. On January 1, 1930, the management of the Exchange was transferred by the Society to the Boston Council of Social Agencies and the service given the yet more accurately descriptive name of the Social Service Index. Responsibility for its management and support now rests upon all the agencies using it. The Social Service Index, or the Central Index, as it is frequently called, is now a file of 800,000 cards housed in the Public Welfare Building, a catalogue of the great library of case histories in the offices of the social service agencies, both voluntary and tax-supported, in Boston and many other cities in the Commonwealth. During the year 1929 the index was consulted 69,000 times, and 43,229 reports were returned to the inquirers telling them where the case histories, if any, could be found. (The corresponding figures for 1931 were 121,944 and 75,176 respectively.)

"Though social service agencies exist in more diverse form than in the beginning of the Central Index, there is this difference—they are more vitally related. The emphasis, too, is no longer so much on the importance of the agency to its friends and supporters, but rather on its duty to foster the interests of the community. . . . The first Annual Report of the Associated Charities of Boston described the object of the Registration Bureau as 'to secure an interchange of information and thereby detect imposture, discourage begging, distinguish the worthy from the unworthy, and promote economy and efficiency in the distribution of relief.' . . . The expression 'Central Index' has its roots in a new logic of organization. It is founded, so to speak, on a self-supporting idea, as opposed to 'Registration Bureau' or 'Exchange' which represents an idea that is negative rather than positive in its implications. The change in the center of interest from the registration of families to the indexing of agency records in a central place is a step in advance in social work. The case history is looked upon, not as a story to be dictated, but as a problem to be solved. Such histories are an index to the quality of the achievement that social case work can render to individuals. They are deposits of educational work."[1]

With the course for the further development of the index thus finely charted, the roots of its immediate problems are found in its size. A few years back, 100 per cent registration of their cases by agencies using the index was advocated. Now those closest to the movement throughout the country are wrestling with the problem of a satisfactory selective process in order that the index file may not be needlessly encumbered.

For two decades or more the Associated Charities remained almost the sole coördinating factor among Boston's charities. In 1891 what was perhaps the first step in the direction of coördination through the methods of conference and association was taken. In that year there was organized a "Conference of Child-helping Societies." The plan, however, had to be abandoned after a few years with only desultory meetings of a steadily diminishing number of people who saw the possibilities of usefulness but could not give the time for steady planning and operation.

Other similar informal groups that functioned for a short while were the Conference of Day Nurseries, organized about 1900; the Committee of Nine, so-called, formed in 1912 and made up of nine persons prominent in child care work; and a Committee on the Care of the Feeble-minded, also formed in 1912. Experience proved, however, that such informal organizations could not maintain continuity, and accordingly a League for Preventive Work was established in 1915. This league federated twenty leading welfare organizations for

---

[1] L. G. Woodberry, *The Central Index*, New York, 1929.

the definite purpose indicated by the name. Its paid secretary planned and carried out studies suggested by an executive committee. It investigated various causes of dependency and demonstrated the importance of continuous, as distinguished from occasional, joint action.

In 1920, the year of the second influenza epidemic, came an experience so convincing to the organizations of this league that they determined that the city should not in the future lack a welding force to unify the action of helping agencies. In this epidemic the League for Preventive Work had tried the experiment of bringing its member agencies together with the head of the City Health Department, Dr. William C. Woodward, to plan for joint action for the protection of afflicted families from unnecessary distress. Definite assignments for service were outlined and accepted by the several agencies, and the result was so impressive that the organizers of the League for Preventive Work became advocates of an even broader, more inclusive undertaking.

Joining forces with them came the group of settlements that since 1900 had been organized in a Boston Social Union (now the Greater Boston Federation of Neighborhood Houses), the Federation for Placement Work, formed in 1919 with a membership chiefly of non-fee-charging employment offices and interested principally in handicapped persons, and, finally, the Boston Health League, also started in 1919 and comprising in its membership all the leading health agencies of the city.

Thus, in 1921, the Boston Council of Social Agencies was organized. The logical culmination of a long process of evolution in Boston, the Council is also part of a country-wide movement for federation and coördination in the field of social work. The movement is exemplified most frequently in joint financing organizations known generally as community chests, the most widely known of which is that of Cleveland, started in 1913. As the result of experiences gained during the war, the central financing movement has grown by leaps and bounds since 1918, so that there are today about two hundred and thirty chests in the United States. To distinguish them from chests or financial federations, the councils of social agencies, community councils, or welfare councils, as they are variously named, are sometimes called functional federations. Some of the chests have councils connected with them. There are also fifteen councils in the country independently established—that is, without connection with community chests. The councils in New York, Philadelphia, and Chicago, as well as that in Boston, are in this category. The question of whether or not a chest should be established in Boston was thoroughly studied by a committee of the Chamber of Commerce, which, in its final report issued in 1925, returned an affirmative recommendation. A majority of the agencies, however, declined to accept the recommendation.

A community council is defined as "a federated group of diversified welfare organizations in a local community, represented by officially appointed delegates and having as its primary purpose the development of an adequate welfare program for the community."[2] It is the present-day manifestation of the charity organization movement of the seventies and eighties and is the most effective instrument so far devised for the coördination of all the units of a highly complex system of welfare activity.

According to the kind of service they render, the member agencies of a council are usually grouped in departments or sections. In Boston there are eight departments (Family, Children, Hospital Social Service, Protective Social Measures, Health, Settlements, Employment and Industrial Conditions, and Character Building) and a Publicity Division. The departments and the Publicity Division, comprising 130 units—all, with very few exceptions, of the larger or more active social agencies in the city, both tax-supported and voluntary, sectarian and non-sectarian—constitute discussion groups on matters of coöperation, standards, and methods of work and have contributed largely to the establishment of the habit of consultation on important moves desired or projected in social work.

As they are made up of groups of specialists, the principal advantage of the departments is the opportunity they provide for discussion of technical problems and matters of special interest and for joint action which might follow such discussion. They do not necessarily foster interest in the broader aspects of community service. This lack is made up in a measure through the general council meetings, but the need of something more has been felt. Accordingly in 1929 a system of district organizations was inaugurated. This plan calls for the bringing together of representatives of all the departments jointly with representatives of local interests for consideration of local community needs and ways of meeting them. There are in the plan values more significant than those of cutting across lines of specialty in social work. If successfully carried through, a district organization should prove a valuable instrument for community organization. It is in effect a council in smaller dimension and consequently more easily unified. Its connection with the city-wide council gives it values that a purely local organization would not possess.

The Council of Social Agencies has direct administrative responsibilities for three services: the Social Service Index, described above; a Purchasing Bureau, through which agencies have made substantial savings by bulking orders; and a Bureau of Research and Studies, just now getting under way.

RESEARCH

Research is an essential part of modern social work, which can no longer act on old beliefs and outworn practices but must proceed, along

---

[2] Arthur Dunham, *Community Councils in Action*, Philadelphia, 1929.

with modern business and with modern medicine, on the basis of fact. Modern business depends, not only for economical management but for its very life, on searching analysis both of its internal processes and of outside competition. Modern medicine bases treatment on scientific research and on skilful diagnosis. It no longer is content to work with symptoms but makes every effort to get at causes.

A pioneer in many lines of social work, Boston finds itself in social research far from the head of the line. To be sure, many studies of outstanding merit have been made here, and not only in Boston itself but at Harvard and the Massachusetts Institute of Technology across the river are to be found some of the country's leaders in social research and allied fields. Boston's splendid equipment in social agencies of all kinds offers a veritable gold mine, as yet unworked, of all kinds of revealing social data. The immediate problem is one of organization. Social research in Boston today is in the same situation as were the city's charities in the seventies, when the Associated Charities and the Confidential Exchange were organized, and as were the social agencies when the Council of Social Agencies was started in 1921. The need is for integration, coördination.

Two steps of primary importance must be taken first of all:

1. A clearing house must be established for all studies in social research;
2. A system must be devised for the uniform recording of statistics.

The setting up of the clearing house would call for an inventory of all studies made within the past ten or fifteen years and a current registering of present and projected studies. This would prevent duplication and overlapping, much as the Social Service Index prevents those things in case work. The background of an adequate system of statistics is the federal census data, the value of which is increased a hundredfold if they be gathered on the basis of small fixed topographical units, known as statistical tracts. As population increases the tracts may be subdivided, but the original boundaries should remain unchanged. The factors that bear closely on the life of the people—population, race, vital statistics, morbidity, unemployment, and the like—could thus be studied with these fixed topographical units as a base. Thus one section of a city could be compared with another at a particular time; or trends in the same section could be followed from year to year as a fund of information about the section is gradually built up.

The Census Bureau in 1910 divided the City of Boston into tracts, but there was not in that year or in 1920 sufficient interest shown to demand the tabulation of the census data on the basis of these tracts. In 1930 this was done. The Boston Health League (the department on health of the Council) has prepared and published a Census Tract

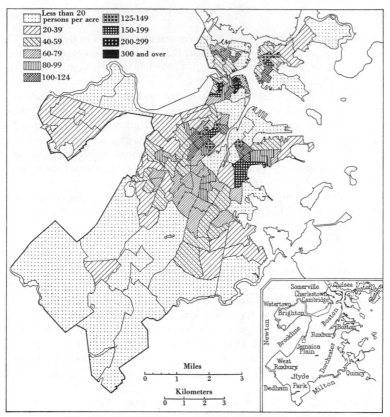

FIG. 1—Density of population, Boston, 1930.

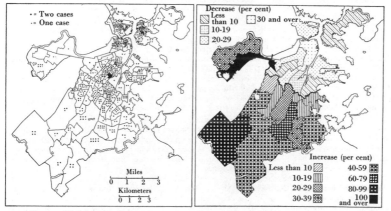

FIG. 2—Diphtheria in Boston, 1930. FIG. 3—Trends of population, Boston, 1915–1930.

FIGS. 1–3—See footnote on p. 440.

439

map of the city and has compiled a comprehensive street list, a necessary adjunct to the map, in order that the position of streets in relation to tracts may be readily disclosed. (This list was published in 1931 by the Boston Health Department.)

With the tract boundaries established and the map and street list available, the next step will be the amalgamation of tracts into districts. Several factors should be borne in mind as these are created: (1) the population of the district (New York uses a unit of population of 25,000); (2) the capitalization of neighborhood spirit and feeling; (3) the existence of present district lines; (4) transportation and communication.

The third step in the process will be to obtain an agreement among social agencies to keep their statistics according to these districts. This does not necessarily mean a realignment of their district work; but it will mean a willingness to do their recording along uniform lines. For example, the City Health Department has led the way in agreeing to record vital statistics by census tracts as well as by wards, as required by law; and the State Board of Probation has already begun to use the tracts in its new statistical department. Once this uniformity is effected it will be possible in any particular district to get significant data that will shed light upon such problems as density of population; racial distribution; death rates, both adult and infant; the incidence of communicable diseases; the distribution of families receiving relief; school attendance; delinquency, both adult and juvenile; and many others.

Three maps of Boston are given on the preceding page. Two of these—Figure 1, showing the density of population in 1930, and Figure 2, showing the distribution of diphtheria cases in 1930—are

NOTES ON FIGURES 1–3

Fig. 1—Density of population in Boston, 1930, plotted from statistics prepared by the Boston Health League from information supplied by the U. S. Census Bureau and the Boston City Street Laying-Out Department; census tract boundaries plotted from Census Tract Map of Boston prepared by the Boston Health League, using base map reproduced by permission of the City Planning Board.

Fig. 2—Diphtheria in Boston in 1930 distributed by census tracts; from unpublished map compiled by the Boston Health League. Detailed maps of this type cannot be compiled on the basis of statistics by wards. Such maps are of great value in the planning of social work programs of all kinds.

Fig. 3—Changes in the population of Boston, 1915–1930, by wards of 1930, plotted from the reports of the decennial census of Massachusetts of 1915 and the U. S. Census of 1930.

On Figures 1 and 2 are shown the boundaries of the 128 statistical tracts into which the city has been divided by the Census Bureau. Figure 3 was compiled on the basis of wards. It may readily be seen how much more revealing than Figure 3 would be a map showing population changes within small, fixed geographical areas such as the census tracts. A ward where a slight increase in population occurred might actually have lost everywhere except in one small section. Furthermore, ward boundaries are constantly changing to suit political exigency.

Figure 1 shows clearly the concentration of population in five main nuclei: (1) the North End and the West End of Boston; (2) Charlestown; (3) East Boston; (4) the South End; and (5) South Boston. The relatively sparse population of the two tracts comprising the business district of old Boston is striking. On Figure 3 we see that the northeastern third of the city as a whole, comprising all the most densely settled areas, declined in population during the fifteen years before 1930. The greatest decrease occurred in old Boston and in parts of Roxbury; the greatest increases in the outlying districts of Brighton, West Roxbury, and Dorchester. Decreases in population occurred in all wards lying northeast of the heavy black line cutting across the city; the wards southwest of this line all gained in population.

based on statistics tabulated by census tracts. The maps illustrate how the keeping of statistics by these tracts will provide, when the practice becomes general, a sure basis for studying many other social phenomena and will be of incalculable advantage in the planning of social work programs of all kinds—relief, recreation, visiting nursing, etc.[3] When Figures 1 and 2 are compared with Figure 3, which shows *by wards* the increase and decrease in population between 1915 and 1930, it is seen at once how much more refined a picture is given when census tracts can be employed. On Figure 3, for example, no distinction is apparent between the crowded North End and the business district with its sparse resident population. The whole of Charlestown and the whole of East Boston each constitute a single unit on Figure 3. The maps based on the census tracts, however, reveal at a glance the wide divergencies that may exist within the limits of a single ward. Thus the third (or old fifth) ward, comprising the north and east side of the peninsula of Boston proper, includes census tracts ranging between the most thickly and the most thinly occupied in the entire city.

When this system of recording information is set up, and not until then, the district or neighborhood plan, described above, can be effectively put into operation. Not only will overlapping be more readily detected, but, what is perhaps more important, bare spots will be disclosed, knowledge of which is so necessary in planning the establishment of new work or the enlargement or development of old.

With these two fundamental preliminary steps accomplished; first, the discovery of what research has gone on before and the setting up of a clearing house of all subsequent studies; and second, the establishment of the machinery for the uniform gathering of statistics, social research could be carried on productively. Studies that might reasonably be undertaken in Boston, with the use of certain classifications of Dr. Neva R. Deardorff, Director of Research in the New York Welfare Council, are of the following general types:

A. *Inventories of Social Resources.* These may relate to the entire community, to neighborhoods, or to socially handicapped or other groups. They deal primarily with quantitative features such as services rendered, personnel, expenditures, etc., although qualitative analyses, using already accepted standards as measures, may be a part of such studies.

B. *Description of Social Problems.* Such inquiries seek to discover the extent, the factors, and the antecedents of each problem. The study of chronic disease made by the Boston Council of Social Agencies in 1926–1927 is typical of this classification. It endeavored to picture the extent of chronic disease in Boston, to measure the facilities for care of the chronically ill, and to reveal needs for added resources. The study of adoptions made in 1926–1927 under the auspices of the Research Bureau on Social Case Work,

---

[3] Census tracts have been used as the basis for extremely detailed analyses of the population of Cleveland, Ohio. See publications of H. W. Green cited on p. 445, below.

since discontinued, is another example. Still a third is the mental hygiene survey of Boston now being carried on jointly by the Massachusetts Society for Mental Hygiene, the Boston Council of Social Agencies, and the Boston Health League.

C. *Continuous Measures of Incidence of Various Forms of Need.* Once the machinery for uniform recording of statistics, as described above, is set up, it will be possible to watch the relationship between need and facilities for meeting it, whether it be for hospital beds, relief, visiting nurse service, playgrounds, or other things.

D. *Demographic studies,* including the human composition, the structure of social relations, and social, geographical, and political boundaries of the community itself, would seem to be fundamental to an understanding of any social condition or problem in it. Such studies would have particular application to the district organization plan, described above.

E. *Studies of Method.* These are likely to be the most painstaking and exhaustive of all the types. The study of interrelationships of social agencies now being made by Miss Ida R. Parker and Miss Alla A. Libbey at the Massachusetts Memorial Hospitals is an illustration.

F. *Studies of Social Causation.* Many agencies now keep their statistics to reveal causes of family dependence, neglect of children, etc. A uniform method of recording statistics would provide more data and consequently increased understanding.

WHAT LIES AHEAD?

When one contemplates the tremendous strides taken by social work in Boston in the past fifty years, one is reluctant to predict what the next fifty years will bring forth. This much is certain: with even stronger coördinating forces at work within its field than there are today, with the course of its development carefully charted on a sound basis of fact and understanding of conditions as they really are, and with an increasingly enlightened interest in its purposes and a growing desire to participate in its varied activities on the part of the people of the city, Boston's social work will justify the assertion of the pioneers of fifty years ago that "the best charity can only flow from a union of science and sympathy, each at its best."

EFFECTS OF THE ECONOMIC DEPRESSION

The foregoing paragraphs were written in 1930. Since then the economic depression, the severity of which has continued to increase up to the present time (July, 1932), has subjected the social agencies of Boston, both tax-supported and voluntary, to a strain never before experienced. Relief, in terms of the elementary requirements for subsistence, has become the most important factor in the program. The Massachusetts system of public welfare, as it operates not only in Boston but generally throughout the state, has proved a veritable bulwark of strength in programs for assisting the unemployed. Boston, with its Department of Public Welfare on the scene with years of experience behind it, was all equipped to meet the repidly increasing demands. It has, so to speak, taken the emergency in its stride. The constantly rising costs of relief have been paid in larger part (well over 90 per cent, in fact) from tax funds. A valuable collateral service requiring large sums in the aggregate, though they appear small when compared with the huge expenditure of the Department of Public Welfare, has been rendered by the private relief and family service agencies. Table I shows the rise in relief costs over a period of two

TABLE I—RELIEF DISBURSEMENTS BY VARIOUS CHARITABLE ORGANIZATIONS
IN BOSTON, JULY, 1930–JUNE, 1932

	JULY–DECEMBER 1930	JANUARY–JUNE 1931	JULY–DECEMBER 1931	JANUARY–JUNE 1932
Overseers of Public Welfare	$1,931,328.26	$3,459,023.70	$3,612,362.74	$6,101,333.30
Soldiers' Relief Department	213,921.23	224,893.78	230,272.98	420,559.24
Family Welfare Society	79,336.23	108,717.10	97,425.23	232,818.20
Boston Provident Association . . .	26,269.59	42,051.32	33,014.88	66,251.86
Associated Jewish Philanthropies . .	46,359.36	51,318.74	52,456.92	60,499.13
Totals	$2,297,214.67	$3,886,004.64	$4,025,532.75	$6,881,461.73

years as reported by the Overseers of the Public Welfare, the Soldiers' Relief Department, and three private societies. It should be noted that the figures cover total relief outlays, not only unemployment relief, although of course unemployment is the primary cause of the increases.

Though material relief is the chief factor in the situation, effort has been constant in the direction of showing the public the necessity of maintaining the services of non-relief agencies. The services given by the hospitals and health agencies and the care of dependent children in certain of its aspects are essentially relief. Those of the educational and recreational agencies—the settlements, the "Y's," and others— are not so easily related to the emergency, although the imperative need of wholesome leisure-time activities for people who have an abundance of leisure time seems obvious.

Needless to say, the public treasury and private philanthropy both have been subjected to a terrific strain to maintain the city's program of social and health services. In January, 1932, Boston essayed its first consolidated fund-raising campaign since the war. The campaign was in no sense of the community-chest type but was wholly for an emergency fund. It was unique in that the Public Welfare Department and the private societies were joined as beneficiaries of the fund. The objective, $3,000,000, was raised by the usual campaign method and was divided—two thirds to the public department and one third to the private societies. The private societies' share was distributed to some 90 agencies of all kinds by a specially appointed Allocating Committee of five citizens. It is generally conceded that another joint campaign, perhaps somewhat differently organized, will be necessary in the winter of 1932–1933.

A few words should be added concerning the two functions especially discussed in the foregoing pages, namely, coördination and research. The validity of the idea of a council of social agencies as the most effective mechanism for coördination in a modern social work set-up has been strengthened by the activity of the Boston Council during the emergency. The Council has been the medium through which common problems have been considered, plans drawn, and joint action effected. Without it the agencies would have found themselves in a state of unrelatedness that could not have been justified and would have seriously impaired their efficiency in meeting the demands the emergency has placed upon them. The Social Service Index, with a load of work in 1931 twice that of 1929, and with figures still mounting, has continued to be the primary factor for the coördination of the work of the relief agencies. Many thousands of dollars must have been saved the agencies through the use of this simple device, at the same time that service to the clients has been improved. Under the guidance of a special committee on the care of the homeless, a central application bureau for homeless men has been established.

The Bureau of Research and Studies, started in 1930 together with several investigations in other fields, has completed two studies of unemployed clients of the social agencies and is now projecting a third. These studies have produced valuable factual data concerning the unemployed of Boston which have been helpful in planning continuing relief programs. The Census Tract project has been developed jointly by the Boston Health League and the Council. Various maps have been produced, and health and welfare districts have been defined and accepted by the city-wide agencies.

REFERENCES

Alphabetical Street Index and Basic Demographic Data for the City of Boston by Census Tracts, compiled by Boston Health League and published by the Boston Health Department, 1931.

Channing, Alice, *A Study of Unemployed Clients of Boston Family and Relief Agencies*, in *Bull. of the Boston Council of Social Agencies*, Vol. 10, December, 1931, p. 11 (also reprinted).

Clapp, M. A., *Further Studies of Unemployed Clients of Boston Social Agencies*, in *Bull. of the Boston Council of Social Agencies*, Vol. 11, June, 1932, pp. 2–14.

A Directory of Charitable and Beneficent Organizations of Boston, The Associated Charities of Boston, 1880.

Directory of Social Agencies of Boston, 8th edit., The Boston Council of Social Agencies, 1932.

Dunham, Arthur, *Community Councils in Action*, Public Charities Association of Pennsylvania, Philadelphia, 1929.

Emerson, Haven, and A. F. Hamburger, *Report on Chronic Disease in Boston*, Boston Council of Social Agencies, Boston, 1927.

Final Report of the Special Committee on Financing of Social Agencies, Boston Chamber of Commerce, Boston, 1925.

Green, H. W., *Facts, Figures and Fiction in Social and Health Statistics: A Description of the Use of Census Tracts as Developed in Cleveland*, in *New England Journ. of Medicine*, Vol. 202, 1930, pp. 771–778.

The same, *Composition and Characteristics of a Typical City* [Cleveland, Ohio] *Analyzed by Census Tracts*, in *Journ. Amer. Statist. Assoc.*, Vol. 27, Mar. 1922, Suppl., pp. 80–91.

The same, *Population Characteristics, by Census Tracts, Cleveland, Ohio, 1930*, Cleveland, 1931.

Hale, G. S., *The Charities of Boston and Contributions to the Distressed of Other Parts*, in Justin Winsor, edit., *The Memorial History of Boston*, Vol. 4, Boston, 1881, Chap. 13.

Kelso, R. W., *The History of Public Poor Relief in Massachusetts, 1620–1920*, Boston, 1922.

Norton, W. J., *The Coöperative Movement in Social Work*, New York, 1927. 373 pp.

Parker, I. R., *Fit and Proper? A Study of Legal Adoptions in Massachusetts*, distributed by the Church Home Society, 41 Mt. Vernon Street, Boston, 1927.

Persons, W. F., *The Welfare Council of New York City: A Report to the Coördination Committee*, New York, 1925.

Then and Now a Friend in Need, The Family Welfare Society of Boston, Boston, 1929.

Truesdell, L. E., *The Tabulation of Population Data by Census Tracts for Cities in the United States*, in *Journ. Amer. Statist. Assoc.*, Vol. 27, Mar. 1932, Suppl., pp. 76–79.

Woodberry, L. G., *The Central Index*, Association of Community Chests and Councils, New York City, 1929.

COAST LAND AND INTERIOR MOUNTAIN VALLEY*

A GEOGRAPHICAL STUDY OF TWO TYPICAL LOCALITIES IN NORTHERN NEW ENGLAND

Derwent Whittlesey

IN contrast with other papers in the volume, which treat particular aspects of man's activities over the whole of New England, this discussion deals with critical interrelations of nature and man in two small, widely separated localities in northern New England, one on the coast of Maine, the other in the Connecticut Valley of New Hampshire and Vermont.

The facts adduced are the tangible, and for the most part visible and "mappable," features and circumstances that give these localities their present-day physiognomy. Such studies as this, belonging to the field of human geography as distinct from physical geography, may for brevity be termed "chorologic," since they have to do with the "science of places." No comprehensive chorologic investigation has been made of New England, nor has an inquiry into any of its larger localities been completed. As a sample of a method of study, therefore, this paper may be of interest. It is believed, however, that the two localities here presented are so representative that their stories are in outline the stories of a large fraction of the thousand localities that make up northern New England.

In journeying through this northeastern corner of the United States, the geographer finds that human occupance of the area is almost certain to be either of one or of a combination of five types: (1) the lowland of specialized farming, (2) the summer resort, (3) the mill town on water power, (4) the mining settlement, and (5) the backwoods. Each mode or combination is linked specifically to local natural resources, and in the two localities dealt with in this paper all five types appear except the mining settlement. Nevertheless, the ingredients are mixed in such different proportions that the two localities present wide contrasts, both in the appearance of the landscape and in the character of occupance. They may also be taken as samples of the two most frequently encountered market-town types of the region: the farming community with a village nucleus to handle farm trade and local manufacturing; and the commercial and manufacturing village, with a periphery of resorts, backwoods, and a few subsidiary farms.

---

*The author's fieldwork in and about Ellsworth in 1930 was made possible by a grant from the "Milton Fund for Research" of Harvard University.

LANCASTER (N. H.) AND ELLSWORTH (ME.) AS CHARACTERISTIC MARKET-TOWN LOCALITIES WITHIN THE REGION

The two market-town localities herein compared are Lancaster, in the upper Connecticut Valley, and Ellsworth, on the Maine coast east of Penobscot Bay (Fig. 1).

Similarities between them are numerous enough to make a comparison of their differences significant. Each is a county seat and market town, containing about 4000 persons. Each lies between 200 and 300 miles from Boston, about half as far from Portland, and only one fourth as far from the Canadian border. They were settled within a year of each other, in the early 1760's, by pioneers from older New England in search of new farm land. Both are in valleys on stream crossings that have always made them centers of the highway system, but neither was reached by rail until late (Lancaster in 1871 and Ellsworth in 1884). The forest is still close enough to be felt, although neither place lies within it. Both possess water power that has been utilized from the beginning and, indeed, determined

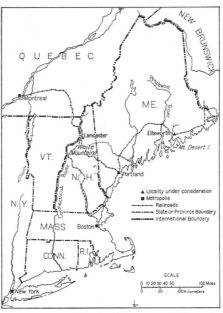

FIG. 1—The regional setting of Lancaster and Ellsworth.

the location of the village centers. Two of the most famous summer resort areas in New England are only fifteen or twenty miles distant—the White Mountains to the southeast of Lancaster, and the Mt. Desert-Penobscot Bay section of the Maine coast to the south of Ellsworth (Fig. 1).

With this background of partial identity, it is not surprising that both places have evolved in much the same way. At the outset subsistence agriculture dominated the life. The locally produced grain was ground in simple mills erected on small power sites which, along with route foci, determined the site of the village center in each case. From very early, however, the products of the forest have been a supplementary source of livelihood. These reached their peak of production in the later decades of the nineteenth century,

during which period they were milled by water power, more completely
developed by this time than in the frontier days. Like extractive
industry everywhere, the production of forest products in time declined, and the water powers have been largely re-utilized to produce

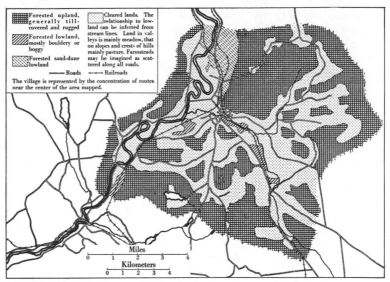

FIG. 2—The Lancaster locality, showing forested areas and cleared lands.

electricity. Synchronous with the decline of forest industry has
been the rise of tourism. Neither locality is sufficiently scenic to vie
with neighboring places in attracting summer residents, although
a few are drawn there by associations of sentiment or by relatively
low costs. But both towns are gateways to more famous regions
and thereby pick up a goodly bit of way business.

The Natural Setting of the Two Localities

Despite all these similarities it must not be supposed that the
Lancaster locality and the Ellsworth locality are counterparts. They
differ both superficially in their appearance and profoundly in their
character. Since both lie within a region economically, socially, and
politically uniform, the key to these differences must be sought
largely in the differences in the natural environment.

At the outset of white settlement the natural setting had not been
much modified by Indian occupation. In the Lancaster locality
(Fig. 2) this comprised the following salient elements: (1) a wide
flood plain overflowed every spring and sometimes in summer, and
therefore treeless, covered with grass which during postglacial time

had somewhat enriched the porous soil of sandy alluvium; (2) a series of river terraces of glacial and postglacial origin, well drained and covered with mixed forest, except on the sandier dune-form stretches, where pines may have been exclusive; (3) low mountains standing

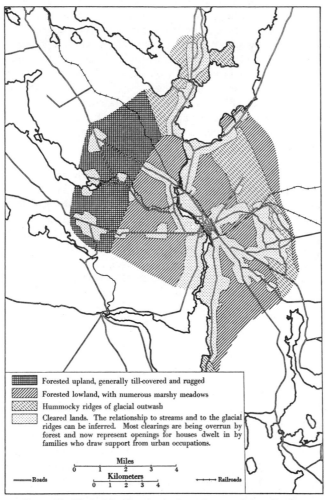

FIG. 3—The Ellsworth locality, showing forested areas and cleared lands.

up from the valley above described, but not too abruptly, their lower slopes averaging not more than 8° or 10°, mantled with many feet of bouldery till derived mainly from the local gneiss and other crystalline rocks, and covered with mixed forest except where seepage created hillside meadows; (4) a considerable left-bank tributary to the main river, reaching the latter near the margin of the master valley by a series of low cascades somewhat less than a mile long; (5) a minor right-bank valley articulating with that from the left, and the two giving access from east and west to that part of the Connecticut Valley above the gorge of the Fifteen Mile Falls (which begin just below Lancaster) and connecting at their heads with other valleys in such a way as to form a continuous pass route across both the White and the Green Mountains; (6) a climate rather continental than coastal, with a growing season of 120 days averaging 66° F., winter temperatures often dropping to −30° F., abundant precipitation (38 inches, of which 14 inches falls as snow), and valley fogs, especially during late summer and autumn; (7) probably some Indian clearings for maize, besides the usual fish, game, and berries of the northern forest.

The Ellsworth locality (Fig. 3) lies on the inner margin of a coastal lowland. Its natural setting at the opening of white settlement was made up of: (1) a series of coast-facing terraces of marine clay which had been altered into a strongly rolling terrain, first by the deposition of crudely assorted glacial débris in the form of glacial deltas and "gravel ridges,"[1] and second by deep erosion; (2) behind the terraces high hills, granite or schist at core, where the bed rock was either exposed to view over numerous stretches of an acre or more or was covered with till in which considerable clay was present, as well as sand, pebbles, and cobbles—this till, however, being strikingly free from boulders except at the bases of the ice-plucked lee slopes of some higher hills; (3) a prevalent mixed forest, with spruce dominant except on wet flats (some at least of these being lacustrine plains where grasses grew and still grow abundantly); (4) a stream, the Union River, fed by numerous lakes, which tumbled for two miles from the hills into high tide over a series of falls, and a tidal estuary, navigable except from December to May (when it was ice-blocked), beginning at the foot of the falls as a narrow stream and widening, three and a half miles below, into a long bay that extended some thirty miles to open ocean; (5) besides the usual berries and inland fish, an abundance of salmon in the river and herring, haddock, cod, lobsters, and clams in salt water; (6) a hill barrier toward the inland unbroken by any convenient gap and accentuated by the wide Penobscot River and its fifty-mile long estuary lying athwart the route to older parts of New England; (7) a climate of definitely modified continental character: few winter snaps marked by temperatures lower than −10° F., a growing season of about 140 days but with an average temperature of only 63° F., numerous sea fogs during

---

[1] G. H. Stone, *The Glacial Gravels of Maine*, Washington, 1894 (*U. S. Geol. Survey Monograph No. 34*).

all the warmer seasons, only half as much snow as in Lancaster, despite an equal amount of precipitation during the year; (8) absence, in all probability, of clearings for maize, because Indians when near the coast were fully occupied in catching and curing fish and game.

EARLY WHITE MAN'S OCCUPANCE

The first stage of white man's occupance[2] found the two settlements evolving along similar lines but with slight variations that early set them on divergent paths.

The object of both groups of settlers was the same—to chop homesteads for themselves out of the free land of the wilderness. Those who trekked up the Connecticut Valley sprang from three generations of inlanders and were bent solely on finding farms. These they already knew were best compounded of meadow on the grassy flood plain, homestead on the well drained terrace, and pasture, wood, and spring on the gentle lower slopes of the mountains. Most of the newcomers to Ellsworth were likewise experienced farmers, but they came from coastal settlements of southwestern Maine and the adjacent parts of New Hampshire and Massachusetts and knew the value of fish as well as the worth of field. When they reached eastern Maine they found neither dictate of nature nor hints from the Indians as to the most suitable constitution of a farm. Having approached their promised land by boat, they settled along the shore; and the evidence offered by clearings even today indicates strongly that there was no agreement as to the ideal arable land. Perhaps the warm soil and abundant well water of the sandy glacial débris was believed to offset the higher fertility and fewer stones of the clay terraces. They learned, however, that while crops were uncertain the sea furnished an apparently limitless supply of food.

Each group of colonists planted its first hamlet on water power, for the sake of a gristmill; each chose unwisely at the start but by trial and error soon found a suitable site. Soon their streams also furnished power to run sawmills. For Lancaster the sawmill was only a local convenience. For Ellsworth it soon became a supplementary source of livelihood, since lumber could easily be shipped by sea to Boston almost from the mill door, whereas exportation of forest products from the Connecticut country had to await the railroad.

DIVERGENT DEVELOPMENT OF THE TWO LOCALITIES

The urbanization of the Atlantic seaboard between Boston and Baltimore created an enhanced demand for lumber, always one of

[2] By "stage of occupance" is meant an epoch during which human occupation of an area remains constant in its fundamental aspects. See Derwent Whittlesey, *Sequent Occupance*, in *Annals. Assoc. of American Geographers*, Vol. 19, 1929, pp. 162–165.

northern New England's prime resources. The industrial revolution signalized by the Civil War compelled northern New England to recast its economic and social life. In the new dispensation local assets turned out to be less uniform than they had appeared in the old. Lancaster and Ellsworth now sharply diverged. Ellsworth is the nodal point for the Union River Basin, the whole of which was originally mantled in a dense stand of excellent trees, notably spruces and white pines. Winter snows encouraged lumbermen to sled the logs down the valley sides to the numerous brooks threading this well watered land. From there the freshets caused by spring melting of the snow took the timber to the master stream. Throughout the summer, in the heyday of lumbering, this became a river of logs awaiting conversion into long lumber, barrel staves, or shingles in one of the dozen mills powered by the stream itself. Once sawed, the lumber was carried by a short haul to the head of the estuary. Here vessels, mostly two- and three-masted schooners, loaded for all the Atlantic ports of the United States from the end of the spring log drive until December, when the estuary became blocked by floating ice. Under the stimulus of strong demand, abundant supply, and ideal environment for cutting, milling, and shipping, Ellsworth became for a time, shortly after the Civil War, the leading lumber-shipping port in the United States. It has not yet ceased to do a small business in miscellaneous lumber, staves, and hardwood lathe products, although the accessible stands of high-grade conifers are now gone.

Under the circumstances it is not surprising that the attention of Ellsworth people became diverted from subsistence farming and fixed upon the lumbering bonanza. The farms lay next door to the woods, which offered a comfortable wage during every winter, the very season when farming was impossible. From winter logging it was a natural transition to summer work in the sawmills or to trucking lumber from mill to wharf—occupations that paid high wages and combined with the winter in the woods to round out the year. By the early 1870's lumber was sustaining the whole community. Work-ingmen spent their high wages with the prodigality of miners or sailors, and merchants profited from this liberality. The hard work of farming appealed to no one, and after the Middle West began to pour its products into Atlantic seaboard cities many farms which had been taken up came to be used only as habitations for villagers. Some of these families had a potato patch, a hay lot, a cow, and a few chickens; but often it was the superannuated father who puttered about the "farm" chores, while the able-bodied son worked at the dominant lumbering business.

In Lancaster the descendants of the farmer-pioneers were not tempted to turn en masse to extractive industry and its concomitants.

True enough, near-by forests of the White Mountains and the Connecticut headwaters offered winter logging jobs to many. Most of the lumber, however, moved to market by direct routes that passed by the locality, and the rest only drifted through on the Connecticut River. Three of the four small water powers of the village were utilized for woodworking and paper mills, but they employed only a few men. Besides, they worked the year round and so did nothing toward providing the complementary industry that so opportunely gave summer jobs to Ellsworth woodsmen.

For those Lancaster men who stayed in the locality during this period of lean years from about 1850 to 1880 there was nothing for it but to stick to the farm despite a dark outlook for farming. The rich soil of the Middle West was populating whole states with farmers emigrant from New England, and the railroad, by bringing to the urban East grain and meat from these rich farms, made even subsistence agriculture unprofitable on the steep, rocky, acid lands of New England. Emigration led to the abandonment of the remotest, steepest, and stoniest acres and to the consolidation of holdings. The corresponding immigration into southern New England in time created a demand for milk so heavy that local farms were unable to meet it. The railroad then made it possible for the Lancaster locality, along with many another, to abandon subsistence farming for specialized dairying. Daily trains now carry the milk and cream to Boston and bring to Lancaster grain feed for the cows and nearly everything used by the people, farmers as well as villagers.

There is no evidence that the upper Connecticut Valley is better adapted to export dairy farming than is the farther Maine coast, except that it is a little nearer to the Boston market. In fact, under the stimulus of tourist demands milk is successfully produced at a number of places near Ellsworth, and ten years ago (1923) a creamery was started in the village to make butter and ice cream. In winter high prices in Boston attract some of the output in the form of fresh cream. Scarcely any milk or cream from Ellsworth itself reaches the creamery, however, although the whole trans-Penobscot region south of Bangor contributes to it—further proof that the locality is not interested in farming. Apparently the favorable combination of forest, power, and water transport at Ellsworth in dominating for two generations the life of the locality stamped the inhabitants with a tradition that they have not yet thrown off. Such farms as once existed have all but disappeared under second-growth scrub. Except for estates supported by city-earned money, only eight or ten men in the locality would call themselves farmers, and of these Lancaster dairymen would recognize as their peers not more than two or three.

Ellsworth, having been preoccupied with lumbering when the new era of specialized farming dawned, found itself unready to take up farming when the exhaustion of superior softwood timber sent lumbering into the discard. By the early years of the twentieth century the easily accessible stands of white pine and clear spruce within the basin of the Union River had been cut, leaving only the unmarketable hardwoods, lightly admixed with inferior conifers. Hence the big spring-freshet drives of logs suitable for long lumber were replaced by drifting short lengths of small timber, staving, and pulpwood. The quinquennium 1915–1920 marked the last trip of a lumber schooner out of Union River. The industry was henceforth moribund, because shipments by rail over the roundabout route to market are overcostly in competition with the water haul of pine from the Gulf states and of redwood and fir from the Pacific Northwest. With no wood to sell, the sawmill power sites fell into disuse, and in 1907 all but the uppermost two were consolidated into a single power unit by the construction of a sixty-foot dam. Here 75,000 horse power of electric energy can be generated, but only to be shipped out of the locality, since the local market absorbs an insignificant fraction of it. With the decline of lumber fell the complementary knitting and shoe factories, which had employed wives and daughters of the lumbermen.

Faced with the swift lapse into desuetude characteristic of extractive industry, and with neither the tradition of farming nor the cleared land on which to establish farms, the economic life of Ellsworth has been refounded on tourism. Like lumbering and dairy farming, tourism sprang from industrialization, this time in its function as creator of a leisure class.

Growth of Tourist Industry

The middle of the nineteenth century saw the beginning of summer resorting among the mountains and along the coast of northern New England. Two of the early centers were the White Mountains and Mt. Desert Island, chosen because of their unmatched beauty in the whole region. Railroad lines, however, linked Boston and New York with the White Mountains, and Mt. Desert was reached by sea. Hence for many years neither Lancaster nor Ellsworth profited from nearness to these celebrated resorts.

Little by little the resort business expanded and intensified. Ranging afield, summer people discovered that the beauties of northern New England were almost coextensive with the region, and taking in summer boarders became general among the permanent inhabitants. Market towns profited from purveying both locally produced and imported foods to neighboring boarding-house and hotel keepers, to cottagers, and to campers. Hotels were built in both Lancaster and Ellsworth to accommodate the passing tourist—capacious, rambling structures of three or four stories, built with the abundant local lumber.

With the coming of the automobile the summer resort industry altered its form, to the advantage of the localities under discussion. All-summer or month-long stays by a select few at a favorite hotel have tended to give place to short stops by nearly everybody in many hotels. Farmers and townsfolk who used to take in boarders now offer overnight accommodation to fleeting auto nomads. Villages still purvey groceries and meats, but they have added to the list ice cream and soda, gasoline and oil, and luncheon and tea. Where cottagers and campers from five or six miles away used to drive in for supplies or entertainment, automobilists now think nothing of running in from fifteen or twenty miles away. Besides enjoying these advantages, which apply with equal force to many market towns of the region, the two localities under consideration have profited especially from a reorientation of routes.

Lancaster, from having been at the tag end of one unimportant rail line from Boston, and a way station on another that led to no congested urban regions, now finds itself at a crossing of automobile roads leading to southern New England, to French Canada, to the White Mountains and Maine, and to Vermont, the Adirondacks, and the Thousand Islands. Ellsworth, an unconsidered inland town during the early days when all summer people traveled by water, and later a way station on the route of the Bar Harbor Express, is now, by virtue of its position on the intersection of the coastal highway with the Mt. Desert Island-Penobscot River road, the distribution point for most visitors to the trans-Penobscot Maine coast, whether they come by rail or by automobile.

Inevitably both communities have become interested in tourism. In the Lancaster locality the interest is confined mainly to certain merchants whose business is increased by the summer visitors or the autumn hunters. Other villagers and most of the farmers are too busy selling milk to Boston to spare much attention to this new means of livelihood.

For Ellsworth, the shift in the incidence of tourism was a godsend. Business along Main Street makes its profits during two, or at most three, summer months. For the rest of the year shops keep open but make little above expenses. During the short season hotels and rooming houses are well patronized by passing motorists, by guests for a month or for the summer, and by business men. During the rest of the year even the traveling salesmen appear but rarely, and most of the other groups are absent. The rural life of the locality is likewise subordinate to tourism, for most of the few farmers are producing special crops for sale to the summer population.

The present stage of occupance in northern New England, although sprung from the specialized industrialization and consequent urbanization of the United States and of the world, is thus seen to have assumed different forms. These have taken shape under the gentle but continuous pressure of a varied natural environment. The two localities, with essentially the same cultural heritage, have become sharply distinct in appearance.

The Contrasting Chorologic Landscapes of the Two Localities

The Lancaster locality is a place of farm lands—meadow at the lowest levels, pasture above—with a nuclear village tucked inconspicuously into a corner of the widest section of lowland (Fig. 2) and forests only on steep hills, sand lands, or bogs. Ellsworth village sprawls along two miles of stream, and clusters of outlying "mill-type" houses extend the urban settlement intermittently along every country road (Fig. 3). Apart from the village, clearings are tiny discontinuous patches fringing the roads, and the forest closes down against the homesteads.

In both localities the architectural forms are similar, and the chief material of construction is wood. But more than half the business blocks in Ellsworth are of brick, and others are faced with stone, compared to a scant half dozen brick buildings in Lancaster village. Village residences in Ellsworth show a larger proportion of story-and-a-half cottages and less fresh paint than Lancaster, where two-story, gleaming white houses predominate. Lancaster, however, has not a single domicile to compare in architectural elegance with three or four older mansions of Ellsworth. These contrasts in the village structures give evidence that Ellsworth was built by people of strongly contrasted wealth—simple wage-earners and men of large fortune—whereas Lancaster represents the solid result of steady effort on the part of a population of equalized wealth. This conclusion is reinforced by a comparison of the habitations outside the villages. In Lancaster commodious, solidly built frame or brick structures, well kept except in the remote hill sections, dot the roads at regular intervals of from forty rods to a mile. In Ellsworth frowsy strings of ill-built and ill-kept houses, many of them cellarless, shingle-sided shacks and others the decrepit relics of sawmill-company construction, line all the roads near the edge of town; isolated cases of the same type are to be found even in the most remote sections of the locality, interspersed with the few farmsteads worthy of the name. Even when allowance is made for summer camps and hunting shacks, an astonishingly large number of the inhabitants live throughout the winter in flimsy huts of a sort that would be uninhabitable in the more rigorous climate of the interior.

The more fugitive aspects of occupance further illuminate the contrasting life of the two localities. In both, winter and spring are the dull seasons, owing to the absence of the tourist and to the difficulty of getting about through snow or slush. In summer and autumn both villages present lively pictures at certain times of the day or week.

In Lancaster milk wagons line up early in the morning before the loading stations, and their drivers are likely to do an errand or two at the stores before returning to the farms. During the day the parking spaces along the main street are used moderately by shoppers from near-by tourist centers and by passing motorists who stop for a soda or a meal. Toward late afternoon farm women may be in for shopping or to attend a social function. In the evening, except on Saturday—when the whole countryside comes in for the movies and to chat with relatives and acquaintances—the business center is very quiet.

The main street of Ellsworth wakes up later, since relatively little milk is brought in. The first real business of the day appears with people in pleasure cars, in station wagons, and in trucks, doing the marketing for summer residents. About ten o'clock it is hard to find a parking space, but the crowd gradually thins out, except on Saturday, when people come from distant hamlets and stay until eight or nine in the evening. Many of these are rare visitors to the market center, if one may judge by their out-of-style clothes and by their half-awed, half-lost expressions. Scarcely a horse is to be seen, however, although in Lancaster buggies and wagons are not uncommon. This only corroborates the impression that an automobile, usually a shiny one, is to be seen in every dooryard of the Ellsworth locality, even where the habitation is a hovel, whereas in Lancaster a number of well-housed farmers do not feel justified in owning a car. Perhaps winter closure of roads in New Hampshire partly explains this difference, for the more open Maine-coast winters permit all-season automobiling. Some part of the explanation, however, must probably be found in the tradition of large wages, uncertain continuance of work, and consequent prodigality of the lumber worker as compared to the sober thriftiness engendered by the small but regular cash income of the dairy farmer.

The Prospect

Both Lancaster and Ellsworth appear to have established themselves as "going concerns" in their present stage of occupance—a significant fact in view of the stagnation in many of their neighboring communities. That the services they render and their appearance possess points in common testifies to similarity in their environmental and social background and in their present activities. This is only

saying that both localities fall within the same chorologic region—
northern New England. But their differences are at least as striking
as their likenesses. This is inevitable in view of the traditions which
their unlike utilization of natural resources has imposed. Ellsworth
represents the coastal zone, while Lancaster represents the interior
lowlands—two of the subregions of northern New England. In both
of these subregions the present stage of occupance has been erected
on a moderately profitable basis of reciprocation with urbanized
parts of the United States. Other market-town localities might be
chosen to represent still other subregions of northern New England.
Bar Harbor, as the type of resort center, and Barre, as the locality
built upon its mineral resource, at once suggest themselves. A third
type, the partially "deserted" town, has already been studied.[3] For
such a locality the present stage of occupance is perilously close to
"unoccupance," except for the occasional presence of hunters and
hikers and a few isolated farm holdings that seem doomed with
the present generation.

These areas of abandonment by people and of reconquest by the
forest disclose the reverse of the shield, the obverse of which is the
composite of Lancaster, Ellsworth, and their like. To a student of
human geography, northern New England is seen to have recently
passed through a vital reorientation in which most of the localities
have altered their appearance and their functions. Prosperity may
differ in degree from that of former times, and it almost certainly
is based on a different organization of environmental and human
resources, but the present status is simply the current phase of an
ever-changing human occupance of essentially unchanging earth
conditions.

---

[3] J. W. Goldthwait, *A Town That Has Gone Downhill*, in *Geogr. Rev.*, Vol. 17, 1927, pp. 527–552.

THE CHANGING GEOGRAPHY OF
NEW ENGLAND

John K. Wright

"OLD NEW ENGLAND"

NEW ENGLAND is more than a mere geographical expression—more than the name of a small portion of the earth's surface between Long Island Sound and Canada. The two words mean very different things to different people—not at all the same, for example, to the Greek mill hand of Lowell or the Polish onion grower of the Connecticut Valley that they do to more articulate exponents of New Englandism.

Americans of the older stocks think of the words "New England" as connoting not only a region but a group of traditions, institutions, and ways of living and of thinking. The frequent use of "New England" as an adjective is evidence of this. We speak of *New England* villages, a *New England* conscience, local government of the *New England* type. Occasionally modern writers have been tempted to disparage or to ridicule the traditional New England—along with Puritanism and the mid-Victorians.[1] Cartoons under the heading "In Old New England" from time to time appear in one of the New York papers. They depict "characters" in typical village settings. Only a distinctive region would be thus singled out.

Ridicule will do New England no harm. If it sometimes takes itself seriously, on the whole there is good reason for it to do so. Its thinkers look with distress upon standardizing tendencies of the times that seem to be undermining some of its cherished customs and ideals and reducing it, perhaps, to the status of a geographical expression after all.[2] Indeed, the traditional New England—even the "Old New England" of the cartoons—has meant too much that is admirable for anyone to view its passing without regret. "The danger is that [New England] will rapidly lose its individual aspect and flavor, and hence lose . . . what actually makes it a rather precious heritage to the nation," writes Walter Prichard Eaton in a recent paper on "Saving New England."[3]

HOMOGENEITY OF NEW ENGLAND

The older New England, however, now counts for little—directly at least—in the lives of the mill hand and onion grower.[4] The New England of the worker in factory and field and shop is not so much the New England of tradition as a more or less homogeneous economic

---

[1] For notes see below, p. 474.

region whose industrial and commercial life is somewhat set off from
that of other sections of the country. It is a region whose several
communities are facing many problems in common and sharing in
many mutual interests, and whose prosperity now depends and will
come to depend in ever increasing measure upon planning and endeavor on a New England-wide rather than on a state-wide or town-
wide base.

Geographical position, the character of topography and natural
resources, and the inheritance of institutions and psychology brought
from the Old World have all contributed to this homogeneity. New
England lies off in a corner of the country. Its western border corresponds roughly to a line of topographical barriers extending from
the Canadian forests almost to Long Island Sound. Partial isolation,
a lack of coal, iron, and other mineral resources of any substantial
value (except possibly marble and granite), and the barriers on the
west have largely determined the course of New England's commercial
and industrial development. They have been serious handicaps under
which the whole region has suffered. Indeed New England's vital
concern in the matter of its external rail and water connections is
comparable with industrial Britain's interest in keeping the sea
roads clear.

SMALL-SCALE TOPOGRAPHY

There are no great open plains in New England, no broad areas
over which uniform types of soil prevail, no mighty river valleys like
those of the Hudson-Mohawk or Ohio or Mississippi to serve as
avenues of commerce into the heart of the continent. New England
is mainly a land of small topographical forms, of disconnected patches
of arable ground and pasture. From an airplane it appears like a
patchwork quilt made up entirely of small pieces of cloth, and of a
pattern homogeneous in the uniformly small scale of its multiform
variations (see p. 14, above).

There is probably a connection between this small-scale topography
and what Dr. Adams in the opening article of this volume calls New
England's "small-enterprise type of life." "The small farm, the
town as the unit of government, the local church governed by its
own local congregation, all trained the New Englander to think and
work in terms of the small and local group" (p. 5, above). Indeed,
one of New England's most serious contemporary problems in the
fields of government and of commerce and industry is whether it
should continue to cling to the small-enterprise type of life when the
rest of the country has turned toward large enterprise and mass
production. Mr. Filene sees the small-enterprise type of mind as
the root of many of New England's recent industrial difficulties,
but Dr. Adams questions the wisdom of mass production for New

England (pp. 69 and 12, above). This difference of opinion illustrates a very large issue that New England manufacturers must face.

NEW ENGLAND CONSCIOUSNESS

That New England actually is a somewhat homogeneous economic region, a unit in relation to many important issues, seems beyond dispute. That its leaders in public and business affairs are becoming more and more acutely conscious of the fact is evident in the rise in recent years of such organizations as the New England Conferences and New England Council, the New England Research Council on Marketing and Food Supply, and the concerted action on many occasions of the governors of the six states. This unity has long existed and springs from the physical and human soil that has given its character to the older New England, but the response to it in the form of an aroused regional consciousness is perhaps more characteristic of the new era in which we live.

CHANGING GEOGRAPHICAL RELATIONSHIPS

Despite its conservatism, contemporary New England, along with all the civilized world, is undergoing a mighty transformation, a symptom as well as a cause of which is a simple mechanical fact—the increasing mobility of men and goods.

Increasing mobility has led to a rapid widening of the economic connections of New England, so that now they extend not only to the farthest corners of the United States but reach over much of the civilized world. Many examples are given in this book of ways in which conditions in New England are affected by circumstances lying beyond its bounds as well as of momentous changes taking place within New England's borders. Let us examine more particularly some of these internal changes.

The automobile is altering the landscape as well as effecting a revolution in our habits. In the paper to which reference has already been made, Mr. Eaton describes the offensive aspects of the great motor highways that cut through the New England countryside from village to village. Take, for instance, the Mohawk Trail (Fig. 2, p. 17, above):

"Most of its length it is a swiftly moving steel and rubber river between banks of 'hot-dog' kennels, fried-clam stands, filling stations, and other odoriferous and ugly reminders of this progressive age. . . . Through the heart of Concord it goes, right through the Mill Dam, trucks rumbling and rattling, buses honking and taking up two thirds of the road, pleasure cars by the thousand. . . . Then on it sweeps, to repeat the same performance in every town it passes through, till it reaches its grand climax on Whitcomb Summit. . . . The human serenity and charm of Cambridge and Concord on the one end, the natural serenity and beauty of the mountain top on the other, alike are gone."[5]

What is true of the Mohawk Trail is true of many of the great through routes. The service of tourists is becoming a large industry. Mr. Eaton points out that visitors will certainly not continue to seek New England if its villages lose their charm, if the beauty of its scenery is disfigured, and if every few miles the traveler is obliged to crawl in second gear through the congested traffic of a town.

He advocates the building of the main highroads straight across the open country between the larger centers and thus the avoidance of the villages and even some of the more populous places. This is his formula for "Saving New England." It is concrete and definite. Whether or not it will "save New England," if carried out it ought at least to eliminate maladjustments due to piecemeal attempts to make over a network of highways originally designed to serve less complex needs than those of the present. It is a program, however, that cannot be put into effect without forethought and research. An ideal trunk highway system for New England cannot be made in a day. Studies of the existing layout of the roads are needed, of different volumes of traffic that now flow over them, of how and where traffic may be expected to increase. For several of the states partial investigations of this sort have been completed and traffic censuses taken[6]; but even were an ideal scheme devised on the basis of surveys of traffic needs, it could not be put into effect immediately. The question would remain as to what changes are needed *first*, how far they are practicable, and how conflicting local interests may be met. To determine these things, local studies would have to be made not only of topography, rock structure, drainage, and distribution of road materials but also of the industrial requirements and political prejudices of the communities through which the roads will pass.

Thus the relatively simple suggestion of Mr. Eaton raises some difficult problems. They are far less difficult than the problems raised by the increasing mobility of men and goods in the field of rural life.

CHANGES IN RURAL LIFE

A generation or so ago much was written of isolation on the lonely farms of New England. Edith Wharton's grim story of Ethan Frome comes to mind. During the long winters the women on hill farms were often shut in for weeks or even months at a time. Social connections were for the most part limited to the immediate neighborhood and were often temporarily broken by snowdrifts or roads turned to mire. The coming of the automobile, telephone, and radio has changed all this. It is now seldom that folks, even in the back districts, are altogether cut off from contact with the outside world. Today we hear little of rural isolation—at least in its older, cruder forms— but it still exists, though the problems it presents are different.

One of these is the problem of medical service. In the old days the doctor in a small community had a steady practice, usually amounting to a monopoly. He seldom had to drive more than ten or twelve miles by buggy in summer or sleigh in winter to reach his most distant patients. Telephone and automobile have immeasurably extended the limits of rural practices. They have made it possible for physicians from the larger towns and cities to visit patients twenty and thirty miles away and for farmers' families to make office calls and patronize clinics and hospitals in town. Village doctors can no longer monopolize practice in their communities. This is one reason why in many a village the doctor's shingle is no longer seen.[7]

Occasionally in times of crisis no doctor can be obtained. In winter and early spring—just the seasons when most illness is abroad —the roads are at their worst. The main roads, even in the snowiest parts of New England, are kept passable for automobiles at all times of year, but this is not true of the side roads leading to remote farmsteads. The doctor from town relying upon his car may find himself stuck in the snow or mud and arrive too late or not at all. Furthermore, many physicians charge for their time or the distance they have to travel.[8] The cost of medical service is likely to be higher in the more isolated sections, and they can least afford it. A few towns are attempting to subsidize resident physicians, but to do so is a severe burden. On the other hand, where several poor towns can combine to maintain a doctor the burden may be distributed.

Another thing to be regretted is the loss of leadership that the disappearance of the old-fashioned rural physician has often entailed. Though the country doctor may not always have kept wholly abreast of his profession, most people regarded him as much more than merely a practitioner of medicine. He was consulted by patients on problems other than medical. He usually knew the community and its interlocking interests as no other man, and his influence was seldom unwise. His passing is but symptomatic of a whole series of related changes in the social life of rural New England.

There would seem to be under way a general weakening of leadership and loosening of bonds. Proximity itself used to be, in rural districts, the main basis of social and economic groupings. Neighborhoods were fundamental units of society. Now when it takes no longer to drive ten miles than it used to take to drive one, neighbors are finding that they have fewer necessary mutual interests, and neighborhoods, perhaps, are tending to become mere topographical terms. Neither church, nor town meeting, nor Grange, nor participation in local social activities plays the part it used to play. How far this loosening and breaking of ties has gone cannot be said, but surveys have shown that it is particularly marked in those parts of southern New England where immigrant stocks have increased rapidly (see pp. 198–203, above).

Urbanization of the Country

The country is becoming more like the city.[9] We are accustomed to think of daily "commuting" from suburbs to office as something associated only with large cities. Commuting, however, has spread into the open country. There are many back farms in New England from which the men or their wives or children drive each morning to town fifteen, twenty, or more miles away to work in shops and mills (see above, p. 40). Some of these farms are operated only part of the time; others serve as residences and are no longer farmed at all. The opportunities furnished by the automobile for part-time work on other jobs, together with the summer boarder, have meant the salvation of many a farm that would otherwise have reverted to forest. On the other hand, the occupants of such farms can hardly feel the same concern in community affairs as in the days when they seldom were drawn away by interests outside of the immediate vicinity of their homes.

The urbanization of rural life is also being accelerated by influences radiating directly from the larger cities. The country, as never before, is deluged by pleasure seekers and high-power salesmen from the cities and by urban ideas carried over the radio. Country folks after visits to town are carrying back to their homes urban views of life—stimulating, perhaps, but often disquieting. Along with the disappearance of the country doctor and minister, there may be passing something of the very essence of the old country life. Country life, Professor Hypes notes, seems to be growing more impersonal (see above, p. 197); and others have pointed to the fact that some of the old-fashioned neighborliness is disappearing with the older type of neighborhood. Whether in the long run the new horizons opening out will compensate for values and amenities that are vanishing is a question for philosophers, but sociologists must find means whereby the evils of the transition may be overcome. Their studies, moreover, must be tied to the earth.

Now that so many families own motor cars a surging tide of humanity sweeps out of the cities and their suburbs and spreads over the landscape in summer. Most of these people have no places of their own to go to, and a grave problem has arisen in the congested parts of southern New England to find outlets into which the currents of this human tide may pour.

If allowed to take their own course without control these floods are a menace. There is a very real danger that they may submerge in a welter of ugliness the little that remains, at least in the environs of the larger centers, of the old New England of quiet villages and tranquil vistas. The sordid character of the highroads is due, more than to any other factor, to this "backwash" from the cities. The private establishments catering to the average Sunday or week-end

tripper may do profitable business, but they are most unlovely—and
it is not wholly the fault of the tripper himself. There are also more
tangible dangers to health and morals, where, as is sometimes the case,
supervision over water, milk, and food supplies, road houses, dance
halls, etc., is inadequate.

Fortunately, these dangers have been recognized—especially in
Massachusetts, Rhode Island, and Connecticut, where the needs
are the greatest. Regional planners and state officials are joining
in the search for means to surmount them. Like the matter of highway policy, the problems of parks and reservations for public use are
eminently problems in applied geography. How much land and
what lands should be taken over by the public, how these lands should
be administered and developed, which tracts should be converted
into resort centers, which ones left as wilderness, how the several
areas should be linked to one another and to the cities—to answer
such questions effectively detailed surveys must be made (as has
been done in part in Connecticut and Massachusetts) of the now
available "open spaces," as well as of their topography and vegetation
and present use and value,[10] and of the people themselves who may
ultimately use them for recreational purposes.

Expansion of Economic Organisms

The tendency of the times in economic enterprise is toward the
organization of larger units of production and distribution. Even
though New England, as compared with other parts of the country,
is still a region of the "small-enterprise type of life," it has been
unable to resist this movement. More people are engaging in single
enterprises under unified management, and broader tracts of country
are being covered than ever before.

Not very many years ago, for instance, Boston received its milk
supply almost exclusively from southern New Hampshire and eastern
Massachusetts. The milk shed of Boston has now spread north-
westward over most of eastern and northern Vermont.[11] Attention
has been called to the broadening of trading areas in New England.
The retail trading areas surrounding the larger towns are growing,
customers are everywhere being drawn to these centers, and many
a small village store that once did a steady business has had to be
closed. The larger wholesale trading areas are likewise expanding.
The trading territories of some individual concerns have been enlarged
too rapidly, and the resulting competition along the frontiers of
rival territories has frequently led to disaster.

The growth of power utilities furnishes another example of the
same movement. From small, isolated networks of transmission
lines, an immense interconnected structure has come into being
covering nearly all New England except Maine. Along with the

enlargement of the physical structure there has been a succession of mergers of the operating corporations and further consolidation of financial control in the hands of holding companies, until a point has been reached at which almost the whole expanse of New England is portioned out between a few large units.

A strictly parallel development has taken place in the railway field. The period of physical extension of trackage came to a close a good many years ago, and it is doubtful if this movement will ever be resumed in the face of competition from the highways. On the other hand, the process of consolidation of ownership and management is not yet completed. The regional unity of New England, as of no other section of the United States, is reflected in the present organization of its railways. With only a few exceptions the lines operating in New England are confined within its borders and controlled in the main by New Englanders.

The Foundation of Geographical Circumstances

These various expanding fields of economic relationships and organizations are of course in no way peculiar to New England; the same sort of thing is going on nearly everywhere. However, they rest, as it were, on a foundation of distinctive geographical circumstances. Unlike what is usually called the "geographical background," this foundation should be conceived as consisting both of natural and of human elements; not only of topographical features, types of vegetation cover, soils and climates, but also of the larger facts in the distribution of population, institutions, industries, and routes of trade and transportation. This foundation changes—the "eternal hills" themselves are worn down by the streams—but the changes that occur in its *natural* elements are almost imperceptible, even to generations of man. In an old, settled community like New England, moreover, the changes in its *human* elements are gradual: channels of trade may broaden and deepen or fall into disuse; cities may grow or decline; new farm lands may be opened to settlement; people may move away from uplands where soils are stony and farming unprofitable. The cumulative effect may be great in the course of time, but after a single year or a decade the alteration is slight. Indeed, the foundation of geographical circumstances may be regarded as essentially static in so far as contemporary issues are concerned. The important point is that man's attitude toward the foundation changes. In 1672 Josselyn described the country beyond the White Mountains as "daunting terrible, being full of rocky Hills, as thick as Mole-hills in a Meadow, and cloathed with infinite thick Woods."[12] The hills and woods are still there, not essentially different from what they were in Josselyn's time, but few today would think of northern New Hampshire as "daunting terrible."

One extremely important element in the foundation of geographical circumstances in New England is the political geography of the region, the system of state, county, and town governments, and the presence in different areas of varying types of political sentiment and of habits of voting. For all practical purposes state and county boundaries are as fixed as the drainage pattern; the party areas, although somewhat more shifting in their outlines and character, are also enduring as human institutions go (Fig. 1).

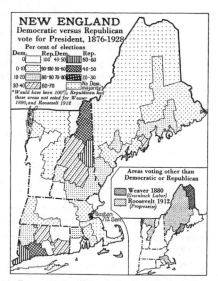

Between the stable mosaic of New England's political structure and the more mobile currents in its economic life there is often no little conflict and friction. This is not an evil in itself when it hinders monopolistic exploitation of natural resources that is to the detriment of the public interest. There are many students who believe in more stringent governmental control of public utilities and in the placing of curbs on the real or imagined capacity of large corporations. As an extreme example of the political obstruction of economic forces may be cited the Fernald Law in Maine prohibiting the export of hydroelectric energy.

But sometimes this conflict and friction may be a drag on legitimate and beneficial enterprise. This often arises from a profound reluctance to

FIG. 1—Voting habits of New England counties in presidential elections, 1876–1928. The main map contrasts Republican with Democratic successes. The inset shows counties that have been carried by candidates of minor parties. For the main map the number of times each county was carried by candidates of the two chief parties was counted. The percentage of Republican—and conversely, therefore, of Democratic successes—was calculated with reference to this total, and this percentage was then plotted for each county on the map. The only counties that were carried by the Democrats in more than half of the elections were Suffolk Co., Mass. (including Boston; carried 10 times out of 14, or in 71 per cent of the elections), New Haven, Conn., and Coös Co., N. H. These maps are based on maps showing votes in presidential elections in C. O. Paullin, *Atlas of the Historical Geography of the United States*, Carnegie Instn. of Washington and American Geographical Society, 1932 (see also J. K. Wright, *Voting Habits in the United States: A Note on Two Maps*, in *Geographical Review*, Vol. 22, 1932, pp. 666–672, where similar maps for the entire United States will be found).

change the forms of government and an unwillingness to erase time-hallowed statutes from the books. Local self-government in New England has not broken down. It preserves too many civic values and protects too many worthy local interests to warrant any such pessimistic view. On the other hand, in many details both local and state government have fallen out of adjustment to pressing needs of the times, and unquestionably—for example, in the case of forest taxation—they tend to place unequal burdens on different communities irrespective of ability to bear these burdens.

Need for Consolidation of Local Governments

Rural Districts. There are parts of New England where common sense suggests that local governments should be consolidated. Sentiment—the desire to preserve things sanctified by historical tradition—is one obstacle in the way of such changes; a larger obstacle is raised by the vested interests of political officeholders and retainers. For this reason the amalgamation of towns seems almost unthinkable to many New Englanders. The "small-enterprise type of mind" is here in evidence. You might almost as well suggest amalgamating Monadnock with Wachusett. It is to be hoped, however, that ultimately research, education, and tactful leadership may accomplish needed reforms, particularly in two special types of area.

These are the back-country districts where population has been falling off[13] and the congested metropolitan districts where it has been increasing most rapidly. On the whole the need is probably more pressing in the former, where many towns now have fewer people than they did a century ago. As population dwindles, the costs of government per taxpayer almost inevitably increase and with them tax delinquency. The thing works in a vicious circle: the more land on which taxes are delinquent, the greater the burden on the remaining occupied land and the greater the chance of this land also becoming delinquent. In sections of rural New York that undoubtedly have their counterparts in northern New England it has been shown that taxes are likely to take a much larger fraction of the poorer farmer's income than that of workers in other industries and that they are a very large factor in rural decline and farm abandonment.[14]

The two main services of town governments are to maintain schools and roads. The automobile has increased the cost of keeping roads in repair and added the item of winter maintenance to the towns' road bills. In the old days when everybody used sleighs only the village streets were plowed and the worst drifts dug out. Now all the main roads are cleared or should be. Population has dwindled most rapidly in the hill towns where the seasons of snow and mud are the longest and where at any season it is costly to keep the roads in decent shape.

Rising standards of education have made schooling more expensive than it used to be. Better buildings and more highly trained teachers are felt to be essential. The urbanization of the countryside has meant that rural folk demand education for their children of a quality comparable to that now received by city children. When they cannot get it families are tempted to leave the rural districts altogether.

The mere fact of a declining population in itself tends to place a heavier tax burden on those who remain behind. The mileage of roads that must be maintained by a town of shrinking population diminishes. If a town of a hundred inhabitants needs ten miles of town road, it does not follow that when the same town has only fifty inhabitants it will need only five miles. The chances are that it will need something like eight or nine miles. It costs a great deal more than half as much to run a school in which there are only ten pupils as it does to run one in which there are twenty pupils. By the same token, two neighboring towns with fifty inhabitants each by consolidating their governments ought to be able to maintain sixteen or eighteen miles of roadway and to educate twenty pupils at much less expense to the taxpayer than if each town were to continue performing these functions separately. The automobile, the telephone, the school bus, and improved road machinery have so far reduced the factor of distance that it is no longer an obstacle in the way of consolidation.

The overhead costs of government in salaries, fees, etc., to town officials could also be substantially reduced by consolidation. Nor would it mean abandoning the town-meeting form of government that has meant so much in New England's civic life. The average New England township covers a tract of country of somewhere around thirty-five square miles in area, a tract from all parts of which the citizens could reach the main village center by using the horse-drawn vehicles of the seventeenth and eighteenth centuries.[15] There is no reason why we should cling to townships of this size in the twentieth century when citizens may just as quickly and conveniently come to town meeting from areas of one or two hundred square miles. There are districts where four or five neighboring towns together now have fewer citizens than any one of them had a century ago.

There is of course no "ideal" size for a township in the areas of declining population. What combinations of existing townships should be made must depend on local circumstances. If consolidation is to be achieved at all and in any other than a haphazard and inefficient fashion, concrete programs must be formulated for large areas as a whole, and such programs must be based upon detailed studies.[16]

Metropolitan Districts. The New England form of town government was devised to serve small communities. When the population of a given township grew beyond a manageable size, the town was usually broken into two or more smaller towns. When, in turn, the population of these became too large, they obtained charters as cities. Further growth in the surroundings of Boston, Hartford, Providence, New Haven, Worcester, and the other large centers has converted these areas into single cities from almost every functional point of view but that of government. In the metropolitan districts of New England the several towns and cities have maintained their independence with mighty singleness of purpose, even though some of them may have delegated specific functions to metropolitan commissions. It seems logical to suppose that consolidation could be carried farther than is now the case.[17] As in the rural towns, the overhead cost of one administration for a given number of people should be less than the overhead cost of five, ten, twenty administrations for the same number of people. Furthermore, with a single administration a more rational distribution of governmental services in relation to the distribution of population should be feasible than where town boundaries have to be considered. All other things being equal, the cost of streets, sewers, fire protection, and other services—and therefore the tax rate—will be higher in a town built partly on rocky, hilly ground than in a town built entirely on level ground. If the two towns were consolidated, this inequality would be ironed out. Towns were originally delimited with little thought of topography, and it seems hardly fair that different sections of a congested metropolitan district should bear unequal tax burdens because certain arbitrary lines were marked out on the ground and drawn on maps a long while ago.

This example shows that there is a topographical aspect to the problem of the government of metropolitan areas even if we assume complete uniformity in wealth, in industrial development, race, and—hardly less important—in political honesty throughout each area. Such uniformity was postulated by the words "all other things being equal." "All other things" never are equal. When local differences in all the variables are considered, the problem becomes enormously complex, and the need for studying it from geographical, legal, economic, social, and other points of view imperative.

A Suggested Survey of Natural and Human Resources

To come back to the foundation of geographical elements, already mentioned, of which the political geography of New England forms a part: this foundation itself changes but slowly, but man's attitude toward it and the uses that he makes of it may often become completely transformed within a short lapse of time. A few critical inventions in the last few years have produced almost a revolution in the New England fisheries industry, both in practices and in outlook. The competition of the automobile has radically altered the uses made of the railroads by New England shippers; it has also created a new public sentiment toward the railroad companies, one in which solicitude has largely replaced fear. In the changing uses both of natural resources and of enduring institutions and in the changing attitudes toward them are rooted many of New England's most critical contemporary problems. The solution of these problems will depend largely on better knowledge than we now possess not only of the processes of change but of the factors that remain relatively fixed—the measurable facts of the geographical foundation.

Concerning these measurable facts much is known but not as much as should be known. What is known, moreover, is recorded in widely scattered and uncoördinated forms, and there are many gaps in this body of information. The federal government has made topographical maps of most of the settled areas of New England, geological and soil maps of relatively limited areas; it has gathered statistical data on population, agriculture, and manufactures in the census reports; it has investigated the commercial and industrial structure of the region. The six state governments, acting in one capacity or another, compile and publish important material of uneven scope and quality. There was a time when Massachusetts conducted a census that rivaled or even excelled that of the federal government in comprehensiveness, but now it does little more than count the number of people in each town. Municipalities, corporations, chambers of commerce, and semi-public associations of various sorts—such as the New England Council—have conducted "surveys" during late years, but many of these have been superficial. A great deal of good work has been done in the colleges and by scholars on their own initiative, but the objectives have necessarily been confined to small areas or relatively limited problems.

The following is quoted from a pamphlet entitled "Why Massachusetts Needs a Survey of Natural Resources," published in 1930 by the Conference on Land Economic Survey:

"In the absence of accurate scientific information we have failed to solve the pressing problems of land utilization on more than half of the area of this state. Scores of declining towns, hundreds of abandoned farms, thousands of idle acres and many decadent industries are monuments to this lack of information and the consequent maladjustment of land use and industry to native resources. A complete inventory of these resources should be made to enable us to rectify these errors and to plan more wisely for the future.

"It was with that purpose in mind that the Massachusetts Forestry Association called a meeting to consider the need of a topographic resurvey and a land economic survey for Massachusetts. From that meeting sprang the Conference on Land Economic Survey. Active leaders in the fields of biology, geology, geography, economics, agriculture, forestry, engineering, business, public health, and town and regional planning presented the needs of their respective interests for the information about our natural resources that would be collected, correlated and made available by such surveys. They pointed to the fact that Massachusetts lags far behind many of the other states in the systematic study of resources and that much money is now being wasted in detached surveys, when the same data should and could be obtained for the whole state at a much lower cost per unit of area by coördinated surveys. The present system corresponds to buying at maximum retail rates commodities that should be purchased at minimum wholesale prices."

Certainly an important principle is stated here, and what is true of Massachusetts is no less true of the other five states. The existence of many common interests binding their citizens together suggests the need of coördinated effort toward the carrying out of systematic studies of the natural resources of *all* New England. Uniform treatment could thus be given to data that are essentially alike in the several states, and comparisons could be made that would be out of the question were each state to tackle the job in its own way. In addition, much could be accomplished in the relatively poorer states that probably would not be accomplished at all if they were left to carry out surveys wholly at their own expense.

In thinking of the advantages of such a survey, need our thought be limited to natural resources? There are many matters relating to population, industry, commerce, politics, and social life about which a more comprehensive and detailed survey could supplement the work of the federal and state governments. The selection of the data collected by the United States Census and the categories under which they are tabulated in the census reports represent an attempt to meet the requirements of a whole nation. They are the result of compromises and adjustments. So far as any one region is concerned they are often inadequate or inappropriate. The proposed New England Survey could conceivably arrange for having census data tabulated systematically by townships or in other forms suited to the special requirements of students of New England problems.

Already a beginning has been made along these lines in the commercial survey of New England carried out by the Department of Commerce in coöperation with the New England Council, but this was an isolated undertaking. The present concept is, rather, of a permanent institution made up of men professionally trained in the natural and social sciences, controlled by a commission of New England men of affairs, and having the official backing and financial support of the states. One of the first tasks of such a comprehensive New England Survey of Natural and Human Resources—as it might be called—could reasonably be the preparation of a *New England Atlas*, in which would appear not only the more usual types of maps of topographical features, natural resources, density of population, racial stocks, industries, and the like, but also maps specially designed to illustrate critical relationships of the sort discussed in the earlier parts of this paper.

Final Observations of the Unity of New England

It has been stated that New England is a somewhat homogeneous economic region, a unit in relation to many important issues, and that consciousness of this unity has been much stimulated of late years. This, however, is by no means to imply that opinion in New

England is united in respect to all of the larger problems that its people are facing or that localism does not still prevail in many quarters. In an unusually pointed newspaper article entitled "Is There One New England or Many?" Mr. F. G. Fassett discusses this problem.[18] He calls attention to evidences of *disunity* in New England opinion. Of especial interest is his reference to a curious case of reaction against recent "all-New England" propaganda. In November, 1930, the president of the Connecticut Manufacturers' Association "made a speech in which he talked of seceding from New England." "As far as his State was concerned, he raised the question whether or not it benefited by talk of 'a united New England front.' . . . He would be compelled to answer 'no' if asked whether there is a New England in the sense of a region actuated by a unity of purpose and opinion." But "there were those in Connecticut who deprecated his position."

Mr. Fassett then adds these observations:

"It is useless to deny that, as far as Connecticut is concerned, there has already been what to many might appear much like a partition. If the State has not been, like all Gaul, divided into three parts, it may be said to have seen a portion of it annexed to New York in the sense that it has become virtually an outlying borough of New York City. When experts there define the New York region, they step over the Connecticut boundary just as they cross the Hudson to reach New Jersey communities. As the traveler through Connecticut nears New York the signs on the factories in Connecticut towns and cities make mention of New York offices. The traveler does not see it, but he crosses the boundary of the New York Federal Reserve district before he crosses the Connecticut line. Summer homes glimpsed along the shore of the Sound belong to New Yorkers rather than to New Englanders. Commuters who sleep in Connecticut spend their working days in New York City."

Mr. Fassett goes on to cite the lack of unity in opinion concerning railroad consolidation and the development of the port of Boston. These are matters touched upon by other contributors to this volume. In opposition to the representatives of the other five states on a committee appointed by the New England Governors to study "all angles of the consolidation problem and to recommend a policy," the Rhode Islanders preferred union with the trunk lines as against a regional form of consolidation favored by the majority (see above, pp. 358–360). The report of the minority from Rhode Island, moreover, was approved by many business organizations both in that state and elsewhere. New England exporters can and do ship their goods through the port of New York more economically than through the New England ports. Propaganda calling for the development of the latter has fallen on deaf ears among a large section of the manufacturers of New England (see above, pp. 384–385). The Fernald Law forbidding the exportation of electric power across the boundaries of the state represents a clash between the supposed interests of Maine and those of southern New England (see above, pp. 315–319).

There are, in short, certain large problems about which opinion in New England is sharply divided. These are problems that cannot be solved on the basis of indiscriminate appeals to New England consciousness and New England pride. The New England survey that has been suggested might well provide specific facts and a point of view that would serve to correct loose thinking and misguided propaganda. The proposed survey might carry further the work of the New England Council toward breaking down provincial attitudes. Fully as important, it might help mark off those economic realms wherein New England is not a unit and wherein frank recognition of this fact offers the way out of perplexing difficulties.

In the long run, what counts for most in New England's prospect is neither the unity nor the internal diversity of the region, neither its local traditions nor any of the things that set it off from the rest of the world. The greatest single fact about New England today, as it has been from the beginning, is the fact that it forms an integral part of the great nation that it helped to build and in whose destiny it must share.

NOTES

[1] For a spirited answer to recent hostile critics of New England life and character see Bernard DeVoto, *New England, There She Stands*, in *Harper's Magazine*, Vol. 164, Mar. 1932, pp. 406–415.

[2] See W. P. Eaton, *New England in 1930*, in *Current Hist.*, Vol. 33, Nov. 1930, pp. 168–173; and C. E. Smith, *Destiny Comes to New England*, in *Century*, Vol. 117, Feb. 1929, pp. 436–444.

[3] W. P. Eaton, *Saving New England*, in *Atlantic Monthly*, Vol. 145, May 1930, pp. 614–621; reference on p. 618.

[4] The changes being wrought in New England by the immigrants are deplored by D. C. Brewer, *The Conquest of New England by the Immigrant*, New York, 1926. An extremely comprehensive study of the immigrants in the United States with many data on New England will be found in the 42 volumes of *Reports of the Immigration Commission*, Washington, 1911 (*61st Congress 2d* [and *3d*] *Sess.*). See also M. L. Hansen, *The Second Colonization of New England*, in *New England Quarterly*, Vol. 2, 1929, pp. 539–560, and Professor Hypes' article entitled *Recent Immigrant Stocks in New England Agriculture* in the present volume, pp. 189–205, above.

[5] Eaton, *op. cit.*, p. 615.

[6] See above, p. 371, note 3.

[7] See Lewis Mayers and L. V. Harrison, *The Distribution of Physicians in the United States*, General Education Board, New York, 1924.

[8] See the same, pp. 64–90; also *Special Report of the Department of Public Health Relative to Health and Medical Service in Sparsely Settled Districts, January, 1925*, Boston, 1925 (Massachusetts, *House, No. 1075*); *Rural Vermont: A Program for the Future*, by Two Hundred Vermonters, Burlington, Vt., 1931, pp. 205–233.

[9] See V. A. Rapport, *Are Rural Services Obsolescent?*, in *Amer. Journ. of Sociology*, Vol. 37, 1931, pp. 266–272 (deals with Connecticut), and C. D. Clark, *Some Indices of Urbanization in Two Connecticut Rural Towns*, in *Social Forces*, Vol. 9, 1931, pp. 409–418.

[10] See *Report of* [Mass.] *Governor's Committee on Needs and Uses of Open Spaces*, Boston, 1929 (with map, 1 : 250,000); P. L. Buttrick, *Public and Semi-Public Lands*

of Connecticut, Hartford, 1930 (Connecticut, *State Geol. and Nat. Hist. Survey Bull. No. 49*) with map, 1 : 250,000.

[11] See cartogram showing milk movements from northern New England to Boston and other cities in E. F. Gerish, *Commercial Structure of New England,* U. S. Dept. of Commerce, Bur. of Foreign and Domestic Commerce, Washington, 1929 (*Domestic Commerce Series No. 26*), p. 193.

[12] John Josselyn, *New England's Rarities . . . , With an Introduction and Notes, by Edward Tuckerman,* Boston, 1865, p. 36.

[13] See the articles by Professors H. C. Woodworth and H. F. Perkins, in the present volume, pp. 178–188 and 206–212, respectively.

[14] See especially R. T. Compton, *Fiscal Problems of Rural Decline: A Study of the Methods of Financing the Costs of Government in the Economically Decadent Rural Areas of New York State,* Albany, 1929 (New York, *Special Report of the State Tax Commission, No. 2*). A situation similar to that discussed in Dr. Compton's monograph undoubtedly prevails in many parts of New England, to which his recommendations would also be pertinent.

[15] The average area of the New England township is 33 square miles; in northern New England the averages are larger (Vermont 37, Maine 36, New Hampshire 35 square miles), and in southern New England smaller (Connecticut 29, Rhode Island 27, and Massachusetts 23 square miles). Only four townships have areas of over 100 square miles (Pittsburg, N. H., 177; Lincoln, N. H., 123; Allegash Plantation, Me., 118; and Waldoboro, Me., 105), and very few exceed 50 square miles. The smallest town is Newcastle, N. H., with less than half a square mile.

[16] Partial consolidation of functions now served by officers in neighboring towns is suggested in the report of the Vermont Commission on Country Life, *Rural Vermont: A Program for the Future,* Burlington, 1931; see also Professor H. F. Perkins' paper in the present volume. Another form of maladjustment of the township organization to the needs of rural communities is suggested in the following passage from a review of *Rural Vermont:*

"One factor in the rural situation, which was not discussed, is the way in which early settlement was made. People bought land they had not seen, tracts spread all over the surfaces of townships six miles square. To be sure, they were often shown pretty little maps with town lots in the center which would make reasonably well-planned villages. But with the lack of roads, and the total failure to adapt these ideal plans to the rugged topography of the townships, the plans were thrown overboard in most cases, and individuals with their large families settled on the lands they had bought, if there was any prospect of making a living out of the soil. Many of these were so isolated that they have been abandoned. And many more, still terribly isolated, continue to be tilled. The advantages of community life, for schools, for recreation, for medical attention, and otherwise, cannot be had for such isolated homes, even though improved roads and means of transportation have lessened some of the hardships. One is inclined to compare this situation with the more fortunate lot of those who live in the villages of Vermont, and the rural villages of such countries as France, where the isolated farmhouse is practically unknown. The tendency in Vermont will be to concentrate the rural population in villages, and overcome the errors of the past, leaving the isolated homes for the summer residents who prefer to spend a part of the year away from their fellows who crowd them so closely in the cities. There is an opportunity here for the newly developed art of planning villages as well as cities, to make them better places to live in." (*Proc. Vermont Historical Soc.,* N. S., Vol. 2, 1931, p. 150.)

[17] See above, pp. 422–424. Mayor Curley of Boston has been a strong advocate of further governmental consolidation in metropolitan Boston (see *Boston Evening Transcript,* Feb. 4, 1931).

[18] *Boston Evening Transcript,* Jan. 26, 1931.

BIOGRAPHICAL NOTES CONCERNING THE AUTHORS

DR. ADAMS is widely known as a writer on American history and on contemporary affairs. In *The Epic of America*, Boston, 1931, he gives a broad review and interpretation of the development of the American nation. Three of his earlier books dealt with the history of New England. *The Founding of New England*, Boston, 1921, won the Pulitzer prize of 1922 for the best book on the history of the United States. This was followed by *Revolutionary New England, 1691–1776*, Boston, 1923, and *New England in the Republic, 1776–1850*, Boston, 1926. In *The Adams Family*, Boston, 1930, he has traced the fortunes of one of the great New England families.

DR. ARTMAN is at present conducting economic studies for the Employment Stabilization Research Institute at the University of Minnesota. He has served on the Extension Staff in Economics at Columbia University and in 1925 carried out for the Port of New York Authority an investigation of the cost of distributing perishable foods in New York City (published in book form by the Columbia University Press under the title *Food Costs and City Consumers*, New York, 1926). From 1926 to 1929 he was in charge of a comprehensive survey of the commercial and industrial life of New England made for the United States Department of Commerce, with the coöperation of the New England Council (see above, p. 62). The results of this survey were published in three parts (or volumes) under the title *Commercial Survey of New England*. Dr. Artman himself wrote Part I, *Industrial Structure of New England*, Washington, 1930 (*Domestic Commerce Ser. No. 28*). He is also the author (with S. H. Reed) of *Foreign Trade Survey of New England*, Washington, 1931 (*Domestic Commerce Ser. No. 40*).

DR. CANCE has been head of the Department of Agricultural Economics of Massachusetts State College since 1910. He is a student of agricultural and industrial conditions in the United States and in European countries, where he has traveled extensively. He served as economist on the United States commission that studied coöperation in Europe in 1913, and was Executive Secretary of the President's Committee on Agriculture and Unemployment in 1922. He has been a member of various committees dealing with economic problems in Massachusetts and in New England. He made a study of immigrants in agriculture for the federal immigration commission (see above, p. 203, note 1) and is the author of many bulletins and articles on agricultural economics.

PROFESSOR CUNNINGHAM has been connected with Harvard University for the last twenty-five years. In 1908 and 1909 he was lecturer on railroad operation; from 1910 to 1916 he served as assistant professor and since 1916 has held the J. J. Hill Professorship of Transportation. He has also filled positions of responsibility on several of the railroads of New England, notably from 1914 to 1916 as assistant to the president of the Boston & Maine. In 1918–1919 he was Assistant Director of Operation of the U. S. Railroad Administration. He is also a former president both of the New England Railroad Club and of the Traffic Club of New England. He is the author of the chapter on railways in *Recent Economic Changes in the United States, Report of the Committee on Recent Economic Changes of the President's Conference on Unemployment, Herbert Hoover, Chairman*, New York, 1929.

MR. CUSHMAN is Executive Secretary of the Boston Council of Social Agencies, a position he has held since 1927. Prior to this he had served as Probation Officer in the Boston Juvenile Court and as Director of Norfolk House Center, a Neighbor-

476

hood House in Roxbury. During the war he organized the home service work under the Red Cross at Camp Devens and after the Armistice had various assignments in the New England Division of the Red Cross, largely relating to the after-care of ex-service men. Before assuming his present position he was for five years Director of the Boston Metropolitan Chapter of the Red Cross.

PROFESSOR DAVIS is professor of agricultural economics and head of the Department of Economics in the Connecticut Agricultural College. He is a student of the history of New England agriculture and of the problem of land utilization in the region. He is the author of a considerable number of articles of a professional character and also of various bulletins of the Storrs Agricultural Experiment Station on land utilization and trends in agricultural development in Connecticut.

MR. DEAN is Chief Engineer of the Massachusetts Department of Public Works. He was first appointed Chief Engineer of the Massachusetts Highway Commission, the predecessor of the present Department of Public Works, in 1910. Prior to that he had been State Engineer in charge of the state highways of New Hampshire from 1904 to 1910. He is Vice-President of the Boston Society of Civil Engineers, a member of the American Society of Civil Engineers, and a former president of the American Road Builders' Association. He has contributed technical papers to the Boston Society of Civil Engineers.

DR. FAIRCHILD, after serving nine years as instructor and assistant professor at Yale University, was appointed to his present position as professor of political economy in that institution in 1913. He has been Director of the U. S. Forest Taxation Inquiry since 1926. He has acted in the capacity of expert on taxation in the U. S. Forest Service from 1908 to 1914 and again since 1925. He has also been adviser on matters of taxation to the Republics of Santo Domingo and of Colombia and to the Territory of Hawaii. In 1929–1930 he was president of the National Tax Association. He is the author of several books and many articles on economics and on problems of taxation, among which may be mentioned: *Taxation of Timberland*, Washington, 1909 (*Report of the National Conservation Commission*) and *Report of a Study of the Connecticut Tax System Conducted for the Connecticut Chamber of Commerce*, Winsted, Conn., 1917.

MR. FILENE, president of Wm. Filene's Sons Company of Boston, is generally recognized as one of the outstanding business leaders of the United States. The great Filene store in Boston is today studied as a model, alike by sociologists and professional employment managers. In the words of Mr. Justice Brandeis, Mr. Filene and his brother "have demonstrated that the introduction of industrial democracy and of social justice is at least consistent with marked financial success." Mr. Filene planned and led the organization of the Boston Chamber of Commerce and was one of the founders of the Boston City Club. In 1919 he established the Twentieth Century Fund, one of a few foundations now devoted to the scientific approach to and solution of economic problems. He has been actively interested in international affairs and was mainly instrumental in organizing the International Chamber of Commerce in 1919. In Europe he played an important rôle in obtaining acceptance of the Dawes Plan.

DR. FISHER has been Director of the Harvard Forest since its establishment in 1908. Its principal contributions to forestry have been the development and demonstration of silvicultural practice and the publication of seventeen bulletins, besides a number of shorter articles embodying the results of special studies in the biology and economics of the forest as well as lessons derived from its management.

MR. FITZGERALD is an associate research chemist on the staff of the Birdseye Laboratories of the General Foods Corporation, which in 1930 absorbed the General Foods Company of Gloucester Mass., with which he had been connected since 1928. After serving as research assistant in bacteriology at the Massachusetts Institute of Technology, he became affiliated in 1924 with the U. S. Bureau of Fisheries at Washington as assistant chemist. In this capacity he investigated the relation of methods of catching and handling fish to their keeping qualities for the purpose of recommending improved methods. This work covered every type of fishing operation on the Atlantic seaboard. First as fisheries engineer for the General Foods Company and subsequently in his present capacity Mr. Fitzgerald has studied problems of plant location, of handling fish on vessels, of refrigerating efficiency of fish-holds, and various chemical and technological problems of fish and fishery products. Since 1930 he has specialized in the chemistry and technology of fruit and fruit products.

MR. GERISH is Chief of the Domestic Regional Division of the Bureau of Foreign and Domestic Commerce, U. S. Department of Commerce. In 1919–1920 he served as instructor in economics, business statistics, and transportation at the College of Business Administration, Boston University. He has been connected with the export, sales, and research departments of several large manufacturing companies. In 1926 he was appointed Senior Business Specialist of the Bureau of Foreign and Domestic Commerce and, while holding this post, helped carry out a comprehensive survey of the commercial life of New England under the direction of Dr. C. E. Artman (see above). In 1930 he was made Chief Business Specialist of the Bureau and in 1931 was appointed to his present position. Besides many articles in scientific periodicals and trade journals, he is the author of several publications of the Bureau of Foreign and Domestic Commerce, notably *The Retailer and the Consumer in New England*, Washington, 1928 (*Trade Information Bull. No. 575*); *Market Data Handbook of New England*, Washington, 1929 (*Domestic Commerce Ser. No. 24*); and *Commercial Structure of New England*, Washington, 1929 (*ibid., No. 26*).

DR. GRAVES is Dean of the Yale School of Forestry. He was engaged in private forestry work from 1896 to 1898, was Assistant Chief of the Division of Forestry in the United States Department of Agriculture from 1898 to 1900, and was then called to Yale to organize and direct the newly established School of Forestry. In 1910 he was appointed Chief of the United States Forest Service, a position which he held until 1920. After two years of private consulting work he resumed his former position at the Yale School of Forestry. He served during the war in the 10th (later the 20th) Engineers in France and upon retirement held the commission of Lieutenant Colonel. Dr. Graves is the author of *Forest Mensuration*, New York, 1906, *Principles of Handling Woodlands*, New York, 1911, and numerous bulletins and scientific articles. He is senior author of: H. S. Graves and C. H. Guise, *Forest Education*, Yale University Press, New Haven, 1932.

MR. GREELEY is a member of the firm of Kilham, Hopkins and Greeley, architects, Boston. He did the housing work for the Massachusetts Homestead Commission and later made the comprehensive plan for the city of Gardner, Mass. For several years he was President of the Massachusetts Federation of Planning Boards and Chairman of the New England Regional Planning League and the New England Association of America. He is Vice-Chairman of the Governor's Committee on the Needs and Uses of Open Spaces in Massachusetts. He has served on the President's Committee on Large Scale Housing Operations and is now a member of the executive board of the Trustees of Public Reservations of Massachusetts and of the Massachusetts Forestry Association. He is a member of the Regional Planning Association of America.

DR. HORMELL is De Alva Stanwood Alexander Professor of Government and Director of the Bureau of Government Research at Bowdoin College. He has served as a city and town consultant on charter making. His publications include articles on state public utilities regulation published annually in *American Political Science Review; Maine Public Utilities*, Brunswick, Me., 1927; *Electricity in Great Britain: A Study in Administration*, New York, 1928; *Control of Public Utilities Abroad*, Syracuse, N. Y., 1930. He has also been a contributor to *Cyclopedia of American Government*, the *American Political Science Review*, the *American City*, and the *National Muncipal Review*.

DR. HYPES is head of the Department of Sociology at the Connecticut Agricultural College and Director of Sociological Research at the Storrs Agricultural Experiment Station. He also serves as Professor of Education and Sociology in the State Board Summer School at Yale University. He has traveled widely in Europe, India, and the Far East studying problems of education and sociology. He is the author of a number of articles in scientific periodicals and also of a monographic study, *Social Participation in a Rural New England Town*, New York, 1927; with J. F. Markey he is joint author of *The Genesis to Farming Occupations in Connecticut*, Storrs, Conn., 1929 (*Storrs Agric. Exper. Sta. Bull. No. 161*).

MR. KEIR is one of the directors of the Dennison Manufacturing Company, Framingham, Mass., and has served as economic adviser to that company since 1925. From 1914 to 1917 he was instructor in economics at the University of Pennsylvania. In 1917 he was appointed head of the Department of Industry at the University of Pittsburgh but resigned to enter military service. From 1920 to 1924 he was professor and head of the Department of Industrial Economics at the Carnegie Institute of Technology, Pittsburgh. In 1923 he served as special investigator for the U. S. Coal Commission. He is a director of the Institute of Management, American Management Association.

DR. McFALL has been Chief Statistician for Distribution, U. S. Bureau of the Census, since 1929. Previously he had served as instructor in economics at the University of Minnesota (1915–1917); chief of the Internal Trade Branch, Dominion Bureau of Statistics, Canada (1917–1920); chief of the Transportation Branch of the same bureau (1919–1920); Chief Statistician, Canada Food Board (1917–1919), Chief Statistician, Canadian Fuel Controller (1918–1919); Cost of Living Commissioner, Labour Department, Canada (1918–1919); professor of agricultural economics, Massachusetts Agricultural College (1920–1927); and in various connections with the United States Department of Agriculture (1920–1925). He was a member of the staff of the Institute of Economics, Washington, D. C., in 1925–1926, and a member of the Domestic Commerce Division, Bureau of Foreign and Domestic Commerce, in 1927–1928. He was editor of *Survey of Current Business*, 1928–1930, and is author of *Railway Monopoly and Rate Regulation*, New York, 1916; *The World's Meat*, New York, 1927; *The External Trade of New England*, Washington, 1928 (*Domestic Commerce Ser. No. 22*), and other government reports, articles, etc., dealing with economic, statistical, and business subjects.

DR. MOREHOUSE was appointed to his present position, that of Chief Economist and Director of the Rates and Research Division, Public Service Commission of Wisconsin, in 1931. Previously he had served as assistant and instructor in economics at the University of Wisconsin (1919–1925) and as assistant professor and associate professor at Northwestern University (1925–1931). From 1923 to 1925 he was research instructor and from 1925 to 1931 research associate in the Institute of Economic Research (formerly the Institute for Research in Land Economics and

Public Utilities). He has been managing editor of the *Journal of Land and Public Utility Economics* since 1925. He is the author of various articles and, with Professor R. T. Ely, joint author of *Elements of Land Economics*, New York, 1924.

DR. PERKINS has been professor of zoölogy at the University of Vermont since 1911 and Director of the University Museum since 1931. In 1925 he organized the Eugenics Survey of Vermont, of which he is director. Dr. Perkins originated the plan for the Vermont Commission on Country Life. It was mainly through his activity that the Commission was established in 1928 and the comprehensive survey of rural Vermont undertaken. He has served as secretary of the Commission.

DR. RADCLIFFE has been Deputy Commissioner of the U. S. Bureau of Fisheries since 1923. In 1907–1908 he served as assistant naturalist on the S.S. *Albatross*, Pacific Islands Expedition. From 1909 to 1912 and again from 1914 to 1916 he held the position of scientific assistant in the Bureau of Fisheries and in 1916 was appointed chief of the Division of Fishery Industries of that bureau. In 1912–1914 he was Director of the Beaufort (N. C.) Biological Laboratory and in 1922–1923 special fisheries investigator for the U. S. Tariff Commission. He has published many papers on fish and on methods and economics of the fisheries, and has contributed to scientific journals, fishery trade journals, the *Encyclopaedia Britannica*, the *American Yearbook*, and the *Americana Annual*.

DR. ROORBACH has been professor of foreign trade at the Graduate School of Business Administration, Harvard University, since 1919. Previously he was assistant professor of economic geography at the University of Pennsylvania. During the early part of the War Dr. Roorbach investigated for the Carnegie Endowment the effects of the war upon industrial and trade conditions in Venezuela; later he was with the Division of Planning and Statistics of the United States Shipping Board. During 1921–1922, he served as Chief of the Division of Statistical Research of the United States Bureau of Foreign and Domestic Commerce and for two summers as special expert with the United States Tariff Commission. He spent 1926–1927 in the Orient studying Far Eastern international trade. In addition to numerous articles on subjects pertaining to economic geography and international trade, he is the author of *Import Purchasing: Principles and Problems*, Chicago, 1927, *International Competition in the Trade of India*, Carnegie Endowment for International Peace, Worcester, Mass., 1931, and *Problems of Foreign Commerce*, New York, 1933. He has been treasurer and vice-president of the Association of American Geographers. He is chairman of the Foreign Trade Committee of the Boston Chamber of Commerce.

DR. SLY has been head of the Department of Political Science and Director of the Bureau for Government Research, West Virginia University, since 1930. Prior to assuming this position he had served as instructor in political sciences at the State University of Iowa (1920–1921), assistant professor of political science at the University of California at Los Angeles (1925–1927), and lecturer on government at Harvard University (1927–1930). He is author of *Town Government in Massachusetts, 1620–1930*, Cambridge, 1930, as well as of many articles on state and local government and of chapters entitled *Geographic Expansion and Town System* and *Massachusetts in the National Government (1776–1781)*, (*1820–1861*), in A. B. Hart, edit., *The Commonwealth History of Massachusetts*, New York, 1927–1930, Vol. 2, pp. 96–119, Vol. 3, pp. 153–179, and Vol. 4, pp. 281–306. He is now engaged upon a systematic study of local government in West Virginia.

DR. WAUGH from 1928 to 1932 held the positions of Executive Secretary of the New England Research Council on Marketing and Food Supply and principal agricultural economist of the U. S. Bureau of Agricultural Economics. Prior to that he had served as specialist in marketing research in the New Jersey Department of Agriculture (1922–1925), extension economist at the Connecticut Agricultural College (1925–1926), and Director of the Massachusetts Division of Markets. He is the author of a number of bulletins on problems pertaining to the marketing and prices of agricultural products and of several articles in scientific publications dealing with these subjects and with statistical methods. At the present time (December, 1932) he is engaged in research in Europe.

DR. WHITTLESEY has been assistant professor and associate professor of geography at Harvard University since 1928. Prior to that he had served as instructor, assistant professor, and associate professor in the University of Chicago. He is the author of many articles dealing with field geography, regional geography, and political geography and joint author with Professor W. D. Jones of *An Introduction to Economic Geography*, of which the first volume appeared in 1925 (the second volume is in preparation). Since 1930 he has been editor of the *Annals of the Association of American Geographers*. He has traveled widely in North America, the Caribbean region, and Europe.

MR. WOODWORTH is agricultural economist in charge of research in agricultural economics for the New Hampshire Agricultural Experiment Station. He came to New Hampshire in 1921 as extension specialist in farm management and worked with individual farmers and groups of farmers in building up better farm enterprises. In traveling over the state in intimate contact with farm people he noted the great difference in the interest and energy of different communities in the management of the farms and has been especially interested in the personnel of the rural community and the influence of the community on the individual. He is the author or co-author of several bulletins published by the New Hampshire Agricultural Experiment Station.

DR. WRIGHT has been librarian of the American Geographical Society of New York since 1920. He is author of *Aids to Geographical Research*, New York, 1923 (*Amer. Geogr. Soc. Research Ser. No. 10*) and *The Geographical Lore of the Time of the Crusades*, New York, 1925 (*ibid., No. 15*) and editor of C. O. Paullin's *Atlas of the Historical Geography of the United States*, Carnegie Institution of Washington and American Geographical Society of New York, 1932.

INDEX

INDEX